HANDBOOK TO EXEGESIS OF
THE NEW TESTAMENT

NEW TESTAMENT TOOLS
AND STUDIES

EDITED BY

BRUCE M. METZGER, Ph.D., D.D., L.H.D., D. Theol., D. Litt.

Professor of New Testament Language and Literature, Emeritus
Princeton Theological Seminary
and
Corresponding Fellow of the British Academy

AND

BART D. EHRMAN, Ph.D.

Associate Professor, Department of Religious Studies
University of North Carolina at Chapel Hill

VOLUME XXV

HANDBOOK TO EXEGESIS
OF
THE NEW TESTAMENT

EDITED BY

STANLEY E. PORTER

BRILL
LEIDEN · NEW YORK · KÖLN
1997

This book is printed on acid-free paper.

ISSN 0077-8842
ISBN 90 04 09921 2

CONTENTS

PART TWO
APPLICATION

PREFACE

This *Handbook to Exegesis of the New Testament* is designed to provide a substantial theoretical and practical guide to the multifaceted discipline of exegesis of the New Testament. Most books on exegetical method are either too short and brief, failing to cover the requisite current topics in sufficient depth, or too technically difficult, failing to provide a useful methodology. I am not sure that this volume has remedied all of the problems of previous volumes, but at least a noble attempt has been made by the contributors. This volume hopes to offer succinct and well-informed essays, each with useful bibliography, written by experts in their respective fields, on many of the most important topics in contemporary exegesis. It is hoped that the volume will serve just as the title states, as a handbook, providing reference to the major tools and topics in the area of New Testament exegesis.

The individual essays have been written so as to provide coverage of the following areas for each topic (although not necessarily in this order): an introduction to the area and its importance for New Testament exegesis, discussion of the major issues of importance with regard to the topic and how they are relevant for exegesis, examples of uses and abuses of the topic in exegesis, and primarily English-language bibliographical references for future reference (often, though not always, in separate bibliographies). Practical examples illustrating the exegetical implications of the topic are also included. Individual contributors have been encouraged to use their essay as a chance to inform both scholars and students, as well as other interested parties, about what they consider to be the best information and approach to the particular topic. Readers will notice, however, that there has been no attempt to impose the same exegetical framework on all contributors, with the result that the multifarious topic of New Testament exegesis has elicited many different models of it demonstrated in this volume. Rather than seeing this as a limitation, I think of this as one of the volume's strengths. If anything, this volume, reflecting recent discussion of the topic of exegesis, well illustrates that it is unwise—if not impossible—to define the term exegesis, apart from seeing it exemplified in the analysis of texts. If the essays included here help in that task, I think that all of us will consider the job to have been worthwhile.

I wish to thank several people and institutions for helping this volume to finally see the light of day. The contributors have been exemplary in their attention paid to the task at hand. Dr David Orton has been exceptionally patient as the volume has worked its way slowly to its final completion. The Faculty of Arts and Humanities of Roehampton Institute London helped to offset some of the expense of producing the manuscript. Brook W.R. Pearson, my colleague, deserves thanks for his help at various stages of this project, including not only his written contribution but his proofreading of the entire manuscript. Most of all, my wife, Wendy, has contributed much effort to getting the manuscript into suitable shape for publication. Her patience with and support for the project have been much more than could have been asked for. Thank you.

Stanley E. Porter
September 1997

ABBREVIATIONS

AAW	Approaching the Ancient World
AB	Anchor Bible
ABD	*Anchor Bible Dictionary*
ABRL	Anchor Bible Reference Library
AGAJU	Arbeiten zur Geschichte des Antiken Judentums und des Urchristentums
AJT	*American Journal of Theology*
AnBib	Analecta biblica
ANRW	*Aufstieg und Niedergang der römischen Welt*
ANTF	Arbeiten zur neutestamentlichen Textforschung
ArBib	The Aramaic Bible
ATR	*Anglican Theological Review*
BBR	*Bulletin for Biblical Research*
BETL	Bibliotheca ephemeridum theologicarum lovaniensium
BI	*Biblical Interpretation*
Bib	*Biblica*
BibOr	Biblica et orientalia
BibSem	The Biblical Seminar
BIS	Biblical Interpretation Series
BJRL	*Bulletin of the John Rylands University Library of Manchester*
BJS	Brown Judaic Studies
BLS	Bible and Literature Series
BT	*The Bible Translator*
BTB	*Biblical Theology Bulletin*
BZ	*Biblische Zeitschrift*
CBQ	*Catholic Biblical Quarterly*
CBQMS	*CBQ* Monograph Series
ConBNT	Coniectanea biblica, New Testament
CRINT	Compendia rerum iudaicarum ad Novum Testamentum
CSR	*Christian Scholar's Review*
CTM	*Concordia Theological Monthly*
DSD	*Dead Sea Discoveries*
ETL	*Ephemerides theologicae lovanienses*
ExpTim	*The Expository Times*
FB	Forschung zur Bibel
FFNT	Foundations and Facets: New Testament
FN	*Filología Neotestamentaria*
FRLANT	Forschungen zur Religion und Literatur des Alten und Neuen Testaments
GBS	Guides to Biblical Scholarship
GTJ	*Grace Theological Journal*
HNTC	Harper's New Testament Commentaries
HTR	*Harvard Theological Review*

HTS	Harvard Theological Studies
HUCA	*Hebrew Union College Annual*
HUT	Hermeneutische Untersuchungen zur Theologie
IBS	*Irish Biblical Studies*
ICC	International Critical Commentary
IDBSup	*Interpreter's Bible Dictionary Supplement*
ITL	International Theological Library
JBL	*Journal of Biblical Literature*
JETS	*Journal of the Evangelical Theological Society*
JR	*Journal of Religion*
JSNT	*Journal for the Study of the New Testament*
JSNTSup	*JSNT* Supplement Series
JSOT	*Journal for the Study of the Old Testament*
JSOTSup	*JSOT* Supplement Series
JSPSup	*JSP* Supplement Series
JTS	*Journal of Theological Studies*
KEK	Kritisch-exegetischer Kommentar
LCL	Loeb Classical Library
LEC	Library of Early Christianity
LT	*Literature and Theology*
MH	*Museum Helveticum*
NCB	New Century Bible
Neot	*Neotestamentica*
NICNT	New International Commentary on the New Testament
NIGTC	New International Greek Testament Commentary
NovT	*Novum Testamentum*
NovTSup	*Novum Testamentum* Supplements
NTAbh	Neutestamentliche Abhandlungen
NTG	New Testament Guides
NTL	New Testament Library
NTOA	Novum Testamentum et Orbis Antiquus
NTS	*New Testament Studies*
NTTS	New Testament Tools and Studies
OBO	Orbis biblicus et orientalis
OTL	Old Testament Library
OTM	Oxford Theological Monographs
PhilAnt	Philosophia Antiqua
PRS	*Perspectives in Religious Studies*
PSTJ	*Perkins (School of Theology) Journal*
QD	Quaestiones disputatae
ResQ	*Restoration Quarterly*
RevQ	*Revue de Qumran*
RILP	Roehampton Institute London Papers
SANT	Studien zum Alten und Neuen Testament
SBEC	Studies in the Bible and Early Christianity
SBG	Studies in Biblical Greek

SBLDS	SBL Dissertation Series
SBLMS	SBL Monograph Series
SBLRBS	SBL Resources for Biblical Study
SBLSBS	SBL Sources for Biblical Study
SBLSP	SBL Seminar Papers
SBLTT	SBL Texts and Translations
SBS	Stuttgarter Bibelstudien
SBT	Studies in Biblical Theology
SCHNT	Studia ad corpus hellenisticum novi testamenti
SCT	Studies in the Classical Tradition
SD	Studies and Documents
SJLA	Studies in Judaism in Late Antiquity
SJT	*Scottish Journal of Theology*
SNTSMS	Society for New Testament Studies Monograph Series
SNTU	Studien zum Neuen Testament und seiner Umwelt
SPB	Studia Post Biblica
SSEJC	Studies in Scripture in Early Judaism and Christianity
SVTP	Studia in Veteris Testamenti Pseudepigrapha
TAPA	*Transactions of the American Philological Association*
TDNT	*Theological Dictionary of the New Testament*
Theol	*Theology*
TJT	*Toronto Journal of Theology*
TLZ	*Theologische Literaturzeitung*
TNTC	Tyndale New Testament Commentaries
TRev	*Theologische Revue*
TS	*Theological Studies*
TTod	*Theology Today*
TU	Texte und Untersuchungen
TynBul	*Tyndale Bulletin*
UBSGNT	United Bible Societies, *Greek New Testament*
VCSup	*Vigilae Christianae* Supplements
VT	*Vetus Testamentum*
WBC	Word Biblical Commentary
WF	Wege der Forschung
WMANT	Wissenschaftliche Monographien zum Alten und Neuen Testament
WTJ	*Westminster Theological Journal*
WUNT	Wissenschaftliche Untersuchungen zum Neuen Testament
ZNW	*Zeitschrift für die neutestamentliche Wissenschaft*
ZTK	*Zeitschrift für Theologie und Kirche*

CONTRIBUTORS

Stephen C. Barton, University of Durham, England

David R. Catchpole, University of Exeter, England

Kent D. Clarke, Roehampton Institute London, England

Eldon Jay Epp, Case Western Reserve University, Cleveland, OH, USA

Craig A. Evans, Trinity Western University, Langley, BC, Canada

David W.J. Gill, University of Wales, Swansea

George H. Guthrie, Union University, Jackson, TN, USA

Thomas H. Olbricht, Pepperdine University, Malibu, CA, USA

John Painter, Charles Sturt University, Canberra, Australia

Brook W.R. Pearson, Roehampton Institute London, England

Tina Pippin, Agnes Scott College, Decatur, GA, USA

Stanley E. Porter, Roehampton Institute London, England

Jeffrey T. Reed, Fuller Theological Seminary, Seattle, WA, USA

Dennis L. Stamps, Queen's Foundation, Birmingham, England

Gregory E. Sterling, University of Notre Dame, Indiana, USA

Paul R. Trebilco, University of Otago, Dunedin, New Zealand

Christopher M. Tuckett, University of Oxford, England

Robert W. Wall, Seattle Pacific University, Seattle, WA, USA

INTRODUCTION

WHAT IS EXEGESIS? AN ANALYSIS OF VARIOUS DEFINITIONS

STANLEY E. PORTER AND KENT D. CLARKE

INTRODUCTION

It is an unseasonably beautiful day in June and a student, wanting much more to be out kicking a football—or anywhere other than where he is—enters to write a final examination paper in biblical studies. With some anxiety he sits down and at the proper moment flings open the exam paper and stares intently at the first question. It innocently reads: 'Biblical Passages: Exegete* fully the prologue to John's Gospel (1:1-18). Remember to make your answer clear and well-organized, showing a coherent train of thought and referring to major scholars and their opinions.' A wry smile crosses our unlikely hero's face, as he remembers several lectures on the prologue, as well as a number of other articles and books he has perused, for he actually knows something about this passage. He begins to formulate an answer. Perhaps the best place to start is with an analysis of the term λόγος. He remembers the lengthy and insightful section in Raymond Brown's commentary on the Jewish background to the concept of 'the Word'.[1] Since Christianity is often considered to be a Jewish sect, closely tied to the Old Testament, this might be the best way to proceed. Besides, it would certainly fill a few pages. But wait. There is also the work of C.H. Dodd on the Greek philosophical background to the concept of 'the Word'.[2] That might be the best way to approach the answer, since the Gospel of John was originally written in Greek, takes notice of other Greek elements in Jesus' ministry, and reflects a religious group that was spread throughout the Greco-Roman world. Then again, perhaps he should answer as do Hoskyns and Davey in their commentary on John, laying out the evidence for both sides.[3] But

---

*   Use of "exegete" as a verb is now common on examination papers.

[1]   R.E. Brown, *The Gospel according to John* (2 vols.; AB, 29, 29A; Garden City, NY: Doubleday, 1966), pp. 519-24.

[2]   C.H. Dodd, *The Interpretation of the Fourth Gospel* (Cambridge: Cambridge University Press, 1954), pp. 263-85.

[3]   E. Hoskyns and F.N. Davey, *The Fourth Gospel* (London: Faber & Faber, 1947), pp. 154-63.

that commentary was, at least in his opinion, a disappointment, for the very reason that it did not make up its mind. A sense of unease comes over our studious friend as small beads of sweat begin to form on his brow and upper lip, and he begins to twist nervously in his seat. 'But this is just background material anyway', he thinks. One of his and other students' most frequent complaints is that the lecturers spend so much time talking about the material behind the text that they never get to the text itself. Perhaps another tack will provide the answer. In a more recent article, Frank Kermode, the literary scholar, picks up long-heard rumblings about the use of the verb 'was' and pursues this as the unifying thread to John's prologue, weaving together various narrative intrusions.[4] But how, our now panicking examinee thinks, does this square with Eugene Nida's structural analysis of John 1:1-5, which uses instead of the verb 'was' a series of repetitions in chiastic order as pivotal points for analysis?[5] Both of these promise interesting answers, but then, hadn't he heard one of the lecturers make the comment that all this new literary stuff was no substitution for exegesis? Glancing at his watch to see how much time he has lost, our now depressed student moves on to the second question: 'Reconstruct the historical background of 1 Corinthians...' and breathes a sigh of relief.

EXEGESIS DEFINED

Broader Definition and Synonyms

Exegesis comprises the most important task of the study of the New Testament (Conzelmann and Lindemann 1988: 1). At the same time, there are few terms in biblical studies like 'exegesis' that are used so freely and represent so many different things to various scholars and students. Thus the plight of our industrious student above. Part of the term's perceived ambiguity may reside in its often synonymous relationship to a number of other words such as 'interpretation' and 'hermeneutics'. Broadly speaking, all three terms fall under the discipline of 'heuristics' (Greek εὑρίσκω which not only meant 'find' or 'come upon', but could also refer to an intellectual discovery based upon reflection, observation, examination, or investigation), that is, the study and development of methods or principles that aid one in

---

[4]   F. Kermode, 'St John as Poet', *JSNT* 28 (1986), pp. 3-16.

[5]   E.A. Nida *et al.*, *Style and Discourse* (New York: Bible Society, 1983), pp. 112-16.

discovering the sense and meaning of a text.

Hermeneutics (Greek ἑρμηνεύω which meant to translate, explain, interpret, or even proclaim) can be widely defined as the attempt to understand anything that somebody else has said or written (Marshall 1979: 11). And, although hermeneutics has classically referred to the science of formulating guidelines, laws, and methods for interpreting an original author's meaning, more recently, the term has been more narrowly restricted to the elucidation of a text's meaning for a contemporary audience. Anthony Thiselton clarifies this point:

> Traditionally hermeneutics entailed the formulation of rules for the understanding of an ancient text, especially in linguistic and historical terms. The interpreter was urged to begin with the language of the text, including its grammar, vocabulary, and style. He examined its linguistic, literary, and historical context. In other words, traditional hermeneutics began with the recognition that a text was conditioned by a given historical context. However, hermeneutics in the more recent sense of the term begins with the recognition that historical conditioning is two-sided: *the modern interpreter, no less than the text, stands in a given historical context and tradition* (Thiselton 1980: 11).[6]

The term exegesis, like hermeneutics, has also been broadly defined as a normal activity in which all of us are engaged from day to day. Hayes and Holladay explain that 'Whenever we hear an oral statement or read a written one and seek to understand what has been said, we are engaging in exegesis' (Hayes and Holladay 1987: 5). The word exegesis itself is derived from the Greek term ἐξηγέομαι, which literally meant 'lead out of'. When applied to written texts the word referred to the 'reading out' of the text's meaning. More generally, exegesis also meant to explain, interpret, tell, report, or describe. And, once again like hermeneutics, exegesis classically referred to the articulation or discovery of a text's meaning based on the understanding of the original author's intentions and goals.

Lastly, the word interpretation (Latin *interpretari* which meant to explain, translate, or understand) is often used interchangeably with the words hermeneutics and exegesis. Such is the case with Gerhard Ebeling who asserts that these three terms are in fact synonyms. Ebeling adds further that 'the words "interpretation" and "hermeneutics" at bottom mean the same', and later goes on to say, 'Hermeneutics therefore, in order to be an aid to interpretation, must

---

[6]   For similar definitions of the term hermeneutics, see Fee 1993: 27; and Osborne 1991: 5.

itself be interpretation' (Ebeling 1963: 321). C.F. Evans takes a similar stance when he states that hermeneutics 'is only another word for exegesis or interpretation'.[7]

Given the close resemblance in meaning of these three terms, it is not surprising that the word exegesis is so diversely applied or that its technical meaning is so difficult to establish. There are, however, a number of helpful distinctions that can be made in order to bring at least some clarification to our discussion and definition of the exegetical task. To begin with, the term interpretation is often used in a less technical and more general sense than either of the words exegesis or hermeneutics. Whereas the objects of interpretation can be various forms of oral, gestural, symbolic, and written communication, the object of exegesis and hermeneutics is more often equated with written data. One might say that interpretation, being the broadest of the three terms, incorporates both hermeneutics and exegesis as sub-categories (see Morgan and Barton 1988: 1-5; and Thiselton 1980: 10). Continuing to work from general to specific, the next term to follow is hermeneutics, which refers to the over-arching theories or philosophies that guide exegesis. And finally, exegesis, the most specific of the three terms, refers to the actual practice, procedures, and methods one uses to understand a text (see Osborne 1991: 5). Exegesis is concerned with the actual interpretation and understanding of the text, whereas hermeneutics is concerned with the nature of the interpretative process and the conditions to which basic understanding is to be subjected (Conzelmann and Lindemann 1988: 1). Exegesis concludes by saying, 'This passage means such and such'; hermeneutics ends by saying, 'This interpretative process is constituted by the following techniques and pre-understandings' (Carson 1984: 22-23).

Traditional Definition

As briefly mentioned, exegesis has been traditionally defined as the process by which a reader seeks to discover the meaning of a text *via* an understanding of the original author's intentions in that text. The classic goal of exegesis has been to articulate the meaning of a passage as the original writer intended it to be understood by his or her contemporary audience. Thus R.T. France (Marshall 1979: 252) understands exegesis as 'the discovery of what the text means in itself,

---

7   C.F. Evans, *Is 'Holy Scripture' Christian?* (London: SCM Press, 1971), p. 31.

that is, the original intention of the writer, and the meaning the passage would have held for the readers for whom it was first intended'. R.P. Martin similarly asserts that 'to 'practice exegesis in regard to the New Testament literature is to enquire what was the meaning intended by the original authors... This is to be the interpreter's primary aim, requiring that his approach to Scripture be one of honest enquiry and a determined effort to find out the intended meaning of the author for his day' (Marshall 1979: 220). And finally, like France and Martin, G.D. Fee explains in his handbook to New Testament exegesis,

> The term 'exegesis' is used...in a consciously limited sense to refer to the historical investigation into the meaning of the biblical text. Exegesis, therefore, answers the question, What *did* the biblical author *mean*? It has to do both with *what* he said (the content itself) and why he said it at any given point (the literary context). Furthermore, exegesis is primarily concerned with intentionality: What did the author *intend* his original readers to understand? (Fee 1993: 27).

Exegesis of this nature has often been called 'grammatico-historical exegesis', or simply 'historical exegesis'. More technically, exegesis that concerns itself solely with historical background, the original author's intentions, and the ancient audience's understanding of these intentions has been termed 'exegesis proper'. The underlying hermeneutical philosophies of grammatico-historical exegesis began to be formulated as early as 1788 by the Leipzig theologian Karl Keil. Keil explained that, to interpret an author meant nothing more than to teach what meaning he intended to convey, or to assure that, when reading a work, the interpreter would think the same things as the author initially conceived. Interpreters were not to concern themselves about the nature of what the original author wrote—whether the words were true or false—but only to understand what was spoken by that author. Keil believed that the function of the interpreter closely resembled that of the historian, for just as the historian seeks to unbiasedly determine what has been done by another, without casting judgment on that event, so too the interpreter must concentrate attention on the author in order that he or she may know and explain to others what was earlier said and written by someone else. That the interpreter differentiates between sacred or profane writers Keil thought was inappropriate, since the writers of Scripture were to be understood in no other way than as human authors. For Keil it was the task of the theologian to consider what value was to be ascribed to the opinions expounded by the sacred writers, what authority was to be attributed to them in the present age, and in what manner they were to be contemporized. In the words of Keil, however, the task of the exegete consisted only in making plain what was handed down by the biblical authors: 'In the case of a sacred no less than a profane author it is the task of the interpreter to bring to light what the author himself thought as he wrote, what meaning is suggested by his own discourse, and what he wished his readers to understand' (Kümmel 1973: 108-109). Grammatico-historical exegesis of this fashion required that a single and definite sense be assigned by the interpreter to the author's words and sentences.

In 1799, soon after Keil wrote, standing on the presupposition that the biblical authors were to be explained just as the profane, without taking the divine revelation of the Scriptures into consideration, and emphasizing a more literal interpretation, G.L. Bauer wrote:

> The only valid principle of interpretation, whether the author be profane or biblical, is this: Every book must be explained in accordance with the linguistic peculiarities that characterize it; this means grammatical interpretation and results in a literal understanding of the text; and the presentation and clarification of the ideas that appear in it, ideas dependent on the customs and the way of thinking of the author himself and of his age, his nation, sect, religion, and so forth, is the task of what is called historical interpretation (Kümmel 1973: 112).

Further separation of the theological from the historical within exegesis can be clearly seen in individuals like Heinrich Meyer, who, in 1829, wrote in his *Critical and Exegetical Commentary* on the New Testament:

> The area of dogmatics and philosophy is to remain off limits for a commentary. For to ascertain the meaning the author intended to convey by his words, impartially and historico-grammatically—that is the duty of the exegete. How the meaning so ascertained stands in relation to the teachings of philosophy, to what extent it agrees with the dogmas of the church or with the views of its theologians, in what way the dogmatician is to make use of it in the interest of his science—to the exegete as an exegete, all that is a matter of no concern (Kümmel 1973: 111).

Although in recent years many of the more radical maxims of grammatico-historical exegesis have been tempered—or at least advocates of the approach have been more willing to admit that a number of larger hermeneutical questions cannot be so easily answered by the method—there remain numerous biblical scholars who wish to preserve the stringent historicity and a-theological stance that grammatico-historical exegesis has promoted. As we shall see below, however, there are a number of difficulties with many of the planks of this interpretative model.

Traditional Definition Questioned

Whereas the emphasis of grammatico-historical exegesis has focused upon what the biblical text originally *meant*, it has been more recently argued that the exegetical task should, and even must, be expanded to include both what the text *has meant* (i.e. its history of interpretation) and what the text *means* (i.e. its relevance for today). Individuals like Werner Stenger divide exegesis into three sub-disciplines: (1) those methods that seek to describe a text's *linguistic form* and underlying structures, (2) those methods that look into the circumstances surrounding a text's *origin* and seek to identify its original addressees, and (3) those methods that investigate the *reception* a text has had in the course of its history and still has in the present. Stenger's close proximity to traditional grammatico-historical exegesis, however, cannot be missed as he claims that

> ...this third group of methods—when the text in question is the New Testament—is the task of every theological discipline, including ethics. Therefore, we must understand the specific discipline of *New Testament* exegesis as obligated in particular to describe the text's linguistic form and investigate the circumstances of its origin. New Testament exegesis is thus directed primarily toward *philological* and *historical* goals, and within this dual focus is called *historical-critical* exegesis (Stenger 1993: 3).

Others, like W.G. Kümmel, still indebted to grammatico-historical exegesis, seem more willing to allow for a balance of interests within the exegetical task. Kümmel emphasizes that New Testament exegetes must keep in mind which of two possible ways of asking questions they will use in dealing with a particular exegetical problem. First, one may intend to learn from the text what it says about the historical circumstances at the time of its composition, its author, the readers for whom it was intended, the intellectual milieu from which it originated, and the external or internal history of primitive Christianity. Secondly, one may intend to discover the objective meaning of the text, that is, to learn from the text what it says about the subject matter discussed in it, and what this means for the interpreter personally (Kaiser and Kümmel 1981: 43-44). Like Kümmel, Dieter Lührmann sees exegesis as the attempt to answer two different questions: 'What is in the text?', and 'What does the text tell me?' (Lührmann 1989: 17).

Alternative Methods of Exegesis

Rather than merely tinkering with the historically-grounded grammatico-historical method, a number of recent biblical interpreters have claimed to overthrow its major assumptions. They have rejected many of its historically-based presuppositions, and have chosen to emphasize other exegetical criteria. We are grouping these exegetical methods together in this programmatic opening chapter, but they are in fact quite diverse, developing in some instances out of reaction to traditional exegesis and in others out of other intellectual disciplines. As a result, several of them have warranted their own separate chapters in this volume, where more comprehensive discussion can take place. The alternative forms of exegesis represented here include discourse analysis, a form of exegesis dependent upon many of the valuable insights of modern linguistics; rhetorical and narratological criticism, with its historical roots in a historically-grounded criticism, but much of its current practice relying upon modern literary conceptions; literary criticism, which remains a tremendously wide and diverse field; ideological criticisms, including such things as liberation and gender-based criticism; social-scientific criticism, taking its cue directly from recent work in the social sciences; and canonical criticism, directly reflecting concerns with the canon not so much in its historical dimensions but as an artifact of the Church. Only a few volumes on exegesis include discussion of these topics (see Hayes and Holladay 1987: 73-82, 110-30), although we suspect that future treatment of the subject of exegesis will need to address directly how these alternative forms of criticism have in fact become part of the mainstream (see Porter and Tombs 1995).

These criticisms deserve to have their place in the mainstream, rather than remaining on the periphery, where they are often viewed as an added extra to interesting exegesis by practitioners of more traditional methods (see Watson 1993). As the following discussion makes clear, there are a number of problem areas in traditional exegesis that these alternative forms of criticism have already or definitionally addressed, and from which traditional exegesis could rightly learn much. For example, literary criticism, as it has been appropriated for New Testament criticism, places exegetical emphasis not on historical origins, but on the final form of the text, attempting to overcome the problem of historical distance through definition.[8]

---

8   See, for example, E. Auerbach, *Mimesis: The Representation of Reality in*

Canonical criticism faces the reality that so little is known about such basic questions as the authorship of even New Testament books, and relies upon the canonical status of these books as its most important interpretative and exegetical context.[9]

ISSUES AND DIFFICULTIES ARISING OUT OF EXEGESIS

Already one can glimpse some of the issues and difficulties inherent to a discussion of the exegetical task. Clearly, reading and understanding the biblical text differs in degree and complexity from how one would read a personal letter from a close friend, the morning newspaper, or the most recent novel to appear on the book stand. A number of the major reasons for this difference in exegetical approach are briefly mentioned below.[10]

The Problem of History

By widening the exegetical task to include both what the text meant in the past and what it means in the present, one introduces a complicated dialectic that is difficult to map out. Related to this is the distinction between 'synchronic' and 'diachronic' exegetical approaches.[11] The goal of the former is to describe a text on the basis of its coherence, structure, and function as it exists in its final form. The goal of the latter is to explain the historical events and processes that brought the text to this form. Exegesis that seeks to answer what the text *means* at present is usually based upon the synchronic

---

Western Literature (trans. W.R. Trask; Princeton: Princeton University Press, 1968).

9   See, for example, B.S. Childs's canonical approach in *Introduction to the Old Testament as Scripture* (London: SCM Press, 1979); and *The New Testament as Canon: An Introduction* (Valley Forge, PA: Trinity Press International, 1994 [1984]).

10   Concerning biblical interpretation, Thiselton groups the majority of hermeneutical and exegetical difficulties into three helpful categories, including (1) the problem of historical distance between ourselves and the biblical writers, (2) problems concerning the role of theology in interpretation, and (3) problems in the relationship between hermeneutics and language (Thiselton 1980: xi, xix).

11   These words draw on the terminology of the Swiss linguist Ferdinand de Saussure (1857–1913) who is generally regarded as the father of modern linguistics. See Part 2 and Part 3 of his *Course in General Linguistics* (trans. R. Harris; London: Duckworth, 1983), pp. 99-187. The most reliable and complete edition is that by R. Engler, *Edition critique du 'Cours de linguistique générale' de F. de Saussure* (Wiesbaden: Harrassowitz, 1967).

condition of the text, that is, *what it is*. On the other hand, exegesis that concerns itself with what the text *meant* relies more heavily upon the diachronic condition of the text, that is, *how it came to be what it is* (Stenger 1993: 26).[12]

The difficulty in bridging this gap exists for a number of reasons. First, the New Testament was not originally written in or to modern society. Instead, it was addressed to specific ancient audiences such as, in the case of Luke–Acts, the individual designated Theophilus; and in the case of the Pauline letters, churches such as those in Galatia, Philippi, and Thessalonica, and individuals such as Philemon, and perhaps Timothy and Titus. Hayes and Holladay rightly state, 'as students interpreting biblical materials we are, in a sense, third-party intruders and suffer from third-party perspectives' (Hayes and Holladay 1987: 15).

Secondly, the original biblical manuscripts were composed in Hebrew, Aramaic, and Greek—all languages very different from contemporary English. Therefore, anyone who comes to the biblical text as an exegete must either rely upon second-hand translations (which are in a very real sense already interpretations) or, ideally, spend the necessary time and effort to learn these ancient languages. Even so, because these ancient languages are no longer spoken or written as they were in biblical times, they become impossible to fully master as a native speaker.

Thirdly, there is an enormous historical separation of almost two-thousand years between the New Testament authors and addressees and our present day. Although this historical distance frees the biblical texts from arbitrary interpretations and allows them to speak with their own voice, it can also prevent them from being relevant for us. Since they are objects from the past, these texts are often made to speak only to the past; therefore, they can fall silent when confronted with modern questions (Stenger 1993: 5). This separation may also result in ambiguity regarding the aims, goals, and intentions of the biblical writers and their audiences. In light of this, some even question the legitimacy of beginning exegesis with the study of the original author's intent:

---

[12]   Stenger makes the interesting point that 'The sequence of synchronic and diachronic modes of observation is not arbitrary: *Before* the question of *how the text has come to be* (diachronic study) stands the question of *what it is* at a given point in time (synchronic study)' (Stenger 1993: 26 and n. 4).

Modern critics increasingly deny the very possibility of discovering the
original, or intended, meaning of a text. The problem is that while the
original authors had a definite meaning in mind when they wrote, that is
now lost to us because they are no longer present to clarify and explain
what they wrote. The modern reader cannot study the text from the ancient
perspective but constantly reads into that passage modern perspectives.
Therefore, critics argue, objective interpretation is impossible and the
author's intended meaning is forever lost to us (Osborne 1991: 7).

Fourthly, not only is there an immense historical gap, but this
historical gap is further compounded by the huge cultural gap that
exists between the New Testament writers and modern day readers,
particularly those in western society. Customs and manners, medicine
and technology, human rights, legal codes, and world and
cosmological views—just to name a few broad cultural constructs—
are considerably different.

Fifthly, the growth and expansion of biblical traditions, the work of
later biblical editors, and the emergence of textual accretions add to
the dilemma. It is well argued that pericopes such as the Markan
resurrection narrative (Mark 16:9-20) and the woman caught in
adultery (John 7:53–8:11) are later expansions of the biblical tradition,
which appeared after the original works of the particular author.
Therefore, it becomes even more difficult to speak of the intentions of
the original writers, and this subsequently serves to further complicate
attempts at traversing the chasm that exists between what a biblical
text meant in its original setting and what it means today. Adding to
this, the oldest biblical manuscripts that we have are copies made
quite some time after the original documents were written. Of the
more than 5000 New Testament biblical manuscripts in our possession
(none of which are identical), the earliest, a small papyrus fragment
containing John 18:31-33 and John 18:37-38, dates to c. 125 CE. The
earliest complete manuscript of the New Testament, Codex Sinaiticus,
dates only to the fourth century CE.

The Problem of Presuppositions

While Lührmann explains that the basic problem of exegesis can be
framed within two questions, 'What happened?' and 'What must I
do?', he adds that one's approach to these questions is shaped by the
traditions from which one comes and in which one has learned to read
the biblical texts, and also by the discussion of these traditions and the
role which the texts play, depending on whether they are felt to be
threatening or liberating. He is correct in saying that this is above all

connected with the question of the status of the biblical texts—whether they are understood as a primary orientation for life; as legitimation of one's own, a group's, one's parents, one's community's, or one's church's ways of life, all of which are open to criticism; as part of the condition of the world in which we live; or any other possibilities one might think of (Lührmann 1989: 17-18). In making these statements, Lührmann introduces another of the difficult issues arising out of exegesis, that of the exegete's presuppositions.

Grammatico-historical exegesis has often been promoted as a method of superlative objectivity. Grammatico-historical exegetes have promoted the idea that they approach the biblical text without any prior understanding of its meaning. The mind of the interpreter is to be a 'blank tablet' (*tabula rasa*), in order that the true and genuine sense of Scripture can show through. The theory is that, by placing themselves into the context, setting, and world of the ancient authors and readers, biblical exegetes are able to view the text from the original perspective, while at the same time suppressing any modern opinions or biases that might affect their interpretation.

Desirability aside, is this type of objective exegesis attainable? In his famous essay, 'Is Interpretation without Presuppositions Possible?', Rudolf Bultmann tackles this complex question. On the one hand, he asserts that exegesis without presuppositions is not only possible but demanded if 'without presuppositions' means 'without presupposing the results of exegesis'. In other words, exegesis must be without prejudice. On the other hand, Bultmann emphasizes that

> *no* exegesis is without presuppositions, inasmuch as the exegete is not a *tabula rasa*, but on the contrary, approaches the text with specific questions or with a specific way of raising questions and thus has a certain idea of the subject matter with which the text is concerned (Bultmann 1960: 289).

The biblical text cannot be read from a neutral stance, regardless of how desirous the exegete is to accomplish this goal. Not only is every exegete determined by his or her own individuality, special biases, habits, gifts and weaknesses, but, in reading a text, the interpreter must formulate an initial understanding of what the text is saying. This must then be verified by the text itself. The reader must have at least some initial idea of or point of reference to the text and what the author is talking about before understanding can take place. Bultmann hastens to add that the historical method of exegesis in itself has several presuppositions, including the presupposition that

history is a unity in the sense of a closed continuum of effects in which
individual events are connected by the succession of cause and effect...
This closedness means that the continuum of historical happenings cannot
be rent by the interference of supernatural, transcendent powers and that
therefore there is no 'miracle' in this sense of the word. Such a miracle
would be an event whose cause did not lie within history (Bultmann 1960:
291-92).

Rather than deny one's presuppositions in the struggle to attain the
facade of ideal objectivity in exegesis, the interpreter must, in the
words of Conzelmann and Lindemann,

> ask (or be asked) about the presuppositions he brings to the text. What
> tradition is in his background? What questions does he expect the text to
> answer? Why indeed does he even deal with this text? It would be wrong
> to move the encounter between exegete and text to a 'neutral zone', as if
> there were, on the one side, a text of timeless value (at any rate) and
> devoid of history (possibly) and, on the other side, an exegete who
> approaches the text free of all presuppositions. There is no exegesis
> without presuppositions. Each interpretation is at least influenced by the
> exegete's own historical setting. Therefore, he must first of all be clear
> about the presuppositions he brings along. One should not understand this
> in terms of psychological introspection. Rather, it is essential to determine
> one's own position, so that the exegete does not yield to an inappropriate
> identification between what the text says and the exegete's predetermined
> expectations (Conzelmann and Lindemann 1988: 2).[13]

The Problem of Theology

Perhaps the most controversial current problem inherent to a
discussion of the exegetical task, and one that has already been
touched upon in the two previous sections concerning history and
presuppositions, is the question of theology and its place within
biblical interpretation. More specifically, this has been referred to as
the dilemma between descriptive (non-confessional) and prescriptive
(confessional) approaches to exegesis. That the Bible is considered by
many to be a sacred religious text hardly needs to be said. However,
for most Christian believers, this 'sacredness' implies a number of
faith assumptions: (1) in some shape or form the Bible is thought to
record the word(s) of God, (2) more so than other writings, the Bible

---

[13]　　The most influential and noteworthy twentieth-century investigation of the
role of prejudice and pre-understanding in the reading of texts is that of H.-G.
Gadamer, *Truth and Method* (New York: Crossroad; London: Sheed and Ward,
2nd edn, 1989).

is considered to embody a truer or better reflection and more accurate representation of reality, (3) the degree of authority attached to the Bible by individuals and communities supersedes that of any other literary text, and (4) the Bible is ascribed a central role in informing and guiding the faith and practice of these individuals and communities. According to a prescriptive approach to exegesis, these assumptions play at least some part in the interpretative process as exegetes seek to explain the biblical text within the context of their faith community. The task of exegesis is not simply to describe the text's historical meaning, but to stand under its authority as well. Unfortunately, this type of special hermeneutic can run the risk of ending up simply pointing out what the exegete already knew, a process often called *eisegesis* ('reading into' the text), rather than *exegesis* ('reading out from' the text). Nietzsche's forceful complaint regarding the theologian applies equally well here:

> Another mark of the theologian is his *incapacity for philology*. Philology is to be understood here in a very wide sense as the art of reading well—of being able to read off a fact *without* falsifying it by interpretation, *without* losing caution, patience, subtlety, in the desire for understanding. Philology as *ephexis* [undecisiveness] in interpretation: whether it be a question of books, newspaper reports, fate or the weather—to say nothing of the 'salvation of the soul'... The way in which a theologian, no matter whether in Berlin or in Rome, interprets a 'word of Scriptures', or an experience...is always so *audacious* as to make a philologist run up every wall in sight.[14]

The descriptive approach to exegesis is best exemplified in the grammatico-historical method's emphasis upon what the text meant. And, as we have already seen, in its attempt to place objective distance between text and reader, the basic tenets of grammatico-historical exegesis are often perceived as being in contention with the more theologically-sensitive concerns of a prescriptive approach. Some of these tenets would include (1) a tendency to emphasize what the text meant while excluding its present meaning, (2) treating the Bible in the same fashion as one would treat any other work of ancient literature, (3) a difficulty in affirming the supernatural or miraculous in the biblical text (although, it must be said, this last point applies more to certain radical forms of grammatico-historical exegesis). Perhaps the classic statement on the problem raised by descriptive

---

14   F. Nietzsche, 'The Anti-Christ', in *Twilight of the Idols and The Anti-Christ* (trans. R.J. Hollingdale; London: Penguin, 1968), pp. 169-70.

exegesis comes from Albert Schweitzer:

> The study of the Life of Jesus has had a curious history. It set out in quest
> of the historical Jesus, believing that when it had found Him it could bring
> Him straight into our time as a Teacher and Savior. It loosed the bands by
> which He had been riveted for centuries to the stony rocks of ecclesiastical
> doctrine, and rejoiced to see life and movement coming into the figure
> once more, and the historical Jesus advancing, as it seemed, to meet it. But
> He does not stay; He passes by our time and returns to His own. What
> surprised and dismayed the theology of the last forty years was that,
> despite all forced and arbitrary interpretations, it could not keep Him in
> our time, but had to let Him go. He returned to His own time, not owing to
> the application of any historical ingenuity, but by the same inevitable
> necessity by which the liberated pendulum returns to its original
> position.[15]

Not only is the Bible an ancient record of past communities, and in
this sense historical, it is also a modern record to present communities,
and in this sense theological. The distinction between the role of the
exegete as a proclaimer of what the text meant, and the role of the
theologian as a proclaimer of what the text means, illustrates the
primary issue at the heart of biblical interpretation today. As Stenger
has said, exegesis 'continually breaks its teeth on this hard nut—to the
extent that it is pursued honestly' (Stenger 1993: 7).

Like our earlier student examinee, it is easy for one to be
overwhelmed by the exegetical task, especially given the above
discussion and in light of the various difficulties that have emerged
from it. However, as Hayes and Holladay point out, one does not
approach the task of biblical exegesis *de nova*:

> Thousands of others throughout the centuries have interpreted the Bible,
> prepared tools available to the contemporary interpreter, and developed
> methods of approaching the problems and issues involved. Probably no
> other book has been so studied as the Bible, and tools for such study have
> been prepared by scholars who have spent their lives engaged in biblical
> exegesis and interpretation (Hayes and Holladay 1987: 18).

CONCLUSION

As this chapter has shown, and as is exemplified throughout this
entire book, exegesis is no one single thing, but rather a complex and

---

[15]   A. Schweitzer, *The Quest of the Historical Jesus* (London: A. & C. Black,
2nd edn, 1945), p. 397.

multifaceted collection of disciplines. The approach or orientation one takes to exegesis, which is most often determined by the particular interests of the interpreter and the questions brought to the text, may only constitute one part of the whole exegetical task. For the linguist, exegesis becomes an analysis of lexis and grammar. For the historical critic, exegesis concerns itself with uncovering ancient backgrounds and original intentions. The theologian embraces exegesis in order to aid in the contemporization of traditions and doctrines that will continually speak in a new and vital way to present believers. The fact is that there are various aspects of a text's meaning and different types of exegesis can address these various aspects. For this reason, the exegete can never hope to present *the* exegesis of a passage as if it were the final word. Rather, one does an exegesis of a passage in which a coherent and informed interpretation is presented, based upon that interpreter's encounter with and investigation of a text at a given point in time.

BIBLIOGRAPHY

Black, D.A., and D.S. Dockery (eds.)
1991   *New Testament Criticism and Interpretation.* Grand Rapids: Zondervan.
Blackman, E.C.
1954   'The Task of Exegesis', in W.D. Davies and D. Daube (eds.), *The Background of the New Testament and its Eschatology.* London: Cambridge University Press: 3-26.
1957   *Biblical Interpretation.* Philadelphia: Westminster.
Brown, R.E.
1985   *Biblical Exegesis and Church Doctrine.* New York: Paulist.
Bultmann, R.
1960   'Is Exegesis without Presuppositions Possible?', in *Existence and Faith: Shorter Writings of Rudolf Bultmann.* Trans. S.M. Ogden. Cleveland/New York: Meridian Books: 289-315.
Carson, D.A.
1996   *Exegetical Fallacies.* Grand Rapids: Baker, 2nd edn.
Carson, D.A., and J.D. Woodbridge (eds.)
1986   *Hermeneutics, Authority, and Canon.* Grand Rapids: Zondervan.
Conzelmann, H., and A. Lindemann
1988   *Interpreting the New Testament: An Introduction to the Principles and Methods of New Testament Exegesis.* Trans. S.S. Schatzmann, Peabody, MA: Hendrickson, 1985.
Danker, F.W.
1970   *Multipurpose Tools for Bible Study.* St Louis: Concordia, 3rd edn.

Doty, W.G.
1972   *Contemporary New Testament Interpretation*. Englewood Cliffs, NJ: Prentice–Hall.

Ebeling, G.
1963   *Word and Faith*. Trans. J.W. Leitch. London: SCM Press, 1963.

Epp, E.J., and G.W. MacRae (eds.)
1989   *The New Testament and its Modern Interpreters*. Philadelphia: Fortress Press.

Fee, G.D.
1993   *New Testament Exegesis: A Handbook for Students and Pastors*. Louisville: Westminster/John Knox Press, rev. edn.

Fee, G.D., and D. Stuart
1993   *How to Read the Bible for All its Worth*. Grand Rapids: Zondervan, 2nd edn.

Fitzmyer, J.A.
1981   *An Introductory Bibliography for the Study of Scripture*. Subsidia Biblica, 3. Rome: Biblical Institute Press, rev. edn.

France, R.T.
1979   *A Bibliographic Guide to New Testament Research*. Sheffield: JSOT Press, 3rd edn.

Furnish, V.P.
1973   'Some Practical Guidelines for New Testament Exegesis'. *PSTJ* 26: 1-16.

Grant, R.M., and D. Tracy
1984   *A Short History of the Interpretation of the Bible*. London: SCM Press, 2nd edn.

Hagner, D.A.
1992   *New Testament Exegesis and Research: A Guide for Seminarians*. Fuller Theological Seminary: D.A. Hagner.

Harrington, D.J.
1979   *Interpreting the New Testament: A Practical Guide*. New Testament Message, 1. Wilmington, DE: Michael Glazier.

Hayes, J.H., and C.R. Holladay
1987   *Biblical Exegesis: A Beginner's Handbook*. London: SCM Press, 2nd edn.

Kaiser, O., and W.G. Kümmel
1981   *Exegetical Method: A Student's Handbook*. Trans. E.V.N. Goetschius and M.J. O'Connell. New York: Seabury, rev. edn.

Keck, L.E., and G.M. Tucker
1976   'Exegesis'. *IDBSup*. Nashville: Abingdon: 296-303.

Kugel, J.L., and R.A. Greer
1986   *Early Biblical Interpretation*. LEC, 3. Philadelphia: Westminster.

Kümmel, W.G.
1973   *The New Testament: The History of the Investigation of its Problems*. NTL. Trans. S. McLean Gilmour and H.C. Kee. Nashville: Abingdon; London: SCM Press.

Lührmann, D.

1989 *An Itinerary for New Testament Study*. Trans. J. Bowden. London: SCM Press; Philadelphia: Trinity Press International.

McKnight, S. (ed.)

1989 *Introducing New Testament Interpretation*. Guides to New Testament Exegesis. Grand Rapids: Baker.

Malherbe, A.J.

1961 'An Introduction: The Task and Method of Exegesis'. *ResQ* 5: 169-78.

Marrow, S.B.

1978 *Basic Tools of Biblical Exegesis*. Rome: Biblical Institute Press.

Marshall, I.H. (ed.)

1979 *New Testament Interpretation: Essays on Principals and Methods*. Exeter: Paternoster.

Mays, J.L.

1960 *Exegesis as a Theological Discipline*. Richmond: Union Theological Seminary.

Mickelson, A.B.

1963 *Interpreting the Bible: A Book of Basic Principles for Understanding the Scriptures*. Grand Rapids: Eerdmans.

Morgan, R., and J. Barton

1988 *Biblical Interpretation*. Oxford: Oxford University Press.

Neill, S., and T. Wright

1988 *The Interpretation of the New Testament 1861–1986*. Oxford/New York: Oxford University Press, 2nd edn.

Osborne, G.R.

1991 *The Hermeneutical Spiral: A Comprehensive Introduction to Biblical Interpretation*. Downers Grove, IL: InterVarsity Press.

Porter, S.E., and D. Tombs (eds.)

1995 *Approaches to New Testament Study*. JSNTSup, 120. Sheffield: Sheffield Academic Press.

Reumann, J.

1969 'Methods in Studying the Biblical Text Today'. *CTM* 40: 655-81.

Riches, J.K.

1993 *A Century of New Testament Study*. Cambridge: Lutterworth.

Sandys-Wunsch, J.

1977 'On the Theory and Practice of Biblical Interpretation'. *JSOT* 3: 66-74.

Scholer, D.M.

1973 *A Basic Bibliographic Guide for New Testament Exegesis*. Grand Rapids: Eerdmans, 2nd edn.

Snodgrass, K.

1976 'Exegesis and Preaching: The Principles and Practice of Exegesis'. *The Covenant Quarterly* 34: 3-30.

Soulen, R.N.

1981 *Handbook of Biblical Criticism*. Atlanta: John Knox, 2nd edn.

Stenger, W.
1993 *Introduction to New Testament Exegesis*. Trans. D.W. Stott. Grand Rapids: Eerdmans.

Tate, W.R.
1981 *Biblical Interpretation: An Integrated Approach*. Peabody, MA: Hendrickson.

Thiselton, A.C.
1980 *The Two Horizons: New Testament Hermeneutics and Philosophical Description with Special Reference to Heidegger, Bultmann, Gadamer and Wittgenstein*. Grand Rapids: Eerdmans.

Turner, G.
1975 'Pre-Understanding and New Testament Interpretation'. *SJT* 28: 227-42.

Voelz, J.W.
1995 *What Does This Mean? Principles of Biblical Interpretation in the Post-Modern World*. Saint Louis: Concordia Publishing House.

Voss, G.
1971 'The Relationship between Exegesis and Dogmatic Theology'. *Concilium* 10: 20-29.

Wagner, G. (ed.)
1982 *An Exegetical Bibliography of the New Testament*. Macon, GA: Mercer University Press.

Watson, F. (ed.)
1993 *The Open Text: New Directions for Biblical Studies?* London: SCM Press.

THE BASIC TOOLS OF EXEGESIS OF THE NEW TESTAMENT:
A BIBLIOGRAPHICAL ESSAY

STANLEY E. PORTER

Bibliographies are helpful tools to provide acquaintance with a subject area, but they are often not as helpful in providing an idea of what a given entry might contain, or the perspective that it takes. An annotated bibliography can often be more helpful, if the comments provided are useful in describing the given sources.[1] However, there is still the question of how these resources might relate to each other, apart from simply falling into the same broad category. This bibliographical essay selects a limited number of sources for comment. It does not attempt to be exhaustive, but to be thorough enough to provide a reasonable idea of the kinds of sources available, and their strengths and limitations in relation to the other possible sources. The essay provides comments on works of exegetical method and those concerned with the basic pillars of exegesis, language and context, placing them alongside works that survey the prior history of interpretation. Sources that build upon these basic sources can be found in the individual essays in the rest of this volume.

1. EXEGETICAL METHOD

The first essay in this volume offers one perspective on the complex task of exegesis. It is notoriously difficult to define exegesis. For those who have attempted a definition of method, this definition has often been too narrow and limited, concentrating upon a restricted number of components. Sometimes these strictures have limited the usefulness of the exegetical conclusions because the methods have failed to confront important historical questions. With the advent of a greater number of critical methods, and re-assessment of the relationship between language and context (and context can be broadly defined), explicit and implicit definitions of exegesis have been reconsidered. This includes reformulating exegesis in such a way that the full range

---

[1] For one recent attempt, with reference to further sources that cannot be included in this essay, see S.E. Porter and L.M. McDonald, *New Testament Introduction* (Grand Rapids: Baker, 1995).

of interpretative models, including traditional higher criticism, have a place. Arguably the best single handbook—though fairly brief at virtually every point—is H. Conzelmann and A. Lindemann, *Interpreting the New Testament: An Introduction to the Principles and Methods of New Testament Exegesis* (trans. S.S. Schatzmann; Peabody: Hendrickson, 1988). Its major limitation is that it does not treat most of the newer methods of interpretation, but it does fully integrate the range of higher criticisms into the exegetical enterprise.

A number of guides have traditionally been available to introduce exegetical method to the student. Most of these are brief even to the point of being simplistic. One of the earliest was O. Kaiser and W.G. Kümmel, *Exegetical Method: A Student's Handbook* (trans. E.V.N. Goetchius and M.J. O'Connell; New York: Seabury, 2nd edn, 1981). It includes discussion of both Old and New Testament exegesis, and the extended example of Romans 5 for New Testament exegesis remains insightful. Similar but more recent is J.H. Hayes and C.R. Holladay, *Biblical Exegesis: A Beginner's Handbook* (Atlanta: John Knox; London: SCM Press, 2nd edn, 1987), which includes brief discussions of literary criticism, structuralism and canon, besides the standard historical criticisms. Fuller discussion of many modern interpretative methods is found in C. Tuckett, *Reading the New Testament: Methods of Interpretation* (London: SPCK, 1987), but proponents of many of these methods may not agree with all of Tuckett's descriptions and assessments. W. Stenger, *Introduction to New Testament Exegesis* (trans. D.W. Scott; Grand Rapids: Eerdmans, 1993), applies brief comments on method to ten New Testament passages, thus exemplifying exegesis. D. Lührmann, *An Itinerary for New Testament Study* (Philadelphia: Trinity Press International; London: SCM Press, 1989), is an attempt at a comprehensive guide, including discussion of several forms of theology. The discussion of exegesis is too brief to provide a useful programme, and hence may not provide the necessary foundation for doing theology. However, comments on theology are not usually found in an introduction to exegesis.

There are also several more theologically conservative guides to exegesis and New Testament interpretation, often with direct application to preaching, including G.E. Ladd, *The New Testament and Criticism* (Grand Rapids: Eerdmans, 1967), S. McKnight (ed.), *Introducing New Testament Interpretation* (Guides to New Testament Exegesis; Grand Rapids: Baker, 1989), G.D. Fee, *New Testament*

Exegesis: A Handbook for Students and Pastors (Louisville: Westminster/John Knox Press; Leominster: Gracewing, 2nd edn, 1993), and W.C. Kaiser, Jr, *Toward an Exegetical Theology: Biblical Exegesis for Preaching and Teaching* (Grand Rapids: Baker, 1981). The best such volume is probably still the one by I.H. Marshall (ed.), *New Testament Interpretation: Essays on Principles and Methods* (Grand Rapids: Eerdmans; Exeter: Paternoster, 1977), because it provides a host of excellent articles by a number of accomplished scholars, arranged in a useful format. A recent attempt to bring discussion up to date is J.B. Green (ed.), *Hearing the New Testament: Strategies for Interpretation* (Grand Rapids: Eerdmans; Exeter: Paternoster, 1995). This volume includes essays on more recent developments not included in Marshall's volume, as well as articles on the expected traditional subjects. Of many volumes in this genre (many of which are best forgotten), one further worth noting is S.L. McKenzie and S.R. Haynes (eds.), *To Each its Own Meaning: An Introduction to Biblical Criticisms and their Application* (Louisville: Westminster/John Knox Press, 1993). Very provocative, as well as highly entertaining, is D.A. Carson's *Exegetical Fallacies* (Grand Rapids: Baker, 2nd edn, 1996). He classifies a range of potential and actual exegetical mistakes under four categories—lexicography, grammar, logic and historical method. This is an intriguing book, not least because it shows how easy it is to make serious exegetical mistakes. Beware that you are not included in a subsequent edition!

2. HERMENEUTICS

One of the most important hermeneutical questions was posed by R. Bultmann in his essay 'Is Exegesis without Presuppositions Possible?', reprinted in *Existence and Faith: The Shorter Writings of R. Bultmann* (trans. S. Ogden; New York/London: Meridian, 1960), pp. 342-51. His answer was that it was not possible, which meant for him that questions of sound historical method were needed as a guard against unsupported bias. Hermeneutics is one of the fastest-changing fields in New Testament studies. What for years was simply a matter of identifying various figures of speech has become a highly technical and philosophically oriented field of discussion. Some of the technical language introduced in these areas can prove daunting, but a rigorous exegete would be well advised to consider seriously the philosophical and hermeneutical implications of the interpretative task. A reasonable guide into some of these issues is V. Brümmer, *Theology and*

Philosophical Inquiry: An Introduction (Philadelphia: Westminster Press, 1982). I limit discussion to those works that directly address New Testament interpretation.

Several of the older volumes are still of merit, including E.C. Blackman, *Biblical Interpretation* (Philadelphia: Westminster Press; London: Independent Press, 1957), who provides a useful history of interpretation; R.W. Funk, *Language, Hermeneutic and Word of God: The Problem of Language in the New Testament and Contemporary Theology* (New York: Harper & Row, 1966); and P. Stuhlmacher, *Historical Criticism and Theological Interpretation of Scripture: Toward a Hermeneutics of Consent* (trans. R.A. Harrisville; Philadelphia: Fortress Press; London: SPCK, 1977). The first is a general survey of the kinds of issues involved in hermeneutics, the second is a collection of highly influential essays, including an introduction to the so-called new hermeneutic, a theologically motivated attempt to come to terms with modern philosophical understanding of the Bible, and the third is a commendable but as yet unrealized attempt to link historical criticism and theology.

The reader would be well advised to note that the modern works on hermeneutics have largely left the earlier treatments behind, however. One of the first volumes in recent times to have a widespread influence on hermeneutical discussion was A.C. Thiselton's *The Two Horizons: New Testament Hermeneutics and Philosophical Description with Special Reference to Heidegger, Bultmann, Gadamer, and Wittgenstein* (Grand Rapids: Eerdmans; Exeter: Paternoster, 1980). This is not easy reading, and may not always seem germane to the exegetical task, but the issues raised by the various thinkers surveyed are essential ones. Thiselton has followed up this work with three others, the first written in conjunction with R. Lundin and C. Walhout, *The Responsibility of Hermeneutics* (Grand Rapids: Eerdmans; Exeter: Paternoster, 1985); the second his *New Horizons in Hermeneutics: The Theory and Practice of Transforming Biblical Reading* (Grand Rapids: Zondervan; London: HarperCollins, 1992), a volume that advances his own interpretative model based upon speech-act theory, a method from recent discussion in linguistic pragmatics; and the third his *Interpreting God and the Postmodern Self: On Meaning, Manipulation and Promise* (Edinburgh: T. & T. Clark, 1995). Thiselton offers many provocative interpretations of many of the most important thinkers on hermeneutics for New Testament exegesis. Also of importance is P. Ricoeur's *Essays on*

Biblical Interpretation (ed. L.S. Mudge; Philadelphia: Fortress Press, 1980), a collection of essays by the French philosopher and literary critic that offers his thoughts on the complexities of biblical interpretation. W. Jeanrond, in *Text and Interpretation as Categories of Theological Thinking* (trans. T.J. Wilson; New York: Crossroad; Dublin: Gill and Macmillan, 1988), offers a highly sensible approach to interpretation, appreciating the processes of textual production and reception, and favoring a textually-based linguistic approach. His *Theological Hermeneutics: Development and Significance* (New York: Crossroad, 1991) develops the theological element of hermeneutics. A quick way into some of the discussion is to be found in the collection of important essays by major writers on the subject, compiled by D.K. McKim (ed.), *A Guide to Contemporary Hermeneutics: Major Trends in Biblical Interpretation* (Grand Rapids: Eerdmans, 1986).

A number of student-oriented introductions to hermeneutics have been recently published. Some of them offer overviews of some of the major issues, often with a distinct slant towards practical exegesis. Volumes that merit mention are those by W.W. Klein, C.L. Blomberg, and R.L. Hubbard with K.A. Ecklebarger, *Introduction to Biblical Interpretation* (Dallas: Word, 1992), a highly practical and common-sensical approach to the subject; G.D. Fee and D. Stuart, *How to Read the Bible for All its Worth: A Guide to Understanding the Bible* (Grand Rapids: Zondervan, 2nd edn, 1993), a genre based discussion that perhaps errs on the side of simplicity; W.R. Tate, *Biblical Interpretation: An Integrated Approach* (Peabody: Hendrickson, 1991), reflecting a literary-critical perspective; and G.R. Osborne, *The Hermeneutical Spiral: A Comprehensive Introduction to Biblical Interpretation* (Downers Grove: InterVarsity, 1991), an exhaustive study that is not always clear on where it comes down on a given issue. A major shortcoming of many of these student-oriented volumes is their tendency to be reductionistic, making it seem as if many of the issues of interpretation are more easily solved than they really are.

3. GREEK LANGUAGE AND LINGUISTICS

The study of the Greek language has made major advances in the last decade, although many of them are still unknown to exegetes. Much of this advance has been predicated upon a re-thinking of previous assumptions in the study of Greek, along with attempts to integrate the best findings of modern linguistic study into an area that has traditionally been controlled by classical philology. The shift has been away from a prescriptive approach based upon only the best literary texts toward description of how language is used in a variety of contexts, especially those that reflect the language of everyday use, such as the documentary papyri of the period. One of the first articles to discuss the place of modern linguistics in biblical exegesis was E.A. Nida, 'The Implications of Contemporary Linguistics for Biblical Scholarship', *JBL* 91 (1972), pp. 73-89. This has now been developed, reflecting more recent research, in S.E. Porter, 'Studying Ancient Languages from a Modern Linguistic Perspective: Essential Terms and Terminology', *FN* 1 (1989), pp. 147-72. There is much work still to be done, and a number of traditional reference tools in the area do not reflect much current thinking. Nevertheless, knowledge of the language of the original text is vitally important for serious exegesis.

There are numerous introductory textbooks available for those who have not yet begun the study of Greek.[2] The basics of the language are, of course, assumed in exegesis of the Greek text, and so discussion here will consider those works that have direct exegetical value. The best book to date on a linguistic approach to exegesis of the Bible, including the New Testament, is probably P. Cotterell and M. Turner, *Linguistics and Biblical Interpretation* (Downers Grove: InterVarsity; London: SPCK, 1989). This volume places linguistic discussion within the demands of the larger hermeneutical task, a framework from which many interpreters could rightly benefit. Also of some value are G.B. Caird, *The Language and Imagery of the Bible* (Philadelphia: Westminster Press; London: Duckworth, 1980), and D.A. Black, *Linguistics for Students of New Testament Greek: A Survey of Basic Concepts and Applications* (Grand Rapids: Baker, 1988). The first volume takes a more common-sense approach to linguistics than many linguists are happy with, and the second is for intermediate level students.

Most will be familiar with the basic grammatical reference tools for the study of the Greek language, but some comment on their relative merit and usefulness may be in order in light of recent linguistic developments. The oldest of the reference grammars still found in regular use is G.B. Winer's, originally published in German early last

---

2   These are surveyed in S.E. Porter, 'Tense Terminology and Greek Language Study: A Linguistic Re-Evaluation', in his *Studies in the Greek New Testament: Theory and Practice* (SBG, 5; New York: Lang, 1996), pp. 39-48.

century and revised several times. It appears in three translations still to be found: *A Treatise on the Grammar of New Testament Greek Regarded as a Sure Basis for New Testament Exegesis* (trans. W.F. Moulton; Edinburgh: T. & T. Clark, 3rd edn, 1882), the mostly widely used, *A Grammar of the New Testament Diction* (trans. E. Masson; Edinburgh: T. & T. Clark, 6th edn, 1866) and *A Grammar of the Idiom of the New Testament* (trans. J.H. Thayer; Andover: Draper, 1870). Winer's grammar reflects a highly logical and rationalistic approach to Greek, in which, for example, a particular tense-form is to be rigidly equated with a particular temporal value. The most widely used reference grammar for the study of the Greek of the New Testament is that of F. Blass and A. Debrunner, originally published by Blass in 1896 and immediately translated into English (*Grammar of New Testament Greek* [trans. J.H. Thayer; London: Macmillan, 1898]). To be preferred is the English translation of the revised tenth edition: *A Greek Grammar of the New Testament and Other Early Christian Literature* (trans. R.W. Funk; Chicago: University of Chicago Press, 1961). The work is still in print in German, edited by F. Rehkopf as *Grammatik des neutestamentlichen Griechisch* (Göttingen: Vandenhoeck & Ruprecht, 17th edn, 1990). It reflects the classical philological thinking of late last century, and tends to dwell on points where the Greek of the New Testament differs from classical Greek. This arbitrary enhancement of classical Greek has a tendency to skew one's perspective negatively against the Greek of the New Testament. In contrast to this approach, J.H. Moulton began his *Grammar of New Testament Greek* early in the century. He introduced to the English-speaking world several important grammatical developments, such as the role that the papyri discovered in Egypt might have in understanding linguistic phenomena in the New Testament, and the category of 'kind of action' (*Aktionsart*) over 'time of action' in discussing the Greek verb. Moulton finished his *Prolegomena* (Edinburgh: T. & T. Clark, 1906; 3rd edn, 1908), but W.F. Howard was enlisted after Moulton's untimely death to finish the second volume, *Accidence and Word-Formation, with an Appendix on Semitisms in the New Testament* (Edinburgh: T. & T. Clark, 1929). Whereas Moulton was quite progressive in his approach, the remaining volumes of the grammar were completed by N. Turner, who had a different approach, treating the Greek of the New Testament as a form of Semitized Greek: *Syntax* (Edinburgh: T. & T. Clark, 1963) and *Style* (Edinburgh: T. & T. Clark, 1976). The largest

Greek grammar, and similar to the perspective of Moulton, is that of A.T. Robertson, *A Grammar of the Greek New Testament in the Light of Historical Research* (Nashville: Broadman, 4th edn, 1934). Although in the course of exegesis one should consult these grammars, one must also be aware that the linguistic perspective represented is now seriously outmoded in light of recent developments in Greek grammar and linguistics. Many areas have benefited from this recent research, such as study of verb tense and mood, phrase structure, and the case system, to name only a few.

There have been a number of intermediate level and handbook-style grammars that have appeared on the market as well. These are designed not only for instructional purposes but for providing a quick survey of a given topic. Three of the earlier grammars are H.E. Dana and J.R. Mantey, *A Manual Grammar of the Greek New Testament* (Toronto: Macmillan, 1927), which is patterned after Robertson's grammar, C.F.D. Moule, *An Idiom Book of New Testament Greek* (Cambridge: Cambridge University Press, 1957; 2nd edn, 1959), and M. Zerwick, *Biblical Greek Illustrated by Examples* (trans. J. Smith; Rome: Pontifical Biblical Institute, 1963). Of the three, Moule's provides the discussion of the most examples and often illustrates their exegetical significance, while Zerwick has the most informed linguistic perspective, and is particularly insightful in his discussion of the Greek verb. More recent works of this sort include J.A. Brooks and C.L. Winbery, *Syntax of New Testament Greek* (Washington, DC: University Press of America, 1979), R.A. Young, *Intermediate New Testament Greek: A Linguistic and Exegetical Approach* (Nashville: Broadman, 1994), S.E. Porter, *Idioms of the Greek New Testament* (Biblical Languages: Greek, 2; Sheffield: JSOT Press, 1992; 2nd edn, 1994), and D.B. Wallace, *Greek Grammar beyond the Basics* (Grand Rapids: Zondervan, 1996). Brooks and Winbery adopt a very traditional approach, with endorsement of a form of sentence diagramming, while Wallace almost shuns advances in modern linguistics. Porter and Young integrate insights from recent linguistic research into their approach, such as on Greek verb structure and discourse analysis.

Experienced exegetes may be aware of many of the Greek grammars mentioned above but may still be unaware of the many important monographs that address specific topics in the study of the Greek of the New Testament. In the same way that thorough exegesis of matters of context requires consultation with specialist monographs, so does Greek language research require study of monographs on pertinent topics, not simply reference to standard grammars. Still important and not yet surpassed is M.E. Thrall's *Greek Particles in the New Testament: Linguistic and Exegetical Studies* (NTTS, 3; Leiden: Brill, 1962), although it reflects a classical-philology approach. N. Turner's *Grammatical Insights into the New Testament* (Edinburgh: T. & T. Clark, 1965) offers occasional exegetically stimulating perspectives on difficult passages. Discussion of select exegetically-significant passages is found in S.E. Porter, *Studies in the Greek New Testament: Theory and Practice* (SBG, 5; New York: Lang, 1996). The influence of the modern linguist Noam Chomsky can be seen in the work of D.D. Schmidt, *Hellenistic Greek Grammar and Noam Chomsky: Nominalizing Transformations* (SBLDS, 62; Atlanta: Scholars Press, 1981), and M. Palmer, *Levels of Constituent Structure in New Testament Greek* (SBG, 4; New York: Lang, 1995). There are other monographs of importance, but these reflect some of the most important that should be consulted in the course of exegesis.

The area where there has been more work than any other, however, is in the study of the Greek verb (see the Chapter on the Greek Language for further discussion). An early study that still has merit is that of E.D.W. Burton, *Syntax of the Moods and Tenses in New Testament Greek* (Chicago: University of Chicago Press, 3rd edn, 1900). His discussion includes many useful insights into Greek verb structure, although it is written outside of the parameters of modern linguistic study. More recently, there have been several monographs that have addressed the question of the relation of Greek verbs to time and to the kind of action they describe. The first monograph in English on this topic was by S.E. Porter, *Verbal Aspect in the Greek of the New Testament, with Reference to Tense and Mood* (SBG, 1; New York: Lang, 1989), followed soon after by B.M. Fanning, *Verbal Aspect in New Testament Greek* (OTM; Oxford: Clarendon Press, 1990), and then by K.L. McKay, *A New Syntax of the Verb in New Testament Greek: An Aspectual Approach* (SBG, 5; New York: Lang, 1993). Although each of these monographs concludes slightly differently regarding the question of how the verbs function in Greek, they are all agreed that the category of verbal aspect is important and needs to be studied further. Verbal aspect is concerned with depicting events as they appear to the language user, rather than relating them to some objective kind of action (or time). A summary of this discussion is found in S.E. Porter and D.A. Carson (eds.), *Greek Language and Linguistics: Open Questions in Current Research* (JSNTSup, 80; Sheffield: JSOT Press, 1993), pp. 18-82. These sources should be consulted, along with the standard reference grammars, when discussing linguistic issues in exegesis of the Greek text.

A further important area of investigation is the area of semantics, or meaning as mediated through language. This is a multi-faceted area that can be extended to include almost every dimension of language use, but is often constricted to the area of lexicography, including dictionary making. J.P. Louw has written a useful introduction to the wider topic of meaning in language, *Semantics of New Testament Greek* (Philadelphia: Fortress Press; Chico: Scholars Press, 1982). Traditional lexicography has often been concerned to provide translational equivalents or glosses for the words of Greek, arranged in alphabetical order. The most widely-used of these lexicons is W. Bauer, *A Greek–English Lexicon of the New Testament and Other Early Christian Literature* (trans. and rev. W.F. Arndt, F.W. Gingrich, and F.W. Danker; Chicago: University of Chicago Press, rev. edn, 1979). This lexicon has many inconsistencies, many of them forced on it by traditional lexicography, including the failure to relate words to each other, but it is full of useful references to extra-biblical Greek examples for comparison. On a smaller scale, with clear reference to the Septuagint, is G. Abbott-Smith, *A Manual Greek Lexicon of the New Testament* (Edinburgh: T. & T. Clark, 3rd edn, 1937). Less useful because it pre-dates appropriation of insights from the Greek papyri, but still cited, is J.H. Thayer, *A Greek–English Lexicon of the New Testament* (New York: American Book Company, 1886). Still of great value because of the evidence from the papyri that is brought to bear on understanding the vocabulary of the New Testament is J.H. Moulton and G. Milligan, *The Vocabulary of the Greek Testament Illustrated from the Papyri and Other Non-Literary Sources* (London: Hodder & Stoughton, 1929). This reference volume makes it clear that understanding of the Greek of the New Testament is enhanced when it is considered within the wider framework of Greek usage of the time.

New Testament lexicography took a sizable step forward, however, with publication of a new form of lexicon based upon semantic fields or domains: J.P. Louw and E.A. Nida (eds.), *Greek–English Lexicon of the New Testament based on Semantic Domains* (2 vols.; New York: United Bible Societies, 1988). Realizing that words are not learned, retained or used in alphabetical order, but rather in relation to other words of related meaning in the language, this lexicon categorizes words according to approximately forty different areas of meaning. One can now see how individual words relate to other words within the same sphere of meaning. In response to criticism (much of it unmerited), the principles of this lexicon are more fully discussed in E.A. Nida and J.P. Louw, *Lexical Semantics of the Greek New Testament* (SBLRBS, 25; Atlanta: Scholars Press, 1992). A basic introduction to the larger topic of semantics is M. Silva, *Biblical Words and their Meaning: An Introduction to Lexical Semantics* (Grand Rapids: Zondervan, rev. edn, 1994). This work relies heavily upon much of the standard theory in lexical semantics in linguistic circles, and is useful for study of the New Testament as well as the Septuagint.

Theological lexicography is a topic that is sometimes introduced into exegesis of the New Testament. Arising out of the Biblical Theology movement earlier in this century, most theological lexicography attempts to link theological concepts with individual words in the language, with the unfortunate result that, often, particular words are said to have special theological meaning in and of themselves and in virtually all contexts. The most widely promoted form of theological lexicography was found in G. Kittel and G. Friedrich (eds.), *Theological Dictionary of the New Testament* (10 vols.; trans. G.W. Bromiley; Grand Rapids: Eerdmans, 1964–76). Apart from providing important lists of extra-biblical references, this source should be avoided for discussion of meaning, in particular in the earlier volumes. Somewhat similar is H. Balz and G. Schneider (eds.), *Exegetical Dictionary of the New Testament* (3 vols.; Grand Rapids: Eerdmans; Edinburgh: T. & T. Clark, 1990–93). C. Spicq, *Theological Lexicon of the New Testament* (3 vols.; trans. J.D. Ernest; Peabody: Hendrickson, 1994), concentrates on New Testament usage, with valuable extra-biblical references. Probably best of this kind of resource is C. Brown (ed.), *The New International Dictionary of New Testament Theology* (4 vols.; Grand Rapids: Zondervan; Exeter: Paternoster, 1975–79), because it is categorized by English concepts, and hence includes a number of Greek words under one general heading. The nadir of this method was perhaps reached in N. Turner, *Christian Words* (Edinburgh: T. & T. Clark, 1980), where he tried to argue on often thin evidence that there was a sizable category of distinctly Christian words. This entire approach has been soundly and rightly criticized by a number of scholars, including J. Barr, *The*

Semantics of Biblical Language (Oxford: Oxford University Press, 1961) and A. Gibson, *Biblical Semantic Logic* (Oxford: Blackwell, 1979). They have shown that there are many persistent logical and linguistic flaws in trying to get meaning out of the history or supposed theological essence of a word, or in trying to transfer one theological meaning to all uses of a word. These critical sources, especially the first, are often cited, but it is still surprising how many such abuses of exegetical method still persist.

4. CONTEXT AND INTERPRETATION

The study of context includes both immediate and remote context, as well as the history of antecedent and ongoing interpretation. Context is an especially difficult concept to define, since it can include such minute structures as a particular place in a letter and such expansive issues as an entire cultural background. In any event, context constitutes one of the major pillars of exegesis. Many of the following chapters in this volume provide useful guides to the topics involved in the study of context, and provide indications of bibliographic resources available in these areas. In this bibliographical essay, several more general sources are discussed. These include volumes that discuss the history of biblical interpretation, and introductions to the New Testament.

A. *History of Interpretation*

The history of New Testament interpretation is often neglected in exegesis, especially much exegesis that purports to return to the original languages and the original text. There is a persistent (mistaken) belief in some circles that one can return to the original text, unaffected by all previous interpretation, and without the influence of modern interpretative constructs. One small example illustrates how fallacious such thinking can be. Much of twentieth-century Pauline interpretation is still conducted as a reaction to the radical re-assessment of the history of the early Church proposed by F.C. Baur. Even those who know something of the history of recent interpretation, however, often overlook earlier periods of thought, such as medieval exegesis.

The most useful guide to recent interpretation is by E.J. Epp and G. MacRae (eds.), *The New Testament and its Modern Interpreters* (Atlanta: Scholars Press, 1989). For the most part, they provide excellent surveys of a host of areas of interpretation in contemporary

New Testament study, along with useful and often extensive bibliographies. There are also a number of earlier works that deal with the history of interpretation. They obviously do not deal with very recent developments, but they are often useful guides to the kinds of questions that were being asked in previous eras of interpretation. One often finds that many of the issues currently being debated have long histories of previous discussion. Some of the more valuable earlier volumes include: M. Jones, *The New Testament in the Twentieth Century* (London: Macmillan, 1924), who discusses the effects of higher criticism on New Testament study, and A.M. Hunter, *Interpreting the New Testament: 1900–1950* (London: SCM Press, 1951), a brief but competent study of the first half of the century, a time vital for development in New Testament studies. There are also a number of more recent treatments of similar issues. For example, W.G. Kümmel, *The New Testament: The History of the Investigation of its Problems* (trans. S.McL. Gilmour and H.C. Kee; Nashville: Abingdon, 1972), offers a detailed compendium of the issues from a distinctly German perspective. His treatment is to be contrasted with that of S. Neill and T. Wright, *The Interpretation of the New Testament 1861–1986* (Oxford: Oxford University Press, 1988), probably the best overview of the topic for the period discussed, although admittedly concentrating on British scholars such as Lightfoot, Westcott and Hort (who can blame them?). Also to be noted are W.G. Doty, *Contemporary New Testament Interpretation* (Englewood Cliffs, NJ: Prentice–Hall, 1972), who discusses more recent trends (at least for that time); R.M. Grant, *A Short History of the Interpretation of the Bible* (Philadelphia: Fortress Press; London: SPCK, 2nd edn with D. Tracy, 1984), a solid short account; B. Lindars on the New Testament in J. Rogerson, C. Rowland, and B. Lindars, *The Study and Use of the Bible* (History of Christian Theology, 2; Grand Rapids: Eerdmans; Basingstoke: Marshall Pickering, 1988); J.C. O'Neill, *The Bible's Authority: A Portrait Gallery of Thinkers from Lessing to Bultmann* (Edinburgh: T. & T. Clark, 1991), who selects a number of individuals for discussion; W. Baird, *History of New Testament Research*. I. *From Deism to Tübingen* (Minneapolis: Fortress Press, 1992), who intriguingly surveys this important early period; and J.K. Riches, *A Century of New Testament Study* (Cambridge: Lutterworth, 1993), which is quite a selective account. The most up-to-date recent account of the rise of modern biblical interpretation, with discussion of several of the recent critical approaches, such as literary criticism and social-scientific criticism, is R. Morgan with J. Barton, *Biblical Interpretation* (Oxford Bible Series; Oxford: Oxford University Press, 1988).

Discussion of earlier biblical interpretation is found in J.L. Kugel and R.A. Greer, *Early Biblical Interpretation* (LEC, 3; Philadelphia: Westminster Press, 1986), in which Greer emphasizes the development of biblical interpretation in the Church Fathers; and K. Froehlich (trans. and ed.), *Biblical Interpretation in the Early Church* (Sources of Early Christian Thought; Philadelphia: Fortress Press, 1984), a useful sourcebook of texts from the early Church.

Surveys of the history of interpretation can serve several useful purposes. For example, they can provide a way into the major intellectual movements that governed the development of various critical perspectives. Furthermore, they can push the reader to explore more detailed accounts of the period or people involved. Perhaps most importantly, however, knowledge of the history of interpretation can help exegetes to avoid making some of the same exegetical mistakes of past interpreters.

B. New Testament Introductions

A final category of bibliography for discussion is the New Testament introduction. The introduction has become a genre in its own right, and one that should not be neglected in exegesis of the New Testament. A good introduction should be able to provide relevant and useful material on the context for the interpretation of a given book, besides establishing the foundation of the biblical documents themselves. It should also include pertinent and relatively current discussion of the major critical issues relevant to study of a given book, and some idea of the various critical methods available for discussion of these issues. Utilizing a New Testament introduction is, of course, not a substitute for full and complete investigation of each of the issues of introduction to be discussed for a given book of the New Testament. Nevertheless, an introduction can often provide a basic framework for understanding the kinds of issues that should be brought to bear in informed exegesis.

New Testament introductions come in a variety of sizes, shapes, lengths and amounts of detail. Reading them soon makes clear that it is difficult to be as inclusive as is needed within the confines of a single volume (or even two). The result is that authors of introductions often reveal a particular perspective. For example, some of them emphasize the Jewish origins and background to the New Testament, while others stress the Greco-Roman context. Some focus almost exclusively upon particular issues related to the given New Testament books, while others introduce a number of important background issues, such as cultural context or canonical formation. Theological perspectives are also often revealed in these introductions, and these almost assuredly have an influence upon a number of critical issues, such as chronology and authorship. The following discussion divides them according to the amount and kind of detail that they provide.

The introductions that will probably be of the most consistent exegetical help are those that have the most detail, including reference to pertinent secondary scholarly literature. There are a number of introductions here that merit examination. H. Koester has written an *Introduction to the New Testament* (2 vols.; Philadelphia: Fortress Press; Berlin and New York: de Gruyter, 1982). The first volume is concerned with the history, culture and religion of the Hellenistic world, and provides useful background information for the interpretation of the New Testament. The second volume treats the history and literature of the New Testament, including apocryphal and pseudepigraphal works. The perspective is that of rigorous German higher criticism, and therefore it is highly predictable (and somewhat skeptical), but it is nevertheless very valuable for understanding the growth and development of the New Testament writings, especially in relation to other sacred literature of the first few centuries, according to this perspective. A far more concise but equally valuable volume is W.G. Kümmel's *Introduction to the New Testament* (trans. H.C. Kee; Nashville: Abingdon; London: SCM Press, 1975). This volume reflects a more moderate German critical perspective. For the most part, the arguments and weighing of them is very fair. From a more conservative British perspective is D. Guthrie's *New Testament Introduction* (Downers Grove and Leicester: InterVarsity, 3rd edn, 1970). This massive volume provides thorough discussion of the various arguments on such issues as authorship, date, opponents, etc. There are also valuable supplemental essays on such things as the Synoptic problem. Even though one can often anticipate Guthrie's conclusions, the marshaling and weighing of arguments is probably the best to be found in a New Testament introduction. None of the introductions above includes discussion of more recent critical methods.

Four other introductions may well prove useful to exegetes. L.T. Johnson has written a highly readable and independent-minded volume, *The Writings of the New Testament: An Interpretation* (Philadelphia: Fortress Press; London: SCM Press, 1986). Johnson does not discuss all of the issues in as much detail as such a volume as Guthrie's does, but he does introduce both historical and theological issues, since he believes that a presentation of the former is inadequate without being informed by the latter. D.A. Carson, D.J. Moo and L. Morris's *An Introduction to the New Testament* (Grand Rapids: Zondervan, 1992) is theologically conservative in its conclusions, but does make useful reference to much primary and secondary literature. Also to be considered is L.M. McDonald and S.E. Porter, *Early Christianity and its Sacred Literature* (Peabody: Hendrickson, forthcoming), a full introduction with reference to much contemporary discussion. B.S. Childs has written an introduction from his canonical-critical perspective in *The New Testament as Canon: An Introduction* (London: SCM Press, 1984; Philadelphia: Fortress Press, 1985). No matter what one thinks of Childs's approach to interpretation, his bibliography and historical survey of the exegetical issues for any given book of the New Testament are worth consulting.

There are several older introductions that should be regularly consulted, because they often marshal incredible amounts of evidence and include detailed argumentation on a given topic. They also show that many of the arguments regarding various positions, such as authorship, have not progressed very far in the last century. Four older introductions are of special note. B. Weiss, *A Manual of Introduction to the New Testament* (2 vols.; trans. A.J.K. Davidson; London: Hodder & Stoughton, 1887), shows an excellent grasp of the primary sources and does not hesitate to use them. T. Zahn, *Introduction to the New Testament* (3 vols.; trans. J.M. Trout *et al.*; ed. M.W. Jacobus; New York: Scribners; Edinburgh: T. & T. Clark, 1909), wrote a massive introduction to stand against the onslaught of F.C. Baur and his followers. G. Milligan, *The New Testament Documents: Their Origin and Early History* (London: Macmillan, 1913), was one of the first to introduce the papyrus finds from Egypt into discussion of New Testament introduction, and hence treats such topics as Greek letter form, one of the first such discussions. Lastly, J. Moffatt, *An Introduction to the Literature of the New Testament* (Edinburgh: T. & T. Clark, 3rd edn, 1918), still provides excellent summaries of the issues, supported from early sources.

Several more modest introductions, some of them written by scholars significant for the history of exegesis, are worth consulting on various individual points. For example, G. Bornkamm's *The New Testament: A Guide to its Writings* (trans. R.H. Fuller and I. Fuller; Philadelphia: Fortress Press, 1973) provides a brief introduction that deals with critical methods. W.D. Davies's *Invitation to the New Testament: A Guide to its Main Witnesses* (Garden City: Doubleday, 1965; repr. Sheffield: JSOT Press, 1993), as the title implies, does not discuss the entire New Testament, but does cover a considerable important part of it. M. Dibelius, *A Fresh Approach to the New Testament and Early Christian Literature* (New York: Scribners, 1936), is of interest to those who wish to trace the origins of form criticism, since he was so important in its development. E.J. Goodspeed, *An Introduction to the New Testament* (Chicago: University of Chicago Press, 1937), provides a volume important in the history of interpretation, especially because of his views of the formation of the Pauline letter corpus at the end of the first century. A.M. Hunter's *Introducing the New Testament* (London: SCM Press; Philadelphia: Westminster Press, 3rd edn, 1972), though dated now, is an excellent first volume for someone unfamiliar with what New Testament introductions are. A.F.J. Klijn, *Introduction to the New Testament* (trans. M. van der Vathorst-Smit; Leiden: Brill, 1980), provides a useful overview of the topic. H. Lietzmann, *The Beginnings of the Christian Church* (trans. B.L. Woolf; 2 vols.; Cambridge: J. Clarke, repr. edn, 1993), is a highly informative introduction by a master of the field of early Christianity. His two volumes take the reader deep into the development of the early Church and the Church Fathers. This source is often neglected, but has a solid linguistic and cultural-historical foundation. E. Lohse, *The New Testament Environment* (trans. J.E. Steely; Nashville: Abingdon; London: SCM Press, 1976), provides an excellent volume on the history and context of early Christianity, and W. Marxsen, *Introduction to the New Testament: An Approach to its Problems* (trans. G. Buswell; Philadelphia: Fortress Press, 1968), provides a very useful introduction to the Greco-Roman background to the New Testament. C.F.D. Moule's *The Birth of the New Testament* (San Francisco: Harper & Row, 3rd edn, 1981; London: A. & C. Black, 3rd edn, 1982) is not a typical introduction, but weaves an intriguing and informative story of the development of the New Testament. N. Perrin, *The New Testament, An Introduction: Proclamation and Parenesis, Myth and History* (rev. D.C. Duling; New York: Harcourt, Brace, Jovanovich, rev. edn, 1982), introduced a fairly radical critical perspective that is retained in this revised edition. A. Wikenhauser, *New Testament Introduction* (trans. J. Cunningham; New York: Herder & Herder; Edinburgh: Nelson, 1958), offers a traditional German Roman Catholic viewpoint, which is well written and sharply focused on the important issues. These very brief summaries make it clear that there are many varying perspectives available in this genre. An exegete would not necessarily want to and certainly would not need to consult all of them to have gained a sufficient grasp of the issues of context in interpretation of the New Testament.

There are also a number of volumes that have individual features that may prove useful. For example, R.F. Collins's *Introduction to the New Testament* (Garden City: Doubleday, 1983) has lengthy introductions to various dimensions of critical methodology, including such things as structuralism. D. Ewert's *From Ancient Tablets to Modern Translations: A General Introduction to the Bible* (Grand Rapids: Zondervan, 1983) provides a lengthy discussion of modern translations. Since translations are important tools in reflecting exegetical understanding, Ewert's assessment of the principles and practices of various translations is much to be welcomed. H.C. Kee's *Understanding the New Testament* (Englewood Cliffs, NJ: Prentice–Hall, 5th edn, 1993) provides useful information on the social context of the beginnings of Christianity. R.P. Martin (*New Testament Foundations* [2 vols.; Grand Rapids: Eerdmans; Exeter: Paternoster, 1975, 1978]) has written two volumes, the first on the Gospels and the second on the rest of the New Testament. There is a wealth of information on topics sometimes not discussed in New Testament introductions, geared for students. J.A.T. Robinson, *Redating the New Testament* (Philadelphia: Westminster Press; London: SCM Press, 1976), is highly concerned with establishing an early (pre 70 CE) date for all of the books of the New Testament, managing to raise along the way most of the important issues of New Testament introduction. C. Rowland's *Christian Origins: From Messianic Movement to Christian Religion* (London: SPCK; Minneapolis: Augsburg, 1985) argues that Jewish life and thought, especially apocalyptic, were clearly the formative influence on early Christianity.

5. CONCLUSION

There are numerous other volumes that could be included in the categories above (new ones are being published all the time), as well as many further categories for potential discussion, such as commentaries. I do not need to list them here, except to say that I do not consider them to be as fundamental to entrance into the exegetical task as have been the works above. That is, of course, not to say that they are unimportant. However, they can more easily and more appropriately be discussed at other points in this volume. This essay provides a starting point for the basic tools of exegesis. In the course of exegesis of a text, there are recurring issues that demand more thorough critical attention. The above sources provide a means of gaining access to many of the more important sources in this discussion. The rest of this volume provides further, more detailed discussion at a number of crucial points, with reference to further bibliography.

PART ONE

METHOD

TEXTUAL CRITICISM IN THE EXEGESIS OF THE NEW TESTAMENT, WITH AN EXCURSUS ON CANON

ELDON JAY EPP

THE ROLE OF TEXTUAL CRITICISM IN NEW TESTAMENT INTERPRETATION

In the broad sweep of biblical interpretation, textual criticism logically and traditionally has preceded 'higher criticism'; hence, textual criticism is known as 'lower criticism'—though these two hierarchical terms, while instructive, are no longer widely used. 'Higher criticism' encompasses all other forms of biblical criticism, interpretation, and exegesis; during the modern period, it culminated in source, form, and redaction criticism and has mushroomed in recent decades as several new modes of criticism and interpretation have emerged, most notably perhaps the various rhetorical, literary, ideological, and sociological methodologies employed to illuminate and interact with the New Testament texts.

This accumulation of interpretative methodologies over the past century and a half has increasingly pushed textual criticism into the background of the exegetical process when, in fact, no hermeneutical procedure that takes seriously the ancient New Testament text can logically or legitimately do so. Part of this eclipse is due to the 'information explosion', which has constantly pushed scholars toward greater specialization and, in turn, toward an increasing neglect of specializations not their own, especially ones as complex as textual criticism. As a result, only a minority of commentators on New Testament writings, for example, *independently* treat text-critical issues in the texts they interpret; rather, if they explore textual variations at all, many rely on the data provided and even the decisions made for them by the popular critical hand-editions of the Greek New Testament, the Nestle–Aland Greek text (27th edn, 1993) and that of the United Bible Societies (4th edn, 1993), both with the same text, but with varying apparatuses of variant readings. In addition to these excellent resources, exegetes commonly, and wisely, use the companion volume to the latter text, *A Textual Commentary on the Greek New Testament* (Metzger [ed.] 1994), which provides text-critical analyses of some 2,050 sets of variation units in the New

Testament that are of both textual and exegetical significance.

That this is a realistic assessment of the use—or non-use—of textual criticism in New Testament scholarship is confirmed by a perusal of the hundreds upon hundreds of books and articles that appear annually on myriad topics across the vast range of New Testament studies, including investigations of the historical Jesus, treatments of biblical theology, literary and sociological studies, and even commentaries, to mention only a few broad categories. How many of these, after all, move beyond the text presented in Nestle–Aland and the *UBSGNT*? How many pause to consider the options and probabilities concerning what the author most likely wrote or, as we usually say, the most likely 'original' text of passages under study? How many stop to ask how the other readings in a given variation unit might disclose different socio-cultural contexts and various ancient interpretations of that text?

Text-critical specialists will have mixed feelings about the shortcuts and compromises made by many exegetes. On the one hand, they will applaud at every turn the utilization of textual variants in interpreting crucial passages, while, on the other, lament the pandemic lack of serious engagement with the theory and principles of New Testament textual criticism, and the consequent infrequence of independent text-critical judgments. Textual critics, of course, are well aware that neither they nor those who emphasize one or another of the numerous sub-specialties in New Testament criticism can master everything, and will continue to offer the requisite handbooks with their principles and examples, all the while hoping to draw more exegetes into those substantive text-critical discussions that would not only enlighten but enliven their interpretative endeavors.

This may appear to be a highly arrogant view of the current situation—a view of textual criticism as a basic discipline that all exegetes should ideally master, yet as an esoteric field that only an elite few will be willing or able to comprehend, let alone practice. In adopting such a stance, are not textual critics isolating themselves and, in the process, encouraging exegetes to ignore them? While discussing the merits and demerits of basic text-critical theory and debating the validity of criteria for determining the priority of readings, should textual critics not be more attentive to the practical needs of exegetes? Should they not be more eager to be servants of exegesis by providing, for example, compendia of predigested decisions on hundreds of variation units?

A quick example may suggest an answer. Mark's opening words as usually given, 'The beginning of the gospel of Jesus Christ, the Son of God', veil a rather evenly divided textual tradition regarding these divine titles. On one hand, Codex Sinaiticus (ℵ) and others have the full phrase, 'Jesus Christ, Son of God', while Codices Vaticanus (B), Bezae (D), and Washingtonianus (W), and other witnesses, have only 'Jesus Christ'. A decision made solely on the basis of manuscript evidence (external evidence) would have to cope with the unsettling fact that the two manuscripts generally deemed 'best', ℵ and B, go their separate ways in this instance. With closely divided manuscript evidence, however, the textual critic would move immediately to internal evidence (evidence from the transcriptional process—how scribes worked—and from the immediate and larger context of the variation unit). Assessing rudimentary transcriptional evidence would support the shorter reading in this case ('Jesus Christ' without 'Son of God'), for Christian scribes, especially when encountering divine names, would be more likely to add the common words 'Son of God' to an existing 'Jesus Christ' than to remove the former phrase if it were in the manuscript being copied. But the larger issue is context, which is here perhaps the *entire* Gospel of Mark! Are the words 'Son of God' likely to have been part of the author's original text because Jesus as 'Son of God' or Jesus' sonship is a major or even a crucial theme of the Gospel? If so, to rule it out by various other text-critical criteria might be to remove from the opening sentence the author's dramatic announcement of a major theme for the entire work that follows. Naturally, whether 'Son of God' serves Mark's Gospel in this way is a question for exegetes to answer, and indeed they have answered it both ways.

The point, however, is that a compendium approach to textual criticism—helpful as the *Textual Commentary*, for example, might be—is not adequate. Just as exegesis often involves and needs textual criticism, so textual criticism often involves and needs exegesis. Decisions frequently cannot be made merely on external evidence, or by using internal criteria such as preference for the harder reading (since scribes tend to smooth out difficulties), or even by assessing the immediate context; rather, larger issues of conformity of a variant to the writing's entire ideological context or to the author's distinctive style or theology, or a reading's conformity to extrinsic heterodox or orthodox doctrinal views must be taken into account.

Another complicating, though nonetheless positive, aspect of the overlap of textual criticism and exegesis that should not be overlooked is that competing readings, even those judged not the most likely original, often have the power to illuminate a text by disclosing alternative 'readings' or interpretations of that text in the early Church. These interpretations (when it can be assumed that they were conscious alterations) may reflect either the solo view of a thinking scribe, or the convictions of a local or regional church or even of an entire doctrinal tradition. Thus, textual criticism, often conceived as having a singular goal of establishing the 'original' text, is in reality a discipline with broader goals, including the display of the variety of opinions and convictions that enlivened the life of the Church throughout its early history. Exegetes, therefore, should never consider the New Testament text to be static or inert, for it was and remains a living text that in turn reveals the living Church that transmits it.

Two additional examples of the intersection of exegesis and textual criticism involve a contemporary issue in much of Christianity. First, the paragraph comprising 1 Cor. 14:34-35 contains the vexing words, 'Women should be silent in the churches', followed by a further statement of submission to husbands and a reinforcement of silence by asserting that 'it is shameful for a woman to speak in church'. Exegetes for generations have observed the difficulties in defending these verses as consistent with Paul's preceding and following arguments, giving rise to a variety of interpretations that attempt, on the one hand, to justify its place in this context and, on the other, to dismiss it as an interpolation into the text—whether by Paul but not belonging here or not Pauline at all. Can textual criticism contribute to a solution?

At first glance, the expected answer might be negative, for these two verses are present in all extant textual witnesses—no divided tradition here and no textual variants in the usual sense. However, a group of Greek and Latin manuscripts including Codex Bezae (the so-called 'Western' manuscripts) place the two verses after v. 40, that is, between the conclusion of a lengthy, connected argument by Paul and the abrupt beginning of a new discussion (ch. 15). Already this dislocation in the textual tradition suggests some uncertainty among scribes about the appropriate place for vv. 34-35 in 1 Corinthians. Moreover, recent investigation shows that vv. 34-35 are invariably treated as a separate paragraph—not connected with v. 33b—in early Greek manuscripts (including 𝔓46 B ℵ A D^P 33). More telling, in the

Latin Codex Fuldensis (F, 547 CE), which contains vv. 34-35 in its usual place, the original scribe placed a siglum after v. 33 that referred the reader to a portion of text in the bottom margin, namely, vv. 36-40 recopied *in toto*. This almost certainly indicates that vv. 34-35 are to be omitted; the scribe (or more likely Bishop Victor, whom we know to have supervised the copying of Fuldensis) had evidence or was otherwise convinced that these verses were not part of the text of 1 Corinthians. More significant still, the original scribe of perhaps our most important uncial manuscript, Codex Vaticanus (B, fourth century), used distinctive sigla to mark vv. 34-35 as a known textual problem, strongly supporting the view that vv. 34-35 is an interpolation and may not be Pauline at all (see Payne 1995). In this striking example, we observe exegesis alerting us to a text-critical problem and textual criticism, in turn, assisting in a solution to the exegetical difficulty. (On the whole issue, see also Fee 1987; Petzer 1993.)

A second example involves the mere difference of a Greek accent in a proper name in Rom. 16:7, which, depending on the decisions made, could offer the one text in which Paul used the word 'apostle' to describe a woman. Again there are both text-critical and exegetical complications. Paul here requests his readers to 'Greet Andronicus and ᾽IOYNIAN [accusative case]...; they are prominent among the apostles'. The accusative singular form ᾽IOYNIAN can be either ᾽Iουνιᾶν (masculine, 'Junias', a hypothetical shortened form of Junianus; but see Cervin 1994: 468-70) or ᾽Iουνίαν (feminine, 'Junia'). Accents, however, seldom occur before the seventh century in New Testament manuscripts, but the second correctors (in the sixth/seventh and ninth centuries, respectively) of two major manuscripts, B (fourth century) and D^p (sixth century), accent the word as feminine, as do many of the later Greek manuscripts, and the Sahidic Coptic (see Plisch 1996) and Chrysostom also understand it as feminine. Indeed, the latter (c. 390 CE) comments on Junia, 'How great the wisdom of this woman that she was even deemed worthy of the apostles' title' (Fitzmyer 1993: 738).

Normal text-critical procedure, such as relying heavily on the earliest manuscripts, is not particularly helpful here because of the lack of accents in these early manuscripts, and Chrysostom's statement becomes the earliest useful witness, affording confirmation of the feminine form that appears as soon as accents come into play.

Contemporary social usage and Greek grammar, however, must also be applied in this case: 'Junias' as a male name is nowhere to be found, but 'Junia' as a Latin woman's name is common in Roman literature and occurs more than 250 times in inscriptions in Rome alone (see Metzger [ed.] 1994: 475; Cervin 1994: 466-69). Grammatically, the rendering, 'they are prominent among the apostles' (i.e. 'as apostles') is preferable to 'they are esteemed *by* the apostles' (but are not apostles) (see Cervin 1994: 470; cf. Fitzmyer 1993: 739-40).

Though evidence for apostleship of women in the early Church is not restricted to this passage, the term 'apostle' applied to a woman is found only here. Elsewhere in the same chapter (16:6, 12), four women are said to have 'worked very hard' (κοπιάω), a term Paul uses of his own apostolic ministry (1 Cor. 4:12; 15:10; Gal. 4:11; Phil. 2:16) and that of others (1 Cor. 16:15-16; 1 Thess. 5:12), and other women are called Paul's 'coworkers' (Rom. 16:3; Phil. 4:2-3) or 'deacon' (NRSV 'minister', Rom. 16:1) (see Scholer 1995). Exegetes must determine what these expressions imply in their various contexts, but the female apostle Junia seems well established through a combination of textual criticism, contemporary evidence from Rome, Greek grammar, and plausibly complementary passages in Paul.

These various examples illustrate the broad scope and extensive relevance of New Testament textual criticism to interpretation, but especially its formidable complexity. Indeed, this complexity of the text-critical enterprise is a prominent reason (1) why textual critics resist the pre-packaging and isolation of most text-critical decisions, why they insist that the panoply of text-critical principles be brought to bear on each case, and why many textual 'decisions' remain open to new evidence, new methods, and new exegetical interpretations; and also (2) why interpreters tend to neglect textual criticism. This scholarly discipline, sometimes viewed as merely mechanical and perfunctory, in reality has both (1) objective, empirical and 'scientific' aspects (quantitative measurement of manuscript relationships, for instance) and (2) subjective and qualitative aspects, aspects of 'art' (such as balancing the probabilities when manuscript evidence is evenly divided or when a reading in a variation unit is both the smoother and yet conforms to the author's style [see further below]). In actuality, therefore, the lengthy history of text-critical studies to date has yielded few if any definitive methods or principles that function independently, much less automatically, and only occasionally provides 'right' or 'wrong' answers in individual cases. Debate is lively between rival brands of eclecticism, on the notions of 'best' manuscripts and 'best' groups of manuscripts, and on the date and even the existence of various major text-types. In fact, text-critics have yet to reach agreement on two very basic matters: the reconstruction of the history of the New Testament text—showing its chronological evolution in relation to extant manuscripts—and the methods by which to do so. If that were not enough, research surprises us with increased complexity when it can be demonstrated, as has been done so well recently, that ancient textual alterations often issued from the will to support not only *heterodox* teaching (a view well established a century ago) but also *orthodox* theology (see Ehrman 1993; and Ehrman and Holmes 1995: 361-79, for many examples).

Thus, rather than merely dispensing simple or simplified principles or operating with 'cut-and-dried' methods—luxuries the discipline does not enjoy—New Testament textual criticism must attempt (1) to determine the most likely original reading through an eclectic and thereby complex methodology, one that utilizes an array of criteria that include both objective and subjective—and at times conflicting—guidelines; and (2) to elicit from variants their scribal or community motivations and their socio-cultural contexts in an effort to illuminate the thought and life of the Church.

This is not to say, however, that New Testament textual criticism is paralyzed and unable to function, or incapable of making useful decisions that will facilitate the exegete's work. It only means that it is often harder than might have been expected and that results are less definitive than might have been wished. A high degree of sophistication in the discipline and a fair measure of courage to apply it are required.

THE NATURE AND MAJOR ISSUES OF NEW TESTAMENT TEXTUAL CRITICISM

In view of these introductory remarks, New Testament textual criticism may be defined as the science and art of assessing the transmission of the New Testament text by (1) evaluating its variations, alterations, and distortions, and then attempting its restoration—its earliest recoverable forms—and (2) seeking to place variants within the history and culture of the early Church, both to determine the age, meaning, and motivation of variants and to extract from them some knowledge of the development and character of early

Christian theology, ecclesiology, and culture.

The requirements for pursuing these goals are essentially twofold: (1) familiarity with the textual transmission process, including the full range of scribal habits and other phenomena of textual variation that influenced it, and (2) knowledge both of the Greek manuscripts that preserve and transmit to us the New Testament text-forms and also of the early versions that delivered these Christian writings to non-Greek-speaking areas. Meeting the first prerequisite will require, in turn, the formulation of criteria for isolating the most likely original readings, while acquaintance with the thousands of manuscripts will require grouping them in some fashion according to shared characteristics. In most of these aspects, New Testament textual criticism is no different from that applied to other ancient literature, but in some ways it presents a special case.

It is well known that numerous writings of classical Greek and Latin authors are preserved in only a small number of manuscripts—often the earliest ones dating some centuries later than the origin of the documents—and that frequently these relatively few textual witnesses can quite conveniently be employed to construct stemmata (or family trees) of the manuscripts, thereby isolating the earliest forms of the text and facilitating the construction of critical editions, though often with the help of considerable textual emendation. However, in the case of the New Testament, or even its individual parts, a different situation dictates a different solution. The difference arises chiefly from the number and age of the extant manuscripts of the New Testament: Greek manuscripts alone run between 5,000 and 5,500 in number; at least one fragment ($\mathfrak{P}$52) dates as early as only a generation after the date of composition, while others, including a fair number extensive in their coverage of text, date from around 200 and into the third century (e.g. $\mathfrak{P}$45 $\mathfrak{P}$46 $\mathfrak{P}$66 $\mathfrak{P}$75). These earliest manuscripts still number fewer than fifty, with about 280 more up to the ninth century, and then the manuscripts burgeon in number so that nearly 4,800 date from the ninth through the sixteenth centuries. Versional manuscripts are also numerous, especially Latin, with about fifty early ones (Old Latin) and more than 10,000 of the Vulgate revision.

This situation—the vast breadth and depth of manuscript materials—affords us both opportunities and difficulties. An opportunity arises from the very mass of extant witnesses, for we may reasonably assume that, somewhere among the estimated 300,000 variant readings, reside virtually all of the original readings. Thus, the necessity for conjectural emendation is almost entirely ruled out (but see Delobel 1994; and cf. Holmes in Ehrman and Holmes 1995: 347-49). Another advantage in the richness of variation is the greater ease with which we should be able to trace out the development and history of the text, as well as the ideological and doctrinal variants that illumine the history of the Church for us. On the other hand, the inherent negatives are obvious enough: the sheer quantity of witnesses and of textual variants vastly complicates the process of determining the most likely original text. For one thing, because of extensive textual mixture among the extant manuscripts, the genealogical method (forming stemmata) is not a viable procedure; hence, it is rarely used in New Testament criticism except, importantly, at the level of an *individual variation unit*, where an attempt is made to identify the one reading in each circumscribed group of variants that best explains the rise of all the others.

What is required (as earlier intimated) is, first, to group manuscripts that share similar textual complexions and to establish time-frames for each group. Smaller groups are called families and the largest groups are called text-types, though the process is not as streamlined as it sounds. In simplest terms, however, if early groupings can be isolated, it is more likely that their readings stand closer, not only in time but also in quality, to those of the original compositions (see further under 'External Evidence' below). Secondly, what used to be called 'canons of criticism', that is, criteria for determining the earliest or most likely original readings, need to be (and currently are being) refined so that they can be applied to individual variant units with more confident results. The massive quantity of variant readings, often with several in an individual variation unit, will, however, on numerous occasions yield closely competitive variants, each of which will command support from one or more criteria that, in a simpler situation, would accredit that particular variant as *the* one most likely original. But now we may have two or three readings, each one meeting different criteria and more than one, therefore, holding a plausible claim to originality. For instance, Luke 10:41-42 (NRSV) reads:

> Martha, Martha, you are worried and distracted by many things; there is need of only one thing. Mary has chosen the better part, which will not be taken away from her.

What words of Jesus to Martha did the author of Luke most likely write? Four basic readings survive: (1) The shortest reading (in the so-called 'Western' textual tradition) omits everything between 'Martha' and 'Mary'. (2) The second (found in one Greek manuscript and some early versions) has 'Martha, Martha, a few things are needed...' This, in the context, is the most difficult reading. (3) The third, 'one thing is needed' (found in two very early papyri and numerous other witnesses), is adopted in the NRSV and selected by several modern critical editions of the Greek text because it has often been judged as best explaining the other variants and hence must have preceded them. (4) However, the fourth reading, 'a few things are needed, or only one' (found in two prominent codices, ℵ and B), is also seen as capable of explaining all the others.

So, at first glance, we have a shortest reading, meeting a long-standing criterion of authenticity (but see below); a most difficult reading, meeting another criterion suggesting authenticity; and two readings thought capable of explaining the others. Where does one turn? In this case, a fuller analysis shows that reading number 1 most likely involves an accidental omission that leaves little sense in the passage, so it drops out of contention. (The 'shorter reading' criterion has recently been questioned, though it never was accorded authority when an accidental omission could be argued.) Externally, reading number 2 is very weakly attested and likely represents a late corruption of either reading 3 or 4—both of which, by the way, are attested both within and outside of Egypt at an early date. The decision rests, then, on whether reading 3 arose from 4 or vice versa, a decision that, in turn, rests on judgments about transcriptional probabilities (what would a scribe most likely write?), on Lukan grammatical usage, and on the degree of sense in the context—an exegetical consideration. Taking these criteria into account, a case can be made that reading 4 is the more difficult of the two yet makes sense, and that reading 3, though the shorter, can plausibly have been derived from 4. Hence, reading 4 may best explain the rise of all the others (see Fee in Epp and Fee [eds.] 1981: 61-75).

New Testament textual critics, then, have to cope with complexity and conflict—and no easy answers—at almost every turn. Yet, they rejoice in the embarrassment of manuscript riches and much prefer that, with all of the complicating factors, to the situation in which their classical colleagues (or those in Mishnah and Talmud studies) find themselves.

THE TRANSMISSION OF THE NEW TESTAMENT TEXT
AND TEXT-CRITICAL PRACTICE

It is clear, however, that neither the grouping of manuscripts nor the clarification of criteria for assessing variants can be accomplished apart from a grasp of the process by which the New Testament text has been transmitted to us. Hence, textual critics—and exegetes— need to rehearse that story of transmission, understand its inner dynamics, and 'get the feel' of it in its ancient context. To do so requires acquaintance with the manuscripts themselves and knowledge of Greco-Roman writing materials, paleography (handwriting), scribal habits, scriptoria (the places where manuscripts were copied), ways that manuscripts were carried from place to place, and a bit of historical imagination.

Though we do not know much about early Christian worship services, except that they would likely follow the format of synagogue services (about which, in turn, all too little is known), we may be sure that early Christian writings were preserved and transmitted in ways that facilitated their use in the worship and life of the Church. Of course, as with all ancient literature, no autographs survive, but we may safely assume that, in the early decades of Christianity, a letter of Paul or, shortly thereafter, portions of a Gospel, would be read in worship services and that, on occasion, visiting Christians would request copies and carry these hitherto unfamiliar documents to their own congregations. At other times, writings would be shared with other churches, sometimes at the request of the writer (cf. 1 Thess. 5:27; Col. 4:16), and we may assume that a natural way to do this would be to produce copies (papyrus was the normal writing material of the ancient world and, at times, it was relatively inexpensive). As New Testament manuscripts were used and reused, and sometimes wore out, they were copied and recopied, whether privately, in churches, or later in scriptoria (c. 200 CE and after). Soon, we may imagine, some churches would possess several of these early Christian writings, and rudimentary collections of Gospels and/or apostolic letters would emerge, some possibly by the conscious act, for example, of a devoted pupil of Paul. In ways such as these, the centuries-long process of Christian manuscript-copying and circulation began, followed by copies of copies of copies, eventually leaving for us the rich, 5,000-plus legacy of widely divergent Greek manuscripts, plus the thousands of versional manuscripts and quotations of New Testament passages in patristic writings.

Beyond this sort of reasonable historical imagination (backed by fragments of evidence), we know precious little about the beginning stages of transmission, though the earliest New Testament manuscripts (as well as Old Testament Scriptures copied for Christian use) were in codex form, that is, our book form as opposed to the scrolls that functioned as the format for Jewish and secular literature prior to Christianity. If Christians did not invent the codex—a debated issue—they at least capitalized upon this recently-invented medium as a more convenient and space-saving format for the preservation and circulation of their writings, thereby enhancing the transmission process.

At times in this process, however, manuscripts were poorly preserved, and numerous early manuscripts are now highly fragmentary. Often a single leaf or only a few leaves remain. Very often, it is only a small portion of a single book. About two-thirds of the papyri and nearly one-third of the uncial manuscripts are preserved in only one or two leaves. Nearly all of the very early, more extensive manuscripts (such as 𝔓45 𝔓46 𝔓72 𝔓75, but not 𝔓66) contain more than one writing. It is significant, however, that, among the fifty-seven earliest manuscripts, four of those that contain no more than two leaves nonetheless contain portions of two New Testament books (𝔓30 𝔓53 𝔓92 and 0171). This opens the possibility, not yet subject to proof, that many, perhaps very many, of the fragmentary papyri originally comprised multiple writings, for when we move away from the third/fourth century, some sixty extant codices contain the entire New Testament, and many other manuscripts demonstrate that early Christian writings circulated in certain quite regular combinations rather than individually. Most often, for example, the four Gospels circulated together in a single codex (as in the third century 𝔓45), as did the Pauline letters (see the very early 𝔓46), though Acts might join either group (as in 𝔓45); or Acts and the general Epistles might form another group (as in 𝔓74); and there were other combinations. (These conventions in the circulation of groups of early Christian writings, as well as the contents of manuscripts and the sequence of books in them, have implications for the lengthy process by which the New Testament canon was formed; see the Excursus below.)

How did documents actually move about in the Greco-Roman world? The New Testament letters confirm what is abundantly evident from many hundreds of private papyrus letters preserved in Egypt, that letter writers frequently utilized secretaries to write for them and then used the informal 'mail service' to secure delivery to their addressees. The latter typically consisted in finding someone sailing up the river or travelling the Roman roads to the destination of one's letter. This process is abundantly illustrated in the everyday Egyptian papyri, but also in the New Testament letters: Paul in his own hand, for example, adds his 'greeting' to letters otherwise written by amanuenses (1 Cor. 16:21; 2 Thess. 3:17; Phlm. 19; cf. Gal. 6:11), and in Rom. 16:22 the amanuensis refers to himself, 'Tertius'. Presumably (*apud* Phlm. 19) Onesimus carried Paul's letter to Philemon; Silvanus carried 1 Peter (5:12); and possibly Phoebe was the carrier for Romans (16:1) and Titus (plus two 'brothers') for 2 Corinthians (8:16-24). Other early Christian writers reflect the same practice: Burrhus carried Ignatius's *Philadelphians*, and Crescens, Polycarp's *Philippians*.

More significant for the transmission of the New Testament, however, is the speed with which private letters (and other documents) travelled in the Greco-Roman world. It can now be documented from extant papyrus letters that show both their date of writing (a customary feature) and their docketed date of receipt (much less commonly done) that letters travelled, for example, 800 miles from Asia Minor to Alexandria in two months; from Transjordan to Alexandria, about 350 miles, in thirty-six days; from Philadelphia to Syria, some 400 miles, in fourteen days; 150 miles from Alexandria to Philadelphia in four days and another in seven days; from Alexandria to another Delta city in nineteen days; and from Memphis to Alexandria, about 125 miles, in three weeks.

This casual but prompt transfer of letters functioned both in the Hellenistic and Roman periods, and operated not only within Egypt (between the Delta, the Fayyûm, and upper Egypt), but also between Egypt and places far removed, such as Ostia in Italy, Cilicia in Asia Minor, Sidon in Syria, and Arabia (taking some actual examples in addition to those cited above).

From data of this kind we can draw important conclusions about the transmission of the early Christian writings and the kinds of text they contained. First, wherever they might have originated in the broad Mediterranean region, the writings that were to form the New Testament could very rapidly have made their way to any other part of the Roman world, and, more significantly, this could have been accomplished in a matter of days, weeks, or a few months. Indeed, it is no longer necessary to assume a long interval of years between the time a New Testament letter or Gospel was written and its appearance in other places, even distant places. The Gospel of John, extant in several very early manuscripts, is a good example; wherever it may have been written, its text (whether in a form like that now in 𝔓52 or 𝔓66 or 𝔓75—all Egyptian papyri) could have reached Egypt quickly; if such a text were then modified during Christian use there, those 'revisions' could rapidly be transported to another part of the Christian world anywhere in the Roman Empire. In view of this situation, it must be granted that various forms of text in the early Christian world could not have been confined to one region for any length of time in any single form. Early Christian writings, regardless of their place of origin, could very quickly move to all other Christian areas, burdened or blessed with all of the unconscious and conscious alterations that accumulated during their active use in a vibrant church.

Secondly, as a consequence of the quick-paced intellectual commerce demonstrable in the Mediterranean area (especially to and from Egypt), we may reasonably assert, although not yet easily prove, that the various textual complexions evident in our very earliest manuscripts, the Egyptian papyri, very possibly and quite plausibly represent texts from that *entire Mediterranean region* (including, of course, forms of text that might have originated in Egypt itself). Thus, in contrast to the common view that the papyri represent only the text of provincial Egypt, it is much more likely that they represent an extensive textual range (if not the full textual spectrum) of earliest Christianity. (On the preceding several paragraphs, see Epp 1989: 8-10; Epp 1991: 43-56; Epp and Fee [eds.] 1981: 274-83; and the detailed documentation provided.)

This is, in many ways, an enlightened and enlightening view of the transmission of the New Testament writings in the period of earliest Christianity, for it brings us into closer touch with the dynamic, vibrant activity within the emergent Church that, in turn, was situated in a real Greco-Roman life-setting that was equally vigorous and robust in its intellectual commerce. We can well imagine the excitement of discovery when Christians of different localities encountered new apostolic letters or Gospels, whether personally while visiting another church, or through the private exchange of letters and documents. We can imagine the strength and comfort that arose from the knowledge that others, near and far, held the same spiritual convictions and doctrinal beliefs and were eager to share the documents in their possession that embodied and expressed those convictions. We can imagine the justifiable pride that congregations would develop as they acquired increasing numbers of these documents, which they would be quick to test by reading from them in services and utilizing them in their teaching, evangelism, and public defense.

This combination of data and scholarly speculation may stretch our minds in other ways. All the New Testament papyri issue from Egypt, but, most of the time, exact geographical locations of their use or even of their discovery elude us. The town of Oxyrhynchus, however, yielded thirty-nine of our current 108 different New Testament papyri; while fragmentary, they contain portions of fifteen of our twenty-seven books; and thirty of them date to the second, third, and early fourth centuries. What do these random discoveries from the rubbish heaps and ruined buildings of this district capital in Upper Egypt tell us about its Christian churches or the role of the Christian writings in those churches? We know from other papyri found there that, in the second century, this small city had twenty temples, a theater accommodating eight to twelve thousand people, and a Roman garrison, and the papyri attest the names of some 5,700 individual inhabitants between 30 BCE and 96 CE. Yet we know virtually nothing about Christianity there, and very little about Christianity in Egypt in general at this time. Does the sizable horde of randomly surviving New Testament papyri indicate many Christians and/or several churches in Oxyrhynchus, a significant collection or even a library of Christian documents, that numerous copies were moving to and from Oxyrhynchus, or perhaps that it was a center of Christian scholarship or even text-critical activity (because we have evidence there of critical editing and annotation of Greco-Roman literary works)? (See Epp 1991: 7-8.) These are tantalizing questions, but currently they do not have answers. Yet, the mere raising of the questions in a real socio-historical context gives a 'feel' for the transmission process of our New Testament text, and provides an agenda for further research.

We do, however, have better knowledge of the technical and mechanical aspects of the process: the nature of scribal activity in copying manuscripts.

1. The Role of Scribes in Textual Transmission

The influence of scribes or copyists was crucial in the whole New Testament transmission process prior to the invention of movable type in the mid-fifteenth century. As these scribes or copyists churned out copies of New Testament writings, both their inadvertent errors and their quite conscious improvements (as they would view them) created the tens upon tens of thousands of textual variants that now present themselves to us for analysis and decision. Scribal 'errors' (better: scribal alterations), however, must be seen in proper perspective because the copying of manuscripts by its very nature is a conservative process (in both meanings of 'conservative') and the overwhelming majority of copying was accurately accomplished. Nonetheless, the most attentive and dedicated scribe, even the slavish scribe, suffered inattentive moments and lapses of connection between eye or mind and hand. Subtle influences such as parallel passages, especially in the Synoptic Gospels, or daily familiarity with liturgical forms of biblical passages led scribes to conform the texts they were producing to those more familiar parallel forms that were fixed in their minds. A greater threat, if that is the appropriate word, to the transmission process, however, was the 'thinking' scribe who felt compelled to assess the meaning or meaningfulness of the text being copied rather than merely to do the job. Some were bold enough to 'correct' the text before them or to include extraneous material familiar to them from other contexts or manuscripts or even from the margins of manuscripts. Numerous variant readings arose in these ways, yet we should not miss noticing that this scribal activity is another vivid piece of evidence that the New Testament text was a living text subject to the vicissitudes of existence—a living, breathing organism reflecting and reacting to its social and theological environment as it moved along in the stream of the vibrant Christian community of which it was a part.

Technically, scribal alterations customarily are placed under the two categories implied above. First, *unintentional scribal alterations* comprise what are often characterized as errors of the eye, of the ear (if copying by dictation), and of the memory or (unthinking) judgment. These include (1) confusion of letters or letter-combinations having similar appearance (or sound); (2) mistaken word division (since uncial manuscripts, including the papyri, were written without spaces or punctuation); (3) misread abbreviations or contractions; (4) interchanges in the order of letters or words (metathesis); (5) substitution of a more familiar word for a less familiar one, or writing a synonym when the meaning but not the exact word is in the copyist's mind; (6) omission of one word when it occurred twice, or skipping material between two similar words or letter-groups (haplography); (7) repetition of a letter, word, or passage when the eye returns to a place already copied (dittography); (8) careless spelling and failure to correct such errors; and (9) unconscious assimilation to similar wording in a parallel passage or lection (on occasion this may be intentional), or harmonization with wording in the immediate context.

Secondly, *intentional scribal alterations*, inevitably *well-intentioned*, correct or otherwise improve the text in accordance with what the scribe believed to be its original or intended form or meaning—or even a meaning more relevant to the scribe's present ecclesiastical context or theological orientation. Thus, sometimes, though still with worthy motives from the scribe's standpoint, changes were made to promote a doctrinal or ideological view not in the text being copied, making the text say what the scribe 'knew' it to mean. These conscious alterations, to be sure, are usually subtle in nature and modest in scope; yet inevitably they shaped the transmission process more than did accidental alterations.

Intentional alterations include (1) changes in grammar, spelling (often proper names), and style; (2) conscious harmonization with parallel passages (often in the Synoptic Gospels, in Old Testament quotations, or in lectionaries), motivated perhaps by the wish to present the 'complete' text in a given context; (3) clarification of geographical or historical points (e.g. time or place; or authorship of Old Testament quotations); (4) conflation of differing readings in two or more manuscripts known to the copyist—again, to be complete; (5) addition of seemingly appropriate material (such as expanding 'Jesus' to 'Jesus Christ' or to the 'Lord Jesus Christ'); and (6) theological or ideological alterations, often small changes in the interest of supporting accepted doctrine, especially issues of Christology, the Trinity, the Virgin Birth, asceticism, etc., or longer additions such as found in manuscripts of the 'Western' textual tradition, where anti-Judaic, anti-feminist, pro-apostle, and other tendencies have been detected.

2. Internal Criteria

Making textual decisions depends very directly on acquaintance with these scribal habits as they functioned in the copying process, for textual critics move from this knowledge to the formulation of *internal criteria* that will assist in distinguishing the most likely original reading among those in a given variation unit. The criteria in this category are labeled 'internal' because they relate to factors or characteristics *within* the text itself (as opposed to 'external' criteria, which relate to the nature of manuscripts, e.g. date and provenance, as something 'outside' or separate from the texts they enshrine). Text-critical criteria have evolved over nearly the whole history of Christianity, for rudimentary 'rules' can be found as early as Origen in the third century, with their modern history beginning in the early eighteenth century. Essentially, the textual critic asks various questions of each variant reading in a variation unit: Can this variant account for the rise of all the others? Does this variant agree with the writer's literary style, or theology? Is this variant 'harder', that is, rough or unrevised when compared with others in the unit? And so forth. Not all criteria will be relevant in all cases, so they are tested for relevance and the results are compared. Not infrequently (as noted earlier) one variant will be supported as the most likely original by one or more of the criteria, while a competing variant is supported by other criteria, or one criterion may support a reading while another discredits it. (An example is Matt. 6:33, where a reading that explains the others competes with one that conforms better to Matthew's style.) At the same time, not all criteria carry the same weight, and the validity of some is now under debate (notably numbers two and six below). So, after analysis, the decision will often have to be made on the basis of 'the balance of probabilities'. There is, however, general agreement on what Constantine Tischendorf noted long ago, that the first criterion below takes precedence over all the others, if it works in a given case. (In general, see Epp in Epp and Fee 1993: 141-73; and Epp 1992; Royse in Ehrman and Holmes 1995: 239-52.)

The criteria that follow are phrased so that, if a criterion accurately describes a textual variant (other things being equal), that variant would have the presumption of being the most likely original.

CRITERIA RELATED TO INTERNAL EVIDENCE

1. A variant's fitness to account for the origin, development, or presence of all other readings in the variation-unit. Such a variant logically must have preceded all others that can be shown to have evolved from it. K. Aland calls this the 'local genealogical method'.

2. A variant's status as the shorter/shortest reading in the variation-unit. Scribes tend to expand the text rather than shorten it, though this is now debated (see Royse in Ehrman and Holmes 1995: 242-43, 246-47; thoroughgoing eclectics, such as Elliott, are inclined to prefer the longer reading; see Elliott in Ehrman and Holmes 1995: 327-28).

3. A variant's status as the harder/hardest reading in the variation-unit. Scribes tend to smooth or fix rough or difficult readings.

4. A variant's conformity to the author's style and vocabulary. The original reading is likely to follow the author's style as observed in the bulk of the writing. (Challenged recently by Petzer 1990.)

5. A variant's conformity to the author's theology or ideology. The original reading is likely to display the same convictions or beliefs found in the bulk of the work. A scribe, however, might 'correct' an author's statement to conform it more closely to that author's theology, thus altering what would have been a 'harder' reading to a smoother reading.

6. A variant's conformity to Koine (rather than Attic) Greek. Scribes show a tendency to shape the text being copied to the more elegant Attic Greek style. (This is now debated; see Martini 1974.)

7. A variant's conformity to Semitic forms of expression. The New Testament authors, being either Jewish or familiar with Septuagint/Greek Old Testament style, are likely to reflect such Semitic expressions in their writings.

8. A variant's lack of conformity to parallel passages or to extraneous items in the context generally. Scribes tend, consciously or unconsciously, to shape the text being copied to familiar parallel passages in the Synoptic Gospels or to words or phrases just copied.

9. A variant's lack of conformity to Old Testament passages. Scribes, who were familiar with the Old Testament, tend to shape their copying to the content of familiar passages.

10. A variant's lack of conformity to liturgical forms and usages. Scribes tend to shape the text being copied to phraseology in the familiar liturgical expressions used in devotion and worship.

11. A variant's lack of conformity to extrinsic theological, ideological, or other socio-historical contexts contemporary with and congenial to a text's scribe. Scribes unconsciously, but more likely consciously, could bring a text into conformity with their own or their group's doctrinal beliefs or with accepted socio-cultural conventions (see Ehrman 1993; and Ehrman in Ehrman and Holmes 1995: 361-79; but contrast Wisse 1989). Naturally, difficulties exist in identifying both the contemporary context and the copyist's time-frame and provenance.

The judicious application of these criteria to competing readings within each variation unit fulfills a major but single part of the twofold methodological process for decision-making: treating phenomena *within* the transmitted text. The *externals* of the matter, the manuscripts themselves as artifacts and each treated as an entity, a 'whole', are the focus of the other major task.

3. The Source Materials of Textual Transmission

Just as 'internal evidence' must be analyzed and evaluated by 'internal criteria', so 'external evidence' must be subjected to 'external criteria'. This involves scrutiny and assessment of the manuscripts, especially with respect to their age, their provenance, the nature of the text they contain, and the manuscript company that they keep: Is the text rough, or smooth and/or revised? Was it copied with care, corrected? Does it share distinctive readings with other manuscripts? Can it be placed into a family or text-type with other similar manuscripts? It is the scribal process just described that has brought us the Greek manuscripts that now constitute the primary sources for establishing the New Testament text—along with the versional manuscripts, which, in their respective traditions, have experienced the same phenomena of shaping and alteration. Only a very brief survey of these primary sources can be provided here.

a. Greek manuscripts of the New Testament. Since the New Testament books were composed in Greek, the Greek manuscripts that preserve them are of primary importance. Unfortunately, some unnecessary complexity has crept into their classification: Greek manuscripts take two forms and are written in two kinds of handwriting on three different writing materials.

1. Format. The two basic forms are *continuous-text* manuscripts, which contain (or originally contained) at least one New Testament writing in continuous fashion from beginning to end, and *lectionary* manuscripts, which developed later and bring together those portions of Scripture appointed to be read in services. Lectionaries do not have the New Testament text in continuous form or in canonical order, but rather provide readings arranged either according to the church year or the calendar year. Often an introductory phrase (called an *incipit*) had to be added to adapt the selected portion to liturgical use (e.g. 'Jesus said...' or 'In those days...').

2. Paleography. As to handwriting, New Testament manuscripts were written in large unconnected letters (uncials or, better, majuscules) into the tenth century, using both papyrus and parchment.

Beginning in the ninth century, smaller (minuscule) and cursive ('running') or connected letters were used, employing parchment and paper.

3. Media. With respect to writing materials, papyrus was used from the beginning into the eighth century, though nearly 75% of New Testament manuscripts were written on parchment (also called vellum)—from the eighth century to the sixteenth; and paper was employed from the twelfth to the nineteenth centuries. Papyrus manuscripts are all continuous-text manuscripts (108), while parchment was the vehicle for both continuous-texts (about 2,400) and lectionaries (about 1,700). Paper manuscripts used for minuscules and lectionaries total about 1,300.

4. Current classifications. To add to the confusion, textual critics ignore some of these categories (continuous-text, parchment, paper) and classify Greek manuscripts using four terms: *papyri, uncials, minuscules,* and *lectionaries.* The papyri are in majuscule script (though not counted among the uncials!), but have been placed in a separate category due to their early date and greater significance, and also for historical reasons: the first was not published until 1868. Reckoned in these categories, different 'papyri' number 108, 'uncials' more than 260, 'minuscules' more than 2,800, and 'lectionaries' nearly 2,300. 'Papyri', 'uncials', and 'minuscules' are all continuous-text manuscripts, while lectionaries are written in both uncial (numbering about 270) and minuscule hands and on both parchment and paper and date from the fourth century on (though only ten originated before the eighth century). To complicate matters further, some manuscripts are bilingual, mainly Greco–Coptic and Greco–Latin (including thirty-four uncials), while others are palimpsests—manuscripts, usually parchment, recovered from a parchment reused by scraping off the original text and writing on the newly prepared surface. There remain more than a hundred New Testament uncials and lectionaries that have been overwritten in this fashion.

In summary, then, the term 'papyri' includes only manuscripts written on papyrus; 'uncial' means only non-papyrus continuous-text manuscripts written in majuscule hand (and does not include the lectionaries so written); 'minuscule' includes only continuous-text manuscripts written in cursive hand (and not the many lectionaries so written); and 'lectionary' means portions for liturgical use regardless of the script or writing material employed. Although many statistics are cited above, the total number of different Greek manuscripts of the

New Testament is difficult to determine, since some thirty papyri and uncials are actually portions of others, as are numerous minuscules and lectionaries. Raw numbers for manuscripts in the latest lists total more than 5,660 (K. Aland 1994), but when duplicates are noted and improperly classified lectionaries are subtracted, the actual total is reduced by perhaps a few hundred, and the safest statement, therefore, is that more than 5,000 different Greek New Testament manuscripts are presently extant.

More important than script, writing materials and format is the value placed on these Greek witnesses. Simply put, beginning in the early eighteenth century and decisively by mid-century, it was agreed that early manuscripts, though fewer, are generally to be preferred to the agreement of a larger number of later manuscripts; hence, the papyri and early uncials assumed the position of prominence. Two groups stand out in importance: first, the fifty-three oldest papyri, plus the four oldest uncials, all of which date prior to the early fourth century; and, secondly, the great uncial manuscripts of the fourth and fifth centuries, primarily Codices Sinaiticus (ℵ, fourth century), Alexandrinus (A, fifth century), and Vaticanus (B, fourth century), which contain all or most of the New Testament, but also Codex Bezae (D, fifth century) containing the Gospels and Acts, and Codex Washingtonianus (W, fifth century) with the four Gospels. The standard handbooks describe these manuscripts and many others of importance (see Metzger 1992; Aland and Aland 1989; cf. in Ehrman and Holmes 1995: Epp on papyri, pp. 3-21; Parker on majuscules, pp. 22-42).

As for the minuscules, about 80% of them are solid representatives of the Majority text (i.e. the Byzantine or Koine text), a text-type that developed in the fourth century and beyond, and become the official ecclesiastical text of the Byzantine Church. While it may contain some early readings, it is a full or conflate text that collected numerous expansive and harmonizing readings and developed over time into a smooth and refined text that has been preserved in hundreds upon hundreds of mostly late manuscripts. However, about 10% of the minuscules are important in establishing the original text, because they preserve elements of the early text (Aland and Aland 1989: 128; in general, see Aland and Wachtel in Ehrman and Holmes 1995: 43-60).

To a high degree, though not exclusively, the lectionaries also represent the Byzantine text-type, and have not been considered of primary importance in establishing the most likely original text. Still, they are likely to have been preserved with a high degree of conservatism because of their official role in church services, doubtless carefully preserving texts much older than their own generally late dates; hence, they assist in tracing the transmission of the New Testament text and cannot be overlooked in seeking the most likely original (see Osburn in Ehrman and Holmes 1995: 61-74).

It will be obvious then—though it took generations of fierce intellectual struggle to reach the conclusion (see Epp in Epp and Fee 1993: 17-25, 144-64; Epp 1992: 427-30)—that textual critics will spend most of their efforts with the readings of the papyri and of the uncials up to about the tenth century, for the presumption is that (1) the most likely original readings are apt to be found here, as are (2) the earliest and most important theological alterations to the text. Always, however, the early versions and patristic citations must be checked in comparison with the Greek witnesses.

b. Versions of the New Testament. Textual criticism would be much simpler, but also much impoverished, if the New Testament text were preserved only in Greek manuscripts. The earliest translations were the Latin, Syriac and Coptic versions (though not necessarily in that order), and they retain the greatest importance. Though their actual origins and early histories are obscure, Latin, Syriac and Coptic versions of the Gospels and other parts of the New Testament were widely circulated in the third century, though the earliest extant Coptic manuscripts date only in the fourth, and late in that century for Latin and Syriac.

Difficulties arise in the use of these and other versions, for no language mechanically reproduces another. For instance, Syriac has no comparative or superlative; Syriac and Coptic have no case endings, and the latter employs strict word order to show subject, object, indirect object, etc.; Gothic has no future form; and even Latin, generally a fine medium for translating Greek, cannot distinguish between the aorist and perfect tenses or the lack of a definite article. Such factors diminish the certainty of recognizing exactly the Greek text behind the versions. Also, some translations are secondary; that is, not translated directly from the Greek text, but from another translation. For example, the Armenian and Georgian possibly have been based on the Greek, but more likely the Armenian stems from Syriac and the Georgian either from Armenian or Syriac or both jointly. In spite of these hindrances, the ancient versions are significant in the search for the most likely original Greek text, especially the three earliest ones, Coptic, Syriac and Latin.

Actually, the earliest version of the Gospels was not a straight-text translation but the famous *Diatessaron* of Tatian, most likely composed in Syriac about 172 CE. It is a harmony of the Gospels with a complex history, since it influenced all further Syriac texts and then appeared in Persian, Armenian, Arabic, and Georgian forms in the east and in Latin, Middle Dutch, Old French, Old and Middle German, Middle English, and Middle Italian in the west (see Petersen 1994a, and in Ehrman and Holmes 1995: 77-96).

The *Latin versions*, the largest tradition of any version, comprise more than 10,000 manuscripts. More than fifty of these (dating from the fourth to the thirteenth centuries) represent the Old Latin version, known from the earliest period in both North Africa and in Europe, and perhaps originating in North Africa in the late second century, though these matters are highly debated. The language of the Old Latin was rough, and no unitary form of text existed; this was recognized already by Jerome, who was asked by Pope Damasus to prepare a revision of these diverse texts, a task which Jerome and others completed in 383. This 'common' version was known as the Vulgate. Old Latin manuscripts continued to be used, however, long after Jerome's time, and these Old Latin texts are particularly useful in understanding the history of the Greek text of the New Testament (see Petzer in Ehrman and Holmes 1995: 113-30).

The *Syriac versions*, like the Latin, have an earlier phase followed by a 'common' edition, the Peshitta (fifth century). Opinions on the date of this version's origin vary from the end of the second century to the mid-fourth. For the Gospels, Acts, and Pauline letters (the limits of the canon in the early Syriac Church), an Old Syriac form survives in continuous-text manuscripts for the Gospels (the Curetonian and the Sinaitic), but virtually only in patristic quotations for the Acts and Paul. Like the Latin, the Old Syriac is more useful in textual criticism than the Peshitta. (See Baarda in Ehrman and Holmes 1995: 97-112.)

The *Coptic versions* are known from third-century Egypt in several dialects: Sahidic, the language of Upper (southern) Egypt; Bohairic from the Delta region of Lower (northern) Egypt; and lesser dialects, such as the Achmimic, sub-Achmimic, Middle Egyptian, and Fayyûmic. The manuscripts are largely fragmentary or late, though a few extensive ones from the fourth–fifth centuries are extant for

Matthew, John, and Acts. (See Wisse in Ehrman and Holmes 1995: 131-41.)

Other early versions of significance include the *Armenian*, probably made in the early fifth century; the *Georgian*, closely akin to the Armenian in origin and character and known from the fifth century; and the *Ethiopic*, perhaps stemming from the fourth or fifth century. Less important ancient versions are in Arabic, Nubian, and Sogdian (Middle Iranian) in the east; and in Gothic, Old Church Slavonic, and Old High German in the west. (See in Ehrman and Holmes 1995: Zuurmond on Ethiopic, pp. 142-56; Alexanian on Armenian, pp. 157-72; Birdsall on Georgian, pp. 173-87.)

c. Patristic Quotations. A final body of source material for establishing the text, and an important source if properly used, is comprised of New Testament quotations found in Church authors of the first several centuries, not only in Greek, but in all relevant languages. They are of special significance for providing closely dated and geographically located textual readings, thus indicating the form that a reading or a text had at a rather definite place and time. A comparison with similar readings in continuous-text manuscripts enables us to specify the antiquity of such readings in the textual tradition and, though less clearly, the possible provenance of the manuscripts containing them. Hence, patristic quotations are valuable evidence in individual cases, and can be especially useful in establishing text-types.

Regrettably, however, the use of patristic quotations is not a simple matter, for the entire text-critical process must first be applied to each of these Church writings to establish the text most likely written. Even the best critical editions, however, do not solve the further problems of determining whether the writer is (a) quoting the text of a New Testament book directly and exactly as it occurs in the text being used (a citation); (b) paraphrasing the text by adapting it to the discussion or to the writer's own syntax while generally maintaining verbal identity with the text being used (an adaptation); or (c) merely alluding to a text's content without substantial verbal correspondence (an allusion). Only when these questions are answered and we know each writer's citing habits and the type of citation in each separate case can patristic quotations be used as evidence for the New Testament text. It is more likely, for example, that long quotations were copied from a manuscript than cited from memory, but it is obvious how complex and difficult the entire matter is. (Lists of

patristic writings cited in critical editions can be found in Nestle–
Aland[27] and *UBSGNT*[4]. On the whole subject, see Fee in Epp and Fee
1993: 344-59 and in Ehrman and Holmes 1995: 191-207; Ehrman
1994; and Petersen 1994b; on Latin patristic writers, North in Ehrman
and Holmes 1995: 208-23; on Syriac, Brock in Ehrman and Holmes
1995: 224-36.)

4. External Criteria

From knowledge of these various sources arise two critical
exercises: First, an attempt to reconstruct the history and evolution of
the New Testament text. This would involve sorting the manuscripts
according to their distinctive textual characteristics and then placing
the groups or clusters of manuscripts into a chronological/historical
continuum, which, in turn, would display temporally the various
textual complexions inherent in each group. Families (such as Family
1 and Family 13) occasionally can be established, followed by
attempts to identify the larger 'text types', classically defined in
quantitative terms as 'a group of manuscripts that agree more than 70
percent of the time and is separated by a gap of about 10 percent from
its neighbors' (Colwell 1969: 59; see Fee in Epp and Fee 1993: 221-
43; Geer in Ehrman and Holmes 1995: 253-67).

Though identifying text-types is a subject of current debate, all
agree on the *Byzantine text type*, or Majority text, represented by
Codex Alexandrinus (A, fifth century)—but only in the Gospels—and
by the vast majority of all our manuscripts. It originated in the fourth
century and, with rare exceptions, does not *exclusively* contain
readings with high claims to represent the original text, though it can
help us trace points of theology and ecclesiology during its long reign
as the official text of the Church (see Fee in Epp and Fee 1993: 183-
208; Wallace in Ehrman and Holmes 1995: 297-320.)

Most agree that two early and therefore highly significant text types
have their roots in the second century and are represented in
identifiable groups or clusters: (1) the *Alexandrian text type* (or B-text,
formerly called 'Neutral'), exemplified predominantly in 𝔓75 (third
century) and Codex Vaticanus (B, fourth century), along with 𝔓66 (c.
200 CE), Sinaiticus (ℵ, fourth century), and later Codex L (eighth
century); and (2) the *'Western' text type* (or D-text), represented by
Codex Bezae (D, fifth century) and by the fragmentary 𝔓29 𝔓38 𝔓48
𝔓69 0171, and later (for Acts) 1739 614 and 383.

In addition, there exists an abortive text type, which we may call the
C-text (formerly called the 'Caesarean') that presents a textual

complexion midway between the Alexandrian and 'Western' (i.e. midway between B and D, hence C-text). It is represented by 𝔓45 (third century) and Codex Washingtonianus (W, fifth century, with origins certainly as early as 𝔓45) in Mark, though its line does not move unambiguously beyond Codex W.

Textual critics, acting on their penchant for early manuscripts and groups, place the most weight on text types B, C, and D, though most recognize B and D as the earliest, even if no definitive decision has been reached as to which of the two had priority. Because of the high quality of text found in the B group in contrast to the often rough form in the D group, most critics favor B as the 'best' kind of text and generally accord to it preeminent authority in textual decisions. Others, recognizing the internal criterion favoring the 'harder' reading, suggest that D's rougher text implies greater antiquity—and the debate goes on. The 1950s discovery of 𝔓75 is often taken, however, as supporting the former view—the superior quality of the B-text: Codex Vaticanus, because of its smooth refined text, had often been viewed as a revised text, but the virtual identity of 𝔓75's text with that of Vaticanus, though 𝔓75 is perhaps a century and a half earlier, automatically ruled out a fourth century revision as the source of the B-text, and pushed the existence of that high quality textual complexion back already to the beginning of the third century.

In summary, and despite much uncertainty and debate, knowledge of the manuscripts permits fairly confident groupings, yielding earlier and later text types, with the presumption of originality *ceteris paribus* resting somewhere in the readings of the early groups, predominantly the B-text, but also the D-text and the 𝔓45-W combination (C-text). This rough reconstruction of the history of the New Testament text and its groupings leads to the second set of criteria for originality of readings, which we call 'external criteria'.

Again, these are phrased so that if a criterion describes the situation of one reading within a variation unit, that reading may be reckoned the most likely original.

CRITERIA RELATED TO EXTERNAL EVIDENCE

1. A variant's support by the earliest manuscripts, or by manuscripts assuredly preserving early texts. Historians of the text conclude that old manuscripts have been less subject to conflation and other scribal alterations.

2. A variant's support by the 'best quality' manuscripts. Manuscripts evidencing careful copying are less likely to have been subject to textual corruption or contamination, and manuscripts that frequently and consistently offer readings accredited as most likely original thereby acquire a reputation of generally high quality—but it must be recognized that internal criteria are utilized to reach the conclusion that certain manuscripts are the 'best'.

3. A variant's support by manuscripts with the widest geographical distribution. Readings attested in more than one locality are less likely to be accidental or idiosyncratic.

4. A variant's support by one or more established groups of manuscripts of recognized antiquity, character, and perhaps location, that is, of recognized 'best quality'. Not only individual manuscripts, but families and text-types can be judged as to age and quality—again, internal criteria contribute to these judgments.

Naturally, what is true of internal criteria is also the case with external criteria: conflicting judgments on a single reading may arise from application of these various external criteria, or two competing readings may be supported by different criteria. More often, however, conflicts arise *between* the internal and external criteria: an external criterion may support one reading as original, while an internal criterion supports another, as when a variant in a very early manuscript or group is also the smoother reading or contains material from a parallel passage. There are many other possibilities. For example, in Matt. 27:17, was Barabbas's name really Jesus Barabbas? There is strong and widespread external support for 'Barabbas' only, but it is highly plausible that the most likely original is 'Jesus Barabbas' even though this reading has weak external support. Why? Because, on internal grounds (reverence for Jesus Christ), 'Jesus' was doubtless dropped from the text because, as Origen in fact says, 'no one who is a sinner [is called] Jesus' (see Metzger [ed.] 1994: 56).

Thus resolution, though rarely simple, is sought once again in the balance of probabilities—by using all relevant criteria and assessing their relative merits in answering the question, What would the author most likely have written? This last sentence describes the method currently dominant: 'reasoned eclecticism'. It represents middle ground between what might be called a 'historical-documentary' method—basically reliance upon documents or manuscripts, that is, external criteria; and 'thoroughgoing eclecticism'—a virtually exclusive reliance upon transcriptional probability, that is, internal criteria. 'Reasoned eclecticism', then, combines the two approaches and employs all relevant criteria for a given case, external and internal, and attempts a resolution by weighing over against one another the various criteria: hence the phrase, relying on 'the balance of probabilities', when trying to decide on the most likely original reading. (On 'thoroughgoing [or rigorous] eclecticism', see Elliott in Ehrman and Holmes 1995: 321-35; on 'reasoned eclecticism', see Holmes in Ehrman and Holmes 1995: 336-60; on both, see Fee in Epp and Fee 1993: 124-40; Epp in Epp and Fee 1993: 141-82; and Epp 1992. Numerous examples of how the various criteria function can be found in Metzger 1992: 207-46; Aland and Aland 1989: 280-316.)

CONCLUSION

In this essay we have journeyed through the relevance of textual criticism for interpreting the New Testament; through the lively story of how its text was transmitted to us, with all of its scribal exigencies that must be understood, evaluated, and often countervailed; through the oft-competing principles that apply both to the internal transcriptional and to the external documentary aspects of manuscripts; and through the description of these documents themselves. As we apply this entire text-critical endeavor to the textual variants of each New Testament writing, we discern multiple voices within the fabric of the text—voices of an ancient author; of the oldest attainable text; of a harmonistic amplifier; of a grammarian or stylist seeking improvement; of a heterodox propagandist or an orthodox 'corrector'; of an otherwise culturally conditioned interpreter; and even the voice of an editor or possibly a revisionist responsible for compositional levels that may lie behind some of our present New Testament writings. Discerning a particular voice is not easy and often nigh impossible, but each attempt is enlightening about the richness, the diversity, and the dynamism of the early Church and its authoritative collection of ancient writings.

EXCURSUS: THE INTERSECTION OF TEXTUAL CRITICISM AND CANON

Certain features of 'New Testament' manuscripts, such as their content and the order and combinations of books they contain, have long been recognized as carrying implications for the lengthy process by which the New Testament canon was formed. Less well recognized are the canonical implications of two other matters related to textual criticism: the mere fact that competing textual variations exist (raising the issue of which text is canonical) and the possibility of discovering compositional levels behind our 'canonical' New Testament books or identifying later formulations of their texts (questioning the meaning of 'original text', among other matters). These three levels of interaction between text and canon deserve exploration, though resolution of the issues they raise is not easily reached.

1. Manuscript Features with Implications for Canon

The presence in manuscripts of books ultimately not retained in the New Testament, the absence in certain manuscripts of books normally expected there, and the sequence in which books are found in manuscripts, as well as the conventional groups and combinations in which early Christian writings circulated, have played a role—not always clearly identifiable—in the formation of the Christian canon. These are all features extraneous to the actual texts of the manuscripts.

A. 'Non-Canonical' Books in 'New Testament' Manuscripts. Some 'New Testament' manuscripts, as is well known, contain writings that did not become part of the Christian canon. As examples: $\mathfrak{P}72$ (3rd/4th century) contains Jude and 1–2 Peter, but they are interspersed among an array of other Christian writings, such as the Nativity of Mary, an Ode of Solomon, the Apology of Phileas, and others. Codex Sinaiticus (ℵ, 4th century) has the Old and New Testaments and, following the latter, the Epistle of Barnabas and the Shepherd of Hermas (part of which is lost—it is not known whether additional works originally were included in the volume). Codex Alexandrinus (A, 5th century) also has the Old and New Testaments as well as 1–2 Clement (again, the manuscript breaks off after a portion of the latter). Codex Boernerianus (G^p, 9th century) of the Pauline Epistles originally contained also the Epistle to the Laodiceans. Curiously, this (obviously spurious) letter can be found in more than a hundred (!) Latin Vulgate manuscripts (including the 6th-century F) and in Arabic and others, and was included in all eighteen German Bibles prior to that of Luther (Metzger 1987: 183, 239-40). As a final example, a twelfth-century Harklean Syriac New Testament contains 1–2 Clement, placing them between the Catholic Epistles and the Pauline epistles (Metzger 1987: 222).

As is known from patristic sources, at certain times in certain places books like 1–2 Clement, the Epistle of Barnabas, the Epistle to the

Laodiceans, and many others, but especially the *Shepherd of Hermas*, were treated as authoritative (or 'canonical'). Three apocalypses, as is well documented, vied over a long period of time for a place among the authoritative writings (the Revelation of John, the *Apocalypse of Peter*, and the *Shepherd of Hermas*). Oddly, the *Apocalypse of Peter* has not been found as part of a New Testament manuscript, though it is included in the canon list attached to Codex Claromontanus (D^p, 6th century, but the list is thought to be earlier); that list, incidentally, also includes the *Shepherd of Hermas*, as well as the *Epistle of Barnabas* and the *Acts of Paul*, though the scribe has placed a dash to the left of these books, as well as the *Apocalypse of Peter*, to note them as in some way exceptional (for the text and discussion, see Metzger 1987: 230, 310-11).

These data raise obvious questions: to what extent do our 'New Testament' manuscripts reflect the status of canon formation in their times? And, did they influence that process? Doubtless, there were effects in both directions, but proof is elusive. For example, in the first two centuries of Christianity, books like *1 Clement*, the *Epistle of Barnabas*, the *Apocalypse of Peter*, the *Shepherd of Hermas*, and others were treated as authoritative by various patristic writers, especially Clement of Alexandria. In the third and fourth centuries— Codex ℵ being produced in the latter—writings such as these were known, used, and valued by the likes of Origen (185–254), Hippolytus (170–235), and Eusebius (c. 265–340). At the same time, Origen is reported to have called 2 Peter 'doubted' and 2–3 John 'questionable', and Eusebius, who designated *Barnabas*, the *Apocalypse of Peter*, and *Hermas* as 'disputed books', also placed James, Jude, 2 Peter, 2–3 John, and perhaps the Revelation of John in this same category. This reveals something of the fluidity still to be found on the fringes of the New Testament canon in the early fourth century—nor was there uniformity across the whole of Christianity on these matters, especially between east and west, and especially on books like Hebrews and Revelation; movement toward our twenty-seven-book canon accelerated as the fourth century closed, but not in all localities (see Gamble 1985: 48-56).

Returning to 'New Testament' manuscripts, it is difficult, therefore, to specify the significance that the presence of *Barnabas* and *Hermas* in the fourth century Codex ℵ has for canon, and the presence of *1–2 Clement* in Codex A in the following century is even less clear.

B. Absence of Expected Books in Manuscripts. Some 'New

Testament' manuscripts do not contain certain books that might have been expected in their particular groupings. For example, 𝔓46 (c. 200) originally had ten letters of Paul, including Hebrews, but not Philemon; it apparently never contained the Pastoral Letters (there is no room). Also, Codex G^p (9th century) lacks Hebrews (though the place of Hebrews in the canon was firm by the end of the fourth century). While three uncials and fifty-six minuscules contain the whole New Testament (that is, our twenty-seven books), two uncial manuscripts and 147 minuscules (including no. 33 of the 9th century) have the whole New Testament *except* the Revelation of John.

Anyone familiar with the history of canon will recognize that the Pastorals (which lack strong early attestation), Hebrews (which could not be linked with any known apostolic author), and especially the Revelation of John (with debated authority and strong rivals) are among those books that were problematic in the canon process (in addition to the perennially difficult, James, Jude, 2 Peter, and 2–3 John). Hebrews is not in the Muratorian Canon (c. 200—though some date it in the 4th century), and Revelation's place in the canon was uncertain for some centuries, especially in Eastern Christianity.

So, again, the extent to which our manuscripts reflect or influenced canon formation is a relevant question, but only rather cautious statements can be made. One can attempt a few under three headings. (1) *Revelation of John*: The very number of extant manuscripts perhaps reflects the uncertainty about the canonicity of Revelation (though there could be other reasons for the phenomenon) in that there are 287 manuscripts of the Revelation of John over against 662 of the Acts and Catholic Epistles, 792 of Paul, and 2,361 of the Gospels (Aland and Aland 1989: 78-79, 83); note also that Revelation has never been a part of the official lectionary of the Greek Church (Metzger 1987: 217). (2) *Hebrews*: While *1 Clement* appears to be the only writing that quotes Hebrews prior to the oldest extant manuscript containing it, namely 𝔓46 (dating c. 200), Hebrews is nonetheless firmly a part of the Pauline collection in that papyrus manuscript because it stands between Romans and 1 Corinthians. This cannot be based on length, because 1 Corinthians is longer than Hebrews, though its proximity to Romans could be based on doctrine (Hatch 1936: 134). (Hebrews, though of unknown authorship, very often circulated with the Pauline letters.) So, the unusual position of Hebrews in this very early manuscript reflects a conviction of Pauline authorship and, in addition, may constitute a canonical claim contemporary with Clement of Alexandria (c. 200), who quotes Hebrews authoritatively and thought that Paul was in some way responsible for its content. (3) *The Shorter Catholic Epistles*: While the history of the canon shows that only 1 Peter and 1 John were quite well established in the third century, but that James, Jude, 2 Peter, and 2–3 John were still striving for acceptance, the history of the text of these Catholic Epistles reveals that there is often no uniform textual character among them in a single manuscript; rather, each epistle may have a text quite different in complexion from the others. This suggests (1) that they had earlier circulated as independent writings and (2) that their differing textual character in a manuscript bringing them together is due to the earlier, most likely separate, manuscripts from which they were copied (Aland and Aland 1989: 49-50). For instance, Jude in $\mathfrak{P}$72 (3rd/4th century), its earliest manuscript, shows a complex textual history (Aland and Aland 1989: 50); moreover, as noted earlier, $\mathfrak{P}$72 contains not only 1–2 Peter and Jude, but an array of other early, 'non-canonical' Christian writings. Thus, not only might a book's absence from a manuscript—where it might be expected—reflect fluidity in canon formation, but fluidity can be inferred also from the varying textual complexions of books in a single grouping or collection, implying, for instance, that writings valued by some were copied and used as individual books until they were more broadly accredited by inclusion in a regular canonical grouping.

Finally, Codex Vaticanus (B, 4th century) is of more than passing interest with respect both to Hebrews and to the shorter Catholic Epistles, even though its New Testament section is assumed to have contained all of our twenty-seven books. The manuscript actually breaks off after Heb. 9:13 (and the 15th-century supplement [= minuscule 1957] that provides the rest of Hebrews and the Revelation of John is of no significance). The Alands (1989: 109) think it probable that, like ℵ and A, Codex B contained writings of the Apostolic Fathers; B has ancient page numbers—a rarity among Greek manuscripts—that permit a calculation of how many pages were lost at the beginning (some 46 chapters of Genesis), but there is no way of telling how many leaves were lost at the end (Gregory 1907: 344-45). Nonetheless, on the assumption that it contained our present New Testament, it has been observed that the order of these books is identical to that of Athanasius's famous list (367 CE)—the first such list we have that contains all and only our New Testament writings. On the surface, then, it might appear that Codex B, especially if (as has been speculated, but by no means substantiated) it were produced in Egypt or in Alexandria itself (where Athanasius was bishop), could be understood as supporting the fourth-century canon documented in Athanasius. Lacking knowledge of its provenance, however, it is safer to say that Codex B documents a fourth-century view of canon, though at some unknown locality or region in Christianity. Specifically, its chapter divisions, some of which show signs of considerable antiquity, permit two observations of interest. First, in the Pauline Epistles—unlike the common practice of separately numbering the sections of each writing—the chapter divisions of Codex B are continuous from Romans on; yet, they reveal that Hebrews, which follows Thessalonians, was placed after Galatians—hence, more firmly in the Pauline group (cf. 𝔓46)—in the manuscript that was the archetype of B (see below on the order of books), suggesting again an earlier conviction of Pauline authorship and perhaps thereby a stronger view of canonicity for Hebrews prior to Codex B. Secondly, and more significantly, is the fact that the 'very old' section divisions in the Catholic Epistles take no account of 2 Peter, suggesting that this often-disputed epistle was rejected also by the maker of these divisions in Codex B (Gregory 1907: 344).

C. Order of Books in Manuscripts. Thirdly, as already illustrated, some manuscripts have New Testament books in an order different from the traditional. For instance, the four Gospels are known in some nine different sequences. Most manuscripts follow the traditional order; the best known deviation occurs in Codices D and W (both 5th century), where the order is Matthew, John, Luke, and Mark. Acts nearly always follows the Gospels, but ℵ (4th century) and the Latin Codex Fuldensis (F, 6th century) place it after the Pauline letters. Hebrews was very frequently included among the Pauline letters and usually followed Philemon, though—as I have already noted—in 𝔓46 (c. 200) it follows Romans, while ℵ, B (both 4th century), and others place it between 2 Thessalonians and the Pastorals. (See Metzger 1987: 295-300.) 𝔓46 also has Ephesians before Galatians. Indeed, Greek and versional manuscripts have the Pauline Epistles in some eight different sequences.

The relevance of these data to canon is more complicated, with more subtle implications. Though arguments can be made that New Testament books were often arranged according to length, usually from the longest to the shortest (it was common to count and record the number of lines, or *stichoi*, in a manuscript), sometimes counting the writings of one author as one work (see Metzger 1987: 296-300), yet it is possible also that fluctuating sequences of books may indicate canonical fluidity or uncertainty. The most plausible example is Hebrews and perhaps, as noted above, an issue is authorship—Pauline or not? Hebrews is found in nine different positions in New Testament manuscripts (see Metzger 1994: 591-92), including a location between Corinthians and Ephesians, between Romans and Corinthians (as in 𝔓46), between Corinthians and Galatians, after Philemon (that is, at the end of the Paulines), but usually between Thessalonians and the Pastorals (א and B) (Frede 1966–71: 292-303). Though the criterion of length appears to be ruled out in all of these combinations, relevant issues might be the uncertainty of the destination or addressees of Hebrews, a desire to place it between the letters to churches and those to individuals, trying to cope with a Pauline Hebrews when it did not fit with the view—well established by the third/fourth centuries—that Paul wrote to seven churches (see Dahl 1962: 261-64 and below), or factors of doctrine. Thus, for whatever reasons, Hebrews was difficult to classify and this, for some early Christians, may have raised questions about its canonicity.

D. Marcionite Prologues. Some manuscripts contain what are generally called Marcionite prologues. They are found in a number of Latin Vulgate manuscripts (including the prominent Codex Fuldensis [F]) and provide, for the Pauline letters, short descriptions of the addressees and reasons for writing—stressing Paul's conflict with false apostles. The current view, however, is that these are not of Marcionite origin, but were written for a Pauline corpus to seven churches that was not connected with Marcion's canon and which later gave way to the fourteen-letter corpus, and that the prologues presuppose an earlier 'seven church' corpus that began with Galatians, 1–2 Corinthians, Romans—the same order found in Marcion's canon, though the order is not to be attributed to Marcion (see Clabeaux 1989: 1-4; Schmid 1995: 287- 89). These manuscript data are difficult to assess, but can potentially assist us in understanding the canon process and the controversies attendant to it, such as the long-standing but elusive role of Marcion, whose differing text of Paul was most likely not a new creation but 'the adaptation of an already existing Pauline Corpus that began with Galatians' (Clabeaux 1989: 4). (The so-called Anti-Marcionite prologues to the Gospels [Mark, Luke, and John only] are found in nearly forty Latin biblical manuscripts [5th–

10th centuries], though the prologue for Luke is also preserved in Greek. They were independently composed, and date in the fourth century, though that for Luke perhaps dates in the second century. Their relevance to canon is negligible, though the early Lukan portion does refer to Luke as a follower of Paul [see Koester 1990: 243, 335-36].)

The four issues treated above are illustrative of the long-standing connection between text and canon, but also of the difficulty of bringing or keeping them together. Natural connections become elusive, and the two disciplines have tended to distance themselves from one another more and more, though scholars like Nils Dahl, Harry Gamble, and John Clabeaux have attempted to clarify again the fruitfulness of their intersection.

2. Textual Variants as 'Canon within the Canon'

There is another level at which textual criticism and issues of canon intersect. One is seldom addressed by textual critics, but raises fascinating if intractable issues, and it may be introduced by invoking an old phrase in a new way: 'A canon within the canon'. This usually refers to defining one's beliefs and practice by relying only upon certain selected books from an authoritative canon (as in Luther's reliance upon Romans and Galatians and his virtual dismissal of James, or Zwingli's rejection of Revelation), though it may also refer to reliance upon selected ideas. If, however, we apply the phrase to the textual variants of an individual variation unit and to the selection of one variant over the others, rather penetrating questions arise: In what sense are competing variant readings canonical? More specifically, when decisions between or among readings are not easily made, in what sense are these competing readings, singly or collectively, canonical? Or, in what sense are readings canonical that are suspected of being theologically motivated—especially when a variant with an 'orthodox' bias can be shown to be secondary?

A. *Manuscript Indications of Textual Problems.* How do the manuscripts themselves deal with recognized textual variations? Scribal sigla have been mentioned above in connection with the 1 Cor. 14:34-35 illustration—a scribe marking a manuscript to alert the reader, in this instance, to a doubtful passage. When manuscripts contain the notable pericope of the adulteress (John 7:53–8:11), often an asterisk (Codices E M Λ) or an obelus (Codex S) accompanies the passage, which are customary signs of a questionable portion of text. Likewise, manuscripts with Mark 16:9-20 often contain such sigla or even comments that older Greek manuscripts do not have the passage (see, for example, minuscule 1) (Metzger 1992: 223-24, 226). Varying locations also alert us to textual-canonical problems. The adulteress pericope is most often found after John 7:52, but sometimes after 7:36 or 21:24, and it can also be found after Luke 21:38, suggesting uncertainty about the pericope among scribes. Another indicator that a scribe's exemplar did not contain a portion of text, but that such texts were known to the scribe, is the use of blank space. Codices L and Δ have a blank space where John 7:53–8:11 would fall, and the scribe of Codex B, completely contrary to his practice when coming to the end of a New Testament book, leaves an entire column blank after Mark 16:8, 'evidently because one or other of the two subsequent endings was known to him personally, while he found neither of them in the exemplar which he was copying' (Hort in Westcott and Hort 1896: I, p. 29 notes). In what sense are these lengthier passages canonical?

B. Authoritative Status of Textual Variants in the Early Church. Some might say that readings clearly rejected on the basis of external and internal criteria should at once be labeled non-canonical. Decisions, however, are not often clear and simple; more importantly, significant variants (that is, those that make sense and are unlikely to be the result of accidental alteration) surely were part of some churches' authoritative Scripture as they were used in worship and as normative for Christian life—whether we now judge them as most likely original or not. To take an example mentioned above, neither appended ending of Mark (that is, beyond γάρ in 16:8) is likely to have been part of the early Gospel of Mark, yet both the so-called 'shorter' and 'longer' endings (and the latter's further expansions) surely were part of the canonical Mark as far as some churches were concerned; even the 'shorter' ending, with its grandiose, obviously non-Markan language, was used in Greek-speaking churches, as well as in churches using Latin, Syriac, Coptic, and Ethiopian (as judged by manuscripts containing it). The same applies to 1 Cor. 14:34-35, which has not only long been considered canonical, but has also played a major role in shaping gender views in Christianity. So, to what extent are variants canonical that were treated as canonical by the early Church, but are now rejected by us?

Or, is the Matthean phrase, 'but rescue us from the evil one' (6:13), canonical also in Luke for the large number of manuscripts that add it to their text of the 'Lord's prayer' (Luke 11:4)? Or, is the final phrase in Matthew's version, 'For the kingdom and the power and the glory are yours forever' (at 6:13), canonical for the many witnesses that carry it—against the clear evidence that it is a later, liturgical addition? What about the added v. 37 in Acts 8? This is another obvious liturgical (baptismal) formula not attested in most of the earliest textual tradition. What of the agraphon in Codex Bezae at Luke 6:4, addressed to a man working on the Sabbath: 'Man, if you know what you are doing, you are blessed; but if you do not, you are accursed and a transgressor of the law'. Again this was canonical for some. Or, if the current revival of the view that the author of Acts wrote two versions of that book were to gain acceptance, would both editions be canonical?

A final example will illustrate an additional problem: Is the doxology in Romans canonical after 14:23, after 15:33, or after 16:23—or after both 14:23 and 16:23, where several manuscripts place it? Or was this doxology never a part of Romans, as other manuscripts and patristic witnesses testify? The further issue is whether Romans originally had 14 chapters, or 15, or 16—as demarcated by the various positions of the concluding doxology—and, more importantly, what does this placement of the doxology tell us about the textual history of Romans and therefore its canonical form? Tracing out the evolution and interrelation of these three forms of Romans is highly complex, to say the least, but it leads (among other matters) to the conclusion that a 14-chapter version of Romans (secondary to the 16-chapter original) was pre-Marcionite and came into existence prior to the collection of a Pauline corpus (see Gamble 1977: 15-35, 96-129; cf. Schmid 1995: 284-94; see Dahl 1962 below). These are issues closely relevant to canon in general and to canon within the canon.

C. Assessing Textual/Canonical Variant Readings. These various kinds of examples from several parts of the New Testament elicit a few observations. First, the Gospels in early Christianity doubtless were read holistically, and not discretely as we tend to do in critical scholarship. (Perhaps the appearance of Tatian's *Diatessaron* c. 172 CE may be viewed as a concrete and dramatic demonstration of such a holistic proclivity.) Therefore, the 'canonical' questions we raise when the 'Lord's prayer' is expanded in Luke by Synoptic harmonization or in Matthew by liturgical influence would not likely have occurred to early hearers of these Gospel passages. Rather, it would appear that canonical issues, to the extent that they were raised at all in the first couple of centuries, focused largely on whole writings ('We accept the following writings...; we reject the following books...', etc.) rather than on what we would call textual variants (cf. Elliott 1993: 353).

A notable exception, however, is Origen, who shows a concern for a 'correct' text of the Old Testament in his *Hexapla* and for that of the 'New Testament'—as far as a New Testament was defined by him— through his numerous text-critical comments on various passages. In addition, his allegorical interpretation demanded a text exact in its details. Hence, he blames the textual aberrations that he finds in various manuscripts on heretics ('Jesus Barabbas' for 'Barabbas' in Matt. 27:16-17—no others would have joined Jesus' name with a sinner), on careless or arbitrary scribes, or on presumably orthodox Christians trying to solve theological or exegetical problems in the text. He himself selects certain readings based on his own investigations of geography (the problems of 'Bethany' or 'Bethabara' in John 1:28, or 'Gadara', 'Gergesa' or 'Gerasa' in Matt. 8:28) or history (preferring in Luke 23:45 'the sun was darkened' to 'the sun was eclipsed', since no eclipse was recorded in Jesus' time), among others (see Pack 1960). It would appear that, for Origen (in the middle of the 3rd century), variant readings did involve questions of a 'canon within the "canon"', though the latter for him was not yet fully defined.

Secondly, still in the context of ancient holistic reading, a larger corpus in the emerging canon may have shaped its individual parts; for instance, the 'longer' ending of Mark 'could have functioned to bring Mark's Gospel into harmony with the fourfold collection', or the inclusion of the Pastoral Epistles in the Pauline corpus could have been motivated by a wish to provide them a broader and more appropriate context (Childs 1985: 52-53). Such a context may also have been sought for the discrete 1 Cor. 14:34-35 segment.

Thirdly, it is commonplace to say that numerous textual variants arose in the early period because these Christian manuscripts were copied by non-professional scribes (for example, Vaganay and Amphoux 1991: 3) or because they did not yet have the status of Scripture (for example, Elliott and Moir 1995: 3). On the latter point, however, Ernest C. Colwell boldly stated forty-five years ago that 'The reverse is the case. It was because they were the religious treasure of the church that they were changed' and 'The paradox is that the variations came into existence because these were religious books, sacred books, canonical books. The devout scribe felt compelled to correct misstatements which he found in the manuscript he was copying' (Colwell 1952: 52-53). Though this cannot account for all variants, and may not have obtained everywhere, it is a more compelling view than the carelessness theory. Undoubtedly, all of the significant variants (as earlier defined) 'are interpretations which were highly enough thought of in some place and at some time to be incorporated into the Scripture itself' (Parvis 1952: 172). On this view, a concept of canonicity has encouraged rather than discouraged textual alterations. Indeed, one may venture the affirmation that, when a scribe effected a theologically-motivated textual alteration, that scribe was making a canonical decision, an independent (or perhaps a community) contribution to the New Testament canon. If so, the process of canon formation was operating at two quite different levels: first, at the level of church leaders of major Christian localities or regions, even as large as the eastern or western church, seeking broad consensus on which books were to be accepted as authoritative for the larger church, and, secondly, also at the level of individual scribes (usually, perhaps, representing a monastic or some other small community) concerned about individual variants that properly expressed their theological or other understanding of the sentences and paragraphs within their already authoritative books.

3. Text/Canon Intersection at the Composition Stages of the New Testament

The issues I have raised go still deeper, to levels behind our canonical New Testament books to pre-canonical, pre-compositional stages in the formation of the early Christian writings.

A. Introducing the Issues from the Four Gospels. These further issues may be introduced and illustrated by referring to a 1988 conference at the University of Notre Dame on 'Gospel Traditions in the Second Century' (see Petersen 1989), where Helmut Koester, facing seven other participants from six countries—all specialists in textual criticism—opened his presentation with the appropriate observation that there is no second century manuscript evidence for the New Testament (except the tiny $\mathfrak{P}52$) and that, therefore, immense problems attend the reconstruction of the textual history of the Gospels in their first century of transmission. Next, he turned on its head the New Testament text-critics' standard claim (imbedded also in my main article above!) that we are fortunate to have so many early manuscripts so close to the time the writings originated; rather, he aptly observed that 'the oldest known manuscript archetypes are separated from the autographs by more than a century. Textual critics of classical texts know that the first century of their transmission is the period in which the most serious corruptions occur'. He adds the provocative note that 'textual critics of the New Testament writings have been surprisingly naive in this respect' (Koester 1989: 19).

Working then from textual agreements between Matthew and Luke when they use Mark, and from comparisons of the *Secret Gospel of Mark* with our Mark, Koester argues that an earlier form of Mark can be discerned behind our canonical Mark; the latter represents a revision, the former becomes our 'oldest accessible text of the Gospel of Mark'—accessible, that is, through the comparisons adduced. He also investigates the Gospel material quoted by Justin Martyr (c. 150), postulating that his aim was to produce '*one* inclusive new Gospel' by harmonizing or by using a harmony of Matthew and Luke; in the process, Justin reveals a freedom to modify this material to demonstrate (as one of his purposes) a more complete fulfillment of prophecy in the events of Jesus. This quick summary cannot do justice to the much more complex study (Koester 1989; 1990: 275-86, 295-302, 360-402; cf. Wisse 1989, who argues against extensive pre-canonical redaction), but, whether these hypotheses are sustained in detail or not, Koester's point is clear and telling:

> ...the text of the Synoptic Gospels was very unstable during the first and second centuries. With respect to Mark, one can be fairly certain that only its revised text has achieved canonical status, while the original text (attested only by Matthew and Luke) has not survived. With respect to Matthew and Luke, there is no guarantee that the archetypes of the manuscript tradition are identical with the original text of each Gospel. The harmonizations of these two Gospels demonstrate that their text was not sacrosanct and that alterations could be expected... New Testament textual critics have been deluded by the hypothesis that the archetypes of the textual tradition which were fixed c. 200 CE...are (almost) identical with the autographs... Whatever evidence there is indicates that not only minor, but also substantial revisions of the original texts have occurred during the first hundred years of the transmission (Koester 1989: 37).

Thus, we are left not only with text-critical questions, such as, which variants of Mark are most likely original, but also penetrating canonical questions, such as, which Mark is original? (See Petersen 1994b: 136-37.) Similar issues pertain to the composition of the other Synoptics, the Fourth Gospel, the Pauline letters, and other portions of the New Testament. One such example is the relation of the well-known Egerton Papyrus 2 (currently dated c. 200) to the Gospel of John. This papyrus usually has been understood as a later excerpt from all four Gospels, but Koester views it as representing a text older than John, because, 'with its language that contains Johannine elements but reveals a greater affinity to the Synoptic tradition, it belongs to a stage of the tradition that preceded the canonical gospels' (Koester 1982: II, p. 182). More recently, Koester has endorsed the view of J.B. Daniels that the Synoptic parallels in Egerton Papyrus 2 represent 'a separate tradition which did not undergo Markan redaction', and that the papyrus's author 'did not make use of the Gospel of John in canonical form' (Koester 1990: 207, quoting the dissertation of Daniels; cf. 206-16). If so, the Gospel of which these papyrus fragments were a part would have been read, without question, as authoritative in some early church or churches, and possibly could have played a role also in the composition of our Gospels. The question arises again: What or where is the original Mark? Or Matthew, or Luke, or John?

B. Introducing the Issues from the Pauline Epistles. When one turns to the (genuine) Pauline letters, it is easier to envision a specific moment at a specific place when a real, identifiable person placed words on papyrus that were to be carried to a congregation in Greece or Asia Minor, but even in these cases, is the 'original' the letter so penned or is it the form each letter had when a Pauline collection was formed? This would take into account the changes that the transmission process had wrought. After all, 'there is no simply "neutral" text from which one can recover a pure textual stream, but the early period reflects highly complex recensional activity from the outset' (Childs 1985: 525).

Two well-known variants, similar in form, raise questions about such recensional activity within the Pauline corpus. At Eph. 1:1, 'in Ephesus' is lacking in a small number of witnesses, but they include the old and venerable 𝔓46 ℵ* and B* (* meaning the original hand, before a later hand 'corrected' the text). Based on the reading of these witnesses and the general or 'catholic' nature of Ephesians, several theories developed, among them that of Archbishop Ussher in the seventeenth century that it was a circular letter intended for several churches and that a blank was left in 1:1 for names of churches using it, and that of E.J. Goodspeed (1933) that 'Ephesians' was written to introduce the first Pauline collection. Nils Dahl takes this textual variant in a different direction, first rejecting the reading of the oldest manuscripts, suggesting that the context within Eph. 1:1 requires a geographical designation, but then allowing the possibility that the letter was originally issued in several copies with a special address in each of them. In any case, the letter must have had a pre-history before it was published as part of the Pauline corpus. The text without any concrete address is to be understood as a result of a secondary 'catholicyzing', to which we have an analogy in the textual tradition of Romans (Dahl 1962: 267).

This is a reference to Rom. 1:7 (and Rom. 1:15), where 'in Rome' is absent from a few witnesses. By an elaborate argument, Dahl contends that the absence of this geographical designation is as well attested as its presence; he then argues that the short, fourteen-chapter version of Romans, ending with 14:23 plus the doxology of 16:25-27 placed there by a number of manuscripts, circulated 'in early days' with no geographical reference and as another 'catholic' epistle of Paul. The complex text-critical problems involving the doxology have been referred to above, and they serve, in Dahl's view, as 'further evidence of the existence of more than one recension of Romans' (1962: 268). Like Ephesians, this fourteen-chapter version of Romans 'will have to be explained as the result of editorial activity...between the times of Paul and Marcion' (1962: 269). Finally, Dahl points out that the earliest patristic references do not easily support 'a standard edition of the Pauline corpus before 100 A.D.' and that 'the question whether our whole textual tradition goes back to one archetypical manuscript of the whole collection will need further investigation' (1962: 271 n. 2). What, then, is the 'original' text of these letters and how is that related to their 'canonical' text as embraced by the church?

C. Various Meanings of 'Original Text' and 'Canon'. So text and canon cross paths at basic and perhaps unsettling levels of inquiry. Whereas traditional textual criticism has contributed much by moving its textual investigations ever closer to the time that the New Testament authors wrote, more recently its tasks have become more intriguing and more challenging as the discipline turns its attention away from the search for merely one 'original' text to an understanding of earlier stages of composition and to earlier 'texts'— earlier 'originals'—that lie behind what we have become accustomed to consider the autographs of our 'canonical' New Testament writings. In addition, various other 'original' texts may have been defined by and during the lengthy canonization process, perhaps, for example, at the point when the Gospels or the Pauline letters were formed into collections, or when writings otherwise achieved a more formal kind of acceptance or canonization in a region of the church. As a result, not only is the process of textual transmission extended farther into the past as the 'original' not only recedes in time but becomes less tangible and thereby more elusive, but the notion of 'original' also advances forward in time beyond what we have usually called the autographs and encompasses later reshapings of the texts. Within this complex tangle of texts and revisions, which finds its life setting in a multifaceted, vibrant, developing church, what, indeed, does 'original' mean? Which 'original' ought we seek? And what meaning or meanings does 'canon' carry?

In short, the question of the 'original' New Testament text has taken on extraordinary complexity. Yet the issue is not new, for aspects of the question were raised pointedly in the middle third of the twentieth century by members of the 'Chicago school' of New Testament textual criticism, who shifted the discipline's emphasis away from the search for the traditional 'original' text. For example, D.W. Riddle affirms:

> The legitimate task of textual criticism is not limited to the recovery of approximately the original form of the documents, to the establishment of the 'best' text, nor to the 'elimination of spurious readings'. It must be recognized that every significant variant records a religious experience which brought it into being. This means that there are no 'spurious readings': the various forms of the text are sources for the study of the history of Christianity (Riddle 1936: 221).

Some years later, M.M. Parvis picked up this theme that there are no spurious readings because:

> All are a part of the tradition; all contribute to our knowledge of the history of the text. And they are significant contributions because they are interpretations which were highly enough thought of in some place and at some time to be incorporated into the Scripture itself (Parvis 1952: 172).

To bring out the real thrust of his position, he adds that, even when we have approached the autographs, we still have only one form of the tradition (Parvis 1952: 173). Thus, there are other authentic forms of the tradition—he might well have said other 'originals'—that enshrine significant stages in the evolution of the New Testament writings or texts.

Brevard Childs, in his programmatic essay on 'The Hermeneutical Problem of New Testament Text Criticism', also wants textual criticism to move away from its traditional goal of attempting to recover the original text, as that term is commonly understood, to a goal of recovering the 'New Testament text which best reflects the true apostolic witness found in the church's scripture', or 'searching for the best received, that is, canonical text'. Such a text, he believes, 'is by definition different from the author's autograph' but lies somewhere between that and the corrupt and uncritical textus receptus (1985: 527-28). Certainly this may qualify as one of the several goals of New Testament textual criticism, but it is unlikely that the discipline will wish to adopt this as its only goal.

Rather, through the examples cited above, various 'originals' or levels of 'originality' come more clearly into view: (1) a 'pre-canonical original' of the text of certain books, representing earlier stages in the composition of what became our New Testament books; (2) an author's 'autograph' of a writing, that is, the textual form as it left the desk of Paul or of a writer of Mark or of the other portions of our New Testament; (3) a 'canonical original', the textual form of a book at the time its canonicity was (perhaps more formally) sought or established, as at the time a collection was made of the Pauline letters or of the four-fold Gospels; and (4) an 'interpretive original', representing each interpretative iteration of a writing, as it was used in the life, worship, and teaching of the Church. This fourth type would not involve extensive rewriting in the New Testament, as might be the case in parts of the Hebrew Bible and its Greek translations (see Tov 1992: 164-80), but rather the creation of individual variant readings that 'clarify' or 'improve' a text, or move it toward or away from orthodoxy, or at most (as possibly in the so-called 'Western' text, if it is deemed secondary) a modestly systematic alteration of a larger text in accordance with an ideological bias. It is important to note also that number two above (an autograph) may really be, as far as we can tell, a number three or a number four kind of 'original'. That is another way of saying that these distinctions, while we may be able to delineate them in a descriptive paragraph like this, are in reality extremely hard to differentiate in any given case. Yet, the reality is that textual criticism can no longer retreat to a position of seeking 'the original' text of the New Testament; rather it must acknowledge and concern itself with multiple 'originals'.

4. Conclusion

Whereas Carl Lachmann (1831) was willing to settle for the New Testament text of the fourth century and Westcott and Hort (1896) for that of the second, the late Kurt Aland quite recently (1981) expressed confidence that the current critical text (N–A[26] and *UBSGNT*[3]) could, for all practical purposes, only a hundred years after Westcott and

Hort, be reckoned as meeting the goal of an edition of the New Testament 'in the original Greek' (Aland 1981: 274-75). Many others, if unwilling to go that far, have been encouraged by our progress in moving from early manuscripts toward an even earlier form of the New Testament text. Now, however, new challenges arise as issues of canon and text intersect in fresh ways.

For one thing, when textual critics consider how the concept of 'canon', that is, 'authority', functioned in earliest Christianity, and especially how it may have influenced a thinking scribe's treatment of the text being copied, they will be the more inclined to view significant variant readings as reflective of real-life situations in the developing Church, and more often than not as events clarifying doctrine and practice within the community of faith. Also, certain sigla, blank spaces, and scribal comments in manuscripts will be examined for the same motivations. At the same time, the competing readings in a given variation unit, as well as varying locations of some lengthier variants, reveal a fluidity of 'canon' at the level of individual variants, just as fluidity at the level of writings and groups of writings is shown by the presence in 'New Testament' manuscripts of books not finally accredited as canon, by the absence of expected books or by the varying order of books in manuscripts.

Not least among the newer issues, however, will be reassessing our goals, including defining what we mean by 'original' and by 'canon', and even devising new approaches that can be utilized to probe into various 'pre-canonical', 'canonical' and 'post-canonical' textual stages of our so-called 'canonical' books.

To be sure, the two disciplines of canon and text parallel one another in that (1) the 'New Testament' canon, during three centuries and more, displays a fair measure of fluidity, and (2) the text of the New Testament evidences a similar fluidity over a similar period, a fluidity, moreover, that persisted at the level of individual variants as long as texts were copied by hand.

Yet, in spite of the interconnections between text and canon that have been highlighted here, the two disciplines are essentially distinct. Canon, by definition, is concerned with authoritative material—in the case of Christianity, with authoritative writings that are normative for faith and practice—and it is concerned with the process that led to canon formation. Canon, after all, involves 'measurement', meeting a standard, and by definition it has limits, even if those limits were not defined immediately or by easily recognized criteria. Yet, in essence and in the final analysis, canon involves authority.

Over numerous generations we have been socialized into thinking of a single original text, and it may appear at first glance that textual criticism also is automatically concerned with authority, for, in simpler times, the original text was not uncommonly identified with the autographs, and the autographs with the canonical, authoritative New Testament text that formed the basis for Christian faith and practice. It has become increasingly clear, however, that the canonical texts of the New Testament are not necessarily the same texts as the autographs. Variants have intruded upon them, including harmonizations, clarifications, and theological alterations toward and away from orthodoxy (whatever that might mean in different times and localities in the early Church), and nothing is simple any longer. Nor are other earlier or later stages of the texts necessarily identical with the autographs, and the earliest attainable text is not necessarily to be identified with one or another of these 'originals'. No longer, in fact, can we expect to arrive at any single, objectively original text that, to some, would automatically be authoritative; even the earliest attainable text in individual variation units frequently falls short of consensus, to say nothing of certainty.

Though some textual *critics* may be searching for such an authoritative 'original' text of the New Testament and may wish to identify it with the authoritative canon (as a normative guide to faith and practice), that purpose is not intrinsic to textual *criticism* as a historical-critical discipline. That is, it is not of the essence or within the domain of New Testament textual criticism to accommodate a theological overlay upon its goals and results. Anyone, of course, may exercise the privilege of placing the discipline within such an ideological framework, but that constitutes a separate and further step, one not intrinsic to the discipline itself. Rather, textual criticism is concerned with the history and transmission of the text of what became and now is the New Testament, and (both at the levels of individual variation units and whole writings) it will still seek an 'earliest attainable' or 'most likely original' text (with all of the misgivings attached to such terms), but will do so only with the recognition that multiple 'originals' must be entertained. Additionally, it will strive to place variant readings within the history and culture of the Church to elicit from them some insights into early Christian theology, church life, and society. These purposes are not immediately, directly, or necessarily involved with issues of authority.

BIBLIOGRAPHY

Aland, B., and K. Aland (eds.)
1993   *Novum Testamentum Graece post. Eberhard et Erwin Nestle.* Stuttgart:
        Deutsche Bibelgesellschaft, 27th edn. (Known as Nestle–Aland[27], its
        additional editors were J. Karavidopoulos, C.M. Martini, and B.M.
        Metzger.)
Aland, B., K. Aland, J. Karavidopoulos, C.M. Martini, and B.M. Metzger (eds.)
1993   *The Greek New Testament.* Stuttgart: Deutsche Bibelgesellschaft/United
        Bible Societies, 4th edn. (Known as *UBSGNT*[4] or *UBS*[4], it contains the
        same text as Nestle–Aland[27]. Both of the preceding editions were
        produced in cooperation with the Institute for New Testament Textual
        Research, Münster.)
Aland, B., and J. Delobel (eds.)
1994   *New Testament Textual Criticism, Exegesis, and Early Church History: A
        Discussion of Methods.* Contributions to Biblical Exegesis and Theology,
        7. Kampen: Kok Pharos. (Five text-critical essays.)
Aland, K.
1981   'Der neue "Standard-Text" in seinem Verhältnis zu den frühen Papyri und
        Majuskeln', in E.J. Epp and G.D. Fee (eds.), *New Testament Textual
        Criticism: Its Significance for Exegesis: Essays in Honour of Bruce M.
        Metzger.* Oxford: Clarendon Press: 257-75.
1994   *Kurzgefasste Liste der griechischen Handschriften des Neuen Testaments.*
        ANTF, 1. Berlin: de Gruyter, 1963; 2nd edn. (The official list of New
        Testament manuscripts.)
Aland, K., and B. Aland
1989   *The Text of the New Testament: An Introduction to the Critical Editions
        and to the Theory and Practice of Modern Textual Criticism.* Grand
        Rapids: Eerdmans, 2nd edn (1st English edn 1987; German original 1982).
        (The latest and most reliable source for data on New Testament
        manuscripts.)
Baarda, T.
1994   *Essays on the Diatessaron.* Contributions to Biblical Exegesis and
        Theology, 11. Kampen: Kok Pharos. (15 text-critical essays.)
Birdsall, J.N.
1970   'The New Testament Text', in P.R. Ackroyd and C.F. Evans (eds.), *The
        Cambridge History of the Bible.* I. *From the Beginnings to Jerome.*
        Cambridge: Cambridge University Press: 308-77.
1992   'The Recent History of New Testament Textual Criticism (From Westcott
        and Hort, 1881, to the Present)'. *ANRW* II.26.1: 99-197.
Cervin, R.S.
1994   'A Note regarding the Name 'Junia(s)' in Romans 16.7'. *NTS* 40: 464-70.

Childs, B.S.

1985   *The New Testament as Canon: An Introduction*. Philadelphia: Fortress
        Press. See 'Excursus I: The Hermeneutical Problem of New Testament
        Text Criticism', pp. 518-30.

Clabeaux, J.J.

1989   *A Lost Edition of the Letters of Paul: A Reassessment of the Text of the
        Pauline Corpus Attested by Marcion*. CBQMS, 21. Washington: Catholic
        Biblical Association.

Colwell, E.C.

1952   *What Is the Best New Testament?* Chicago: University of Chicago Press.

1969   *Studies in Methodology in Textual Criticism of the New Testament*. NTTS,
        9. Leiden: Brill. (11 text-critical essays.)

Dahl, N.A.

1962   'The Particularity of the Pauline Epistles as a Problem in the Ancient
        Church', in W.C. van Unnik, *Neotestamentica et Patristica: Eine
        Freundesgabe, Herrn Professor Dr. Oscar Cullmann zu seinem 60.
        Geburtstag überreicht.* NovTSup, 6. Leiden: Brill: 261-81.

Delobel, J.

1994   'Textual Criticism and Exegesis: Siamese Twins?', in B. Aland and J.
        Delobel (eds.), *New Testament Textual Criticism, Exegesis, and Early
        Church History: A Discussion of Methods*. Contributions to Biblical
        Exegesis and Theology, 7. Kampen: Kok Pharos: 98-117.

Ehrman, B.D.

1993   *The Orthodox Corruption of Scripture: The Effect of Early Christological
        Controversies on the Text of the New Testament*. New York: Oxford
        University Press.

1994   'The Use and Significance of Patristic Evidence for New Testament
        Textual Criticism', in B. Aland and J. Delobel (eds.), *New Testament
        Textual Criticism, Exegesis, and Early Church History: A Discussion of
        Methods*. Contributions to Biblical Exegesis and Theology, 7. Kampen:
        Kok Pharos: 118-35.

Ehrman, B.D., and M.W. Holmes (eds.)

1995   *The Text of the New Testament in Contemporary Research: Essays on the
        Status Quaestionis*. SD, 46. Grand Rapids: Eerdmans. (22 text-critical
        essays.) The relevant chapters of this important volume should be
        consulted in connection with the various topics covered in the present
        essay (titles slightly abbreviated): E.J. Epp, 'Papyrus Manuscripts', pp. 3-
        21; D.C. Parker, 'Majuscule Manuscripts', pp. 22-42; B. Aland and K.
        Wachtel, 'Minuscule Manuscripts', pp. 43-60; C.D. Osburn,
        'Lectionaries', pp. 61-74; W.L. Petersen, 'Diatessaron of Tatian', pp. 77-
        96; T. Baarda, 'Syriac Versions', pp. 97-112; J.H. Petzer, 'Latin Version',
        pp. 113-30; F. Wisse, 'Coptic Versions', pp. 131-41; R. Zuurmond,
        'Ethiopic Version', pp. 142-56; J.M. Alexanian, 'Armenian Version', pp.
        157-72; J.N. Birdsall, 'Georgian Version', pp. 173-87; G.D. Fee, 'Use of
        the Greek Fathers', pp. 191-207; J.L. North, 'Use of the Latin Fathers', pp.
        208-23; S.P. Brock, 'Use of the Syriac Fathers', pp. 224-36; J.R. Royse,

'Scribal Tendencies', pp. 239-52; T.C. Geer, Jr, 'Analyzing and Categorizing Greek Manuscripts', pp. 253-67; R.A. Kraft, 'Use of Computers', pp. 268-82; M. Silva, 'Modern Critical Editions and Apparatuses', pp. 283-96; D.B. Wallace, 'Majority Text Theory', pp. 297-320; J.K. Elliott, 'Thoroughgoing Eclecticism', pp. 321-35; M.W. Holmes, 'Reasoned Eclecticism', pp. 336-60; B.D. Ehrman, 'New Testament Manuscripts and Social History', pp. 361-79.

Elliott, J.K.

1992   *Essays and Studies in New Testament Textual Criticism*. Estudios de Filología Neotestamentaria, 3. Cordoba, Spain: Ediciones el Almendro. (13 text-critical essays.)

1993   'Non-Canonical Sayings of Jesus in Patristic Works and in the New Testament Manuscript Tradition', in R. Gryson (ed.), *Philologia Sacra: Biblische und patristische Studien für Hermann J. Frede und Walter Thiele zu ihrem siebzigsten Geburtstag*. Freiburg: Herder: 343-54.

Elliott, J.K. (ed.)

1990   *The Principles and Practice of New Testament Textual Criticism: Collected Essays of G.D. Kilpatrick*. BETL, 96. Leuven: Leuven University Press/Peeters. (69 of Kilpatrick's text-critical essays.)

1976   *Studies in New Testament Language and Text: Essays in Honour of George D. Kilpatrick on the Occasion of His Sixty-fifth Birthday*. NovTSup, 44. Leiden: Brill. (20+ text-critical studies.)

Elliott, J.K., and I. Moir

1995   *Manuscripts and the Text of the New Testament: An Introduction for English Readers*. Edinburgh: T. & T. Clark. (A brief manual.)

Epp, E.J.

1991   'New Testament Papyrus Manuscripts and Letter Carrying in Greco-Roman Times', in B.A. Pearson, A.T. Kraabel, G.W.E. Nickelsburg and N.R. Petersen (eds.), *The Future of Early Christianity: Essays in Honor of Helmut Koester*. Minneapolis: Fortress Press: 35-56.

1989   'The New Testament Papyrus Manuscripts in Historical Perspective', in M.P. Horgan and P.J. Kobelski (eds.), *To Touch the Text: Biblical and Related Studies in Honor of Joseph A. Fitzmyer, SJ*. New York: Crossroad: 261-88.

1992   'Textual Criticism: New Testament'. *ABD* 6: 412-35.

Epp, E.J., and G.D. Fee

1993   *Studies in the Theory and Method of New Testament Textual Criticism*. Grand Rapids: Eerdmans. (17 essays on the history of the New Testament text and on various text-critical methodologies. Chapters 2, 3, 5, 8, and 14 by Epp and 1, 4, 7, 12, 13, and 17 by Fee are the most relevant to the present essay.)

Epp, E.J., and G.D. Fee (eds.)

1981   *New Testament Textual Criticism: Its Significance for Exegesis: Essays in Honour of Bruce M. Metzger*. Oxford: Clarendon Press. (29 essays on textual variation in specific New Testament texts and on textual transmission and translation.)

Fee, G.D.

1983   *New Testament Exegesis: A Handbook for Students and Pastors.* Philadelphia: Westminster Press: 51-60.

1987   *The First Epistle to the Corinthians.* NICNT. Grand Rapids: Eerdmans: 699-708.

1981   '"One Thing is Needful?" Luke 10:42', in E.J. Epp and G.D. Fee (eds.), *New Testament Textual Criticism: Its Significance for Exegesis: Essays in Honour of Bruce M. Metzger.* Oxford: Clarendon Press: 61-75.

Finegan, J.

1974   *Encountering New Testament Manuscripts: A Working Introduction to Textual Criticism.* Grand Rapids: Eerdmans.

Fitzmyer, J.A.

1993   *Romans.* AB, 33. New York: Doubleday: 733-44.

Frede, H.J. (ed.)

1966–71 *Epistulae ad Philippenses et ad Collosenses.* Vetus Latina, 24.2. Freiburg: Herder: 292-303.

Gamble, H.Y., Jr

1977   *The Textual History of the Letter to the Romans: A Study in Textual and Literary History.* SD, 42. Grand Rapids: Eerdmans.

1985   *The New Testament Canon: Its Making and Meaning.* GBS. Philadelphia: Fortress Press.

1989   'The Canon of the New Testament', in E.J. Epp and G.W. MacRae (eds.), *The New Testament and its Modern Interpreters.* Philadelphia: Fortress Press; Atlanta: Scholars Press: 201-43.

1995   *Books and Readers in the Early Church: A History of Early Christian Texts.* New Haven: Yale University Press.

Goodspeed, E.J.

1933   *The Meaning of Ephesians.* Chicago: University of Chicago Press.

Gregory, C.R.

1907   *Canon and Text of the New Testament.* ITL. Edinburgh: T. & T. Clark.

Hatch, W.H.P.

1936   'The Position of Hebrews in the Canon of the New Testament'. *HTR* 29: 133-51.

Koester, H.

1982   *Introduction to the New Testament.* II. *History and Literature of Early Christianity.* Philadelphia: Fortress Press; Berlin/New York: de Gruyter.

1989   'The Text of the Synoptic Gospels in the Second Century', in W.L. Petersen (ed.), *Gospel Traditions in the Second Century: Origins, Recensions, Text, and Transmission.* Christianity and Judaism in Antiquity, 3. Notre Dame: University of Notre Dame Press: 19-37.

1990   *Ancient Christian Gospels: Their History and Development.* London: SCM Press; Philadelphia: Trinity Press International.

Martini, C.M.

1974   'Eclecticism and Atticism in the Textual Criticism of the Greek New Testament', in M. Black and W.A. Smalley (eds.), *On Language, Culture, and Religion: In Honor of Eugene A. Nida.* The Hague: Mouton: 149-56.

Metzger, B.M.

1977   *The Early Versions of the New Testament: Their Origin, Transmission, and Limitations*. New York: Oxford University Press. (A comprehensive work; the treatment of each version concludes with a statement, by a noted expert, on that version's 'limitations in representing Greek'.)

1987   *The Canon of the New Testament: Its Origin, Development, and Significance*. Oxford: Clarendon Press.

1992   *The Text of the New Testament: Its Transmission, Corruption, and Restoration*. New York/Oxford: Oxford University Press, 3rd edn (1st edn 1964; 2nd edn 1968). (Long the standard manual in English. The appendix in the first two editions listing Greek papyri has been replaced by a chapter on advances in the field from 1964 to 1990.)

Metzger, B.M. (ed.)

1994   *A Textual Commentary on the Greek New Testament: A Companion Volume to the United Bible Societies' Greek New Testament (Fourth Revised Edition)*. Stuttgart: Deutsche Bibelgesellschaft/United Bible Societies. (A report of the reasons for the adoption/rejection of readings in the *UBSGNT*[4] text; it covers about 2,050 sets of variants.)

Pack, F.

1960   'Origen's Evaluation of Textual Variants in the Greek Bible'. *ResQ* 4: 139-46.

Parvis, M.M.

1952   'The Nature and Tasks of New Testament Textual Criticism: An Appraisal'. *JR* 32: 165-74.

Payne, P.B.

1995   'Fuldensis, Sigla for Variants in Vaticanus, and 1 Cor 14.34-5'. *NTS* 41: 240-62.

Petersen, W.L.

1994a *Tatian's Diatessaron: Its Creation, Dissemination, Significance, and History in Scholarship*. VCSup, 25. Leiden: Brill. (A comprehensive work.)

1994b 'What Text Can New Testament Textual Criticism Ultimately Reach?', in B. Aland and J. Delobel (eds.), *New Testament Textual Criticism, Exegesis, and Early Church History: A Discussion of Methods*. Contributions to Biblical Exegesis and Theology, 7. Kampen: Kok Pharos: 136-52.

Petersen, W.L. (ed.)

1989   *Gospel Traditions in the Second Century: Origins, Recensions, Text, and Transmission*. Christianity and Judaism in Antiquity, 3. Notre Dame: University of Notre Dame Press. (8 text-critical articles.)

Petzer, J.H.

1990   'Author's Style and the Textual Criticism of the New Testament'. *Neot* 24: 185-97.

1993   'Reconsidering the Silent Women of Corinth—A Note on 1 Corinthians 14:34-35'. *Theologia Evangelica* 26: 132-38.

Plisch, U.-K.
1996   'Die Apostelin Junia: Das exegetische Problem in Röm 16.7 im Licht von Nestle–Aland[27] und der sahidischen Überlieferung'. *NTS* 42: 477-78.

Riddle, D.W.
1936   'Textual Criticism as a Historical Discipline'. *ATR* 18: 220-33.

Schmid, U.
1995   *Marcion und sein Apostolos: Rekonstruktion und historische Einordnung der marcionitischen Paulusbriefausgabe*. ANTF, 25. Berlin/New York: de Gruyter.

Scholer, D.M.
1995   Paul's Women Coworkers in Ministry'. *Theology, News and Notes* 42.1. Pasadena, CA: Fuller Theological Seminary: 20-22.

Tov, E.
1992   *Textual Criticism of the Hebrew Bible*. Minneapolis: Fortress Press; Assen/Maastricht: Van Gorcum. [See pp. 164-80 on the issue of 'original' text.]

Vaganay, L., and C.-B. Amphoux
1991   *An Introduction to New Testament Textual Criticism*. Cambridge: Cambridge University Press, 2nd edn (1st English edn, 1937; French original by Vaganay, 1934). (A brief manual, now brought up to date.)

Westcott, B.F., and F.J.A. Hort
1896   *The New Testament in the Original Greek*. 2 vols. Cambridge/London: Macmillan, 2nd edn (1881–82).

Wisse, F.
1989   'The Nature and Purpose of Redactional Changes in Early Christian Texts: The Canonical Gospels', in W.L Petersen (ed.), *Gospel Traditions in the Second Century: Origins, Recensions, Text, and Transmission*. Christianity and Judaism in Antiquity, 3. Notre Dame: University of Notre Dame Press: 39-53.

THE GREEK LANGUAGE OF THE NEW TESTAMENT

STANLEY E. PORTER

1. THE HISTORY AND DEVELOPMENT OF THE GREEK OF THE NEW TESTAMENT

Writers such as Homer, who probably wrote in the eighth century BCE, Herodotus, who wrote in the fifth century BCE, and Plato, Thucydides, and the tragedians Aeschylus, Sophocles and Euripides, who wrote in the fifth and fourth centuries BCE, wrote in a Greek different from that of the New Testament.[1] The Greek of the New Testament represents the non-literary Greek used throughout the Greco-Roman world of the first century. The first century falls in the middle of the period in history often referred to as the Hellenistic period, which extended roughly from the late fourth century BCE to the fourth century CE (some divide the period into two parts, the Hellenistic followed by the Roman period). Greek is but one language of the group called the Indo-European languages.

The earliest recognizable forms of Greek go back to the Myceneans, a group of people who came to occupy what are known today as the Greek islands and mainland. Mycenean civilization reached great heights in the late second millennium BCE (on Crete and mainland Greece). This great civilization declined or was destroyed by approximately 1200–1100 BCE, however, throwing that region into what has been called a dark age—a period of which very little is

---

[1]   For a history and discussion of Greek, including description of grammatical features, see L.R. Palmer, *The Greek Language* (London: Duckworth, 1980), esp. pp. 3-198; and G. Horrocks, *Greek: A History of the Language and its Speakers* (London: Longmans, 1997), esp. pp. 3-127, who provides sample texts along with analysis. Palmer, former Professor of Comparative Philology in the University of Oxford, and Horrocks, the newly-appointed Professor of Comparative Philology in the University of Cambridge, approach the question of the language of the New Testament without the kinds of presuppositions that seem to influence the work of many biblical scholars. See also P.W. Costas, *An Outline of the History of the Greek Language, with Particular Emphasis on the Koine and the Subsequent Periods* (Chicago, 1936; repr. Chicago: Ares, 1979); R. Browning, *Medieval and Modern Greek* (Cambridge: Cambridge University Press, 2nd edn, 1983).

known, especially linguistically. In the nineteenth century, a number of tablets and other inscriptions were found, especially at the remains of a city called Pylos on the Greek mainland. These tablets and inscriptions were written in what scholars today call Linear B, the written script of the Myceneans. Deciphered in 1952, Linear B is an earlier, syllabic form of writing what is recognizably Greek.[2]

The Greek islands and mainland emerged out of their dark age in approximately 800 BCE, and such records as exist indicate that there were a number of dialects of Greek in use by varying people groups; as a result, this era has been called the 'dialect period'. The traditional view regarding the re-birth of Greek civilization was that various waves of settlement from outside resulted in several different Greek regional dialects on the Greek islands and mainland. More recently, the position has been advocated that the various regional dialects can be attributed to linguistic developments by indigenous people groups, originally perhaps divided into eastern and western Greek language varieties. These dialects are related in a complex way, with several different systems used to describe them. The major regional dialects of Greek discussed by scholars are Attic-Ionic, in which Attic was a fairly conservative variety of Ionic (see below), Arcado-Cypriot, Doric and other west Greek varieties, and Aeolic. These dialects were distinguished by such linguistic features as differences in vowel length, varying sound changes, whether and how contraction of vowels occurred, differences in declensional endings for both nouns/adjectives and verbs, the use of particles, occasional differences in case relations, and some differing vocabulary. In some instances, the dialects may have been unintelligible to each other due to significant sound changes, but it appears that the written forms of the languages were more easily understood (cf. Herodotus 8.144.2, who, writing in the early fifth century BCE, says that the Greeks were of one blood and of one tongue). The Homeric or epic dialect was based upon a form of Ionic, but with influence from other dialects. It was not

---

2   On the history of its decipherment, see J. Chadwick, *Linear B and Related Scripts* (London: British Museum Publications, 1987); and his more technical *The Decipherment of Linear B* (Cambridge: Cambridge University Press, 2nd edn, 1967). For an excellent account of this and the subsequent period in Greek language history, see L.R. Palmer, *Mycenaeans and Minoans: Aegean Prehistory in the Light of the Linear B Tablets* (London: Faber & Faber, 1961). Linear A, a script in many ways similar to that of Linear B, and found along with it, remains undeciphered.

a spoken language as such, but reflected a poetic form of language adapted by region as the poems were recited and later written.

During the fifth century BCE there emerged what is called the 'classical period', describing the ascendance of Athenian military and economic power, culture, philosophy, literature, and the arts. The economic prosperity of Athens led to achievements that transformed a relatively insignificant city into a place of central importance. Its language underwent a similar transformation. Because of persistent Athenian cultural dominance, its particular variety of the Ionic dialect of Greek came to be widely used, and much of the literature from this period is written in it. The conservative and even archaic earlier form of Attic gave way to a more progressive form of language used by various writers. This form of language, reflecting many of the more innovative features of the Ionic dialect, became the literary and then administrative language of Athens, with wider influence and use throughout Greece. This is the variety of Greek that formed the basis of the common written language of the Hellenistic world.

The remains that we have of ancient Greek, including the Athenian variety, come to us in the form of written texts. We obviously do not have any instance of the spoken language. What we do know of the spoken language, however, is based upon reconstructions from the evidence of various written texts, including inscriptions, and later papyri. The confusion of spelling of words, for example, gives us some idea of how certain letters and words were pronounced at the time. At the most, probably only 20 to 30% of the men of classical Athens could read or write, with arguably lesser percentages throughout the Greco-Roman world.[3] For the most part, people had to have public inscriptions read to them. The language that was actually spoken by classical Athenians was not the literary language of the best writers and most highly educated of the time, but a variety that was not characterized by the same intricacies of syntax.[4] This is not to say that their spoken language was necessarily simple, but that it did not maintain the same artificiality as typifies much Athenian prose and

---

[3]   See W.V. Harris, *Ancient Literacy* (Cambridge, MA: Harvard University Press, 1989), p. 141 and *passim*, for discussion of the levels of literacy throughout the Greek and Roman worlds.

[4]   See S.-T. Teodorsson, 'Phonological Variation in Classical Attic and the Development of Koine', *Glotta* 57 (1979), esp. pp. 68-71; cf. his *The Phonology of Attic in the Hellenistic Period* (Götheborg: Acta Universitatis Gothoburgensis, 1978).

certainly poetry of the time. This is consistent with what is known of the general relationships between the written and spoken forms of any given language.

A major turning point in the development and dissemination of the Greek language (all languages develop as they are used, though not according to some pre-determined rate or pattern) was the rise to power of the Macedonian conqueror Alexander the Great.[5] One of the most influential people at any time in the ancient world, his love of Greek culture had more to do with the New Testament being written in Greek than probably any other single factor. Due to the relationship between Macedonia and Greece, exemplified by the love of Alexander's father, Philip II of Macedon, for things Greek and Alexander's own education by Aristotle, when Macedonia exerted its hegemony in the fourth century BCE over the Greek mainland, it in turn adopted Athenian Greek as its administrative language.

When Alexander undertook his conquest of the Persians, he gathered around him an army of 50,000 Greek soldiers. Consequently, Alexander instigated a very important linguistic movement at the same time as he inaugurated his military conquests. Wherever Alexander went, he took the Greek language with him. The result of his widespread conquests was that Greek was established as the common language of communication, coming to dominate local and regional indigenous languages as various people groups were conquered and submitted to Alexander's rule. This Attic-Ionic form of Greek, which we now call Hellenistic Greek, was used both as a written and as a spoken language. Through the process of widespread dissemination, especially as Greek came into contact with a variety of other languages, and as the various dialects of the soldiers and others mixed, the process of linguistic change was accelerated away from many of the regional peculiarities, to a more universally used common dialect (or *koine*). This pattern of development was consistent and in harmony with other Hellenistic cultural dissemination—the four Hellenistic Greek kingdoms, including the Ptolemies and the Seleucids, and later the Romans continued the same patterns.

As a result, Hellenistic Greek became *the* prestige language of the Greco-Roman world, and remained so even after Latin established itself as a significant language of the empire in the second century CE.

---

5   See R. Lane Fox, *Alexander the Great* (London: Allen, 1974); P. Green, *Alexander to Actium: The Historical Evolution of the Hellenistic Age* (Berkeley: University of California Press, 1990).

In linguistic terms, this means that Greek was the language that those who had cultural and economic superiority used, and that those who wished to attain such status or to carry on effective interaction with such people had to know Greek. This language is to be found in a wide range of authors and texts, from the most ephemeral business contracts and receipts, as recorded in the Greek papyri, to the numerous literary writers of the times (e.g. Polybius the historian). Even though the works of a good number of the most famous and popular writers of the time have disappeared without much trace (e.g. Epicurus, whose 300 volumes have all vanished apart from quotation by others), there is still an abundance of material to be examined.[6] The domination of this form of Greek was not without several reactions, however. Several poets rejected the common language and chose to write poetry in forms of earlier Greek dialects. Something similar happened in the third century BCE with the rise of what is called Asianism, which was a reaction against the balanced and measured style of the literary form of Hellenistic Greek, and so indulged in a more exuberant style. In the second century CE, somewhat in reaction to Asianism, a movement called Atticism developed, in which some writers rejected what they perceived to be the corruption of the language, and advocated a return to the standards of vocabulary and style of the best classical writers of Athens.[7] None of these movements ever had much influence apart from on certain literary authors (including some later Christian writers).

What is noteworthy and in some ways surprising about the linguistic situation of the first century is the significant consistency of Hellenistic Greek across the span of the Greco-Roman world. Even in Phrygia and Lycaonia, in the interior of Asia Minor, where regional dialects had a better chance of survival (as they did in some places, especially with the lower classes),[8] Greek was the common language, although perhaps with some regional differences in pronunciation (see Acts 14:11). As Palmer says of this common language, it 'smothered and replaced the ancient local dialects'. He states: 'Profound linguistic consequences might have been expected from the adoption of what was basically the Attic dialect by users of not merely non-Attic, but

---

6   See K.J. Dover *et al.*, *Ancient Greek Literature* (Oxford: Oxford University Press, 1980), pp. 134-76, esp. pp. 134-36.

7   See Horrocks, *Greek*, pp. 50-51 on these reactive movements.

8   See Horrocks, *Greek*, pp. 63-64.

non-Greek speech. In fact the changes were remarkably slight.'[9] This level of usage is also exemplified by a wealth of non-literary texts, one of the most important of which is the New Testament. This language can also be found in the papyri from Egypt, as well as the papyri found more recently in the Roman east. These documents, most of which were discovered in the last century and the early part of this century, comprise thousands of examples of the use of the Greek language over the span of the Hellenistic period in a variety of contexts, most of which reflect day to day life.[10]

The major linguistic features of Hellenistic Greek, in distinction from earlier forms of Greek, include the following (apart from instances of retention or revival of earlier features by Atticists): regularized features of pronunciation, vowel reduction, declensional endings of nouns/adjectives and verbs regularized and simplified, with regular first aorists replacing irregular second aorist endings, final ν used more frequently, especially in instances where the third declension was being formed like the first/second declensions, increased use of certain prepositions, disappearance of some particles, μι verbs being regularized into ω verbs, the optative virtually disappearing, the dual, already restricted, being completely eliminated, the middle voice being reduced in importance (often replaced by the passive), the subjunctive with ἵνα beginning to replace the infinitive, the dative case under pressure as the role of the accusative case was expanded, the use of ἄν increased, and periphrasis in a variety of contexts increased in frequency.

---

[9]   Palmer, *Greek Language*, pp. 175, 176.

[10]   See E.G. Turner, *Greek Papyri: An Introduction* (Oxford: Clarendon Press, 2nd edn, 1980), and R.S. Bagnall, *Reading Papyri, Writing Ancient History* (AAW; London: Routledge, 1995) on the papyri. Collections of texts useful for New Testament study are in A.S. Hunt and C.C. Edgar, *Select Papyri* (LCL; vols. 1–2; London: Heinemann; Cambridge, MA: Harvard University Press, 1932, 1934); G.H.R. Horsley and S. Llewelyn, *New Documents Illustrating Early Christianity* (7 vols. to date; New South Wales: Macquarie University, 1981–); J.L. White, *Light from Ancient Letters* (FFNT; Philadelphia: Fortress Press, 1986). Cf. also S.E. Porter, 'The Greek Papyri of the Judaean Desert and the World of the Roman East', in *The Scrolls and the Scriptures: Qumran Fifty Years After* (ed. S.E. Porter and C.A. Evans; RILP, 3; JSPSup, 26; Sheffield: Sheffield Academic Press, 1997), pp. 292-316.

2. DEBATE OVER THE KIND OF GREEK IN THE NEW TESTAMENT

On the basis of what has been said above, it would appear that the question of the kind of Greek found in the New Testament[11] would be a relatively straightforward one to answer—it is written in a form of non-literary Greek of the Hellenistic period. However, discussion of the Greek of the New Testament has been anything but straightforward. The issues raised relate to the complex theological, ethnic and cultural environment in Palestine in which many of the books of the New Testament originated. Because the Egyptian papyri mentioned above had yet to be assessed in terms of the New Testament, before the turn of this century there was a widespread belief in many circles that the language of the New Testament constituted a special biblical dialect of Greek, possibly even a divinely inspired or 'Holy Ghost' Greek. This theory, not advanced in a highly systematic way, grew out of noting significant differences between the Greek of the New Testament and the Greek found in the literary writers of the Hellenistic period, and certainly of the classical period. The periodic style of Thucydides, or even the Hellenistic literary language of Polybius, is not the style of the Greek New Testament. Consequently, for example, one of the leading Greek–English lexicons of the day had a list of several hundreds of words that supposedly had meanings in the Greek Bible (both testaments) that were unattested elsewhere.[12]

Two men were primarily responsible for showing the inadequacy of the view that the Greek of the New Testament was a special form of Greek, as emotionally and theologically satisfying as that view may have been. Adolf Deissmann from Germany and James Hope Moulton from England were two of the most important scholars for discerning and disseminating the importance of the recent papyrological discoveries for the study of the New Testament. Deissmann's chance notice of the similarities between a papyrus text and the Greek of the New Testament led to his investigation of the vocabulary of the New Testament. His several major books on the topic are still highly

---

11 See S.E. Porter (ed.), *The Language of the New Testament: Classic Essays* (JSNTSup, 60; Sheffield: JSOT Press, 1991), esp. pp. 11-38 for further bibliography, and for selections from major texts mentioned in the following discussion.

12 See H. Cremer, *Biblico-Theological Lexicon of New Testament Greek* (Edinburgh: T. & T. Clark, 4th edn, 1895), pp. 693-98.

valuable tools for study of the Greek New Testament.[13] In them, Deissmann shows abundantly how the Greek of the papyri and inscriptions from the Hellenistic period help to elucidate the Greek of the New Testament. The lengthy list of words with supposedly unattested meanings was reduced to a small handful, one that certainly could not justify a theory of the Greek of the New Testament constituting a unique dialect of Greek. Moulton, and his colleague George Milligan, wrote a still-valuable lexicon illustrating how the vocabulary of the Greek Bible could be elucidated by the papyri, but his even greater accomplishment was to show the *grammatical* significance of the papyri for understanding the Greek of the New Testament.[14] In response to the argument that various constructions in the Greek of the New Testament are odd or unusual Greek, or even heavily influenced by Semitic languages such as Hebrew and Aramaic, the papyri were said to show that most, if not virtually all, of these phenomena were possible, if not regular, constructions in the Greek of the day. For example, it has been claimed that the use of the present tense in narrative in some of the Gospels reflects their Aramaic origins. In fact, the frequency of this kind of tense usage within the Gospels falls well within the parameters of use of the form in other historical writers of the period who have no connection to Semitic influence upon their writings. Moulton, who was tragically killed during World War I while crossing the Mediterranean on the way back from a missionary trip to India, was unable to complete the major task of writing an entire grammar of the Greek New Testament according to the principles illustrated above.

After the death of Deissmann, Moulton and others who had appreciated the importance of the papyri, there was a backlash against their position. In light of the Jewish origins of Christianity, it is perhaps understandable that a number of scholars assumed that the

---

[13]   E.g. A. Deissmann, *Bible Studies* (trans. A. Grieve; Edinburgh: T. & T. Clark, 1901; 2nd edn, 1909), esp. pp. 61-267; *Light from the Ancient East* (trans. L.R.M. Strachan; London: Hodder & Stoughton, 1910; 4th edn, 1927).

[14]   See J.H. Moulton, *Prolegomena*, vol. 1 of *A Grammar of the Greek New Testament* (Edinburgh: T. & T. Clark, 1906; 3rd edn, 1908); cf. his 'New Testament Greek in the Light of Modern Discovery', in *Essays on Some Biblical Questions of the Day: By Members of the University of Cambridge* (ed. H.B. Swete; London: Macmillan, 1909), pp. 461-505. The lexicon is J.H. Moulton and G. Milligan, *The Vocabulary of the Greek Testament Illustrated from the Papyri and Other Non-Literary Sources* (London: Hodder & Stoughton, 1914–29).

language of the New Testament—even though it is Greek—was also Semitic in some form. Several different Semitic hypotheses were advanced to explain the Greek of the New Testament. In its earliest forms, it is perhaps best illustrated by the work of Charles Torrey, who argued that the Gospels, the first half of Acts, and Revelation were all translated from Aramaic (some have argued that Hebrew was the original language of composition for some of the books of the New Testament, although this view is even more difficult to sustain than the Aramaic hypothesis).[15] Whereas many have pointed out grammatical deficiencies in the Greek New Testament, Torrey took these as indications not of linguistic deficiencies on the part of the text, but as a reflection of their being translations (in reality, many of these are simply failures to conform to the artificial standards of classical Greek as used by Athenian writers). Rather than being sloppy or badly done translations, these translations, according to Torrey, were done with the intent of preserving fidelity to their original language and meaning. This first generation of Semitic hypotheses came under severe attack, even by advocates of other forms of Semitic hypotheses. The major lines of criticism revolved around the failure of Torrey and fellow advocates to show that supposed instances of translation were in fact best explained in this way as opposed to being examples of Hellenistic Greek. The next generation of Semitic-language advocates made a much more modest set of claims regarding the Greek New Testament.[16] Rather than arguing that the Gospels or other New Testament books were originally Aramaic documents, they conceded that they were Greek documents, but that they reflected authors whose native tongues were Aramaic, or that they recorded words spoken by Jesus and others that were translated out of Aramaic. This is not to say that the author simply made a wooden translation of the Aramaic words, but that an Aramaic substratum lay behind these Greek texts. This is indicated not only by what is generally known about the linguistic character of Palestine at the time (according to this position) but by various occasional oddities in the wording or concepts that indicate the Semitic original (see the Chapter on the Life

---

15   C.C. Torrey, *Our Translated Gospels: Some of the Evidence* (London: Hodder & Stoughton, 1936); *The Composition and Date of Acts* (HTS, 1; Cambridge, MA: Harvard University Press, 1916); *The Apocalypse of John* (New Haven: Yale University Press, 1958).

16   A well-known representative is M. Black, *An Aramaic Approach to the Gospels and Acts* (Oxford: Clarendon Press, 1946; 3rd edn, 1967).

of Jesus by Craig Evans). This position is clearly correct in recognizing that at least some if not most of the original words of Jesus were in Aramaic. Nevertheless, this position sometimes works from an improper estimation of the linguistic climate in Palestine. The linguistic situation was not one of simply two languages, Aramaic and Greek, competing on an even footing. Greek was the prestige language of Palestine, and anyone wishing to conduct business on any extended scale, including any successful fishermen from the Hellenistic region of Galilee and probably any craftsmen or artisans who would have come into contact with Roman customers, would have needed to have known—indeed, would have wanted to know— Greek. In this kind of situation, it is the non-prestige language that will usually show the influence of the prestige language, not the other way around (of course, the grammar of the language, especially its syntax, remains unaffected, even if a given user shows signs of being affected). The evidence is that Palestine, including the Jerusalem area, was part of the Greek-speaking Hellenistic world, and had been since the conquests of Alexander—more than three hundred years before the time of the New Testament.[17]

The supposed confrontation between Aramaic and Greek noted above has led a few scholars to posit that the mix of the two languages led to the development of a special dialect of Semitic Greek.[18] For some, this dialect was a temporary language created when the two came into initial confrontation, while for others, this constituted an independent variety of Semitic Greek that continued to be used in the early Church. The influence of this Semitic-Greek hypothesis has been widely felt. It appeals to those with a predisposition for wishing to find special characteristics about the language of the New Testament, appreciating the Jewish background of Christianity. This is a position usually based on theological rather than linguistic criteria,

---

[17]   See P. van der Horst, *Ancient Jewish Epitaphs: An Introductory Survey of a Millennium of Jewish Funerary Epigraphy (300 BCE–700 CE)* (Kampen: Kok Pharos, 1991), pp. 24-32.

[18]   See, for example, H. Gehman, 'The Hebraic Character of Septuagint Greek', *VT* 1 (1951), pp. 81-90; N. Turner, 'The Language of the New Testament', in *Peake's Commentary on the Bible* (ed. M. Black and H.H. Rowley; London: Nelson, 1962), pp. 659-62; *idem, Syntax*, vol. 3 of *A Grammar of New Testament Greek*, by J.H. Moulton (4 vols.; Edinburgh: T. & T. Clark, 1963), esp. pp. 1-9; *idem, Grammatical Insights into the New Testament* (Edinburgh: T. & T. Clark, 1965), pp. 174-88.

however. This view, advocated by Turner, who was responsible for writing one of the few reference grammars of New Testament Greek, has had a surprisingly long currency in spite of its numerous shortcomings. First, there is little linguistic basis for this theory. Although it seems like a possible linguistic situation, this kind of a creole or composite Greek cannot be found in any other place except, allegedly, the New Testament (which of course is the body of literature being examined, so it hardly constitutes suitable independent evidence to prove the case). Secondly, it introduces an implausible linguistic situation, in which, for example, Paul would use this form of Greek even though he was writing to be understood in Greek-speaking cities spread throughout the Greco-Roman world, such as Rome, Corinth or Ephesus (to cite three very different locales).

In the last twenty years or so, there has been a return to support of the Greek hypothesis of Deissmann and Moulton in the work of Mosés Silva and Geoffrey Horrocks.[19] Silva has been especially instrumental in this return because of his close attention to matters of linguistic method. Supported by recent work in the papyri by Horsley, Silva has shown that the linguistic distinction between *langue* (the language system) and *parole* (a particular writer's use of it) clarifies the linguistic situation in Palestine in the first century. Although one's individual *parole* may have had peculiarities brought about through knowledge of a Semitic language, the *langue* in use was clearly Hellenistic Greek. Horrocks recognizes both that the writers of the New Testament, because of their lack of higher education, avoided Atticistic characteristics, and that Aramaic may have been the first language of the majority of them. He also recognizes that there has been a longstanding dispute over which characteristics may or may not reflect Semitic influence. Nevertheless, most of these features, Horrocks maintains, can either be paralleled in the Septuagint, which he views as one of the most important examples of Hellenistic vernacular literature, or in low-level *koine* (i.e. Hellenistic) Greek texts such as are found in Egypt. Thus, for understanding the Greek of the New Testament, one needs to be most attentive not so much to the

---

[19]   M. Silva, 'Bilingualism and the Character of New Testament Greek', *Bib* 61 (1978), pp. 198-219; Horrocks, *Greek*, pp. 92-95, and pp. 56-59 on the Septuagint. See also G.H.R. Horsley, 'Divergent Views on the Nature of the Greek of the Bible', *Bib* 65 (1984), pp. 393-403; C.J. Hemer, 'Reflections on the Nature of New Testament Greek Vocabulary', *TynBul* 38 (1987), pp. 65-92.

Semitic sources, but rather to the Greek of the papyri and other contemporary writers.

3. THE LANGUAGES OF JESUS

Related to the issue of the Greek of the New Testament is the question of what language or languages Jesus spoke. Although there have been some who have discussed the possibility that Jesus spoke Hebrew, and there is some evidence that he did from Luke 4:16-20, the vast majority of scholars rightly believe that Jesus' primary language was Aramaic.[20] This hypothesis seems very well founded. Jesus was born to a Palestinian Jewish family, and was apparently well-versed in the institutions related to the Jewish people, including the use of Aramaic, the language of the Jews since their return under the Persians from exile in Babylon. Not only did Aramaic remain a low-level vernacular in Syria during the time of the Seleucids and after, but Aramaic continued to be used by Jews during the first century (contrary to some earlier hypotheses that it was not widely used at this time), as is well attested from the Dead Sea Scrolls finds and other related documents. Jewish worship during this time was often carried on in Aramaic, with an interpretative translation into Aramaic (known as a 'targum') of the biblical text being offered.

The portrait of Jesus is in harmony with this scenario. In the Gospels, Jesus communicates on numerous occasions with members of the Jewish religious establishment, participates in various Jewish religious observances in Palestine, and is recorded as using Aramaic on several different occasions (e.g. Mark 5:41; 7:34; 15:34 = Matt. 27:46, where there are direct quotations). Thus it is consistent with his linguistic milieu to suppose that on many, if not the vast majority of, occasions Jesus not only spoke but taught those who gathered around him in Aramaic, and that the words of Jesus recorded in the New Testament, although rendered into Hellenistic Greek, were at one time translated out of Aramaic. Nevertheless, because of the difficulties of translation, including the extreme difficulty in finding word-for-word

---

[20]   The classic statement on Jesus' use of Aramaic is G. Dalman, *Jesus–Jeshua: Studies in the Gospels* (trans. P.P. Levertoff; London: SPCK, 1929), esp. pp. 1-37. See also J.A. Fitzmyer, 'The Languages of Palestine in the First Century A.D.', in *Language of the New Testament*, pp. 126-62 (a corrected version of an article that first appeared in *CBQ* 32 [1970], pp. 501-31). On Hebrew and Jesus, see H. Birkeland, *The Language of Jesus* (Oslo: Dybwad, 1954).

equivalence between languages, and the fact that the words of Jesus are found in the sustained narratives of the Gospels, one must be cautious in attempting to reconstruct these Aramaic words. As Black, an advocate of the Aramaic hypothesis, states with regard to at least the longer parables,

> the 'translation' is not literal but literary; in other words, it is doubtful if it can be justly described as translation at all in some cases, even where the evidence points to the existence and use of an Aramaic source. The Evangelists, that is to say, are for the most part writing Greek Gospels, even where they are dependent upon sources.[21]

There is also good evidence for thinking that Jesus knew and used Greek, however, possibly even using it on occasions when he taught. Many scholars recognize this fact in theory, but hesitate to specify particular instances where this may have occurred. Jesus came from an area that had been highly influenced by Hellenism. Nazareth was a small village, but it was on the same trade route as an excellent example of a Greek city in Palestine, Sepphoris, where both Greek and Aramaic were spoken, and near the primarily Gentile Decapolis, ten Hellenistic cities or villages in the region of Galilee. Jesus was involved in a trade where it is reasonable to assume that he would have had contact with others than simply his local townspeople, possibly including Romans, or others who spoke Greek. In the course of his itinerant ministry, Jesus also traveled to various parts of Palestine where he may have had contact with Greek speakers. In fact, several of his disciples, including Andrew, Philip, and even possibly Peter, had Greek names, despite being Jewish.

In the Gospels, there are at least five episodes that point to Jesus using Greek at least on occasion.[22] The first and most important is Mark 15:2-5 (= Matt. 27:11-14; Luke 23:2-5; John 18:29-38). In this passage, Jesus is interrogated by Pilate. In their conversation, in which there is no indication of a translator being present, it is unreasonable to think that Pilate spoke Aramaic or that they conducted their conversation in Latin. The Roman procurator of such an area of the

---

21   Black, *Aramaic Approach*, p. 274. On translation from Aramaic, see L.D. Hurst, 'The Neglected Role of Semantics in the Search for the Aramaic Words of Jesus', *JSNT* 28 (1986), pp. 63-80.

22   See S.E. Porter, 'Did Jesus ever Teach in Greek?', *TynBul* 44.2 (1993), pp. 223-35; cf. R.A. Horsley, *Archaeology, History and Society in Galilee: The Social Context of Jesus and the Rabbis* (Valley Forge, PA: Trinity Press International, 1996), esp. pp. 154-71.

empire would have scorned the idea of learning that people's indigenous language, especially when so many of them spoke Greek (55 to 60% of all Jewish funerary inscriptions in Palestine are in Greek, including about half of the inscriptions found in Jerusalem itself),[23] and Latin was reserved for official Roman business. On the basis of this evidence, as well as the Gospel criteria of multiple attestation (i.e. a tradition is found in two or more independent sources), redactional tendencies (i.e. a feature cannot be attributed to the editorial tendencies of a writer), and especially historical coherence (i.e. a feature coheres with what we know of the historical context), it can be argued that Jesus and Pilate spoke Greek to each other in their conversation. In the course of Pilate's questioning of Jesus, he asks him, 'Are you the king of the Jews?'. And Jesus answers, 'You say so'. On the basis of the criteria mentioned above, there is good reason to think that these are the actual words of the conversation in Greek. In four other passages, there is not enough evidence to establish the actual wording of Jesus (Mark 7:24-30; John 12:20-28; Matt. 8:5-13 = Luke 7:2-10), but the historical coherence and linguistic evidence are strong enough to suggest that on these occasions Jesus also spoke in Greek. This allows for the possibility that Jesus may have even taught in Greek, something that perhaps took place in Matt. 16:13-20 at Caesarea Philippi. In light of the scene involving Jesus' disciples, the location in a Hellenistic context, and the Synoptic tendencies, a plausible case can be made that Jesus conducted this dialogue with his disciples in Greek.

4. GRAMMATICAL STUDY

In this brief section, a complete introduction to the Greek language cannot be offered. That must be reserved for formal study, supplemented by consultation of reference grammars, lexicons and important monographs and articles on various dimensions of the Greek language. What is provided here is a brief discussion of two features of the language, areas where grammatical study has direct bearing on exegesis. This section is written from the assumption that the reader has already studied the Greek language sufficiently to understand its basic workings, although some of the ideas presented below may challenge some previously held assumptions.

---

[23]   See van der Horst, *Ancient Jewish Epitaphs*, pp. 23-24.

A. A Linguistic Approach to the Greek of the New Testament

Virtually all reference grammars for the study of the Greek of the New Testament were written before the insights of modern linguistic study were applied to analysis of the language (see the Bibliographical Essay, above). It is only within the last twenty or so years that New Testament study has benefited from what can be considered a modern linguistic approach.

Before discussing dimensions of the Greek language itself, several of the principles of modern linguistics bear repeating, since they offer a different perspective than is often found in studies of the Greek of the New Testament.[24] The best way to proceed may be first to dispel some of the misconceptions regarding what a modern linguistic approach is. Modern linguistics is not the ability to speak many languages, nor is it the ability to necessarily know more languages than simply the biblical languages concerned (such as various cognate Semitic languages, Coptic, etc.). A modern linguistic approach is not to be equated with studying the history of a language, and certainly not isolating and studying the development of only one element in the language. Modern linguistics is certainly not a matter of studying etymologies (the histories of words). Modern linguistics is not classical philology, with its concern for studying a select few of the best preserved literary texts as the standard by which all language usage is judged. One of the major shortcomings of the grammar by Blass, revised by Debrunner, is that it assumes knowledge of classical Greek and uses it as the point of reference for comparison and evaluation of the Greek of the New Testament. Modern linguistics is not to be equated with traditional grammar, which is often dependent upon the categories of ancient Latin. A modern linguistic approach is not to be equated with ability to translate a language, since translation is only one among many indications of one's understanding of a language, and not always the best one.

To the contrary, a modern linguistic approach to a language views the language as a self-referential system, in which all of the various elements of the language are interconnected and form a co-ordinated structure. Thus, verbal usage in Greek is related to other linguistic

---

24   See S.E. Porter, 'Studying Ancient Languages from a Modern Linguistic Perspective: Essential Terms and Terminology', *FN* 2 (1989), pp. 147-72, for elucidation of the following concepts; cf. J. Lyons, *An Introduction to Theoretical Linguistics* (Cambridge: Cambridge University Press, 1968), for an excellent introduction to the topic.

elements, such as case. The verbal system itself is structured, since selection of a present or perfect tense-form means that other tense-forms have not been selected (see below). This systematic and structural dimension to language is crucial to understanding the use of language in context, and hence its meaning. Description and analysis of the language should begin from empirical data and present these data in an explicit fashion, open to analysis by others. Thus estimation of the function of, for example, participles, is determined on the basis of a complex set of definable factors, such as tense-form, case, syntax and even context. Furthermore, synchronic analysis takes precedence over diachronic analysis, although the two are inter-related. That is, any given synchronic state is the result of diachronic change. For example, the Greek four/five case system (five, if one counts the vocative as an independent case, four if one does not) may earlier have had eight cases, but it is the four/five cases that must be defined in terms of their use in the New Testament (see below). Diachronic information may be interesting and even informative, but it is not to be equated with or elevated above synchronic description and analysis. A modern linguistic analysis is descriptive rather than prescriptive. Thus, one may observe that a New Testament writer does not use the optative as did the Attic Greeks, but that should not form the basis of a judgment regarding the quality of the Greek involved, but should instead form the basis of a description of modal usage.

These brief principles of differentiation should help to put the following short grammatical studies in their proper linguistic context.

B. Grammatical Studies

A number of issues with exegetical implications have been subjects of longstanding debate in Greek grammatical study, but which have recently had light shed upon them by a modern linguistic approach. This is the place not to discuss all of these issues in detail, but to survey two of them briefly so as to make the reader aware of the limitations of previous research and of possibilities for continuing research.

1. Verb Structure. Study of Greek verb structure has undergone radical changes in the last almost two-hundred years.[25] The first period of modern study has been called the rationalist period. This period,

---

[25] See S.E. Porter, *Verbal Aspect in the Greek of the New Testament, with Reference to Tense and Mood* (SBG, 1; New York: Lang, 1989), pp. 50-65, for a survey of approaches to Greek verb structure.

perhaps best represented by the influential grammarian G.B. Winer, analyzed Greek verbal structure in terms of a logical framework. In this framework, tense-forms were said to be equated with temporal values. As a result, Winer says that

> the aorist refers to the past simply (the simple occurrence of an event at some past time, considered as a momentary act)...the imperfect and the pluperfect always have reference to subordinate events which stood related, in respect of time, with the principal event (as relative tenses); and last, the perfect brings the past into connexion with the present time, and represents an action as a completed one, in relation to the present time.

Winer goes on to say that 'Strictly and properly speaking, no one of these tenses can ever stand for another...'[26] This kind of framework, in which tense-form and time are rigidly equated, is still reflected in a number of elementary or teaching grammars, whose frameworks students and scholars tend to take with them in their exegesis of the text.[27] However, a moment's reflection will show that this framework is inadequate to explain what actually occurs in the language. For example, Winer cannot adequately account for instances of the historic present, such as in Mark's Gospel where the present tense is used in a narrative context, that is, where a present form appears to have past reference (e.g. Mark 14:12-25); neither can he account for the gnomic use of the aorist tense, where the aorist is used for events that are not, strictly speaking, past but are recurring events of nature (e.g. Jas 1:11). Winer's grammar is of limited use in terms of understanding the Greek verbal system.

The next stage in Greek verbal study applied the results of the findings of comparative philology in the late nineteenth century. Great advances were made in the study of languages when it was realized that many languages had family resemblances. As a result of this discovery, new categories of thought were applied to analysis of languages ancient and modern. One of the most important of these grammarians was Karl Brugmann, who elucidated the theory of

---

26   G.B. Winer, *A Treatise on the Grammar of New Testament Greek Regarded as a Sure Basis for New Testament Exegesis* (trans. W.F. Moulton; Edinburgh: T. & T. Clark, 3rd edn, 1882), pp. 330-31.

27   See S.E. Porter, *Studies in the Greek New Testament: Theory and Practice* (SBG, 6; New York: Lang, 1996), pp. 39-48, for a review of elementary and intermediate grammars.

Aktionsart.[28] This theory stated that verb structure is related not only or exclusively to temporal categories, but to the kind of action or the way that an event occurs. *Aktionsart* theory stated that a language has various means, including the use of verb tenses, verbal roots, and affixing of prepositions, to express the ways in which action occurs. This theory was adapted for New Testament study first by Friedrich Blass in his grammar, which, expanded by Albert Debrunner, has been translated into English and continues to be the most widely-cited New Testament Greek reference grammar, and then by James Hope Moulton, the first to introduce *Aktionsart* terminology into New Testament study.[29] *Aktionsart* theory made a distinctive contribution to Greek grammatical study in that it frees the tense-forms from strict reference to time, especially promoting the recognition by most grammarians that non-indicative verb forms did not refer to time. However, this theory also had severe limitations. The first was in its attempt to objectify a conception of how events transpire, and then to equate these conceptions with particular grammatical forms. It was soon seen that action is multifarious, and that there is no such thing as a punctiliar action or a linear action in and of itself, only insofar as a given observer chooses to describe it as such, and certainly no easy way to equate this to tense-forms.[30] Thus, lightning striking could be described using a present tense verb (Luke 17:24), and the Temple could be described with an aorist verb as having taken forty-six years to build (John 2:20). Nevertheless, most reference grammars of Greek utilize this model of verbal description, including those of A.T. Robertson, C.F.D. Moule, and Nigel Turner.[31]

The third and final stage in discussion of Greek verbal structure is a logical continuation from that of *Aktionsart* theory, and recognizes

---

[28]   K. Brugmann, *Griechische Grammatik* (ed. A. Thumb; Munich: Beck, 1885; 4th edn, 1913), esp. pp. 538-41.

[29]   F. Blass and A. Debrunner, *A Greek Grammar of the New Testament and Other Early Christian Literature* (trans. R.W. Funk; Chicago: University of Chicago Press, 1961), pp. 166-81; Moulton, *Prolegomena*, pp. 108-51.

[30]   See F. Stagg, 'The Abused Aorist', *JBL* 91 (1972), pp. 222-31, who brought this to vivid attention; cf. also C.R. Smith, 'Errant Aorist Interpreters', *GTJ* 2 (1981), pp. 205-26.

[31]   A.T. Robertson, *A Grammar of the Greek New Testament in the Light of Historical Research* (New York: Doran; London: Hodder & Stoughton, 1914; Nashville: Broadman, 4th edn, 1934), pp. 821-910; C.F.D. Moule, *An Idiom Book of New Testament Greek* (Cambridge: Cambridge University Press, 2nd edn, 1959), pp. 5-19; Turner, *Syntax*, pp. 59-89.

that verbs are not primarily concerned either with time or with objectified action, but with a subjective perspective on action. This has come to be called aspect theory. The first full-scale treatment of aspect theory to appear in English, written from a modern linguistic perspective, was published in 1976,[32] and since that time there have been a number of other valuable treatments published, including several applying aspect theory in various ways to the Greek of the New Testament. Early studies using the terminology of aspect tended simply to equate it with *Aktionsart*, apart from the innovative study by Maximilian Zerwick, which contained many useful insights.[33] The major studies worth mentioning, however, are those by Buist Fanning, K.L. McKay and Stanley Porter.[34] There is still significant disagreement among these three proponents, regarding such matters as whether Greek verbs are timeless when used in the indicative mood, and what the relationship is between semantics (the meanings of the verb tense-forms in and of themselves simply as part of the Greek verbal network) and pragmatics (the meanings of the verb tense-forms when used in context).[35] Nevertheless, there is a growing consensus among these scholars, and being utilized by others, that verbal aspect theory of the verb forms (synthetic verbal aspect) is an interpretative framework with higher descriptive powers regarding Greek verbal function than previous theories.

The implications of aspect theory for exegesis are extensive, including at least the following: Each verb tense-form is not to be equated with a single temporal value or an objective description of action. Each tense-form is instead to be seen in relation to putting into

---

[32]   B. Comrie, *Aspect: An Introduction to the Study of Verbal Aspect and Related Problems* (Cambridge: Cambridge University Press, 1976).

[33]   See M. Zerwick, *Biblical Greek Illustrated from Examples* (trans. J. Smith; Rome: Pontifical Biblical Institute, 1963), pp. 77-99.

[34]   B.M. Fanning, *Verbal Aspect in New Testament Greek* (OTM; Oxford: Clarendon Press, 1990), followed to some extent by D.B. Wallace, *Greek Grammar beyond the Basics* (Grand Rapids: Zondervan, 1996); K.L. McKay, *A New Syntax of the Verb in New Testament Greek: An Aspectual Approach* (SBG, 5; New York: Lang, 1993), reflecting earlier work by him especially in journal articles; Porter, *Verbal Aspect*, followed by *idem, Idioms of the Greek New Testament* (Biblical Languages: Greek, 2; Sheffield: JSOT Press, 1992; 2nd edn, 1994), pp. 20-49, where further examples are provided.

[35]   See the discussion in S.E. Porter and D.A. Carson (eds.), *Biblical Greek Language and Linguistics: Open Questions in Current Research* (JSNTSup, 80; Sheffield: JSOT Press, 1993), pp. 18-82.

grammatical form a particular view of an action, as described by the author. How the verbal aspects are defined is still a matter of debate, but one set of terminology that has been adopted is to use the terms perfective aspect for the aorist tense-form, imperfective aspect for the present/imperfect tense-form, and stative aspect for the perfect/pluperfect tense-form. These labels are fairly descriptive, relating to whether an action is seen as complete in itself, in progress, or representing a complex state of affairs. The tense-forms are also weighted (on the basis of their formal features, frequency, regularities in their paradigms, and semantic values), so that the author may choose to give relative emphasis or stress to one event over another by the choice of verb tense-form. Related to this is a greater amount of flexibility in estimating the contribution of the verb tense-form to establishing the meaning of a passage, not just the temporal placement and ordering of events. This has placed a greater emphasis upon the study of context, including an appreciation of the importance of discourse analysis (see the Chapter on Discourse Analysis by Jeffrey Reed).

Greek verb choice becomes one of several contributing elements in describing the structure of a discourse. For example, Mark 11:1-11 provides a good illustration of how the perfect tense-form (stative aspect), among the use of a number of aorist (Mark 11:4, 6, 7, 8, 11) and present/imperfect tense-forms (Mark 11:2-3, 5, 7, 9), is used to draw grammatical attention to certain features of the text that other commentators have noticed for other, non-grammatical reasons. For example, the perfect participle is used to describe the colt as being tied up (Mark 11:2, 4; cf. also vv. 5, 9, 10). This draws attention to the state of the colt. The colt might seem to be a strange item to emphasize, until it is realized that the author seems to be drawing attention to two factors. The first is that this part of the story is directly related to the prophetic importance that the colt was to play in the entrance of the messiah,[36] and the second is that this is the object of Jesus' own prophecy to his disciples, both of which prophecies are

---

[36]   See W.L. Lane, *The Gospel according to Mark* (NICNT; Grand Rapids: Eerdmans, 1974), p. 395, who comments: 'The attention given to this phase of the action and the explicit reference to "a colt tied", with its allusion to Gen 49:11, points to a *deeper significance* supplied by the Oracle of Judah, Gen 49:8-12. The allusion to Gen 49:11 confirms the messianic character which the animal bears in Ch. 11:1-10' (italics added).

fulfilled.[37] The perfect tense-form, in conjunction with other tense-forms, is used by the author to help to make this point, and an exegete will want to pay attention to such grammatical markers.

2. *Case Structure.* Greek is an inflected or synthetic language, which means that various classes of words (such as nouns, pronouns, adjectives and verbs) take meaningful endings that help to establish the relations between meaningful units of the language. The cases have been one of the most widely discussed inflected features of Greek. Traditional discussion of the cases is concerned with two questions. The first is the number of cases in New Testament Greek. A number of New Testament Greek grammarians work from the framework that Greek maintains an eight-case system, consisting of nominative, vocative, genitive, ablative, dative, locative and instrumental. A good example of this approach is found in Robertson's grammar, where he makes a distinction between the ablative and genitive cases. He rejects the term 'ablatival genitive', because 'That implies that the [ablative] case is after all a kind of genitive. That is only true as to form, not as to sense, and causes some confusion. In Greek the ablative is not a live case in form, but in sense it is.'[38] This reveals the major problem with the eight-case system, and that is the supposed ability to differentiate legitimate functions of these cases. As Robertson admits, this is a functional distinction, not a formal one, in other words, there is no difference in form in the Greek of the New Testament between the genitive and ablative cases. Robertson defines around ten different senses of the genitive case and seven or eight senses of the ablative, yet he maintains only his two functional categories. Regardless of the origins of the forms, it seems better to argue for a restricted number of case forms. Hence, there are four formal cases in Greek—nominative, accusative, genitive and dative—with the vocative, often treated as a fifth case, being restricted

---

37   See S.E. Porter and J.T. Reed, 'Greek Grammar since BDF: A Retrospective and Prospective Analysis', *FN* 4 (1991), pp. 154-56, for this and other examples.

38   Robertson, *Grammar*, p. 514. A similar kind of analysis is found in H.E. Dana and J.R. Mantey, *A Manual Grammar of the Greek New Testament* (Toronto: Macmillan, 1955), pp. 65-95; and J.A. Brooks and C.L. Winbery, *Syntax of New Testament Greek* (Washington, DC: University Press of America, 1979), pp. 2-59, but who compound difficulties by how they treat cases with and without the prepositions.

to select instances in the singular, and probably best viewed as a sub-category of the nominative case.

The second issue is related to defining the cases. The traditional theory is what may best be described as a localist theory. That is, various literal spatial or local categories are equated with each of the case-forms and extended to include the various uses of the particular form. This is the kind of analysis found in many discussions of case in the grammars of New Testament Greek.[39] There are a number of criticisms of this theory of case, however. The first is that these figurative extensions of the literal spatial or local category often seem to show significant over-extension, making it difficult to find the original image in the extended definition of the case. A second criticism is that various criteria are sometimes applied to the individual cases, as well as being further applied to defining the cases in relation to each other. A second way of defining the cases is in terms of syntactical differentiation. In other words, the cases are defined according to how the case is used in a particular arrangement of words, for example, which case follows which verb and when, and is used with which preposition.[40] Another way of defining the cases is by means of a set of functional criteria drawn from instances of contextual usage.[41] A surprisingly large number of grammarians, however, do not bother to define the cases, but simply list and exemplify individual categories of usage.[42] Sometimes these lists of usage become quite large and unwieldy. This situation certainly has caused frustration for those attempting to define the Greek cases, since no consistent or simple definition of the individual cases can be found.

One recent response to this situation is the proposal of Simon Wong, based upon recent work in linguistics on what is called semantic case theory.[43] In this analysis, case is not a form-based

---

[39]   See, for example, Robertson, *Grammar*, pp. 453-54; Dana and Mantey, *Manual Grammar*, pp. 68-69.

[40]   Brooks and Winbery, *Syntax*, p. 2.

[41]   Moulton, *Prolegomena*, p. 69.

[42]   See, for example, Blass and Debrunner, *Greek Grammar*, pp. 79-109; Turner, *Syntax*, pp. 230-48; Moule, *Idiom Book*, pp. 30-47.

[43]   See S. Wong, 'What Case is This Case? An Application of Semantic Case in Biblical Exegesis', *Jian Dao* 1 (1994), pp. 49-73. He is using the work of C.J. Fillmore, 'The Case for Case', in *Universals in Linguistic Theory* (ed. E. Bach and R.T. Harms; London: Holt, Rinehart and Winston, 1968), pp. 1-88; *idem*, 'The Case for Case Reopened', in *Syntax and Semantics. VIII. Grammatical Relations* (ed. P. Cole and J.M. Sadock; New York: Academic, 1977), pp. 59-81.

category, but a semantic category, one concerned to define meaningful relations between participants in events. As a result, Wong tries to provide a more consistent theory for Greek on the basis of the function of each semantic case. The result is an identification of fifteen semantic cases. These include: agent, experiencer, patient, range, reference, benefactive, locative, source, goal, path, instrument, comitative, manner, measure, and time. As one example that Wong gives, in 1 Thess. 2:14-15, the Jews are the agents who cause the death of Jesus and the prophets, agent being defined as an animate entity that instigates an event. Wong is to be commended for introducing an important set of categories into the linguistic discussion, one that has proven significant for the wider field of linguistic discussion. More particularly, he has forced discussion to move beyond simply speaking about linguistic forms and introduced potentially useful semantic categories.

Despite these strengths, however, Wong's theory is probably not the solution to the problem of case that is being sought. There are several problems with his theory that deserve brief mention.[44] One is that even in Wong's re-definition their remains ambiguity regarding the word 'case'. Sometimes he seems to be speaking of a set of formal categories, other times a set of semantic categories specific to Greek, and other times a set of universal cases that seem to exist apart from any particular language. A further problem is the relationship between any set of formal cases and semantic cases. Wong has defined fifteen semantic cases, but there are only four or five formal cases in Greek. Of course, he would want to include any set of relations in which a verbal action lies at the center, but this simply illustrates further the potential difficulty in defining terms adequately. A final weakness is that Wong is utilizing universal semantic categories, from which linguistic discussion has moved away in favor of typological categories. In other words, linguists are less concerned with defining universal categories that are thought to exist across languages (sometimes called notional roles), and more concerned with the similarities and differences that exist between languages (on the basis of grammatical roles). Notional roles have proved frustrating to define precisely, since they cannot be applied in an unambiguous way to any language, and they can always be re-defined to make further

---

[44]   See S.E. Porter, 'The Case for Case Revisited', *Jian Dao* 6 (1996), pp. 13-28, for a fuller summary and critique of Wong's proposal, as well as the positive solution sketched out below.

distinctions. Besides this, they are at least in part based on grammatical roles, undermining the mentalist framework upon which they are based.[45]

Any notional roles regarding case must be seen in relation to grammatical roles, which shift analysis to the phenomena of the language itself, before consideration of any hypothetical universals.[46] Grammatical roles are specific to a language on the basis of grammatical marking, and are finite in number for any specific language. For an inflectional language such as Greek, one must begin with the meanings indicated by the case markings themselves (synthetic case marking). Meaning must also be extended to include the immediate syntax (or co-text) and the larger context (concepts defined more fully in the Chapter on Discourse Analysis). Like many other languages, Greek uses prepositions to make finer distinctions than its inflectional system can make, although Greek also evidences 'complementary distribution', to use Blake's term, in which a single case can express different functions. Rather than using the methods of the traditional grammarians (many of whom were mentioned above), however, an approach as outlined by Blake may be the most productive. He states:

> cases are seen as a system, each one having a single, general meaning. These general meanings are not self-sufficient; one cannot predict from the generalised meaning to the set of contexts in which a case can be used. However, generalised meanings, or at least generalised characterisations, can form the basis for a componential analysis of case which enables one to capture similarities between sets of cases.[47]

In light of Blake's comments, it seems that there is still a place for what might appear to be a traditional analysis, though one with a linguistically informed understanding of case.

There are several further factors that can help to define the Greek cases in a systematic way. The first is that, as in other systems of Greek, there is a hierarchy of case usage. This hierarchy can be

---

[45]   See F.R. Palmer, *Grammatical Roles and Relations* (Cambridge: Cambridge University Press, 1994), esp. p. 1 and *passim*.

[46]   See B.J. Blake, *Case* (Cambridge: Cambridge University Press, 1994); Palmer, *Grammatical Roles*, pp. 5-6, 8; J.P. Louw, 'Linguistic Theory and the Greek Case System', *Acta Classica* 9 (1966), pp. 73-88. This framework is already reflected in part in Porter, *Idioms*, pp. 80-100.

[47]   Blake, *Case*, p. 11; cf. Louw, 'Linguistic Theory', p. 82; Porter, *Idioms*, p. 140.

established on the basis of the distribution of the cases with regard to frequency of usage, their material markedness (i.e. the amount of morphological substance to the forms), implicational markedness (i.e. the regularities and irregularities of the forms), and semantic markedness. On the basis of these factors, a distinction can be made between the nominative and the oblique (or non-nominative) cases (those that are syntactically governed). The nominative case is the most restricted and the genitive the most diverse in usage. In Hellenistic Greek, the dative already shows signs of restriction, since it is under pressure from the other cases. This set of semantic priorities is reflected in the emphasis in Greek on subjects and objects in case usage, with less emphasis on peripheral grammatical relations such as location or instrumentality, which are often expressed with the help of prepositions, especially in the dative case. In exegesis of the cases, one should perhaps begin with the following single or general meanings of the cases.

The nominative case is the nominal case, that is, it simply denotes an entity, not a relation between an entity and a predicate. It can be used in isolation, and is morphologically relatively unmarked (note, for example, the neuter gender forms). The nominative case is used as the subject or predicate, and can be used appositively to define itself. As a result, the subject is usually encoded by the nominative, and the subject is associated with the topic of a proposition. There are also a number of independent uses of the nominative case, and these would include its use for direct address and as a temporal indicator.

In the oblique or syntactically restricted cases, the accusative case is the oblique nominal case, and hence is often used as the object of the verb, sometimes in the form of the double accusative or appositionally. The so-called 'accusative of respect' is a category that in some ways describes most uses of the accusative, since the accusative case is a syntactically limited form with only loose semantic relations to the verb, as seen for example in the accusative case with passive verbs (Rom. 3:2). The genitive is the case of restriction. It places a limitation on the element in the genitive or restricts another item. In Greek grammars, the number of classificatory schemes for the genitive is legion. This well exemplifies the pattern in which more heavily marked cases that are removed from the fundamental case—the accusative of the oblique cases or the nominative for the entire case system—have the most diffuse usage, such as what are called subjective and objective genitives. The dative case is the case of relation. Under pressure from other cases, it is not now as diverse in usage as it once was, and its usage often tends to be formulaic, for example, the use of the dative case in letter openings, even where the dative is misused in other places in the letter. This situation is reflected in prepositions often being used to help define the function of the dative case.

5. LANGUAGE AND MENTALITY

A persistent problem in exegesis is the fact that a number of stereotypes about the biblical languages and those who used them still persist. One of those concerns supposed differences between Hebrew and Greek mindsets, and this is often linked to supposed differences between the grammars of the respective languages.[48] For biblical studies, this issue came to the fore in the 1950s and 1960s, linked to the Biblical Theology movement, in conjunction with its views about how God was working in unique ways in the biblical writers. There was a swift and decisive response to the contrasts drawn between Hebrew and Greek mindsets in the early 1960s, but contrasts drawn between the Greek and Hebrew minds and languages continues to influence exegesis in a way that they should not.[49]

The major issue is that, in the past, some scholars have argued that there is a close relationship between language and thought patterns, and that these relationships also apply, in a biblical context, to the minds of ancient Hebrew and Greek speakers. According to this

---

[48] This section builds upon material first presented in S.E. Porter, 'Two Myths: Corporate Personality and Language/Mentality Determinism', *SJT* 43 (1990), pp. 299-306; 'Problems in the Language of the Bible', in *The Nature of Religious Language: A Colloquium* (ed. S.E. Porter; RILP, 1; Sheffield: Sheffield Academic Press, 1996), pp. 29-33.

[49] Advocates of a decisive relation between language and cognitive processes include T. Boman, *Hebrew Thought Compared with Greek* (trans. J.L. Moreau; London: SCM Press, 1960), esp. pp. 17-23, 123-92, who was the major proponent of the kinds of characterizations offered in the next two paragraphs; O. Cullmann, *Christ and Time* (trans. F.V. Filson; London: SCM Press, 1951); and more recently M.R. Wilson, *Our Father Abraham: Jewish Roots of the Christian Faith* (Grand Rapids: Eerdmans, 1988). The most noteworthy response in biblical studies came from J. Barr, *The Semantics of Biblical Language* (Oxford: Oxford University Press, 1961), pp. 8-106; *idem, Biblical Words for Time* (London: SCM Press, 1962; 2nd edn, 1969). On the Biblical Theology movement, see B.S. Childs, *Biblical Theology in Crisis* (Philadelphia: Westminster Press, 1970), pp. 44-47.

analysis, the Greeks are stereotypically defined as static and contemplative, but the Hebrews as dynamic; the Greeks as abstract and the Hebrews as concrete in their thinking; the Greeks as dualistic and the Hebrews as monistic in their view of the person. Such stereotypes become problematic when such characterizations begin to influence exegesis, most notably when estimations of the supposed thought-patterns of the biblical writers are attributed to differences in the grammars of their languages.

As a result, it has not been unknown to find support for differences in the way Hebrew and Greek speakers think on the basis of the Hebrew verbal system establishing their dynamism, while the noun-based structure of Greek accounts for their static nature. Furthermore, the Hebrews supposedly had a special understanding of time on the basis of their verbal system, such that the future had the same certainty as the past, since the Hebrew perfect tense-form is often translated with either past or future English and German forms. It was further posited that, since Hebrew word order was verb–subject, with the 'action' word first in the sentence, the Hebrews had a clear sense of history based around their two verb tenses, the present and past-future. The Greeks, however, did not have such a clear sense of history, but were given to subtle nuance, undoubtedly because of their numerous verb tenses, with Greek a language of elaboration, subtlety and richness. These kinds of examples could be elucidated further, but provide a sufficient amount of data to grasp the theory being proposed.

The perspective upon which such characterizations as noted above were constructed was derived from principles first defined in the nineteenth century and then later elucidated in the twentieth century.[50] The German nationalistic scholar Wilhelm von Humboldt first argued for the relationship between language and mentality. His ideas were developed in this century most notably by the linguists Edward Sapir and his student Benjamin Lee Whorf, probably under the influence of the American anthropologist Franz Boas, and by a few others.[51] They

---

[50]   See J. Lyons, *Language and Linguistics: An Introduction* (Cambridge: Cambridge University Press, 1981), esp. pp. 302-12; and A.C. Thiselton, *The Two Horizons* (Grand Rapids: Eerdmans, 1980), pp. 133-39, for brief summaries of this position.

[51]   See E. Sapir, *Language: An Introduction to the Study of Speech* (New York: Harcourt Brace, 1921); *idem, Selected Writings in Language, Culture, and Personality* (ed. D.G. Mandelbaum; Berkeley: University of California Press,

made popular a combination of linguistic relativity and linguistic determinism that has become known as the Sapir-Whorf hypothesis, which also made its way into biblical studies.

Whorf defines the major presupposition of this approach when he says that

> the background linguistic system (in other words, the grammar) of each language is not merely a reproducing instrument for voicing ideas but rather is itself the shaper of ideas, the program and guide for the individual's mental activity, for his analysis of impressions, for his synthesis of his mental stock in trade.

He goes further and states that

> We dissect nature along lines laid down by our native languages... We cut nature up, organize it into concepts, and ascribe significance as we do, largely because we are parties to an agreement to organize it in this way— an agreement that holds throughout our speech community and is codified in the patterns of our language.

Linguistic relativity states that each language has its own unique structure that does not necessarily reflect some sort of linguistic universals. But as Whorf also says, the agreement is not an explicit one but an implicit one, and 'ITS TERMS ARE ABSOLUTELY OBLIGATORY',[52] that is, there is linguistic determinism. The most inflexible form of this theory is the one that is often found in biblical studies. It states that, in our thinking, we cannot experience anything apart from the categories and distinctions encoded in our language. These categories in a given language are unique to that system and incommensurable to those of any other system.

The implications of such a theory for exegesis are noteworthy. If the inflexible form of the theory is accurate, exegesis would appear to be almost an impossibility, since, without sharing the language of the biblical speaker, one cannot hope to penetrate the thought processes that gave rise to the text, since they are wholly conditioned by the language and thus only accessible to speakers of that language, in this case an ancient language with no first-hand access to it. Perhaps it is true that all modern exegesis is without basis, since there are no

---

1984); B.L. Whorf, *Language, Thought and Reality* (ed. J.B. Carroll; Cambridge, MA: MIT Press, 1956); and F. Boas, *Handbook of American Indian Languages* (Washington, DC: Smithsonian Institute, 1911).

[52] Whorf, 'Science and Linguistics', in *Language*, pp. 212, 213, 213-14 (emphasis his).

moderns who have native competence in the ancient languages, and hence cannot hope to penetrate the real workings of the text. It is difficult to imagine how one might go about proving such a hypothesis, however. It appears rather that, although one must confront very real difficulties in understanding ancient languages as they were used in their original cultural and historical contexts (and these difficulties should not be minimized), sufficient progress has been made to suggest that real understanding is being gained. Thus, the hard form of the Sapir-Whorf hypothesis must be dismissed, if for no other reason than that it is not quantifiable.[53]

There are further difficulties with this hypothesis that warrant examination, however. One is with regard to the descriptions of the biblical languages cited above. These must clearly be established before one could hope to test the viability of a weaker form of the Sapir-Whorf hypothesis. Whereas previous interpreters may have thought of the Hebrew verbal system as time-oriented, the major theory of Hebrew verb structure from late in the nineteenth century to the present argues for an aspectual system, in which Hebrew verbs are used according to a view of the kind of action rather than the time of action.[54] This makes it very difficult to characterize the Hebrew language as conveying a clear sense of history on the basis of its two verb tenses, since the time-based nature of the tenses has been eliminated. If recent work on the Greek verbal system proves correct—that the Greek verbal structure is also aspectually-based, rather than time-based—then the two languages seem to have a common verbal foundation, regardless of how one sees this as influencing Hebrew and Greek mentality.

It is also difficult to quantify the differences in mentality influenced or in some way caused by the differences in linguistic structure. One notices that much of the previous work has been done apart from an explicit method or methodological controls on the gathering and interpretation of data. For example, what would constitute evidence that the Hebrews had a keen sense of history and the Greeks did not? The fact that the first writers of history are often cited as being Greek speakers is apparently disregarded. The fact that there are few if any

---

53   See J.A. Lucy, *Grammatical Categories and Cognition: A Case Study of the Linguistic Relativity Hypothesis* (Cambridge: Cambridge University Press, 1992), pp. 153-54.

54   For a brief survey of Semitic verb structure, see Porter, *Verbal Aspect*, pp. 157-59.

histories in the strict sense in the Hebrew Bible does not seem to have been taken into account either. In a similar vein, temporal reference in the Japanese language is not based upon verbal forms, even though the Japanese are characterized as being very time-oriented.[55] This evidence would seem to mitigate the kinds of evidence often appealed to in the Sapir-Whorf hypothesis.

Recent linguistic work with regard to the Sapir-Whorf hypothesis confirms the analysis above. Some of Whorf's research, upon which the hypothesis was based, has been called into question. Whorf argued, for example, that since the Hopi language did not have a time-based tense system, the Hopis perceived of the world differently from those who did have such a time-based tense system, such as many Indo-Europeans.[56] Whorf was not able to substantiate what that difference in behavior was, however. As Crick has stated, when he noted that the Sapir-Whorf hypothesis was not based on field work, 'It is therefore doubly appropriate that the whole area now be recast. There should be no more facile pronouncements on the relations of language and culture.'[57] In his recent work, John Lucy has taken up the challenge of developing a suitable means of testing the hypothesis. His criteria designate that the study must be comparative, with data from two or more languages, that the comparison should involve a 'non-linguistic reality' as the standard by which to judge the hypothesis's validity, that the languages used must have a contrast in how they construe this reality, and that there must be a way to articulate the differences that the linguistic difference makes for thought.[58] Lucy's study goes on to conduct such a study, and offers support for a modest form of the Sapir-Whorf hypothesis on the basis of contrasting ways of marking number in Yucatec Mayan, a language of Mexico, and American English. Differences in the two languages seem to have an influence on the way speakers of the languages think about the entities involved. However, Lucy is cautious about his findings. He notes that further studies must be conducted to test the reliability of his results, that further work needs to be done to show whether the results can be generalized, that the issue of causality has

---

[55]   See E.A. Nida, 'The Implications of Contemporary Linguistics for Biblical Scholarship', *JBL* 91 (1972), p. 83.

[56]   Whorf, 'Some Verbal Categories of Hopi', in *Language*, pp. 112-24.

[57]   M. Crick, *Explorations in Language and Meaning: Towards a Semantic Anthropology* (London: Malaby, 1976), pp. 59-63 (63).

[58]   Lucy, *Grammatical Categories*, pp. 1-2.

not been proved, since other factors may be involved, and that there may be other factors still to be examined, such as the educational levels of those involved.[59]

One can see that, in light of the most recent research into the Sapir-Whorf hypothesis, we are a long way from proving the hypothesis with regard to the biblical languages and their users. The difficulties that must be addressed include the fact that we do not have native speakers for whom linguistic studies can be devised, and we must find new and different ways of assessing any data. Some of the data cited above indicate that there may be greater similarities in some fundamental linguistic structures of Greek and Hebrew than previously noted, which minimizes some of the possible points of contrast. There is, of course, the very difficult—perhaps even insurmountable—task of attempting to assess the difference that linguistic differences may have made on the thought patterns of the ancients. In light of these difficulties, it may be better simply to acknowledge that language has some influence on thought patterns, without pressing what those differences might be in the case of the biblical languages.

6. CONCLUSION

The fortuitous linguistic situation created by the widespread use of Greek can be readily appreciated. Greek played a major sociological role in uniting together a vast territory that had a wide variety of differing indigenous cultural, social, economic and religious backgrounds represented. The conquest of Alexander and his bringing of things Greek to the wider Mediterranean world helped to provide the basis for the later *pax Romana* (Roman peace), begun during the reign of Augustus, which was characterized by social, political and economic stability, besides linguistic stability and unity. Into this Greco-Roman world, Jesus, Paul and the other New Testament writers were born. Although Jesus predominantly used Aramaic, he apparently used Greek as well, and it was Greek that became the language of the early Church. This linguistic unity was an important factor in helping to create ecclesial unity. Paul and others wrote letters to churches located throughout the Greco-Roman world, with the full expectation that they would be able to read and understand the letters. Although there is plenty of evidence that the audiences did not always

---

[59]   Lucy, *Grammatical Categories*, pp. 158-59.

appreciate what was said in the letters, there is nothing to suggest that the problem was caused by their failure to understand the language itself in which the letters were written. It was in Greek that the writings not only of the Greek New Testament were preserved, but of virtually all of the apocryphal New Testament materials as well, not to mention the Septuagint and Greek pseudepigrapha, which formed such important sources for the New Testament and early Church writers. The earliest Church Fathers were Greek writers. Thus, knowledge of this language provides an important prerequisite to exegesis of the Greek New Testament (for further bibliography, see the Bibliographical Essay above).

THE GENRES OF THE NEW TESTAMENT

BROOK W.R. PEARSON AND STANLEY E. PORTER

INTRODUCTION: WHAT IS GENRE?

Genre has long been a subject of debate in both literary theory and criticism. Perhaps not surprisingly, it has also become an important issue in the realm of New Testament studies, with much weight being placed on identifying the particular literary species of the various books of the New Testament. Although there is much more at stake in this discussion than the mere identification of the genres of the New Testament documents, this has dominated most of the discussion of genre, as the following pages make amply clear. A more fundamental question, however, is that of what role genre should play in exegesis.

Perhaps the most illuminating study of this question is that of E.D. Hirsch in his *Validity in Interpretation*. Hirsch was concerned with showing how works are better examined by the material intrinsic to themselves than by that which is drawn from a document's extrinsic 'context'. So, while he makes a statement as bald as 'All understanding of verbal meaning is necessarily genre-bound',[1] he goes on to drastically qualify this by drawing a distinction between 'intrinsic genre' and 'extrinsic genre':

> We can...define quite precisely what an intrinsic genre is. It is that sense of the whole by means of which an interpreter can correctly understand any part in its determinacy...[2]

This definition of genre greatly modifies our understanding of his earlier words to the effect that all interpretation is bound by genre. Unfortunately, Hirsch's first statement about genre is often taken out of context to make genre, as an external characteristic, a determinative factor in interpretation (that is, suggesting that a particular document

---

[1]   E.D. Hirsch, Jr, *Validity in Interpretation* (New Haven: Yale University Press, 1967), p. 76. Although Hirsch's treatment of genre is one of the most salient available, there are other aspects of his literary-philosophical program that are less convincing, especially his credulity toward the idea of 'objective' interpretation. Reliance in this chapter upon his treatment of genre should not be seen as endorsement of such aspects of his program.

[2]   Hirsch, *Validity in Interpretation*, p. 86.

or part of a document may or may not mean in a particular way because other documents with a similar genre do or do not do so).[3] With regard to this, Hirsch goes on,

> If an intrinsic genre is capable of codetermining any partial meaning, there would seem to be left small *Spielraum* for that useful, catchall term, 'the context'. Ordinarily we cannot do without the term... [By this term] We mean the traditions and conventions that the speaker relies on, his attitudes, purposes, kind of vocabulary, relation to his audience, and we may mean a great many other things besides. Thus the word 'context' embraces and unifies two quite different realms. It signifies, on the one hand, the givens that accompany the text's meaning and, on the other, the constructions that are part of the text's meaning... My purpose is to show that we use 'context' to signify two necessary but distinct functions in interpretation. By 'context' we mean a construed notion of the whole meaning narrow enough to determine the meaning of a part, and, at the same time, we use the word to signify those givens in the milieu which will help us to conceive the right notion of the whole. In certain situations, certain types of meaning are very likely to occur. In addition to usage traits, therefore, we can have situation traits which help us to guess what kind of meaning we confront. But the givens of a situation do not directly determine verbal meanings. They help suggest a probable *type* of meaning, and it is this *type* idea which determines the partial meaning of which we defend when we invoke the word 'context'. In other words, the essential component of a context is the intrinsic genre of the utterance. Everything else in the context serves merely as clue to the intrinsic genre and has in itself no coercive power to codetermine partial meanings. Those external clues may be extremely important, but often (as in some anonymous texts) they are almost entirely absent. To know the intrinsic genre and the word sequence is to know almost everything. But the intrinsic genre is always construed, that is, guessed, and is never in any important sense given... One of the main tasks of interpretation can be summarized as the critical rejection of extrinsic genres in the search for the intrinsic genre of a text.[4]

We have chosen to give this quotation rather than a summary because this is perhaps the most succinct statement on the subject of genre that has been made, and summary would simply do it no justice. However, some explanation may be in order. The idea of genre, according to Hirsch's formula above, is not one that is drawn from *outside* the text

---

3   A good example of this is found in D.E. Aune, 'The Problem of the Genre of the Gospels: A Critique of C.H. Talbert's *What is a Gospel?*', in *Gospel Perspectives*. II. *Studies of History and Tradition in the Four Gospels* (ed. R.T. France and D. Wenham; 6 vols.; Sheffield: JSOT Press, 1981), p. 9.

4   Hirsch, *Validity in Interpretation*, pp. 86-89.

(for example, in the case of one who suggests that, as *Hamlet* is a tragedy, all of the characteristics of tragedy, ancient and modern, must be understood before one can appreciate the significance of the action in the play), but rather something that is drawn from reading the work itself (continuing the same example, understanding that the action in *Hamlet*, while similar to other works often labeled as tragedies, is unique to itself and can only be understood by a thorough examination thereof). While this does not do justice to the breadth of implication of Hirsch's formulation of the problem, it does highlight the essential dichotomy with which he confronts us.

When it comes to the question of the genres of the New Testament, much of the discussion has been concerned more with the question of *extrinsic* genre than *intrinsic*. Genre criticism has been touted as an important key to the determination of meaning in texts,[5] but it is probably best understood simply as a helpful tool to discover the situational circumstances within which the document came into being (i.e. *Hamlet* was not written so much as a tragedy as it was written as *Hamlet*, and, in the same way, we can expect that the Gospels were written not so much as Gospels as they were as Matthew, Mark, etc.).

The place of a particular work within the history and development of a genre is also significant. As Heather Dubrow puts it: 'writing in a genre can be a highly polemical gesture, a way of attempting to initiate a new chapter of literary history through the act of creating a single work of art'.[6] 'In other words, it is by overturning our generic expectations that a writer can induce in his reader a series of intellectual reflections and emotional experiences very like those being enacted in and by the work itself.'[7]

When it does come to drawing broad classifications, however, which is what most work on genre is concerned to do, we need to

---

5   See G.D. Fee and D. Stuart, *How to Read the Bible for All its Worth* (Grand Rapids: Zondervan, 2nd edn, 1993), p. 19: 'To interpret properly the "then and there" of biblical texts, one must not only know some general rules that apply to all the works of the Bible, but one needs to learn the special rules that apply to each of these literary forms (genres)'. Also, A.Y. Collins, *The Beginning of the Gospel: Probings of Mark in Context* (Philadelphia: Fortress Press, 1993), p. 2: 'The decision about the genre of Mark is not merely a matter of taxonomy or academic scholarship. One's assumptions about the literary form of Mark affect the way this work is allowed to function in the lives of the readers, in the life of the church, and in society.'

6   H. Dubrow, *Genre* (Critical Idiom, 42; London: Methuen, 1982), p. 30.

7   Dubrow, *Genre*, p. 37.

drastically switch theoretical tracks and look to the work of the formalist literary critics, René Wellek and Austin Warren. Although such a formulation as Hirsch's obviates the need for genre as an important interpretative tool, he still suggests that it is helpful as a key to seeking the meaning of a text. Unfortunately, his theoretical program does not drive him to provide much in the way of practical suggestions for how such an external feature could be found. Wellek and Warren, however, do provide us with a helpful working definition:

> Genre should be conceived, we think, as a grouping of literary works based, theoretically, upon both outer form [common formal characteristics]...and also upon inner form (attitude, tone, purpose—more crudely, subject and audience). The ostensible basis may be one or the other...but the critical problem will then be to find the *other* dimension, to complete the diagram.[8]

It is this definition which will be utilized throughout the rest of this chapter to determine the specific genre of the various books of the New Testament, turning back to Hirsch for discussions of the exegetical implications of genre.

The Distinction between Literary Genre and Literary Form

The distinction between smaller units within complete works and the larger wholes of which they are constituent parts is something important to be aware of at the outset. As Wellek and Warren state: 'complex literary forms develop out of simpler units'.[9] So, we do not talk of, for example, the parable as a *genre*, but rather as a literary *form*,[10] which works of many genres may include.[11]

Ancient Definition of Genre Versus a Modern One

Genre has been a subject of discussion in the western literary tradition since its earliest days. Aristotle and Horace are our main sources for the early views of genre theory, but the line of speculation and classification has continued throughout the following millennia. This, however, begs the question of whether we should utilize ancient

---

8   R. Wellek and A. Warren, *Theory of Literature* (New York: Harcourt, Brace & World, 3rd edn, 1956), p. 231.

9   Wellek and Warren, *Theory*, p. 236, citing André Jolles.

10   A good example of the confusion of these two is J.L. Bailey and L.D. Vander Broek, *Literary Forms in the New Testament* (London: SPCK, 1992).

11   See D.E. Aune, *The New Testament in its Literary Environment* (LEC; Philadelphia: Westminster Press, 1987), p. 13.

theories of genre which are at least roughly contemporary with the writings of the New Testament, or make use of modern genre theory which is based not so much on historical precedent and context as it is on hermeneutical philosophy and literary theory. There are two considerations with regard to this question. The first is the relative usefulness of ancient genre theory, and the second is whether or not much of what we do have in the way of ancient genre theory is actually contemporary or relevant to the writings of the New Testament. On the first point, Wellek and Warren again offer some insight:

> Anyone interested in genre theory must be careful not to confound the distinctive differences between 'classical' and modern theory. Classical theory is regulative and prescriptive, though its 'rules' are not the silly authoritarianism still often attributed to them. Classical theory not only believes that genre differs from genre, in nature and in glory, but also that they must be kept apart, not allowed to mix...

> Modern genre theory is, clearly, descriptive. It doesn't limit the number of possible kinds and doesn't prescribe rules to authors... Instead of emphasizing the distinction between kind and kind, it is interested...in finding the common denominator of a kind, its shared literary devices [forms] and literary purpose.[12]

As to the second point, D.A. Russell, in his monograph on the subject of ancient criticism, has a lengthy discussion on the question of ancient genre theory, and, in parallel with much work currently being done on the application of ancient rhetorical categories to the interpretation of the New Testament,[13] he concludes that, as the material that we have from antiquity is almost uniformly concerned with the *production* of literature, and not its *interpretation*, 'It follows that [its] value as evidence either of poetic practice or of "genre theory" is limited and uncertain'.[14]

---

12   Wellek and Warren, *Theory*, pp. 233-34.
13   See the chapter in this volume on rhetorical criticism, and the articles by S.E. Porter, J.T. Reed, and C.J. Classen in *Rhetoric and the New Testament: Essays from the 1992 Heidelberg Conference* (ed. S.E. Porter and T.H. Olbricht; JSNTSup, 90; Sheffield: JSOT Press, 1993), pp. 100-122, 292-324 and 265-91, as well as the relevant portions in S.E. Porter (ed.), *Handbook of Classical Rhetoric in the Hellenistic Period (330 B.C.–A.D. 400)* (Leiden: Brill, 1997).
14   D.A. Russell, *Criticism in Antiquity* (Berkeley: University of California Press, 1981), p. 158.

So, we suggest that, in the application of genre theory to the New Testament texts, while taking into account works and categories of works that could have a bearing on understanding the meaning of the New Testament writings,[15] it should be understood that there is no such thing as an ancient genre theory. Thus, ancient writings on generic categories should be used with great caution, as they are generally concerned with the *creation* of literature, not its *interpretation*. To interpret literature along the lines delineated in ancient authors is a misuse of the original purposes of those discussions. However, if for no other reason, this practice should be avoided from a practical point of view, as Wayne Meeks has pointed out:

> There was a time when nearly every New Testament scholar had been trained in the Greek and Latin classics. Comparing the genres and styles of the early Christian writings with other ancient literature was for them natural and obvious, though such comparisons did not always produce better understanding. The differences between the New Testament books and the literary works of the Golden Age were so great that often the result of comparing the two was that the Christian documents were put in a class by themselves.[16]

Of course, as Meeks goes on to suggest, the discovery of the papyri and increased availability of other Greco-Roman literature have made possible the comparison of the New Testament documents with others of the same time period, but this process of discovery has still not taken us any closer to discovering an ancient 'genre theory' that was, or could be, used for interpretative purposes.

Pseudonymity and the Investigation of Genre

The question of pseudonymity is an important and crucial question for the study of the New Testament documents.[17] That the Gospels, Hebrews, the Petrine and Johannine epistles are all formally *anonymous* is a well-known and recognized fact, with obvious exegetical consequences and limitations imposed as a result. However, it is also often assumed or asserted that a good deal of the Pauline literature and much of the remaining *antilegomena* are *pseudonymous*, which has exegetical consequences that are not so

---

[15] For which the most complete and accessible survey available is Aune, *The New Testament in its Literary Environment*.

[16] W.A. Meeks, 'Foreword', in Aune, *The New Testament in its Literary Environment*, p. 7.

[17] See the Chapter in this volume on the Pauline Letters for further comment.

often discussed. As far as genre goes, we must recognize that, if, for example, the Pastoral Epistles are pseudonymous, then their genre becomes a very sticky question. Both their form and content indicate that, while somewhat dissimilar from Paul's other, undisputed letters, they are still letters, and they are all obviously superscripted by Paul. But, if they are not letters, then what are they? They are obviously mimicking true letters, and the idea of their inclusion in the early Christian scriptural canon suggests that they must have been seen as genuine—but what does this do to our interpretation of them? If we begin from our external 'evidence' that indicates pseudonymity and use that as a directional finder that will help us determine the intrinsic genre of these documents, we must be aware that, if this is so, we are dealing with something totally other than a 'true' letter, and which stands as, in some ways, a parody of that genre. If, though still taking into account this extrinsic factor, we rely instead on intrinsic factors to be our ultimate guide to the meaning of these documents, then such questions will not prevent us from interpreting the documents themselves.[18]

THE GENRES OF THE NEW TESTAMENT

Gospels

The Gospels have been the most hotly contested New Testament documents insofar as their genre is concerned. The most difficult factor in establishing the genre of the Gospels is that, on first examination, they seem to have no close parallels in the ancient world. This is not to say that they are entirely without parallel, but the very fact that there is a *great deal* of similarity among the canonical four (and especially among the three Synoptics) makes them seem as if they somehow sprang from the early Christian communities that produced and used them as a wholly new form of literature (often called *sui generis*). This was indeed the conclusion of many of the early form critics, such as Rudolf Bultmann, Martin Dibelius, and K.L. Schmidt.[19]

Most of the subsequent discussion of the genre of the Gospels has,

---

18   For further discussion, see S.E. Porter, 'Pauline Authorship and the Pastoral Epistles: Implications for Canon', *BBR* 5 (1995), pp. 105-23.

19   See the survey of this period in R. Guelich, 'The Gospel Genre', in *The Gospel and the Gospels* (ed. P. Stuhlmacher; Grand Rapids: Eerdmans, 1991), pp. 173-208, esp. pp. 186-94.

however, revolved around their similarity with various forms of ancient biography. Ancient biography was not, of course, what we may think of as biography—many of the concerns of modern biography were simply not the concerns of the ancients,[20] and subjects for biography often included even the gods. Thus, when asserting that the Gospels are most similar to biography, this is not tantamount to calling them 'histories', as we shall see, although this is certainly one of the possibilities.

There have been other attempts to determine the genre of the Gospels,[21] but the overwhelming trend has been towards seeing the Gospel genre as some kind of biography. Indeed, the idea that the Gospels are biographies has been discussed in modern times at least since Clyde Votaw's programmatic essays published in 1915.[22] Indicative of the wide variety of modern approaches to the Gospels as biographies are the works of Charles Talbert, Philip Shuler, and Richard Burridge.

---

[20]   Such as the interior, psychological development of the character in question.

[21]   G.G. Bilezikian, *The Liberated Gospel: A Comparison of the Gospel of Mark and Greek Tragedy* (Grand Rapids: Baker, 1977). Even though Bilezikian uses Aristotle's *Poetics* as the basis of his assessment, he admits that Mark was not trying to write a Greek tragedy, but rather to put together a new literary work (genre?) to promote a unique religious message (p. 109). This, however, merely amounts to the *sui generis* hypothesis in different clothing. Another view that has been promoted, although not widely followed, is that the Gospels were written in the form of Jewish lectionaries, carrying on in the tradition of the synagogue, if not within the synagogues themselves. The most recent proponent of this view is M.D. Goulder, *The Evangelists' Calendar: A Lectionary Explanation of the Development of Scripture* (London: SPCK, 1978). Another divergent view, though quite popular in the late sixties and early seventies, has dropped almost completely from sight. This is the idea that the Gospels are *aretalogies*, biographies which were written to establish the divine nature of a human being, often referred to as 'divine man' biographies or myths. This was most strongly put forward by M. Hadas and M. Smith in their *Heroes and Gods: Spiritual Biographies in Antiquity* (New York: Harper & Row, 1962). The most telling criticism of this position is that, as Hadas and Smith themselves admit, we simply 'have no complete text surviving from the past specifically labeled aretalogy' (p. 60). It is almost certain that this never constituted a genre in and of itself.

[22]   Originally published as C.W. Votaw, 'The Gospels and Contemporary Biographies', *AJT* 19 (1915), pp. 45-73, 217-49, they have been re-issued in *The Gospels and Contemporary Biographies in the Greco-Roman World* (Philadelphia: Fortress Press, 1970).

Charles Talbert: The Gospels as Varied Mythical Biographies.
Talbert has published two monographs on the subject of the Gospel
genre. His first, published in 1974, suggests that the genre of Luke–
Acts is patterned after such things as the lives of the eminent Greco-
Roman philosophers, but adapted by Luke into a cultic function to
show his readers '*where* the true tradition was to be found in his
time...and *what* the content of that tradition was'.[23] In his second
monograph on the issue, published three years later, he expanded this
initial survey of the genre of Luke–Acts to a survey of all the
canonical Gospels. In this second monograph, Talbert moves more
strongly in the direction of his 1974 book, and, though classifying all
four Gospels as biographies, assigns them to the realm of myth, rather
than historiography.[24]

On the basis of a typology of Greco-Roman biographies which he
began in his 1974 work and continued in his later book, Talbert claims
that Mark, Luke–Acts (taking them as a single work with a single
generic form) and Matthew are all 'written in terms of the myth of the
immortals', with Luke–Acts having the additional feature of being a
'myth of origins for an early church', and Matthew being written
exclusively for a 'cultic setting'. John is seen as a 'myth of a
descending-ascending redeemer figure', unlike anything else in
Greco-Roman biography.[25] The essential bifurcation Talbert identifies
in Greco-Roman biography is between didactic and non-didactic
biography, and, according to Talbert, all of the Gospels are examples
of the former. He further splits didactic biography into various sub-
types, all of which he finds reflected to some degree in his
characterizations of the Gospels. An additional point which is
important in his analysis of the issue of genre revolves around his
placement of the didactic type of biography in a cultic setting.

Talbert's work, while initially received with some warmth, received
a shattering blow from David Aune in his thorough and complete
assessment and debunking of Talbert's hypothesis.[26] Aune's
thoroughgoing critique of *What Is a Gospel?* pointed out quite well
one of the continuing problems in New Testament studies, namely

---

23   C.H. Talbert, *Literary Patterns, Theological Themes and the Genre of
Luke–Acts* (SBLMS, 20; Missoula, MT: Scholars Press, 1974), p. 135.
24   C.H. Talbert, *What is a Gospel? The Genre of the Canonical Gospels*
(Philadelphia: Fortress Press, 1983).
25   Talbert, *What is a Gospel?*, pp. 134-35.
26   Aune, 'Genre of the Gospels', pp. 9-60.

that, when disciplinary boundaries are crossed, as in this case into the territory of classical philology, it is often done in a haphazard manner. As Aune puts it, 'the author roams the breadth and length of Graeco-Roman literature...virtually unencumbered [by] modern classical philology... While this guarantees a "fresh" approach, it also conjures up our image of a blindfolded man staggering across a minefield.'[27] Aune's assessment most certainly does not suffer from such a short-coming. His final conclusions on the question of the Gospels' relationship with Greco-Roman biography do, however, leave one disappointed. In several pages demonstrating that Talbert's for-mulation of the problem is impossible, he offers only a single piece of evidence that the Gospels could not be biographies, namely that they are anonymous, and, according to this early formulation, 'with few exceptions, *all ancient biographies of the Graeco-Roman world were written in the names of real or fictitious/pseudonymous authors*'.[28] However, in his later work on the subject, Aune drops this singular objection, and agrees with what is swiftly becoming a scholarly consensus, that the Gospels are examples of Greco-Roman biography.[29]

In a paper subsequent to the two volumes discussed here, Talbert, perhaps feeling the weight of such criticisms, suggests that 'It is among the biographical literature of antiquity that one finds the greatest affinities with the canonical Gospels. Exactly how the Gospels fit into the *bios* literature remains for future study to clarify.'[30] This is exactly what both Philip Shuler and Richard Burridge have attempted to do, albeit in two significantly different manners.

Phillip Shuler: Matthew as Encomium Biography. Shuler wrote in 1982, too late, apparently, to have the benefit of Aune's damaging review of Talbert's thesis, or for his warnings concerning improper appropriation of classical material. Perhaps as a result of this unfortunate timing, his attempt to situate the Gospels in the milieu of

---

27   Aune, 'Genre of the Gospels', p. 17.
28   Aune, 'Genre of the Gospels', p. 44 (emphasis his).
29   Aune, *The New Testament in its Literary Environment*, pp. 17-76, esp. pp. 63-66.
30   C.H. Talbert, 'Seminar on Gospel Genre: Introduction', in *Colloquy on New Testament Studies: A Time for Reappraisal and Fresh Approaches* (ed. B.C. Corley; Macon, GA: Mercer University Press, 1983), p. 200.

Greco-Roman biography has also not met with an overwhelmingly positive response.[31]

Shuler has several key presuppositions which seem to color his particular solution to the problem. These presuppositions are compounded by a misunderstanding of the literary theory of genre. The most important presupposition which Shuler brings to his discussion is that the Gospels, while containing some historical information, 'were apparently not primarily conceived for the purpose of conveying historical information'.[32] This assertion (which he characterizes as an observation) leads him to search for an ancient genre which would allow the Gospels to have some other function than strict historical documentation. For such a genre he turns to what he calls *'epideictic oratory...*more specifically the *encomium'*.[33] The most telling blow to Shuler's work is that he *never demonstrates that such a genre existed*. He uses several words which he sees as synonyms for 'encomium', but does not show that they have any connection, other than the fact that he draws them together to create his fictitious genre.

The analysis in Shuler's book relies on Matthew, making the title of the book somewhat misleading, probably because the dissertation upon which this book is based did deal with all of the Synoptics (although he states in his conclusion that the application of his idea to the other Gospels awaits further research). It is perhaps not surprising that, no matter how persuasive his reasoning may be, the fact that there is little or no evidence for the claims he makes has left this as merely another example of an unsuccessful attempt to establish the genre of the Gospels.

Richard Burridge: The Gospels as Biographies. Burridge's monograph on this topic, *What Are the Gospels? A Comparison with Graeco-Roman Biography*,[34] has come as a breath of fresh air in this

---

[31]   For a thorough review, see that by S.E. Porter in *JETS* 26 (1983), pp. 480-82.

[32]   P.L. Shuler, *A Genre for the Gospels: The Biographical Character of Matthew* (Philadelphia: Fortress Press, 1982), pp. 36-37.

[33]   Shuler, *A Genre for the Gospels*, p. 37. Encomium, loosely defined, is a biography told for the purpose of flattery or praise, usually highly exaggerated and full of apocryphal stories inserted for the purpose of reinforcing the image of the subject.

[34]   R.A. Burridge, *What Are the Gospels? A Comparison with Graeco-Roman Biography* (SNTSMS, 70; Cambridge: Cambridge University Press, 1992).

discussion. He carries out with gusto the program which was suggested by Aune in his attack on Talbert's position, using a macro-level approach to determine a 'family resemblance' between the Gospels and other Greco-Roman biography. Rather than focusing on the individual items of dissimilarity between the Gospels and other biography, Burridge focuses on the widespread similarities. He discusses and analyzes such features as the opening, the degree to which the subject of the biography is also the subject of the verbs in the piece, mode, setting, size, structure, topic and character. He finds a high degree of similarity between the Gospels and their biographical counterparts in the use and presence of such features, leading him to be able to assert with confidence that 'the time has come to go on from the use of the adjective "biographical", for *the gospels are bioi!*'[35]

The establishment of a generic category for the Gospels is not, however, the end of the debate. There are further questions that need to be more fully examined, each with their pursuant exegetical implications. Such questions might include examination of the implications of the relationships between the various Gospel writers as they made use of each other's work,[36] and investigation of the social implications of the appropriation of the biographical genre, among others.

Acts

The genre of Acts is often treated along with the genre of Luke. This is not surprising, given the close relationship which is almost universally recognized between the two writings. However, it must be recognized that, no matter that they both probably had the same author, or that they form two parts of the same story, they are different works.[37] We will thus treat Acts as a separate work in this chapter, with the recognition that the investigation of the genre of Acts may very well have implications for the genre of Luke, and *vice versa*, but that that will have to be a subject for further study.

There are three major views concerning the genre of Acts. The first two, attractive for their possible exegetical pay-off, have not, unfortunately, met with overwhelming acceptance. The final one, the

---

[35]   Burridge, *What Are the Gospels?*, p. 243.

[36]   A subject treated briefly in Aune, *The New Testament in its Literary Environment*, pp. 65-66.

[37]   See Burridge, *What Are the Gospels?*, pp. 244-47.

idea that Acts is most properly defined as history, while not on the surface having the same potential for quick exegetical pay-off, does, in our opinion, do the most justice to the text of Acts.

One thing that must be noted at the outset of any discussion of the genre of Acts is that there are several factors that often influence scholars to choose one genre over another, but that really have little to do with genre at all. A good example of this is found in the work of Gerd Lüdemann,[38] whose redactional approach aims to separate 'tradition' from 'redaction' in Acts. This is an attempt on his part to cut away that material which does not reflect a 'historical' situation, or at least to find what he sees as the earliest strands of tradition in the book. The problem with this approach, as with much historical criticism, is that there are un-provable presuppositions at the bases of such a program that distinctly color the results. The single most damaging presupposition is that the supernatural and miraculous events described in the book simply cannot be historical. As with the investigation of many of the central events of the New Testament, while it is quite true that such events and themes are not perhaps historically *quantifiable*, neither is it possible to disprove them on a historical basis. However this debate moves back and forth, it is important to realize that it really has nothing to do with the *genre* of Acts. If genre is to be found, according to the working definition from Wellek and Warren that we adopted above, as a combination of form and content/subject matter, then questions about the *character* of that subject matter must be left to one side when attempting to determine genre. Suggesting that Luke wrote history does not obviate the question of whether or not that history is reliable, nor, for that matter, does asserting that Luke was a novelist mean that he did not relate historical matters. Genre is not a question that can be settled simply on the grounds of how reliable or unreliable the material of a particular work may be. We would do well to remember this when discussing all of the generic questions which relate to the New Testament, but especially when approaching the question of the genre of Acts, which

---

[38]   G. Lüdemann, *Early Christianity according to the Traditions in Acts: A Commentary* (trans. J. Bowden; Philadelphia: Fortress Press, 1987). Lüdemann is, of course, not the only one to approach Acts redactionally. See also H. Conzelmann, *Acts of the Apostles* (Hermeneia; Philadelphia: Fortress Press, 1988).

so often seems to boil down to scholars' beliefs about the reliability of Luke's historical information.[39]

Acts as a Romance or Novel. This view, defended most strongly by Richard Pervo,[40] essentially posits that Acts was written in the form of an ancient novel (or romance), and that the themes and patterns found in Acts are very similar to other such works in the Greco-Roman world. The exegetical implications of such a 'discovery' seem obvious: if we were able to determine such a relationship, we would be able to examine Acts in light of several other works that contain similar material. (Or, alternatively, such an association would allow us to side-step some of the more difficult historical questions which attend the study of Acts.) We would be able to see where Acts was similar to other such works, and, perhaps more importantly, we would be able to determine where Acts differed—where it was making a special point. We would be able to understand, so the reasoning goes, more about the implicit contract that the writer of Acts had with his audience, and could use this to interpret the flow of action in the book of Acts.

As seductive as such an idea is, the identification of Acts with the

---

[39]   Further, the genre of Acts is not affected by discussions of the date of Acts. If one places Acts in the second century or the first, it does not affect either the form or subject matter of the book. Neither do questions concerning the authorship of Acts have any bearing on its genre, as the book is formally *anonymous*, not pseudonymous.

With regard to the question of pseudonymy, much has been made of the so-called 'we-passages', that is, if the 'we-passages' reflect an attempt on the part of the author to give the impression that he was present during the events he describes in those sections, then this, assuming a late date for Acts, would amount to pseudonymous authorship. This, of course, relies on several tenuous assumptions, most notably that of a late date for Acts. No matter what one believes about the date of Acts, however, S.E. Porter ('The "We" Passages', in *The Book of Acts in its First Century Setting*. II. *Graeco-Roman Setting* [ed. D.W.J. Gill and C. Gempf; Grand Rapids: Eerdmans, 1994], pp. 545-74) has demonstrated that the 'we-passages' form one continuous source which the writer of Acts has employed in the construction of his narrative. Thus, no matter what the date or who the author of Acts, they have no real bearing on the genre.

[40]   R.I. Pervo, *Profit with Delight: The Literary Genre of the Acts of the Apostles* (Philadelphia: Fortress Press, 1987); see also R. Hock, 'The Greek Novel', in *Greco-Roman Literature and the New Testament: Selected Forms and Genres* (ed. D.E. Aune; SBLSBS, 21; Atlanta: Scholars Press, 1987), esp. pp. 138-44.

ancient novel or romance runs into some extremely difficult ground. The study of the ancient novel has received much attention from classicists in recent times, which has been a positive step away from the elevation of the more popular and 'high-brow' writers of the classical period towards a broader appreciation of the spectrum of ancient literature.[41] As positive as this attention has been for our overall understanding of Greco-Roman culture, it simply does not do much to illuminate the genre of Acts. Pervo has sought to establish several parallel features between ancient novels and Acts, and comes up with a genre for Acts which he calls the 'historical novel'.[42] Unfortunately, such a category does not actually seem to exist, even among the texts which Pervo himself cites. In another place, he defines Acts as 'a theological book and a presentation of history, [which] also seeks to entertain'.[43] It is arguable whether this definition does much to place Acts within the category of the ancient novel, since the functions which he lists are quite natural ones for historical writings, as well.[44] Pervo's failure to place Acts in the category either of the novel or of history means that his genre of the 'historical novel' is not reflective of the ancient literature which he cites, and leaves the reader wondering exactly what it is that he is trying to prove. Indeed, the features which he does point out as parallel with ancient novels (such as imprisonments, shipwrecks, travel narratives, etc.) are all paralleled not only in novels, but also in non-fictive writing. There are also several elements of Acts that must be minimized to make an identification with the novel possible,[45] the most serious of which seems to be the fact that one of the distinguishing features of the ancient novel was its predictable ending, something quite definitely not present in Acts' somewhat abrupt and, from a literary standpoint, unsatisfactory ending.[46]

---

41   See T. Hägg, *The Novel in Antiquity* (Berkeley: University of California Press, 1983); B.E. Perry, *The Ancient Romances: A Literary-Historical Account of their Origins* (Berkeley: University of California Press, 1967).

42   Pervo, *Profit with Delight*, p. 136.

43   Pervo, *Profit with Delight*, p. 86.

44   On the entertainment value of ancient historical writing, see B.L. Ullman, 'History and Tragedy', *TAPA* 73 (1942), pp. 250-53; F.W. Walbank, 'History and Tragedy', *Historia* 9 (1960), pp. 216-34.

45   See L. Alexander, *The Preface to Luke's Gospel: Literary Convention and Social Context in Luke 1.1-4 and Acts 1.1* (SNTSMS, 78; Cambridge: Cambridge University Press, 1993) for a recent, if dated, summary of such elements.

46   A point recognized by Pervo himself, *Profit with Delight*, pp. 48-50.

Pervo's assessment suffers most seriously, perhaps, not so much from his analysis as from his faulty reasoning. A good deal of weight is placed on the similarities which he finds between Acts and the subsequent apocryphal acts of the various apostles. The fact that these works are late and clearly derivative does not seem to bother him, since he reasons that, if the first Acts was fictive, then it can be assessed on the basis of all subsequent fictive 'acts'. The logic of such an exegetical move escapes us, but is, unfortunately, not universally rejected.[47]

All-in-all, the case for the novel being the basis for the genre of Acts has not been well enough argued to date. Unfortunately, this has not meant that it has been rejected as a category for the study of Acts, and Pervo continues to be cited as evidence and support for this idea, regardless of the relative weakness of his position.[48] Until further evidence is brought forward which builds a more convincing case, we would do much better to leave the idea of the novel to one side in terms of the question of a genre for Acts.

Acts as a Travel Narrative or Sea Voyage. From the standpoint of genre, the idea that Acts, with its problematic 'we-passages', is in the 'conventional' form of an ancient account of a sea voyage is attractive for one reason in particular: it makes the questions of date and authorship, often seen to be integral to the interpretation and implications of the 'we-passages', irrelevant, for, if the passages are simply conventional, then there can be no question of deception or pseudonymy on the part of the author. Of course, this also means that their value as historical sources comes into question. This position is advocated most strongly by Vernon Robbins.[49] Robbins bases his

---

[47]   See, e.g., W. Bindemann, 'Verkündigter Verkündiger: Das Paulusbild der Wir-Stücke in der Apostelgeschichte: Seine Aufnahme und Bearbeitung durch Lukas', *TLZ* 114 (1989), pp. 705-20.

[48]   Indicative of this continuing trend is a recent volume of essays from a conference on Luke–Acts, in which, of the three essays dealing even tangentially with the genre of Acts, two of the three rely on Pervo's classification of Acts as a novel (L. Alexander, '"In Journeyings Often": Voyaging in the Acts of the Apostles and in Greek Romance', pp. 17-49, and G. Downing, 'Theophilus's First Reading of Luke–Acts', pp. 91-109, both in *Luke's Literary Achievement: Collected Essays* [ed. C.M. Tuckett; JSNTSup, 116; Sheffield: Sheffield Academic Press, 1995]).

[49]   V.K. Robbins, 'By Land and Sea: The We-Passages and Ancient Sea Voyages', in *Perspectives on Luke–Acts* (ed. C.H. Talbert; Edinburgh: T. & T. Clark, 1978), pp. 215-42.

assessment on a wide variety of parallels which he draws from literature spanning the spectrums of time (1800 BCE to 300 CE), space (Egyptian, Greek, and Latin), and generic form (epic, poetry, prose narrative, oratory, fantasy, autobiography, romance/novel, scientific prose, etc.). Unfortunately, while this breadth may be seen by Robbins as corroborative of his assertion that there was a convention in describing ancient sea voyages, it is better seen as an obvious case of 'parallelomania'. There are simply no controlling criteria by which the examples he includes have been selected. One gets the impression that his results are highly selective and perhaps not entirely representative. A further problem is the inclusion of so many different forms of writing. There is simply no cohesiveness in the examples Robbins cites.[50] It is probably much better to see the use of the first person plural in ancient texts where sea voyages are described as a natural pattern functioning whenever conveyances with multiple passengers are included in narratives.[51] This 'solution' to the genre of Acts is probably best seen as a side-issue regarding the provenance of the 'we-passages', having little to do with the over-all genre of Acts.

Acts as History. Acts has been understood as a historical document for most of its life in the Church, as well as within most critical dialogue. That it has been recently interpreted in different ways (as above) does not, however, mean that the essential features which originally led most to think of it as a historical document have disappeared. We must re-iterate, however, that we are not speaking here of the historical *reliability* of the document, only of its genre. In terms of form, Acts has many features which recommend it as ancient history. These include its historical preface,[52] the author's claim to be using

---

50   For analysis of Robbins's various examples, see Porter, 'The "We" Passages', pp. 554-58; J.A. Fitzmyer, *Luke the Theologian: Aspects of his Teaching* (New York: Paulist Press, 1989), pp. 16-22; and W.S. Kurz, 'Narrative Approaches to Luke–Acts', *Bib* 68 (1987), pp. 216-17.

51   As C.K. Barrett states, 'It is simply that in any vehicle larger than a bicycle there may well be a number of passengers who become, for a time, a community' ('Paul Shipwrecked', in *Scripture: Meaning and Method* [ed. B.P. Thompson; Festschrift A.T. Hanson; Hull: Hull University Press, 1987], p. 53).

52   Although Alexander has argued that the preface is similar to scientific prose of the ancient world (*The Preface to Luke's Gospel* and 'Luke's Preface in the Context of Greek Preface-Writing', *NovT* 28 [1986], p. 69), she makes the mistake, from a generic point of view, of focusing almost entirely on form, and not enough on content. It is probably better to see it as similar to the prefaces of other Hellenistic historians. See D. Earl, 'Prologue-Form in Ancient

sources in the compilation of his account, its chronologically linear movement, and its episodic nature, among others.[53]

It seems that the best position with which to go forward is that Acts is a form of historiography common to the ancient world. While this does make the best sense of the evidence, it does not, unfortunately, provide the exegete with a great deal of exegetical 'fire power'. It does not allow esoteric new documents and literary traditions to be brought to bear on the problem. It does not eliminate the need for further historical work to be done concerning the nature of the history contained in Acts. In short, seeing Acts as history leaves one in much the same position in which scholars have always been—needing to go to the text itself to understand its ins and outs, its patterns and purposes. The fact that Acts is best seen as history means that the exegete has a great deal of difficult work to do, because, although its form and content seem best related to the historical genre, the genre of history is very wide indeed. As with most writings, one cannot deduce meaning from genre. One can only begin the task from this point.

Pauline and Other Letters

The Pauline and the so-called 'Catholic' or General Epistles or letters have had perhaps the least discussion from the point of view of genre, although they have had their share of the limelight. While literary genre theory is perhaps least equipped from a theoretical standpoint to deal with epistolary literature (as letters are seldom seen as 'literary' creations, but rather mundane, functional documents), Wellek and Warren's working definition of genre, involving form and subject matter or content, is still helpful in placing them within the Greco-Roman literary world.

Epistle versus Letter. There has really only been one serious question raised concerning the genre of the Pauline letters. This relates to a

---

Historiography', *ANRW* I.2 (ed. H. Temporini; Berlin: de Gruyter, 1972), pp. 842-56.

[53]   An excellent survey of the similarity of Acts to other works of Greco-Roman historiography can be found in M.A. Powell, *What Are they Saying about Acts?* (New York: Paulist Press, 1991), pp. 80-83. See also C.J. Hemer, *The Book of Acts in the Setting of Hellenistic History* (WUNT, 49; repr. Winona Lake, IN: Eisenbrauns, 1990), *passim*; Aune, *The New Testament in its Literary Environment*, pp. 80-111; W.C. van Unnik, 'Luke's Second Book and the Rules of Hellenistic Historiography', in *Les Acts des Apôtres: Traditions, rédaction, théologie* (ed. J. Kremer; BETL, 48; Gembloux: Duculot, 1979), pp. 37-60; and C.K. Barrett, *Luke the Historian in Recent Study* (London: Epworth, 1961).

distinction between the *letter*, or the *true letter*, and the *literary letter*, or the *epistle*. This distinction is largely the result of Adolf Deissmann's important investigations around the turn of the century in his *Bible Studies* and *Light from the Ancient East*.[54] Deissmann was among the first of the New Testament scholars to recognize the value of the papyri for New Testament study, and to utilize them in his work. At the time only recently discovered, the treasure-trove of documents from a stratum of society that had been previously almost entirely hidden from view sent shock waves throughout the world of New Testament studies. Deissmann's famous bifurcation between the two forms of epistolary writings is based primarily on an identification of especially the Pauline letters with many of the newly discovered letters of the ancient Egyptian villages and towns which had yielded their rubbish heaps and archive deposits. Indeed, much of the lexical and grammatical information that has been gleaned from the Egyptian papyri has provided an incredible amount of comparative data for the study of the Greek of the New Testament, but Deissmann's work was based on more than just a recognition of the *koine* of New Testament Greek. He also had a very distinct and Romantic picture of the social world into which Christianity first erupted. In Deissmann's writings, there is a strict delineation between the 'literary' world and the 'unliterary' world which has more to do with his rather naive Romantic sociological approach, than with distinctions necessarily drawn from in-depth study of the New Testament literature. In his own words,

> Christianity...does not begin as a literary movement. Its creative period is non-literary.

> Jesus of Nazareth is altogether unliterary. He never wrote or dictated a line.[55] He depended entirely on the living word, full of a great confidence that the scattered seed would spring up... He had no need to write letters...the new thing for which He looked came not in a book, formulae, and subtle doctrine, but in spirit and fire.

> Side by side with Jesus there stands, equally non-literary, His apostle. Even from the hand of St. Paul we should possess not a line, probably, if he had remained, like his Master, in retirement. But the Spirit drove the cosmopolite back into the Diaspora...

---

54   G.A. Deissmann, *Bible Studies* (trans. A. Grieve; Edinburgh: T. & T. Clark, 1901), pp. 1-59; *Light from the Ancient East* (trans. L.R.M. Strachan; London: Hodder & Stoughton, 4th edn, 1927), pp. 146-251.

55   Leaving aside the passage in John 8:6-8.

Such sayings of the non-literary Jesus as have been reported to us by others, and such non-literary letters as remain to us of St Paul's, show us that Christianity in its earliest creative period was most closely bound up with the lower classes and had as yet no effective connexion with the small upper class possessed of power and culture...

The creative, non-literary period is followed by the conservative, literary period, but this receives its immediate stamp from the motive forces of the former epoch.[56]

Deissmann puts this assessment at the end of his discussion of the letter form of the Pauline writings, as if it were a discovery of his analysis, rather than its true motivation. In truth, as Stanley Stowers has stated,

Deissmann's antithesis between the natural and the conventional was typical of nineteenth- and early twentieth-century Romanticism popularized in Deissmann's day by the writings of Leo Tolstoy and others. Now, however, theorists of literature and culture are widely agreed that there is a conventional dimension to all intelligible human behavior.[57]

Deissmann's contention concerning the Pauline letter form was perhaps the inevitable result of such a strong delineation between 'literary' and 'unliterary'. Of course, this delineation really had more to do with the perceived social make-up of society at the time of the New Testament writings, reflecting contemporary German Romantic ideas of natural religion and the stagnancy of the Church at the time, against which the idealized New Testament Church was held up as an example. Had Paul been shown to be 'literary' (meaning 'upper class', 'conventional' or 'hierarchical'), then the whole contention that there was an ideal pattern of an early Church which could be emulated in modern times would have disappeared. And so, Paul's letters, which are different in form and character from many of the other New Testament epistles or letters, became elevated (or lowered) to a position of the 'true letter', while letters such as James, 1 and 2 Peter, and Jude are seen as 'literary letters', or 'epistles'. The designation of these as 'epistles' has largely to do with the fact that their content is somewhat universally accessible, and that their addressees (such as Jas 1:1, 'to the twelve tribes of the dispersion') are seen to be a 'public'

---

56   Deissmann, *Light from the Ancient East,* pp. 245-47.
57   S.K. Stowers, *Letter Writing in Greco-Roman Antiquity* (LEC; Philadelphia: Westminster Press, 1986), p. 19. See pp. 17-26 for a thorough analysis of Deissmann's position and an overview of recent epistolary theory.

(Christian) audience. In contrast to these, Paul's letters are seen to be more circumstantial, contextual, and spontaneous, as well as all being relatively private (that is, to a limited, known group of people, or to an individual. Even Galatians, probably a circular letter to the churches in the whole region of Galatia, would have been to a limited group of people that Paul would have largely known, and, in addition, addresses a very particular situation).

In some ways, Deissmann's distinction is valid—there is no point in defending the thesis that the undisputed Pauline epistles are the same in either form or content to some of the Catholic Epistles, or even to the often disputed Pastoral Epistles (the difference in form and content being one of the reasons they are disputed). However, rather than such a distinction as Deissmann draws, it is probably better to see features such as audience, situation, and the character of the content as differentiating one set of letters from another set of letters, rather than as differentiating letters from epistles. One could take Deissmann's two categories (between which even he admits some variation, even if he does see everything which is not actually a 'true letter' as a poor approximation thereof) as poles on a continuum of letter writing, one pole being the personal, completely private letter, the other pole being the public, 'literary' letter intended to be read by a wide variety of people, none of which the author may necessarily know. Between the two poles there is room for great diversity, and, of course, an incredible range of possible subject matter, the only limit being perhaps that the material is something which someone separated for some reason from another person wants that person to know.

The Structure of the Letter: Three, Four, or Five Parts. Concerning the 'form' part of our working definition of genre, that is, what sort of structures we might expect to see if we are to classify something as a letter, there is widespread agreement with a slight bit of variation. The differentiation of opinion is simply over how *many* parts a letter had in the Greco-Roman world. Three-part,[58] four-part,[59] and five-part[60] letter structures have been proposed. While it is quite true that most ancient Greek letters can be divided into three parts (the opening, the

---

[58]   See J.L. White, 'Ancient Greek Letters', in Aune (ed.), *Greco-Roman Literature*, pp. 85-105, esp. p. 97.

[59]   See J.A.D. Weima, *Neglected Endings: The Significance of the Pauline Letter Closings* (JSNTSup, 101; Sheffield: JSOT Press, 1994), p. 11.

[60]   See W.G. Doty, *Letters in Primitive Christianity* (GBS; Philadelphia: Fortress Press, 1973), pp. 27-43.

body, and the closing), Paul seems to have been a bit of an innovator in his letter writing. While still very much a Greco-Roman letter writer, some have posited that Paul developed the standard thanksgiving, usually seen as transitionary from the opening to the body-opening of Greco-Roman letters, into a part of its own. Similarly, perhaps because of the specific use of the letter form under which most of Paul's extant letters fall, namely the letter to a church, a part of the body of the letter in which Paul develops his moral, ethical, or practical teaching seems to have become a distinct portion of his letter form all of its own. This is usually called the 'paraenesis', and is often seen by those who advocate a three- or four-part Pauline letter form as simply being a part of the body of the letter. Paul does seem to have developed this part of his letter form to the point where it is a distinct portion of the letter on its own, but one should not let such an innovation suggest that Paul's letters are not typical, Greco-Roman letters. Even the disputed Pauline epistles, including the Pastorals, evince much the same pattern as the undisputed ones. If, however, as we have discussed above, they are pseudonymous, this raises serious questions concerning their genre, as they then become, perhaps as strongly (and as negatively) as even Deissmann would put it, 'literary letters', but this because of their fictive nature, rather than their social class.

The other letters in the New Testament all have some of these parts, but none has the breadth or consistency of the Pauline letters (although Paul does not even always have all five parts). This should not suggest that the other letters are defective in some way, merely that they are different. Even Deissmann allowed that the last two Johannine letters were 'true letters',[61] and it is indeed true that, along with Philemon, these two letters seem to have the most in common with the papyri letters we have in our possession. However, many of the other Catholic/General Epistles such as 1 John, 1 and 2 Peter, and Jude all carry some of the features of the typical Greco-Roman letter.

Hebrews and James. Hebrews and James are often separated from the other Catholic/General Epistles because they seem to be the least like letters of them all. Indeed, Hebrews is without an epistolary opening (although, due to the rather abrupt beginning of the document, some have speculated that there was an opening that has been lost in the transmission process), and it is quite unlike any of the other New

---

61   Deissmann, *Light from the Ancient East*, pp. 241-42.

Testament letters that have a body, often composed of doctrinal teaching or discourse, followed by a paraenetic section. In fact, the only epistolary feature of Hebrews, other than its later title, is the epistolary-like ending (which actually seems quite Pauline in nature). As a result of this disparity between Hebrews and either the specific Pauline or the wider Greco-Roman letter form, some have suggested that Hebrews is not a letter at all. Other genres that have been suggested include a homily or sermon, or a collection of such addresses.[62] Evidence garnered in support of this position includes the reference within the body of Hebrews to itself as a 'word of exhortation' (13:22); the common stance throughout the book reminiscent of that which a preacher might take, for example, in the continual references to the audience as 'brethren' (3:1, 12), as well as the references to the author as 'speaker' (2:5; 6:9; 8:1); and, finally, the pattern of citations of Scripture being followed by explanations thereof.

A similar position is that the text of Hebrews is in the form of a classical rhetorical oration. Hebrews does indeed evince several of the characteristics of classical rhetoric, and some take the presence of such features to mean that Hebrews was composed as an oration. While divided on the exact category of rhetoric under which Hebrews would fall,[63] those convinced of this position at least agree that Hebrews does employ stylistic features of Greco-Roman rhetoric. There is, however, a problem with this view. The classification of Hebrews as a particular species of rhetoric is often seen (as with much of rhetorical criticism) as a kind of magic key which will unlock the meaning of the book. This is, unfortunately, not possible, as the controversy over its particular species of rhetoric shows us.

Whether seen as an oration, as a homily or as a collection of homilies, Hebrews is probably best analyzed on the basis of its internal structure, rather than one imposed from outside that may or may not be entirely appropriate to the book itself. Where elements of such external structures can be discerned in the text of the book, they

---

62   See J. Moffatt, *An Introduction to the Literature of the New Testament* (Edinburgh: T. & T. Clark, 3rd edn, 1918), pp. 428-29; and S. Stanley, 'The Structure of Hebrews from Three Perspectives', *TynBul* 45.2 (1994), pp. 247-51.

63   B. Lindars ('The Rhetorical Structure of Hebrews', *NTS* 35 [1989], pp. 382-406) suggests deliberative (concerned with future action); and Aune (*The New Testament in its Literary Environment*, p. 212) suggests epideictic (concerned with the reinforcement of beliefs already held by the audience).

should by all means be appropriated, as long as that does not mean the wholesale importation of other criteria that have not been discerned from within the text itself.

Another position advocated regarding the genre of Hebrews posits that the exegetical technique used in the book is closest to the technique of midrash, and that, rather than just utilizing this technique, the book is itself a midrash on Psalm 110. Midrash (from the Hebrew verb meaning 'to seek') is a Jewish exegetical technique that is essentially an extended explanatory commentary on a portion of Scripture. Midrash is a quite fashionable topic at the present moment in New Testament scholarship, and has been applied to almost all of the New Testament writings in one form or another. Here it is posited that, because of the continued references throughout the book to Psalm 110, and the elucidation of the meaning of this text at Heb. 7:11-28, the whole book is a midrash on this psalm.[64] This position is probably best left to one side, as it does little to explain anything but the sections of Hebrews that discuss Psalm 110, and does not cohere in significant and sustained ways with other examples of the midrashic genre.

The genre of Hebrews is perhaps one of the most difficult to ascertain in the entire New Testament, but, if we remember that genre is merely a tool that we as interpreters can use to help us into the lowest level of meaning of a particular work, this should not be too daunting a problem. It simply means that there is more work to be done to ascertain what Hirsch calls the *intrinsic genre* of the book— we may not know under which circumstances the book was written, but we do have the book, and it is long enough and well enough structured that we can use internal criteria to determine what the book is trying to do and say. Beyond that, we are at somewhat of a loss concerning the genre of Hebrews.

James has been another book which has been debated in terms of its generic character. It was one of Deissmann's so-called 'literary letters', and it has often been seen as such in modern criticism.[65] The

---

64   See G.W. Buchanan, *To the Hebrews* (AB, 36; Garden City, NY: Doubleday, 1971), p. xix. For an earlier demonstration that Psalm 110 is not discussed in Hebrews in a way commonly expected in midrash, see D.M. Hay, *Glory at the Right Hand: Psalm 110 in Early Christianity* (SBLMS, 18; Nashville: Abingdon Press, 1967).

65   Two basic ways of construing James as a 'literary letter' are (1) that it is a form of Hellenistic diatribe (J.H. Ropes, *A Critical and Exegetical Commentary*

move towards seeing James as a 'literary letter' revolves primarily around the audience addressed ('the twelve tribes in the dispersion'), and the general ethical nature of much of the material in the letter itself which would all be easily understood, so the argument goes, in a general, Greco-Roman context, not necessitating any specific situational setting. The source of this general teaching is, of course, not an issue for the determination of genre, nor is the fact that the audience addressed is a large one that cannot possibly have been known by the author. In fact, as James does exhibit standard epistolary features (opening, two-part body, closing), it is probably best, in terms of genre, to leave it at that.

Revelation

The determination of the genre of Revelation presents us with two distinct problems: (1) the relationship of Revelation to other, Jewish, apocalyptic literature, and (2) how to classify and identify such apocalyptic literature. The first problem is somewhat dependent on the solution to the second, so it will be to this that we turn first.

Views of Jewish Apocalyptic. The word 'apocalyptic', derived from the Greek word for 'revelation', connotes more than just a form of literature. Indeed, the literary genre we call 'apocalypse' is only a part of the overall matrix of belief, eschatology, philosophy, history, and social setting of the wider concept of apocalyptic thought. As John Collins has defined it, 'recent scholarship has abandoned the use of "apocalyptic" as a noun and distinguishes between apocalypse as a literary genre, apocalypticism as a social ideology, and apocalyptic eschatology as a set of ideas and motifs that may also be found in other literary genres and social settings'.[66] It is true, however, that older scholarship focused more closely on 'apocalyptic' as a form of literature. In this phase of the study of 'apocalyptic', it was usual to have a list of things that were seen as indicative of the apocalyptic genre, and then to measure different pieces against that 'yard-stick'

---

on the Epistle of St James [ICC; Edinburgh: T. & T. Clark, 1916]), and (2) that it is a form of paraenesis, closely linked to the Jewish wisdom tradition (M. Dibelius, *James* [ed. H. Greeven; Hermeneia; Philadelphia: Fortress Press, 1975], pp. 3-11). James has also been seen, similarly to Hebrews, as a sermon or homily, or a collection thereof. Regardless of its original form, however, it is quite clearly now in the form of a letter, and all that remains from the standpoint of genre is to determine what kind of letter.

66   J.J. Collins, *The Apocalyptic Imagination: An Introduction to the Jewish Matrix of Christianity* (New York: Crossroad, 1992), p. 2.

list.[67] Although D.S. Russell does admit that 'These various "marks" belong to apocalyptic not in the sense that they are essential to it or are to be found in every apocalyptic writing, but rather in the sense that, in whole or in part, they build up an *impression* of a distinct kind which conveys a particular *mood* of thought and belief',[68] it was not until more recent scholarship that the implications of his admission have been fully felt.

This newer phase of scholarship, instead of enumerating various characteristics of 'apocalyptic', concentrates on the overall *matrix* of belief and thought out of which apocalyptic literature flowed. Thus the definition above.[69] This has given a tremendous impetus to the study of the apocalypse as a literary genre, and has given us a more useful way of classifying works that seem to fall under this generic term without having to resort to endless enumerations of the content that apocalypses may have.

It has long been recognized that the term 'apocalypse' is not given as the actual title of a book until the end of the first century or beginning of the second.[70] However, the general matrix of the literary genre that became known as the 'apocalypse' was well in place by at least the third century BCE with the writing of portions of *1 Enoch*.[71]

---

[67]   L. Morris, *Apocalyptic* (Grand Rapids: Eerdmans, 1972), pp. 34-67 lists 13 different characteristics of apocalyptic, while D.S. Russell, *The Method and Message of Jewish Apocalyptic: 200 BC–AD 100* (OTL; Philadelphia: Westminster Press, 1964), p. 105 lists 19.

[68]   Russell, *The Method and Message of Jewish Apocalyptic*, p. 105.

[69]   Other important works in this newer, matrix phase of apocalyptic scholarship include D. Hellholm (ed.), *Apocalypticism in the Mediterranean World and the Near East* (Tübingen: Mohr–Siebeck, 1983); and J.J. Collins (ed.), *Apocalypse: The Morphology of a Genre* (*Semeia* 14 [1979]). However, the most recent survey of the language surrounding 'apocalyptic' by R.B. Matlock ('"Apocalyptic" Interpretation and Interpreting "Apocalyptic": A Critique', in his *Unveiling the Apocalyptic Paul: Paul's Interpreters and the Rhetoric of Criticism* [JSNTSup, 127; Sheffield: Sheffield Academic Press, 1996], pp. 247-316) brings together and raises several of its own criticisms of the whole discussion, most notably, the use of a concept of 'apocalyptic' to interpret the very writings out of which the concept ostensibly sprang—we have no source for 'apocalyptic' or 'apocalypticism' other than apocalypses!

[70]   See J.J. Collins, *Maccabees, Second Maccabees: With an Excursus on the Apocalyptic Genre* (Wilmington, DE: Michael Glazier, 1981), p. 130; *idem, The Apocalyptic Imagination*, p. 3.

[71]   Collins, *Maccabees, Second Maccabees*, p. 132. The portions of *1 Enoch* found at Qumran, written in Aramaic, namely the Book of the Watchers (1–36)

Continuing with our definition of genre as a combination of formal characteristics and subject matter or content, the following are the formal characteristics thought now to be typical of apocalypses in general, with, of course, some variation between the various books themselves:[72] (1) An apocalypse is a revelation. It will thus include 'a narrative framework that describes the manner of revelation'. (2) 'The main means of revelation are visions and otherworldly journeys, supplemented by discourse or dialogue and occasionally by a heavenly book.' (3) 'The constant element is the presence of an angel who interprets the vision or serves as guide on the otherworldly journey. This figure indicates that the revelation is not intelligible without supernatural aid.' (4) 'In all Jewish apocalypses the human recipient is a venerable figure from the distant past, whose name is used pseudonymously.' (5) 'The disposition of the seer before the revelation and his reaction to it typically emphasize human helplessness in the face of the supernatural.' This list of formal characteristics cuts across the whole of the apocalyptic genre, with few exceptions. One additional characteristic which we should like to posit is the frequent command on the part of the explaining angel to the recipient of the vision or otherworldly traveler to seal up or hide the contents of the vision or the journey which he has taken.

On the other side of the generic coin, the question of subject matter or content, Collins also has a helpful set of guidelines:[73] 'The content of apocalypses...involves both a temporal and spatial dimension, and the emphasis is distributed differently in some works'. (1) 'Some, such as Daniel, contain an elaborate review of history, presented in the form of prophecy and culminating in a time of crisis and eschatological upheaval.' (2) 'Others, such as *2 Enoch*, devote most of their text to accounts of the regions traversed in the otherworldly journey.' (3) 'The revelation of a supernatural world and the activity of supernatural beings are essential to all apocalypses.' (4) 'In all there are also final judgement and a destruction of the wicked.' (5) The eschatology of the apocalypses differs from that of the earlier prophetic books by clearly envisaging retribution beyond death.' (6)

---

and the Astronomical Book (72–82), have pushed back the dating of the earliest apocalyptic literature quite significantly. Previously, the earliest apocalypse was thought to be Daniel 7–12 (Collins, *Maccabees, Second Maccabees*, p. 132).

[72]   The following list is adapted from Collins, *The Apocalyptic Imagination*, pp. 4-5.

[73]   This list is also adapted from Collins, *The Apocalyptic Imagination*, p. 5.

'Paraenesis occupies a prominent place in a few apocalypses (e.g. *2 Enoch, 2 Baruch*), but all the apocalypses have a hortatory aspect, whether or not it is spelled out.'

Together, these two lists contain many of the elements that the former phase of apocalyptic scholarship enumerated, but this arrangement eliminates the confusion between form and content, as well as allowing elements that properly belong in the category of 'apocalypticism' or apocalyptic belief to be left out of the discussion of genre.

There have, indeed, been other attempts to classify the genre of the apocalypses, but they have not proved convincing. Bruce Malina's recent *On the Genre and Message of Revelation*[74] is an attempt to identify Revelation with the wider genre of 'astral prophecy', which is essentially a way of pulling together all literature with an astrological 'bent' under one umbrella term. Malina is quite right to point out the many astrological elements in Revelation, and he is also probably correct that a good deal of apocalyptic imagery was drawn from popular Hellenistic literature, but his wide ranging (both temporally and spatially) review of this literature (not limited to a Hellenistic context) must surely argue in itself for a more specific identification of the genre of the apocalypse. If indeed astrological speculation was as widespread as Malina would have us believe, then it cannot, by definition, help us too much in the search for a genre, as it is not a *distinguishing* feature. This, of course, assumes that his presentation of the evidence is even-handed, which is far from sure. Another attempt, this time aimed at the entire genre of the apocalypse, also widens the field quite drastically. Christopher Rowland's *The Open Heaven*[75] argues that we should view apocalyptic simply as literature in which heaven is opened up and a revelation is given, ignoring the content of that revelation.[76] The impetus behind this definition is the wish to eliminate eschatology from the discussion of apocalyptic, and, as with Malina's later attempt to broaden the genre drastically, bring information from many different kinds of texts into play when interpreting apocalyptic.[77] These two solutions ignore opposite sides

---

[74]   B.J. Malina, *On the Genre and Message of Revelation: Star Visions and Sky Journeys* (Peabody, MA: Hendrickson, 1995).

[75]   C. Rowland, *The Open Heaven: A Study of Apocalyptic in Judaism and Christianity* (New York: Crossroad, 1982).

[76]   Rowland, *The Open Heaven*, p. 14.

[77]   For the wish to do away with eschatology in the definition of the genre of

of the generic formula: Malina ignores formal characteristics, and Rowland ignores content. As such, they should both be rejected on purely methodological grounds.

How Much is Revelation like Jewish Apocalyptic Literature? The question remains, however, concerning how well Revelation fits within the apocalyptic genre. According to the definition we have here adopted, following Collins, Revelation fits all of the formal characteristics save for the fact that Revelation is not (likely) pseudonymous. If one accepts the additional formal element we have suggested, namely that concerning the issue of secrecy of the contents of the revelation, then Revelation also does not accord with this characteristic. It also contains most, if not all, of the elements of content from Collins's list. It seems that, according to Collins's definition, we can safely place Revelation in the genre of the apocalypse.

However, in terms of both form and content, Revelation contains many things which other apocalypses do not. These elements include the incredibly large amount of visual imagery (as opposed to other forms of revelation, such as conversation), the commissioning of a prophet (1:17-19; 10:8–11:2), prophetic oracles (1:7, 8; 13:9-10; 14:12-13; 16:15; 19:9-10; 21:5-8), oaths (10:5-7), seemingly liturgical music of various forms (hymns, 4:11; 5:9-14; 7:10-12, 15-17; 11:15-18; 12:10-12; 15:3-4; 16:5-7; 19:1-8; and a dirge, 18:2-24), and lists of virtues and vices (9:20-21; 14:4-5; 21:8, 27; 22:14-15). In addition to these elements, the letters to the seven churches that form the first section of the book after the introduction are also unparalleled in other apocalypses.

While these are not major elements that would necessitate a redefinition of the genre of Revelation, they do lead us to think that there is perhaps more at work in Revelation on the level of genre than that of apocalypse. Richard Bauckham has suggested three different genres at work in Revelation: letter, prophecy and apocalypse.[78]

The letters to the seven churches, the epistolary-like greeting in 1:4, and the short epistolary closing (22:18-21) have led some to believe

---

apocalypse, see Rowland, *The Open Heaven, passim*; and J. Carmignac, 'Qu'est-ce que l'Apocalyptique? Son emploi à Qumran', *RevQ* 10 (1979), pp. 3-33.

[78] R. Bauckham, *The Theology of the Book of Revelation* (New Testament Theology; Cambridge: Cambridge University Press, 1993), pp. 1-17. See also G.R. Beasley-Murray, *Revelation* (NCB; Grand Rapids: Eerdmans, 1974), pp. 12-29.

that Revelation was originally a circular letter to these places. This hypothesis is interesting from a generic point of view, and may have some bearing on the generic sub-category (i.e. 'an apocalypse sent as a letter'), but really does little to affect the overall character of the book. That Revelation would have been produced, according to this view, for specific audiences is in no way different than the supposition concerning other apocalyptic literature.

The other category in Bauckham's three-fold generic category for Revelation is prophecy. We have noted some of the prophetic characteristics above, but we add here the fact that John refers to the contents of the book as prophetic both at the beginning (1:3) and at the end (22:6), together with the famous injunction against addition or subtraction therefrom. Speculation concerning the relationship of Revelation to early Christian prophecy, and indeed, the relationships between early Christian prophecy, ancient Jewish prophecy, and apocalypticism in general is fascinating, but, in the end, inconclusive. It is probably sufficient to note that there was a prophetic tradition within early Christianity, and that Revelation must have had some connection with this tradition. Barring further information, however, we should not lean too heavily on this supposition in the exegesis of the book, unless we can identify the prophetic characteristics from within the text.

The most important and fascinating ways in which Revelation does differ from the rest of Jewish apocalypses are the non-pseudonymous nature of the book,[79] and the fact that, rather than being commanded to shut up the contents of the book, John is ordered to write what he sees and send it to the seven churches (1:11; 22:10). It is true that, in 10:4, John is commanded not to write down the contents of the seven thunders, but this is quite paltry when compared to the commands to seal up entire books (which, oddly enough, have all been 'broken', or we would not have been able to read the books themselves!). It is probably best to see the command for sealing in the earlier apocalypses as part of the convention of pseudonymity. It is uncertain whether or not the authors of these books expected their audiences to be taken in by such a convention, but the fact that John is first of all ordered to *not* seal the words of his prophecy, and then is ordered to seal up a small portion of what he has heard, *and does*, argues that this

---

[79]   Assuming that the 'John' mentioned in the book is the same person who had the visions, as there is no attempt to identify this person with any hero of the past.

was an important feature of the apocalyptic genre for John, the manipulation of which should alert us to possible exegetical capital to be made. The motivation given in 22:10, 'Do not seal up the words of the prophecy of this book, for the time is near', suggests that this formal element had influenced the eschatological content of the book.

While Revelation has both striking similarities and dissimilarities with other apocalyptic literature, we would do well in our exegesis to pay attention to both, for it is in precisely this way that genre can be the most helpful in exegesis, showing us both where a book is similar and where it differs from those that have gone before.

CONCLUSION: THE EXEGETICAL IMPLICATIONS OF GENRE

This examination of the various generic categories under which the New Testament books fall has concentrated mostly on the *identification* of their genres. However, this is by far the least important question of genre criticism. The more important questions concern the *implications* of genre for the reading and interpretation of literature. As we have seen, there are those who would make it a determinative factor—know the genre and know the meaning—but this is simply not the way that genre criticism can be responsibly employed. Hirsch's definition of understanding being genre-based, so often misunderstood, provides us with the best entrée. It is by the identification of the *intrinsic* genre—the overall structure and characteristics of a book—that we will go a long way towards understanding that book. In conclusion, then, let us remember that 'One of the main tasks of interpretation can be summarized as the critical rejection of extrinsic genres in the search for the intrinsic genre of a text'.[80]

BIBLIOGRAPHY

Genre Theory/Overview
Aune, D.E.
1987   *The New Testament in its Literary Environment*. LEC. Philadelphia: Westminster Press. (The standard reference tool concerning the genres of the New Testament and many other aspects of the literary environment of the Greco-Roman world.)

---

[80]   Hirsch, *Validity in Interpretation*, p. 89.

Dubrow, H.

1982   *Genre*. Critical Idiom, 42. London: Methuen. (An excellent summary and investigation of the whole idea of modern genre theory.)

Hirsch, E.D., Jr

1967   *Validity in Interpretation*. New Haven: Yale University Press: 68-126. (This is one of the classic and most important discussions of genre from a literary perspective, but must be read in its entirety to avoid misconstrual of its ideas and over-dependence on Hirsch's credulous approach to 'objective' interpretation.)

Russell, D.A.

1981   *Criticism in Antiquity*. Berkeley: University of California Press: 148-58. (A brief but thorough treatment of the several classical texts dealing with genre.)

Wellek, R., and A. Warren

1956   *Theory of Literature*. New York: Harcourt, Brace and World, 3rd edn: 226-37. (The classic of formalist literary criticism, very helpful in the practicalities of assessing the genres of particular works.)

Genres of the New Testament
Gospels

Aune, D.E.

1981   'The Problem of the Genre of the Gospels: A Critique of C.H. Talbert's *What is a Gospel?*', in R.T. France and D. Wenham (eds.), *Gospel Perspectives*. II. *Studies of History and Tradition in the Four Gospels*. 6 vols. Sheffield: JSOT Press: 1-60.

Burridge, R.A.

1992   *What Are the Gospels? A Comparison with Graeco-Roman Biography*. SNTSMS, 70. Cambridge: Cambridge University Press. (Perhaps the best treatment of the subject thus far.)

Collins, A.Y.

1993   *The Beginning of the Gospel: Probings of Mark in Context*. Philadelphia: Fortress Press.

Guelich, R.

1991   'The Gospel Genre', in P. Stuhlmacher (ed.), *The Gospel and the Gospels*. Grand Rapids: Eerdmans: 173-208. (Good overview of the topic, but somewhat dated, as it was published before Burridge's work came out.)

Shuler, P.L.

1982   *A Genre for the Gospels: The Biographical Character of Matthew*. Philadelphia: Fortress Press.

Talbert, C.H.

1974   *Literary Patterns, Theological Themes and the Genre of Luke–Acts*. SBLMS, 20. Missoula, MT: Scholars Press.

1983   *What is a Gospel? The Genre of the Canonical Gospels*. Philadelphia: Fortress Press.

Votaw, C.W.
1970   *The Gospels and Contemporary Biographies in the Greco-Roman World.*
       Philadelphia: Fortress Press. (The classic modern statement concerning the
       relationship of the Gospels to biography. Reprints his original
       programmatic articles on the topic first printed in 1915.)

Acts
Hägg, T.
1983   *The Novel in Antiquity.* Berkeley: University of California Press. (An
       excellent study of the ancient novel form by a classical scholar.)
Hemer, C.J.
1990   *The Book of Acts in the Setting of Hellenistic History.* WUNT, 49.
       Tübingen: Mohr–Siebeck. Repr. Winona Lake, IN: Eisenbrauns.
Hock, R.
1987   'The Greek Novel', in D.E. Aune (ed.), *Greco-Roman Literature and the
       New Testament: Selected Forms and Genres.* SBLSBS, 21. Atlanta:
       Scholars Press. (Argues for the novel as the generic category of Acts.)
Perry, B.E.
1967   *The Ancient Romances: A Literary-Historical Account of their Origins.*
       Berkeley: University of California Press. (An earlier treatment of the novel
       form by a classical scholar, still quite useful.)
Pervo, R.I.
1987   *Profit with Delight: The Literary Genre of the Acts of the Apostles.*
       Philadelphia: Fortress Press. (Argues for the novel as the genre of Acts.
       The most rigorous, if unconvincing, defense.)
Powell, M.A.
1991   *What Are they Saying about Acts?* New York: Paulist Press. (Suggests that
       Acts should be read as both literature and history.)
Unnik, W.C. van
1979   'Luke's Second Book and the Rules of Hellenistic Historiography', in J.
       Kremer (ed.), *Les Acts des Apôtres: Traditions, rédaction, théologie.*
       BETL, 48. Gembloux: Duculot: 37-60.

Pauline and Other Epistles
Deissmann, G.A.
1901   *Bible Studies.* Trans. A. Grieve. Edinburgh: T. & T. Clark: 1-59. (The
       introductory essay to Deissmann's beliefs about the sociological
       development of the early Church, the 'unliterary' character of Jesus and
       Paul, and the distinction between the letter and the epistle/literary letter.)
1927   *Light from the Ancient East.* Trans. L.R.M. Strachan. London: Hodder &
       Stoughton. 4th edn: 146-251. (Develops the ideas from the essay in *Bible
       Studies* with some significant changes and re-statements, although the
       essential thesis remains unchanged.)
Doty, W.G.
1973   *Letters in Primitive Christianity.* GBS. Philadelphia: Fortress Press.

Stowers, S.K.

1986   *Letter Writing in Greco-Roman Antiquity*. LEC. Philadelphia: Westminster Press. (Includes an assessment of Deissmann's distinction between letter and epistle/literary letter.)

White, J.L.

1986   *Light from Ancient Letters*. FFNT. Philadelphia: Fortress Press.

Hebrews and James

Buchanan, G.W.

1971   *To the Hebrews*. AB, 36. Garden City, NY: Doubleday. (Suggests that Hebrews is a midrash on Psalm 110.)

Dibelius, M.

1975   *James*. Ed. H. Greeven. Hermeneia. Philadelphia: Fortress Press. (Sees James as a form of paraenesis, closely linked to the Jewish Wisdom tradition.)

Hay, D.M.

1967   *Glory at the Right Hand: Psalm 110 in Early Christianity*. SBLMS, 18. Nashville: Abingdon. (Demonstrates that Hebrews cannot be a midrash on Psalm 110.)

Ropes, J.H.

1916   *A Critical and Exegetical Commentary on the Epistle of St James*. ICC. Edinburgh: T. & T. Clark. (Views James as a form of Hellenistic diatribe.)

Stanley, S.

1994   'The Structure of Hebrews from Three Perspectives'. *TynBul* 45.2: 247-51. (Defends the view that Hebrews is a homily or collection of homilies.)

Revelation

Bauckham, R.

1993   *The Theology of the Book of Revelation*. New Testament Theology. Cambridge: Cambridge University Press. (Examines the prophetic, epistolary, and apocalyptic features of Revelation.)

Collins, J.J.

1992   *The Apocalyptic Imagination: An Introduction to the Jewish Matrix of Christianity*. New York: Crossroad. (The most thorough statement of the newer, matrix approach to Jewish and Christian apocalypticism.)

Collins, J.J. (ed.)

1979   *Apocalypse: The Morphology of a Genre*. Semeia 14. (Contains many helpful essays on the topic, with several dissenting opinions.)

Hellholm, D. (ed.)

1983   *Apocalypticism in the Mediterranean World and the Near East*. Tübingen: Mohr–Siebeck. (A collection of essays on the various aspects of the newer approach to apocalypticism.)

Morris, L.

1972   *Apocalyptic*. Grand Rapids: Eerdmans. (A very short, but quite thorough examination of Jewish apocalyptic from the older perspective.)

Russell, D.S.

1964 *The Method and Message of Jewish Apocalyptic: 200 BC–AD 100*. OTL. Philadelphia: Westminster Press. (The classic expression of the older approach to Jewish apocalyptic.)

SOURCE, FORM AND REDACTION CRITICISM
OF THE NEW TESTAMENT

DAVID R. CATCHPOLE

INTRODUCTION

It was a finished product—a letter, a gospel, or whatever—that each New Testament writer put together, and which each recipient—an individual, a community, or whoever—received. The recipients may or may not have been aware of the process that lay behind that finished product, may or may not have had first-hand experience of any of the raw material that the writer adopted and perhaps adapted. Unless writers for their own reasons specifically drew attention to earlier material—thus, Luke in his preface (Luke 1:1-2), or Paul in his tactical appeal to tradition (1 Cor. 15:1-3)—those recipients were expected to do one and only one thing, namely, make sense of the finished product. The writer was bound to assume that they would, and the recipients were expected to show that they could.

A preoccupation with the finished product is wholly legitimate, and such a preoccupation undoubtedly enjoys widespread favour in New Testament studies at the present time. 'The synchronic rules, OK?' is more or less the triumphant cry of those who have lost faith in the older tradition-historical disciplines and the ability of those disciplines to cope with the complexities within the texts, or who have lost hope that anything new could possibly result from persevering with the tools of yesterday, or who, for their own conservative reasons, never had any faith in those tools to lose in the first place. For such persons, wishing to write their own griefless *In Memoriam* after what they believe to be the death of diachronic studies, the words of Alfred Lord Tennyson could scarcely be bettered: 'Our little systems have their day; they have their day and cease to be...'

Yet, without retreating an inch from the need for synchronic studies; without resisting in the slightest degree their concern to enter sensitively into the intellectual transaction—the meeting of the minds of original writers and original readers; without reducing the kaleidoscopic variety of ways in which a text may evoke a response in readers of every era and any situation, it remains important to resist an unhelpful polarization. On the one hand, diachronic studies at their best have not failed to respect the synchronic approach, and that respect needs to be reciprocated. The ideal goal must be such insights as can be made available by the mutual correction and enrichment of both together. On the other hand, diachronic studies, which probe the prehistory of the finished product, are based on evidence within the text itself. That evidence calls insistently for attention and explanation. It establishes the principle that tradition-history is no optional extra. Source criticism, form criticism and redaction criticism, which together bring tradition-history to light, have not outlived their usefulness, and we cannot suppose that they will ever cease to be. And that which does not cease to be cannot possibly cease to be relevant and indeed essential to the task of exegesis.

The last observation can be made even more pointed. Exegesis has to find appropriate ways of being conditioned by, and showing respect for, all the facts of the life of the texts under scrutiny. It involves work, not just on the final stage, but also on all other recoverable stages, in the development of the material. It involves the exercise of sympathetic identification with the processes as well as with the product.

At this point, some definitions need to be put in place:

Source criticism is the process of bringing to light the earlier resources available to an author. Although used conventionally of documents, written resources, and tending to be concerned with literary relationships, there is, it must be said, no reason in principle why it should not include the study of unwritten or oral resources.

Form criticism recognizes that source material may have been in written form, but that it was not necessarily so. It aims therefore to separate out the distinct units of material that the compilers of the sources selected, to establish the earliest forms of those units, to classify them on the basis of 'family likeness', and, by the exercise of informed imagination, to posit for each a setting and a purpose in the life of a community.

Redaction criticism is the study of the theological significance of editorial activity on the part of an evangelist or any other source-using writer. Such editorial activity is most visible in changes made to the content of an individual unit of material, but it also extends to the process of arrangement of plural units, the setting up of sequences, and the use of juxtapositions.

As parts of the overarching whole of the study of tradition-history, each of these three critical methods has opened up perspectives that enhance the process of exegesis. In combination, they provide evidence of a developing and dynamic process. At the beginning of its life, a distinct unit has a meaning and a function. To analyse its structure, to classify it, and to define its purpose will be a gesture of respect for its integrity. Through the subsequent stages of its internal growth and modification, including its association with other units, whether as immediate neighbours or as one of a set of literary building blocks that form a total building, a change in meaning and function may or may not take place. Exegesis at its best will take all such change into account. To respect and exploit the integrity of the material at each of these stages, and to preserve a sense of the distinctness of each of them, is the opportunity and also the responsibility of exegesis. To compress the process so that developments are ignored would be the very opposite—a failure to recognize an opportunity, and a lack of respect for the individuality of the persons or groups who participated in the generation, the adaptation and the reception of that unit.

The three named 'criticisms' have a quite distinct history within the development of the study of the New Testament. Although by no means restricted in application to the Gospels, their contribution and their essential complementariness have nevertheless been especially clearly exemplified in the area of Gospel criticism. In that area, form criticism (cf. Bultmann 1963) emerged shortly after World War I as a corrective of the supposed one-sidedness of source criticism, while redaction criticism (cf. the survey in Rohde 1968) emerged shortly after World War II as a similar corrective of form criticism. In the first case, Gospel sources needed to be understood in oral and not exclusively documentary terms, and the corollary was that they also needed to have their roles in their presumed communities exposed to the light of day. In the second case, Gospel writers needed to be recognized as theologically creative writers, again in a social and community setting, and not as mere collectors and compilers. In supplementing and complementing, but not displacing or undermining, its predecessor, each method extended and enriched the tradition-historical or diachronic approach to the Gospels. It remains the case that each needs and, at its best, integrates with the others, and similarly, that the diachronic and synchronic approaches need and, at their best, integrate with one another.

Each of the three methods has established itself as an essential part of the New Testament specialist's equipment. To say this is not to forget that even among those who accept all three in principle there remains considerable space for the exercise of individual judgment in practice, and therefore, wholly unsurprisingly, plenty of disagreement. These disagreements underline the need to be aware, not simply of the great advances and insights that have been achieved, but also of the series of decisions, some of them debatable, that the process of tradition-historical reconstruction includes. Exegesis, drawn along in the wake of tradition-history, cannot be unaffected by the outcome of those decisions. Not only so, but after those decisions have been made, exegesis finds itself faced with further testing questions arising from the sheer fact of the hard and unyielding reality of development that *any* tradition-historical reconstruction exposes. At this point, two things are required: first, to clarify some of the typical decisions that tradition-history, building on the three criticisms, requires, and secondly, to exhibit in a series of examples the serious questions posed for exegesis by the phenomenon of development.

MAJOR ISSUES

Source critical activity quickly brings to the fore the matter of criteria, presuppositions and procedures.

Each and every text, ancient or modern, has first to be read in its own terms and assumed to be coherent and consistent. Source criticism gains its first foothold when lapses in coherence and consistency become apparent. Thus, in the Gospel of Mark, the erratic distribution of secrecy/silence commands suggests that earlier stories have received later emendation. Similarly in the Gospel of Luke, three beatitudes dealing tersely and economically with problems that are characteristically human and by no means restrictedly religious (6:20b-21), presently co-exist with another beatitude, itself both lengthy and emphatically religious (6:22-23). In the Gospel of Matthew, encouragement to persons so resourceless as to be racked by worry about the supply of food and clothing (6:25a, 26, 28-30, 31, 32b) has mixed into it a saying that functions better as a warning to the prosperous (6:25b) and other sayings employing a quite different underlying logic (6:27, 32a). Something seems to be going on that calls for a source-critical solution! Similarly, in the Gospel of John, a reference to a single perplexing 'work' on a sabbath (7:22) establishes a direct connection between 7:15-24 and 5:1-18, but ignores the series of very remarkable events in the intervening chapter. Such inconsistency is sometimes substantial, sometimes stylistic, sometimes both. Thus, there is manifestly a change of style in John 1:6-8 after 1:1-5; John 1:15 'interrupts' 1:14, 16-17; unusual language and ideas occur in John 1:1-5, 14, 16-17; there is, as it happens, precedent for a book's beginning as John 1:6 does (cf. 1 Sam. 1:1, Job 1:1). Do John 1:1 and 1:6, someone might ask, represent alternative beginnings for this Gospel? All in all, then, the text itself poses questions, the seriousness of which source criticism has to attempt to answer. Of course, in the light of everything one can discover from the whole of an author's work, a judgment has to be made as to whether these really are dislocations and not evidence that the authorial technique employed just happens to be different from the one we would have used.

When more than one document is involved, and a literary relationship involving direct contact or dependence between them has proved convincing on the basis of, say, extensive verbal overlap or common order of disparate component parts, the question is then one of how that relationship would be defined. While debate has not ceased over the so-called tendencies of the Synoptic tradition (Sanders 1969), where such literary relationships are conceded by all but a few, there are certain typical principles that have commended themselves widely. One is that 'the general tendency of early Christology...was from the lesser to the greater' (Davies and Allison 1988: 104). Another related principle is that it is easier to understand the removal than the deliberate insertion of details which might cast a shadow across the figure of Jesus. These principles can be seen at work in the following way:

A synchronic reading of the Gospel of Mark makes clear without a doubt that the term 'Son of God' is set at the heart of his Christology: affirmed in 1:1, acknowledged by demons who as supernatural beings recognize an equally supernatural being in 3:11-12, 5:6 (Wrede 1971: 25), accepted by Jesus himself (14:61-62), and admitted by the representative of the execution squad (15:39), this is gospel truth for Mark. That being so, it defies credibility and demands intolerable credulity that Mark, possessed of Matthew, should scale down the Petrine confession, itself located at the high point of his narrative, from 'You are the Messiah, the Son of the living God' (Matt. 16:16) to 'You are the Messiah' (Mark 8:29).

In similar vein, the risks involved in painting a picture of Jesus as aggressively impatient (Mark 1:41, 43), possibly illegitimate (Mark 6:3), limited in power (Mark 6:5), and not necessarily as good as God

(Mark 10:18), were patently obvious. Equally obvious and understandable would be a common strategy on the part of Matthew and/or Luke to eliminate or reduce those risks. Hardly persuasive would be any source-critical scheme that required us to envisage Mark as deliberately turning the safe into the unsafe, or the risk-free into the risky.

The much-debated Q hypothesis for the explanation of common Matthew/Luke traditions can be defended by using similar arguments (cf. Catchpole 1993: 1-59; Tuckett 1996: 1-39). The main rival, Luke's use of Matthew (cf. Goulder 1989: 3-71), is jeopardized by variations in wording and ideas which suggest that frequently Luke has an earlier version. Can Luke really have been willing to scale down a 'Jesus = Wisdom' Christology to a 'Jesus < Wisdom' Christology (Matt. 11:2-19//Luke 7:18-35)? Would the scale of a miraculous cure (Matt. 12:22-24//Luke 11:14-16) be reduced or the passion of the Jonah-like Son of man be eliminated (Matt. 12:38-40//Luke 11:29-30)?

If the Synoptic Gospels exhibit to the satisfaction of most specialists the phenomenon of direct literary relatedness, the question of principle concerning when similar relatedness may be presumed is raised in acute form if the fourth Gospel is set alongside the other three. Opinion, it has to be said, remains sharply divided. Over against direct literary relatedness (advocated, for example, by Neirynck in a series of studies, 1991: 571-711) the most favoured alternative remains common Johannine and Synoptic dependence on earlier pre-Johannine and pre-Synoptic tradition, which in turn gives rise to the hypothesis of a signs source with or without a passion narrative attached (cf. Fortna 1970, 1988). The latter hypothesis can appeal with some conviction to the numbering of some of the Johannine 'signs' (2:12; 4:54), the alleged unsuitability of 20:30-31 as an ending for and summary of the Gospel as a whole, and above all to the presence of dislocations or *aporias* within the text (e.g. 14:31). The division of opinion serves to highlight the urgent need for a consensus concerning criteria and presuppositions, perhaps along the following lines. First, the inference that John used the Synoptics should not depend upon the requirement that he should have used them in the same way as they used one another. Secondly, where there is a Johannine/Synoptic overlap there ought to be some features of the Johannine version that appear to be earlier, as well as others that appear to be later, than those in the parallel Synoptic version, if we are to posit the existence of a version of the tradition that is prior to both. Thirdly, Johannine inclusion of features that are clearly redactional in one of the Synoptic Gospels ought, by and large, to be sufficient to prove Johannine dependence, not on pre-Synoptic tradition, but on that Synoptic Gospel.

Someone might ask whether a source-critical decision on any of these contentious issues matters one way or the other to the exegete. The answer is that it does, since the foundations on which redaction-critical activity may build will have been laid differently, the developments from sources to finished products measured differently, and the intentions of the editor of a given work defined differently.

Form-critical activity has immense potential for an understanding of how texts grow and how their functions may correspondingly change. It also has to be put into effect with care and an awareness of the risks involved. The perils are, however, heavily outweighed by the potential for important insight.

First, in the case of material for which an oral stage of transmission is posited, it is wholly appropriate to respect the norm that the earliest version of a tradition is likely to be, as it were, lean and economical. Sometimes a later written version may be more economical than an earlier one, but when that is the case, it may well serve as a pointer to the substance of what underlies and antedates the earlier one.

The tradition of Jesus' reception of the children is a case in point. Matthew's version (19:13-15) is later, in the sense that it depends on Mark's version (10:13-16). But it is a witness to, without having direct access to, an earlier pre-Markan version, in that only one declaration by Jesus is retained in the story tradition (Matt. 19:14//Mark 10:14), while the other is moved elsewhere (Matt. 18:3//Mark 10:15).

Secondly, the use of parallel and precedent with a view to classification of material into families has an important bearing on how the logic of a tradition actually works, as well as where its origin may be located. This may be a hedge against misunderstanding by virtue of clarifying the necessary interpretative framework. It may also expose the setting within which it is or is not appropriate to treat material.

The tradition of the walk to Emmaus (Luke 24:13-15) is a case in point. It abounds in Lukanisms but, in view of Luke's tendency to paraphrase the wording of his sources, it is not thereby shown to be a Lukan creation. Its approximate pre-Lukan form can be recovered by exploiting the presence of, and then removing, some formally disruptive elements. Thus, shorn of the interrupting material in Luke 24:21b-24, the story is able to reappear as an independent unit, unconnected to Luke 24:1-12 (cf. Fuller 1972: 105). Again, shorn of the intrusive announcement of the appearance to Peter in Luke 24:33-35 (cf. Fuller 1972: 111-13), itself introduced in the same way as Acts 10:1–11:18 is introduced in advance of Acts 11:19-21 in order to connect a decisive event in Christian history with the experience of an ecclesiastical heavyweight, Peter, the tradition can be seen to have just *one* climax and *one* major concern, its aetiological role as an expression of the community's eucharistic experience of the risen Christ. The pre-Lukan tradition can now be classified. It belongs to the family of journey-type epiphany stories (cf. Gen. 18–19; Tobit 5–12; Mark 6:45-52), which is very important indeed, for the classification of the story has the effect of classifying the Jesus who appears in it. By the choice of this form of story, his risenness is defined in angelic terms, a view which happens to be firmly resisted by Luke. Not for nothing did the evangelist have the risen Jesus eating in emphatically non-angelic fashion (Luke 24:41-43, cf. Tob. 12:19; Josephus, *Ant.* 1:11:2 §197; Philo, *On Abraham* 23 §118)!

Thirdly, in following up the last point, an insistence upon a community setting and on a correspondingly useful purpose is usually extremely helpful. Negatively, if a community setting and purpose cannot easily be envisaged in a particular case, it may well be that creative writing is the explanation nearest to hand. Positively, this insistence recognizes the essentially social character of human life in general, and the early Christian movement in particular.

Redaction critical activity also needs to be hedged in by some cautions or caveats. First, as has often been observed, there is a danger that it may overplay the differences between two versions of a given tradition and fail to give appropriate weight to overlaps, that is, to upset the balance between the changes that were made and those that were not made (cf. Tuckett 1987: 120-21). The latter represent an author's decision just as much as the former. As with the application of the criterion of dissimilarity in historical Jesus studies, there is a danger of substituting the distinctive for the characteristic. Once again, therefore, the method requires that it be supplemented by other disciplines that emphasize the finished product.

Secondly, there is a related danger that all the traditions in a Gospel might be forced violently into one single mould, thus causing an unrealistic consistency to be 'discovered'. After all, any given writer may or may not have thought through all the issues he intended to discuss, and he may or may not have subordinated all his resources to a single purpose. As mentioned above, the charitable presumption when reading any text must be that the writer was consistent, but critical realism occasionally requires the recognition of inconsistent thinking. One recalls here the vexatious non-uniformity that seems to characterize Luke's presentation of eschatology (Mattill 1979), or the inconsistency of Mark's superimposition of the secrecy motif (Wrede 1971: 11-23). One thinks also of Matthew's handling of worldwide mission, with a perplexing juxtaposition of requirement (Matt. 28:19) and prohibition (Matt. 10:5-6), or his treatment of the Pharisees, with unguarded endorsement of the content of their teaching (Matt. 23:2-3) alongside swingeing denunciation of the alleged discrepancy between that teaching and the divine word (Matt. 15:6-9). Quite clearly, therefore, redaction criticism needs always to be operated with care and to be allowed to disclose a trend in a writer's thinking rather than an entirely homogeneous and consistent product. It must also allow for the possibility that the status and function of different constituent parts of the whole may vary. Thus, for example, it is well known that Matthew intends certain traditions to function as models with ongoing applicability in conduct or belief in a community whose life is disclosed ('transparency'), while other traditions preserve a non-repeatable situation without ongoing relevance to conduct or belief ('historicization') (Strecker 1995: 81-101).

These three traditional and unshakable criticisms form part of the stable foundation upon which exegesis must be built, for all that the use of each is not free from risk. However, if the methods are used, notwithstanding the risks, then the major issue that the exegete must confront again and again is the reality of development. These texts had not reached a final and static state, for they share in, indeed they condition and are conditioned by, the dynamism of early Christian experience. That being so, the exegete has to keep apart the different stages in the development and, above all, must not synthesize them.

USES IN EXEGESIS

Since it is important to remember that the Gospels are not the only texts that pay rich dividends to those who invest in these methods, I shall begin by considering some Pauline material.

No other Pauline passage can hold a candle to Phil. 2:6-11 in respect of theological profundity and influence through the centuries of Christian history. With the aid of the three critical methods one is able to reach back to an earlier text (source criticism), recover its original purpose and life setting (form criticism), and note the distinct changes of meaning brought about by Pauline editorial work (redaction criticism). How much one would miss by playing the synchronic card alone!

That said, one ought, of course, to play it. Lines of connection between this passage and its wider context are firmly established by the call to be of the same mind (v. 2) and also to share the mind of Christ (v. 5); the request for humility (v. 3) in view of the self-humbling conduct of Christ (v. 8); the critique of 'empty glory' (κενοδοξία, v. 3) in the light of the self-emptying of Christ (v. 7) and the ultimate achievement of God's glory (v. 11); and the strengthening of the demand for obedience (v. 12) by the reminder of the unswerving obedience of Christ (v. 8) (Hooker 1975: 152-53). In other words, the 'story of Christ' is intended to provide a paradigm (Fee 1995: 191-97), deliberately and skillfully directed at a local situation made problematic by sub-Christian 'mindsets' (Fee 1995: 174-97). It is at home in its context. Nevertheless, vv. 6-11 stand out from their context in view of the awkward connection (ὅς) with v. 5; their poetic and rhythmic 'feel'; and the lack of, or at best the limited, correlation between the content of vv. 9-11 and the situation of fractured relationships in the Philippian community. The presence of ideas and terms atypical of Paul, that is, the grasping (ἁρπαγμός), Christ as servant (δοῦλος), Christ's receiving a gift from God (ἐχαρίσατο αὐτῷ), and his high exaltation (ὑπερύψωσεν), gives further support to the existence of pre-Pauline material. One needs therefore to play the diachronic card as well. This will reinforce the results of synchronic interpretation by isolating some Pauline redaction, but it will also enable one to get back to an earlier stage and a non-identical set of meanings. Paul not only adopted, but also adapted, this 'song of Christ's glory'. Adaptation took the form of three widely agreed editorial insertions:

First, 'even death on a cross' (θανάτου δὲ σταυροῦ, v. 8). The originality of this phrase is not secured by a recollection of crucifixion as the mode of death prescribed for slaves (*contra* Hengel 1977: 62-63), for the servant Christ is not a slave. The phrase itself matches Paul's conviction about the cross as the centre of the Christian gospel (cf. 1 Cor. 1:18; 2:2; Gal. 3:1; Phil. 3:18) (Martin 1983: xvi, 220-22), and its insertion is readily understandable in those terms. Without it, the preceding statement comes to a fine climax in 'to the point of death' (μέχρι θανάτου). That being so, the emphasis is now on the whole of the preceding life, and how from beginning to end it was a life of obedience, cf. *3 Macc.* 7:16, where μέχρι θανάτου describes committed faithfulness up to the point of being willing to die, though death does not in fact take place.

Secondly, 'in heaven and on earth and under the earth' (ἐπουρανίων καὶ ἐπιγείων καὶ καταχθονίων, v. 10). The insertion of this phrase would fit with Pauline statements in Phil. 3:20-21, where the subordination of 'all things' (τὰ πάντα) by the exalted Christ is presented as the exercise of the power which will also establish the resurrection body. The same pattern is apparent in 1 Cor. 15:20-28, where the present reign of Christ over all but one of the hostile powers culminates in the defeat of the last one, death, and the arrival of the era of general resurrection.

Confirmation of the correctness of removing 'in heaven and on earth and under the earth' comes from a form-critical direction. Its omission leaves a neat chiastic structure in vv. 10-11:

> so that at the name of Jesus
>> every knee should bend,
>> and every tongue should confess
> that Jesus Christ is Lord.

The recognition of this underlying form has a further advantage: it enables the knees that bend and the tongues that confess to be recognized as exclusively human, and then one remembers that Isa. 45:23, which is unmistakably echoed in that ending, is part of a call *to the whole world* of humankind to recognize the sovereignty of the one God:

> Turn to me and be saved, all the ends of the earth! For I am God, and there is no other. By myself have I sworn...: 'To me every knee shall bend, every tongue shall swear'.

So the pre-Pauline poem/hymn sees the sovereignty of God being recognized through an acknowledgment of the lordship of Jesus *by all of humankind, Jews and Gentiles*. That means that the material was produced, not in a restrictedly Jewish Aramaic-speaking context (as some have supposed) but in a community brought to birth by the worldwide Christian mission.

Finally, 'to the glory of God the Father' (εἰς δόξαν θεοῦ πατρός, v. 11). A good deal of raw material is already assembled that can demonstrate the secondariness of this phrase. First, the form of vv. 10-11 is better without it. Secondly, its presence protects the sole and lonely eminence of the one God, which might be put at risk by placing Christ in the position of God; cf. Paul's usage of Isa. 45:23 elsewhere, with God as the focus of attention (Rom. 14:11). Thirdly, there are similar references elsewhere to the achieving of the glory of God; cf. Rom. 15:7; 2 Cor. 4:15; Phil. 1:11, including the call for the imitation of Paul as a means of imitating Christ in a Jew/Gentile setting and all εἰς δόξαν θεοῦ (1 Cor. 10:31–11:1). Fourthly, the reference to God as Father introduces a Sonship Christology, which is entirely absent from the earlier part of the hymn. It does, however, correspond to the Pauline view of the subordination of the Son to the Father after the final triumph, to quote 1 Cor. 15:27-28 again.

So we can compare and contrast the two stages, the pre-Pauline and the Pauline, in the development of this 'song of Christ's glory'. At the pre-Pauline stage, the exaltation of Christ was a response of divine grace to a whole *life* of obedience. The reality of the exaltation was intended to be acknowledged universally in faith by the whole of humankind—that is, the spread of confessing persons is set out on a horizontal line, as it were. At the Pauline stage, the interest shifted from the life of obedience to the ending of life in death. The reality of the exaltation was intended to be acknowledged by the supernatural powers. These beings are distributed along a vertical line, as it were. Their rule enslaves humankind until the last enemy, death, is destroyed. Then the sovereignty of the Son will give way to the final sovereignty of the Father. Most strikingly, the acknowledgment of the lordship of Jesus changes from a confession of faith to an admission of defeat.

To sum up, source criticism uncovers the pre-Pauline material. Form criticism defines its character, a poem or even a hymn, and provides a setting, a worshipping Christian community of mixed ethnic background. Redaction criticism gives insight into the mind of Paul, acting as a theologically energetic adapter, and strengthens synchronic studies of the contribution of the hymn to the totality of the letter to the church at Philippi.

Consider now some evidence from the Gospels. The basic and most irreducible unit of Gospel tradition is the isolated saying. It may or may not have been transmitted with a setting, and if it has been, the setting may or may not be original. While that setting will disclose something of the human context in which the saying was put to work, it may or may not be insightful or legitimate.

Take, for example, the saying 'Give to the emperor the things that are the emperor's, and to God the things that are God's' (Mark 12:17). Two things may be said of the so-called pronouncement story in which it is embedded (Mark 12:13-17). First, its life setting must be that of Jewish Christianity in Palestine, where the payment of tribute posed the question of 'tolerating mortal masters, after having God for their Lord' (Josephus, *War* 2:8:2 §118). Secondly, the logic of the narrative, which hinges on ownership of a coin, and the politically very conservative position it adopts, require Jesus only to say, 'Give to the emperor the things that are the emperor's'. This suggests that the saying, with its two foci of the emperor and God, was probably separate and not embedded in its present context. As such a separate saying, its content is much less conservative, much more enigmatic, much more demanding of a decision by the responsive and responsible listener—more in tune, can one say, with the prophetic Jesus and with the politics of change and hope that were central to his mission? To ask that question is implicitly to answer another question as to the legitimacy and defensibility of the secondary development that embedded such a saying in such a setting. Once the narrative setting is in place, enigma is absent, prophecy is silent, the possibility of change is nowhere to be seen. Methodologically, what is important is that the concerns of form criticism with life setting, aided by an internal dislocation, give insight into the history of a tradition: two stages, two settings, two meanings.

Take another isolated saying, 'But I say to you that (a) if you are angry with your brother you will be liable to judgment; (b) and if you say *raca* to your brother you will be liable to the council; (c) and if you say, "You fool", you will be liable to the hell of fire' (Matt. 5:22). Once again, internal dislocation enables us to reach back source-critically to an earlier version, v. 22ac, which satisfies basic form-critical requirements, and then to come forward redaction-critically to an understanding of the role of the saying in the Gospel of Matthew.

First, within v. 22 as it stands, there is a serious tension. Two equivalent and very mild insults (Luz 1990: 282) have two far from equivalent consequences. In the first case, it is liability to the council (ἔνοχος τῷ συνεδρίῳ) and in the second case, liability to the hell of fire (ἔνοχος εἰς τὴν γέενναν τοῦ πυρός). By 'the council' is meant not a regular Jewish court, still less the Jerusalem sanhedrin, for no ordinary Jewish court would judge the offence described—indeed, 'if such a law were ever implemented, the courts would be swamped with a flood of cases and the judicial system would be paralyzed' (Betz 1995: 221)! So, the term should be understood in formal but not conventionally Jewish terms as referring to some sort of assembly, which its earlier usage makes wholly natural (cf. Lohse 1971: 861-62). Yet the tension remains: answerability to a human assembly *versus* liability to a divine punishment. This tension suggests that v. 22b does not belong to the same stratum of tradition as v. 22c, with both making concrete an initial demand in v. 22a (*contra* Luz 1990: 281). Nor does the content of v. 22b encourage the thought that an original saying consisting of v. 22ab has received a Matthaean editorial addition in v. 22c (thus Davies and Allison 1988: 515-16). Rather preferable is a reconstruction based on the match between v. 22b and Matt. 18:15-17. Both address the problem of tensions and offences between Christians, and both envisage an assembly (συνέδριον = ἐκκλησία) which will deal with it. All of this is probably what v. 22b has in mind, which suggests Matthaean redaction as the best explanation. Placing v. 22b alongside v. 22c reflects the same mindset as placing 18:18 after 18:15-17: the decision of the συνέδριον or ἐκκλησία is the decision of God!

Secondly, v. 22ac is an entirely satisfactory saying in respect of both form and content. Formally, it uses synonymous parallelism, saying the same thing twice in different ways. Content-wise, v. 22c clarifies v. 22a very appropriately: that which stems from the heart (anger) expresses itself openly in dismissive speech. There is also a good match between the two definitions of the consequences of offending: 'the hell of fire' stands for divine punishment, and so too can judgment (κρίσις). Moreover, there are plenty of Jewish parallels for 5:22ac, especially in the wisdom literature (Sir. 1:22; 27:30–28:7).

At the pre-Matthaean stage, therefore, there existed a saying voiced by someone who stood four-square within the wisdom tradition:

If you are angry with your brother you will be liable to judgment;
and if you say, 'You fool', you will be liable to the hell of fire.

The speaker would have had a positive concern with inter-personal harmony, and that alone. Matthew introduced a quite different concern, to dispel the suspicion that Jesus had 'come to abolish the law and the prophets' (Matt. 5:17). So along with his aim of adjusting the saying for use in the discipline-cum-conciliation procedures of his Christian community, he also wished to use it under the general heading provided by Matt. 5:17-19, that is, to demonstrate the continuity between Moses and Jesus. The 'higher righteousness', set polemically over against Pharisaic piety in Matt. 5:20, is described in 6:1-18, but not in the six paragraphs that make up Matt. 5:21-48. Matt. 5:21-22 dominates the first of the six paragraphs, exemplifying the principle set out in 5:17-19. The mission of Jesus (5:17) and the conduct of Jesus' disciples (5:19) are, or should be, conditioned by the classic Jewish position on Scripture. So, with an exact quotation of one Mosaic passage (Exod. 20:13) and a summary of several other passages referring to human judicial process (Exod. 21:12; Lev. 24:17; Num. 35:12; Deut. 17:8-13), Matthew defines the Mosaic base. By adding here (as in Matt. 5:31, 38, 43) the antithetical and authoritative introduction, 'But I say to you...', he formalizes the position of Jesus. And the upshot is the sharpest possible attack on anyone who espouses a Christian theological position that undercuts Moses. In the light of what is said later about Christian prophets, charismatic in practice and (from the point of view of the arch-conservative Matthew) liberal in theology, the attack looks like a confrontation with real people representing an actual and not a theoretical threat. So here is another piece of raw material for exegesis: source criticism and form criticism combining to expose a saying whose setting is within the wisdom tradition of the Jewish community, while redaction criticism exposes the saying's adoption and then adaptation to problems faced by a Christian community— partly problems of strained personal relationships, and partly problems caused by itinerant charismatic Christian prophets. In Matthew's view, their dangerous liberalism would be branded, and they themselves banished, by the judge. Even the identity of the judge has been altered in the process: Matt. 5:22ac by itself had in mind no one but God, but Matt. 5:22 in context has in mind no one other than Jesus.

The third example takes the parables as its focus. It is beyond all doubt that parables played a central role in the prophetic strategy of the historical Jesus. Also clear is the fact that there are many different sorts of parables. The reconstruction of the history of some of the parabolic traditions requires a decision in each case about the sort of parable that is under scrutiny. It can then lead to important insights into that parable's original function, as well as showing how sometimes significant adaptation for later and quite different purposes has occurred. Here are two parables which serve to illustrate both the process of tradition-history and the nature of the resultant exegetical task.

Perhaps the best known of all the parables in popular parlance is the parable of the good Samaritan. Redaction criticism notices some salient features of the setting provided for this parable by Luke, involving a remodeling of the question and answer concerning the first of all the commandments (Luke 10:25-28//Mark 12:28-34). A changed question is posed at the outset, 'Teacher, what must I do (ποιήσας) to inherit eternal life?', and the idea of doing (ποιεῖν) then becomes a thread running through the whole unit as Luke has edited it (cf. τοῦτο ποίει καὶ ζήσῃ, v. 28; ὁ ποιήσας τὸ ἔλεος μετ' αὐτοῦ—πορεύου καὶ σὺ ποίει ὁμοίως, v. 37). The question itself belongs in the setting of the Gentile mission as understood by Mark (10:17) and then by Luke (Acts 16:30), but by no means in the Palestinian setting of Jesus. Jesus' referral of the questioner to the law reminds us again of the rich young man episode (Mark 10:19//Luke 18:20), though this time the commandments are quoted by the questioner (Luke 10:27). This is important for Luke, for what a person says 'from his own mouth' constitutes a binding commitment (cf. Luke 4:22; 19:22; 22:71). Then there follows from Jesus himself the parable in devastating answer to the extremely theoretical question, 'And who is my neighbour?'.

What does one need to know to feel the force of the parable that answers that question? Three things. First, it was plain for all to see that the word 'neighbour' in Lev. 19:18 stands for a fellow member of the Jewish people; cf. 'anyone of your own kin...any of your people'. Secondly, it was plain in advance to all who listened that, after the priest, and then the Levite, there would come down the road an Israelite lay person (Jeremias 1963: 204). After all, the three formed a quite conventional trio (cf. *m. Git.* 5.8 on the order of reading the Torah in the synagogue: 'A priest reads first, and after him a levite, and after him an Israelite'. Similarly, *m. Kid.* 4.1; cited by Meyer 1967: 239-41). Only in this case, what was plain in advance to the listeners turned out to be quite wrong, for the person who showed love was the dreaded and detested Samaritan. Thirdly, the Samaritan, indeed any Samaritan, exposed to the light the shadow side of Jewish experience, the prejudice, the grudges nurtured by historical memory and fed by contemporary provocation. No one can understand the parable without knowing all this, and no Jewish person could hear it without being hurt. But the deeply disturbing meaning of love could then be drawn out, love embodied in an action which refuses to let the past or the present, race or religion, erect a boundary fence.

The authenticity of this parable is virtually beyond question (though cf. Goulder 1989: 487-91), but on what level does it work, and what is its life setting? Almost certainly it must be the real social and political world of the Jewish people. Can we seriously suppose that the fractured relationships between Jewish and Samaritan people could be passively tolerated by either speaker or attentive hearer of this parable? And can we seriously suppose that the religious establishment as represented by priest and Levite was one with which the speaker of this parable was at home and in sympathy? If that is so, and if the parable was originally set in that rather earthy and realistic world of Jewish society, it follows that Luke has taken a liberty in setting it somewhere else, that is, in a world remote from the need to do something about Jewish/Samaritan racial and religious prejudice, a world in which salvation needed to be sought anxiously rather than presumed gratefully (cf. Sanders 1977). The distinction between the two worlds in which the pre-Lukan and the Lukan parable belong is a distinction that is formative for the exegetical enterprise.

The parable of the mustard seed is preserved in three alternative versions (Matt. 13:31-32//Mark 4:30-32//Luke 13:18-19). Exegesis of a synchronic sort will naturally take account of each evangelist's sequence. In Matthew, the parable is the third in a sequence of four, all carefully linked together by similar introductions, 'he put before them another parable', all taking the form of anecdotes, and all clamped together by scripturally reinforced explanations of the reason and purpose of parable telling (Matt. 13:14-15, 35). In Mark's case, synchronic exegesis will note the particular closeness of this parable to the preceding parable of the seed growing secretly (Mark 4:26-29), with a slightly greater distance between both and the all-controlling parable of the sower being brought about by a collection of separate sayings (Mark 4:21-25). Comparable exegesis of the Lukan sequence will maximize the significance of the pairing of the parables of mustard seed and leaven (Luke 13:18-21) in a setting where no other parables are present. Given that the evangelists have probably been hard at work to produce these sequences, synchronic and composition-critical insights overlap very considerably. But what about the redaction-critical, the source-critical and the form-critical?

Alongside Mark 4:30-32, the existence of another underlying version of the parable is indicated by a series of 'minor agreements' between Matthew and Luke against Mark. This series comprises the introduction, 'the kingdom...is like...'; the words 'that someone took...' followed by a verb in indicative form, which have the effect of making the parable into a story of something that happened *once*, rather than (as in Mark) a 'similitude' describing something which *always* happens; the location of the sowing in land which belongs to the person whose experience is described (field/garden); the use of the verb 'to grow' (αὐξάνω); the outcome of the process as a tree (δένδρον) rather than a shrub (λάχανον); the nesting of the birds in the branches of the tree rather than under the shadow of the shrub; and finally the pairing of this parable with that of the leaven (Matt. 13:33//Luke 13:20-21), which does not appear at all in Mark.

The Q version is apparently preserved very carefully by Luke 13:18-19, because, when the Markan elements are pruned away from Matthew's version, what is left matches Luke's version! So there are two versions to play off against one another, one telling a quite unique and indeed amazing story, and the other attempting to describe what always happens and is commonplace. Of the two, the Q version looks the more original for two reasons. First, it is less 'heavy' in its explanation of the significance of the mustard seed. It may well be right to say that the mustard seed is the smallest of all the seeds, but the less elaborate and explicit version is likely to be the earlier in this case. Secondly, the nesting of the birds of the heaven is a feature of both versions, and must therefore be original, but, while it hardly fits with the 'shrub' scheme, it fits well with the 'tree' scheme.

The predominant features of the parable are, first, the mustard seed, which is proverbially tiny (cf. Matt. 17:20//Luke 17:6); secondly, the unexpected outcome of the process of sowing; and thirdly, the size of the end product, the tree, which is demonstrated by the nesting of the birds of the heaven. It is the image of the tree with birds' nests in its branches which requires exegetical attention, for it is a familiar biblical image, and it always conveys a message about one nation's sovereignty over all others. The sovereignty may be that of Israel over all non-Israelite nations (Ezek. 17:22-24), or that of Egypt over all non-Egyptian nations (Ezek. 31:5-7), or that of Babylon over all non-Babylonian nations (Dan. 4:10-12). That being so, the life setting of the parable must have been one of high political hope. The ancient expectation of the sovereignty of the Jewish people was being reaffirmed, while the choice of the proverbially minute mustard seed reflected a sense that sovereignty for such an apparently trivial nation might seem almost unbelievable. The use of an anecdotal form enabled something almost unbelievable to be described, but that simply demonstrates that God's kingly intervention to produce something abnormal was an essential factor in the story.

Exegesis of the parable, recovered by source criticism, and isolated and contextualized by form criticism, would be firmly and unequivocally political. The complexion of the exegesis of that first stage of tradition-history may have been maintained at the second stage, its use in Q as one of a complementary pair of anecdotes describing what a man did (Luke 13:18-19), and then what a woman did (Luke 13:20-21). Q was interested in the political prospects of the Jewish people (Matt. 19:28//Luke 22:30) and the social turn-around which God's kingship would effect (Luke 6:20b-21). But, we may ask, how political was the complexion of the parable when incorporated by the three later evangelists into their Gospels? The answer is 'probably very little, if at all'. The community context for Mark is obviously Christian, and probably incipiently sectarian, for this parable is brought firmly under the control of the all-conditioning parable of the sower (Mark 4:13). That parable is in turn dominated by the notion of the insider/outsider distinction (Mark 4:10-12, 33-34), so helpful to those who search for divine legitimation and the assurance that they—and they alone—have received and understood a revelation from God (cf. Watson 1985: 62-63). The community context for Matthew is much more strongly sectarian, for the Gospel reflects the breakdown in relations between Christians and the parent Jewish community. The Lukan situation is less clear: all that can be said with a fair degree of assurance is that the parable has nothing like its original full-blooded political message.

The final example comes from the Gospel of John. In John 6, there is a remarkable agreement between John and Matthew/Mark in the sequence involving the feeding of thousands of hungry people, the walking on the water, the refusal of a sign, a discourse about food, and the confession by Peter. Since Mark has long been recognized as an author who made his own decisions about order, John's order looks dependent on the earlier Markan redaction. Such dependence is made all the more probable by the firm likelihood that the tradition of Peter's confession is a Markan creation (Catchpole 1984: 326-28). John 6:60-71 depends upon that Markan creation, and it exhibits no arguably pre-Markan features. By inference, the fourth Gospel depends upon Matthew/Mark. In that case, what has the author of that

Gospel done with his source material? What does redaction criticism reveal?

The vital clue is the fact that Peter's confession of Jesus has been remodeled and set in a new context. The sermon on Exod. 16:4, 15 in John 6:31-58 had caused consternation among 'the Jews' and also division among 'the disciples'. Jesus had spoken of himself in extremely strong and realistic terms as God's gift in word and sacrament. This proved just too much. Jesus' question, 'Do you also wish to go away?', enables Peter's answer to be the confession of those continuing loyalists who stay with Jesus. Note in this connection four considerations, each of which treats the Johannine text as 'transparent', that is, as a window through which we may observe the situation of the community for which that text is written (cf. Martyn 1979).

First, Jesus speaks surprisingly and paradoxically about some disciples who do not believe (v. 64), and he explains their position by an appeal to predestination. An appeal to predestination is a sectarian reflex, a typical theological reaction on the part of those who belong to a small breakaway group which feels threatened. John's Christian community is like that (cf. 9:22; 12:42; 16:2), but this breakaway group from the Jewish community has the additional problem that some of their own number also go back to where they came from, that is, to the Jewish synagogue community. Their reason for doing so seems to be that they cannot tolerate the sacramental theology that the Johannine community has developed.

Secondly, the devil is not speaking through Peter, as was the case in Mark 8:33. He is at work in Judas (6:70) and in those former Christian Jews who have now defected and returned to the non-Christian community. To associate the former members of the Christian group with Judas (6:64) is bad enough—to associate them with Satan is ferocious indeed. Such fierce polemic is again typically sectarian.

Thirdly, not 'You are the Messiah' (Mark 8:29), says Peter, but 'We have come to believe and know that you are the Holy One of God' (John 6:69). Why the change of terminology? Answer: The language of holiness is the language of heavenliness and of Sonship. It presents Jesus as a person who belongs essentially to the divine world, the world of the angels in which he is unique (cf. 10:36). That is the essence of Johannine belief about him: he is 'the one coming into the world' (11:27; cf. 3:13).

Fourthly, with the problem of defection from the Johannine

community in mind we ought to take seriously the internal connection between 'we have come to believe and know (ἡμεῖς πεπιστεύκαμεν καὶ ἐγνώκαμεν)' in John 6:69 and the reading 'that you may continue to believe...' (πιστεύητε) in John 20:31. The writer is concerned to keep the Jewish Christians from lapsing back into becoming Christian Jews, that is, members of the Jewish synagogue community who hold a low view of Jesus or, worse still, non-Christian Jews who regard Jesus as someone who led Israel astray (cf. 7:12).

Thus it emerges that the traditional disciplines—source, form and redaction criticism—encourage the exegete to develop a sensitivity to the text as the final stage in a multi-stage development. Each of those stages witnesses to the capacity of highly prized material to be both adopted and adapted, to influence and be influenced by changing challenges, circumstances and convictions. The final stage is readily accessible and vitally important: the earlier stages are sometimes less easily accessible but never less important. The conclusion is therefore clear: between the synchronic and the diachronic there can be, there must be, a complementary and mutually enriching harmony.

BIBLIOGRAPHY

Betz, H.D.
1985   *The Sermon on the Mount.* Hermeneia. Minneapolis: Fortress Press.
Bultmann, R.
1963   *The History of the Synoptic Tradition.* Oxford: Blackwell.
Catchpole, D.R.
1984   'The "Triumphal" Entry', in E. Bammel and C.F.D. Moule (eds.), *Jesus and the Politics of His Day.* Cambridge: Cambridge University Press: 319-34.
1993   *The Quest for Q.* Edinburgh: T. & T. Clark.
Davies, W.D., and D.C. Allison, Jr
1988   *The Gospel according to Saint Matthew.* Vol. 1. Edinburgh: T. & T. Clark.
Fee, G.D.
1995   *Paul's Letter to the Philippians.* Grand Rapids: Eerdmans.
Fortna, R.T.
1970   *The Gospel of Signs.* Cambridge: Cambridge University Press.
1988   *The Fourth Gospel and its Predecessor.* Edinburgh: T. & T. Clark.
Fuller, R.H.
1972   *The Formation of the Resurrection Narratives.* London: SPCK.
Goulder, M.D.
1989   *Luke: A New Paradigm.* Sheffield: JSOT Press.
Hengel, M.
1977   *Crucifixion.* London: SCM Press.

Hooker, M.D.

1975 'Philippians 2:6-11', in E.E. Ellis and E. Grässer (eds.), *Jesus und Paulus. Festschrift W.G. Kümmel*. Göttingen: Vandenhoeck & Ruprecht: 151-64.

Jeremias, J.

1963 *The Parables of Jesus*. London: SCM Press.

Lohse, E.

1971 'συνέδριον'. *TDNT* 7: 860-71.

Luz, U.

1990 *Matthew 1–7*. Edinburgh: T. & T. Clark.

Martin, R.P.

1983 *Carmen Christi*. Grand Rapids: Eerdmans.

Martyn, J.L.

1979 *History and Theology in the Fourth Gospel*. Nashville: Abingdon.

Mattill, A.J., Jr

1979 *Luke and the Last Things*. Dillsboro, NC: Western North Carolina Press.

McKenzie, S.L., and S.R. Haynes (eds.)

1993 *To Each its Own Meaning: An Introduction to Biblical Criticisms and their Application*. London: Chapman.

Meyer, R.

1967 'Λευίτης'. *TDNT* 4: 239-41.

Neirynck, F.

1991 *Evangelica*. Vol. 2. Leuven: Peeters.

Perrin, N.

1970 *What is Redaction Criticism?* London: SPCK.

Porter, S.E., and D. Tombs (eds.)

1995 *Approaches to New Testament Study*. JSNTSup, 120. Sheffield: Sheffield Academic Press.

Rohde, J.

1968 *Rediscovering the Teaching of the Evangelists*. London: SCM Press.

Sanders, E.P.

1969 *The Tendencies of the Synoptic Tradition*. Cambridge: Cambridge University Press.

1977 *Paul and Palestinian Judaism*. London: SCM Press.

Sanders, E.P., and M. Davies

1989 *Studying the Synoptic Gospels*. London: SCM Press.

Strecker, G.

1995 'The Concept of History in Matthew', in G.N. Stanton (ed.), *The Interpretation of Matthew*. Edinburgh: T. & T. Clark.

Tuckett, C.M.

1987 *Reading the New Testament*. London: SPCK.

1996 *Q and the History of Early Christianity*. Edinburgh: T. & T. Clark.

Watson, F.

1985 'The Social Function of Mark's Secrecy Theme'. *JSNT* 24: 49-69.

Wrede, W.

1971 *The Messianic Secret*. Cambridge: James Clarke.

DISCOURSE ANALYSIS

JEFFREY T. REED

Discourse analysis (less frequently referred to as Textlinguistics or Text Grammar) is a sub-discipline of modern linguistics that seeks to understand the relationships between language, discourse, and situational context in human communication. Consequently, it draws upon the insights of several other academic disciplines, in its early years including linguistics, anthropology, sociology, philosophy (see van Dijk 1985), and in more recent years, communication theory, social psychology (Potter and Wetherell 1987), and artificial intelligence. Discourse analysis is, therefore, an interdisciplinary approach to language and human communicative behaviour and cannot, or should not, be reduced to simplistic definition. My goal here is to highlight some of the guiding tenets and major approaches of discourse analysis so as to provide an overall framework that may be useful in the exegesis of the New Testament. In addition, the select bibliography will guide the reader into more detailed models and applications of discourse analysis.

GUIDING TENETS OF DISCOURSE ANALYSIS

A. Analysis of the Production and Interpretation of Discourse

Discourse analysts investigate the roles of the author, the audience, and the text (and its language) in the production and consumption of communicative acts. On the one hand, discourse analysts seek to *interpret a speaker's or author's rôle in the production of discourses*. In addition to the speaker's role, discourse analysts also seek to *interpret the listener's or reader's comprehension(s) of and response(s) to the discourse*. Every discourse eventually has an audience who will listen to or read it, ponder it, and likely respond to it in some way. Even monologue is based on dialogue. We rarely communicate with ourselves. We communicate with others. We communicate to be heard.

These two sides of the communicative process, and the language used to mediate between them, make discourse analysis a complex undertaking. For example, what is said is not always what is meant, and what is meant is not always what is understood. The speaker, the

language, and the listener each have a certain degree of independence
in the communicative act. As P. Cotterell notes,

> ...the speaker may be either unaware of the real message he [or she] was
> encoding, or unwilling to admit to the message, so that he can disown the
> message... In the same way the listener, possibly because of his
> relationship to the speaker, may 'perceive' a message that cannot be
> detected by anyone else. If he claims to perceive it, on what grounds can
> anyone else deny that it is there? Certainly not by analysing the offending
> utterance as though it were a cold sentence.[1]

Despite this always possible impediment to communication, readers
want to interpret the symbols set before them: 'Hearers and readers
have a powerful urge to make sense out of whatever nonsense is
presented to them' (Stubbs 1983: 5). They may not 'get it right', but
they attempt to understand and, more than that, to understand
'correctly' (i.e. to understand the intended purpose of a given
discourse).

The fact that the same message may invoke multiple interpretations
presents another dilemma for discourse analysis. The analyst again
may look to the actual language of the discourse, the situation and
knowledge of the participants involved, and the responses invoked by
the message in order to account for multiple interpretations. The
'why' of multiple interpretations, not the 'fact' of them, is important
to the discourse analyst.

Brown and Yule summarize this two-part tenet aptly:

> We shall consider words, phrases and sentences which appear in the
> textual record of a discourse to be evidence of an attempt by a producer
> (speaker/writer) to communicate his message to a recipient (hearer/reader).
> We shall be particularly interested in discussing how a recipient might
> come to comprehend the producer's intended message on a particular
> occasion, and how the requirements of the particular recipient(s), in
> definable circumstances, influence the organization of the producer's
> discourse. This is clearly an approach which takes the communicative
> function of language as its primary area of investigation and consequently
> seeks to describe linguistic form, not as a static object, but as a dynamic
> means of expressing intended meaning (Brown and Yule 1983: 24).

B. Analysis beyond the Sentence

The discourse analyst is also guided by the tenet to *examine*

---

1   P. Cotterell, 'Sociolinguistics and Biblical Interpretation', *Vox Evangelica*
16 (1986), p. 64.

language at a level beyond the sentence (cf. Stubbs 1983: 6-7). This is perhaps the most distinguishing, if not best known, doctrine of discourse analysis. The long-lived taboo in linguistics that grammar is confined to the boundary of the sentence has been forsaken by discourse analysts. Grammar, they claim, is influenced by linguistic levels beyond the sentence, namely, the 'discourse'. J.P. Louw's prediction that linguistics in the 1970s would direct its attention to units larger than the sentence was already being fulfilled between the late 50s and the early 70s (Louw 1973: 102). K.L. Pike noted in 1964 that '*beyond the sentence* lie grammatical structures available to linguistic analysis'.[2] This change in perspective arose from the observation that words or sentences are rarely used in isolation, but typically as part of an extended discourse of sequenced sentences (esp. in the case of written texts). T. Givón criticizes those who do not observe this aspect of language:

> It has become obvious to a growing number of linguists that the study of the syntax of isolated sentences, extracted, without natural context from the purposeful constructions of speakers is a methodology that has outlived its usefulness.[3]

S. Wallace is even more trenchant:

> That linguistic categories contribute significantly to the structure of an extrasentential text, indeed, that one does not truly understand the meaning of a linguistic category until one comprehends its function in a text, are suggestions that mainstream twentieth-century linguistics has all but ignored.[4]

The study of larger discourse units, however, does not eliminate the need for investigating words and clauses. Discourse analysts advocate a bottom-up and top-down interpretation of discourse. The analyst might begin at the bottom with the analysis of morphology, moving up through words, phrases, clauses, sentences and paragraphs (i.e. sequences of sentences and embedded sequences of sentences) until reaching the top, the discourse. From here the direction is reversed to

---

2   K.L. Pike, 'Beyond the Sentence', *College Composition and Communication* 15 (1964), p. 129.

3   T. Givón, 'Preface', in *Syntax and Semantics. XII. Discourse and Syntax* (New York: Academic Press, 1979), p. xiii.

4   S. Wallace, 'Figure and Ground: The Interrelationships of Linguistic Categories', in *Tense-Aspect: Between Semantics and Pragmatics* (ed. P.J. Hopper; Amsterdam: Benjamins, 1982), p. 201.

see how the larger discourse influences paragraph construction and on down.[5] In this framework, the analysis of words and clauses is important, but only from the perspective of the larger discourse, as J.L. Lemke puts it:

> Language is not simply used to produce word-meaning or clause-meaning, it is used to produce text-meaning, and texts, by co-patterning many word-choices and clause formations, can make meanings that words and clauses cannot. That is why we make texts. Text-meaning realizes social functions…and among the most important social functions of texts is the maintenance and modification of social value systems.[6]

C. Analysis of Social Functions of Language Use

A third tenet of discourse analysis is that *discourse should be analyzed for its social functions and, thus, in its social context* (see esp. Gumperz 1982). The result has been a strong marriage between discourse analysis and *sociolinguistics and pragmatics*. As Brown and Yule state,

> Any analytic approach in linguistics which involves contextual considerations necessarily belongs to that area of language study called *pragmatics*. 'Doing discourse analysis' certainly involves 'doing syntax and semantics', but it primarily consists of 'doing pragmatics' (Brown and Yule 1983: 26).

Discourse is not simply a set of propositions (logical, literal, conceptual, or cognitive) with a certain factual content, but rather social, communicative interaction between humans. As N. Fairclough theorizes, 'Discourse is a mode of action, one form in which people may act upon the world and especially upon each other' (Fairclough 1992: 63). This has led discourse analysts away from abstract formalisms of language and into the realm of the interpersonal and functional roles of language. This focus is based in part on the principle that increasingly larger units of language are less and less constrained by grammar and more and more by the communicative context. Consequently, both the immediate context (Malinowski's 'context of situation') and the broader culture ('context of culture') factor into a discourse analysis, since language and language behaviour 'cannot be acquired in isolation, but rather can only be

---

5   On the notions of 'bottom-up' and 'top-down' analysis, see Brown and Yule 1983: 234-36.

6   J.L. Lemke, 'Semantics and Social Values', *Word* 40 (1989), p. 48.

learnt and are only available for one's use in situational contexts'.[7] M.A.K. Halliday has made this tenet central to his theory of language: 'Language is as it is because of its function in social structure'.[8]

D. Analysis of Cohesiveness

That there is a relationship formally, semantically, and pragmatically between the various parts of a given text and that there is some thematic element which flows through it, in part allows a listener/reader to recognize it as a *cohesive* piece of communication rather than a jumble of unrelated words and sentences. How is it, then, that speakers go about forming texts into cohesive units? How do they combine relatively unrelated words and sentences into meaningful wholes? Discourse analysts repeatedly seek answers to such questions, attempting to identify how language is used to create cohesive and coherent communication. Labov describes the task similarly: 'The fundamental problem of discourse analysis is to show how one utterance follows another in a rational, rule-governed manner—in other words, how we understand coherent discourse'.[9] When attempting to answer such questions, it is important to note that the structural cohesiveness of texts should be viewed as a continuum. At one pole of the continuum are texts with a high degree of unity and cohesiveness. At the opposite pole are texts which can be quickly recognized as a jumble of words and sentences with little 'textuality'. Although a text might be elegantly unified or grossly fragmented, most texts lie somewhere between these two poles—neither altogether cohesive nor altogether incohesive.

Whereas the first tenet of discourse analysis emphasizes the speaker's role in the production of discourse, this tenet recognizes the important role that specific languages (i.e. linguistic codes) play in the production of discourse. Granted, humans are the ones who communicate, who interact with others, who convey 'meaning'. Nevertheless, language (i.e. shared symbols), as it has been formulated and agreed upon by cultural groups, significantly determines the ways in which speakers/authors are expected to construct their message. To put it differently, successful

---

7   R. Wodak, 'Discourse Analysis: Problems, Findings, Perspectives', *Text* 10 (1990), p. 126.

8   M.A.K. Halliday, *Explorations in the Functions of Language* (London: Edward Arnold, 1973), p. 65.

9   W. Labov, *Sociolinguistic Patterns* (Philadelphia: University of Pennsylvania Press, 1972), p. 252.

communication implies shared grammar. Or as Gumperz maintains,

> It seems clear that knowledge of grammatical rules is an essential component of the interactive competence that speakers must have to interact and cooperate with others. Thus if we can show that individuals interacting through linguistic signs are effective in cooperating with others in the conduct of their affairs, we have prima facie evidence for the existence of shared grammatical structure (Gumperz 1982: 19).

In conclusion, many New Testament commentaries say little about the grammatical structure of the text as a whole (though they often comment on the grammar of particular parts of the text) and, conversely, most Greek grammars treat language as an abstract system and not as a system in a particular text (though they often cite examples from particular texts). Discourse analysis of the New Testament should attempt to bring the grammarian and the commentator or exegete more in line with one another. Discourse analysis appraises the language of the text as a whole, keeping in perspective both the language of the text as a system and the individual message(s) of the text. My proposal is that this is what discourse analysis, especially discourse analysis of the New Testament, should be about. It is a reading of discourse based on comprehensive linguistic models of language structure and cohesiveness.

DOING DISCOURSE ANALYSIS

The following discussion represents one possible framework for 'doing' New Testament discourse analysis. It is not intended to be comprehensive, but if combined with the many studies in the select bibliography, it may serve as a springboard into more detailed models of New Testament language and discourse. The discussion is organized around four sections: (a) distinguishing the various linguistic and extra-linguistic levels which influence discourse production and interpretation, (b) analyzing the semantic content of discourse, (c) investigating the interpersonal dimensions of discourse, and (d) studying the cohesive structures of discourse.

A. Levels of Discourse

The first step in discourse analysis, although seemingly obvious, is to identify the text to be investigated. This will preferably be an entire discourse, from beginning to end, or if only part of a discourse, it should be explicitly studied in relation to the larger discourse. In addition, it is necessary to clarify what aspect of the discourse is going to be analyzed. This question involves what are termed here the *levels of discourse* or boundaries of discourse. Discourse analysts often try to account for the various linguistic and contextual factors which constrain the production and especially the interpretation of texts. These constraints range from the smallest meaningful unit—the morpheme—to the broadest meaningful unit—the speaker's culture. A discourse, then, pertains to these two communicative levels and all of those in between. These levels of discourse may be categorized under two headings: co-text and context. *Co-text* refers to linguistic units that are part of a discourse and, more specifically, linguistic units that surround a particular point in the discourse. *Context* refers to extra-linguistic factors that influence discourse production and interpretation, and it may be broadly categorized in terms of the *context of situation*,[10] that is, the immediate historical situation in which a discourse occurs, and the *context of culture*, that is, the 'world view(s)' in which a discourse occurs. See the following diagram.

Standard Language/Code Variety of Language/Dialect Idiolect	*Context of Culture*
Genre/Register	*Context of Situation*
Discourse (Paragraph) Sentence (Clause) Phrase/Group Word	*Co-text*

At the bottom level is the word. Though admittedly problematic to define, *word* is denoted here as 'sound with *sense*' (i.e. attributed meaning)—this includes the combination of meanings contributed by the 'morphemes' which make up the word. *Phrase* includes the function of *attribution*, the ascribing of a quality or characteristic to a central linguistic item or head term. An adjective phrase, for example, contains a nominal element which is ascribed some quality by an

---

10   M.A.K. Halliday, *Language and Social Man* (London: Longman, 1974), pp. 28-29: 'Essentially what this implies is that language comes to life only when functioning in some environment... The "context of situation" does not refer to all the bits and pieces of the material environment... It refers to those features which are relevant to the speech that is taking place.'

adjective. In the phrase τυφλὸς προσαίτης ('blind beggar'; Mark 10:46), the head term is προσαίτης ('beggar') and the adjective τυφλός ('blind') attributes meaning to it. The level of *sentence* adds the function of *transitivity*, that is, processes (aspect and modality), participants (voice, person, number), and often circumstances (when, in what manner, etc.). The largest linguistic level, *discourse*, adds the function of communicative *task*, that is, the overarching purpose(s) or role(s) of the author's communication (e.g. speech acts)—this is roughly equivalent to the notion of genre or register. The clause and paragraph are subsets of the sentence and discourse. However, both the clause and paragraph share the function of *relation* (i.e. the ability to signal ties between stretches of language), since they often contain discourse markers that relate them to their co-text. *Clauses* are often combined by conjunctions to form complex sentences. Similarly, *paragraphs* are often combined by discourse markers to form larger parts of discourse. This is typically accomplished by particles (e.g. γάρ, οὖν, διὰ τοῦτο, ὅθεν, ἄρα, διό, δέ, νῦν), but can also be signaled by generic formulas (e.g. 'I want you to know...' epistolary formulas), grammatical person, number, tense, case, and semantically-signaled shifts in topic.

With these co-textual levels of discourse in mind, the discourse analyst turns to the text at hand ready to inspect how the speaker/author has combined smaller linguistic forms (and their functions) to form a larger discourse. The question is not primarily whether the speaker has done it well, but how it has been done. An incoherent discourse often reveals just as much about discourse structure as a coherent discourse. But where does the interpreter begin when analyzing the various levels of discourse? The concepts of *bottom-up* and *top-down analysis* provide a starting point. To read from the bottom-up is to begin by analyzing the smaller units of discourse and how they are combined into increasingly larger units. The discourse analyst starts with the smallest unit, the word and its morphemes, and concludes with the largest unit, the discourse. To read from the top-down is to begin with an understanding of larger discourse functions (e.g. register/genre) and then to interpret the meaning of smaller units in terms of those functions. Bottom-up analysis may be likened to inductive reasoning, in which the analyst arrives at a theory (e.g. appraisal of a text's theme) based on separate, individual facts (e.g. microstructures). Top-down analysis, on the other hand, is comparable to deductive reasoning, in which a person reasons from a known principle (e.g. the function of a certain genre) to an unknown (e.g. the meaning of a particular use of a word)—from a premise to a logical conclusion.

Whereas the previous levels of discourse concern explicit linguistic forms, the following have to do with extra- or non-linguistic factors of communication.

Standard Language/Code Variety of Language/Dialect Idiolect	*Context of Culture*
Genre/Register	*Context of Situation*

Sociolinguistic studies have shown that the idea of an isolated, fixed language does not do justice to the facts. Rather, *varieties of language* exist within and across various societies. Only in the case of *standard languages*, perhaps such as Hellenistic Greek, may we think of a *language* in contrast to what is typically termed *dialect*. A standard language, or *code*, is shared by a group of people, either because they are part of the same culture or because they have the need to communicate despite differing cultural backgrounds. Such linguistic codes provide a way to communicate despite regional and social dialects. Each language user not only learns the standard language and varieties of language needed to communicate, but he or she acquires language based on personal experience, resulting in a somewhat idiosyncratic *idiolect* or personal variety of language. All the experiences and events of the individual's life give rise to a unique usage of the linguistic code, a sort of fingerprint. For example, a certain individual might have his or her own pronunciation, intonation, rate of delivery, vocabulary, or sentence structure. More importantly, each language user would recognize the idiolects of others and attach social significance to them. Paul's idiolect, both written and spoken, surely evoked certain types of cognitive and emotive responses from his audiences (cf. 2 Cor. 10:10).

Whereas standard languages and varieties of languages are determined by broad sociological factors, *registers* or *genres*[11] have to do with more narrow, limited sociological factors. A variety of

---

11   The terms are used interchangeably here, perhaps the only difference being that register specifically concerns the social context of a 'way of speaking' and genre has more to do with the spoken or written manifestation of that context.

language refers to *language according to user*,[12] but register refers to *language according to use*. More specifically, the term *register* refers to *a configuration of meanings that is associated with a particular situation* (Halliday and Hasan 1989: 38-39).[13] Registers are the linguistic expressions of various types of social activities commonly undertaken by social-groups (e.g. telephone conversations; teacher–pupil interchange; doctor–patient appointments; or ancient letters). They are a means of 'doing things' with language. Consequently, registers are one of the most important ways of relating the language of a particular New Testament text to its context of situation.

To summarize the various levels of discourse, words are part of a linguistic code shared by a group of people, but they are also part of a variety of language shared by various subgroups of a society. Furthermore, these words reflect the idiolect of a particular author. This overall semiotic system reflects the context of culture influencing the production and interpretation of discourse. In addition, every discourse is part of a unique historical context (Halliday and Hasan 1989: 42)—a context of situation—which is revealed generically by the register and particularly by its own lexico-grammatical composition. The co-textual levels affect discourse production and interpretation as soon as the first word is written or read. This initial word then influences the possible combinations of other words and in turn the resulting clause influences construction of the ensuing clause. These clauses may be grouped semantically into a paragraph, which in turn influences other formations of paragraphs. Both co-textual (inter-linguistic) and contextual (extra-linguistic) factors, therefore, play a role in the discourse analysis of a particular grammatical item in a text. Consequently, discourse analysis is an attempt at understanding language beyond the level of the sentence (paragraph, discourse, register/genre), but without neglecting the semantic importance of the sentence itself (word, phrase, clause).

B. Analysis of Semantic Content

Halliday, a leading contributor to the field of discourse analysis, proposes two essential functions of language: (1) to understand the environment (ideational), and (2) to act on the others in it

---

12   R.A. Hudson, *Sociolinguistics* (Cambridge: Cambridge University Press, 1980), pp. 48-49.

13   Halliday further specifies this 'configuration of meanings' in terms of the Firthian contextual categories of field, tenor, and mode.

(interpersonal).[14] The first part of Halliday's theory, *ideational meanings* (sometimes referred to as *experiential meanings*), concerns the real world as it is comprehended by human experience.[15] 'Language...gives structure to experience, and helps us to determine our way of looking at things.'[16] Much of discourse analysis of the New Testament involves studying such ideational features of discourse.

To be more specific, ideational meanings have to do with what is 'going on' in the text in relation to what is going on outside of the text, that is, the use of language to represent 'doings, happenings, feelings, and beings' in the real or imagined world (Halliday 1985b: 101). This is what people usually have in mind when they talk about what a word or sentence 'means'—the 'semantic content' of language. This function of language enables humans to build a mental portrait of a discourse. It enables them to relate language to what goes on around them (the context of situation and the context of culture) and to what they have individually experienced in the course of their lives.[17] The grammar of the clause accomplishes this by means of *processes*,

---

14   Halliday 1985b: xiii. Halliday's model of language is serviceable for the discourse analyst in that it attempts to relate the meanings of language to the context of situation, thus dealing with two of the major tenets of discourse analysis (see tenets one and three discussed above). In addition, although the sentence plays an important role in Halliday's functional grammar, his theory moves grammatical study into the realm of the discourse (tenet two above). Halliday's notion of textual meanings of language directly relates to discourse cohesion (tenet four).

15   Halliday and Hasan 1976: 238. Other terms used to describe this phenomenon include 'representational', 'cognitive', 'semantic', and 'factual-notional'.

16   M.A.K. Halliday, 'Language Structure and Language Function', in *New Horizons in Linguistics* (ed. J. Lyons; Harmondsworth: Penguin Books, 1970), p. 143.

17   The notion of ideational meanings may give the impression that discourse simply represents external reality. This, of course, would be a narrow and incomplete understanding of discourse and the processes involved in comprehension. A significant amount of discourse describes non-real (fictive) people and events, and sometimes quite outlandish ones (e.g. the dancing elephants in Disney's film *Fantasia*). Nevertheless, the world of the text is frequently comprehended with reference to the real world (i.e. experiences) of the reader. For example, the ability to draw analogies from a text results in a proportionate level of discourse comprehension (cf. the *principle of analogy* in Brown and Yule 1983: 64-67).

participants in the process, and *circumstances* associated with the process (Halliday 1985b: 101). In Hellenistic Greek, processes are typically expressed by a verbal phrase, participants by a nominal phrase, and circumstances by adverbial or prepositional phrases: for example, Gal. 1:18 ἔπειτα (circumstance) μετὰ τρία ἔτη (circumstance) ἀνῆλθον (process/participant) εἰς Ἱεροσόλυμα (circumstance) ἱστορῆσαι (process [of subordinate clause]) Κηφᾶν (participant [of subordinate clause]). These three ideational functions of Greek may be further subdivided, as seen in the following chart which summarizes the five types of processes (i.e. verbal events) in New Testament discourse along with their corresponding participants.

Process	Function	Participants

material:
   action
   event
	'doing'
	'doing'
	'happening'
		Actor, Goal[18]

mental:
   perception
   affection
   cognition
	'sensing'
	'seeing'
	'feeling'
	'thinking'
		Senser, Phenomenon[19]

verbal:	'saying'	Sayer, Target, Verbiage

relational:
   attribution
   identification
	'being'
	'attributing'
	'identifying'
		Carrier, Attribute
		Identified, Identifier

existential:	'exists'	existent

Process Types and Their Participants

One way of treating the ideational content of a New Testament discourse would be to analyze each clause in terms of the above process and participant types, searching for patterns in the text.

Besides participants and processes, most Greek clauses use *circumstances* to express additional ideational meanings. For example, adverbs, prepositions, and case-forms are all used in Hellenistic Greek to specify functions of extent, location, manner, cause, accompaniment, and role. These functions are summarized in the following chart.

---

[18]   *Actor* = logical subject, and *Goal* = patient.

[19]   The *Senser* is the conscious participant that is feeling, thinking, or perceiving. The *Phenomenon* is the participant that is being felt, thought, or perceived.

Extent	duration (temporal) distance (spatial)	how long? how far?
Location (Realm)	time (temporal) place (spatial)	when? where?
Manner	means quality comparison	how? with what? in what way? like what?
Cause	reason/purpose/result behalf	why? what for? what result? for whom?
Accompan- iment	comitation addition	with whom/what? who/what else?
Matter		about what? regarding whom?
Role		what as?

Circumstantial Functions

The above discussion of participants, processes, and circumstances primarily deals with the *grammatical* forms of ideational meanings. A more obvious way of representing ideational meanings is by means of lexis or word choice. Indeed, an important part of determining the ideational functions of discourse is by analyzing the lexical choices of the author. Some linguists and psychologists have attempted to set forth stereotypical mental representations of human knowledge of the world, variously termed *scripts, scenarios, mental frames,* and *schemata*.[20] The various theories share the belief that knowledge is organized in memory according to contextual scenarios or schemata; the theories are, thus, cognitive-psychological approaches to discourse comprehension. Understanding discourse is, in this sense, essentially a process of retrieving stored information from memory and relating it to the encountered discourse. This remembered framework may then be adapted to fit reality by changing details as necessary.

> The theories emphasise that cognition is central to the act of communication. In order to understand the world 'out there' people organise it into meaningful categories. As an individual's experience increases so does his or her schemata of the world (Brown and Yule 1983: 236).

In the light of work being done on mental schemata, the vocabulary or lexis of a language plays a significant role in conveying the

---

20 See, for example, D. Tannen, 'What's in a Frame? Surface Evidence for Underlying Expectations', in *New Directions in Discourse Processing* (ed. R.O. Freedle; Norwood, NJ: Ablex, 1979), pp. 137-81.

ideational meanings of discourse. Because of the importance of vocabulary for the analysis of ideational meanings, a tool like J.P. Louw and E.A. Nida's *Greek–English Lexicon* is invaluable for the discourse analyst. Despite the title, this work offers much more than the standard lexicon. It seeks to partition New Testament words into their semantic domains and subdomains, that is, the various categories of meaning (usually cultural categories) which distinguish words from one another.[21] This lexicon is characterized by functional categories, making it especially beneficial for the discourse analyst. For example, rather than listing words in their alphabetical order, Louw and Nida order them according to meaningful categories such as Geographical Objects and Features, Maritime Activities, and Household Activities. Under each category or domain, further subdomains may also be delineated. Under the category of Geographical Objects and Features, for example, are the subcategories or subdomains of Universe/Creation, Regions Below the Surface of the Earth, Heavenly Bodies, Atmospheric Objects, The Earth's Surface, Elevated Land Formations, Depressions and Holes, and so on. By grouping words according to functional categories, Louw and Nida reveal an essential function of words, namely, a means of storing and communicating human knowledge of culture and experience. More importantly, under each category (domain or subdomain) words are listed according to a hierarchy, that is, words with the most general meaning are listed first and those with the most narrow meanings last (from generic to specific). For example, under the category of Household Activities, οἰκονομέω/οἰκονομία ('to manage and provide for a household') is listed first and σαρόω ('to sweep by using a broom') last. In other words, sweeping with a broom conveys a more specific household activity. Though the lexicon is far from perfect (e.g. it needs to be supplemented with extra-biblical literature), it is clearly a move in the right direction for approaching lexis in terms of cognitive schemas of culture rather than isolated and abstracted meanings.

C. Analysis of Interpersonal Dimensions of Discourse

Interpersonal meanings, sometimes referred to as *interactional meanings*, concern the use of language to establish and maintain social

---

[21]   On the theoretical moorings of the lexicon, see J.P. Louw and E.A. Nida, 'Introduction', in *Greek–English Lexicon of the New Testament Based on Semantic Domains* (2 vols.; New York: United Bible Societies, 1988), I, pp. vi-xx.

relations (Halliday and Hasan 1976: 26-27). Whereas ideational meanings may be likened to 'language as reflection', interpersonal meanings may be likened to 'language as social action'. Through them the speaker expresses his or her own comments, attitudes, and evaluations on the surrounding environment. In addition, interpersonal meanings are used to act on the others in it (Halliday 1985b: xiii). Consequently, interpersonal meanings also reveal 'how the speaker defines how he sees the person with whom he is communicating'.[22]

There are four essential interpersonal functions in Hellenistic Greek—offers, commands, statements, questions—as illustrated in the following four-cell diagram.

commodity exchanged / role in exchange	goods-and-services	information
giving	OFFER Matt. 4:19 ποιήσω...	STATEMENT John 6:48 ἐγώ εἰμι ὁ ἄρτος
demanding	COMMAND Rom. 13:12 ἀποθώμεθα...	QUESTION Heb. 2:6 τί ἐστιν ἄνθρωπος ὅτι...

Behind all four of these interpersonal functions are two roles being played by the speaker: *giving* and *demanding*.

> Either the speaker is giving something to the listener (a piece of information, for example) or he is demanding something from him...giving means 'inviting to receive', and demanding means 'inviting to give'. The speaker is not only doing something himself; he is also requiring something of the listener (Halliday 1985b: 68).

These two speech roles are done with respect to two kinds of commodities, what Halliday calls 'goods-and-services' and 'information'. *Goods-and-services* include any speech event with the aim of getting the audience to perform an action ('open the door!') or give an object ('send the letter!'). The other commodity is the exchange of *information*, which implies a verbal response from the listener—'I am the bread of life' may invoke a 'No, you are not'. The intersection of the two speech roles (giving and demanding) and the two commodities exchanged (goods-and-services and information) result in the four interpersonal meanings found in discourse.

By studying the interpersonal functions of each clause of a

---

22   Hudson, *Sociolinguistics*, p. 49.

discourse, the New Testament interpreter may gain a better overall perspective on how an individual author chooses to interact with the reader. The following chart may guide such an analysis of an entire New Testament discourse, highlighting the grammatical forms which commonly serve certain speech roles.

Commodity exchanged	Speech function	Common expressions	Example
information	statement or question[23]	indicative	Rom. 5:21 ἵνα ὥσπερ ἐβασίλευσεν ἡ ἁμαρτία ἐν τῷ θανάτῳ, οὕτως καὶ ἡ χάρις
		subjunctive	βασιλεύσῃ διὰ δικαιοσύνης εἰς ζωὴν αἰώνιον...
		optative	1 Pet. 3:17 κρεῖττον γὰρ ἀγαθοποιοῦντας, εἰ θέλοι τὸ θέλημα τοῦ θεοῦ, πάσχειν ἢ κακοποιοῦντας
		modal adjunct	Rom. 3:9 τί οὖν;...
goods-and-services	command	imperative	1 Pet. 5:2 ποιμάνατε τὸ ἐν ὑμῖν ποίμνιον τοῦ θεοῦ...μὴ ἀναγκαστῶς ἀλλὰ ἑκουσίως κατὰ θεόν, μηδὲ αἰσχροκερδῶς ἀλλὰ προθύμως
		subjunctive	Luke 2:15 διέλθωμεν δὴ ἕως Βηθλέεμ καὶ ἴδωμεν τὸ ῥῆμα τοῦτο
		lexis	1 Thess. 4:1 ...τὸ πῶς δεῖ ὑμᾶς περιπατεῖν καὶ ἀρέσκειν θεῷ!
	offer	future	2 Cor. 12:15 ἐγὼ δὲ ἥδιστα δαπανήσω καὶ ἐκδαπανηθήσομαι ὑπὲρ τῶν ψυχῶν ὑμῶν
		subjunctive	Luke 6:42 ἄφες ἐκβάλω τὸ κάρφος
		modal adjunct	Rom. 11:14 εἴ πως παραζηλώσω μου τὴν σάρκα καὶ σώσω τινὰς ἐξ αὐτῶν

---

23 Statements and questions are not always grammatically distinguished; however, the interrogative pronoun is one way of distinguishing the two.

D. Analysis of Discourse Cohesiveness

That there is a relationship, both *semantically and grammatically*, between the various parts of a text (cohesive ties), and that there is some *thematic element* that flows through it (information flow), results in cohesive discourse rather than a jumble of unrelated words and sentences.[24] Cohesion 'occurs where the *interpretation* of some element in the discourse is dependent on that of another. The one *presupposes* the other, in the sense that it cannot be effectively decoded except by recourse to it' (Halliday and Hasan 1976: 4). These cohesive relationships may occur between words and phrases or even between sentences and paragraphs (i.e. thematically-organized sequences of sentences). That such relationships occur in texts is not an overly sophisticated observation, but the question remains: How is language used to create these cohesive relationships? Or, for the New Testament interpreter: What criteria may be used to discuss the relative cohesiveness of a text? The notion of cohesive ties has been one linguistic approach to such questions. *Cohesive ties* refer to a language system's ability to form relations between linguistic items of the various levels of discourse. The nature of this relationship is primarily semantic, that is, the ties are related in a meaningful way. Cohesive ties consist of two types: organic and componential.

Organic ties primarily concern the conjunctive systems of language, such as particles which serve as markers of transition (e.g. γάρ, ἀλλά, δέ, καί). Organic ties are also signaled by prepositions, grammatical structure (e.g. genitive absolute using γίνομαι), and conventionalized lexical items (e.g. λοιπόν). Organic ties make up the 'logical' system of natural language and consist of two functional systems: (1) interdependency or 'taxis' (parataxis and hypotaxis), which is found at all levels of language, and (2) expansion and projection, which is limited to the levels of clause and paragraph (see Halliday 1985b: 192-251, 302-309). *Hypotaxis* is the logico-semantic relation between a dependent element and the element on which it is dependent (dominant element). *Parataxis*, on the other hand, is the logico-semantic relation between two linguistic elements of equal status and, thus, either could stand independently of the other (e.g. 'I am going to the store' '...and I will buy some soup').

---

24   Halliday often treats a fourth function of language under the rubric of textual meanings, namely, *logical* meanings (e.g. the rhetorical functions of 'and', 'because', 'if...then', and 'or').

In both types of clause structures, the logico-semantic relation between the primary and secondary clause may be one of *projection* or *expansion*. In the case of *expansion*, the secondary clause 'expands' the primary clause in one of three ways: (1) elaboration, (2) extension, or (3) enhancement. In *elaboration*, the secondary clause or phrase expands upon the primary by 'elaborating' on it or some portion of it, that is, restating, specifying, commentating, or exemplifying. In *extension*, the secondary clause 'expands' the primary clause by moving beyond it, that is, adding to it, giving an exception, or offering an alternative. In *enhancement*, the secondary clause 'expands' the primary clause by qualifying it with a circumstantial feature of time, place, cause, or condition. For example, in Greek a preposition plus infinitive may be used to expand a primary clause, with the preposition specifying the type of expansion. By way of simile, the three types of expansion may be likened to enriching a building: (1) *elaborating* the existing structure of a building; (2) *extending* it by addition or replacement; (3) *enhancing* its environment. The following chart may serve as a reference tool for analyzing these three types of organic ties in New Testament discourse. One benefit of such study is that we may gain a better understanding of how an author builds an argument from one clause to the next or how a story develops from one section to the other.

ELABORATION (+)	
Apposition	(restate or re-present; epexegetical)
expository	ὅτι, ἵνα, τοῦτο ἐστιν (in other words, that is, I mean, to put it another way)
exemplifying	οὕτως, οὕτω, γέγραπται, ῥητῶς (for example, for instance, thus, to illustrate)
Clarification	(summarize or make precise)
corrective	μᾶλλον, μενοῦν, μενοῦνγε, ἀλλά, οὐχ ὅτι (or rather, at least, to be more precise, on the contrary, however)
particularizing	μάλιστα (in particular, more especially)
summative	λοιπόν, οὖν (in short, to sum up, in conclusion, briefly)
verifactive	ὅλως, ὄντως (actually, as a matter of fact, in fact)

EXTENSION (=)	
Addition	
positive	καί, δέ, τέ, πάλιν, εἶτα, ἐπί, καί...καί, τε...καί, τε...τε, μέν...δέ (and, also, moreover, in addition)
negative	οὐδέ, μηδέ (nor)
Adversative	ἀλλά, δέ, μενοῦν, μενοῦνγε, μέντοι, πλήν, παρά (but, yet, on the other hand, however)
Variation	
replacive	ἀντί, τοὐναντίον, μέν...δέ (on the contrary, instead)
subtractive	ἐκτός, εἰ μή (apart from that, except for that)
alternative	ἤ, ἤ...ἤ, ἤτοι...ἤ (alternatively, or)

ENHANCEMENT (x)	
Spatio-Temporal	
following	καί, δέ, κατά (then, next, afterwards)
simultaneous	ὡς, ὅτε, ὅταν, πότε, ποτέ, καθώς, ἅμα, ἐφάπαξ (just then, at the same time)
preceding	πρό, πρίν, πρῶτον, ἤδη, πάλαι (before that, hitherto, previously)
conclusive	λοιπόν (in the end, finally)
immediate	εὐθύς, εὐθέως (at once, immediately, straightaway)
interrupted	ταχύ, ταχέως, αὔριον, μέλλω (soon, after a while)
repetitive	ἄνωθεν, πάλιν, εἰς τὸ πάλιν (next time, on another occasion)
specific	μεταξύ, σήμερον, αὔριον (next day, an hour later, that morning)
durative	ἐν τῷ μεταξύ (meanwhile, all that time)
terminal	ἕως, ἄχρι, μέχρι (until then, up to that point)
punctiliar	νῦν, δεῦρο (at this moment)
Comparative	
positive	ὅμοιος, ὁμοίως, τοιοῦτος, ὅμως, ὡς, ὡσεί, ὥσπερ, καθώς, καθά, καθό, ὡσαύτως (likewise, similarly)
negative	ἤ, ἤπερ, negated 'positive forms' (in a different way)

Causal-Conditional	
(1) causal	
result	διό, πρός, εἰς, ἵνα, οὖν, τοίνυν, τοιγαροῦν, ὡς, ὥστε (in consequence, as a result)
purpose	ἵνα, ὅπως, ὥστε, μήποτε, μή πως (for that purpose, with this in view)
reason	ὅτι, γάρ, διά, διότι, χάριν, ἕνεκεν, ἐπεί (on account of this, for that reason)
basis	ἐπί, νή (on the basis of, in view of)
(2) conditional	
positive	εἰ, εἴπερ, ἐάν, ἐάνπερ, εἴτε...εἴτε, ἄν, πότερον (then, in that case, if, under the circumstances)
negative	εἰ μή, ἐὰν μή (otherwise, if not)
concessive	καίπερ, καίτοι, καίτοιγε, κἄν [καί + ἐάν] (yet, still, though, despite this, however, even so, nevertheless)
Respective	
positive	ὧδε, ἐνθάδε (here, there, as to that, in that respect)
negative	ἀλλαχοῦ (in other respects, elsewhere)

The other type of cohesive tie involves *componential* relationships in discourse. Whereas organic ties generally concern various paratactic and hypotactic, logico-semantic relationships between clauses and paragraphs, *componential ties* generally concern the meaningful relationships between individual linguistic components in the discourse (e.g. repetition of words). In order to account for the various semantic relationships between discourse components, Halliday and Hasan appeal to three types of componential ties: (1) co-reference; (2) co-classification; and (3) co-extension (see Halliday and Hasan 1980: 43-59). These are akin to the distinctions of reference, denotation, and sense often discussed in semantic theory.

Co-reference or reference refers to the cohesive ties between linguistic items of the same identity. In the sentence 'John bought the suit, which he gave to his brother', the relative pronoun 'which' refers to the entity 'suit'. Both lexical items—'suit' and 'which'—share the same identity. The same is true of ὁ ἀστήρ and ὅν in Matt. 2:9. *Co-classification* or denotation—the second type of componential tie—refers to cohesive ties between linguistic items of the same class or genus. One way to create this type of tie is by *substitution*, as in 'I want the children to draw with crayons' and 'I want the teenagers to draw with pencils'. By substituting 'teenagers' for 'children' and 'with pencils' for 'with crayons' the two sentences form a cohesive tie of co-classification with respect to who should do the drawing and how it should be done. A co-classificational tie (of 'sinning') is created in Rom. 2:12 by substituting ἀνόμως with ἐν νόμῳ (ὅ σοι γὰρ ἀνόμως ἥμαρτον...καὶ ὅσοι ἐν νόμῳ ἥμαρτον). Another way to convey co-classification is by *ellipsis* or zero-anaphora. For example, an individual might say to another, 'I hit the ball so hard it went over the parking lot. How hard did you [hit the ball]?' A cohesive relationship exists between these sentences because of the elided element 'hit the ball'. Both sentences do not refer to the same event; rather, they fall into the class of 'ball-hitting'. Similarly, in Phil. 2:4 (μὴ τὰ ἑαυτῶν ἕκαστος σκοποῦντες ἀλλὰ τὰ ἑτέρων ἕκαστοι) the participle, σκοποῦντες, is elided after ἀλλά, creating a co-classificational tie of 'considering'. *Co-extension* or sense—the third type of componential tie—refers to cohesive ties between linguistic items of the same semantic field, but not necessarily of the same class. In the sentences 'John ate the pizza' and 'Susie gobbled down the cake' the linguistic pairs 'John' / 'Susie', 'ate' / 'gobbled down', and 'pizza' / 'cake' do not refer to the same entities nor do they refer to the same class (e.g. pizza is not a kind of cake). Co-extensional ties are one of the most common ways of creating cohesiveness in texts and interpreting cohesive links in texts. These ties are primarily lexical. By using words with similar senses, speakers talk about similar things in similar ways.

Co-extensional ties may be further subdivided into (1) instantial and (2) general types. *Instantial lexical relationships* arise from the particular demands of the text (Halliday and Hasan 1980: 43-59). For example, the author of 1 Timothy may be referring to the specific individual Τιμόθεος when he uses the vocative ὦ ἄνθρωπε θεοῦ in 1 Tim. 6:11. However, this understanding is based on shared knowledge between the author and reader and not gained from the Greek language itself. That is, ὦ ἄνθρωπε θεοῦ, as a Greek expression, is not a unique referent for Timothy. Instantial ties often prove difficult for the modern reader because their interpretation is based on knowledge of the immediate text or the context of situation; a study of other contemporary literature or of Greek semantics is of little or no help.

General lexical relationships originate from the language system itself; thus, they are shared by a group of language users. General co-extensions take five forms: reiteration, synonymy, antonymy, hyponymy, and meronymy. *Reiteration* occurs when both members of the cohesive tie consist of the same lexical item. This is one of the more obvious forms of cohesive ties. However, the simple repetition of a lexical item does not imply total synonymy nor does it leave out the possibility that the same (spoken or written) lexical items have two quite different meanings with the same spelling (a monetary 'bank' or a river 'bank') and/or pronunciation ('meet' and 'meat'). Furthermore, the repetition of some words, such as the article ὁ, does not necessarily indicate cohesiveness. That is, repetition is not a phenomenon of the code itself but of the code as it is used by a speaker/author; hence, its presence in discourse as a cohesive device must be argued for by the interpreter, not simply asserted (this is an important point for debates over literary integrity of New Testament texts). *Synonymy* refers to cohesive ties created by lexical items sharing similar meanings (but not necessarily totally synonymous), that is, words from the same semantic domain. *Antonymy* refers to cohesive ties created by lexical items opposite in meaning. It is not that antonyms are unrelated in meaning but that the antonyms differ in one or more semantic features but share others—there is negativity and similarity. Thus 'dog' and 'kite' are not antonyms, because they do not share anything in common that would allow the listener to recognize a semantic tie between the two. But a cohesive tie might be intended between 'hot' and 'cold' (when used in the same text) because they share the semantic notion of temperature. *Hyponymy* refers to cohesive ties created by an inclusive semantic relationship between lexical items. One lexical item is included in the total semantic range of another item (but not vice-versa). This allows for a hierarchy of meanings in lexical systems. For example, 'Labrador' is a hyponym of 'dog', 'dog' is a hyponym of 'animal', 'animal' is a hyponym of 'living beings', and so on. Similarly, οὖς is a hyponym of μέλος. The one is included in the semantic range of another, which in turn is included in the semantic range of another, and so on. Hyponymy may be further distinguished according to contracting types (e.g. '*People* got on and off. At the news-stand *businesspersons*, returning to Paris, bought that day's papers.') and expanding types ('*Tulips* are cheap even in January. But then, *flowers* seem to be necessary to Scandinavians during the darkest season.'). *Meronymy* refers to part-whole relationships between lexical items. For example, the word 'fur' is a meronym of 'dog' or 'cat'. Similarly, κόμη is a meronym of κεφαλή. The one is a part of the other. Because it is part of the other, it may be used to create a semantic relationship between the words.

Through the analysis of co-referential ties (e.g. pronouns, demonstratives), co-classificational ties (e.g. substitution, ellipsis), and co-extensional ties of both instantial (i.e. those tied to the situational context) and general types (repetition, synonymy, antonymy, hyponymy, and meronymy), the discourse analyst is able to demonstrate a major component of textual cohesiveness. As seen above, co-reference and co-classification are primarily expressed by *grammatical* networks in the language and co-extension is primarily expressed by *lexical* networks.

A nagging question remains: What makes one text seemingly more cohesive than another? Or, for the New Testament interpreter: What criteria may be used to discuss the relative cohesiveness of a New Testament text? The notion of *semantic chains*, primarily discussed in systemic-functional linguistics, provides a reasonable set of criteria for such questions. A chain is formed by a *set* of discourse lexemes, each of which is related to the others by a semantic relation of co-reference, co-classification and/or co-extension. If a text, for example, contains a discourse participant who is identified using pronouns ('he preached...'), demonstratives ('that one healed...'), or the person's name ('Jesus said...'), then these elements form a chain of co-reference. There are two types of chains: identity chains and similarity chains. *Identity chains* are expressed by co-referential ties and *similarity chains* are expressed by co-classificational and co-extensional ties. Exposing the identity and similarity chains of a text, nevertheless, proves less than adequate when attempting to speak about the relative cohesiveness of a text. In order to determine relative textual cohesiveness, the discourse analyst should differentiate between peripheral, relevant, and central tokens. *Peripheral tokens* include those linguistic items which do not take part in a chain. This happens, for example, when a topic is brought up in a clause and then subsequently dropped from the discussion. It is isolated from other chains and, hence, is peripheral to the author's larger argument. *Relevant tokens* include all linguistic items in the text which are part of one or more chains. It should not be concluded, however, that a high proportion of relevant tokens to peripheral tokens necessitates greater textual cohesiveness (although it may play some role). *Textual cohesiveness is primarily occasioned by central tokens. Central tokens* refer to linguistic items in chains that interact with linguistic items in other chains. If the two chains interact in more than one part of the text (especially in close contexts), it is likely that the author is 'on about' a similar topic, thus creating cohesiveness and potential coherence in the text. He is establishing a thread in the discourse, and using language in an organizing manner.

'The minimum requirement for chain interaction can be phrased as follows: for two chains x and y to interact, at least two members of x should stand in the same relation to two members of y' (Halliday and Hasan 1980: 57). In other words, two lexical items (the same or different) of the same chain must be used in conjunction with at least two other lexical items (the same or different) of another chain.[25] Typically, chain interaction involves a chain of *participants* (e.g. 'the Philippian Christians') and a chain of *events* (e.g. 'think...'); however, chain interaction may occur when one chain of participants interacts repeatedly with another chain of participants (e.g. 'Paul' says, hopes, sends 'the Philippians...'). The theory of cohesive ties is based on the view that a key factor for creating coherence lies in similarity. Chain interaction is a theory of similarity in texts—the view that cohesiveness is created by speakers saying similar kinds of things (e.g. chain 1) about similar kinds of phenomena (e.g. chain 2). In non-technical terms, chain interaction is the speaker's *being 'on about' similar kinds of things.* This understanding of language use is closely related to the principle of linguistic *redundancy*, that is, texts will typically transmit less information than the sum of their linguistic parts. Redundancy 'serves to reduce the likelihood of an error in the reception of the message resulting from the loss of information during the transmission'.[26] By repeating certain semantic content, the author better enables the reader to correctly understand the intent of the discourse.

---

[25]   To limit chain interaction to 'two' may seem arbitrary, but it is the necessary lowest boundary since if only 'one' chain interaction were required then every clause of discourse would necessarily be a central token—a problematic conclusion. Admittedly, Halliday and Hasan are after a relative (scalar), not absolute, set of criteria for speaking about the cohesiveness of discourse.

[26]   J. Caron, *An Introduction to Psycholinguistics* (trans. T. Pownall; New York: Harvester Wheatsheaf, 1992), p. 5.

CONCLUSION

The tenth anniversary issue of the journal *Text* (1990), volume eleven of *Annual Review of Applied Linguistics* (1990), and the International Congress of Linguists in Berlin (1987)—where discourse analysts formed the largest contingent—all testify to this model's popularity among both theoretical and applied linguists. In 1989, W.A. Beardslee prophesied about the potential alliance between discourse analysis and biblical studies,

> It may well turn out to be the case that another type of linguistic interpretation [discourse analysis], making much less extensive hermeneutical claims, will come to be even more fruitful for actual exegesis than structuralism or Güttgemanns's generative poetics (Beardslee 1989: 188).

Despite such promising words, it can hardly be claimed that discourse analysis has presently been established as a widespread hermeneutic in mainstream biblical scholarship. Its reputation is, however, growing. If it is to be as successful in biblical studies as it has been in linguistics, we need more New Testament exegetes to set forth clearly defined methods of discourse analysis which are then applied to New Testament texts. Furthermore, if modern linguistics is to have a lasting impact on New Testament studies, there will need to be a revival of interest in grammatical study. And, although Greek grammar still requires further study with respect to morphology or its formal units of meaning (e.g. verbal aspect and tense-forms), it surely requires even more research with respect to the discourse functions of the language. Although the present study is decidedly cursory in scope, an attempt has been made to provide an overall map which may guide the reader into further study and prompt thoughtful interaction especially with modern linguistic theory.[27]

BIBLIOGRAPHY

The following (very) select bibliography lists key works in discourse analysis belonging to the fields of (1) general linguistics and (2) biblical scholarship. In addition to the works cited, several linguistic journals and series are worth consulting, including *Text, Discourse Processes*, and *Annual Review in Applied Linguistics*, and the two series *Papiere zur Textlinguistik/Papers in Text-linguistics* (New York/Hamburg: H. Buske) and *Untersuchungen zur*

---

[27]   A more detailed discussion of this model of New Testament discourse analysis may be found in Reed 1997: 16-122.

Textlinguistik/Research in Text Linguistics (Berlin/New York: de Gruyter). Several biblical studies journals which often include works on discourse theory include *Bible Translator, Selected Technical Articles Related to Translation, Journal of Translation and Textlinguistics* (formerly *Occasional Papers in Translation and Textlinguistics*), *Notes on Translation, Neotestamentica, Filología Neotestamentaria* and *Linguistica Biblica*.

1. Linguistics

Beaugrande, R. de
1980   *Text, Discourse and Process: Toward a Multidisciplinary Science of Texts.* Advances in Discourse Processes, 4. Ed. R.O. Freedle. Norwood, NJ: Ablex.
1990a   'Text Linguistics through the Years'. *Text* 10: 9-17.
1990b   'Text Linguistics and New Applications'. *Annual Review of Applied Linguistics* 11: 17-41.

Beaugrande, R. de, and W. Dressler
1981   *Introduction to Text Linguistics.* Longman Linguistics Library, 26. London: Longman.

Brown, G., and G. Yule
1983   *Discourse Analysis.* Cambridge: Cambridge University Press, 2nd edn.

Coulthard, M.
1985   *An Introduction to Discourse Analysis.* London: Longman, 2nd edn.

Crusius, T.W.
1989   *Discourse: A Critique and Synthesis of Major Theories.* New York: Modern Language Association of America.

Dijk, T.A. van
1972   *Some Aspects of Text Grammars.* The Hague: Mouton.
1977a   *Grammars and Descriptions: Studies in Text Theory and Text Analysis.* Berlin: de Gruyter.
1977b   *Text and Context: Explorations in the Semantics and Pragmatics of Discourse.* London: Longman.
1980   *Macrostructures: An Interdisciplinary Study of Global Structures in Discourse, Interaction, and Cognition.* Hillsdale, NJ: Lawrence Erlbaum.
1985   'Introduction: Discourse as a New Cross-Discipline', in T.A. van Dijk (ed.), *Handbook of Discourse Analysis.* I. *Disciplines of Discourse.* New York: Academic Press: 1-10.

Dijk, T.A. van (ed.)
1985   *Handbook of Discourse Analysis.* 4 vols. London: Academic Press.

Dressler, W.
1972   *Einführung in die Textlinguistik.* Tübingen: Niemeyer.

Fairclough, N.
1992   *Discourse and Social Change.* Cambridge: Polity Press.

Freedle, R.O. (ed.)
1977   *Discourse Production and Comprehension.* Norwood, NJ: Ablex.
1979   *New Directions in Discourse Processing.* Norwood, NJ: Ablex.

Grimes, J.E.
1975   *The Thread of Discourse*. The Hague: Mouton.

Gumperz, J.J.
1982   *Discourse Strategies*. Studies in Interactional Sociolinguistics, 1. Cambridge: Cambridge University Press.

Halliday, M.A.K.
1985a   'Dimensions of Discourse Analysis: Grammar', in T.A. van Dijk (ed.), *Handbook of Discourse Analysis*. II. *Dimensions of Discourse*. London: Academic Press: 29-56.
1985b   *Introduction to Functional Grammar*. London: Edward Arnold; 2nd edn, 1994.

Halliday, M.A.K., and R. Hasan
1976   *Cohesion in English*. London: Longman.
1980   'Text and Context: Aspects of Language in a Social-Semiotic Perspective'. *Sophia Linguistica* 6: 4-90.
1989   *Language, Context, and Text: Aspects of Language in a Social-Semiotic Perspective*. Oxford: Oxford University Press.

Kinneavy, J.L.
1971   *A Theory of Discourse*. New York: Norton.

Longacre, R.E.
1983   *The Grammar of Discourse*. New York: Plenum.

Petöfi, J.S., and H. Rieser (eds.)
1973   *Studies in Text Grammar*. Dordrecht: Reidel.

Polyani, L. (ed.)
1987   *The Structure of Discourse*. Norwood, NJ: Ablex.

Potter, J., and M. Wetherell
1987   *Discourse and Social Psychology: Beyond Attitudes and Behavior*. London: Sage Publications.

Schiffrin, D.
1994   *Approaches to Discourse*. Oxford: Blackwell.

Sinclair, J.McH., and R.M. Coulthard
1975   *Towards an Analysis of Discourse*. Oxford: Oxford University Press.

Stubbs, M.
1983   *Discourse Analysis: The Sociolinguistic Analysis of Natural Language*. Language in Society, 4. Oxford: Blackwell.

Tannen, D. (ed.)
1984   *Coherence in Spoken and Written Discourse*. Advances in Discourse Processes, 12. Norwood, NJ: Ablex.

2. Biblical Studies

Beardslee, W.A.
1989   'Recent Literary Criticism', in E.J. Epp and G.W. MacRae (eds.), *The New Testament and its Modern Interpreters*. Atlanta: Scholars Press: 175-98.

Bergen, R.D.

1982 *Discourse Criticism: Introduction, Methodology, and Application to Genesis 1:1–2:3*. Fort Worth, TX: Summer Institute of Linguistics.

Black, D.A. (ed.)

1992 *Linguistics and New Testament Interpretation: Essays on Discourse Analysis*. Nashville: Broadman Press.

Boers, H.

1994 *The Justification of the Gentiles: Paul's Letters to the Romans and Galatians*. Peabody, MA: Hendrickson.

Callow, K.

1974 *Discourse Considerations in Translating the Word of God*. Grand Rapids: Zondervan.

Cotterell, P., and M. Turner

1989 *Linguistics and Biblical Interpretation*. Downers Grove: InterVarsity Press.

Dawson, D.A.

1994 *Text-Linguistics and Biblical Hebrew*. JSOTSup, 177. Sheffield: JSOT Press.

Fryer, N.S.L.

1984 *Discourse Analysis and Exegesis*. Kwadlangerzwa: University of Zoeloeland.

Guthrie, G.

1994 *The Structure of Hebrews: A Text-Linguistic Analysis*. NovTSup, 73. Leiden: Brill.

Hellholm, D.

1980 *Das Visionenbuch des Hermas als Apokalypse: Formgeschichtliche und texttheoretische Studien zu einer literarischen Gattung. I. Methodologische Vorüberlegungen und makrostrukturelle Textanalyse*. ConBNT, 13. Lund: Gleerup.

Johanson, B.

1987 *To All the Brethren: A Text-Linguistic and Rhetorical Approach to 1 Thessalonians*. ConBNT, 16. Stockholm: Almqvist & Wiksell.

Levinsohn, S.H.

1992 *Discourse Features of New Testament Greek: A Coursebook*. Dallas: Summer Institute of Linguistics.

Louw, J.P.

1973 'Discourse Analysis and the Greek New Testament'. *BT* 24: 101-19.

1979 *A Semantic Discourse Analysis of Romans*. 2 vols. Pretoria: University of Pretoria Press.

1982 *Semantics of New Testament Greek*. Philadelphia: Fortress Press.

1992 'Reading a Text as Discourse', in D.A. Black (ed.), *Linguistics and New Testament Interpretation: Essays on Discourse Analysis*. Nashville: Broadman Press: 17-30.

Olsson, B.

1974 *Structure and Meaning in the Fourth Gospel: A Text-Linguistic Analysis of John 2:1-11 and 4:1-42*. ConBNT, 6. Lund: Gleerup.

Pickering, W.

1980 *A Framework for Discourse Analysis*. Arlington, TX: Summer Institute of Linguistics and University of Texas at Arlington.

Porter, S.E., and D.A. Carson (eds.)

1995 *Discourse Analysis and Other Topics in Biblical Greek*. JSNTSup, 113. Sheffield: JSOT Press.

Porter, S.E., and J.T. Reed

1991 'Greek Grammar since BDF: A Retrospective and Prospective Analysis'. *FN* 4: 143-64.

Reed, J.T.

1993 'To Timothy or Not: A Discourse Analysis of 1 Timothy', in S.E. Porter and D.A. Carson (eds.), *Biblical Greek Language and Linguistics: Open Questions in Current Research*. JSNTSup, 80. Sheffield: JSOT Press: 90-118.

1995 'Modern Linguistics and the New Testament: A Basic Guide to Theory, Terminology, and Literature', in S.E. Porter and D. Tombs (eds.), *Approaches to New Testament Study*. JSNTSup, 120. Sheffield: JSOT Press: 222-65.

1997 *A Discourse Analysis of Philippians: Method and Rhetoric in the Debate over Literary Integrity*. JSNTSup, 136. Sheffield: Sheffield Academic Press.

Schenk, W.

1984 *Die Philipperbriefe des Paulus*. Stuttgart: Kohlhammer.

Snyman, A.H.

1991 'A Semantic Discourse Analysis of the Letter to Philemon', in P. Hartin and J. Petzer (eds.), *Text and Interpretation: New Approaches in the Criticism of the New Testament*. Leiden: Brill: 83-99.

Werner, J.R.

1982 'Discourse Analysis of the Greek New Testament', in J.H. Skilton and C.A. Ladley (eds.), *The New Testament Student and his Field*. Phillipsburg, NJ: Presbyterian and Reformed.

RHETORICAL AND NARRATOLOGICAL CRITICISM

DENNIS L. STAMPS

INTRODUCTION

It may seem odd linking rhetorical and narratological criticism, as they represent two different interpretative perspectives, but at a number of significant points, the two interpretative approaches converge to share similar foundations. In addition, the two have been linked as distinguishing two sides of one coin in terms of the two main critical tasks of discourse theory: narrative demarcating the textual ways and means; rhetoric the effects of such textual devices.[1] In order to introduce the significance and importance of rhetorical and narratological criticism, it is helpful to examine their common foundations and their relationship to a common critical task.

Exegesis includes understanding the biblical text in its final form. The final form of a biblical text is that form of the text which results from the conclusions of textual criticism, source criticism and tradition criticism. In addition, when biblical critics refer to the final form of a text, they generally mean the complete literary (and canonical) form of the text that a reader reads without necessary reference to the literary origins and development of the text. Rhetorical and narratological criticism are two critical approaches to the New Testament that are concerned with the final form of the text.

Within the bounds of the final form of New Testament texts, rhetorical and narratological criticism also are concerned with examining the modes and effects of literary arrangement. Terry Eagleton, in his revision of literary theory as discourse theory, suggests a link between rhetorical and literary criticism by defining the interpretative critical task as follows: 'What would be specific to the kind of study I have in mind...would be its concern for the kinds of *effects* which discourses produce, and how they produce them...this is, in fact, probably the oldest form of "literary criticism" in the world,

---

[1]   J.H. Hayes and C.R. Holladay, *Biblical Exegesis: A Beginner's Handbook* (London: SCM Press, 2nd edn, 1987), pp. 73-80.

known as rhetoric'.[2] Wayne Booth also explicitly links rhetoric with narrative in his work, *The Rhetoric of Fiction*: 'My subject is the technique of non-didactic fiction, viewed as the art of communicating with readers—the rhetorical resources available to the writer...as he tries, consciously or unconsciously, to impose his fictional world upon the reader'.[3] Eagleton and Booth as critics of literature are both concerned to examine the way literary texts affect the reading event and the reader. From this larger literary perspective, both rhetorical and narratological criticism, as forms of biblical criticism, are concerned to discover and analyze the 'formal devices of language' or the imbedded textual strategies that operate within a text. But both critical methods conceive the operation of these textual strategies in different ways: rhetorical criticism in terms of argumentation; narrative criticism in terms of the story.

As mentioned above, within the scope of the examination of textual strategies comes a concern for the effects of such. Rhetorical criticism is concerned with how the arrangement of the components of argumentation work towards proof or persuasion. Narratological criticism examines the way the narrative components work to create a story. This concern for the effects of textual strategies can, in both cases, be called a rhetorical concern. M.A. Powell distinguishes between the two approaches as follows: rhetorical criticism is concerned with the rhetoric of persuasion, that is, how the textual components work together to persuade the reader to adopt particular theses presented within the text for their assent; narrative criticism is concerned with the rhetoric of narrative, that is, how the components of story-telling work together to create narrative coherence.[4]

An interesting aspect of both rhetorical and narratological criticism is their concern for a unified text or the ways the parts cohere to make the whole. Biblical historical criticism often leaves a text in disparate parts, showing how different parts of a biblical text relate to different origins, literary and situational. With regard to Gospel criticism in particular, form, tradition and redaction criticism often atomize the

---

[2]   T. Eagleton, *Literary Theory: An Introduction* (Oxford: Blackwell, 1983), p. 205.

[3]   W.C. Booth, *The Rhetoric of Fiction* (Chicago: University of Chicago Press, 2nd edn, 1983), p. xiii.

[4]   M.A. Powell, *What is Narrative Criticism? A New Approach to the Bible* (London: SPCK, 1993), pp. 14-15.

story into unrelated literary pieces.[5] Rhetorical and narratological criticism acknowledge that a text has many parts (devices, components, etc.), but assumes an internal textual connectedness or integration. Rhetorical and narratological criticism assumes that biblical texts can be understood in terms of a holistic overarching purpose, whether that purpose is to persuade or to tell a meaningful story.

In sum, rhetorical and narratological criticism represent a kind of final-form criticism of the biblical texts which is neither solely nor primarily occupied with the historical origin and development of the text. As interpretative perspectives, they are interested in analyzing the text in terms of textual components or devices which cohere with respect to an overarching communicative intention. The critical agenda is to discover and examine the textual components and to analyze how they work together to create a purposeful effect.

THEORETICAL AND INTERPRETATIVE ISSUES AND THEIR RELEVANCE FOR EXEGESIS

Having examined the foundational interpretative issues that rhetorical and narratological criticism share, it is necessary to look at each separately and examine what is distinctive to each interpretative approach with respect to the exegetical task. In so doing, it is also important to have some sense of how each critical perspective developed into a recognized distinctive interpretative method. The development and theory of rhetorical criticism will be discussed first, then narratological (or narrative) criticism.

Rhetorical Criticism

The application of rhetorical criticism to the New Testament has a long history.[6] It extends back to the early Church Fathers who, trained in rhetoric, read many New Testament texts in order to analyze the persuasive style of the New Testament so that contemporary preachers could imitate this biblically-sanctioned rhetoric; a good example of this is St Augustine's *On Christian Doctrine* (Book 4). The 'revival'

---

[5]   N.R. Petersen, *Literary Criticism for New Testament Critics* (GBS; Philadelphia: Fortress Press, 1978), pp. 11-20.

[6]   A handy summary of the history of rhetorical criticism in biblical studies is D.F. Watson and A.J. Hauser, *Rhetorical Criticism of the Bible: A Comprehensive Bibliography with Notes on History and Method* (BIS, 4; Leiden: Brill, 1994), pp. 101-109.

of rhetorical criticism in biblical criticism in the late twentieth century has occurred through a number of influences. The writings of three scholars, James Muilenburg,[7] Amos N. Wilder,[8] and E.A. Judge,[9] have been particularly important. Modern application of rhetorical criticism in New Testament studies, however, is better known for that critical perspective initiated by H.D. Betz. In 1974, he suggested that the whole of Galatians should be interpreted and analyzed as a rhetorical discourse, an apologetic letter, which utilizes traditional ancient rhetorical categories of speech.[10] Then in the mid-1980s, a classicist, G. Kennedy, applied Greco-Roman rhetorical criticism to the whole range of New Testament literature in his book, *New Testament Interpretation through Rhetorical Criticism*, suggesting a formulaic procedure for analyzing textual units according to the theories of ancient rhetoric.[11] His easily applicable procedure for rhetorical criticism has spawned numerous rhetorical analyses of New Testament texts, and is a watershed manual in New Testament rhetorical criticism. Like Betz, Kennedy attempts to show how the New Testament texts are examples of the art of ancient Greco-Roman rhetoric and/or function in a manner similar to ancient rhetorical categories. Kennedy states the rhetorical critical task as follows:

> What we need to do is try to hear his [Paul's] words as a Greek-speaking audience would have heard them, and that involves some understanding of classical rhetoric... The ultimate goal of rhetorical analysis, briefly put, is the discovery of the author's intent and of how that is transmitted through a text to an audience.[12]

From this perspective, the New Testament supposedly was written and read in the context of Greco-Roman rhetoric and one can reconstruct that historical dimension in the text by identifying the classical rhetorical units, classifying them, and thereby discerning their

---

[7]   J. Muilenburg, 'Form Criticism and Beyond', *JBL* 88 (1969), pp. 1-18.

[8]   A.N. Wilder, *The Language of the Gospel: Early Christian Rhetoric* (New York: Harper & Row, 1964).

[9]   E.A. Judge, 'Paul's Boasting in Relation to Contemporary Professional Practice', *Australian Biblical Review* 16 (1968), pp. 37-50.

[10]   H.D. Betz, 'Literary Composition and Function of Paul's Letter to the Galatians', *NTS* 21 (1975), pp. 353-79; *Galatians: A Commentary on Paul's Letter to the Churches in Galatia* (Hermeneia; Philadelphia: Fortress Press, 1979).

[11]   G.A. Kennedy, *New Testament Interpretation through Rhetorical Criticism* (Chapel Hill, NC: University of North Carolina Press, 1984).

[12]   Kennedy, *New Testament Interpretation*, pp. 10, 12.

rhetorical function and intent in relation to the original situation, the original author, and the original audience.

W. Wuellner also has been influential in the application of rhetorical criticism to the New Testament. In particular, his appropriation of the New Rhetoric and modern communication theory in his most recent writings has extended New Testament rhetorical criticism so that it includes any communication theory that helps illumine the way a text works to create its effect.[13] Wuellner posits a form of rhetorical criticism that corresponds with the movement for a rhetoric revalued or rhetoric reinvented. From this perspective, rhetoric is understood as a practical performance of power inseparable from the social relations in which both the rhetorical act is situated and the rhetorical critic is situated. Wuellner states his position as follows:

> ...as rhetorical critics (rhetorics as part of literary theory) we face the obligation of critically examining the fateful interrelationship between (1) a text's rhetorical strategies, (2) the premises upon which these strategies operate (gender in patriarchy or matriarchy; race in social, political power structures), and (3) the efficacy of both text and its interpretation; of both exegetical practice and its theory (= method).[14]

While Wuellner's definition of rhetoric is far from clear, his move away from rhetoric as the application of Greco-Roman categories to the New Testament or as a way to excavate the historical meaning is obvious.

As implied in the survey of the development of recent New Testament rhetorical criticism, there is no single overarching methodology that can be found in the current practice of rhetorical criticism of the New Testament. Critical practice depends on whether one understands rhetoric as a purely historical phenomenon identified with ancient Greco-Roman rhetorical convention, as a universal communicative perspective identified with modern analyses of argumentation, or as some combination of the two.[15] Based on the previous survey, several of the different rhetorical-critical approaches to the New Testament will be examined.

The first rhetorical-critical approach is the historically-based

---

13   W. Wuellner, 'Where is Rhetorical Criticism Taking us?', CBQ 49 (1987), pp. 448-63; 'Hermeneutics and Rhetorics: From "Truth and Method" to "Truth and Power"', *Scriptura S* 3 (1989), pp. 1-54.

14   Wuellner, 'Hermeneutics and Rhetorics', p. 38.

15   Watson and Hauser, *Rhetorical Criticism*, pp. 109-15.

rhetorical criticism. Since the historical paradigm still governs exegesis of the New Testament in the guild of New Testament studies, it is not surprising that rhetorical criticism with a historical emphasis, as advocated by Betz and Kennedy, dominates most rhetorical-critical studies of the New Testament. This stream of rhetorical criticism seeks to correlate the text with its supposed original historical context, specifically ancient Greco-Roman rhetoric.

This particular approach is interested in reconstructing the rhetorical form and function of the biblical text in its historically-reconstructed situation. The text is analyzed as a piece of ancient Hellenistic rhetoric according to the historical-rhetorical categories gleaned from ancient rhetorical handbooks and ancient rhetorical compositions.[16] The rhetoric of the text, from this historical perspective, is a recovery of the original author's use of Greco-Roman rhetoric to persuade the original readers in the context of the original historical setting or rhetorical situation. M. Mitchell's book, *Paul and the Rhetoric of Reconciliation*, provides one of the clearest examples of this approach.[17]

The second historically-based perspective, the 'Kennedy' school, while remaining historical in perspective, seeks to restate the interpretative goal in exclusively rhetorical terms, and according to classical or Greco-Roman rhetorical terms. He adopts a five-step approach to analyze any rhetorical argument: (1) determine the rhetorical unit, either a self-contained textual unit or an entire book; (2) define the rhetorical situation, that is, the person, events and exigence which precipitated the rhetorical response; (3) determine the species of rhetoric (judicial, deliberative or epideictic) and the rhetorical problem or stasis; (4) analyze the invention (argument by ethos, pathos and logos), arrangement (the ordering of the argument according to the components such as the *exordium* or introduction, the *narratio* or statement of facts, the *probatio* or main body of the argument, and the *peroratio* or the conclusion), and style (the use of

---

16 Greco-Roman rhetorical theory based on the handbooks and compositions, in general, dealt with five aspects of the practice of rhetoric: invention, arrangement, style, memory and delivery. A convenient explanation and definition of these five aspects can be found in B. Mack, *Rhetoric and the New Testament* (GBS; Minneapolis: Fortress Press, 1990), pp. 25-48.

17 M.M. Mitchell, *Paul and the Rhetoric of Reconciliation: An Exegetical Investigation of the Language and Composition of 1 Corinthians* (Louisville: Westminster/John Knox Press, 1991).

figures of speech and other such devices to shape the speech according to the needs of the invention); and (5) evaluate the rhetorical effectiveness of the rhetorical response in addressing the rhetorical situation.[18]

D. Watson, in his book, *Invention, Arrangement and Style*, provides an application of Kennedy's methodology to the epistles of Jude and 2 Peter.[19] He first sets forth an amplification and simplification of Kennedy's rhetorical theory, which also draws heavily on ancient rhetorical handbooks to provide clarification and definition of the rhetorical terms and categories he uses.[20] Watson then analyzes Jude in the following way. The rhetorical unit is the letter as a whole. The situation is identified as 'the infiltration of the church or churches by a doctrinally and ethically divergent group'.[21] He classifies the species of rhetoric for Jude as deliberative, and analyzes the invention or argument of the letter as follows: the *exordium* (v. 3); the *narratio* (v. 4); the *probatio* with three proofs (vv. 5-16); the *peroratio* (vv. 17-23). Interestingly and questionably, he labels the epistolary prescript as 'quasi-exordium' (vv. 1-2) and the letter closing, a doxology, as 'quasi-peroratio' (vv. 24-25); these two literary units of letters do not easily conform to the classical oral rhetorical model Watson uses as the basis of his analysis. Through the application of his rhetorical-critical theory, Watson not only wants to illumine the rhetorical nature of the argument, but to solve the problems of literary integrity and dependency between Jude and 2 Peter.

As mentioned, another rhetorical-critical perspective practised in New Testament studies is advocated in the work of Wuellner. Wuellner advocates the priority of rhetoric over hermeneutics. This re-prioritization not only constitutes the reinvention of rhetoric, but also the complete abandonment of the interpretative task as presently practised in New Testament studies:

> It made a revolutionary difference to take the familiar notion, that human beings in general, and religious persons in particular, are hermeneutically constituted, and replace it with the ancient notion familiar to Jews and Greeks alike, that we are rhetorically constituted. We have not only the capacity to understand the content or propositions of human signs and

---

18   Kennedy, *New Testament Interpretation*, pp. 33-38.
19   D.F. Watson, *Invention, Arrangement, and Style: Rhetorical Criticism of Jude and 2 Peter* (SBLDS, 104; Atlanta: Scholars Press, 1988).
20   Watson, *Invention*, pp. 1-28.
21   Watson, *Invention*, p. 29.

symbols (= hermeneutics); we also have the capacity to respond and interact with them (= rhetorics). [22]

For Wuellner and others like him, the rhetoric of a text is the power of a text to effect social identification and transformation in every act of reading. The operative rhetoric is dependent upon the immediate social context of any reading (whether ancient or modern) and of the readers, emphasizing the ideology of the text as a practical exercise of power. A helpful example of this approach is A.C. Wire, *The Corinthian Women Prophets*.[23]

With regard to exegetical procedure, the different rhetorical-critical practices in New Testament interpretation suggest an essential rhetorical-critical method. Whether or not an exegete correlates the New Testament text with Greco-Roman oratorical rhetorical practice, rhetorical criticism is about analyzing a text in order to assess and evaluate the modes and means of the argumentation and the effect(s) of that argumentation in terms of its power to persuade. In order for an exegete to classify the forms of argumentation being utilized, the exegete will have to adopt some kind of theory of argumentation. The options available are numerous, and include Greco-Roman rhetorical theory, the New Rhetoric of Chaim Perelman,[24] and more general theories of argumentation, often based on a theory of rhetoric.[25] Assessing and evaluating the persuasive power of the argumentation is a more subjective procedure and will often depend on the context in and to which the rhetorical-critical task is being addressed.

In terms of application to Scripture, a biblical critic needs to identify a textual unit that has some integrity (a beginning, middle and conclusion). Then, using the theory of rhetoric adopted, to identify and analyze the rhetorical components or devices of this unit which work to persuade the audience to assent to the ideas and beliefs presented in the text. The rhetorical-critical task also includes evaluation of the effectiveness of the devices, of the consequences of

---

[22] Wuellner, 'Hermeneutics and Rhetorics', p. 38.

[23] A.C. Wire, *The Corinthian Women Prophets: A Reconstruction through Paul's Rhetoric* (Philadelphia: Fortress Press, 1990).

[24] C. Perelman and L. Olbrechts-Tyteca, *The New Rhetoric: A Treatise on Argumentation* (trans. J. Wilkinson and P. Weaver; Notre Dame: University of Notre Dame Press, 1989).

[25] W.J. Brandt, *The Rhetoric of Argumentation* (New York: Bobbs-Merrill, 1970); W. Nash, *Rhetoric: The Wit of Persuasion* (Oxford: Oxford University Press, 1989).

the way the argument is presented, and of the effect the point-of-view might have upon the audience in view.

Within this very general theory of rhetorical criticism, there are several important assumptions which need further explanation. First, critics must identify the rhetor in their theory of rhetoric. For most biblical rhetorical critics, the rhetor is the original historical author, but notionally it is possible to identify that historical author with the implied author who is limited to the authorial identity entextualized within the discourse.[26] Secondly, rhetorical criticism can work on almost any size unit of text down to a sentence, possibly even a clause or phrase, and up to a whole discourse like a Gospel or epistle or even the whole Bible. The problem is whether rhetorical criticism, in analyzing a unit of text, discerns a textual integrity which was intentionally created, or critically imposes a pattern of coherence as an analytical procedure. Thirdly, identifying, analyzing and evaluating the rhetorical components depends a great deal upon the situation the rhetoric is perceived to be addressing. For many biblical critics, the situation in view is the original historical occasion in which the writer addresses the original audience (whether hearers or readers of the text), but rhetorical criticism can work equally in the situation of the canonical text addressing a modern audience (or any variant of this type of situation).

Rhetorical criticism is a very helpful critical perspective, which provides a methodological approach for analyzing and evaluating the argumentation of a biblical text based on a particular theory of rhetoric adopted by the biblical critic.

Narratological Criticism

Examining the biblical text in terms of its literary qualities is not a new critical practice. What is more recent is the sustained effort to apply modern 'secular' literary-critical theories of narrative to the Gospel literature. In actual practice, this effort has been complex and complicated and cannot be fully comprehended apart from an attempt to relate modern literary criticism to contemporary biblical-literary criticism.[27] For the sake of brevity, only the particular practice of

---

26   The implied author is the author (re)constructed by the reader from the textual traces of the author within the narrative; see Booth, *Rhetoric*, pp. 66-77.

27   Reliable guides for such are S.D. Moore, *Literary Criticism and the Gospels: The Theoretical Challenge* (New Haven: Yale University Press, 1989); and S.E. Porter, 'Literary Approaches to the New Testament: From Formalism to Deconstruction and Back', in S.E. Porter and D. Tombs (eds.), *Approaches to*

narrative criticism that has emerged in biblical studies will be examined.

The development of narrative criticism in biblical studies in recent years has a twisted route. The dominance of historical-grammatical criticism since the Enlightenment in biblical studies is well documented.[28] Alongside this development there has occurred the occasional literary reading of the Bible, but for the most part, these two distinct approaches have occurred without any mutual interaction. With reference to the Gospels, this means that historical critics focus on the development and transmission of the Gospels from their sources to their present canonical form. The reconstruction of this historical process is always also done in relation to a reconstruction of the individuals and communities who were associated with each step of the development, writing, editing and transmission of each Gospel.

From the 1940s onwards, an approach developed which was essentially identified with the study of literature. In schools and universities it was known as 'the study of the Bible as literature'.[29] As secular literary criticism fragmented into different interpretative methods beginning primarily with the New Criticism and going up to and including deconstructionism and New Historicism, the biblical texts were occasionally read using these different methods. On the whole, biblical critics took no notice.

However, in the 1960s there was an avenue of study that examined the parables from a modern literary perspective. From this and the growing inter-disciplinary nature of the study of the humanities at this time, in the 1970s there erupted a concerted effort in biblical studies to apply modern literary-critical methods to the biblical text, primarily the Gospels. The pioneering work of William Beardslee, David Rhoads, Jack D. Kingsbury, R. Alan Culpepper and Robert C. Tannehill meant that, by the 1980s, there was a substantive literary analysis of each of the five New Testament narratives by a recognized biblical critic.[30] As of today, there is a well-established discipline

---

New Testament Study (JSNTSup, 120; Sheffield: Sheffield Academic Press, 1995), pp. 77-128.

[28] R. Morgan with J. Barton, *Biblical Interpretation* (Oxford: Oxford University Press, 1988), pp. 44-200.

[29] The classic text is M.E. Chase, *The Bible and the Common Reader* (London: Macmillan, 1952).

[30] W.A. Beardslee, *Literary Criticism of the New Testament* (GBS; Philadelphia: Fortress Press, 1969); D. Rhoads and D. Michie, *Mark as Story: An*

within biblical studies of the literary and narratological interpretation of Scripture.

It is important to recognize, however, that narrative criticism as it is practised in biblical studies has no parallel in secular literary criticism. It resembles in many ways some of the developments that are associated with New Criticism and the subsequent developments within the reader-oriented perspectives in secular literary studies.[31] In order to understand the practice of narrative criticism in biblical studies, it is necessary to examine both the essential literary principles which are assumed and the elements of narrative analysis which are employed. However, like rhetorical criticism, there is no universal agreement as to what exactly comprises narrative criticism in biblical studies, but there is far more agreement in this interpretative approach than with rhetorical criticism.

In the introduction, some of the basic assumptions that narrative criticism shares with rhetorical criticism were noted. In its focus upon the final form of the text, narrative criticism not only concentrates on the coherence of the text but on the text as an end in itself.[32] In this sense, the text is not primarily a source to recover the events and persons associated with the original writing and reception of the text, but an event in itself. The focus is on the experience of the text as a communication event within a specified context. In this regard, the text's reference to the world outside the text is one of the components or devices of narrative that must be analyzed. It is out of this assumption that narrative critics interpret a text with a second essential understanding, that a text be interpreted in reference to the implied author and the implied reader as opposed to the real author and the real reader. The implied author and reader are figures within the narrative, implicitly or explicitly, which are presupposed and constructed by the narrative itself:

> The implied author is a hypothetical construction based on the requirements of knowledge and belief presupposed in the narrative. The

---

Introduction to the Narrative of a Gospel (Philadelphia: Fortress Press, 1982); J.D. Kingsbury, *Matthew as Story* (Philadelphia: Fortress Press, 1986); R.A. Culpepper, *Anatomy of the Fourth Gospel: A Study in Literary Design* (Philadelphia: Fortress Press, 1983); R. Tannehill, *The Narrative Unity of Luke–Acts: A Literary Interpretation* (2 vols.; Philadelphia and Minneapolis: Fortress Press, 1986, 1990).

31　Porter, 'Literary Approaches', pp. 83-120.
32　Powell, *What is Narrative Criticism?*, pp. 7-8.

same is true of the implied reader. The implied author is the one who would be necessary for this narrative to be told or written. The implied reader is the one who would be necessary for this narrative to be heard or read.[33]

A third basic principle is the assumption of a writing and reading process which undergirds any narrative interpretation. Literary texts are a product of a composition process in which the written text is a form of communication through which a message is passed from the author to the reader(s). In terms of the reading process, a reader encounters a text in sequential order, and generally understands the narrative as a unified whole, connecting the parts to a larger narrative scheme.

With these basic literary assumptions, narrative criticism examines various narrative elements or devices and considers their role and effect in constructing a narrative whole (the story) and their effect upon how the story is told or the rhetoric of the story (the discourse).[34] The various narrative elements are related to the more general narrative concepts of structure or plot, characterization, point-of-view and setting. Each of these general concepts can be broken down into several narrative features or devices.[35]

Narrative structure is the pattern of the narrative elements or of the narrative components of the story. In particular, structure relates to the order of the events. Events may be ordered chronologically or topically, by using prediction or foreshadowing or flashback. Structural patterns include devices like repetition, chiasm, contrast or comparison, and summary, which are used to organize and develop the story and shape the discourse. In addition, the duration and frequency of the events are part of the structure; duration refers to the amount of 'ink' an incident is given over other incidents; frequency refers to the number of times an incident is referred to in the story. In

---

[33]   E.S. Malbon, 'Narrative Criticism: How Does the Story Mean?', in J.C. Anderson and S.D. Moore (eds.), *Mark and Method: New Approaches in Biblical Criticism* (Minneapolis: Fortress Press, 1992), p. 27.

[34]   The distinction between story and discourse stems from S. Chatman, *Story and Discourse: Narrative Structure in Fiction and Film* (Ithaca, NY: Cornell University Press, 1978), pp. 19-22.

[35]   Useful discussions of narrative features are found in Powell, *What is Narrative Criticism?*, pp. 23-82; *idem*, 'Narrative Criticism', in J.B. Green (ed.), *Hearing the New Testament: Strategies for Interpretation* (Grand Rapids: Eerdmans, 1995), pp. 244-48; Malbon, 'Narrative Criticism', pp. 26-36; also Chatman, *Story and Discourse*, pp. 43-262.

John's Gospel, John the Baptist foreshadows the events to come by his declaration, 'Behold the Lamb of God who takes away the sin of the world (John 1:29). A key to the structure of Acts is tied to a geographical progression foreshadowed in Acts 1:8. In Mark's Gospel, the repetition of the three passion predictions (Mark 8:31; 9:31; 10:33-34) all occur after a climactic recognition of who Jesus is by the disciples in Mark 8:27-30. Two events, the healing of Jairus's daughter and the healing of the woman with a haemorrhage, are intercalated to provide a comparison and contrast about faith in Mark 5:22-43. Summary provides important transitions in the story of Acts (1:43-47; 4:32-35; 6:7; 9:31).

Plot relates directly to narrative structure, but is often concerned with the specific causal links between events. Jesus' conflict with evil and with the religious authorities propels Mark's story forward and explains the 'why' for many of the events (see Mark 3:6). The martyrdom of Stephen and the consequent persecution of Christians is the cause of Christians leaving Jerusalem for Judea and Samaria (Acts 1:8). When no explicit cause is given to an event, it is the element of plot which suggests that a reader implicitly seeks a connective link between events. The seemingly designed pattern of miracles, parables, exorcisms and teaching in Mark 1–8 provides a fruitful example of the need to try to discern an implicit plot.

Character and characterization refer to the way persons are presented in the story. Presentation includes what a person says and the way a person acts. Characterization is also developed by what others say about them, how they function in the plot and what the narrator says about them. Characters are generally crucial to the development of the story. The disciples in Mark's Gospel are consistently portrayed as misunderstanding Jesus and his mission even at the resurrection. Judas is a complex character in Mark's Gospel, but fairly flat or one-dimensional in John's Gospel. Philip, Peter and Paul in Acts provide interesting examples of characterization which is linked vitally to the plot.

Point-of-view is a pervasive narrative technique, in that the story is always being presented or told from some perspective which has an evaluative consequence. Most narratives are dominated by the narrator, who is generally related to the implied author, and is usually considered to have a reliable perspective. The change in point-of-view in Mark's Gospel when the author moves from narration to direct commentary, particularly in the incident when Jesus teaches about what comes from the heart of a person (Mark 7:16, 19), provides a very significant comment within the story. Sometimes the narrator is identified with a character, thus when different characters speak, we are hearing their point-of-view. The divine voice from heaven in Mark 1:11 and 9:7 is an example of a reliable point of view that contributes to the plot; equally, when the demons speak in Mark's Gospel, they speak with supernatural insight that is absent in humans.

Setting refers to the where and when or the spatial, temporal and social locations of narrative events. Different settings have implications for the plot and rhetoric of the narrative. Luke's Gospel clearly manipulates setting for significant narrative purposes. Jerusalem and the Temple (Luke 2:22-38), the wilderness and the forty days (Luke 4:1), the mountain (Luke 6:12; 9:28)—all evoke a sense of prophetic significance when an event occurs in these settings. The controversies with religious leaders in Mark 2:23–3:12 are heightened because they occur on the Sabbath.

Other important narrative devices include symbolism, irony and intertextuality. The use of water in John's Gospel assumes symbolic meaning at points representing Christian baptism. Irony, in which the reader knows that the proper response is contrary to that which is stated in the text, may be the operative device in the ending of Mark's Gospel when, after seeing the empty tomb, the women said nothing for they were afraid. In Matthew's Gospel, intertextuality is at work with the Old Testament allusions and quotations that riddle the story and provide implicit commentary on the significance of the events of the plot.

Narrative criticism is important for the interpretation or exegesis of the New Testament narratives. Narrative criticism assists the exegetical task by suggesting the relationship between different textual units in the Gospels and Acts. But it primarily provides an interpretative perspective which can evaluate the purpose or significance of the what and why (structure and plot), the who (characters), the when and where (setting), and the wherefore (point-of-view) of the events in a biblical narrative.

THE USES AND ABUSES OF RHETORICAL AND NARRATOLOGICAL CRITICISM IN EXEGESIS

There are some significant issues which must be confronted in the use of rhetorical and narrative criticism for exegesis. The exegetical issues with regard to these two interpretative approaches centre around the matters of genre, history and textual integrity.

With regard to both rhetorical and narrative criticism there is the problem of application with respect to different genres in the biblical corpus. Rhetorical criticism, especially the school of rhetorical criticism that employs a form of ancient Greco-Roman rhetorical theory, is best suited for speech-like texts such as the New Testament epistles, homilies and the prophetic oracles found in Revelation. There have been no satisfactory rhetorical-critical analyses of the Gospel as a whole or of significant portions.[36] The most effective rhetorical analyses of the Gospel tradition have been with respect to the smaller textual units that make up pronouncement stories or *chreiai*. The exegetical question persists: should rhetorical criticism be applied to narrative texts which are far more removed from speeches than even the didactic epistles?

In fact, there is much debate as to the appropriateness of using ancient rhetorical categories even for analyzing New Testament epistles.[37] The ancient rhetorical handbooks of the first century CE which are extant were prescriptive for the construction of the appropriate speech for a defined social situation. They did not include instructions for writing letters. In fact, letters appear to have been recognized in categories other than rhetorical speech. The debate over the rhetorical analysis of Galatians well represents the problem.[38] What type of rhetorical species is Galatians? What is the rhetorical invention or pattern of argumentation for Galatians? It appears that no two rhetorical critics agree. At best, the rhetorical analysis of New Testament letters using Greco-Roman rhetorical theory is a heuristic device for identifying and analyzing patterns of argumentation.

A similar concern applies to narrative criticism. As would be expected, most narrative criticism has been applied to the Gospels. Can narrative criticism be applied to New Testament epistles? An interesting example is N. Petersen's literary-sociological analysis of

---

[36] For an expanded discussion of this matter, see D.L. Stamps, 'Rhetorical Criticism of the New Testament: Ancient and Modern Evaluations of Argumentation', in Porter and Tombs (eds.), *Approaches to New Testament Study*, pp. 129-51.

[37] Stamps, 'Rhetorical Criticism', pp. 141-48.

[38] See the insightful discussion in S.E. Porter, 'Paul of Tarsus and his Letters', in S.E. Porter (ed.), *Handbook of Classical Rhetoric in the Hellenistic Period (330 B.C.–A.D. 400)* (Leiden: Brill, 1997), pp. 533-85.

Philemon.[39] In this treatment, he takes a letter and transforms it into a story utilizing narrative elements like plot, characters, setting and point-of-view. The principal objection to this exegetical procedure is that it requires a generic transformation in order to work: the letter is transformed into a narrative before it is analyzed. This seems to violate some of the literary assumptions of narrative criticism, which accepts the final form of a text. While Petersen provides one of the most interesting and provocative readings of a New Testament letter, his method implicitly assumes all discourse is narrative at one level and can be analyzed as such. This assumption begs too many questions with regard to genre and exegetical procedure (but deserves further consideration).

The matter of genre and narrative criticism goes to the heart of the exegesis of the Gospels and Acts. Is there a sense in which narrative criticism assumes a modern literary phenomenon, the novel, as the basis for its critical assumptions? And if so, does this impose upon the ancient writings a literary perspective that is inappropriate? Indeed, are the Gospels even narratives at all? Does the recognition of the Gospel genre as *bios* or kerygma and Acts as history put a question over the application of narrative criticism to these texts? On the other hand, narrative criticism provides some of the most exciting and insightful analyses of the Gospels. Some critics would argue that narrative criticism is more appropriate than the historical-critical method, because it respects the coherent story and biographical nature of the texts.[40] This debate is, however, far from closed.

A second matter which applies to both narrative and rhetorical criticism is the relationship of each method to history. Narrative criticism is often criticized for being non-historical or a-historical. This stems from its concern for the text as an event in itself and not the historical occasion in which and to which the text is addressed and its concern for the implied author and reader(s) versus the historical author and reader(s). Certainly, narrative criticism is not the appropriate method to ascertain answers to historical questions one might ask in relation to an ancient document like the Bible, but this does not mean that it vitiates historical concerns. Narrative critics respond to this charge by stating that a narrative critic must be conversant with the historical information the implied reader is meant

---

[39]   N.R. Petersen, *Rediscovering Paul: Philemon and the Sociology of Paul's Narrative World* (Philadelphia: Fortress Press, 1985).

[40]   Powell, 'Narrative Criticism', p. 254.

to have, that body of common knowledge assumed in the world of the story.[41] For modern narrative critics of the Bible, this will include historical and cultural information not generally known today, thus requiring some historical investigation on the part of the narrative critic.

The more difficult historical concern with regard to narrative criticism is how it conceives of the referentiality of the text in regard to the historical context. Narrative criticism eschews the premise that the biblical texts are the primary evidence for the historical situation in which they were written and to which they were written, or at least the premise that this perspective has the primary claim on the meaning of the text. It is one thing to say that narrative criticism cannot be used to extract this historical information; it is another thing to say that such information is unimportant to the interpretation of the text or, more radically, that the text by its very nature as narrative cannot answer such historical questions. Good exegesis cannot ignore historical concerns, even if narrative criticism chooses to.

Rhetorical criticism has the opposite problem. Much rhetorical criticism, especially the kind that utilizes Greco-Roman oral rhetorical categories, assumes a direct correlation between the original historical situation that prompted the response, and the form of rhetoric and kinds of rhetorical devices used in the response. Equally, this form of rhetorical criticism presumes a direct relationship between the rhetorical analysis and the author's intention, that is, the rhetorical critic's analysis of the rhetoric of a biblical text is an effort to discover, in a one-to-one correspondence, the original author's compositional intention. It is this commitment to historical concerns which has prompted some historical critics to suggest rhetorical criticism is simply one more critical tool in the historical critic's bag.[42] But this form of historical rhetorical criticism falls prey to much of the same criticism that traditional historical criticism has received. On the other hand, there are those rhetorical critics like Wuellner who look to other interpretative goals than history, and who adopt a less direct correspondence between the rhetoric of a text and the situation behind it. The hermeneutical question of how well an interpretative method can recover, even reconstruct, the historical context of a text's

---

41   Powell, *What is Narrative Criticism?*, p. 20.

42   For a fuller discussion of how rhetorical criticism has been assimilated into the historical-critical method, see D.L. Stamps, 'Rhetorical Criticism and the Rhetoric of New Testament Criticism', *LT* 6 (1992), pp. 268-79.

composition is still open for discussion among rhetorical critics.

Another interesting problem which both narratological criticism and rhetorical criticism have attempted to address as part of their critical task is the integrity of a text. As both methods operate with an underlying assumption that a text in all its parts has an overarching unity, this methodological assumption has been used to counter arguments for compositional incoherence. For instance, a rhetorical-critical analysis of Philippians by Watson suggests that the rhetorical cohesion of the argument of the canonical text of Philippians contradicts any partition or multiple-letter theories for the letter.[43] However, simply because an interpretative method can discern a literary integrity for a text does not mean that the text originated as a coherent whole. Both narrative criticism and rhetorical criticism have the means for integrating discourse digression and disjunction into the larger discourse purpose. It should be equally possible that rhetorical and narratological criticism might assess a text as so disjointed in argument or as a story that it could not be considered as an integrated textual whole. The simple problem is that rhetorical and narratological criticism cannot necessarily solve a problem like textual integrity when, by presupposition, both methods assume textual wholeness or unity.

CONCLUSION

Rhetorical and narratological criticism are two interpretative approaches that focus on the final form of the text in order to analyze the literary arrangement of the textual components or devices and to assess the effect of this arrangement. Rhetorical criticism particularly analyzes a text in order to evaluate the argument and its persuasiveness. Narratological criticism assesses the way a narrative text tells a story. Both critical approaches use diverse and particular interpretative methods to classify and evaluate the literary techniques employed within a text. Both methods are particularly useful in the exegetical task in seeing how a text works as a whole to present a coherent (or incoherent) argument or story.

---

[43]   D.F. Watson, 'A Rhetorical Analysis of Philippians and its Implications for the Unity Question', *NovT* 30 (1988), pp. 57-88. For a more balanced approach to the issue, see J.T. Reed, *A Discourse Analysis of Philippians: Method and Rhetoric in the Debate over Literary Integrity* (JSNTSup, 136: Sheffield: Sheffield Academic Press, 1997), pp. 124-52, 406-18.

BIBLIOGRAPHY

Rhetorical Criticism

Betz, H.D. 'Literary Composition and Function of Paul's Letter to the Galatians'. *NTS* 21 (1975), pp. 353-79.

_____. *Galatians: A Commentary on Paul's Letter to the Churches in Galatia.* Hermeneia. Philadelphia: Fortress Press, 1979.

Brandt, W.J. *The Rhetoric of Argumentation.* New York: Bobbs-Merrill, 1970.

Hughes, F. *Early Christian Rhetoric and 2 Thessalonians.* JSNTSup, 30. Sheffield: JSOT Press, 1989.

Judge, E.A. 'Paul's Boasting in Relation to Contemporary Professional Practice'. *Australian Biblical Review* 16 (1968), pp. 37-50.

Kennedy, G.A. *New Testament Interpretation through Rhetorical Criticism.* Chapel Hill, NC: University of North Carolina Press, 1984.

Mack, B. *Rhetoric and the New Testament.* GBS. Minneapolis: Fortress Press, 1990.

Mitchell, M.M. *Paul and the Rhetoric of Reconciliation: An Exegetical Investigation of the Language and Composition of 1 Corinthians.* Louisville: Westminster/John Knox Press, 1991.

Muilenburg, J. 'Form Criticism and Beyond'. *JBL* 88 (1969), pp. 1-18.

Nash, W. *Rhetoric: The Wit of Persuasion.* Oxford: Oxford University Press, 1989.

Perelman, C., and L. Olbrechts-Tyteca. *The New Rhetoric: A Treatise on Argumentation.* Trans. J. Wilkinson and P. Weaver. Notre Dame: University of Notre Dame Press, 1969.

Porter, S.E. (ed.). *Handbook of Classical Rhetoric in the Hellenistic Period (330 B.C.–A.D. 400).* Leiden: Brill, 1997.

Porter, S.E., and T.H. Olbricht (eds.). *Rhetoric and the New Testament: Essays from the 1992 Heidelberg Conference.* JSNTSup, 90. Sheffield: JSOT Press, 1993.

_____. *Rhetoric, Scripture and Theology: Essays from the 1994 Pretoria Conference.* JSNTSup, 131. Sheffield: Sheffield Academic Press, 1996.

_____. *Rhetorical Analysis of Scripture: Essays from the 1995 London Conference.* JSNTSup, 146. Sheffield: Sheffield Academic Press, 1997.

Stamps, D.L. 'Rhetorical Criticism and the Rhetoric of New Testament Criticism'. *LT* 6 (1992), pp. 268-79.

_____. 'Rhetorical Criticism of the New Testament: Ancient and Modern Evaluations of Argumentation', in S.E. Porter and D. Tombs (eds.), *Approaches to New Testament Study.* Sheffield: JSOT Press, 1995, pp. 129-69.

Watson, D.F. *Invention, Arrangement, and Style: Rhetorical Criticism of Jude and 2 Peter.* SBLDS, 104. Atlanta: Scholars Press, 1988.

Watson, D.F. (ed.). *Persuasive Artistry: Studies in New Testament Rhetoric in Honor of George A. Kennedy.* JSNTSup, 50. Sheffield: JSOT Press, 1991.

Watson, D.F., and A.J. Hauser. *Rhetorical Criticism of the Bible: A Comprehensive Bibliography with Notes on History and Method.* BIS, 4. Leiden: Brill, 1994.

Wilder, A.N. *The Language of the Gospel: Early Christian Rhetoric.* New York: Harper & Row, 1964.

Wire, A.C. *The Corinthian Women Prophets: A Reconstruction through Paul's Rhetoric.* Philadelphia: Fortress Press, 1990.

Wuellner, W. 'Where is Rhetorical Criticism Taking us?', *CBQ* 49 (1987), pp. 448-63.

_____. 'Hermeneutics and Rhetorics: From "Truth and Method" to "Truth and Power"'. *Scriptura S* 3 (1989), pp. 1-54.

Narratological Criticism

Beardslee, W.A. *Literary Criticism of the New Testament.* GBS. Philadelphia: Fortress Press, 1969.

Berlin, A. *Poetics and Interpretation of Biblical Narrative.* BLS, 9. Sheffield: Almond Press, 1983.

Booth, W.C. *The Rhetoric of Fiction.* Chicago: University of Chicago Press, 2nd edn, 1983.

Chatman, S. *Story and Discourse: Narrative Structure in Fiction and Film.* Ithaca, NY: Cornell University Press, 1978.

Culpepper, R.A. *Anatomy of the Fourth Gospel: A Study in Literary Design.* Philadelphia: Fortress Press, 1983.

Eagleton, T. *Literary Theory: An Introduction.* Oxford: Blackwell, 1983.

Frei, H. *The Eclipse of Biblical Narrative: A Study in Eighteenth and Nineteenth Century Hermeneutics.* New Haven: Yale University Press, 1974.

Funk, R.W. *The Poetics of Biblical Narrative.* Sonoma, CA: Polebridge Press, 1988.

Kingsbury, J.D. *Matthew As Story.* Philadelphia: Fortress Press, 1986.

McConnell, F. (ed.). *The Bible and the Narrative Tradition.* Oxford: Oxford University Press, 1986.

Malbon, E.S. 'Narrative Criticism: How Does the Story Mean?', in J.C. Anderson and S.D. Moore (eds.), *Mark and Method: New Approaches in Biblical Studies.* Minneapolis: Fortress Press, 1992, pp. 23-49.

Moore, S.D. *Literary Criticism and the Gospels: The Theoretical Challenge.* New Haven: Yale University Press, 1989.

Petersen, N.R. *Literary Criticism for New Testament Critics.* GBS. Philadelphia: Fortress Press, 1978.

_____. *Rediscovering Paul: Philemon and the Sociology of Paul's Narrative World.* Philadelphia: Fortress Press, 1985.

Porter, S.E. 'Literary Approaches to the New Testament: From Formalism to Deconstruction and Back', in S.E. Porter and D. Tombs (eds.), *Approaches to New Testament Study.* JSNTSup, 120. Sheffield: Sheffield Academic Press, 1995, pp. 77-128.

Powell, M.A. *What is Narrative Criticism? A New Approach to the Bible.* London: SPCK, 1993.

_____. 'Narrative Criticism', in J.B. Green (ed.), *Hearing the New Testament: Strategies for Interpretation.* Grand Rapids: Eerdmans, 1995, pp. 239-55.

Rhoads, D., and D. Michie. *Mark as Story: An Introduction to the Narrative of a Gospel.* Philadelphia: Fortress Press, 1982.

Tannehill, R. *The Narrative Unity of Luke–Acts: A Literary Interpretation.* 2 vols. Philadelphia and Minneapolis: Fortress Press, 1986, 1990.

NEW TESTAMENT LITERARY CRITICISM

BROOK W.R. PEARSON

INTRODUCTION

Literary theory has, over the past three decades, become a very important contributor to the field of New Testament exegesis, and has gained a fairly wide following in current New Testament criticism. This is not surprising when one takes into account the many highly stylistic portions scattered throughout the New Testament, such as the Beatitudes (Matt. 5:1-7) or the Christ 'hymn' of Phil. 2:6-11. These sections seem naturally to lend themselves to literary, aesthetically sensitive treatments that traditional historical criticism has been unable to provide. To put it bluntly—the existence of traditional 'literary' devices within the different genres of New Testament literature simply invites literary treatment.[1]

As obvious as this need for literary treatment of New Testament texts may seem, literary criticism has actually been somewhat of a latecomer to the scene of New Testament study. Although it has taken little time to become popular in New Testament exegesis, literary methodology took much longer to catch on in New Testament studies than it did in the study of the Old Testament. This lag between the widespread use of literary criticism in the study of the Old Testament and that of the New Testament is telling. It can probably be explained by three main factors, each of which, when reversed, poses a problem for the practitioner of New Testament literary criticism: (1) The historical information regarding the New Testament literature—all of which was written within, at most, a hundred year period only two millennia ago—is, to most scholars, much clearer and more prodigious than the information we have regarding the Old Testament. This older collection is literature of often indeterminate date, extensive editorial influence, and, at the least, between a millennium

---

[1]   In the Gospels there is everything from simile (Matt. 13:31-33) and extended metaphor (Mark 12:1-12) to foreshadowing (Mark 8–10); some of the Pauline letters have obvious hymnic/poetic portions (Phil. 2:6-11; Col. 1:15-20; 2 Tim. 3:16); and Revelation is, if nothing else, incredibly image-laced (e.g. ch. 18 with the whore of Babylon).

and two centuries older than the New Testament. (2) A much higher proportion of the Old Testament is in what we traditionally see as 'literary' form, such as the poetry of the Psalms and the proverbial statements of the wisdom literature. There seem to be only small portions of the Old Testament that do not lend themselves to literary treatment. (3) Very soon after the formation of the modern state of Israel, the study of the Old Testament was placed within the literary faculties of its universities, and some important western universities, while not going quite that far, actively applied literary methodology in the study of the Old Testament fairly early on. The New Testament, beyond the acclaim garnered by the King James Version as a classic of the English language in English departments, has stayed resolutely in the religious studies or theological faculties of western universities. Certain biblical studies faculties have indeed turned to a more literary approach, but this has not had the same effect on the field as the literary appreciation of the Old Testament.

These same three factors that have encouraged the use of literary methods in the study of the Old Testament, when reversed, act as obstacles to the use of literary method in New Testament study. In direct contrast to the practice of literary criticism in the study of the Old Testament, the New Testament literary critic has three problems that must be addressed: (1) The New Testament documents are able to be placed much more clearly within specific historical settings; (2) The bulk of the New Testament books are not in a recognizable literary form;[2] (3) The field of New Testament criticism is not one that has historically supported literary methodologies. One additional factor that blocks the undiminished use of literary criticism in the study of either the New Testament or the Old Testament is the fact that the historical nature of the events reported therein is of utmost importance to the followers of at least one of the world's major religions, and is, in many ways, the most significant factor that has been threatened by traditional historical criticism. Literary criticism, which is largely a-historical in theoretical or methodological orientation, does not usually ask or answer the historical questions that

---

[2]   Of 27 New Testament 'books', only the Revelation, the four Gospels, and Acts are not in epistolary form (although the Revelation does have epistolary qualities). This leaves 21 'books' not fitting into a normal 'literary' form, since letters have traditionally not been considered as literature per se, but rather as functional literary forms or types. See the Chapter in this volume on Genre in the New Testament.

are so important for, among others, confessional reasons. Some find this aspect of literary treatments of the New Testament threatening.

However, as much as these obstacles are real ones, the promise of exegetical 'payoff' with the use of literary-critical methods has drawn many practitioners of New Testament criticism to experiment with their usefulness for exegesis. Unfortunately, one of the damaging characteristics of most New Testament literary criticism has been its 'appropriative' nature. Much New Testament literary criticism has felt free to pick and choose from the various methodologies that are available to the secular literary critic, but this appropriation means that New Testament literary criticism has not necessarily gone through the same theoretical and methodological 'growing pains' that the field of literary criticism has over the course of the last approximately one hundred years. Some literary methods have thus become very popular in New Testament exegesis to the exclusion of others, but without the theoretical and historical underpinnings that they have in literary criticism. This 'appropriative' character of New Testament literary criticism is one of the issues that needs to be addressed in future literary work in New Testament study.

The most popular literary methodologies currently in use in New Testament criticism are: formalism, with its close relative, the New Criticism; reader-oriented criticisms; post-structuralism and de-constructionism; and anthropological structuralism.[3] The appeal of these particular methodologies is easy to understand—they seek access to the center of meaning in the experience of reading (or, in the case of deconstructionism, the lack of a center). This search for access to meaning and significance is perhaps the most important element that literary methodologies can add to the discipline of New Testament criticism. This is especially true when one considers that traditional historical criticism has not typically had the search for the significance of the text as its *raison d'être*, and has at times even denied the possibility of finding a text that could be understood. Each of these three methods of literary criticism that have typically been utilized by New Testament critics is part of the search for a center of meaning, and, hopefully, access to understanding.

---

[3]   Other methodologies that have been utilized, but which have not yet proved themselves, are biographical criticism, genre criticism, and archetypal criticism, among others. The method of anthropological structuralism is not discussed in this chapter because, although it often appears under the title 'literary criticism', it is much more of a social-scientific approach than a literary one.

USES AND ABUSES OF NEW TESTAMENT LITERARY CRITICISM

Textual Intercourse: Post-Structuralism and Deconstruction

Post-structuralism, while by definition not a monolithic methodology, is that which is based (sometimes more closely than at other times) on the work of several loosely connected philosophers. Jacques Derrida, Michel Foucault, Julia Kristeva, Harold Bloom, Roland Barthes, Paul de Man and Jacques Lacan are the key figures in the field of post-structural thought, and their work comes from, and has been applied to several different disciplines.

'Post-structuralism' is often seen as a synonym for 'deconstructionism', but the relationship between the two is in fact a one-sided one. Deconstructionism is more properly thought of as the work by and patterned after the post-structuralist thinker Jacques Derrida. The term is, however, often applied to much that should simply fall under the broader title of 'post-structuralism'.

The literature that this movement has spawned has been prodigious—to even attempt to distill the thought of any one of these thinkers would take, and has taken, several thick volumes. Because of this, and because my interest here is with the application of this criticism to the New Testament, I will instead rely upon the methodological description of self-confessed New Testament practitioners of post-structuralist and deconstructionist approaches.

The most prolific New Testament post-structuralist is Stephen D. Moore, whose several books and articles are the most thorough-going examples of deconstructive New Testament criticism. Moore's distillation of post-structuralism is based on several quotations from Paul de Man and Jacques Derrida:

> 'The paradigm for all texts consists of a figure (or a system of figures) and its deconstruction' (de Man).

> 'A deconstruction always has for its target to reveal the existence of hidden...fragmentations within assumedly monadic totalities' (de Man)

> 'The text...tells the story, the allegory of its misunderstanding' (de Man)

> 'It has been necessary to...set to work, within the text...certain marks ...that...I have called undecidables...that can no longer be included within philosophical (binary) opposition, but which, however, inhabit philosophical opposition, resisting and disorganizing it' (Derrida)

'I do not "concentrate", in my reading…either exclusively or primarily on those points that appear to be the most "important", "central", "crucial". Rather, I de-concentrate, and it is the secondary, eccentric, lateral, marginal, parasitic, borderline cases which are "important" to me and are a source of many things, such as pleasure, but also insight into the general functioning of a textual system' (Derrida)

'Deconstruction is inventive or it is nothing at all; it does not settle for methodical procedures, it opens up a passageway, it marches ahead and marks a trail…it produces rules—other conventions' (Derrida).[4]

This smorgasbord of quotations from the two most well-known practitioners of the deconstructive (anti-)project gives a good idea of what deconstructive criticism is about. Moore has summarized well. Essentially, the deconstructive/post-structuralist critic looks for places that texts' binary oppositions—what Derrida calls 'undecidables'— (such as spirit/flesh, light/dark, etc.) break apart. This is, however, not like looking for breaks in the text as redaction critics do—perceived cracks in the finished surface of a text that point to an earlier stage of production. Rather, it is looking for where the philosophy of the text breaks down—where the system that ostensibly holds the text together can be shown to be unstable. By pointing out these cracks and working on them as if with a crowbar, the critic hopes to deconstruct the hegemony or integrity of the (repressive) text.

Part of the deconstructive project is the idea of the relatedness of all texts—intertextuality—that asserts that all texts are connected to all other texts. This concept, first developed by Kristeva, allows the critic to creatively demonstrate this connectedness in the empty space that has been provided by the deconstructive efforts. We will see below an example of this 'intertextuality' when we examine some of Moore's work.

Much of the work that has been associated with Foucault and his particular version of post-structuralism has focused on the power structures inherent in texts, and the way that they have both created and maintained actual power structures. The work that has followed this recognition has often sought to subvert those power structures by pulling texts to pieces in a hope that this will have a similar effect on the actual power structures upon which they rely. In essence, the post-

---

4   S.D. Moore, 'Deconstructive Criticism: The Gospel of the Mark', in J.C. Anderson and S.D. Moore (eds.), *Mark and Method: New Approaches in Biblical Studies* (Minneapolis: Fortress Press, 1992), p. 85.

structural/deconstructive project offers new texts in place of the old.

Post-structuralist exegetical techniques allow critics to assert themselves in the space they have created by pulling down old texts. This is often accomplished through the use of complicated word-plays, innuendoes (often sexual), interlinguistic etymologies (often in reverse chronological order), and outright re-writing of the text. These are all more than amply demonstrated in Moore's treatments of the New Testament. Perhaps the best example is to be found in the introductory essay from which I quoted earlier, which is actually a distillation of the first half of an earlier book entitled *Mark and Luke in Poststructuralist Perspectives: Jesus Begins to Write*.[5] In the section of the essay that bears the same title as both the essay and the first part of the earlier book,[6] Moore writes,

> Mark's theology is commonly said to be a theology of the cross, a theology in which life and death crisscross. Jesus' crucifixation... In Mark, the signature of the disciple can only ever be that of a crisscross or Christcross, which my dictionary defines as 'the figure or mark of a cross in general; esp. that made in "signing" his name by a person that cannot write' (*OED*). But a person unable to write is generally unable to read, and in Mark, the disciples, generally at cross-purposes with Jesus, are singularly unable to read. Jesus must speak cross words to his puzzled disciples...
>
> A cross is also a chiasmus, a crosswise fusion in which the order established in the first instance...is inverted in the second instance... Central to Mark is the fact of the crucifiction, a fiction structured like a cross or chiasmus.
>
> Chiasmus comes from the Greek verb *chiazein*, 'to mark with the letter c', pronounced *chi*. And *chi* is an anagram of *ich*, which is German for the personal pronoun *I*, and the technical term in Freud (whose appearance here is anything but accidental)[7] that English translators render as *ego*. And Jesus, who identifies himself to his terrified disciples in Mark 6.50 with the words *egō eimi* ('I am,' or 'it is I'), himself possesses a name that is an echo of the French *Je suis* ('I am'), the single superfluous letter being the *I* (or ego), which is thus marked out for deletion: 'Father not what I [*egō*] want, but what you want' (14.36).

---

5   S.D. Moore, *Mark and Luke in Poststructuralist Perspectives: Jesus Begins to Write* (New Haven: Yale University Press, 1992).

6   'The Gospel of the Mark' where 'Mark' is crossed through with a large 'X' in Moore, 'Deconstructive Criticism', p. 95.

7   Much of the work of J. Lacan is based on the work of Freud.

To be marked with the c, the cross, is painful, for *chiazein* also means 'to cut'. Another meaning of *chiasma* is 'piece of wood'. And the *chiasma* on which Jesus writ(h)es is a lectern as well as a writing desk. Dying, he opens up the book to Psalm 22 and reads the opening verse... *Chi*, the first letter of *Christos* ('Christ'), is also the twenty-second letter of the Greek alphabet.[8]

The purpose of this lengthy (and almost entirely continuous) quotation is to demonstrate just how counterproductive the results of this methodology can be. Moore is, however, a faithful practitioner of deconstructive methodologies and programs—there is no question about that. My contention is simply that the methodology has not yet produced, and gives no hint that it ever will produce, anything of lasting value to the field of New Testament study.[9]

While Moore's three full-length books on various aspects of literary criticism and deconstruction do at least make for some interesting reading if one is interested in post-structuralism, this is not always true of criticism that claims to be 'deconstructive'.

David Seeley's *Deconstructing the New Testament*[10] is a good example of work that illustrates methodological confusion—it bears the title 'deconstructive', but probably should not. Its title and introduction seem to suggest that it will be a work of deconstructive criticism, but it ultimately fails to consistently implement any of the major tenets of the various post-structuralist agendas. It is, in many

---

8   Moore, 'Deconstructive Criticism', pp. 95-96.

9   Perhaps one of the problems is that the actual exegetical work done by Moore is limited by the fact that much of it seems to make multiple appearances. See 'Are there Impurities in the Living Water that the Johannine Jesus Dispenses? Deconstruction, Feminism and the Samaritan Woman', *BI* 1 (1993), pp. 207-27, *Literary Criticism and the Gospels: The Theoretical Challenge* (New Haven: Yale University Press, 1989), pp. 159-70, and *Poststructuralism and the New Testament: Derrida and Foucault at the Foot of the Cross* (Minneapolis: Fortress Press, 1994), pp. 43-64 for a triple treatment of John 4 and the theme of living water in John's Gospel. In one incarnation of this he states, 'What remains unquestioned in [previous] readings, however, is Jesus' superiority to the Samaritan woman. He retains his privileged role as the dispenser of knowledge...while the woman retains her traditional role as the compliant recipient of knowledge, a container as empty as her water jar, waiting to be filled. The hierarchical opposition of male and female—the male in the missionary position, the female beneath—remains essentially undisturbed' (*Poststructuralism and the New Testament*, p. 50). This is a good example of the innuendo that is often found sprinkled amongst the kind of deconstruction that Moore practises.

10   D. Seeley, *Deconstructing the New Testament* (Leiden: Brill, 1994).

ways, a work of historical criticism in the guise of literary treatment, and ends up being a good example of neither. This, as we have mentioned, is a recurrent problem with many so-called 'literary treatments' of the New Testament—work is labeled one way, but carried out according to a different set of presuppositions.

Recourse to the Text: Formalism

On the other end of the literary scale stands formalism. Formalism has been perhaps the most significant contributor to the field of New Testament exegesis.[11] The reason for its genesis in the field of 'secular' literary criticism may help to explain its popularity in New Testament exegesis. Formalism began in the early part of the twentieth century primarily as a response to the historicism and psychologism that had dominated literary studies up until that point. The name of formalism's most popular and influential manifestation, the 'New Criticism', hints at the way in which this theoretical stance affected the field of literary criticism. Its hegemony in literature departments lasted for around forty years, but its influence is by no means completely dissipated. It continues to be tacitly taught by many literature teachers, and it is the theory against which much deconstructive and reader-oriented theory is practised.

In reacting to the historicism and psychologism that had held sway in various permutations since the Enlightenment, the New Criticism (and its formalist cousins) asserted that the text was sufficient in and of itself for the process of interpretation, and that the goal of interpretation was the understanding of the text itself. Thus, rather than merely pointing to historical facts or the author's psychological development, the text was asserted to be important *in and of itself*. The text took over the primary role for determining its meaning, and reference to 'extrinsic' material such as history or biography was kept to an absolute minimum.[12] This was coupled with a tacit belief that the text itself was enough to guide the interpreter to an understanding that more or less coincided with that of the author.

New Testament practitioners who have been frustrated with the

---

[11]   This is arguably true for literary criticism as a whole in this century.

[12]   Some claim that the New Criticism disallows *any* recourse to so-called 'extrinsic' factors, but this is not borne out by reading the most important New Critical thinkers, such as T.S. Eliot in 'Tradition and the Individual Talent', in *Selected Essays* (London: Faber & Faber, 1932; 3rd edn, 1951), pp. 13-22, and R. Wellek and A. Warren, *Theory of Literature* (New York: Harcourt, Brace & World, 3rd edn, 1956 [1942]), pp. 39-40.

endless stream of seemingly unanswerable questions posited by historical criticism, or the lack of regard for the text in its final form except as it points to its earlier stages of production, can probably understand the attractiveness that this theory has had for both its original proponents and those New Testament exegetes who have recently discovered it.

Unfortunately, perhaps because of the greater perceived import of the history surrounding the New Testament texts, much that has taken the title 'formalist' or 'New Critical' in New Testament exegesis has not been able to shed its historical-critical presuppositions and agendas. This has led, again, to pseudo-literary/pseudo-historical treatments that serve merely to reinforce older historical-critical work, with little new material added to the discussion.

Not all the New Testament New Critical work, however, has had this failing. Most notable amongst the successful New Critical treatments of New Testament texts has been that of David Rhoads and Donald Michie, *Mark as Story*.[13] It is unique in that it is co-written by both a New Testament scholar and a 'secular' literary critic. It reads more like a work of 'secular' literary criticism than a work of New Testament exegesis, and the authors are very clear about their presuppositions and goals both in the introduction and throughout the book:

> The purpose of this book is to aid in recovering the experience of the Gospel of Mark as unified narrative, to better understand the story as a whole and to appreciate its impact...
>
> The study of narrative emphasizes the unity of the final text. Such a study of the formal features of Mark's gospel tends to reveal the narrative as a whole cloth. The narrator's point of view in telling the story is consistent throughout. The plot is coherent: events that are anticipated come to pass; conflicts are resolved; predictions are fulfilled. The characters are consistent...the unity of the gospel is apparent in the remarkable integrity of the story it tells. Although scholars know little about the origin of this gospel, a literary study of its formal features suggests that the author succeeded in creating a unified narrative.[14]

A good example of this method at work is found in their discussion of one of the structural features of the Gospel—the way Mark

---

13   D. Rhoads and D. Michie, *Mark as Story: An Introduction to the Narrative of a Gospel* (Philadelphia: Fortress Press, 1982).

14   Rhoads and Michie, *Mark as Story*, pp. 2-3.

arranges episodes in concentric patterns:

> In the concentric pattern...related episodes form rings around one central
> episode. A comparison of the paired episodes illuminates and enriches
> many aspects of these stories.
>
> The five conflicts between Jesus and the authorities in Galilee show a
> concentric relationship of A, B, C, B^1, and A^1. Paired episodes A and A^1
> along with B and B^1 form an outer and inner ring around the central
> episode C. Episode A (the healing of the cripple) and episode A^1 (the
> healing of the withered hand) reflect each other in structure, content, and
> theme: both occur indoors, involve the healing of the body, and include
> the same characters (Jesus, the authorities and the person healed); both
> healings are delayed while the narrator reveals unspoken accusations
> against Jesus (blasphemy in A and healing on the Sabbath in A^1); and both
> involve serious legal penalties. Furthermore, in both episodes Jesus
> responds to the unspoken accusations with rhetorical questions. Cleverly
> he avoids indictment by healing instead of pardoning sins (thus avoiding
> the charge of blasphemy) in episode A, and by not touching the withered
> hand (thus avoiding the charge of doing work on the Sabbath) in episode
> A^1.
>
> Episodes B (eating with sinners) and B^1 (picking grain on the Sabbath)
> are also related: both are concerned with eating and with uncleanness
> (from toll collectors in B and from violation of the Sabbath in B^1). The
> form of both episodes includes an action, the authorities' objections and
> Jesus' explanation of the action. Both involve the same characters (Jesus,
> disciples, and the authorities). In both cases, Jesus answers with a proverb
> and then with a statement of his purpose and authority.
>
> These four episodes (A, B, B^1, A^1) form two concentric patterns
> around episode C in which Jesus teaches about fasting (in contrast to the
> eating theme of B and B^1). By contrast with other episodes, the setting is
> indefinite and the questioners are not specified. Nor are the questioners
> hostile. As a result, this central episode focuses on Jesus' response rather
> than on conflicts or actions, and Jesus' response illuminates all five of the
> episodes that make up the concentric pattern...
>
> These five 'conflict' episodes create a dramatic experience for the
> reader.[15]

One can see immediately the potential exegetical significance of this
kind of approach. Indeed, this illustrates what is probably the greatest
strength of the formalist approach (and much reader-oriented

---

15   Rhoads and Michie, *Mark as Story*, pp. 51-53.

criticism), namely that it deals with the text and its form *as it has been received*, which is patently *not* the point of most historically oriented criticism.

Exegetically, formalism and the forms of reader-oriented criticism related to it are probably the most significant methodologies. They have the most to offer to an exegete who is interested in an interpretation that is somewhat *text* oriented. One point must be noted, however. Both formalism and reader-oriented criticism (see below) are well past their prime in 'secular' literary studies. The forms of these criticisms that still have significant voices have worked through many methodological problems and issues, responded to many theoretical challenges, and incorporated many new ideas. New Testament literary criticism must make an effort both to catch up to and to stay abreast of these changes and developments, so as to avoid falling into methodological problems that have already been addressed by 'secular' literary critics.

Textual Discourse: Reader-Oriented Criticism

Reader-oriented criticism is perhaps the hardest to define of the three criticisms at which we are looking. In both New Testament study and 'secular' literary criticism, reader-oriented criticism swings from pseudo-deconstructionist[16] to pseudo-formalist,[17] and everywhere in between.

Reader-oriented criticism rests to varying degrees on the work of several different theorists. The most notable of these are Wolfgang Iser and Stanley Fish, whose work has been at the forefront of the two major schools of reader-oriented criticism. Iser's work has been a mediating position between formalism and a more radical form of reader-response. He recognizes that there is much that is stable in a text, but allows that there is enough that is indeterminate so as to allow for the reader to have a hand in creating the 'work' (as opposed to the simple 'text', which acts as a guide to the reader in the act of

---

16 Moore's earliest work exhibits this mixture of reader-oriented ideas and deconstructionist ones. See especially the permutation of his treatment of John 4 and the theme of living water in the fourth Gospel as it appears in *Literary Criticism and the Gospels*, pp. 131-70.

17 See J.A. Darr's *On Character Building: The Reader and the Rhetoric of Characterization in Luke–Acts* (Literary Currents in Biblical Interpretation; Louisville: Westminster/John Knox Press, 1992) and R.A. Culpepper's *The Anatomy of the Fourth Gospel* (Minneapolis: Fortress Press, 1983), esp. pp. 3-11 and 203-28, discussed below.

reading, and which, in combination with the experience of the reader, forms the 'work').[18] The second school of thought, largely following the lead of Stanley Fish, is more radical, and goes so far as to assert that, without the reader, there is no text.

In New Testament criticism, John Darr and Alan Culpepper are perhaps the two best examples of practitioners of the kind of reader-oriented criticism espoused by Iser. Culpepper is a self-confessed formalist, but his chapter on the reader in *The Anatomy of the Fourth Gospel* goes a long way towards a reader-oriented criticism, while Darr's methodology is more overtly reader-oriented. Both of them emphasize the *implied* reader.[19] Darr's overt reliance on Iser's work puts him firmly in the reader-oriented camp, as the following passage more than amply demonstrates:

> Our search for 'the reader' of Luke–Acts must begin with a good long look in the mirror, for, to a greater or lesser extent, we tend to create readers in our own image. Critics cannot escape the circularities of interpretation by positing a neutral, 'zero degree', objective, transcendent reader, or by appealing to some pristine original audience. To some degree, *the* reader is always *my* reader, a projection of my own experience of reading the text. And, of course, my particular cultural horizon—shaped by factors like gender, class, social setting, education, age, vocation, and ideological orientation—colors that reading.
>
> The imaging of readers is always conditioned by the critic's individual experience and cultural environment. It would be wrong to conclude from this fact, however, that we must simply identify the modern interpreter as *the* reader of Luke–Acts. Indeed, if our treatment of Lukan characters and characterization is to be truly *text-specific*, then the audience to which we

---

[18] W. Iser's view, as his 1972 paper entitled 'The Reading Process: A Phenomenological Approach' (*New Literary History* 3 [1972], pp. 279-99) suggests, owes much to the phenomenology of Martin Heidegger. This may be why it also comes very close to his student, H.-G. Gadamer's concept of 'horizons' in reading, the fusion of which is the essence of interpretation (see *Truth and Method* [New York: Crossroad; London: Sheed and Ward, 2nd edn, 1989], pp. 302-307).

[19] This terminology is drawn from the communications model put forward by the formalist linguist R. Jakobson, later modified by S. Chatman, *Story and Discourse: Narrative Structure in Fiction and Film* (Ithaca, NY: Cornell University Press, 1978), p. 267. Culpepper reproduces the diagram of this model to help facilitate his discussion and demonstrate which parts of the model he finds important for criticism and understanding of texts (see *Anatomy of the Fourth Gospel*, pp. 6-8).

refer should fit the cultural profile of the readers for whom the account was written. That is, we must reconstruct—to the fullest extent possible—the extratextual repertoire, literary skills and basic orientation of the original audience. In doing so, our ultimate purpose is hermeneutical, not historical: we are less concerned with discovering the identities of intended addressees than with ascertaining the type and degree of 'cultural literacy' the author seems to have assumed for his audience. In other words, the question is not 'Who is the reader *per se*?' but rather, *'What did a reader have to bring to a text in order to actualize it competently?'*[20]

A good example of this formalistic reader-oriented criticism at work is found in the following page from Darr's *On Character Building*:

> Luke's story is but a part of a much larger, ongoing story in which God plays the major role.
>
> But how, then, is the reader made aware of God's actions and will? How does one determine what God—this invisible, mysterious super-agent—has done? The answer, of course, is that the readers are provided with the carefully authenticated oracles which explicate how the divine impinges on personages, events, and natural forces. It has long been noted that the author was very careful to establish precise lines of authority among characters, and to confirm every major new phase in the progression of Christianity. . . .
>
> Readers of Luke–Acts soon recognize that the divine impinges on this narrative world in certain carefully designated ways. The sources of divine accreditation and approbation are delimited and specified meticulously. Much like the narrator's perspective, the divine frame of reference provides the audience with a consistent and highly authoritative guide for constructing and/or evaluating characters and their roles in the action.[21]

In ostensible contrast to the Iserian method adopted by Darr, Robert Fowler places his work on the other end of the reader-oriented scale, following Stanley Fish.[22] Unfortunately, Fowler's work is not entirely

---

20   Darr, *On Character Building*, pp. 25-26, emphasis on the last sentence added.

21   Darr, *On Character Building*, pp. 51-53.

22   Fish's work underwent a major shift over time—whereas he started out with the idea of 'affective stylistics', which was very close to the approach espoused by Iser, his later work went in a much more radical direction, epitomized by his assertion that, without readers, there are no texts. It is this later Fish that Fowler attempts to follow. See S. Fish, *Is there a Text in this Class? The Authority of Interpretive Communities* (Cambridge, MA: Harvard University Press, 1980).

successful at leaving his formalistic and historical-critical roots behind. He asserts that

> once the author finishes the text and gives it to the world, she [sic] no longer has control over it; thereafter the text has a life of its own. Once out of the author's hands, the text is totally dependent on its readers. Such life as it continues to enjoy flows from them. Unless the text is read and comes to life in the reading experience, it is simply a lifeless assemblage of paper, binding, and dried ink. The text has no life or meaning unless life and meaning are conferred upon it by a reader.

This makes good Fishian sense, but seems to be at odds with his following paragraph on the same page:

> Although perhaps indeed 'readers make everything', such slogans over-simplify. Saying that the reader is everything, the way some reader-response critics do, is misleading. Practically speaking, the text is important...[23]

Here, not even a sentence later, Fowler seems to be retreating from the theory that 'the text has no life or meaning unless life and meaning are conferred upon it by a reader', to a more formalist-oriented criticism such as that which we saw in Darr and even in Rhoads and Michie.

Reader-oriented criticism is perhaps the most flexible of all literary criticisms currently being practised in New Testament exegesis. As noted above, it can theoretically range from pseudo-formalistic to pseudo-deconstructionistic work. This range of possibilities may be a strength, but it more often than not displays itself as a weakness—the problem with having so much leeway is that it becomes very difficult to measure the results of one's criticism against the theory one is purportedly following. This is obviously a problem for someone like Fowler, who sounds alternatively formalistic and radically Fishian, but this problem is by no means limited to Fowler's work.

Indeed, as I mentioned above, this is one of the largest problems in New Testament literary exegesis as a whole—its appropriative and hybrid character. Methodological confusion often leads to confused, mis-labeled exegetical results. Seeley, as we saw above, is an example of a critic who has perhaps become enamored with the idea of a particular brand of literary criticism, but who fails to carry it out in any measurable, legitimate way. This is perhaps the key problem to be overcome by New Testament exegetes who wish to make use of

---

[23]   R.M. Fowler, *Let the Reader Understand: Reader-Response Criticism and the Gospel of Mark* (Minneapolis: Fortress Press, 1991), p. 26.

literary criticism, and one which, until it can be addressed, will continue to hamper the establishment and development of literary criticism as a major force in New Testament exegesis.

APPLICATION: A FORMALIST READING OF MATTHEW

This chapter has thus far dealt with a variety of different literary criticisms, showing how some of the major methods have been applied in the study of New Testament texts. As suggested above, however, not every criticism has been equally well received, nor, in my opinion, is equally well-suited to the task of exegesis. My belief is that the formalist-motivated approaches probably have the most potential for exegetical 'pay-off'. The following few pages are an example of a formalist reading of a portion of Matthew's Gospel.

Matthew has long been recognized as a highly organized and well structured piece of literature. This organization and structure has, perhaps, been the most frustrating aspect of the Gospel for those historical critics eager to discern the *ipsissima verba* or 'actual words' of Jesus. And so, hoping to strip away the detritus which the author layered on top of the earliest strands of tradition which he wove into the final form of the Gospel, source and form critics dismantled the structure of the text, interested only in the left-over pieces (pericopes). Later, scholars began to realize that the way in which the Gospel writers put together the different blocks of tradition may have had some significance, and so redaction criticism was born to determine what those significant over-all features might be. The development of redaction criticism brought the Gospel as a whole back into view, but it focuses its lenses on the *seams* between the pieces, which, though a step beyond just looking at the individual pieces, still leaves the Gospels as essentially patchwork blankets made up of unrelated pericopes, and anything which did relate the pieces is seen as revealing 'redactional tendencies'. In a sense, redaction criticism is just source criticism from a different perspective.

And so the turn to a formalist approach to the Gospels (what has often been identified with 'narrative criticism' in Gospel studies). Formalist literary criticism is concerned with studying the Synoptics not so much in the light of the other Synoptics, but rather as finished products in and of themselves. In many ways, the similarities between the Synoptic Gospels have clouded the fact that each one is a complete work of its own, self-referential, and deserving of examination in its own right. Perhaps the Gospel of John has been lucky in this respect, in that, possibly because it is so unlike the others, a great deal of 'literary' work has been done on it. The Synoptics have also begun to garner this kind of attention, as we saw in the first part of this chapter.

Matthew has long been recognized to be very keen to portray Jesus as the replacement of several elements of the national experience and practice of Israel. The place where this Matthean trend is perhaps the most obvious is in ch. 12. There, Jesus asserts that he is greater than, in turn, the Temple (v. 6), Jonah (v. 41), and Solomon (v. 42). One cannot help but think of the early Christian appellation of Jesus as Prophet, Priest, and King, or even, perhaps, the prominence of these three as the trio of pre-Christian loci of messianic expectations.[24] This much is obvious, and has been mentioned many times before, but how does this theme fit in with the developing plot of Matthew's Gospel?

The plot that Matthew establishes from his very first chapter is driving and relentless. From the formal genealogy that introduces this 'book of the generations of Jesus Christ, son of David, son of Abraham' (1:1) until the end of the Gospel, the movement of the plot-line is the most important and significant factor of the work. One manner in which Matthew develops the plot-line and characterization of Jesus is with the language of seeing, especially with imperatives of sight.

Throughout the Gospel we the readers are implored to 'behold...'[25] many things. The 'behold...' idiom is one that is frequent in the longer Synoptic Gospels—59 times in Matthew and 55 in Luke. It is somewhat less frequent in Mark and John, with seven and four occurrences respectively. However, this idiom seems to have special significance for Matthew. His most common use of this word is as a narrative marker, which sets off either the introduction of or conclusion to significant events in the Gospel.[26] This usage as a clear

---

[24]   See, especially, *T. Levi* 18:2, where the offspring of Levi is called prophet, priest and king. This is often suggested to be the person of Alexander Janeus, the only Hasmonean ruler (who were all both kings and priests) who was also known as a prophet, thus being the only figure in the history of Israel to bring these three together.

[25]   ἰδού, the particle formed from the frozen aorist active imperative of εἶδον.

[26]   Examples of this are numerous. Some of the more significant are through-out the infancy narrative at 1:20, 23; 2:1, 9, 13, 19; at Jesus' baptism and temptation in 3:16, 17; 4:11; as well as throughout the rest of the Gospel, often in the context of miracle stories, 8:2, 24, 29, 32, 34; 9:2, 3, 10, 18, 20, 32; 12:2, 10, 46; 15:22; 17:3, 5; 19:16; 20:30. Perhaps the most noticeable areas in the Gospel

marker of narrative development, which is the most common use of the word throughout the Gospel, forms a backdrop against which the more striking usages occur, when it is almost always on the lips of Jesus, with only three exceptions: Gabriel in 1:23, the Pharisees at 12:2, and Peter at 19:16.[27] This idiom, while it may very well relate a usual pattern of speech for those of the time, on the basis of the fact that Matthew includes it at places that the other Synoptics do not, even when there is a parallel passage, seems indeed to hold special significance for him.

In the first sixteen chapters of Matthew, up to the point in the plot where Jesus begins 'to show his disciples that he must go to Jerusalem and suffer many things...' (16:21), there is an element of tension that builds up for the reader, because it becomes patently clear early on that the confrontations between the teacher Jesus and the Pharisees are such that they will not end happily. The fact that the readers can see this quite clearly, while the characters in the narrative do not, works well for the development of the tension of this first part of the Gospel's plot. One gets the sense that the characters in the Gospel are being swept along, with Jesus, the protagonist, being the only character who is aware of the consequences of his actions. Of course, as the readers are also aware of this tension, we must be aware that any audience or readers of this book would have been (and are still) assumed to have been aware of the end of the story, knowing what the outcome of Jesus' seemingly flagrant disregard for these authorities will be. Matthew was quite aware of the fact that the readers knew the ending already, and thus the point of the book is not to keep the readers in the dark, but rather to help them understand the significance of and reasons for the ending. However, until this fact is made clear by Jesus himself, right after Peter's confession, no one else seems to understand the import of the events that are taking place. This process

---

where this usage occurs (largely unparalleled in the other Synoptic Gospels) are the passion, resurrection and resurrection appearances: 26:47, 51; 27:51; 28:2, 7, 9. ἰδού is also found on the lips of Jesus in several parables, and as a part of several Old Testament quotations. Although it is not my purpose here to discuss the relationships between the Gospels, it is interesting to note that, of the 34 usages as a narrative marker, where the narratives are paralleled in one or both of the other Synoptics, Matthew's use of ἰδού is only paralleled four times by Luke, twice by Mark using the form ἴδε, and once by Mark using ἰδού.

27   This list does not include the occurrence in 12:47, as it seems that, on the basis of both the external textual evidence and the lack of parallel for this type of usage in Matthew for ἰδού, it should be excluded.

of hinting on Matthew's part skillfully adds to the tension which builds up until the secondary climaxes[28] of Peter's confession and the subsequent revelation by Jesus of his future in Jerusalem. The theme of replacement in the Gospel is very important in building up this dramatic tension, so that, when Matthew tells us that Jesus begins to instruct his disciples regarding his death, we the readers are not surprised that death is at the end of this chain of events.

The three usages of ἰδού ('behold') which stand out in this first half of the Gospel, and which firmly establish the theme of replacement, are all found within ch. 12. The first, on the lips of the Pharisees in 12:2, culminates with Jesus saying, '...I say to you that one greater than the Temple is here' (12:6). The second two, both in response to the demand by the scribes and Pharisees for a sign, are in vv. 41 and 42: '...behold, one greater than Jonah is here', and, 'behold, one greater than Solomon is here'. It is significant that these three occurrences in this narrative[29] begin with a question from Jesus' frequent interlocutors in this Gospel, the Pharisees. It is an integral part of Matthew's irony that some of the most significant observations and revelations concerning Jesus come from the mouths of those most antagonistic to him.[30] This pattern of ironic admissions continues at the beginning of this chapter when the Pharisees point out to Jesus that his disciples are not acting in accordance with their idea of the Law. This is, although they do not realize it, an admission that something special is going on when it comes to Jesus. Otherwise, why would they merely ask him about it, rather than *do* something about it? Why use it as an excuse to question Jesus? If there was not some tacit understanding that Jesus was a teacher to be reckoned with, then the disciples would have been handled on their own, which they are obviously not in this case. Instead, *Jesus* is made to answer for his

---

[28]   By a 'secondary climax', I mean a resolution of tension in the plot-line which is not that which forms the pivotal development in the book. The primary climax of this Gospel is not until the end, when Jesus is resurrected from the dead.

[29]   Set off at the opening with the formulaic, 'In that time...' (12:1), and, at its closing, with 13:1, 'In that day...'

[30]   The most striking example of this is in the infancy narrative, when the unsuspecting Magi tip Herod off to the fact that they have astrological proof that a king of the Jews has been born, to which he replies, 'Where is *the Christ* to be born?' (2:4, emphasis added). The fact that this admission of Jesus' messiahship is on the lips of his first human enemy is easily overlooked by those already convinced of this fact, but to one not so convinced, or to those newly initiated to the story of Jesus' life, what a striking admission!

disciples' perceived misdeeds, which gives him the opportunity to tell the Pharisees why he has allowed them to do such a thing. Throughout, he is seen as the one in control, and his statement that one greater than the Temple has come is the height of the replacement theme in Matthew.

The scene has been set for some fairly tense words to pass between Jesus and the Pharisees by the time we reach ch. 12, and we the readers are not disappointed. This time, in contrast to an earlier exchange in ch. 9, the Pharisees know to ask Jesus first, rather than his disciples, and they are rewarded with the fairly clear statement that Jesus is antagonistic both to them and to their conception of the Law. Instead of offering a rival interpretation of the Law, Jesus argues that the Law itself is broken by the priests in the process of the Temple worship (something which was seen as inviolate, the center of Jewish religious and cultural identity), but even that is meaningless, because, as he says, 'I tell you, something (or, someone) greater than the Temple is here' (12:6). This claim on Jesus' part, whether it is to be understood as a claim which he makes for himself, or a claim that he makes concerning the kingdom of heaven which he has been proclaiming (the verb is without an expressed subject, and is sufficiently ambiguous to allow either reading), is beyond anything that he has said before in the Gospel. And then, concluding an inclusio[31] begun at 9:13 during the earlier exchange of hostilities between Jesus and the Pharisees, he says to them, 'But if you knew what it is, "I desire mercy and not sacrifice", you would not have condemned the blameless, for the son of man is lord of the Sabbath' (12:7, 8). In contrast to their claim to merely have the proper *interpretation* of the Law, he, Jesus, 'the son of man', is over all of it, Sabbath, Law, and, most importantly, Temple.

The last set of confrontations was over the fact that Jesus and his disciples ate with sinners and tax-collectors. This time, they do not question Jesus, but rather his disciples, exactly the opposite of the pattern in ch. 12. In fact, they never ask Jesus a question at all in ch. 9, but rather he voluntarily offers the words of Hosea, 'Go and learn what this means, "I desire mercy and not sacrifice"' (Matt. 9:13; cf.

---

[31] 'Inclusio' is a term used to refer to a section of a particular work that is set off from the rest, often by a formulaic expression at either end. From an exegetical standpoint, such things are quite important, as they can provide important keys to understanding what the author is conveying by the way that he has arranged the material within the delineated section.

Hos. 6:6), after overhearing their question to the disciples. Significantly, this previous exchange also follows an ἰδού phrase, which introduces the fact that 'many tax-collectors and sinners, coming, reclined with Jesus and his disciples' (9:10). In the intervening narrative, among other things, John's disciples question Jesus about the differences between his disciples and himself, and the Pharisees. This follows directly on from the run-in over eating with undesirables, and allows Jesus the chance to discourse on the very differences to which the reader was just introduced in narrative format. The reaction of the Pharisees to Jesus' subsequent healings and the acclaim he receives as 'Son of David' (9:27), as well as being something that has never been seen before in Israel (9:33), is that, 'By the ruler of demons he casts out demons' (9:34). This exchange gains significance and completion in ch. 12.

After this exchange, the calling of the Twelve, and discourses on future persecutions, troubles, and rewards, John's disciples reappear. This time they have been sent directly from John, and are there to ask him if he is indeed the Christ. Jesus' cryptic response may very well be an admission on his part of his status as messiah that would only be able to be fully understood by John's disciples,[32] but the continuing discourse that sets up those who are 'least in the kingdom of heaven' (11:11) to be greater than John is clear in its intention to place Jesus' followers (and himself) on a higher plane than those who have gone before.

Back in ch. 12, as with the earlier cycle of confrontation vignettes in ch. 9, following rather quickly on the primary confrontation is another, regarding the permissibility of healing on the Sabbath. This confrontation is also introduced with an ἰδού phrase: 'and behold, a man having a withered hand' (12:9). Jesus apparently heals the man, although the healing is not done by any word or command, but merely seems to have taken place while Jesus was debating with the Pharisees about the lawfulness of doing good on the Sabbath. This event causes the Pharisees to plot 'how to destroy him' (12:14).

Jesus' healing continues after this first run-in with the Pharisees in ch. 12, which is followed by the programmatic quotation of Isa. 42:14 (Matt. 12:18-21). Then we encounter the second of the triad of

---

[32]   It is possible that this passage makes reference to a tradition shared by a document from Qumran (4Q521), which may have also been known by the disciples of John the Baptist. For a discussion, see C.A. Evans, *Jesus and his Contemporaries: Comparative Studies* (Leiden: Brill, 1995), pp. 127-29.

replacement statements in the chapter. In 12:22, a blind and dumb demoniac is brought to Jesus for healing. Jesus heals him, restoring both his sight and his ability to speak. This causes many who witness this event to wonder, out-loud, whether this could be the 'Son of David' (12:23), a significant term in Matthew (starting even with the genealogy in ch. 1), probably having much to do with Jesus' status as the messiah. However, the Pharisees' response to this is that Jesus is casting out demons by 'Beelzebul, the prince of demons' (12:24). The previous incident in ch. 9, where these two elements (both 'Son of David' and the accusation of Jesus' ability to cast out demons coming from Beelzebub) are also in close collocation to each other, comes to a conclusion in this passage. Left open there, its themes are drawn together and interpreted in this passage. It is exactly the same thing that Jesus has done here, as in ch. 9, which has caused the crowds to marvel, and they have marveled in exactly the same way as before, wondering if Jesus could be the son of David. This may very well have something to do with the tradition that Solomon, David's son, had become, during the intertestamental period, associated with the control and use of demons (see the *Testament of Solomon*), but, regardless of this possible connection, it is a connection with Jesus that the Pharisees are loathe for the crowds to make, and so they attempt to turn this marvel into a horror. Jesus, however, is said to be 'knowing their thoughts' (12:25—'knowing' is a perfect participial form of the verb translated 'see' in many circumstances cited in this chapter, from the same root as ἰδού), and he responds to them with an argument concerning the absurdity of such a concept, and then provides us with the clearest evidence that the opposition that has formed between him and the Pharisees is final:

> the one not being with me is against me, and the one not gathering with me scatters. On account of this I say to you, every sin and blasphemy will be forgiven people, but the blasphemy of the spirit will not be forgiven. And whoever should speak a word against the son of man, it will be forgiven him, but whoever should speak against the holy spirit, it will not be forgiven him either in this age, or in the one about to [come] (Matt. 12:30-32).

Immediately after this exchange we come to the final two replacement sayings. They come as a result of a request on the part of the scribes and Pharisees for a sign from Jesus (12:38). He responds almost violently with the assertion that they will be given nothing but the sign of Jonah. This, to the readers, is a clear parallel with, indeed, almost a description of the final climax of the book—Jesus' death and resurrection. However, the import of the sign goes further than this—those in Nineveh will rise and judge 'this generation' (12:41), because they (though Gentiles?) repented at the preaching of Jonah, 'and behold, something (or someone) greater than Jonah is here' (12:41). This is followed by a further condemnation for 'this generation', as the Queen of the South will also judge them at the final judgment, because she came to hear the wisdom of Solomon, 'and behold something (or someone) greater than Solomon is here' (12:42). These last two replacement sayings cinch the case against the Pharisees, the scribes, and any others contained in the appellation 'this generation'. Jesus is *almost* saying that he is the replacement for these people, but not quite. He has been hailed twice as Son of David, but said nothing, now he says that something greater even than the Son of David is here. He has preached and taught throughout this first part of the Gospel, but those contained in 'this generation' have not heard. He has embodied the very essence of the three strains of Jewish national experience, and those who should be able to understand do not. The parable that follows on these two replacement sayings may be a reference to the priesthood that had existed since Hasmonean times, and stands as a very direct, though still veiled attack upon it. If this is so, then this would hark back to the first replacement saying at 12:6, and form a direct link between this discourse and Jesus' attack on the religious leaders at the beginning of the chapter.

This language of seeing that drives the plot forward in the Gospel is one of the primary ways in which Matthew structures his work in such a way that the reader is tipped-off that something significant either is happening, is about to happen, or has just concluded that will provide part of the key that will unlock the reasons, the motivation for Jesus' death. After all of the focus on the replacement by Jesus of the most important and cherished parts of the Jewish national experience in ch. 12, ch. 13 provides a string of closely packed references that focus on the seeing language in a new way. The first is the often debated quotation of Isaiah in 13:14 and 15.[33] Here, Jesus explains why he teaches in parables, and answers that the reason he does this is because it fulfills the words of the prophet Isaiah who said,

---

[33]   Often debated because Mark introduces this with ἵνα, probably with a sense of purpose, while Matthew seems to soften it by dropping the ἵνα and introducing it as an explanation, not some sort of prophetic requirement.

hearing, you will hear, but will not understand; seeing, you will see, but you will not see (or perceive), for the heart of this people has been dulled, and they hear with heavy ears, and they close their eyes, lest they should see with [their] eyes and they should hear with [their] ears and understand with [their] heart and they should turn, and I heal them (Matt. 13:14, 15; cf. Isa. 6:9, 10).

This quotation serves as an indictment of all those who have missed the significance of the events of the first part of the Gospel, and as an explanation as to why they have done so. It is important that this reason be given, as this now begins to make sense of what has been taking place. It is followed by the next occurrence of the language of sight, vv. 16 and 17: 'But blessed are your eyes because you see, and your ears because you hear. Truly I say to you that many prophets and righteous ones longed to see what you see, and did not see [it], and to hear what you hear, and did not hear [it].' The disciples, reasonably minor characters in the Gospel up until this point, are explained as the true seers. In a sense, this blessing is similar to the function (although with a dissimilar content) of that at the end of John's Gospel (20:24-29) after the confession of Thomas. In this case, the reader is also one who has seen, and who has heard. The status of the disciples is, in a sense, being conferred on the reader.

Space has allowed this to only be a small and cursory example of how awareness of the literary features of the New Testament writings can aid in their interpretation, and the job is not done. It is important that, in future literary work on the New Testament, we pay attention to the objections that have been and continue to be raised concerning the use of literary criticism to interpret New Testament texts.[34] As Craig Evans puts it, 'there is a danger inherent in the employment of these new methods, if conventional modes of exegesis are neglected. An exegesis that cares little about history...is in danger of misunderstanding the text and distorting the distinctive motifs the respective evangelists may have wished to convey.'[35] In my exegesis

---

[34]   An excellent, if somewhat demanding, overview of the problems with much New Testament literary criticism is S.E. Porter, 'Literary Approaches to the New Testament: From Formalism to Deconstruction and Back', in S.E. Porter and D. Tombs (eds.), *Approaches to New Testament Study* (JSNTSup, 120; Sheffield: Sheffield Academic Press, 1995), pp. 77-128.

[35]   C.A. Evans, 'Source, Form and Redaction Criticism: The "Traditional" Methods of Synoptic Interpretation', in *Approaches to New Testament Study*, p. 19.

of Matthew in this chapter, I hope it is quite obvious that literary methods by no means have to reject the findings of historical criticism, and are indeed illumined by recourse to them. If literary criticism is to become anything but a side-show in future biblical criticism, it is important that this link with both history and historical criticism be maintained, and this will potentially lead to the results of both criticisms benefiting from each other's results.

BIBLIOGRAPHY

General Overviews and Introductions to Literary Criticism

Moore, S.D. *Literary Criticism and the Gospels: The Theoretical Challenge.* New Haven: Yale University Press, 1989. (A work written at the tail-end of Moore's reader-oriented phase, it is valuable as an overview, especially if the reader is aware of Moore's radical reader-oriented, almost deconstructionist approach.)

Porter, S.E. 'Literary Approaches to the New Testament: From Formalism to Deconstruction and Back', in S.E. Porter and D. Tombs (eds.), *Approaches to New Testament Study.* JSNTSup, 120. Sheffield: Sheffield Academic Press, 1995, pp. 77-128. (A critical, if slightly over-skeptical, appraisal of the various permutations of New Testament literary criticism containing a manifesto of issues that need to be addressed in future work.)

Scott, W. (ed.). *Five Approaches of Literary Criticism: An Arrangement of Contemporary Critical Essays.* New York: Collier, 1962. (This volume, although somewhat dated, puts together in one place many of the classic essays by the representatives of many of the older styles of criticism [moral, psychological, sociological, archetypal], and includes several essays on formalist criticism.)

Walhout, C., and L. Ryken (eds.). *Contemporary Literary Theory: A Christian Appraisal.* Grand Rapids: Eerdmans, 1991. (This book gives critical reviews of several of the major 'brands' of contemporary literary criticism from a conservative perspective. It is a quite valuable overview.)

Formalist Criticism

Culpepper, R.A. *The Anatomy of the Fourth Gospel.* Minneapolis: Fortress Press, 1983. (Culpepper's examination is both an excellent treatment of the text of John, and a good primer in the basics of formalist, with a little reader-oriented, criticism.)

Eliot, T.S. 'Tradition and the Individual Talent', in *Selected Essays.* London: Faber & Faber, 1932; 3rd edn, 1951, pp. 13-22. (This is the classic essay on the relationship between literary works and the tradition in which they are found.)

Rhoads, D., and D. Michie. *Mark as Story: An Introduction to the Narrative of a Gospel.* Philadelphia: Fortress Press, 1982. (Perhaps the best example of sustained formalist criticism of any New Testament text.)

Ruthven, K.K. *Critical Assumptions.* Cambridge: Cambridge University Press, 1979. (Ruthven's approach to criticism, while not 'formalist' in the strictest sense of the word, incorporates many of the strengths of this particular approach. It remains free from an overly theoretical character while providing many practical helps for the critic.)

Wellek, R., and A. Warren. *Theory of Literature.* New York: Harcourt, Brace & World, 1942; 3rd edn, 1956. (Wellek and Warren is still the basic text of formalist literary criticism.)

Poland, L.M. *Literary Criticism and Biblical Hermeneutics: A Critique of Formalist Approaches.* AAR Academy Series, 48. Chico, CA: Scholars Press, 1985. (A very insightful examination of formalist approaches to New Testament exegesis.)

Reader-Oriented Criticism

Darr, J.A. *On Character Building: The Reader and the Rhetoric of Characterization in Luke–Acts.* Literary Currents in Biblical Interpretation. Louisville: Westminster/John Knox Press, 1992. (A very even-handed and well presented work in the tradition of more formalist-oriented reader-oriented criticism.)

Fish, S. *Is there a Text in this Class? The Authority of Interpretive Communities.* Cambridge, MA: Harvard University Press, 1980. (The basic text of more radical reader-oriented criticism.)

Fowler, R.M. *Let the Reader Understand: Reader-Response Criticism and the Gospel of Mark.* Minneapolis: Fortress Press, 1991. (Although an uneven attempt at applying a Fishian style of reader-oriented criticism to Mark, this reflects the state of play in much reader-oriented New Testament criticism.)

Iser, W. *The Implied Reader: Patterns of Communication in Prose Fiction from Bunyan to Beckett.* Baltimore: Johns Hopkins University Press, 1974. (Iser's basic introduction to his more formalist-oriented kind of reader-oriented criticism.)

_____. *The Act of Reading; A Theory of Aesthetic Response.* Baltimore: Johns Hopkins University Press, 1978. (This book pushes Iser's theoretical conclusions to new heights, with more attention to theoretical rigor than his earlier work.)

Staley, J.L. *Reading with a Passion: Rhetoric, Autobiography, and the American West in the Gospel of John.* New York: Continuum, 1995. (A radical reader-oriented method, bordering on deconstructionism, which shows us how important understanding the American West [or anything from the reader's life] is for the interpretation of John.)

Tompkins, J.P. (ed.). *Reader-Response Criticism: From Formalism to Post-Structuralism.* Baltimore: Johns Hopkins University Press, 1980. (An edited volume containing 12 essays by various practitioners spanning the whole spectrum of reader-oriented criticism. Good for introductions to the various permutations.)

Post-Structural/Deconstructionist Criticism

Bloom, H. *A Map of Misreading*. Oxford: Oxford University Press, 1975. (One of the classics of American deconstructionism.)

De Man, P. *The Resistance to Theory*. Minneapolis: University of Minneapolis Press, 1986. (The most representative example of de Man's criticism.)

Derrida, J. *Of Grammatology*. Trans. G.C. Spivak. Baltimore: Johns Hopkins University Press, 1976. (The basic [if anything in this particular brand of criticism can have such a title] introduction to Derrida's critical enterprise.)

Foucault, M. *The Archaeology of Knowledge*. Trans. A.M. Sheridan Smith. World of Man. New York: Pantheon, 1972. (The most complete presentation of Foucault's post-structuralist approach.)

Moore, S.D. *Mark and Luke in Poststructuralist Perspectives: Jesus Begins to Write*. New Haven: Yale University Press, 1992. (Written in the James Joycean mode, this is a good example of why deconstruction should be avoided as a critical method. Does a very good job of applying and explaining, as much as such can be done, the tenets of deconstructionism.)

_____. *Poststructuralism and the New Testament: Derrida and Foucault at the Foot of the Cross*. Minneapolis: Fortress Press, 1994. (More 'exegetical' than his previous book, this, too, shows us why deconstruction can never be an important force in New Testament exegesis. The creativity and faithfulness to poststructuralist criticism are to be commended. Includes an extended annotated bibliography.)

Norris, C. *Deconstruction: Theory and Practice*. New Accents. London: Routledge, rev. edn, 1991. (A recent, thorough, and accessible introduction and examination of deconstructionist phenomena.)

IDEOLOGICAL CRITICISMS, LIBERATION CRITICISMS, AND WOMANIST AND FEMINIST CRITICISMS

TINA PIPPIN

INTRODUCTION TO THE AREA AND ITS IMPORTANCE FOR NEW TESTAMENT EXEGESIS

During the last half of the twentieth century, the world began to shift out of the colonial empires of Europe and the United States. Independence movements and revolutions reshaped the map, but these changes did not initially have much of an effect on academic biblical scholarship in the countries of the former colonizers. Missionary movements and translations of the Bible continue to uphold the hegemony of the 'West'. In a postmodern age, however, multiple, marginal voices are becoming more prevalent. The debates about the 'original' context of the New Testament are shifting from a myopic focus on historical 'facts' and what the text 'means' to an opening of the conversation with and about the text to multiple readers and meanings. Reading the New Testament is no longer considered a neutral or innocent act; issues of power and domination are being revealed. Part of this revelation includes the importance of the ethics and politics of interpretation and the ethical responsibility of the New Testament scholar in the web of past, present and future relationships between the text and lived experience. New Testament exegetes are finding themselves in a larger interpretative world, where the history of the New Testament as both an oppressive and liberatory text is gaining strength.

The main voices of liberation in New Testament exegesis come from the liberation theologies in the broadly defined areas of Latin America, Asia and Africa. In the United States, African-American biblical hermeneutics and feminist, womanist and mujerista readings are also under the category of liberation hermeneutics. Liberation hermeneutics is a general term for all these interpretative strategies that link theory and practice and emphasize social and cultural location in reading the New Testament. More specifically, liberation criticisms call into question the authority of the biblical canon and the notion of Scripture. Liberation criticisms arise in response to the oppressive systems of racism, sexism, heterosexism, classicism, colonialism and christo-fascism (a term from Dorothee Soëlle). In the 'Third World' (or two-thirds world) and in the 'First World' (or one-third world), those who have traditionally been excluded from power and voice create their own structures for reading the New Testament.

The theoretical base for ideological criticisms comes from the class analysis of Karl Marx. For Marx, ideology was false consciousness, and the ideology of the ruling classes could be revealed using reason and scientific methods. Marxist literary readings attempt to uncover the 'reality' of the text: the discursive practices of ideology present in narrative. The idea of discursive, signifying practices (between human subjects) comes from both Antonio Gramsci and Louis Althusser, and Marxist literary critics such as Fredric Jameson and Terry Eagleton utilize their approaches. Every text and every reading is ideological; even the way one talks about ideology is ideological. Catherine Belsey offers a summary definition of these approaches, stating that ideology is

> the sum of the ways in which people both live and represent to themselves their relationship to the conditions of their existence. Ideology is inscribed in signifying practices—in discourses, myths, presentations and re-presentations of the way 'things' are—and to this extent it is inscribed in the language (1980: 42).

Ideology is about 'lived experience' (Althusser) and about power (Michel Foucault). Texts represent the struggle for power and the complex relations of power. Foucault takes further the Marxist definition of ideology as the mystification or illusion of the values of the ruling classes. Ideology as it relates to power is '...a partial truth, a naturalized understanding or a universalistic understanding or a universalistic discourse...' (Barrett 1991: 168). Ideological criticisms (also called 'ideology critique'; I am using the plural here to emphasize the different types of these criticisms) push against the partial truths in narratives to its 'twin aspirations of emancipation and exposure' (Billig and Simons 1994: 1). Strictly speaking, ideological criticisms are those interpretative methods that use the critical theory of Marxist literary criticism. In a broader sense, all liberation hermeneutics are part of ideological criticisms, because they want to unmask the power relations in writing and interpreting. Also, ideological criticisms provide the theoretical foundation to much liberation hermeneutics, including the Marxist–Christian dialogue, materialist, feminist, postmodern and postcolonial readings of the Bible. Ideological criticisms in the narrow sense are more often found in Hebrew Bible scholarship, but in the broad sense New Testament studies has a wealth of liberatory readings of texts; the readings at Solentiname are perhaps the most comprehensive readings from the oppressed.

Furthermore, in New Testament studies the presence of ideological and liberative criticisms brings new conversation partners and previously neglected aspects of the text into the exegetical discussion. One example is that, while introductory textbooks on the New Testament are beginning to make space for feminist and liberation hermeneutics, this inclusion is still minimal (cf. Pregeant's section, 'Theological and Ideological Interpretation', 1995: 19-21). New Testament exegesis is becoming more interdisciplinary and global, and these criticisms point to the shape and content of future debates.

THE MAIN ISSUES

History, meaning, truth and reality are all terms used in ideological criticisms, and the idea is to subvert the traditional notions of these terms. Whose history, meaning, truth and reality is being represented? In ideological criticisms, the search for cracks in the dominant structure is of fundamental importance. There are relationships in the text—personal, political, structural—but ideology is not linear. Rather, there is a clash of ideologies in a text which forces the reader to make theoretical and practical choices. Who controls the professional and publishing aspects of New Testament studies? What are the ideological commitments of the translators of the New Testament into English and other languages? What is at stake in the interpretative process? For two thousand years the dominant agenda in Christianity has been keeping women submissive to men (and out of the priesthood), arguing that homosexuality is a sin, supporting the physical disciplining of children, accepting the death penalty, legitimizing warfare and Christian participation in it, and anticipating a violent end of the world. Readers have used the New Testament to argue for and against these beliefs and actions. Which interpretations are ethical? Are any and all interpretations allowable? Certain texts have been made central and others, such as, 'sell what you own, and give the money to the poor' (Mark 10:21), have been rationalized. The choices made and the makers of these choices are a focus in liberatory criticisms. Any interpretation that has 'canonical' place in New Testament scholarship is called into question. Different voices engage in a conversation with their own contexts and with traditional, historical modes of interpretation.

Clarice Martin shows the issues of ideological critical readings of the New Testament as connected to race and gender. In her reading of Acts 8, Martin points to the existence of the 'politics of omission' in biblical scholarship that omits Africa and Africans from the discussion of New Testament texts (Martin 1989). From her womanist perspective she concretely encourages African-American biblical hermeneutics to '...encourage black males and black females to assume an advocacy stance in identifying liberatory biblical traditions that promote ideological and existential empowerment for black women at every level of ecclesiastical governance' (Martin 1991: 230). Here the connection between ideological texts and readings is clear as Martin points to the effects of the household codes on the lives of black women in the Church. Interpretation is a political act that has multiple effects on and in the lives of people.

In liberatory readings there is a search for liberatory texts (especially previously neglected ones) and the confrontation with oppressive texts or texts that have an oppressive history of interpretation. Often the text may be oppressive, but as Sheila Briggs relates, there is 'the voice of the oppressed under the text' (Briggs 1989: 137), when the oppressed claim and subvert oppressive texts to liberatory ends. The New Testament is a product of its times, but the dominant readings are questioned and resisted. The voices of the marginalized or the oppressed provide the hermeneutical key to reading the New Testament.

Reconstructive strategies are prevalent in liberatory readings. Mainstream feminist hermeneutics is basically reconstructionalist, claiming a positive place for women in the New Testament. Elisabeth Schüssler Fiorenza developed an important feminist reading of the New Testament that accepts the texts that are liberating to women (and men) as authoritative as the word of God and that rejects the oppressive texts as patriarchal inventions. Schüssler Fiorenza relates: 'Reclaiming the Bible as a feminist heritage and resource is only possible because it has not functioned only to legitimate the oppression of all women...' (1984: xiii). She sets up four reading strategies in feminist biblical hermeneutics, which are: hermeneutics of suspicion, hermeneutics of remembrance, hermeneutics of evaluation and proclamation, hermeneutics of liberative vision and imagination (1992: 52-76). Schüssler Fiorenza uses these strategies to interpret Luke 10:38-42. This text is traditionally positive for women, but the hermeneutic of suspicion shows that the silent woman (Mary) is the one traditionally honored, and Jesus as Lord is still at the center of the story (1992: 62). A hermeneutic of remembrance shows the struggles of Mary and Martha as reflecting the struggles of women in the early Church (1992: 68). The hermeneutics of evaluation and proclamation reveals the paradox of the concept of 'service' and brings forth '...the need to re-envision women's ministry as such a practice of solidarity and justice' and not subordination and self-sacrificial service (1992: 73). The hermeneutics of imagination calls for feminist reinterpretation in which contemporary women retell the story from their own contexts and experiences (1992: 73-76). With these critical tools the reader is to explore the oppressive and liberative parts of the text and work toward a historically reconstructive, liberative paradigm of reading. Both women and men can share in the liberating power of the New Testament and work toward dismantling oppressive structures.

USES AND ABUSES OF THE TOPIC IN EXEGESIS

Ideological criticism of the New Testament is about how one reads and appropriates the text. Stephen Moore traces the significance of the term ideology as used in relation to point of view in narratological readings of the New Testament (1989: 56-63). One example is Alan Culpepper's use of the term 'ideological point of view' to describe the narrator's 'stereoscopic view', but partial telling, in the Gospel of John. The narrator leads the audience toward belief in Jesus as the preexistent Logos (1983: 32-34; based on the poetics of Boris Uspensky). This idea of the ideology/point of view of the authors, narrators and characters of a story is the prominent usage of the term ideology by New Testament critics. This definition keeps ideology in the realm of literary devices and structures. Fred Burnett takes this narratological idea further to disclose the ideology of the implied author in the Gospel of Matthew. Burnett argues that the reader is to take sides with Jesus against 'the Jews', thus producing an anti-Jewish ideology in the Gospel: 'The formation of "the Jews" as a negative topos, rejecting Jesus and thus separated from their father-God, is an ideological construction. I contend that real readers through the centuries have read Matthew correctly because they have been manipulated by the anti-Jewish norm of the text...' (1992: 175). Burnett is pointing to the existence of multiple readings of the text across time and the hermeneutical effects of this anti-Jewish ideology in 'lived experience'.

The Bible and Culture Collective pushes the use of ideology even further into the realm of social and political relations. The definition is that 'ideological reading...is a deliberate effort to read against the grain—of texts, of disciplinary norms, of traditions, of cultures' (1995: 275). Ideological criticism involves acts of reading that are both resisting and engaging (cf. Sugirtharajah 1995: 316). Examples of New Testament readings come from materialist readings of the Gospel of Mark from Fernando Belo and Ched Myers (see the discussion in The Bible and Culture Collective, 1995: 293-300). Belo focuses his semiological reading of Mark on the subversive political ideology that he calls 'materialist ecclesiology' (1981: 5). Belo's interest is in the social formation and transformation and uses a logical, semiological method to reveal how ideology works in the text. Myers has a similar concern, but focuses more on political hermeneutics in determining that Mark is a subversive Gospel of liberation of the poor from the dominant Roman power. Mark's Gospel holds the discourse of liberation in ways that contemporary oppressed people can utilize in their struggles for justice.

R.S. Sugirtharajah gathers a group of marginal voices together in his collection of essays. His main interest is in relating postcolonial theory to global experiences of the Bible. In his own exegesis, he shows different readings of Paul's conversion experience and then offers a 'dialogical approach' based on interfaith experiences. This approach '...acknowledges, the validity of the varied and diverse religious experiences of all people and rules out any exclusive claim to the truth by one religious tradition...every religion is worthy of love and respect' ([ed.] 1995: 310). Sugirtharajah sees conversion in a broader sense—that one might not be converted from Hinduism to Christianity but be able to combine elements of both religions, as Paul did with Judaism and belief in Jesus. Thus, Sugirtharajah finds Paul's conversion as a transformative experience ([ed.] 1995: 312). This approach has radical ramifications for New Testament exegesis, for it is open to including sacred Scripture from other religious traditions (e.g. the story of Rama from the Ramayana used in different Hindu groups in different ways) and different cultural experiences (visiting the Hindu temple) ([ed.] 1995: 314). There is no hegemony of Christianity in Sugirtharajah's liberatory method. He states: 'All religions contain liberative as well as oppressive elements and the hermeneutical task is to enlist the liberative aspects to bring harmony and social change to all people' ([ed.] 1995: 310). This idea echoes Eagleton: 'If a theory of ideology has value at all, it is in helping to illuminate the processes by which such liberation from death-dealing beliefs may be practically effected' (1991: 224). There is a revolutionary, egalitarian and transformative nature to liberatory criticisms, and the effect on New Testament exegesis is to bring new contextual readings to the text.

Another approach to an interfaith global perspective has been made by Fernando Segovia and Mary Ann Tolbert in two workshops they organized on social location criticism. Basically, the social location of the interpreter influences the interpretation. Exegesis occurs in the context of struggle—predominantly of the struggle against (white, male EuroAmerican) meta- or master-narratives, since these narratives have historically excluded any global conversation (Segovia 1995: 32). Social location is also called the 'politics of location' (Tolbert 1995: 306), a term from feminist poet Adrienne Rich. Individuals often have multiple identities and experience multiple struggles that affect their reading of the New Testament.

In conclusion, ideological criticisms lead to careful, committed readings and provide a critical edge. When New Testament scholars read the Bible, they invent ideologies. Liberatory readings are creations of new (utopian) narratives. Does the reader submit to or revolt against the ideologies of a text? Ideological and liberatory criticisms allow the readers choices and the chance to break out of any hegemonic interpretative discourse. The old stories live and function in new ways, converging with readers' lives and stories. Ideological criticisms shake New Testament exegesis from its scientific, historical-critical base and can lead to what Schüssler Fiorenza calls '"the dance of interpretation" as a critical rhetorical process' (1992: 75). The interpretative process opens up to a wealth of possibilities. Rather than focusing on the impossibilities of what an exegete cannot know (e.g. the 'meaning' of a text), the emphasis is on possibilities for dialogues—and for liberation.

BIBLIOGRAPHY

Barrett, M.
1991   *The Politics of Truth: From Marx to Foucault*. Stanford, CA: Stanford University Press.

Belo, F.
1981 *A Materialist Reading of the Gospel of Mark.* Trans. M.J. O'Connell. Maryknoll: Orbis.

Belsey, C.
1980 *Critical Practice.* London: Methuen.

The Bible and Culture Collective
1995 *The Postmodern Bible.* New Haven: Yale University Press.

Billig, M., and H.W. Simons
1994 'Introduction', in Simons and Billig (eds.), *After Postmodernism: Reconstructing Ideology Critique.* London: Sage Publications: 1-11.

Briggs, S.
1989 'Can an Enslaved God Liberate? Hermeneutical Reflections on Philippians 2:6-11'. *Semeia* 37: 137-53.

Burnett, F.W.
1992 'Exposing the Anti-Jewish Ideology of Matthew's Implied Author: The Characterization of God as Father'. *Semeia* 59: 155-91.

Cannon, K.G., and E. Schüssler Fiorenza (eds.)
1989 *Interpretation for Liberation. Semeia* 47.

Culpepper, R.A.
1983 *Anatomy of the Fourth Gospel: A Study in Literary Design.* Philadelphia: Fortress Press.

Eagleton, T.
1991 *Ideology: An Introduction.* London: Verso.

Eagleton, T. (ed.)
1994 *Ideology.* New York: Longman.

Felder, C.H. (ed.)
1991 *Stony the Road we Trod: American Biblical Interpretation.* Minneapolis: Fortress Press.

Gottwald, N.K., and R.A. Horsley (eds.)
1993 *The Bible and Liberation: Political and Social Hermeneutics.* Maryknoll: Orbis.

Jameson, F.
1981 *The Political Unconscious: Narrative as a Socially Symbolic Act.* Ithaca, NY: Cornell University Press.

Jobling, D., and T. Pippin (eds.)
1993 *Ideological Criticism of Biblical Texts. Semeia* 59.

Keohane, N.O., M.Z. Rosaldo, and B.C. Gelpi (eds.)
1983 *Feminist Theory: A Critique of Ideology.* Chicago: University of Chicago Press.

Martin, C.J.
1989 'A Chamberlain's Journey and the Challenge of Interpretation for Liberation'. *Semeia* 47: 105-35.
1991 'The Haustafeln (Household Codes) in African American Biblical Interpretation: "Free Slaves" and "Subordinate Women"', in Felder (ed.) 1991: 206-31.

Moore, S.D.
1989 *Literary Criticism and the Gospels: The Theoretical Challenge.* New Haven: Yale University Press.

Myers, C.
1988 *Binding the Strong Man: A Political Reading of Mark's Story of Jesus.* Maryknoll: Orbis.

Newsom, C.A., and S.H. Ringe (eds.)
1992 *The Women's Bible Commentary.* Louisville: Westminster/John Knox Press.

Pregeant, R.
1995 *Engaging the New Testament: An Interdisciplinary Introduction.* Minneapolis: Fortress Press.

Rowland, C., and M. Corner
1989 *Liberating Exegesis: The Challenge of Liberation Theology to Biblical Studies.* Louisville: Westminster/John Knox Press.

Schüssler Fiorenza, E.
1983 *In Memory of Her: A Feminist Theological Reconstruction of Christian Origins.* New York: Crossroad.
1984 *Bread Not Stone: The Challenge of Feminist Biblical Interpretation.* Boston: Beacon Press.

Schüssler Fiorenza, E. (ed.)
1993 *Searching the Scriptures.* I. *A Feminist Introduction.* New York: Crossroad.

Segovia, F.F.
1995 '"And They Began to Speak in Other Tongues": Competing Modes of Discourse in Contemporary Biblical Criticism', in Segovia and Tolbert (eds.) 1995a: 1-32.

Segovia, F.F., and M.A. Tolbert (eds.)
1995a *Reading from this Place.* I. *Social Location and Biblical Interpretation in the United States.* Minneapolis: Fortress Press.
1995b *Reading from this Place.* II. *Social Location and Biblical Interpretation in Global Perspective.* Minneapolis: Fortress Press.

Sugirtharajah, R.S.
1995 'Inter-Faith Hermeneutics: An Example and Some Implications', in Sugirtharajah (ed.) 1995: 306-18.

Sugirtharajah, R.S. (ed.)
1995 *Voices from the Margin: Interpreting the Bible in the Third World.* Maryknoll: Orbis.

Tamez, E. (ed.)
1989 *Through her Eyes: Women's Theology from Latin America.* Maryknoll: Orbis.

Tolbert, M.A.
1995 'The Politics and Poetics of Location', in Segovia and Tolbert (eds.) 1995a: 305-17.

Zizek, S. (ed.)
1994 *Mapping Ideology.* New York: Verso.

SOCIAL-SCIENTIFIC CRITICISM

STEPHEN C. BARTON

INTRODUCTION: ISSUES OF DEFINITION AND BACKGROUND

Social-scientific criticism of the New Testament is best understood as a development of historical criticism (Barton 1995). As such, it is part of the overall task of interpreting the New Testament texts in the context of the first-century Mediterranean world from which they come. However, whereas historical criticism traditionally focuses on questions of dating, authorship, language, genre, historical background, the history of the tradition, and the particularity of historical events narrated in the texts, social-scientific criticism asks questions of a different kind, to do more with the typical social patterns and taken-for-granted cultural conditions most likely to have characterized the New Testament world. Howard Kee (1989: 65-69) has grouped these social-scientific questions in seven categories: boundary questions, authority questions, status and role questions, ritual questions, literary questions with social implications, questions about group functions, and questions concerning the symbolic universe and the social construction of reality. The claim of 'sociological exegesis' is that, by asking a different set of questions, aspects of the text often left hidden from view by traditional methods are allowed to come to the surface (cf. Garrett 1992: 89-90).

Putting it another way, whereas historical criticism focuses diachronically on relations of cause and effect over time, social-scientific criticism focuses synchronically on the way meaning is generated by social actors related to one another by a complex web of culturally-determined social systems and patterns of communication. This difference may be compared to that between interpreting a motion picture, in which meaning arises in the viewer's response to a succession of frames in sequence over time, and interpreting a single frame, where meaning is sought in the relation of the subjects to each other and their environment as they are caught in a single moment. The shift is from a simple, linear, cause-and-effect model of interpretation to one which tries to engage in what anthropologist Clifford Geertz (1973: 3-30) refers to as 'thick description' in interpretation.

A useful definition is the one given recently by a leading North American exponent of the method, John H. Elliott (1995: 7):

> Social-scientific criticism of the Bible is that phase of the exegetical task which analyzes the social and cultural dimensions of the text and of its environmental context through the utilization of the perspectives, theory, models, and research of the social sciences. As a component of the historical-critical method of exegesis, social-scientific criticism investigates biblical texts as meaningful configurations of language intended to communicate between composers and audiences. In this process it studies (1) not only the social aspects of the form and content of texts but also the conditioning factors and intended consequences of the communication process; (2) the correlation of the text's linguistic, literary, theological (ideological), and social dimensions; and (3) the manner in which this textual communication was both a reflection of and a response to a specific social and cultural context—that is, how it was designed to serve as an effective vehicle of social interaction and an instrument of social as well as literary and theological consequence.

Social-scientific criticism has made a considerable impact on interpretation of the New Testament in the past twenty-five years, as a number of bibliographies make clear (e.g. Harrington 1988; Theissen 1989; May 1991; Elliott 1995: 138-74). The reasons for this impact are numerous and of various kinds. They include: the rise to prominence of the social sciences from the late nineteenth century on, and the impact of the sociology of knowledge in a wide range of academic disciplines; the influence on interpretation theory of the hermeneutics of suspicion represented by such intellectual giants as Nietzsche, Durkheim, Marx and Freud; the exhaustion of the historical-critical method as traditionally understood, and the failure of form criticism to fulfil its promise of identifying the *Sitze im Leben* of the New Testament texts; shifts in historiography generally away from the 'great man' view of history typical of Romanticism to one more attentive to history 'from below', with a much stronger popular and social dimension; the influence of the discovery of texts and archeological remains, as at Qumran, which provide important new comparative data for social history and sociological analysis; and the surfacing of different kinds of questions to put to the New Testament in the light of developments in twentieth-century theology, not least, the failure of liberal theology and the urgent concerns (often of a social and political kind) raised by liberation and feminist theologies.

THE STRENGTHS AND WEAKNESSES OF SOCIAL-SCIENTIFIC CRITICISM

One major strength of the method, implicit in the foregoing, is that social-scientific criticism has revitalized historical criticism of the New Testament by enlarging the agenda of interpretation, allowing a different set of questions to be put to the text, and providing methods and models to help answer these new questions in a controlled and accountable way. Now the reality to which the New Testament texts bear such profound and brilliant witness is able to be grasped more fully by the interpreter: that the texts have a social and political dimension as well as an individual and religious dimension; that the transformation involved in becoming a follower of Jesus is a transformation of body as well as soul; and that incorporation into Christ through repentance and baptism involves taking on a new identity and participating in a new society. Robin Scroggs (1980: 165-66) put the point well in a programmatic address to New Testament scholars in Paris in 1978:

> To some it has seemed that too often the discipline of the theology of the New Testament (the history of *ideas*) operates out of a methodological docetism, as if believers had minds and spirits unconnected with their individual and corporate bodies. Interest in the sociology of early Christianity is no attempt to limit reductionistically the reality of Christianity to social dynamic; rather it should be seen as an effort to guard against a reductionism from the other extreme, a limitation of the reality of Christianity to an inner-spiritual, or objective-cognitive system. In short, sociology of early Christianity wants to put body and soul together again.

Thus, social-scientific criticism offers the possibility of enlarging our understanding both of the world behind the text and the narrative world within the text, as well as of ourselves as culturally-embedded interpreters of the text. It makes possible what Wayne Meeks (1986) has called 'a hermeneutics of social embodiment'. The creative outworking of this kind of approach can now be seen in a very wide range of studies on every New Testament text (surveyed in Barton 1992). Classic amongst these are John Gager's analysis of the social world of early Christianity as millenarian (Gager 1975), Gerd Theissen's pioneering work on the Palestinian social setting of the Jesus movement (Theissen 1978), J.H. Elliott's sociological exegesis of 1 Peter (Elliott 1981), Bruce Malina's anthropological approach to 'the New Testament world' (Malina 1981), and Wayne Meeks's study of the urban setting and ethos of Pauline Christianity (1983, indebted to Theissen 1982). This work is increasing rapidly in sophistication. In Pauline studies, for example, Theissen (1987) has experimented more recently with psychological models, Margaret Mitchell has drawn on rhetorical analysis (Mitchell 1991), and Dale Martin has drawn upon a wide range of anthropological data (ancient and modern) to interpret 1 Corinthians (D.B. Martin 1995).

Of course, such work is not without its potential (or real) weaknesses, nor its critics. Some argue that the danger of anachronism in using models from a quintessentially modern discipline like sociology is too great, and will have the disastrous result of giving a reductionist account, allowing the interpreter to find in early Christianity only what the interpreter is looking for already or only what the sociological tools are equipped to discover. The widespread use of the Weberian church-sect typology may be a case in point. In spite of refinements by Bryan Wilson and others (cf. Esler 1987: chap. 3), it may just be too blunt a tool of analysis to do sufficient justice to the startling novelty and historical particularity of the movement inaugurated by Jesus. On the other hand, it may be the case that the typology of the sect or the study of millenarian movements or Weber's theory of the routinization of charisma may draw attention to features of early Christian social dynamics which might otherwise go unnoticed (cf. Barton 1993).

A related concern arises from an awareness of the genealogy of the social sciences in post-Enlightenment atheistic positivism. Recently, John Milbank has argued powerfully that, historically-speaking, the social sciences are attempts to 'police the sublime'. They are parasitic on Christian orthodoxy and represent modern heretical deviations grounded in an ideological and methodological atheism (Milbank 1990: 51-143). However, not all theologians share Milbank's hostility to the social sciences (e.g. Flanagan 1992; Roberts 1993), and it is worth noting that some of the most significant analyses of biblical material from a social-scientific perspective have come from sociologists and anthropologists who are themselves religiously committed (e.g. Douglas 1966, 1973). For such as these, it is a matter of accepting that the social sciences offer an interestingly different map of the same ground. Such a map may be illuminating in providing certain kinds of information not otherwise so readily available, but it need not be the only map there is. Sociologist of religion David Martin puts the point sharply (D. Martin 1995: 40):

[S]ociology can have nothing whatever to say about the Incarnation. Sociology might consider the long-term impact of Jesus Christ on human history, or analyse the struggles between groups which surrounded this or that formulation of Christian doctrine, but it cannot trespass directly on who He is. You may remember the conclusion of Schweitzer's *Quest of the Historical Jesus* where Schweitzer says that those who follow Him will *find out* who He is. Sociology is not concerned with that *kind* of finding out. It may identify Christ as a bearer of charisma, that is, as anointed by a powerful grace, but the Incarnation is not within its scope. You cannot even imagine a sociological argument the conclusion of which triumphantly vindicates or disproves the Christian claim concerning Christ.

It may be that Martin overstates his case here, as if social-scientific investigation could have no possible bearing on the truth claims of Christian faith. Since this is not so of historical investigation—the findings of which, it has always been held, can and do bear on Christian doctrine—it is hard to see why social-scientific investigation should be hermetically sealed off from Christian doctrine as Martin suggests. Nevertheless, the basic thrust of his comment helps to allay some of the concerns raised by Milbank that the social sciences are inimical *per se* to the theological and spiritual dimensions of New Testament interpretation.

Perhaps the best way to test this out and to see in general what social-scientific insights have to offer is to take a case study. Since it is probably true to say that most sociological exegesis so far has concentrated on the letters of Paul (cf. Neyrey 1990), the example which follows is a case study from the Gospels.

SOCIAL-SCIENTIFIC METHOD IN PRACTICE: JESUS' REJECTION AT NAZARETH (MARK 6:1-6)

The story of Jesus' rejection in his hometown (*patris*) is a critical story in Mark's Gospel (cf. Barton 1994: 86-96). It brings to a climax the theme of the misunderstanding and rejection of Jesus by his own kith and kin (cf. 3:20-35) and anticipates Jesus' rejection by his people as a whole, a process which culminates in the passion. Strikingly, this is the only occasion in Mark where Jesus' power to heal is thwarted almost completely (6:5). It is also the only occasion when Jesus is said to be 'amazed' (*thaumazein*)—one of a group of terms normally used for the natural response to a revelation or epiphany (e.g. 5:14, 20, 42). Ironically, however, what comes to him as a revelation is the unbelief (*apistia*) of those native to his own locality, people who should have been on Jesus' side. It is no coincidence then that this is the last episode in which we hear of Jesus' kinsfolk in Mark's account.

But how may we account for this crisis in Jesus' hometown? Why is it here, among those familiar to him, that his authority as a wise teacher is challenged and that 'he could do no mighty work'? Why, when his wisdom and miraculous powers are acknowledged (6:2) does his presence nevertheless generate such hostility: 'And they took offense (*eskandalizonto*) at him' (6:3b)? What is the significance of the list of Jesus' brothers and sisters (6:3)? Such questions may be answered quite properly at a number of levels. At the level of Markan theology, for example, we have here a case-study in the nature of unbelief and the need for faith (cf. Marshall 1989: 189-95), where this negative example contrasts powerfully with the two positive examples—the faith of the woman with the haemorrhage (5:25-34, esp. v. 34a) and the faith of Jairus (5:22-24, 35-43, esp. v. 36)—immediately preceding. At the level of Markan poetics, we have a striking instance of Mark's use of irony, where those closest to Jesus fail to recognize him. In spite of the force of their own threefold confession (6:2b), they are like those of whom Jesus spoke earlier who 'see but do not perceive and hear but do not understand' (4:12). At the historical-doctrinal level, it is quite common for the biographical information in 6:3 to be interpreted above all as an aid to discerning the status of the Catholic doctrines of the virginal conception and the perpetual virginity of Mary (cf. Brown 1978: 59-67).

However, while the theological, literary and historical approaches are adequate so far as they go, social-scientific critics would suggest that there are likely to be elements in the narrative which may become intelligible or be thrown into sharper relief if insights from the social sciences are drawn in also. Of particular interest for this approach is the verbal exchange between the townsfolk and Jesus at the very heart of the episode (6:3-4). The 'many' people present in the synagogue express their offense at Jesus by saying, '...Is not this the carpenter, the son of Mary and brother of James and Joses and Judas and Simon, and are not his sisters here with us?'. The sharp riposte of Jesus follows, in proverbial form: 'A prophet is not without honour, except in his own country, and among his own kin, and in his own house'.

From a social-scientific perspective, a number of points are worth attention. First, there is the importance of conflict, since conflict situations bring to the surface usually hidden assumptions about norms, values and things taken-for-granted (Coser 1956). This episode is one of many episodes of conflict in Mark, not a few of which occur in the synagogue and/or on the sabbath (e.g. 1:21-28; 2:23-28; 3:1-6). Such conflicts show that the breaking in of 'the kingdom of God' with the coming of Jesus (1:15) is a social as well as a spiritual reality. Traditionally significant places like the synagogue and the Temple and traditionally important times like the sabbath or the festivals are seen in a new light and reinterpreted in such a way as to make possible novel patterns of action and sociability (cf. Kelber 1974; Malbon 1986). One such novel pattern is referred to explicitly in the opening of this very episode: 'He went away from there and came to his own country; *and his disciples followed him*' (6:1). It seems very likely, from a sociological point of view, that the offense generated by Jesus' appearance in his hometown is related, at least in part, to the challenge to a settled, Galilean peasant community represented by Jesus' itinerant lifestyle in the company of twelve chosen followers (3:13-19; cf. 1:16-20; 2:13-14). Noteworthy in this connection is the fact that, after the rebuttal in Nazareth, Jesus resumes his itinerancy straight away and even sends out the twelve in pairs as an extension of his own work (6:6b-13). It is as if the rebuttal in Nazareth consolidates, not only the hostility of Jesus' kith and kin (cf. 3:20-21, 31-35), but also the alternative pattern of sociability developing around Jesus.

A second point of importance in social-scientific terms is that the conflict focuses on the inter-related issues of identity and authority and the recognition of the same by the giving or withholding of 'honour' and 'faith' (cf. Moxnes 1993). In traditional societies, personal identity is ascribed more than acquired. It is a matter not so much of 'Who am I?', but more of 'To whom do I belong?'. In other words, it is a matter, not so much of individual existential self-discovery (so characteristic of modernity), as of what is given in group membership (Malina 1981: chaps. 3, 5). The most significant group for defining identity in antiquity is the family or (extended) household (*oikos* in Greek, *familia* in Latin) (bibliography in Hanson 1994).

Precisely this conception lies behind the challenge to Jesus in the question put by the people in the synagogue (6:3). They see him in traditional terms where identity and authority are ascribed according to occupation ('the carpenter'), kinship group ('the son of Mary, and brother of James and Joses...'), and accepted location ('and are not his sisters here *with us*?'). Over against this, the identity and authority of Jesus are conveyed in different terms: his unannounced appearance with a retinue of disciples in train (6:1), his adopting the role of teacher in the synagogue (6:2a), and his reputation for wisdom and miracle-working, a reputation which both precedes him and which he seeks to confirm in the people's presence by his words and by the ritual of the laying on of hands (6:2b, 5b). His identity and authority are implicit also in his self-designation (in proverbial terms) as a 'prophet' (6:4).

It is this divergence over the terms for identifying and acknowledging Jesus which lies at the heart of the conflict and which social-scientific analysis helps to clarify. To use categories from Max Weber's analysis of ideal types of authority (Weber 1964), it is a divergence between seeing Jesus in the traditional, kinship and household terms of Galilean village life and seeing him in charismatic terms as the Spirit-inspired Son of God (1:1, 9-11, 12-13, etc.) bringing a new order ('the kingdom of God') into being. Significantly, the novelty of the social dimension of this alternative order is characterized in part by the relativization of ties of natural kinship in favour of ties of fictive kinship. Hence, Jesus' earlier declaration: 'Whoever does the will of God is my brother, and sister, and mother' (3:35; cf. 10:28-30).

We can, however, take the social-scientific analysis of this passage a stage further. The issue from the townspeople's point of view is not just the identity and authority of Jesus: it is a question of their own identity and authority as well. Their question about the source of Jesus' wisdom and power ('Where did this man get all this?') and their refusal to look beyond the horizon of Jesus' occupation and kith and kin for an answer represents a reaffirmation of their own traditional way of seeing things. It is an attempt to reclaim Jesus and to limit his charismatic authority by making him 'one of them' once more. Their 'offense' is strongly interpersonal, an offense directed 'at him' (*en autō*) (6:3b). As such, it is an attempt to shame Jesus by putting him in his place, which is the place ascribed above all by his kin group. To acknowledge that Jesus has another identity and an authority legitimated from some other (supernatural) source would be to acknowledge a new order of things, along with the corollary that they belonged to him instead of him belonging to them.

That Jesus recognizes the response of his compatriots as an attempt to put him in his place is clear from his reply which, in its tripartite form, is an intensifying expansion of the standard proverb (cf. Luke 4:24; John 4:44) and powerfully conveys the strength of his disaffection: 'A prophet is not without honour, except in his own country, *and among his own kin, and in his own house*' (6:4). In consequence, a mutual distancing in social relations takes place. If the people's response is one of 'offense' at him (6:3b), his response is one of 'amazement' at their unbelief (6:6a).

There is one final, remarkable point that invites comment: the fact that Jesus was able to do 'not even one mighty work' (6:5a). If we approach this statement christologically, especially if our Christology is the traditional Chalcedonian 'two natures' orthodoxy, there is an obvious problem stemming from the admission here of a limitation on Jesus' supernatural power (cf. 13:32 also!). Awareness of this problem is reflected, for example, in Charles Cranfield's explanation: 'The point...is not that Jesus was powerless apart from men's faith, but that in the absence of faith he could not work mighty works *in accordance with the purpose of his ministry*' (Cranfield 1959: 197; his emphasis). This may be a legitimate gloss on the narrative which helps to soften the christological dilemma. But perhaps Christology is not the main point here, and the dilemma is an artificial one.

In fact, a social-scientific perspective would suggest that the main point is the breakdown of reciprocity in relations between Jesus and the people. Their refusal to ascribe honour to him on the basis of his wisdom and supernatural powers—and indeed, there is the further possibility that they are attributing Jesus' wisdom and power to a demonic source, as has happened earlier (cf. 3:22-30)—means that there exists no longer a basis in sociability for Jesus to confer the grace which flows from him. It is not that Jesus cannot work a miracle (as the exception in 6:5b shows), but that the basis in human reciprocity and sociability which would make a miracle mean anything does not exist (cf. Pilch 1992). We are talking, in other words, not so much about the nature of Christ, as about the nature of (Palestinian) society and what it is that permits or inhibits positive, life-giving reciprocity. If this is so, then a significant corollary is that the 'unbelief' identified in 6:6a is not just (what we might call) a spiritual failure, it is a social and relational failure as well.

CONCLUSION

The above case-study demonstrates in miniature the way in which social-scientific criticism complements traditional historical and theological concerns in New Testament interpretation by allowing a new set of questions to be put to the text. The potential of this method for revitalizing historical criticism has become apparent in many recent publications (e.g. Neyrey 1991; Theissen 1992; Esler 1995). The discipline has reached a sufficient level of maturity to make it possible now for new 'lives of Jesus' to appear (e.g. Crossan 1991), and new biblical commentaries to be written (e.g. Malina and Rohrbaugh 1992). It remains to be seen, perhaps, whether social-scientific criticism will help revitalize New Testament theology and ethics as well. Certainly, some promising beginnings have been made (e.g. Countryman 1989; Meeks 1993).

BIBLIOGRAPHY

Barton, S.C.
1992   'The Communal Dimension of Earliest Christianity'. *JTS* 43: 399-427.
1993   'Early Christianity and the Sociology of the Sect', in F. Watson (ed.), *The Open Text: New Directions for Biblical Studies?* London: SCM Press: 140-62.
1994   *Discipleship and Family Ties in Mark and Matthew*. Cambridge: Cambridge University Press.
1995   'Historical Criticism and Social-Scientific Perspectives in New Testament Study', in J.B. Green (ed.), *Hearing the New Testament: Strategies for Interpretation*. Grand Rapids: Eerdmans: 61-89.
Brown, R.E. (ed.)
1978   *Mary in the New Testament*. Philadelphia: Fortress Press.
Coser, L.A.
1956   *The Functions of Social Conflict*. London: Routledge & Kegan Paul.
Countryman, L.W.
1989   *Dirt, Greed and Sex*. London: SCM Press.
Cranfield, C.E.B.
1963   *The Gospel according to St Mark*. Cambridge: Cambridge University Press.
Crossan, J.D.
1991   *The Historical Jesus: The Life of a Mediterranean Jewish Peasant*. Edinburgh: T. & T. Clark.
Douglas, M.
1966   *Purity and Danger: An Analysis of the Concepts of Pollution and Taboo*. London: Routledge & Kegan Paul.

1973   *Natural Symbols, Explorations in Cosmology*. London: Barrie & Jenkins, 2nd edn.

Elliott, J.H.

1982   *A Home for the Homeless: A Sociological Exegesis of I Peter: Its Situation and Strategy*. London: SCM Press.

1995   *Social-Scientific Criticism of the New Testament*. London: SPCK.

Elliott, J.H. (ed.)

1986   *Social-Scientific Criticism of the New Testament and its Social World*. Semeia, 35. Decatur, GA: Scholars Press.

Esler, P.F.

1987   *Community and Gospel in Luke–Acts*. Cambridge: Cambridge University Press.

1994   *The First Christians in their Social Worlds*. London and New York: Routledge.

1995   *Modelling Early Christianity*. London and New York: Routledge.

Flanagan, K.

1992   'Sublime Policing: Sociology and Milbank's City of God'. *New Blackfriars* 73: 333-41.

Garrett, S.

1992   'Sociology of Early Christianity'. *ABD* 6: 89-99.

Holmberg, B.

1990   *Sociology and the New Testament: An Appraisal*. Minneapolis: Fortress Press.

Gager, J.G.

1975   *Kingdom and Community: The Social World of Early Christianity*. Englewood Cliffs, NJ: Prentice–Hall.

Geertz, C.

1973   *The Interpretation of Cultures*. New York: Basic Books.

Hanson, K.C.

1994   'BTB Readers Guide: Kinship'. *BTB* 24: 183-94.

Harrington, D.J.

1988   'Second Testament Exegesis and the Social Sciences: A Bibliography'. *BTB* 18: 77-85.

Kee, H.C.

1989   *Knowing the Truth: A Sociological Approach to New Testament Interpretation*. Minneapolis: Fortress Press.

Kelber, W.H.

1974   *The Kingdom in Mark: A New Place and a New Time*. Philadelphia: Fortress Press.

Malbon, E.S.

1986   *Narrative Space and Mythic Meaning in Mark*. San Francisco: Harper & Row.

Malina, B.J.

1981   *The New Testament World: Insights from Cultural Anthropology*. Atlanta: John Knox.

Malina, B.J., and R.L. Rohrbaugh
1992   *Social-Scientific Commentary on the Synoptic Gospels*. Minneapolis: Fortress Press.

Marshall, C.D.
1989   *Faith as a Theme in Mark's Narrative*. Cambridge: Cambridge University Press.

Martin, D.
1995   'Jesus Christ and Modern Sociology', in W.R. Farmer (ed.), *Crisis in Christology*. Livonia, MI: Dove: 39-46.

Martin, D.B.
1995   *The Corinthian Body*. New Haven: Yale University Press.

May, D.M.
1991   *Social-Scientific Criticism of the New Testament: A Bibliography*. Macon, GA: Mercer University Press.

Meeks, W.A.
1983   *The First Urban Christians*. New Haven: Yale University Press.
1986   'A Hermeneutics of Social Embodiment'. *HTR* 79: 176-86.
1993   *The Origins of Christian Morality*. New Haven: Yale University Press.

Milbank, J.
1990   *Theology and Social Theory: Beyond Secular Reason*. Oxford: Blackwell.

Mitchell, M.M.
1991   *Paul and the Rhetoric of Reconciliation*. Louisville: Westminster/John Knox Press.

Moxnes, H.
1993   'Honor and Shame'. *BTB* 23: 167-76.

Neyrey, J.
1990   *Paul, In Other Words: A Cultural Reading of his Letters*. Louisville: Westminster/John Knox Press.

Neyrey, J.H. (ed.)
1991   *The Social World of Luke–Acts: Models for Interpretation*. Peabody: Hendrickson.

Pilch, J.J.
1992   'Understanding Healing in the Social World of Early Christianity'. *BTB* 22: 26-33.

Roberts, R.H.
1993   'Transcendental Sociology? A Critique of John Milbank's *Theology and Social Theory: Beyond Secular Reason*'. *SJT* 46: 527-35.

Scroggs, R.
1980   'The Sociological Interpretation of the New Testament: The Present State of Research'. *NTS* 26: 164-79.

Theissen, G.
1978   *The First Followers of Jesus*. London: SCM Press.
1982   *The Social Setting of Pauline Christianity*. Edinburgh: T. & T. Clark.
1987   *Psychological Aspects of Pauline Theology*. Edinburgh: T. & T. Clark.

1989   'Auswahlbibliographie zur Sozialgeschichte des Urchristentums', in *Studien zur Soziologie des Urchristentums*. Tübingen: Mohr–Siebeck, 3rd edn.

1993   *Social Reality and the Early Christians*. Edinburgh: T. & T. Clark.

Weber, M.

1964   *The Theory of Social and Economic Organization*. New York: Free Press.

CANONICAL CRITICISM*

ROBERT W. WALL

1. INTRODUCTION

The dramatic rise of scholarly interest in the canon of the New Testament in recent years has two focal points—historical and hermeneutical. Historians of the biblical canon are primarily interested in its formation within early Christianity, whether as a theological notion or a literary collection. Although the questions addressed often imply substantial theological problems, sometimes recognized and considered, most of these studies specialize in the historical features of the Bible's formation or the ideological freight which guided the canonizing process. Thus, for example, the relationship between a book's authorship and its canonization, while theologically interesting, is typically discussed in terms of how attribution of authorship influenced the reception of a particular book both within the earliest Church and then into the biblical canon.

Some interpreters of the biblical canon are especially interested in the *idea* of a biblical canon, which then provides the conceptual freight for various interpretative strategies, typically articulated under the rubrics of 'canonical criticism' (James A. Sanders) or 'canonical approach' (Brevard S. Childs). Not only are practitioners of canonical criticism joined by a common orientation toward Scripture which provides a touchstone for their interpretation, but they also share a common criticism of the historical-critical enterprise, although to different degrees and with different concerns. Generally, however, it is thought that the methodological interests of historical criticism demote the Church's more theological intentions for the Christian Bible. Thus, while historical-critical analysis is primarily concerned with the circumstances that shaped particular biblical writings at their diverse points of origin, the orienting concern of canonical criticism is the theological purpose of each stage of the Bible's compositional

---

*   Portions of this essay are excerpted from R.W. Wall, 'Reading the New Testament in Canonical Context', in J.B. Green (ed.), *Hearing the New Testament: Strategies for Interpretation* (Grand Rapids: Eerdmans, 1995), pp. 381-404.

history—from the moment of composition to the moment of canonization. The issue of Scripture's referentiality and intentionality, then, is decisive in forging the *Gestalt* of canonical hermeneutics, which supposes that the very act of interpretation enables and empowers the rendering of the Christian Bible as the word of God for today's canonical audience.

Actually, the idea of a biblical canon includes two integral ingredients: the Christian Bible is both a canonical collection of writings and a collection of canonical writings. In the first case, emphasis is placed upon the Bible's final literary form (*norma normata*), and in the second case, emphasis is placed upon its ongoing religious function (*norma normans*).[1] The methodological interests of canonical criticism follow along the lines of these two emphases, introduced by the work of Old Testament scholars, B.S. Childs and J.A. Sanders. Their disagreements over what constitutes agreed hermeneutical essentials have charted the territory of canonical criticism for the guild of biblical scholars.

In brief, the 'canonical approach' of Childs posits hermeneutical value in the Bible's final literary form (*norma normata*), which supplies the normative written witness to Jesus Christ.[2] The Bible's role as Christianity's 'rule of faith' presumes its trustworthy (or 'apostolic') witness to him whose incarnation ultimately provides the norm for the community's 'rule of faith'. Only in this christological sense can one say that Scripture supplies both the subject matter for the Church's theological reflection as well as the theological boundaries or context within which Christian theology and ethics take shape. An interpretative emphasis on the Bible as a specific and limited body of sacred writings not only values its subject matter for theological reflection and confession, but also envisages the very ordering of the Bible's sub-units as the privileged, permanent

---

[1]   Cf. J.A. Sanders, 'The Integrity of Biblical Pluralism', in J.P. Rosenblatt and J.C. Sitterson, Jr (eds.), *'Not in Heaven': Coherence and Complexity in Biblical Narrative* (Bloomington: Indiana University Press, 1991), pp. 154-69, esp. pp. 154-57.

[2]   Without question, Childs's most influential work is his *Introduction to the Old Testament as Scripture* (Philadelphia: Fortress Press, 1979); in my opinion, he has not advanced his discussion of the 'canonical approach' since its publication. See, however, Gerald Sheppard's fine essay on 'Canonical Criticism', *ABD* 1 (1992), pp. 861-66.

expression of an intentioned, dynamic interaction between the faithful and their written rule of faith.

The canonical approach to biblical interpretation is less interested in lining up behind the reconstructed historical or linguistic intentions of a pre-canonical stage in the formation of a particular composition or collection. The 'synchronic' interest of Childs is rather posited in a subsequent period during which the Christian Scriptures took their final literary shape and at the same time stabilized certain theological convictions as true in a more universal or catholic sense.[3]

---

3   I recognize the contested nature of what 'synchronic' interpretation intends to accomplish in biblical and literary analysis; see M.G. Brett, *Biblical Criticism in Crisis: The Impact of the Canonical Approach on Old Testament Studies* (Cambridge: Cambridge University Press, 1991), pp. 104-15. Further, there are multiple definitions of the 'canonical process' within the field of canonical criticism. For Childs, the idea of a canonical process is vaguely historical and refers to the final stage in the formation of the biblical canon when the believing community 'recognized' its 'rule of faith' in the shape and content of a discrete form (i.e. the 'final form') of its Scripture. I would agree with Childs that this recognition of a biblical canon took place within history and resulted in the 'fixing' of a particular shape of biblical literature; but this final stage in the formation of a discrete Scripture was largely guided by impressions of its truthfulness or intuitions of its ongoing religious utility rather than the outcome of some positivistic or rational judgment. Nor did some final redactor (or God, according to the fundamentalists) wave an 'editorial wand over all the disparate literature', to use Sanders's phrase, to create the Church's Bible. In fact, the primacy Childs grants to the final stage of the canonical process is really an appeal to a useful metaphor for the primacy he grants to the final form of the canon. Although Brett successfully, in my view, provides Childs with the necessary epistemology to anchor his methodological interests, Sanders's notion of canonical process complements Childs's approach in a different way. Sanders's point is to describe the hermeneutics of the canonical process by which we understand more adequately *how and why* Jewish ('prophetic') and Christian ('apostolic') writings were preserved, collected and canonized into biblical form. First of all, the canonizing process was a 'monotheizing process' by which biblical writings became the 'Word of God', brought near to God's people in relevant response to their ever-changing needs; cf. Sanders's superb summary of his account of canonical criticism in 'Integrity'. Secondly, however, biblical writings became God's Word by the act of biblical (i.e. rabbinical or midrashic) interpretation, so that 'what got picked up and read again and again, and was recommended to the children and to other communities nearby, and continued to give value and to give life, was what made it into the canon' (Sanders, 'Integrity', p. 168). For Sanders, the biblical canon 'norms' are the community's hermeneutics by which biblical texts are resignified into theologically relevant

No one is entirely clear why these various writings and collections, so different in theological conception and sociological origination and so fluid during their early history, eventually stabilized into the Christian Bible. Certainly, one probable reason is aesthetic: over time, different communions of believers came to recognize one particular arrangement of books as more useful for a variety of religious services, even as the number of alternative arrangements (or 'canon lists') was eventually narrowed by disuse. In other words, a specific form of biblical literature triumphed because it facilitated or better served its intended role within the faith community.[4] Thus, according to Childs, the final shape of the Christian Scriptures best combines and relates its subject matter to serve the Church as the literary location where theological understanding is well founded and soundly framed.

The 'canonical criticism' of Sanders posits value in the act of interpretation which enables the Bible to function canonically in shaping the theology and guiding the praxis of the Church (*norma normans*). The methodological interests of Sanders are more intuitive than those of Childs, emphasizing rather the interpretative calculus found at the composition's point of origin, during the canonical process, and throughout the history of interpreting the biblical canon. For Sanders, 'canonical process' is not concentrated by a specific historical moment or literary product as it is for Childs; hermeneutics is not synchronic in this sense. Rather, the canonical approach of Sanders is more 'diachronic', and involves the entire history of the Bible's interpretation, whenever the faith community draws upon its Scriptures to provide a norm for its faith and life. Beginning even before biblical texts were written and continuing today, faithful interpreters contemporize the meaning of their Scriptures so that the faith community might better understand what it means to be and do what God's people ought.

For Sanders, canonical function antedates and explains canonical form, even as final form facilitates those functions the faith community intended for its canon. In my view, Childs has offered no compelling response to the objection that his interest in the Bible's

---

teachings, which help to form the community's particular identity amidst the ambiguities and vicissitudes of human life and history.

4   This point draws upon H.-G. Gadamer's idea of 'classical' literature; cf. *Truth and Method* (New York: Crossroad; London: Sheed and Ward, 2nd edn, 1989), esp. pp. 285-90.

final literary form is too parochial, elevating the final form of the Protestant Bible over the various other biblical canons within the Christian Church. On the other hand, by shifting his attention from the Bible as *norma normata* to the Bible as *norma normans*, from its literary form to its ecclesial function, Sanders relativizes the hermeneutical importance of the Bible's final form. Since, for him, canonical function takes precedence over canonical form, the literary shape (or translation!) of a particular community's Bible is subsumed under the interpreter's more important vocation of adapting Scripture's meaning to the community's ever-changing life situation.

Canonical criticism, then, concentrates on how a biblical text becomes canonical in the act of interpretation, when different interpreters pick up the same text again and again to 'comfort the afflicted or afflict the comfortable'. In the hands of faithful interpreters, past and present, Scripture acquires multiple meanings. Of course the aim of relating the canon to the faith community is to form a people who worship and bear witness to the one true God.[5] Thus, the Christian Bible is more than a canonical collection of sacred writings, shaped by religious intentions and insights into a discrete literary anthology that itself envisions patterns of hermeneutical engagement. The Bible is canonical primarily in a functional sense, with an authorized role to provide a norm for the worship and witness of all those who belong to the 'One Holy, Catholic and Apostolic Church'. Under the light of this perspective toward the Bible, interpreters are led to ask additional questions about the meaning of every biblical text that attends first of all to the *theological shape* of the Church's faith (in both confession and conflict) rather than to the literary shape of its biblical canon.[6]

In this sense, Sanders reminds Childs that the history of the Bible's formation did more than settle on the shape of a canonical collection

---

5   See J.A. Sanders, *Canon and Community* (Philadelphia: Fortress Press, 1984).

6   While Sanders contends that the biblical canon is characterized by its textual 'stability' and contextual 'adaptability', his principal methodological interest has always been the Bible's adaptability (even as Childs's methodological interest has always been the Bible's stability). For Sanders, the fluidity of the biblical canon is a matter of the historical record; yet, it is also the constant experience of faithful interpreters, whose task it is to find new meanings in the same biblical texts for their new situations. It is this *experience* of interpretation that justifies this interest in Scripture's characteristic of adapting itself to new hearers and readers.

of sacred writings to delimit the Church's 'official' theology and ethics; it also evinced a species of hermeneutics that contemporizes the theological quotient of biblical teaching to give it an authoritative voice for today's community whose worship and witness is again undermined by similar theological crises. What got picked up again and again and reread over and over were those same writings that could interpret the present crisis of faith and resolve it in a way that maintained faith and empowered life.

In fact, biblical writings were first preserved because they were sufficiently ambiguous in intent for different interpreters to mediate truth to their different audiences. At the same time, other writings were filtered out as being too narrow in sociological context or semantic intent to have a life beyond their first readers. According to Sanders, the elevation of a scriptural writing to canonical status required an inherent capacity to be reinterpreted over and again in spiritually profitable ways by different interpreters for different situations. This sort of unrecorded hermeneutics envisages the same canonical function found in the Bible's final literary form: the Bible is formed to inform the community's understanding of God.

My own work has sought to combine and extend these insights of Sanders and Childs.[7] In doing so, I recognize the contested nature of canonical criticism within the guild of biblical scholarship. Nevertheless, the present chapter does not seek to defend the methodological interests of canonical criticism against its main competitors. Nor does it intend to provide critics with the proper epistemological credentials to lend support to my exegetical conclusions. This important work has already been undertaken by others, so that the methodological interests of canonical criticism can now be more fully exploited for fresh insight into the meaning of Scripture for today.[8]

---

[7]   See R.W. Wall and E.E. Lemcio, *The New Testament as Canon: A Reader in Canonical Criticism* (JSNTSup, 76; Sheffield: JSOT Press, 1992).

[8]   See especially Brett, *Biblical Criticism*. Brett's work requires supplementation in two ways: (1) to distinguish between a canonical approach to Old Testament studies and New Testament studies, where some of the methodological problems Brett raises and responds to are not quite as important (e.g. the duration of the canonical process) but where other problems are (e.g. the relationship between the two testaments); and (2) to show more carefully and critically how the 'canonical approach' of Childs is different from and complemented by the 'canonical criticism' of Sanders. This latter point has been recently taken up in a helpful essay by M.C. Parsons, 'Canonical Criticism', in

2. THE METHODOLOGICAL INTERESTS OF CANONICAL CRITICISM

Biblical Exegesis

Theological reflection on the Bible integrates two discrete tasks—biblical exegesis and theological interpretation. The foundational task of the hermeneutical enterprise is exegetical, which aims at a coherent exposition of Scripture's 'plain meaning'.[9] My use of the catchphrase 'plain meaning' is metaphorical, indicating a primary interest in the final form of the biblical canon, rather than in the literary or sociological environs at its point of origin, its author, or any of its sub- or pre-texts (however important these constructions might be to achieve a holistic meaning). Neither do I view the exegetical task as interested in privileging one particular meaning as 'canonical' for all believers for all time.[10]

D.A. Black and D.S. Dockery (eds.), *New Testament Criticism and Interpretation* (Grand Rapids: Zondervan, 1991), pp. 253-94.

9   My use of the controversial term, 'plain meaning', is neither naive nor courageous. It seeks rather to exploit two discussions, one medieval and another modern, the first Jewish and the second Christian. The first source for defining 'plain meaning exegesis' is the medieval rabbinate, whose commentaries on Scripture typically distinguished between *peshat* ('straightforward') and *derash* ('investigation') as two integral exegetical modes. If the aim of hermeneutical inquiry is *peshat*, the interpreter is concerned with a closely reasoned description of what the text actually says. In this first mode, the interpreter responds to the hermeneutical crisis of the text's incomprehensibility within a congregation of believers for whom that text is canonical. If the aim is *derash*, the interpreter is concerned with an imaginative interpretation of what the text means for its current audience. This second task, while rooted in the first, responds to a different and more important hermeneutical crisis, which is the perception of the text's theological irrelevance for its current readers. If the biblical canon intends to facilitate theological reflection, then the ultimate aim of exegesis is not *peshat* but *derash*. My second source is the work of R.E. Brown who reintroduced the idea of Scripture's *sensus plenior* into the scholarly debate over biblical hermeneutics ('The History and Development of the Theory of a *Sensus Plenior*', *CBQ* 15 [1953], pp. 141-62; *The Sensus Plenior of Sacred Scripture* [New York: Paulist Press, 1960]). According to Brown's more modern (and positive) definition, the *sensus plenior* or 'plenary sense' of a biblical text agrees with the theological aspect of the entire biblical canon. My use of 'plain meaning' includes this sense, so that the single meaning of any text bears witness to the Bible's witness to God.

10   See R.W. Wall, 'The Relevance of the Book of Revelation for the Wesleyan Tradition', *WTJ*, forthcoming.

Moreover, I view the exegetical task in a collaborative way: it is the shared task of a community of interpreters, whose different interests in the biblical text expose its multiple contours in pursuit of a 'thickened' or holistic description of meaning. However, a methodological interest in the plain meaning of a particular text is constricted by compositional and canonical contexts within which specific texts acquire their distinctive literary and theological meaning. Plain meaning exegesis aspires to a 'standard' meaning, since texts do not gather together an inclusive community of infinite meanings. Common sense and critical attention to words and patterns of words point the exegete to specific meanings. Exegetical strategies are prioritized, then, that are concerned with the meaning and arrangement of words and pericopes as well as the theological content they convey.

Of course, Scripture has a profoundly intertextual texture, which is exploited in canonical criticism. The careful interpreter is naturally sensitive to the citations, allusions, and even echoes of other 'subtexts' heard when reading a biblical text. And the canonical critic is inclined to value these, especially biblical, subtexts hermeneutically: that is, they provide an implied yet normative context for the writer's own theological reflection on the events being narrated or the spiritual crisis being resolved. There is a sense in which New Testament writers are viewed as interpreters of their Scripture and their compositions as commentaries on Scripture. More importantly, this exegetical sensitivity to the author's intended meaning, in turn, enhances the exegete's understanding of the text's plain meaning.[11]

The scholar's search for the plain meaning of a biblical text or tradition does not mark a return to a fundamentalistic literalism, which denies both the historical process that formed the Christian Scriptures and the theological diversity found within it. Rather, a concern for plain meaning guards against hermeneutical supersession. Thus, the community at work on biblical texts pursues meaning with ideological blinders on, without immediate regard for the integral wholeness of Scripture: critical exegesis seeks to restore to full volume the voice of every biblical writer so that the whole meaning of Scripture can then

---

[11]   In canonical criticism, this exegetical sensitivity takes on a theological cast when speculating on the relationship between the two testaments of the Christian Bible: the New Testament is a midrash on the Old Testament, for it bears witness that the salvation promised in the first is fulfilled by the Jesus of the second.

be vocalized as a chorus of its various parts. To presume the simultaneity between every part of the whole, without also adequately discerning the plain meaning of each in turn, undermines the integral nature of Scripture and even distorts its full witness to God. Finally, however, the aim of critical exegesis, which has successfully exposed the pluriformity of Scripture, is 'to put the text back together in a way that makes it available in the present and in its (biblical) entirety—not merely in the past and in the form of historically contextualized fragments'.[12] In this sense, then, the plain meaning of individual writings or biblical traditions, although foundational for scriptural interpretation, has value only in relationship to a more holistic end.[13]

Even though the search for the plain meaning of Scripture concerns itself with stable texts and standard meanings, the exegetical history of every biblical text is actually quite fluid. This limitation is deepened by recognition of the inherent multivalence and intertextuality of texts. Further changes in the text's 'plain meaning' result from new evidence and different exegetical strategies and from interpreters shaped by diverse social and theological locations. In fact, the sort of neutrality toward biblical texts that critical exegesis envisages actually requires such changes to be made. Our experience with texts tells us that the ideal of a 'standard' meaning cannot be made absolute, whether as the assured conclusion of the scholarly guild or as some meaning ordained by (and known only to) God. Thus, the fluid nature of exegesis resists the old dichotomy between past and present meanings, and between authorial and textual intentions.

As a practical discipline, plain meaning exegesis clarifies the subject matter of Scripture, which supplies the conceptual freight of those theological norms and ethical principles that form Christian faith. Simply put, the straightforward meanings of the variety of biblical writings, considered holistically, help to delimit the range and determine the substance of the Church's current understanding of what it means to believe and behave as it must. Yet, whenever biblical theology is still attempted, it remains (with a few notable exceptions) exclusively an exegetical enterprise as though a careful description of the Bible's theology is sufficient to perform its canonical roles. It is in response to this misconception that I claim exegesis is the means but

---

12   J.D. Levenson, *The Hebrew Bible, The Old Testament, and Historical Criticism* (Louisville: Westminster/John Knox Press, 1993), p. 79.

13   Esp. B.S. Childs, *Biblical Theology of Old and New Testaments* (Minneapolis: Fortress Press, 1992), pp. 719-27.

not the end of the hermeneutical enterprise: the plain meaning of Scripture must come to have contemporary meaning for its current readers before it can function as their Scripture.

Theological Interpretation

The interpreter's second task is *interpretation*, which, in my definition, aims to give the subject matter of Scripture its canonical significance for today. That is, if exegesis locates canonical authority in biblical texts, then interpretation re-locates religious authority in the social contexts of the faith community where the Word of God is ultimately heard and embodied. Biblical interpretation, as I understand it, is fully contextual and aims at an imaginative (i.e. analogical) reflection on the subject matter of biblical teaching. The purpose of such reflection is to 're-canonize' biblical teaching so that the faith community might know who it is as God's people and how it is to act as God's people within a new situation. While critical exegesis aims to restrict the plain meaning of a biblical text to a single standard (at least in theory), the interpretative task seeks an application of that meaning for a people whose faith and life are in constant flux. Of course, the problem to which the act of interpretation responds is the recognition that biblical writings are all occasional literature, written by particular authors for particular audiences in response to crises of a particular time and place. No biblical writing was composed for the biblical canon nor for the universal readership it now enjoys.

In fact, the interpretative presumption is that current readers will not draw out the very same meaning from a composition that might have been intended by its author or understood by its first readers. Times and places change the significance of texts for new readerships. Rather than decanonizing certain Scripture as 'irrelevant' or imposing a biblical world-view upon a contemporary readership, an interpretative strategy must be engaged that seeks to relate the whole witness of the biblical canon and the whole life of the faith community in fresh and meaningful ways.

In this sense, the crisis of biblical authority is the propriety of prior interpretations of Scripture—including those of the biblical writers— for a 'new' situation. This is ultimately a theological crisis, since the subject matter of biblical revelation fails to convey God's Word to a particular people with clarity and conviction, either because they cannot understand what Scripture says, or because they cannot understand its immediate relevance for life and faith.[14] In this case, then, imagination is required by the interpreter to exploit more easily the inherent polyvalency of biblical teaching in order to find new meanings for new worlds.

Thus, the interpreter presumes that the agreed plain meaning of a biblical text embodies a community of analogical meanings, while at the same time recognizing that not all of these meanings hold equal significance either for a particular interpreter or for the interpreter's faith community. The interpreter's interpretations of Scripture seek to clarify and contemporize the Bible's subject matter for those who struggle to remain faithful at a particular moment in time and place. In this regard, then, the act of interpretation imagines an analogue from a range of possible meanings that renders the text's subject matter meaningful for a people who desire to remain faithful to God within an inhospitable world.

The Role of the Interpreter

All of what has been said to this point about the exegetical and interpretative tasks implies something about the interpreter's 'authority'. Perhaps because its pioneers are theologically located within Reformed Protestantism, canonical criticism has always emphasized the authority of the Christian Bible. However, whether an interpretation satisfies the Church's intentions for its Bible depends to a significant degree upon the interpreter's 'individual talent'. The talented interpreter has the capacity to make coherent and contemporary the meaning of diverse biblical traditions, each singly and together within the whole; and then to relate the canon to the faith community in ways that facilitate the hearing of God's word.

To be sure, the interpreter's talent to facilitate a meaningful conversation between canon and community is determined in part by one's vocation, whether 'prophetic' or 'priestly'. On this basis, creative and compelling interpretations of biblical texts are made that relate the plain meaning of the biblical text to the current social context in ways that actually produce theological understanding (and so a more vital faith in God) and moral clarity (and so more faithful obedience to God's Word). In this sense, the talented interpreter renders Scripture in ways that empower the community's worship of and witness to God in the world. Thus, the interpreter imagines what

---

14   For this point, see M. Fishbane, *The Garments of Torah* (Bloomington: Indiana University Press, 1989), pp. 16-18.

'analogical meaning' can be made of the text's 'plain meaning' for the community's formation as God's people, whether to 'correct and rebuke' a distorted faith (prophetic hermeneutic) or to 'teach and train' a developing faith (priestly hermeneutic).

Further, the interpreter's talent is shaped by time and place. Not only does the interpreter bring a particularized perspective to the biblical text; the interpreter also brings one's own 'special' texts to the text, to participate in a conversation already under way.

A Model for Canonical Interpretation

Under the light of these methodological interests, the framework for an interpretative model can now be constructed as a sequence of three discrete although integral parts: canonical context, content and conversations. What follows is a brief description of the task *apropos* to each part.

Canonical Context. An interest in the final literary form of the New Testament leads the interpreter to an initial set of hermeneutical clues derived from consideration of both the placement and titles of New Testament writings, which are properties of their canonization. Quite apart from authorial intentions, the literary design of the biblical canon suggests that particular units of the New Testament canon (Gospel, Acts, Letter, Apocalypse) have particular roles to perform within the whole. This consideration of the structure of the New Testament orients the interpreter to the subject matter found within each of those canonical units. Often the title provided for each unit by the canonizing community brings to clearer focus what particular contribution each unit makes to a fully Christian faith.

In this regard, the sequence of these four units within the New Testament envisages an intentional rhetorical pattern—or 'canon-logic' to use Albert Outler's apt phrase[15]—that more effectively orients the readership to the New Testament's pluriform witness to God and to God's Christ. By the logic of the final literary form of the New Testament canon, each unit is assigned a specific role to perform within the whole, which in turn offers another explanation for the rich diversity of theology, literature, and language that casts Scripture's subject matter. Thus, the Gospel is placed first within the New

---

15   A.C. Outler, 'The "Logic" of Canon-Making and the Tasks of Canon-Criticism', in W.E. March (ed.), *Texts and Testaments: Critical Essays on the Bible and Early Church Fathers* (San Antonio, TX: Trinity University Press, 1980), pp. 263-76.

Testament because its narrative of the person and work of the Messiah when taken as a fourfold whole, is theologically and morally foundational for all that follows.

Along with the final placement of writings and collections within the biblical canon, new titles were provided for individual compositions, sometimes including the naming of anonymous authors. These properties of the canonizing stage shed additional light on how these compositions and collections, written centuries earlier for congregations and religious crises long since settled, may continue to bear witness to God and God's Christ for a nameless and future readership. The importance of any one biblical voice for theological understanding or ethical praxis is focused or qualified by its relationship to the other voices that constitute the whole canonical chorus. Extending this metaphor, one may even suppose that these various voices, before heard only individually or in smaller groups, became more impressive, invigorating, and even 'canonical' for faith only when combined with other voices to sing their contrapuntal harmonies as the full chorus.

Canonical Content. A biblical text, once placed within its distinctive canonical context, acquires a potential for enhanced meaning that should help to guide the exegetical task. A canonical approach to exegesis is never solely concerned with an 'objective' description of the biblical text in isolation from other biblical texts; rather, the analysis of a writer's literary artistry or theological tendencies serves the overall canonical project. The description of the text's plain meaning results from a close and critical analysis of its compositional and theological aspects (see under 'Biblical Exegesis' above). In many ways, this part of the canonical-critical enterprise is the most traditional. *Canonical criticism does not sponsor any new exegetical strategy; rather, it sponsors a particular orientation toward the biblical text whose principal methodological interests are its final literary form and canonical functions.* Naturally, the canonical interpreter is first of all drawn to those exegetical strategies that seek to make meaning out of the biblical text itself rather than its prehistory or the historical circumstances that occasioned its writing.

Canonical Conversations. The intended role of the biblical canon is to adapt its ancient teaching to contemporary life; this is also the primary objective of biblical interpretation. Under this final rubric, the results of the first two tasks are now gathered together as the subject matter of two formative and integral 'conversations' about the community's life of faith. The first conversation is *intercanonical* (i.e. conversations between different biblical traditions/writers) and the second is *intercatholic* (i.e. conversations between the Bible and different faith traditions); the first provides a norm and guidance for the second.

While a number of metaphors work well to express the Bible's theological plurality coherently and constructively, my preference for the interpreter's practical task is *conversation*. Naturally, there are different kinds of conversations between people. A canonical approach to the New Testament's pluriform subject matter envisages a conversation that is more complementary than adversarial. In one sense, the *intercanonical* conversation is very much like an intramural debate over the precise meaning of things generally agreed to be true and substantial. The purpose or outcome of debate is not to resolve firmly fixed disagreements between members of the same community or panel as though a normative synthesis were possible; rather more often, it is the sort of debate that clarifies the contested content of their common ground. Likewise, the biblical canon stabilizes and bears continuing witness to the historic disagreements between the traditions of the Church's first apostles, which were often creative and instructive (cf. Acts 15:1-21; Gal. 2:1-15). Not only do these controversies acquire a permanent value within Scripture, but Scripture in turn commends these same controversies to its current readers who are invited to engage in a similar act of what Karl Popper calls 'mutual criticism',[16] in order to provide more balance to parochial interests or supply instruction to clarify the theological confession of a particular faith tradition.

In fact, the point and counterpoint of this sort of conversation sometimes works better than those that seek agreement, in that they more readily expose the potential weakness of any point made *to the exclusion* of its counterpoint. In this sense, I presume that a more objective and functional meaning emerges that is neither the conception of any one biblical writer—a 'canon *within* the canon'— nor the presumption of any one expositor—a 'canon *outside* of the canon'. Rather the canonical interpreter seeks to relate the different ideas of particular biblical writers and canonical units together in contrapuntal yet complementary ways, to expose the self-correcting (or prophetic) and mutually-informing (or priestly) whole of New

---

[16]   I learned of Popper's helpful categories for determining textual objectivity as a good reason for both receiving and preserving literary texts from Brett, *Biblical Criticism*, pp. 124-27.

Testament theology. In this way, the diversity of biblical theologies within the New Testament fashions a canon of 'mutual criticism', resulting in a more objective interpretation of Scriptural teaching. A New Testament theology thus envisaged underscores what is at stake in relating together the individual parts, whose total significance is now extended beyond their compiled meaning: the New Testament's diverse theologies, reconsidered holistically as complement witnesses within the whole, actually 'thicken' the meaning of each part in turn.

The midrashic character of biblical interpretation compels the contemporizing of texts, so that 'new' meanings are not the result of textual synthesis, but rather arise from contextual significance. Thus, by reconstituting these intercanonical disagreements into a hermeneutical apparatus of checks-and-balances, the interpreter may actually imagine a comparable dialogue which aids the Church's awareness of how each part of the New Testament canon is important in delimiting and shaping a truly biblical religion. In fashioning a second conversation under the light of the first, therefore, the checks-and-balances are re-imagined as *intercatholic* conversations which continue to guide the whole Church in its various ecumenical conversations.

How the intercanonical conversations are arranged and then adapted to a particular faith tradition is largely intuitive, and depends a great deal upon the interpreter's talent and location (see above). It should go without saying that my particular adaptation of Acts owes a great deal to who and where I am when coming to this text and its current socio-ecclesial context, so I must try to listen to other interpreters, believing that true objectivity emerges out of a community of subjectivities. Thus informed, a close reading of biblical texts and ecclesial contexts can be more easily linked together, particular communions with particular New Testament writers, in order to define the normative checks-and-balances of a complementary conversation that maintains and legitimizes traditional distinctives on the one hand, with the prospect of correcting a tendency toward triumphalist sectarianism on the other.

3. THE CASE OF THE ACTS OF THE APOSTLES

The following section of the present chapter seeks to illustrate the importance of locating the book of Acts within its 'canonical context' for exegesis, where the interpreter elevates the significance of a book's *intra*canonical relationships with collections of other biblical books in forming Scripture's full witness to God. No one disagrees anymore that Scripture's theology is at the very least the sum of its various theologies; our point is rather to underscore their *synergy* so that their whole is actually greater than their mere sum when factoring in the theological importance of these intracanonical relationships which are fixed by the final form of the New Testament. As argued in a previous study, the placement and title of Acts provide substantial clues for proceeding in this regard.[17]

The Placement of Acts in Canonical Context

Sharply put, the strategic placement of Acts between the Gospels on the one hand and the apostolic letters on the other is suggestive of the transitional role it performs within the New Testament: the narrative of Acts both *concludes* the prior fourfold narrative of Jesus and *introduces* the subsequent twofold collection of apostolic letters that follow. This placement of Acts within the New Testament is even more strategic if P. Achtemeier is correct in noting that the relationship between the Gospels and letters is roughly analogous to the relationship between the Lord and his disciples: that is, even as the disciples follow the Lord's lead, so also the advice and instruction of the biblical letters follow the lead of Jesus tradition.[18] In this way, Acts may well function within the New Testament as a 'bridge' which connects the collections of Gospels and letters in meaningful dialogue by providing a paradigmatic narrative that explores the continuing relationship between disciples and their risen Lord.

The Relationship between Acts and the Fourfold Gospel. The variegated relationship between Luke and Acts is a topic of longstanding interest among critical scholars. Our interest is similar although concentrated differently by the relationship between the fourfold Gospel and Acts within the New Testament. In this regard, the close relationship between Acts and the Gospels is indicated by the formal features of a succession narrative found in the prologue to Acts (1:1-14). (1) The Evangelist first recalls the public ministry of Jesus (1:1) and indicates that the apostolic successors will continue this ministry in his absence (1:2). The convenient opening phrase,

---

17 See R.W. Wall, 'Acts of the Apostles in Canonical Context', *BTB* 18 (1988), pp. 15-23.

18 P.J. Achtemeier, 'Epilogue: The New Testament Becomes Normative', in H.C. Kee, *Understanding the New Testament* (Englewood Cliffs, NJ: Prentice–Hall, 4th edn, 1983), p. 369.

'began (ἤρξατο) to do and teach', and common address (cf. Luke 1:4), 'Theophilus', underscore this robust sense of continuity between the narrative of Acts and the antecedent narrative of Jesus' earthly ministry; indeed, we anticipate that the word of God, which Jesus proclaimed and enacted, will now be articulated by the speeches and deeds of his apostolic successors (cf. Mark 1:1, 14). The overall canonical effect of this relationship is rather similar to the author's own intention, even though the biblical Acts now qualifies a fourfold narrative of Jesus' earthly ministry: the revelation of God through Jesus continues to be disclosed through the earthly mission of his immediate successors, whose names are listed for the reader (1:12-14), and ultimately through the congregations they founded.

(2) The narrative and theological importance of the ascension of Jesus (1:9-11; cf. Luke 24:50-53) has been variously considered.[19] As a feature of the transitional role Acts performs within the New Testament, Jesus' departure from earth marks the 'official' ending of his earthly ministry (and its narrative in the fourfold Gospel) and the beginning of his apostolic succession (and its narrative in Acts). As such it fashions the mid-point of the New Testament's continuing narrative about the doings and sayings that disclose God's reign within history, which Jesus (= Gospel) had begun. In this sense, Jesus' departure from earth is also his departure from the narrative, his place within salvation's history now to be occupied by the apostles who will also be empowered by God's word and Spirit until Jesus returns.

(3) Central to this succession story is the Lord's commissioning of his apostles (1:8), which establishes the Church's identity and obligation as a missionary community and the geographical index by which the narrative of the Church's mission is framed in Acts. The final phrase, 'to the end of the earth (= Rome?)', echoes Isa. 49:6, where the servant of Yahweh brings God's salvation to the nations. Yet, according to the Gospel, God's messianic Servant offered God's salvation only to Israel, even though a universal salvation is predicted at his birth (Luke 2:29-32). Not until Acts is God's salvation extended to the nations, thus completing the Gospel narrative. Significantly, the narrative ends ambiguously in Rome, with Paul awaiting the Caesar's audience and his fate unknown. From a canonical perspective, the narrative ending functions to commission the readership to succeed

---

19   Esp. M.C. Parsons, *The Departure of Jesus in Luke–Acts* (JSNTSup, 21; Sheffield: JSOT Press, 1987).

Paul in bearing witness to God's reign by word and deed.

Two features of this commission in particular explain the nature of the continuity between Jesus and the Church. (a) The apostolic vocation is to bear 'witness' to the risen Lord, whose messianic ministry culminating in the resurrection testifies to the triumph of God over sin and death. Not only do the apostolic speeches of Acts repeat—more or less—the principal events that compose the story of Jesus, but their acts of 'signs and wonders' typically envisage the triumph of the resurrection as continuing confirmation that the story of Jesus is true. (b) More importantly, this missionary vocation is empowered by the Spirit of the risen Christ. The Lord's promise of the Spirit and its eventual fulfilment at Pentecost respond to the theological crisis provoked by his departure: what is the current status of the 'word' that bears witness to God's reign on earth now that God's Messiah has left? The incomprehension, even uncertainty, of the disciples even after Easter, clearly indicated by their questioning of Jesus (1:6), envisages this present crisis. Only after Pentecost, when the Spirit fills the community (2:4), is the full status of the risen Lord grasped (2:22-36). Even the Baptist's witness to Jesus' 'greatness', which is measured by the baptism by Spirit and fire rather than by water (Luke 3:16), is not yet realized until the Spirit's arrival. Sharply put, the New Testament witness to God's triumph in Christ is incomplete without the narrative of the Spirit found in Acts. In fact, the absence of parousia hope in the speeches of Acts may well be intended to underscore the fundamental importance of Pentecost, since the arrival of the 'Day of the Lord' as the great and manifest day of salvation (Acts 2:20-21) occurs at the Pentecost of the Spirit rather than at the parousia of the Lord. In this sense, this story of the Spirit more than continues the story of Jesus: in fact, Acts concludes and completes the Gospel about Jesus by providing the final and clearest confirmation of his ongoing importance for God's people.

The Relationship between Acts and the Multiple Letter Canon. The intracanonical relationship between Acts and the following two collections of letters is more difficult to 'stage-manage'. On the one hand, epistolary literature is generically different than narrative; differences of all sorts between Acts and the letters seem even more apparent as a result. For example, the deeper logic of narrative moves from the fact of experience to theological conclusion rather than moving the other way as is more often the case with letters. Further, the purposes and orienting concerns of the various authors are also different. For example, Luke's idealized *Paulusbild* appears rather contrary to Paul's own self-understanding.[20] In fact, while Luke seems to know a great deal about Paul, his story of Paul has very little basis in the Pauline Letters. Yet, on the other hand, there is an obvious connection between Acts and the letters that the Church has always recognized: Acts offers readers of the New Testament a theological (rather than a chronological or historical) introduction to the letters that follow.[21]

For example, (a) Acts offers biographical introductions to the authors of the letters. In canonical context, such biographies serve a theological purpose by orienting readers to the authority (religious and moral) of apostolic authors as trustworthy carriers of the word of God. While the historical accuracy of Luke's narrative of Paul and other leaders of earliest Christianity may be challenged,[22] their rhetorical and moral powers only confirm and commend the importance of their letters. Even the unstoppable expansion of Christianity into the pagan universe through apostolic preaching, which Acts narrates with profound optimism, serves to underscore the anticipated result of reading and embracing what these same agents of the divine word have written and now read as canonical. Again, the issue is not that Acts fails us as a historical resource; rather, that its narrative succeeds as a theological resource which orients us to the literature that follows. In this case, Luke's intention to defend Paul and his Gentile mission, which especially shapes the second half of his narrative, serves well the overarching canonical intention to introduce his writings as theologically normative.

Further, (b) a reading of Acts fashions a narrative context within which to better understand the diverse theologies of *both* collections of letters, Pauline and those from the 'pillars' of the Jewish mission, 'James, (1–2) Cephas and (1–3) John' (so Gal. 2:9). Acts retains and approves of the theological diversity found within the apostolic witness (cf. Acts 15:1-21). Even though the modern discussion has

---

20   Cf. J.C. Lentz, Jr, *Luke's Portrait of Paul* (SNTSMS, 77; Cambridge: Cambridge University Press, 1993).

21   See R.W. Wall, 'Israel and the Gentile Mission According to Acts and Paul: A Canonical Approach', in I.H. Marshall (ed.), *The Theology of Acts* (The Book of Acts in its First Century Setting, 6; Grand Rapids: Eerdmans, forthcoming).

22   However, see C.J. Hemer, *The Book of Acts in the Setting of Hellenistic History* (WUNT, 49; Tübingen: Mohr–Siebeck, 1989).

emphasized how a catholicizing narrator softens the disagreements between the leaders of earliest Christianity, yet, what is often overlooked in making this point is that the Church eventually collected and canonized a Pauline corpus whose principal letters were often polemical and potentially divisive. The question is never raised why these letters were included in the canon of a catholic Church if the aim was to shape theological uniformity.

Might it not be the case that the canonizing process looked to Acts not to smooth Paul's polemical edges, as Baur insisted, but to interpret them? Might the canonical intention of Acts be to explain rather than temper the diversity, even divisiveness, envisaged by those very letters that follow it in the Second Testament canon? According to Acts, the Church that claims its continuity with the first apostles tolerates a theological pluralism even as the apostles did; yet, not without controversy and confusion. What is achieved at the Jerusalem Synod is a kind of theological understanding rather than a theological consensus. The divine revelation given to the apostles according to Acts forms a pluralizing monotheism which in turn informs two discrete missions and appropriate proclamations, Jewish and Gentile (cf. Gal. 2:7-10). Thus, sharply put, Acts interprets the two collections of letters in a more sectarian fashion: the Pauline corpus reflects the gospel of the Gentile mission, while the non-Pauline collection reflects the gospel(s) of the Jewish mission. However, rather than causing division within the Church, such a theological diversity is now perceived as normative and necessary for the work of a God who calls both Jews and Gentiles to be the people of God. As a context for theological reflection, Acts forces us to interpret the letters in the light of two guiding principles: first, we should expect to find kerygmatic diversity as we move from Pauline to non-Pauline letters; and secondly, we should expect such a diversity to be useful in forming a single people for God. Against a critical hermeneutic which tends to select a 'canon within the canon' from among the various possibilities, the Bible's own recommendation is for an interpretative strategy characterized by a mutually-informing and self-correcting conversation between biblical theologies.

Finally, (c) the 'orienting' theological commitments of Acts guide theological reflection upon the letters. The point here is not that a theology of Acts determines or even anticipates the theological ideas found in the letters; rather, the point is that Acts shapes a particular perspective, a practical 'worry', an abiding interest that influences the interpretation of the letters. For example, one may contend that the primary orienting concern of Acts is the missionary advancement of the word of God to the 'end of the earth'. This concern then functions in theological reflection as an implicit way of thinking about and organizing the subject matter of the letters that follow. If the orienting concern is the Church's Spirit-empowered succession to Jesus' messianic mission, then a reading of the letters under the light of Acts will bring to sharper focus the identity and praxis of a missionary people who respond to the Lord's demand to be his witness to the end of the earth.

This orienting concern is even true of the non-Pauline letters which do not seem to be missionary writings. For example, the faith community addressed by the non-Pauline letters is typically cast in terms of its marginal status in the world rather than in terms of its missionary vocation. How does this orienting concern provided by Acts, then, finally deepen the rather contrary understanding of God's people as a community of 'aliens and strangers'? The canonical approach presumes the connection is complementary rather than adversarial. In this case, a missionary Church, which may be inclined to accommodate itself to the mainstream of the world system in order to more effectively spread the gospel (cf. 1 Cor. 9:12b-23), is reminded by the non-Pauline witness that it must take care not to be corrupted by the values and behaviors of the world outside of Christ (cf. Jas 1:27). That is, the synergism effected by the orienting concern suggests that the diverse theologies that make up the whole biblical canon compose a dynamic self-correcting apparatus which prevents the reader from theological distortion.

The Title, 'The Acts of the Apostles', in Canonical Context

The modern study of the title, 'The Acts of the Apostles', typically reflects an interest in the intentions of the author or in the genre of his narrative. This is mistaken if, as likely, the title is a property of the canonical process rather than of the author. That is, the title envisages the intended role of the narrative *within the biblical canon* for nurturing theological understanding, whether or not this New Testament role agrees with the literary or historical intentions of the author for his first readers. The significance of the canonical title involves two interrelated observations. First, the canonical process moved the Evangelist's more particular intention for his narrative to Theophilus to perform a more universal role in nurturing the Church's understanding of God. Secondly, the effect of the title's reference to 'the apostles' is to shift the reader's attention from the Spirit (and a more 'charismatic' theology) to the apostles (and a more 'institutional' theology).

The first idea presumes that, sometime during the canonical process, the narrative of Acts became associated with the ancient literature of 'acts' (*pracheis*), setting aside its original function, like Luke's Gospel, of a διήγησις (Luke 1:1), a genre of historical 'narrative'. On the other hand, an 'acts' is yet another genre of historical narrative consisting of stories of persons (real or fictive) with exceptional powers who act in mighty ways. Significantly, the literary 'acts' is a kind of aretalogy—a 'folk' narrative about the wondrous powers of someone who participated significantly in a community's or nation's history. Indeed, the canonical process recognized the importance of a narrative about the powerful words and deeds of the apostles whose witness to the risen Christ founded the Church and formed its rule of faith.

Significantly, such a narrative about heroic powers scores a deeply religious point as well, since these mighty deeds were not of one's own making but rather testified to divine favor. Not only was the hero divinely blessed, but the narrative's readers were typically insiders who linked their own destiny with that of their heroes whose favored status indicated their own. In this regard, the second half of the title, 'of the apostles', envisages a similar clue for reading Acts in the context of the Christian Scriptures. Given the importance of the Spirit's work in enabling witness to the risen Jesus, the credit of mighty 'acts' to the apostles is something of a misnomer—from the author's pentecostal perspective they are in truth 'acts of the Spirit'. What theological significance attends to the title's shift of focus from Spirit to the apostles?

Perhaps such a shift during the second century reflects an interest in defending 'mainstream' Christianity's claims against rivals (e.g. Judaism, Gnosticism, Montanism), but, as a canonical marker, it orients the current reader to Acts for interpreting its message. That is, the reader of a narrative who focuses on the story of apostles rather than on the 'signs and wonders' of the Spirit is naturally drawn to the authority of these Spirit-filled persons, who exemplify particular commitments and values for subsequent generations of believers who confess their loyalty to the 'One Holy Catholic and Apostolic Church'. The role of the canonical narrative is to shape identity into the next generation.

HELLENISTIC PHILOSOPHY AND THE NEW TESTAMENT

GREGORY E. STERLING

In his presidential address to the Society of New Testament Studies which he delivered in 1993, Martin Hengel correctly affirmed that 'a New Testament scholar who understands only the New Testament, *cannot* at all correctly understand this'.[1] What else should he or she understand? Ideally, as much as she or he can about the Hellenistic, Roman, and Jewish worlds; realistically, choices have to be made. I suggest that one of the more promising choices is Hellenistic philosophy.

At first, this might seem strange. New Testament writers rarely mention Hellenistic philosophers or their works explicitly. When they do, they reveal divergent judgments. The author of Colossians warns the community against 'someone' taking them prisoner 'through philosophy and empty deception' (Col. 2:9). 'Empty deception' is probably the author's way of describing the Colossians' 'philosophy' (see below). On the other hand, the author of Acts offers a positive assessment. He sets the scene for Paul's *Aereopagetica* by presenting him in debate with certain Epicurean and Stoic philosophers who charge the Christian missionary with the crime for which Socrates was executed (Acts 17:18, 20; Xenophon, *Mem.* 1:1:1; cf. also Justin Martyr, *1 Apol.* 5:3; *2 Apol.* 10:5). This is not the first time in Acts that a disciple or group of disciples appears in a role reminiscent of Socrates (cf. Acts 4:19; 5:29; and Plato, *Apol.* 29d). The speech which follows is an argument that Greek philosophy is a forerunner to Christianity. The author even cites a line from Aratus of Soli who learned his Stoicism from Zeno, the founder of the Stoa (Acts 17:28; Aratus, *Phaen.* 5). In this way, the author anticipates the more famous formulation of Clement of Alexandria who argued that Greek philosophy was for the Greeks what the law was for the Jews (*Strom.* 1.5.28; cf. also Philo, *Virt.* 65, for an earlier Jewish version). Such a view hardly swept the field; there were always opponents. Clement's counterpart on the southern shore of the Mediterranean, Tertullian,

---

[1]   M. Hengel, 'Aufgaben der neutestamentlichen Wissenschaft', *NTS* 40 (1994), p. 321.

expressed his dissent in an often cited *bon mot*: 'What in fact does Athens have to do with Jerusalem?' (*Praes.* 7:9).

These statements—both the rejections and the recommendations—point to the fact that early Christians did not avoid Hellenistic philosophy. Within the context of the first two centuries, it would be difficult to see how they could. There are several factors which naturally led early Christians to appropriate Hellenistic philosophy. First, early Christians' monotheistic understanding of an imageless God finds a counterpart in Greek philosophy. It is not at all surprising that, when Greeks first encountered groups of Christianity's parent religion, they naturally compared them to philosophers (e.g. Theophrastus in Porphyry, *De abst.* 2:26; Megasthenes in Clement, *Strom.* 1:15:72:5; and Clearchus of Soli in Josephus, *Apion* 1:176–83). Jewish authors later cultivated this image by presenting themselves as a philosophical movement. The most obvious example of this is the practice of presenting sectarian groups as philosophical schools who either devote themselves to contemplation (e.g. Philo's portrait of the Therapeutae [*Contempl.* 26, 28, 67, 69, 89] and Essenes [*Prob.* 88]) or differ in ways analogous to the Hellenistic philosophical schools (e.g. Josephus's presentation of Jewish sects [*War* 2:119–66; *Ant.* 18:11–25]). Jewish authors such as Aristobulus, the author of the Wisdom of Solomon, and Philo used Hellenistic philosophy to restate their own understandings of the divine. It should hardly occasion surprise to discover Christians appropriating concepts from Hellenistic philosophy to present their evolving christologies, for example, Origen's understanding of the incarnation (*Prin.* 2:6:3). Secondly, during the Hellenistic and Roman periods, Hellenistic philosophy invited this appropriation by becoming more religiously oriented. This is clearly evident in Middle Platonism when Eudorus, following Plato, defined the purpose of life (τέλος ἀγαθῶν) as 'likeness to God' (ὁμοίωσις θεῷ [Plato, *Tht.* 176a-b; Eudorus in Stobaeus 2:7:3 = 2:49:8-12 Wachsmuth; Philo, *Fug.* 63). This proclivity became so enticing in some instances that someone like Philo of Alexandria thought Moses and Plato both grasped the same realities, although Moses more fully (e.g. *Virt.* 65; *Spec.* 2:164-67). Similarly, Justin Martyr argued that Socrates was a Christian since he lived according to the Logos (*1 Apol.* 46:3). Thirdly, the moral emphasis of Christian paraenesis finds its closest Greco-Roman counterpart in moral philosophy. Seneca described the function of philosophy to Lucilius in these words: 'it forms and fashions the soul, sets life in order, rules over actions, demonstrates what should be done and what should be given up...' (*Ep.* 16:3). In another letter he pointedly asks: 'Is philosophy not the law of life?' (*Ep.* 94:39). Jewish predecessors had already learned the value of casting Jewish ethics in the form of Greek virtues (e.g. *Testaments of the Twelve Patriarchs*; *4 Maccabees*; Pseudo-Phocylides; Philo, *Virt.*). Later Christians would make this connection explicit by christianizing pagan philosophers such as Seneca (Tertullian, *De anima* 20; Jerome, *Ad Joven* 1:49), Epictetus (Origen, *Ag. Celsus* 6:2), and Musonius Rufus (Justin Martyr, *2 Apol.* 8:1; Origen, *Ag. Celsus* 3:66). So great was the attraction of Seneca's moral outlook that a fourth-century Christian (or Christians) composed a set of fourteen fictitious letters between Paul and Seneca.[2]

These observations help us to pose the question of the importance of Hellenistic philosophy for the interpretation of New Testament texts in a historical framework. We have uncontested Jewish precedents and unambiguous patristic evidence for Jewish and Christian use of Hellenistic philosophy. Do the authors of the New Testament stand within this tradition, or do they represent an alternative perspective?

STATUS QUAESTIONIS

While there have been many individual attempts to answer this question, there have been three sustained efforts. The initial attempt came in the seventeenth century in the form of *Observationes* and *Annotationes*, two closely related forms of commentaries which provide parallels to New Testament texts. It reached its apex in Johann Jakob Wettstein's (1693–1754) edition of the New Testament which supplied both an *apparatus criticus* for the text and an apparatus listing parallels. Wettstein explained the rationale for the latter in his accompanying essay 'On the Interpretation of the New Testament'. He wrote: 'If you want to understand the books of the New Testament more clearly and more fully, clothe yourself in the person of those to whom they were first delivered by the apostles for reading'. He continued: 'Transfer yourself in thought to that time and that place where they were first read' (Wettstein 1962: II, p. 878). The parallels he listed were offered as a means of recreating that lost

---

2   For the texts, see E. Hennecke and W. Schneemelcher, *New Testament Apocrypha* (2 vols.; Louisville: Westminster/John Knox Press, rev. edn, 1991, 1992), II, pp. 46-53.

world, largely—although not exclusively—through lexical material. Wettstein was so successful that his collection has not yet been superseded in a single source, although there are currently several efforts underway to do so. One of these is an effort to present parallels to the New Testament from a history-of-religions perspective. The initial publication came in Germany (Berger and Colpe 1987), but has recently been seconded by an English counterpart (Boring, Berger, and Colpe 1995). There is another project underway to revise Wettstein's New Testament, the *Neuer Wettstein* (Strecker and Schnelle 1997). Although the scope of interest for these projects extends beyond the philosophical material, it is easily one of the richest sources of parallels.

The enduring value as well as the limitations of Wettstein's New Testament have long been recognized. In the early decades of this century, C.F. Georg Heinrici launched a revision effort. Like the contemporary project, he labeled his 'a new Wettstein'; however, the name was later altered to *Corpus Hellenisticum Novi Testamenti* (CHNT).[3] Although the project had a well defined objective, the task of the project and the political difficulties created by two world wars have forced the project to move in fits and starts. There are currently three centers working on the two major branches of material: the Hellenistic Jewish at Halle, Germany, and the pagan at both Utrecht, The Netherlands, and the Divinity School of the University of Chicago in the USA. The admirable but extremely ambitious goal of the project to investigate everything from antiquity which is of significance for an understanding of the New Testament forced the heads of the project to rethink the feasibility of issuing a new Wettstein. They wisely chose to publish the conclusions of their research in a series of interim articles and monographs. To date they have published six volumes in the *Studia ad Corpus Hellenisticum Novi Testamenti* series, and a number of monographs and articles elsewhere. The project is especially important because the initial publications of those working on the pagan materials concentrated on Hellenistic moral philosophers. These include many of the major figures: Apollonius of Tyana (Petzke 1970), Dio Chrysostom (Mussies 1972), Plutarch (Almquist 1946; Betz 1975 and 1978), Musonius Rufus (van der Horst 1974), Hierocles (van der Horst

---

3   For a recent summary of the project by one of its leaders, see P.W. van der Horst, 'Corpus Hellenisticum', *ABD* 1 (1992), pp. 1157-61.

1975), and Lucian (Betz 1961). Unlike Wettstein, who worked from the New Testament to Greco-Roman parallels, publications within this project set up their comparisons in numerous ways: from the New Testament to Greco-Roman parallels, from Greco-Roman texts to the New Testament, and thematic arrangements.

The third collaborative effort has concentrated on a more restricted corpus than the previous two. During his career at the Divinity School of Yale University, Abraham Malherbe worked on and promoted the study of Hellenistic moral philosophers. The work which he has inspired has progressed in two stages. In the first, he served as teacher and *Doktorvater*. He published his own work in articles (Malherbe 1987, 1989, 1992), and successfully encouraged a number of students to write and publish their dissertations or revised dissertations (Hock 1980; Balch 1981; Stowers 1981; Fiore 1986; Fitzgerald 1988). This process has now reached a second generation with his students producing students in the same area (Glad 1995). The second stage began when several of his former students, under the leadership of John T. Fitzgerald, organized the Hellenistic Moral Philosophy and Early Christianity Group of the Society of Biblical Literature. While Malherbe's influence continues to be felt, the group has become more diverse and taken on an identity of its own. In contrast to previous efforts which have primarily worked from one text to other sets of texts, this group has worked on producing translations of obscure texts (Clay, Glad, Konstan, Thom, and Ware forthcoming) and *topoi* common to both moral philosophy and Christian paraenesis (Fitzgerald 1996 and 1997). In the latter case, New Testament texts are but a small part of the larger effort to understand the topos in various philosophical traditions.

AREAS OF RESEARCH

The diversity of the major projects and their range of interests indicate the potential Hellenistic philosophy has for understanding the New Testament. The following are *suggestions* based on some of the larger areas of past and potential research. I have not made any attempt to be exhaustive. The material naturally falls into several major (overlapping) divisions.

Paradigms: Prophets, Pastors, or Philosophers?

At the end of the third century CE, a governor of lower Egypt named Hierocles wrote a treatise entitled *Philalethes* ('Lover of

Truth') comparing Apollonius of Tyana, the first century CE Neopythagorean, to Jesus of Nazareth. The work generated enough excitement that Eusebius of Caesarea felt compelled to write a response. Heriocles had a case: there are a number of striking similarities between the two, especially in the miracles they performed (see Petzke 1970). While the thrust of the controversy was not whether Jesus was a philosopher but whether Apollonius was divine, the debate points out Jesus' similarities to a philosophical figure.

In recent years, the specific point of comparison has been with the Cynics. One of the most famous descriptions of Cynics comes from the Stoic Epictetus. This student of Musonius Rufus opens his description of the ideal Cynic, an ideal many Stoics did not consider personally attainable, with a question: 'How is it possible for someone who has nothing, is naked, without home, without hearth, unbathed, without servant, without city to live comfortably? Look, God has sent you one who will demonstrate in practice that it is possible.' He then quotes his imaginary Cynic: 'Look at me. I am without home, without city, without possession, without a servant. I sleep on the ground. I have no wife, no child, no lousy governor's mansion, but only the earth, sky, and one lousy threadbare cloak.' He then challenges: 'Yet what am I lacking? Am I not without pain? Am I not without fear? Am I not free? Which of you has ever seen me fail to get what I want or fall into what I would avoid?' He then turns to interpersonal relationships: 'When have I ever censured either God or human, or accused anyone? None of you has ever seen me depressed, have you? How do I deal with those whom you fear and hold in high regard? Isn't it as though they were slaves?' He comes to the climax: 'Who has seen me and not thought that he saw his king and master?' Epictetus then urges his audience: 'Look at these Cynic words! Look at the character! Look at the commitment!' He does so because he knows that not everyone accepts this ideal depiction: 'No, but a lousy wallet, staff, and great jaws [make a Cynic]' (3:22:45-50).

It would be hard for those familiar with the New Testament to miss some of the similarities between this description and various New Testament texts. One of the most obvious is the Q text containing Jesus' responses to would-be followers. Jesus' reply to the first volunteer echoes the text above: 'The foxes have holes and the bird have nests, but the Son of Man does not have anywhere to lay his head'. The second response, 'Let the dead bury their own dead' (Matt. 8:18-22//Luke 9:57-60 [61-62]), sounds very much like the Cynic disdain for burial conventions (Lucian, *Dem.* 66; Diogenes Laertius 6:79). In the same way Jesus sent the disciples on an itinerant mission charging them: 'Carry no money-bag, no wallet, no sandals. Greet no one in the way' (Luke 10:4//Matt. 10:10). While the specifics of the Q text differ from the distinctive features of the Cynics, the ethos is the same, that is, homeless itinerants who are reduced to living by the generosity of others. Such analogies have led several scholars in recent years to argue that the closest parallel to Jesus and the Jesus movement which produced Q is Cynicism (e.g. Theissen 1975 [for Q]; Downing 1988 and 1992; Crossan 1991 and 1994; Mack 1988 and 1993). Certainly there were Cynics in the general area, for example, Menippus, Meleager, and Oenomaus all hailed from Gadara in Syria and Meleager spent his adult life in Tyre. It is not, however, clear that the villagers of rural Galilee would have perceived Jesus and his followers as identical with the urban Cynics who began to resurface in the first and second centuries CE after an apparent hiatus. The identification is even more problematic if we compare the essence of the messages. 'The kingdom of God', a concept squarely anchored in Judaism, stood at the heart of Jesus' message. This is radically different than 'living according to nature' which lies at the center of Cynic preaching. We should also remember that Jesus formed a movement which came to include communities, a social phenomenon at odds with the Cynics as we know them. In short, I find it difficult to conceive of Jesus of Nazareth in terms that are not principally Jewish. This does not mean that he and his immediate followers did not share some aspects in common with Cynics. It is, however, one thing to share common life-styles and rhetorical techniques; it is quite another to argue that a Jewish prophet was a Cynic philosopher.[4]

A much stronger case can be made for Paul's indebtedness to

---

4   There are a significant number of critiques of the Cynic hypothesis from a broad spectrum of perspectives. Some of the more important include: C.M. Tuckett, 'A Cynic Q', *Bib* 70 (1989), pp. 349-76; H.D. Betz, 'Jesus and the Cynics: Survey and Analysis of a Hypothesis', *JR* 74 (1994), pp. 453-75; R. Horsley, 'Jesus, Itinerant Cynic or Israelite Prophet?', in *Images of Jesus Today* (ed. J.H. Charlesworth and W.P. Weaver; Faith and Scholarship Colloquies, 3; Valley Forge, PA: Trinity Press International, 1994), pp. 68-97; J.M. Robinson, 'The History-of-Religions Taxonomy of Q: The Cynic Hypothesis', in *Gnosisforschung und Religionsgeschichte: Festschrift für Kurt Rudolph zum 65. Geburtstag* (ed. H. Preißler and H. Seiwert; Marburg: Diagonal, 1994), pp. 247-65; P.R. Eddy, 'Jesus as Diogenes? Reflections on the Cynic Jesus Thesis', *JBL* 115 (1996), pp. 449-69.

popular philosophy. The discussion began in earnest with efforts to
discover the history-of-religions background for an apostle. Walter
Schmithals stated the issue in these words: 'The question is whether
there is not at least an *institution* to be found which could be
compared with the primitive Christian apostolate'. Citing Epictetus's
statements as his principal evidence, he affirmed that the Cynic-Stoic
sage who was also divinely commissioned as a messenger/proclaimer
was the closest analogy.[5] In recent years, the discussion has become
much more nuanced. Malherbe has pointed out Paul's familiarity with
the traditions of popular moral philosophers, especially the Cynics, in
a series of publications (Malherbe 1987 and 1989). For example, he
pointed out the striking parallels between Paul's defense of his
ministry in Thessalonica (1 Thess. 2:1-12) and Dio Chrysostom's
description of an ideal Cynic (32:11-12) (Malherbe 1989: 35-38). He
did, however, recognize a fundamental difference between Paul and
the Cynics: 'Paul...was a founder of communities, of which the
Cynics had none. In his communal concern, Paul was more like the
Epicureans, although we know little about contemporary Epicurean
communities' (Malherbe 1989: 8). The study of the Herculaneum
papyri, and the identification of some of the writings as Epicurean, are
now changing that. Clarence Glad has recently argued that Pauline
psychagogy ('guidance of souls') finds its closest analogy in the
Epicurean communities of Athens, Naples, and Herculaneum. These
communities were headed by Zeno of Sidon, the scholiarch of the
Epicurean school at Athens, and two of his students, Siro at Naples
and Philodemus at Herculaneum. Glad argues that Paul's apparent
inconsistencies in dealing with the Corinthians were the result of his
practice of psychagogic adaptability (cf. 1 Cor. 9:19-23). In particular,
he contends that the shift from harsh to gentle responses within a
community setting is best illuminated by the treatises of Philodemus
from Herculaneum. Unlike some of the recent publications on Jesus
and the Jesus movement which tend to identify Jesus and his followers
with Cynics, Malherbe and Glad prefer to point out that Paul is
simultaneously *Paulus christianus* and *Paulus hellenisticus*.

There is an important distinction which needs to be made in all
assessments of early Christians and Hellenistic philosophers: we must
distinguish between our analyses of ancient figures as witnesses to

---

5   W. Schmithals, *The Office of Apostle in the Early Church* (Nashville/New
York: Abingdon, 1969), pp. 111-14.

philosophical practices/traditions and their self-identities. For example, Philo of Alexandria is a witness to Middle Platonism; he was not, however, a professional philosopher working in the Platonic tradition in the same sense that Alcinous was. Philo's principal commitment was to Moses, even if his Moses was a Platonized Moses. Similarly, Jesus of Nazareth, his immediate followers, and early Christians may share a great deal in common with different philosophical traditions; we must not, however, forget their primary loyalty. Such allegiances often result in modifications to the material they appropriate.

This limitation does not, however, negate the importance of working comparatively with philosophical materials. There is still a good deal of work to do on the traditions in the Gospels. Detailed analyses of the sayings material is limited. Hans Dieter Betz's recent commentary on the Sermon on the Mount is perhaps the most comprehensive work on a significant textual base.[6] I think that, in the case of a Gospel such as Luke, it would be worth examining how philosophy shapes the larger narrative. For example, I am suspicious that the consistent elimination of fear and strong emotion in the portrayal of Jesus' death in Luke is modeled on accounts of the death of Socrates (e.g. Luke 22:39-46//Mark 14:32-42; Luke 23:27-31; Luke 23:48//Mark 15:33-39).[7] The same need exists for the epistolary literature. Malherbe has worked primarily in the Thessalonian correspondence and Pastorals; and Glad in 1 Corinthians. While these are the most obvious beginning points, they do not exhaust the possibilities.

Hellenistic Moral Philosophy and Christian Paraenesis

This previous work does, however, point to the most promising area of research, the formation of individuals and communities through established paraenetic practices. For the sake of clarity I will group these into larger analytical subdivisions.

Modes of Discourse. Within the twentieth century, researchers have explored three modes of discourse which are specifically related to popular moral philosophy. Although these have at times been confused with genres, they are best considered as modes of discourse

---

6   H.D. Betz, *The Sermon on the Mount* (Hermeneia; Minneapolis: Fortress Press, 1995).

7   J. Kloppenborg, 'Exitus Clari Viri: The Death of Jesus in Luke', *TJT* 8 (1992), pp. 106-20, is a beginning point for research.

rather than literary categories. By classifying these as philosophical modes of discourse, I do not mean to imply that they were restricted to philosophical circles. They were, however, carefully cultivated within the philosophical tradition of education.

Diatribe (διατριβή). Rudolf Bultmann launched his career with a thin but famous dissertation in which he summarized previous research on the diatribe and applied it to Paul (Bultmann 1910). The older view which he inherited was that Bion of Borysthenes created the diatribe. Later Cynics and Stoics developed it as a form of a philosophical sermon for popular consumption. More recently, Stanley Stowers has demonstrated that the diatribe was intimately associated with school instruction among philosophers (Stowers 1981). It is attested among numerous philosophical traditions: Cynics (Teles, Dio Chrysostom), Stoics (Seneca, Musonius Rufus, Epictetus), Epicureans (Philodemus), and Platonists (Plutarch, Maximus of Tyre). One of the clearest ways in which we can understand the significance of the term is to remember that the oldest manuscripts of Arrian's notes of Epictetus's lectures give them the title 'diatribes'. Diatribe thus refers to the dialogical or give-and-take mode of classroom discourse which uses the Socratic method of censure and persuasion. It was not, however, restricted to philosophical circles, as Thomas Schmeller has shown (Schmeller 1987). In his latest assessment, Stowers suggests that the term should be used 'for moral lectures and discussions in philosophical schools, written records of that activity, and literary imitations of that kind of pedagogical discourse'.[8] Both Jews and Christians found the method to be useful. In Alexandria, the author of the Wisdom of Solomon and Philo of Alexandria employ the diatribe (Wendland 1895). Paul uses it extensively in Romans (e.g. interlocutor [2:17-29; 3:1-9; 3:27–4:2], address in the second person singular [2:1-5, 17-29; 8:2; 9:19-21; 11:17-24; 14:4, 10], and objections [6:1, 15; 7:7, 13; 9:14, 19; 11:1, 11, 19]) and less frequently in other letters (e.g. 1 Cor. 6:12-20; 15:29-35). The only other New Testament author to make clear use of it is the author of James (e.g. address in second person [2:19-23; 4:13–5:6], objection [2:18], and rhetorical questions [2:2-7, 14-16; 3:20-21; 4:4, 12]).

The Paraenetic Style (ὁ παραινετικὸς χαρακτήρ). Pseudo-Libanius, the ancient epistolographer, describes the paraenetic style in

---

8   S. Stowers, 'Diatribe', *ABD* 2 (1992), p. 191. Cf. also his discussion, 'The Diatribe', in *Greco-Roman Literature and the New Testament* (ed. D.E. Aune; SBLSBS, 21; Atlanta: Scholars Press, 1988), pp. 71-83.

these words: 'The paraenetic style is that style by which we exhort (παραινοῦμεν) someone by urging him to undertake something or to avoid something'. He suggests that it is divided into two parts: encouragement and dissuasion. There was, however, a problem in the ancient world: some confused paraenesis which only encourages what is self-evident with advice which must persuade.[9] Unfortunately, the understanding of paraenesis is still problematic. One of the complicating factors which needs attention is the relationship between paraenesis as a form of discourse and paraenesis as a literary category. For example, within the New Testament we can point to three different applications of paraenesis: paraenetic letters (see below), paraenetic sections of letters (e.g. Rom. 12:1–15:13; Gal. 5:1–6:10; 1 Thess. 4:1–5:25; Eph. 4:1–6:20; Col. 3:1–4:6), and letters which scatter paraenetic sections and techniques throughout (e.g. 1 Corinthians and Hebrews). Since paraenesis is not restricted to a distinct literary genre or genres, I think that we should distinguish between a paraenetic mode of discourse and paraenetic forms of discourse.

Some of the most important features of the paraenetic mode of discourse which have echoes in the New Testament are: the use of the language of exhortation, the appeal to tradition or what the hearers already know, the use of examples to be imitated and an antithetical style which contrasts what should be avoided with what should be emulated (Fiore 1986: 10-21; Malherbe 1989: 49-66 and 1992: 278-93). The best New Testament examples of these features come from 1 Corinthians, 1 Thessalonians, and the Pastorals. Paul and his later student(s) frequently place the language of exhortation/advice on the apostle's lips (e.g. (δια-)μαρτύρομαι [1 Thess. 2:12; 4:6; 1 Tim. 5:21; 2 Tim. 2:14; 4:1]; νουθετέω [1 Cor. 4:14]; παραγγέλλω/παραγγελία [1 Cor. 7:10; 11:17; 1 Thess. 4:2, 11; 1 Tim. 1:5, 18; 6:13]; παρακαλέω/παράκλησις [1 Cor. 1:10; 4:13, 16; 16:15; 1 Thess. 2:3, 17; 4:1, 10; 5:14; 1 Tim. 1:3; 2:1]; and παραμυθέομαι [1 Thess. 2:12]). Nor is this list complete: it could be expanded significantly if we included the references to Paul's charges to his deputies or to mutual exhortation. Paul's use of 'you know' or 'just as you know' in 1 Thessalonians (2:1; 3:3, 4; 4:2; 5:2 and 1:5; 2:2, 5, 11 respectively) is strikingly similar to Seneca's anaphoric use of 'you know' in his

---

9   I have used the edition of A. Malherbe, *Ancient Epistolary Theorists* (SBLSBS, 19; Atlanta: Scholars Press, 1988), p. 69 (Pseudo-Libanius 5).

defense of advice as exhortation (*Ep.* 94:25-26). In the same way that the Pseudo-Socratic Cynic epistles appeal to Socrates as an example, Paul and his disciples appeal to his life as a model (e.g. 1 Cor. 4:16; Gal. 4:12; Phil. 3:17; 1 Thess. 1:6; 2 Thess. 3:7; 1 Tim. 1:16; 2 Tim. 1:13; 3:10-11; cf. also 2 Tim. 4:6-8 [for details see Fiore 1986]). Finally, like Epictetus and many others, Paul likes to state things antithetically, that is, 'not...but' (e.g. Epictetus 2:12:14; 1 Thess. 2:3-4).

The Protreptic Style (ὁ προτρεπτικὸς χαρακτήρ). Another factor which increases our difficulty in understanding paraenesis is the confusion over whether protreptic (an exhortation to take up the philosophic life) and paraenetic refer to distinct rhetorical traditions or whether protreptic is subsumed beneath paraenesis. Like paraenesis, protreptic can refer to either a mode of discourse or a distinctive literary form. Unlike paraenesis, no rhetorician or epistolographer defined a protreptic literary work. Perhaps this is due to the antipathy between rhetoricians and philosophers who cultivated the protreptic style. One of our best descriptions of the style is found in Epictetus's defense of the protreptic style against an interlocutor who wants to defend the epideictic style. Epictetus maintains that a philosopher's task is to improve the hearers, not entertain them: 'Men, a philosopher's school is an operating room. You should not leave in a state of happiness but of pain' (3:23:30). His interlocutor then asks whether there is a protreptic style. Epictetus, on affirming there is, goes on to describe it: 'It is the ability to demonstrate to one and many the battle in which they are thrown about and that they think about everything except what they want'. He explains: 'For they want the things which produce happiness, but they are looking for them in all the wrong places' (3:23:34). The protreptic style thus consists of at least two components: negatively, it is pointing out the problems with the hearer's present state; and positively, it is offering a solution through an invitation to take up the philosophic life.

This form of philosophical rhetoric could and did assume literary shape. While Plato criticized the Sophists for their protreptic speeches (*Euthd.* 278e–282d, 288b–307c), he also wrote several himself (*Phaedo* and *Epinomis*). His most famous student and his successors also composed *protreptikoi* (Aristotle [Diogenes Laertius 5:22 and Stobaeus 4:32:21 = 5:786:1-4 Hense]; Theophrastus [Diogenes Laertius 5:49]; Demetrius of Phaleron [Diogenes Laertius 5:81]; and Aristo of Ceos [Diogenes Laertius 7:163]). Cynics (Antisthenes

[Diogenes Laertius 6:16] and Monimus [Diogenes Laertius 7:83]) and Stoics (Persaeus [Diogenes Laertius 7:36]; Cleanthes [Diogenes Laertius 7:175]; Chrysippus [Plutarch, *Mor.* 1041e]; and Poseidonius [Diogenes Laertius 7:91, 129]) also wrote invitations to their philosophical traditions. One of the most famous is Cicero's *Hortensius* which is now lost, but which exercised a profound influence over Augustine (*Conf.* 3:4). Such a genre had a natural appeal to Jews (Wisdom of Solomon) and Christians (Justin Martyr, *Dialogue*; Clement, *Protrepticus*; Minicius Felix, *Octavius*; and the *Epistle to Diognetus*). Paul's letter to the Romans is probably a letter drawing from his protreptic preaching but modified to suit the specific requirements of the occasion.[10] This may help to explain why he opens with a severe censure and then moves on to offer hope through a new life.

Literary Forms. These examples point out that New Testament authors, particularly Paul and his disciples, knew and used the language and techniques of moral exhortation. They also used the larger forms which were typical of such discourse.

Paraenetic Letters. The largest such form is actually a type of letter. Pseudo-Libanius offers the following sample of a παραινετικὴ ἐπιστολή: 'My good friend, always be a follower of virtuous men. For it is better for the follower of good men to enjoy a good reputation than following the bad to be shamed by all.' This short sample points out several important features. First, ancients recognized the paraenetic letter as a distinct form. Secondly, the essence of exhortation is captured in the gnomic encouragement to imitate worthy models. Thirdly, reputation is the motivating factor. Fourthly, style and form are inseparable. This is unmistakable in the use of imitation and contrast. The function of such a letter is not to teach anything new, that would be advice; rather, it is to reinforce what the hearers already know but have not incorporated into their lives fully. There are several letters within the New Testament which should probably be considered paraenetic: 1 Thessalonians, 1 Timothy, 2 Timothy, Titus, James, and 1 Peter.

Lists of Virtues and Vices. A common literary form in moral instruction is lists of vices and virtues. The Stoics and those

---

10   D.E. Aune, 'Romans as a *Logos Protreptikos*', in *The Romans Debate* (ed. K.P. Donfried; Peabody, MA: Hendrickson, 2nd edn, 1991), pp. 278-96, has argued Romans is a *logos protreptikos*.

influenced by them were particularly fond of such lists. So, for example, Dio Chrysostom has more than 80 of these lists. The Stoics frequently formed virtue lists by subordinating appropriate virtues beneath Plato's four cardinal virtues ('prudence' [φρόνησις], 'moderation' [σωφροσύνη], 'justice' [δικαιοσύνη], and 'courage' [ἀνδρεία]) (Plato, *Phd.* 69c; *Rep.* 427e; *Leg.* 631c). They sometimes did the same for the corresponding vices ('folly' [ἀφροσύνη], 'profligacy' [ἀκολασία], 'injustice' [ἀδικία], and 'cowardice' [δειλία]) (for examples see *SVF* 3.262-94). Jewish authors both appropriated lists and created their own. We have numerous examples of the four cardinal virtues common in Platonic and Stoic circles (e.g. *4 Macc.* 1:2-4, 18; 5:23; Wis. 8:7; and Philo, *Leg.* 1:71-72) as well as other lists, some of which can be incredibly long (e.g. Philo, *Sacr.* 32). They are also common in the New Testament: there are approximately 18 independent vice lists (Matt. 15:19; Mark 7:21-22; Rom. 1:29-31; 13:13; 1 Cor. 5:10-11; 6:9-10; 2 Cor. 12:20-21; Eph. 5:3-5; 1 Tim. 1:9-10; 6:4-5; 2 Tim. 3:2-4; Titus 3:3; 1 Pet. 2:1; 4:3, 15; Rev. 9:21; 21:8; 22:15), 16 independent virtue lists (2 Cor. 6:6-7a; Eph. 4:2-3; 5:9; Phil. 4:8; 1 Tim. 3:2-4, 8-10 and 12, 11; 4:12; 6:11, 18; 2 Tim. 2:22-25; 3:10; Titus 2:2-10; Heb. 7:26; 1 Pet. 3:8; 2 Pet. 1:5-7) and four compound lists (Gal. 5:19-21 and 22-23; Eph. 4:31 and 4:32–5:2; Col. 3:5-8 and 12; Titus 1:7 and 1:8). Interestingly, in the compound lists, the vices always precede the virtues. These lists can assume several different forms: most lack connectives (asyndetic [e.g. Gal. 5:19-21, 22-23]) but some use multiple connectives (polysyndetic [e.g. 1 Cor. 6:9-10]). The traditions that stand behind New Testament lists are problematic. A list such as Matt. 15:19, which specifies the sins of the Decalogue, clearly comes from a Jewish tradition. On the other hand, many—although not all—of the virtues and vices are common to the moral philosophers as well. Perhaps more intriguing is the function of such lists. They are frequently used to illustrate virtue and vice (e.g. Mark 7:21-22). They can serve protreptically to point out the morally unacceptable condition of the hearer in need of moral conversion (e.g. Rom. 1:29-31), paraenetically to encourage hearers to continue their moral improvement by reminding them of how far they had come through contrasting lists (e.g. Gal. 5:19-23; Eph. 4:31–5:2; Col. 3:5-8, 12) or by reminding them of either where they once were (e.g. 1 Cor. 6:9-10) or need to be (e.g. 2 Pet. 1:5-7). A vice list can function polemically to characterize an opponent (e.g. 2 Tim. 3:2-4), while a virtue list can spell out qualifications for a Church office (e.g. 1 Tim. 3:2-4, 8-10 and 12, 11).

Hardship Lists (περιστάσεις). These are not the only lists which are largely indebted to the moral philosophers. Another list is the so-called hardship catalogues (περιστάσεις, e.g., Rom. 8:35-39; 1 Cor. 4:9-13; 2 Cor. 4:8-9; 6:4-10; 11:23-28; 12:10; Phil. 4:11-12; 2 Tim. 3:11). The term περίστασις means both circumstance and difficult circumstance. From this, some writers began to use the term as a comprehensive phrase for a list of difficult circumstances (Fitzgerald 1988: 33-46). One of the most striking New Testament examples is Paul's use of four contrasting clauses in 2 Cor. 4:8-9 to describe how God has made evident the presence of the divine treasure (the message of Jesus Christ) in clay pots (the apostles):

> put in a tight situation but not crushed,
> at a loss but not without a hint,
> hounded but not abandoned,
> thrown down but not out.

The apostle's description is similar to Plutarch's later paradoxical characterization of the Stoic sage (*Mor.* 1057e):

> although confined is not hindered,
> although thrown down a cliff is not forced,
> although stretched on the rack is not tortured,
> although mutilated is not made lame,
> although he falls in a wrestling match is unbeaten,
> although surrounded is impregnable,
> although sold by his enemies is untaken ...

John Fitzgerald (1988) and Martin Ebner (1991) have shown how Paul's hardship catalogues are part of his apostolic self-understanding. His use of such catalogues is particularly striking in his relationship with the Corinthians. The specific function of each catalogue varies with contextual concerns: sometimes Paul offers his own hardships as a model (1 Cor. 4:9-13 [see also 14-16]), at other times, he uses his hardships to demonstrate how God is at work in him (2 Cor. 4:8-9; 6:4-5), and at other times he uses a list polemically to distance himself from his opponents (2 Cor. 11:23-28). In all cases, the paradox of battered but not beaten which we find in the philosophers is at the fore. As we have learned to expect, Jewish authors had already appropriated such catalogues (e.g. Philo, *Det.* 34; *Jos.* 26; *T. Jos.* 1:3-7 [which contains a Christian interpolation]). Like Paul, some of these attribute the power to endure directly to God (e.g. *T. Jos.* 1:3-7).

However, this is not an exclusively Jewish-Christian feature: a Stoic like Seneca can also recognize the presence of divine power in suffering (*Ep.* 41:4-5). What I find most intriguing about Paul's use of these lists in his Corinthian correspondence is that they function as a means of authenticating his ministry. In this way, the lists impinge on Paul's self-understanding; yet, it is his self-understanding as an apostle of Jesus Christ, not a sage.

Haustafeln. Another form of a list or catalogue is the group of texts which set out the responsibilities of members of a household, which Martin Luther appropriately called *Haustafeln* (Eph. 5:21–6:9; Col. 3:18–4:1; 1 Pet. 2:13–3:17). These are based on the three pairs set out by Aristotle: master–slave, husband–wife, father–child (*Pol.* 1:1253b1-14; *N.E.* 1134b9-18; 1160a23–1161a10; cf. also Pseudo-Aristotle, *M.M.* 1:1194b5-28). Hellenistic moralists, especially Stoics, developed codes of behavior around these three pairs (e.g. Chrysippus in Pseudo-Plutarch, *Mor.* 7e; Aristo, who opposes the arrangement in Seneca, *Ep.* 94:1-2; Arius Didymus [in Stobaeus 2:7:26 = 2:148:5-149:24 Wachsmuth]). Others expanded the relationships in various directions (e.g. Hierocles, *On Duties*). The same expansion is evident in the New Testament and early Christian texts (1 Tim. 2:8-15; 6:1-2; Titus 2:1-10; *1 Clem.* 1:3; 21:6-9; Ignatius, *Pol.* 4:1–6:1; Polycarp, *Phil.* 4:2–6:1).

The source from which early Christians drew their *Haustafeln* has been the occasion of an extended debate in the twentieth century.[11] The main contours of the discussion are as follows. Early in the century, Martin Dibelius argued that Col. 3:18–4:1 was a Christianized version of a Stoic household code. Karl Weidinger (Dibelius's student), David Schroeder, and James Crouch have subsequently all pointed out that Greek-speaking Jews had already adopted household codes (Pseudo-Phocylides 175–227; Philo, *Dec.* 165–67; *Hypoth.* 8:7:3; Josephus, *Apion* 2:189–209). More recently, Dieter Lührmann, Klaus Thraede, and David Balch have argued that the discussions derive from the Hellenistic discussion of the topos *On Household Management* (περὶ οἰκονομίας) which derives from Aristotle's earlier presentation. The strength of the last position is the way the New Testament texts function contextually. It appears that New Testament authors are encouraging early Christians to live the

---

[11]   For summaries, see D. Balch, 'Household Codes', in *Greco-Roman Literature and the New Testament* , pp. 25-50; *idem*, 'Household Codes', *ABD* 3 (1992), pp. 318-20; and J.T. Fitzgerald, 'Haustafeln', *ABD* 3 (1992), pp. 80-81.

basic values of the larger world in order to avoid unnecessary criticism (e.g. 1 Pet. 2:11-12). This suggests that the appropriation may have been direct.

Topoi. Like several of the other categories we have mentioned, there is a debate about the meaning of *topos*. The ambiguity begins with Aristotle, who used τόπος to refer to both the contents of an argument and the form (*Rh.* and *Top.*). He made a further distinction between stereotypical arguments which are useful in specialized areas (ἴδιοι τόποι) and those which are useful in all areas (κοινοὶ τόποι or *loci communes*). The result has been a great deal of confusion both in antiquity and in modern scholarship. Alexander Pope expressed his disdain for the bewilderment with a barbed satire: 'I therefore propose that there be contrived with all convenient dispatch, at the public expense, a Rhetorical Chest of Drawers, consisting of three stories, the highest for the Deliberative, the middle for the Demonstrative, and the lowest for the Judicial'. He then adds the punchline: 'These shall be divided into Loci or Places, being repositories for Matter and Argument in the several kinds of oration or writing' (*Peri Bathous*, chap. 12). New Testament scholars have not helped the situation by using the term to refer to a literary category.[12] I prefer to follow Malherbe in this instance and understand the term to refer to 'conventional subjects' when applied to the moralists. There are a number of set themes which philosophers across a wide spectrum of views discuss. The easiest way to discover these is to compare the headings of moral essays, diatribes, or sections for our major sources, for example, Cicero, Seneca, Musonius Rufus, Epictetus, Hierocles, Plutarch, and Stobaeus.

The most widely studied *topos* in recent research is *On friendship* (περὶ φιλίας). Betz has shown how Paul draws on friendship motifs in his argument in Gal. 4:12-20.[13] Peter Marshall has examined Paul's relationship to the Corinthians from this perspective (Marshall 1987). A number of scholars in the SBL Hellenistic Moral Philosophy and Early Christianity Group have examined Philippians in light of friendship (L. Michael White in Balch, Ferguson, Meeks 1990: 201-

---

12   See D.G. Bradley, 'The *Topos* as Form in the Pauline Paraenesis', *JBL* 72 (1953), pp. 238-46 and the critiques of T.Y. Mullins, 'Topos as a New Testament Form', *JBL* 99 (1980), pp. 541-47 and J.C. Brunt, 'More on the *Topos* as a New Testament Form', *JBL* 104 (1985), pp. 495-500.

13   H.D. Betz, *Galatians* (Hermeneia; Philadelphia: Fortress Press, 1979), pp. 220-37.

15; John Reumann, Ken Berry, Abraham Malherbe, and John Fitzgerald in Fitzgerald 1996: 83-106, 107-24, 125-39, 141-60 respectively). Although I think it would be a mistake to suggest that early Christians adopted the philosophical model of friendship as a basis for their interpersonal relationships—fictive kinship is more appropriate—they clearly knew and used the concept.

Hellenistic Philosophy and the Beginnings of Christian Theology

It is widely recognized that it was not until the second century that Christians began extensively using Hellenistic philosophy to write Christian theology. There are, however, some exceptions which are worth noting. We should not think of these as systematic appropriations of metaphysical systems as is true with Clement and Origen, but as popular appropriations of metaphysical thought in exegetical or liturgical contexts.

Platonic Ontology and Metaphysics. Augustine thought that Neoplatonism was the philosophy best suited to Christianity, although he had some reservations about it (*City of God* 8:12). Some New Testament authors and communities found its predecessor to be attractive. This is somewhat surprising since there is a fundamental tension between the Platonic worldview and the eschatological/ apocalyptic worldview characteristic of most New Testament authors. The former operates with an atemporal ontological distinction between the world of being and the world of becoming. The latter moves along temporal lines in which the present is headed towards the future inauguration of the eternal reign of God. Yet not all Jews and Christians found the tension insurmountable. The author of the Wisdom of Solomon managed to combine Middle Platonism with a pronounced eschatology, although it was not apocalyptic. Similarly, Origen found it possible to work with Middle Platonism and Christian eschatology, even if some later found his eschatology objectionable. We should not therefore posit the two as impossible contradictories, but as two systems which stand in varying degrees of tension. I will offer four examples: two of these are commonly recognized, although disputed (Hebrews and John); two are more controversial (1 Corinthians and Colossians).

The Corinthians. The earliest significant influence of Platonic views appears to come from members of the Corinthian community who were influenced by Platonizing interpretations of Genesis 1–2 emanating from Jewish circles. The clearest example is in 1 Cor. 15:44-49 where Paul's eschatological orientation leads him to argue against the Corinthians' understanding of Gen. 1:26-27 and Gen. 2:7. The latter became the focal point of the controversy. Paul quotes it, but reverses the order of clauses c and b (1 Cor. 15:45). Nor was his reversal accidental, as his explanation makes clear: 'The spiritual is not first, but the natural'. Since Paul's comments are polemical in nature, the Corinthians appear to believe otherwise. The most likely explanation of the Corinthians' position is that they identified the spiritual with the human in Gen. 1:26-27 and the natural with the human in Gen. 2:7. Paul's christological eschatology leads him to identify the natural with Adam and the spiritual with Christ. The closest analogy to the Corinthians' view is that of Philo, who makes a Platonic distinction between the intelligible human of Gen. 1:26-27 who is in the image of God and the sense-perceptible human of Gen. 2:7 who is molded. For example, after citing Gen. 2:7 in *On the Creation of the World*, he comments: 'Through this statement he indicates that there is an enormous difference between the *anthropos* who has now been molded and the *anthropos* in the image of God who previously came into being...' (*Opif.* 134–35; cf. also *Leg.* 1:31-32; *Plant.* 18-19; *Det.* 83). It is probably the influence of this type of Platonizing exegesis which values the immortal soul and denigrates the corruptible body that led the Corinthians to deny the resurrection.[14]

Hebrews. Until the discovery of the Dead Sea Scrolls, virtually all New Testament scholars recognized a strong Platonic perspective in Hebrews. The scrolls, however, have led to a reappraisal of the influence of Platonism, beginning with a famous essay of C.K. Barrett.[15] Today, the relationship between the vertically oriented Platonism and the horizontally oriented apocalypticism within the letter is debated.[16] It appears to me that both perspectives are undeniably present. I can best illustrate this in two texts which use the

---

14   For details and bibliography, see G.E. Sterling, '"Wisdom among the Perfect": Creation Traditions in Alexandrian Judaism and Corinthian Christianity', *NovT* 37 (1995), pp. 355-84.

15   C.K. Barrett, 'The Eschatology of the Epistle to the Hebrews', in *The Background of the New Testament and its Eschatology* (ed. D. Daube and C.H. Dodd; Cambridge: Cambridge University Press, 1956), pp. 363-93.

16   Two important representatives in recent discussions are J.W. Thompson (1982), who argues for a Platonic background, and L.D. Hurst, *The Epistle to the Hebrews: Its Background of Thought* (SNTSMS, 65; Cambridge: Cambridge University Press, 1990), who argues against it in favor of apocalyptic traditions.

famous Platonic metaphor of 'shadow' (*Rep.* 7:515a-b), but in slightly different ways. The first is in the discussion of the tabernacle in chapter eight when the author refers to the priests on earth 'who serve in a shadowy copy (ὑποδείγματι καὶ σκιᾷ) of the heavenly (tabernacle)' (8:5). Although some have challenged the Platonism of this statement in recent years, several factors lead me to conclude it is present: the use of the Platonic image ('shadow'), the earthly/heavenly contrast, and the citation of Exod. 25:40 as a textual basis for the distinction. Interestingly, Philo of Alexandria makes the same Platonic distinction from the same text (*Leg.* 3:102-103; *Q.E.* 2:82). It may have been a well known interpretation in some circles. The second text uses identical imagery, but juxtaposes it with an eschatological perspective which operates temporally: 'For the law has a shadow (σκιάν) of the good things to come, not the very image of the things (οὐκ αὐτὴν τὴν εἰκόνα τῶν πραγμάτων)...' (10:1). Once again the imagery of the contrast is Platonic: 'shadow' (*Rep.* 7:515a-b) versus 'image' (*Crat.* 439a). As with the earlier text, the author considers the Mosaic cult and law to be but a shadowy reflection. What is surprising is that the reality ('image') is situated temporally rather than ontologically. I suggest that the audience and author both accept the Platonic distinction, but that the author adds the eschatological twist in keeping with his christological understanding of history. In this way, I think that the dynamics between author and community are similar to those between Paul and the Corinthians.

The Colossians. The shadow imagery appears in another New Testament document. The Colossian heresy is one of the most difficult problems of New Testament exegesis. The key evidence that it might have some basis in Platonism is in two phrases from the second of four warnings (2:8):

> Watch out lest someone take you captive
> through philosophy (διὰ τῆς φιλοσοφίας)
> and empty deception
>
> according to the tradition of humans,
> according to the elements of the cosmos (κατὰ τὰ στοιχεῖα τοῦ κόσμου)
> and not according to Christ.

In each of the two pairs of clauses following the warning, the author cites a phrase from the Colossians and qualifies it with a matching pejorative. As we have already pointed out, the first set of clauses suggests that the Colossians are appealing to 'philosophy'. The third warning provides a couple of specific hints about the identification of the philosophy: 'Therefore do not let anyone judge you in what you eat and drink or with respect to a feast or a new moon or a Sabbath celebration. These things are a shadow (σκιά) of what is to come, the reality (σῶμα) belongs to Christ' (2:16-17). This statement presupposes that the readers are familiar with an allegorical reading of the LXX along Platonic lines, since the author has no need to explain it. As with the Corinthians, the closest parallel is a statement of Philo of Alexandria who exhorted those who read the story of Babel literally 'not to stop with these things, but to go on to figurative readings; realizing that the words of the oracles are like certain shadows of the realities (σκιάς τινας ὡσανεὶ σωμάτων), but the meanings which are revealed are the true and underlying entities' (*Conf.* 190). The second clause of Col. 2:8 suggests that the Colossians are appealing to a system which includes 'the elements of the cosmos'. These appear to refer to the basic four or five elements; however, 2:20 suggests that the Colossians also understand these to mean elemental spirits. I think that the Colossians knew a system which correlated the elements with elemental spirits. The best example we have of such a system is Philo's demonology/angelology where he—in keeping with Middle Platonism—presents a *scala naturae* which posits a direct correspondence between the elements and their *genera*. The agreement in Philo's presentation in *Gig.* 6–18, *Plant.* 12–14, and *Somn.* 1:133-45 with Calcidius, *Com. in Tim.* 127–36 suggests that both the Jewish author and his later Christian counterpart drew on a Middle Platonic handbook. The Colossians apparently knew either some Greek-speaking Jews from outside the community or some Greek-speaking Jews who had become members of the Christian community who had introduced the community to an allegorical reading of the Scriptures which incorporated a Middle Platonic demonology.[17]

John. A final example occurs in the hymnic prologue of John. The language of the prologue clearly echoes the language of the creation story of Genesis 1. One of the echoes is the verb shift between the chaotic primeval world ('the earth was [ἦν]...' [LXX Gen. 1:2]) and the orderly created world ('let there be...and there was [γενηθήτω...

---

17   For details and bibliography, see G.E. Sterling, 'A Philosophy according to the Elements of the Cosmos: Philo of Alexandria and Colossian Christianity', in *Philon d'Alexandrie et le langage de la philosophie* (ed. C. Lévy; Turnhout: Brepols, forthcoming).

ἐγένετο]' [LXX Gen. 1:3 κ.τ.λ.]). The prologue, however, goes beyond this to make a clear distinction between the eternal Logos and the temporal creation: 'In the beginning was (ἦν) the Logos and the Logos was (ἦν) with God and the Logos was (ἦν) God. He was (ἦν) in the beginning with God. Everything became (ἐγένετο) through him and not one thing became (ἐγένετο) without him.' The shift in tenses is not accidental: it is maintained throughout the prologue (the Logos *was* [1:1, 2, 3, 9, 10, 15, 18] versus the world *became* [1:3, 6, 10, 14, 17]) and possibly in the main text itself (8:24, 28, 58; 13:19). This shift is reminiscent of Plato's famous question 'whether the cosmos always was (ἦν), having no beginning, or became (γέγονεν), having begun from a certain beginning' (*Tim.* 28b). Middle Platonists such as Philo of Alexandria use this grammar to make the same distinction between the two worlds that the prologue of John makes (*Opif.* 12; *Post.* 30; *Gig.* 42).

There are other New Testament texts which use Platonic language and thought, for example, 2 Cor. 4:16–5:10 which combines Platonic and apocalyptic categories of thought and language. These point to the attraction Platonism had for early Christians, an attraction which would develop into a lasting contribution at a later date. I think that there are numerous reasons why first- and second-century Christians found Middle Platonism inviting. First, it offered a sense of the transcendent which naturally appealed to their understanding of faith. Secondly, within this transcendence Platonists developed a hierarchy of being. Most importantly, they found ways to bridge the gap between the intelligible and sense-perceptible worlds. While solutions varied, they all posited an intermediary. Early Christians found this intermediary extremely useful for christological reflection. Thirdly, the Platonic definition of 'end of the goods' as 'likeness to God' aligned with early Christian morality and spirituality. Fourthly, this was coupled with Middle Platonic demonology which posited an ascent of the soul, a view which has continually appealed to mystics. The appeal of philosophical ontology/metaphysics was not, however, limited to these larger conceptual frameworks. It could also become quite specific.

Prepositional Metaphysics. Hymns or texts which use liturgical language in the New Testament often make use of the common philosophical practice of expressing causality through prepositions. Willy Theiler gave the name 'metaphysics of prepositions' to the practice of using prepositions to denote different causes.[18] The discussion goes back to Aristotle, who distinguished material, formal, efficient, and final causes (*Ph.* 194b–95a; cf. also *Metaph.* 933a-b). Middle and Neoplatonists regularly aligned three prepositional phrases with corresponding causes (αἰτίαι). Aetius preserves the clearest formulation of the Middle Platonic position: 'Plato held there were three causes. He says: "by which (ὑφ' οὗ), out of which (ἐξ οὗ), to which (πρὸς ὅ)". He considers the by which (ὑφ' οὗ) to be the most important. This was that which creates, that is the mind' (*Placita* 11:2). The first is Aristotle's efficient cause; the second is his material cause; and the third is the Stagirite's formal cause. Others expanded the list (e.g. Seneca, *Ep.* 65:8-10). The tendency to increase the causes led Heinrich Dörrie to posit the existence of a rival interpretation which collapsed causes to a single principle, even though multiple prepositional phrases continued to be used, especially 'out of which (ἐξ οὗ), in which (ἐν ᾧ), for which (εἰς ὅ)'.[19] He called this the 'Stoic-Gnostic series'. Jewish interpreters such as Philo of Alexandria exploited the Platonic series openly (*Q.G.* 1:58; *Cher.* 124–27; *Prov.* 1:23).[20] Did early Christians?

There are a number of texts in the New Testament which use 'prepositional metaphysics' (e.g. John 1:3-4; Rom. 11:36; 1 Cor. 8:6; Col. 1:16-17; Heb. 1:2). Interestingly, there is not a consistent pattern. christological hymns tend to collapse all prepositional phrases into christological statements. For example, consider the hymn in Col. 1:16-17:

For in him (ἐν αὐτῷ) all things in heaven and on earth were created...
all things have been created by him (δι' αὐτοῦ) and for him (εἰς αὐτόν).
He is before all things (πρὸ πάντων)
and in him (ἐν αὐτῷ) all things exist.

The same happens when the phrases are used in doxologies addressed to God, for example, Rom. 11:36. There are, however, exceptions such as 1 Cor. 8:6:

---

18   W. Theiler, *Die Vorbereitung des Neuplatonismus* (Berlin/Zürich: Weidmann, 1964), pp. 17-34.

19   H. Dörrie, 'Präpositionene und Metaphysik: Wechselwirkung zweier Prinzipienreihen', *MH* 26 (1969), pp. 217-28.

20   For details and bibliography, see D.T. Runia, *Philo of Alexandria and the Timaeus of Plato* (PhilAnt, 44; Leiden: Brill, 1986), pp. 171-74.

But for us there is one God, the Father,
out of whom (ἐξ οὗ) are all things and for whom (εἰς αὐτόν) we exist,
and one Lord, Jesus Christ,
through whom (δι' οὗ) are all things and through whom (δι' αὐτοῦ) we
exist.

In this instance, there is a distinction between the source (God) and
the agent of life (Christ). Early Christians extended such metaphysical
usages to include soteriological applications. So the author of
Ephesians writes: 'Blessed be the God and Father of our Lord Jesus
Christ who blessed us with every spiritual blessing in the heavenly
places in Christ (ἐν Χριστῷ), just as he chose us in him (ἐν αὐτῷ)
before the foundation of the world to be holy and blameless before
him in love'. The Paulinist continues: 'He predestined us for adoption
through Jesus Christ (διὰ 'Ιησοῦ Χριστοῦ) for him(self) (εἰς
αὐτόν)...' (Eph. 1:3-5; cf. also Col. 1:19-20). Once again we find a
distinction. It appears that early Christians were aware of the
philosophical use and adapted it as the occasion demanded. There is,
however, a good deal of work which needs to be done in this area.[21]

Hellenistic Philosophy. A final area of research for students of the
New Testament is Hellenistic philosophy itself. Our knowledge of
Hellenistic philosophy is still more limited than we would prefer (see
below). We need editions and translations of particular authors,
detailed analyses of specific texts, as well as larger comparative
analyses of themes. New Testament scholars have already made a
contribution to the field by contributing a number of text and
translation projects (Attridge 1976; Malherbe 1977; Fitzgerald and
White 1983), yet there is a great deal of work which remains. For
example, we now have a collection of the fragments of Eudorus, a
pivotal figure in the emergence of Middle Platonism in Alexandria;
however, they are buried in a somewhat obscure Italian journal.[22] We
need a collection with an English translation. We also need an edition
and English translation of Hierocles, the second-century CE Stoic who
wrote an elementary handbook. Surprisingly, there is still no English

---

[21]   See now G.E. Sterling, 'Prepositional Metaphysics in Jewish Wisdom
Speculation and Early Christological Liturgical Texts', *The Studia Philonica
Annual* 9 (1997), pp. 219-38.

[22]   C. Mazzarelli, 'Raccolta e interpretazione delle testimonianze e dei
frammenti del medioplatonico Eudoro di Alessandria', *Rivista de Filosofia
Neoscolastica* 77 (1985), pp. 197-209, 535-55.

translation of Maximus of Tyre, even though several have discussed undertaking it.[23] We also have no English translation for von Arnim's collection of early Stoic material or of Stobaeus, although the length of both of these makes the lacunae understandable.

DIFFICULTIES

The above examples have already indicated some of the difficulties in using Hellenistic philosophy. It is, however, important to deal with them more directly and fully. I will only touch on the most crucial.

Hellenistic Philosophy. The task of comparing two different bodies of literature requires control of both. While access to the world of New Testament scholarship is relatively easy, entrance into the world of Hellenistic philosophy is more daunting. Yet it requires the same care and attention to nuance as New Testament documents do. In fact, as the complexities of the material and sophistication of the authors rise, so must the sophistication of the interpreters. This means that we must spend a significant amount of time reading philosophical texts until we can read them with precision. As an entree into this world I have provided a chart of the major philosophical figures at the end of this chapter. The chart is designed as a pedagogical tool, not an exhaustive listing of philosophical schools or philosophers within those schools. I have used the following criteria for inclusion. First, I have only included philosophical schools/traditions which have direct relevance for the New Testament. I have not thought it important to include the Cyrenaic, Dialectical, Eretrian, or Megarian schools whose spheres of influence were largely limited to the early Hellenistic world. Secondly, I have included philosophers on the basis of their importance for the tradition he or she represents and the potential relevance of the author for students of the New Testament . My goal is to provide a guide for locating figures whose views or contributions are of interest to students of the New Testament. I have placed an asterisk beside the name of those who served as scholiarchs of recognized schools. Thirdly, I have only included figures whose primary allegiances are to a specific philosophical tradition. This means that I have omitted writers like Philo of Alexandria and Lucian

---

23   There is an old English translation based on the Latin tradition: T. Taylor, *The Dissertations of Maximus Tyrius* (1804; repr. Thomas Taylor Series, 6; Rome: Prometheus Trust, 1994).

of Samosata, even though their works are significant for understanding the period.

There are several limitations which must be kept in mind in handling philosophical texts in this period. First, the extant material is frustratingly fragmentary. For example, Stoicism is generally divided into three periods: the Old Stoa, the Middle Stoa, and the Late Stoa. We have important representatives for the Late Stoa in the works of Seneca, Epictetus, and Marcus Aurelius; however, we do not have a single treatise extant in its entirety from representatives of either of the first two periods—everything must be reconstructed from secondary citations and summaries. This is not unique: the same state of affairs holds true for the vast majority of works in Hellenistic philosophy. Secondly, our understanding of Hellenistic philosophy is still in flux, even in some important areas. For example, it was not until recent years that scholars recognized Middle Platonism as a distinct stage in the development of the Platonic tradition (Dillon 1977). Even though this stage is now widely recognized, the specific contours of Middle Platonism continue to be debated. The consequences of such shifts may be extremely important. For example, Harry Wolfson wrote his monumental two volume analysis of Philo's thought prior to the recognition of Middle Platonism. His basic method was to compare Philo to Plato, Aristotle, and the Stoics.[24] He failed to recognize that Philo's understanding of Plato was shaped by Middle Platonic interpretations, which is now a presupposition of contemporary scholarship. This is another way of saying that an interpreter needs to know the history of the discussion within the philosophical tradition in order to use a concept properly. Thirdly, this period of philosophy is characterized by 'eclecticism'. By 'eclecticism' I do not mean a potpourri of incompatible concepts thoughtlessly thrown together, but rather the effort to combine what were considered different aspects of a larger unity of thought (Dillon and Long 1988). This means, however, that the task of using the views of a specific philosopher is often complex. Let me illustrate. Some philosophical figures are extremely difficult to place in a specific tradition. Was Pseudo-Cebes a Platonist, Stoic, Cynic, Neopythagorean, or simply eclectic? Was Dio Chrysostom a Stoic or a Cynic? Was Numenius a Neopythagorean with some Platonic leanings

---

[24]   H.A. Wolfson, *Philo: Foundations of Religious Philosophy in Judaism, Christianity, and Islam* (2 vols.; Cambridge, MA: Harvard University Press, 2nd edn, 1948).

or a Pythagoreanizing Middle Platonist? A case can be made for each position, because the author uses material which points in more than one direction. Even when we do know the specific school loyalty of a philosopher, he or she may and probably did appropriate concepts from other philosophical traditions. The issue then arises whether the presuppositions underlying the concept are also brought over, or whether they are incompatible with the larger system of the author, thus forcing a change in the thought. For example, Philo of Alexandria cites the widely known Stoic understanding of the two principles in creation: active and passive (*Opif.* 8–9; cf. Diogenes Laertius 7:134). For the Stoics these are two complementary causes; however, for Philo, only the active principle (God) is a cause, the passive (matter) is an object set over against the active cause. Philo's Jewish monotheism has thus altered his use of technical philosophical concepts. Similarly, when Paul condemns the Gentile world and says that 'God delivered them over to a worthless mind to do the things which are not proper functions (ποιεῖν τὰ μὴ καθήκοντα)', he uses a technical Stoic term (e.g. Diogenes Laertius 7:107-109; Cicero, *Fin.* 3:17:20-22). However, it is difficult for me to believe that Paul accepted the anthropology which underlay the Stoic understanding of the term. I think rather that this is but another example of the ubiquity of Stoic language and concepts in the Roman world.

Greek-Speaking Judaism. There is another major paradigm issue. How did early Christians acquire their knowledge of Hellenistic philosophy? Did they learn it directly from pagans and then make their own applications? Or did they learn it indirectly through Greek-speaking Jews who had already made the appropriations? Or should we imagine a more complex situation in which early Christians sometimes adapted what they had themselves learned about Hellenistic philosophy and at other times used what they had learned in a Greek-speaking synagogue?

Let me illustrate the difficulty one often faces. One of the unique concerns of Luke–Acts is its emphasis on 'repentance' (μετάνοια). The author understands this as a turning to God involving a reformation of life (e.g. Acts 26:20). While the terms generally denote a sense of regret in the Greek world, there are several philosophical figures who use it to describe moral improvement (e.g. Pseudo-Cebes, *Tabula* 10:4-11:1-2; Dio Chrysostom 34:18-19; Plutarch, *Mor.* 26d, 27a, 204a, 551d, 712c). Some Second Temple Jewish authors found this to be a natural way to speak of conversion from paganism to

Judaism (*Jos. Asen.* 9:2; 15:6-8; 16:7 and Philo, *Virt.* 175–86). Did the author of Luke–Acts make the same appropriation, or simply apply what he had already learned in a synagogue? While both are possible, I am inclined to think the latter is more probable. The author was probably a Greek-speaking Jew (perhaps a God-fearer) who had a long-standing relationship with the synagogue. More importantly, the author's twofold understanding of the process as turning to the one true God and then living a reformed life (Acts 26:20) matches the presentation we have in Philo (*Virt.* 175–79, 180–86). Thus, while it is possible that the author of Luke–Acts directly appropriated the concept from moral philosophers, it is more likely that he simply applied to Christianity what he had earlier learned in Judaism.

The above example as well as those which I have cited earlier illustrate the complexities of the issue. I will offer a couple of principles as controls for exploring this question. First, we must weigh each instance independently. We can neither assume that Greek-speaking Judaism was the sole conduit of classical culture to early Christianity, nor that it had no role. Similarly, we should not assume that, if one author borrows a literary tradition from a Jewish source, that all New Testament authors did so. Social situations and contextual demands are too complex for such simplistic generalizations. Secondly, as we have seen, there are good reasons for believing that, in some cases, Christians inherited existing Jewish adaptations of Hellenistic philosophy. We should, however, weigh these on a sliding scale. *Certainty*—understood in historical terms— only exists when we can demonstrate that there are unique Jewish-Christian concerns, for example, when a tradition is anchored in an exegesis of a text from the Torah. We may posit *probability* if there is substantial agreement in the details, as is the case with μετάνοια. In a case where the material or perspective is common to both the Jewish and Greco-Roman sources, we may only speak of a *possibility*. Thirdly, possibilities do not mean, however, that we should automatically discount the role of Greek-speaking Judaism, since Greek-speaking Jewish adaptations of Hellenistic philosophy established a *precedent* for early Christians. In short, the synagogue not only provided early Christians with specific concepts, but demonstrated what could be done with Hellenistic thought and moral exhortation.

The best example of both processes is Paul of Tarsus. No one questions Paul's attachment to the synagogue in the early years of his life. If we can believe the tradition of Acts 21:39—the fact that it runs counter to the tendency of Acts suggests that we can—Paul was a citizen of Tarsus. His citizenship in a Greek city would have required not only a primary education, but passing the *ephebeia*, and possibly advanced education. Since Tarsus was famous for philosophy (Strabo 14:5:13), especially for her Stoic philosophers (Dio Chrysostom 33:48 and Lucian, *Octogenarians* 21), and Paul's letters betray acquaintance with philosophy, it is possible that he received some advanced training in philosophy. This would at least explain why he is so adept at incorporating popular philosophy in his letters. It also suggests that Paul, like Philo of Alexandria, had the requisite training to create his own applications. While Philo's knowledge of Hellenistic philosophy is more profound than Paul's, the apostle has the more creative mind. In any case, whether we posit a genealogical or an analogical relationship, Greek-speaking Judaism is a *sine qua non* for understanding the early Christian use of philosophy (for details see Sterling forthcoming).

Parallels. These observations should warn us against the naive use of parallels. Each text must first be interpreted in its own right, not as a parallel to another text, that is, it must be contextualized literarily, historically, and socially. Years ago, Samuel Sandmel delivered a presidential address to the Society of Biblical Literature in which he warned against 'parallelomania'.[25] We need to remind ourselves of this in an age where we can search entire corpuses of texts electronically in a matter of a few minutes. The purpose of research is not to list analogous expressions of the same thought, but to understand the ancient texts. This means weighing differences as well as similarities. We must also remember that this is a bilingual tradition. Latin is especially important for the Late Stoa, although its value is hardly restricted to a single tradition. Finally, we need to remember the social location of the representatives. Professional philosophers were not typically in the same social position as artisans. We must ask how philosophy circulated in popular forms as early Christianity was far from elitist.

CONCLUSIONS

As long as this chapter is, I have not touched upon a number of relevant areas of research. For example, I have not attempted to

---

25   S. Sandmel, 'Parallelomania', *JBL* 81 (1962), pp. 1-13.

explore some of the more obvious points of comparison: christological concepts such as the Logos, Paul's anthropology (e.g. conscience), Paul's ecclesiology (e.g. the community as a body), or specific virtues or vices. Although I have paid some attention to literary forms, I have not begun to exhaust the possibilities. Other literary forms include *chreai*, which play such a large role in the Synoptic Gospels, *symposia*, which are important to Luke, *epitomes*, which may have served as models for collections like the Sermon on the Mount (e.g. Hierocles, *On Duties*), and *gnomes*/gnomologies (e.g. *Gnomologium Vaticanum*) and doxographies (e.g. Arius Didymus and Aetius), which may have served as the source for many early Christians' knowledge of Hellenistic philosophy. I have also not attempted to deal with a number of significant issues of social history, such as the locale for Paul's public ministry and the entire issue of whether there were schools (e.g. the Pauline and Johannine schools). What I have tried to do is to underscore the importance of reading philosophical texts if we are to understand the New Testament. If I have said more about Paul than any other New Testament author, it is because his letters are the most obvious beginning point; however, it would be a mistake to stop with the Pauline corpus.

The relationship between Christian faith and theology on the one hand and philosophy on the other is extraordinarily complex. The divergent attitudes toward philosophy which surface in the New Testament continue to find echoes. For those who attempt to bring the human experience of God to articulation through critical reflection, philosophy is a natural resource; at least a number of New Testament writers thought so.[26]

BIBLIOGRAPHY

Primary Sources

I have attempted to list texts and English translations whenever possible. I have not always listed the *editio major* for major authors. These can almost always be found in the Budé (now Les Belles Lettres), Oxford Classical Texts, or Teubner series. When this is not the case, I have made an attempt to be more complete.

---

[26]   I wrote this chapter while doing research for a larger related project supported by the Institute for Scholarship in the Liberal Arts of the College of Arts and Letters at the University of Notre Dame. I want to express my appreciation for their support. John T. Fitzgerald was kind enough to read the manuscript for me. I greatly appreciate his suggestions.

Neopythagoreans
Collections
Städele, A.
1980   *Die Briefe des Pythagoras und der Pythagoreer.* Meisenheim am Glan: Hain.
Thesleff, H.
1965   *The Pythagorean Texts of the Hellenistic Period.* Acta Academiae Aboensis, Ser. A. Humaniora 30.1. Åbo: Åbo Akademi.
Apollonius of Tyana
Conybeare, F.C.
1912   *Philostratus, The Life of Apollonius of Tyana.* 2 vols. LCL. Cambridge, MA: Harvard University Press.
The Golden Verses
Thom, J.C.
1995   *The Pythagorean, Golden Verses.* Religions in the Greco-Roman World, 123. Leiden: Brill.

Epicureans
Diogenes of Oenoanda
Smith, M.F.
1993   *The Epicurean Inscription.* La Scuola di Epicuro, Sup. 1. Naples: Bibliopolis.
Lucretius
Rouse, W.H.D.
1982   *Lucretius, De rerum natura.* Rev. M.F. Smith. LCL. Cambridge, MA: Harvard University Press.
Philodemus
Clay, D., C.E. Glad, D. Konstan, J.C. Thom, and J. Ware
forthcoming *Philodemus: On Frankness of Speech.* SBLTT. Atlanta: Scholars Press.
Indelli, G., and V. Tsouna-McKirahan
1995   *Philodemus: On Choices and Avoidances.* Scuola di Epicuro, 15. Naples: Bibliopolis.
Obbink, D.
1995   *Philodemus on Piety.* Oxford: Clarendon Press.
Oliveri, A.
1914   *Philodemi Περὶ Παρρησία.* Leipzig: Teubner.

Academics/Middle Platonists
Academics
Cicero
Caplan, H. *et al.*
1912–58 *Cicero.* 28 vols. LCL. Cambridge, MA: Harvard University Press.

Middle Platonists
Alcinous
Dillon, J.
1993   *Alcinous: The Handbook of Platonism.* Oxford: Clarendon Press.
Whittaker, J.
1990   *Alcinoos: Enseignement des doctrines de Platon.* Paris: Les Belles Lettres.
Apuleius
Beaujeu, J.
1973   *Apulée: Opuscules philosophiques (Du Dieu de Socrate, Platon et sa Doctrine, Du monde).* Paris: Les Belles Lettres.
Atticus
Des Places, É.
1977   *Atticus, Fragments.* Paris: Les Belles Lettres.
Maximus of Tyre
Koniaris, L.
1995   *Philosophumena-dialexeis.* Berlin/New York: de Gruyter.
Trapp, M.B.
1994   *Maximus Tyrius Dissertationes.* Leipzig: Teubner.
Numenius
Des Places, É.
1973   *Numenius: Fragments.* Paris: Les Belles Lettres.
Plutarch
Babbitt, F.C. *et al.*
1927–76 *Plutarch's Moralia.* 16 vols. LCL. Cambridge, MA: Harvard University Press.

Cynics
Collection
Paquet, L.
1988   *Les Cyniques Grecs: Fragments et Témoignages.* Philosophica, 35. Ottawa: Editions de l'Université d'Ottawa, 2nd edn.
Epistles
Attridge, H.W.
1976   *First-Century Cynicism in the Epistles of Heraclitus.* HTS, 29. Missoula, MT: Scholars Press.
Malherbe, A.J.
1977   *The Cynic Epistles.* SBLSBS, 12. Missoula, MT: Scholars Press.
Bion
Kindestrand, J.F.
1976   *Bion of Borysthenes: A Collection of the Fragments with Introduction and Commentary.* Stockholm: n.p.
Pseudo-Cebes
Fitzgerald, J.T., and L.M. White
1983   *The Tabula of Cebes.* SBLTT, 24. Chico, CA: Scholars Press.

Dio Chrysostom
Cohoon, J.W., and H.L. Crosby.
1932–51 *Dio Chrysostom.* 5 vols. LCL. Cambridge, MA: Harvard University Press.
Oenomaus
Hammerstaedt, J.
1988 *Die Oralkelkritik des Kynikers Oenomaus.* Beiträge zur klassischen Philologie, 188. Frankfurt am Main: Athenäum.
Teles
O'Neil, E.
1977 *Teles (The Cynic Teacher).* SBLTT, 11. Missoula, MT: Scholars Press.

Stoics
Collection
Arnim, I. von
1905–24 *Stoicorum veterum fragmenta.* 4 vols. Leipzig: Teubner. Repr. Dubuque, IA: Brown, n.d.
Epictetus
Oldfather, W.A.
1925–28 *Epictetus.* 2 vols. LCL. Cambridge, MA: Harvard University Press.
Hierocles
Arnim, H. von
1906 *Hierokles: Ethische Elementarlehre (Papyrus 9780) nebst den bei Stobäus erhaltenen ethischen Exzerpten aus Hierokles.* Berliner Klassikertexte, 4. Berlin: Weidmann.
Bastianini, G., and A.A. Long
1992a *Hierocles' 1.1:268-451 in Corpus dei papiri filosofici Greci e Latini.* Florence: Olschki.
1992b 'Dopo la nuova edizione degli *Elementa di etica* di Ierocle Stoico', in *Studi su codici e papiri filosofici: Platone, Aristotele, Ierocle.* Accademia Toscana di Scienze e Lettere 'La Colombaria,' 'Studi', 129. Florence: Olschki: 221-49.
Marcus Aurelius
Haines, C.R.
1916 *Marcus Aurelius.* LCL. Cambridge, MA: Harvard University Press.
Musonius Rufus
Lutz, C.E.
1947 'Musonius Rufus: "The Roman Socrates"'. *Yale Classical Studies* 10: 3-147.
Seneca
Basore, J.W. *et al.*
1917–72 *Seneca.* 10 vols. LCL. Cambridge, MA: Harvard University Press.

General Collections
Ancient
Aetius and Arius Didymus
Diels, H.
1965   *Doxographi Graeci.* Berlin: de Gruyter, 4th edn (Berlin: Reimer, 1st edn, 1879).
Diogenes Laertius
Hicks, R.D.
1925   *Diogenes Laertius.* 2 vols. LCL. Cambridge, MA: Harvard University Press.
Lucian of Samosata
Harmon, A.M., K. Kilburn, and M.D. Macleod
1913–67 *Lucian.* 8 vols. LCL. Cambridge, MA: Harvard University Press.
Stobaeus
Wachsmuth, C., and O. Hense
1894–1912 *Ioannis Stobaei: Anthologium.* 5 vols. Berlin: Weidmann. Repr. 1974.
Modern
Long, A.A., and D.N. Sedley
1987   *The Hellenistic Philosophers.* 2 vols. Cambridge: Cambridge University Press.

Hellenistic Jewish Authors
Josephus
Niese, B.
1887–89 *Flavii Iosephi opera.* 7 vols. Berlin: Weidmann. Repr. 1955.
Thackeray, H.StJ., R. Marcus and L. Feldman
1926–65 *Josephus.* 10 vols. LCL. Cambridge, MA: Harvard University Press.
4 Maccabees
Hadas, M.
1953   *The Third and Fourth Books of Maccabees.* Jewish Apocryphal Literature, 3. Philadelphia: Dropsie College for Hebrew and Cognate Learning. Repr. New York: Ktav, n.d.
Philo
Arnaldez, R., J. Pouilloux, and C. Mondésert
1962–92 *Les œuvres de Philon d'Alexandrie.* 34 vols. Paris: Cerf.
Cohn, L., P. Wendland, S. Reiter, and I. Leisegang
1962   *Philonis Alexandrini opera quae supersunt.* 7 vols. Berlin: Reimer, 2nd edn (1st edn, 1896–1930).
Colson, F.H., G.H. Whitaker, and R. Marcus
1929–62 *Philo.* 12 vols. LCL. Cambridge, MA: Harvard University Press.
Pseudo-Phocylides
Derron, P.
1986   *Pseudo-Phocylide: Sentences: Texte établi, traduit et commenté.* Paris: Les Belles Lettres.
Horst, P. van der
1978   *The Sentences of Pseudo-Phocylides.* SVTP, 4. Leiden: Brill.

Testaments
The Testament of Abraham
Schmidt, F.
1986   *Le Testament Grec d'Abraham: Introduction, édition critique des deux recensions grecques, traduction.* Texte und Studien zum Antiken Judentum, 11. Tübingen: Mohr–Siebeck.
Stone, M.E.
1972   *The Testament of Abraham: The Greek Recensions.* SBLTT, 2. Missoula, MT: SBL.
The Testament of Job
Brock, S.P.
1967   *Testamentum Iobi,* with J.-C. Picard, *Apocalypsis Baruchi Graece* PVTG, 2. Leiden: Brill.
Kraft, R.A. *The Testament of Job.* SBLTT, 5. Missoula, MT: SBL and Scholars Press, 1974.
Testaments of the Twelve Patriarchs
Hollander, H.W., and M. de Jonge
1985   *The Testaments of the Twelve Patriarchs.* SVTP, 8. Leiden: Brill.

Collections of Parallels
Berger, K., and C. Colpe
1987   *Religionsgeschichtliches Textbuch zum Neuen Testament.* Göttingen: Vandenhoeck & Ruprecht.
Boring, M.E., K. Berger, and C. Colpe
1995   *Hellenistic Commentary to the New Testament.* Nashville: Abingdon.
Malherbe, A.J.
1986   *Moral Exhortation: A Greco-Roman Sourcebook.* LEC. Philadelphia: Westminster Press.
Strecker, G., and U. Schnelle (eds.)
1997   *Neuer Wettstein: Texte zum Neuen Testament aus Griechentum und Hellenismus.* 2 vols. Berlin: de Gruyter.
Wettstein, J.J.
1751–52 *Novum Testamentum Graecum.* 2 vols. Amsterdam. Repr. Graz, Austria: Akademische Druck und Verlagsanstalt, 1962.

Secondary Sources
Hellenistic Philosophy
Armstrong, A.H. (ed.).
1967   *The Cambridge History of Later Greek and Early Medieval Philosophy.* London: Cambridge University Press.
Billerbeck, M. (ed.).
1991   *Die Kyniker in der modernen Forschung: Aufsätze mit Einführung und Bibliographie.* Bochumer Studien zur Philosophie, 15. Amsterdam: Grüner.

Dillon, J.M.
1977   *The Middle Platonists: 80 BC to AD 220.* Ithaca, NY: Cornell University Press. 2nd edn forthcoming.
Dillon, J.M., and A.A. Long (eds.).
1988   *The Question of 'Eclecticism': Studies in Later Greek Philosophy.* Hellenistic Culture and Society. Berkeley/Los Angeles: University of California Press.
Dudley, D.R.
1937   *A History of Cynicism from Diogenes to the 6th Century.* London: Methuen.
Flashar, H.
1994   *Die hellenistische Philosophie.* 2 vols. Die Philosophie der Antike, 4. Basel: Schwabe.
Gersh, S.
1986   *Middle Platonism and Neoplatonism: The Latin Tradition.* 2 vols. Publications in Medieval Studies, 23.1-2. Notre Dame: University of Notre Dame Press.
Haase, W. (gen. ed.).
1987–94 *Philosophie, Wissenschaften, Technik. ANRW,* 2:36:1-7. Berlin/New York: de Gruyter.
Long, A.A.
1986   *Hellenistic Philosophy: Stoics, Epicureans, Sceptics.* Berkeley/Los Angeles: University of California Press, 2nd edn.
Rist, J.M.
1969   *Stoic Philosophy.* Cambridge: Cambridge University Press.
Zeller, E.
1923   *Die Philosophie der Griechen in ihrer geschichtlichen Entwicklung.* 3 vols. in 6 parts. Leipzig: Reisland, 5th and 6th edn.

Hellenistic Philosophy and the New Testament

With a few exceptions, I have only listed monographs, and only those monographs which are either entirely devoted to the topic or have made a major impact on the field in recent years.

Almquist, H.
1946   *Plutarch und das Neue Testament: Ein Beitrag zum Corpus Hellenisticum Novi Testament.* Uppsala: Appelberg.
Balch, D.L.
1981   *Let Wives be Submissive: The Domestic Code in 1 Peter.* SBLMS, 26. Chico, CA: Scholars Press.
Balch, D.L., E. Ferguson, and W. Meeks (eds.).
1990   *Greeks, Romans, and Christians: Essays in Honor of Abraham J. Malherbe.* Minneapolis: Fortress Press.

Betz, H.D.
1975 *Lukian von Samosata und das Neue Testament: Religionsgeschichtliche und paranetische Parallelen. Ein Beitrag zum Corpus Hellenisticum Novi Testamenti.* TU, 76. Berlin: Akademie-Verlag.

Betz, H.D. (ed.).
1975 *Plutarch's Theological Writings and Early Christian Literature.* SCHNT, 3. Leiden: Brill.
1978 *Plutarch's Ethical Writings and Early Christian Literature.* SCHNT, 4. Leiden: Brill.

Bultmann, R.
1910 *Der Stil der paulinischen Predige und die kynisch-stoische Diatribe.* FRLANT, 13. Göttingen: Vandenhoeck & Ruprecht.

Crossan, J.D.
1991 *The Historical Jesus: The Life of a Mediterranean Jewish Peasant.* San Francisco: HarperSanFrancisco.
1994 *Jesus: A Revolutionary Biography.* San Francisco: HarperSanFrancisco.

De Witt, N.W.
1954 *St Paul and Epicurus.* Minneapolis: University of Minnesota Press.

DeMaris, R.E.
1994 *The Colossian Controversy: Wisdom in Dispute at Colossae.* JSNTSup, 96; Sheffield: JSOT Press.

Dey, L.K.K.
1975 *The Intermediary World and Patterns of Perfection in Philo and Hebrews.* SBLDS, 25. Missoula, MT: Scholars Press.

Downing, F.G.
1988 *Christ and the Cynics: Jesus and Other Radical Preachers in First-Century Tradition.* JSOT Manuals, 4. Sheffield: JSOT Press.
1992 *Cynics and Christian Origins.* Edinburgh: T. & T. Clark.

Ebner, M.
1991 *Leidenslisten und Apostelbrief: Untersuchungen zu Form, Motivik und Funktion der Peristasenskataloge bei Paulus.* FB, 66. Würzburg: Echter Verlag.

Fiore, B.
1986 *The Function of Personal Example in the Socratic and Pastoral Epistles.* AnBib, 105. Rome: Biblical Institute Press.

Fitzgerald, J.T.
1988 *Cracks in an Earthen Vessel: An Examination of the Catalogues of Hardships in the Corinthian Correspondence.* SBLDS, 99. Atlanta: Scholars Press.

Fitzgerald, J.T. (ed.).
1996 *Friendship, Flattery, and Frankness of Speech: Studies on Friendship in the New Testament World.* NovTSup, 82. Leiden: Brill.
1997 *Greco-Roman Perspectives on Friendship.* SBLRBS. Atlanta: Scholars Press.

Freedman, D.N. (ed.).

1992   *The Anchor Bible Dictionary.* 6 vols. New York: Doubleday.
        Hellenistic Philosophies
        R. Hock, 'Cynicism', 1: 1221-26.
        E. Asmis, 'Epicureanism', 2: 559-61.
        J. Dillon, 'Platonism', 5: 378-81.
        J. Thom, 'Pythagoreanism', 5: 562-65.
        T. Schmeller, 'Stoics, Stoicism', 6: 210-14.
        Modes of Speech/Literary Forms
        S. Stowers, 'Diatribe', 2: 190-93.
        J. Fitzgerald, 'Haustafeln', 3: 80-81.
        D. Balch, 'Household Codes', 3: 318-20.
        B. Fiore, 'Parenesis and Protreptic', 5: 162-65.
        J. Fitzgerald, 'Virtue/Vice Lists,' 6: 857-59.

Glad, C.E.

1995   *Paul and Philodemus: Adaptability in Epicurean and Early Christian Psychagogy.* NovTSup, 81. Leiden: Brill.

Hock, R.F.

1980   *The Social Context of Paul's Ministry.* Philadelphia: Fortress Press.

Horst, P.W. van der

1973   'Macrobius and the New Testament: A Contribution to the Corpus Hellenisticum'. *NovT* 15: 220-32.

1974   'Musonius Rufus and the New Testament'. *NovT* 16: 306-15.

1975   'Hierocles the Stoic and the New Testament: A Contribution to the Corpus Hellenisticum'. *NovT* 17: 156-60.

1980   *Aelius Aristides and the New Testament.* SCHNT, 6. Leiden: Brill.

1981   'Cornutus and the New Testament'. *NovT* 23: 165-72.

Koskenniemi, E.

1994   *Apollonios von Tyana in der neutestamentlichen Exegese: Forschungsbericht und Weiterfuhrung der Diskussion.* WUNT, 2.61. Tübingen: Mohr–Siebeck.

Mack, B.L.

1988   *A Myth of Innocence: Mark and Christian Origins.* Philadelphia: Fortress Press,.

1993   *The Lost Gospel: The Book of Q and Christian Origins.* San Francisco: HarperSanFrancisco.

Malherbe, A.J.

1987   *Paul and the Thessalonians: The Philosophic Tradition of Pastoral Care.* Philadelphia: Fortress Press.

1989   *Paul and the Popular Philosophers.* Minneapolis: Fortress Press.

1992   'Hellenistic Moralists and the New Testament'. *ANRW* 2.26.1: 267-333.

Marshall, P.

1987   *Enmity in Corinth: Social Conventions in Paul's Relations with the Corinthians.* WUNT, 2.23. Tübingen: Mohr–Siebeck.

Martin, T.W.
1996   *By Philosophy and Empty Deceit: Colossians as Response to a Cynic Critique.* JSNTSup, 118. Sheffield: Sheffield Academic Press.

Mussies, G.
1972   *Dio Chrysostom and the New Testament.* SCHNT, 21. Leiden: Brill.

Petzke, G.
1970   *Die Traditionen über Apollonius von Tyana und das Neue Testament.* SCHNT, 1; Leiden: Brill.

Sevenster, J.N.
1961   *Paul and Seneca.* NovTSup, 4. Leiden: Brill.

Schmeller, T.
1987   *Paulus und die 'Diatribe': Eine vergleichende Stilinterpretation.* NAbh, 19. Munster: Aschendorff.

Stowers, S.K.
1981   *The Diatribe and Paul's Letter to the Romans.* SBLDS, 57. Chico, CA: Scholars Press.

Theissen, G.
1975   'Itinerant Radicalism: The Tradition of Jesus Sayings from the Perspective of the Sociology of Literature'. *Radical Religion* 2: 84-93.

Thompson, J.W.
1982   *The Beginnings of Christian Philosophy: The Epistle to the Hebrews.* CBQMS, 13. Washington: Catholic Biblical Association.

Vögtle, A.
1936   *Die Tugend- und Lasterkataloge im Neuen Testament.* NTAbh, 16.4-5. Münster: Aschendorff.

Hellenistic Philosophy, Greek-Speaking Judaism and the New Testament
Crouch, J.E.
1972   *The Origin and Intention of the Colossian Haustafel.* FRLANT, 109. Göttingen: Vandenhoeck & Ruprecht.

Horst, P.W. van der
1978   'Pseudo-Phocylides and the New Testament'. *ZNW* 69: 187-202.

Sterling, G.E.
forthcoming *The Jewish Plato: Philo of Alexandria, Greek-Speaking Judaism, and Christian Origins.* Peabody, MA: Hendrickson.

Thomas, J.
1992   *Der jüdische Phokylides: Formgeschichtliche Zugänge zu Pseudo-Phokylides und Vergleich mit der neutestamentlichen Paränese.* NTOA, 23. Freiburg: Universitätsverlag; Göttingen: Vandenhoeck & Ruprecht.

Thyen, H.
1955   *Der Stil der Jüdisch-Hellenistischen Homilie.* FRLANT, 65. Göttingen: Vandenhoeck & Ruprecht.

Wendland, P.
1895   *Philo und die kynisch-stoische Diatribe.* Beiträge zur Geschichte der griechischen Philosophie und Religion. Berlin: Reimer.

SIGNIFICANT HELLENISTIC PHILOSOPHERS
(FOURTH CENTURY BCE—SECOND CENTURY CE)

	Pythagoreans	Epicureans	Academics / Platonists	Peripatetics	Skeptics/ Pyrrhonists	Cynics	Stoics
4th BCE							
	Early Pythagoreanism Archytas of Tarentum (*fl.* c. 380)		Plato* (c. 429–347)			Antisthenes (c. 445–c. 360)	
			Old Academy Speusippus* (c. 407–339)	Aristotle* (384–322)		Diogenes of Sinope (c. 400–c. 325)	
			Xenocrates* (*fl.* 339–314)	Theophrastus* (c. 370–c. 287)	Pyrrhon of Elis (c. 365–c. 270)	Crates of Thebes (c. 365–c. 285)	
	The Golden Verses			Demetrius of Phaleron (b. c. 350)		Hipparchia (Wife of Crates)	
		Epicurus* (341–271)	Polemo* (*fl.* 314–c. 276)			Onesicritus (*fl.* 325)	

3rd BCE							
							Early Stoa
		Metrodorus of Lampsacus (c. 331–c. 278)	Crates* (fl. c. 275?)	Strato of Lampsacus* (fl. c. 287–c. 269)	Timon of Phlius (c. 320–230)	Bion of Borysthenes (c. 325–c. 255)	Zeno of Citium* (334–262)
		Polyaenus of Lampsacus (fl. c. 300)		Lyco* (c. 302–c. 224)		Menippus of Gadara (fl. 300–250)	Dionysius of Heraclea (c. 328–248)
		Hermarchus of Mytilene* (fl. 315–c. 265)	Crantor (fl. c. 275?)			Leonidas of Tarentum (fl. 300–250)	Aratus of Soli (c. 315–c. 239)
						Pseudo-Anacharsis (c. 300–250)	Persaeus (c. 306–c. 243)
		Colotes (fl. c. 310–260)				Menedemus (fl. 3rd cent.)	Herillus of Carthage (fl. c. 270)
							Aristo of Chios (fl. c. 250)
							Cleanthes* (331–232)
			New Academy/ Middle Academy Arcesilaus* (fl. c. 273–c. 242)				

			Lacydes* (*fl.* c. 242)			Teles of Megara (*fl.* c. 235)	
				Aristo of Ceos* (*fl.* c. 225)			Chrysippus* (c. 280–206)
2nd BCE							
			Carneades* (c. 214–129)	Critolaus* (*fl.* 200–150)			Zeno of Tarsus* (*fl.* c. 200)
							Diogenes the Babylonian* (c. 240–152)
		Demetrius Lacon (*fl.* 2nd cent.)					Antipater of Tarsus* (*fl.* c. 152–c. 129)
							Apollodorus of Seleucia (Student of Diogenes)
							Archedemus of Tarsus (Student of Diogenes) *Middle Stoa* Boethius of Sidon (Cont. w/ Panaetius)

			Clitomachus* (fl. 128–110)				Panaetius* (c. 185–110)
			Metrodorus of Stratonicia (fl. late 2nd–early 1st cent.)				Mnesarchus* (fl. c. 110)
		Zeno of Sidon* (c. 155–75)	Philo of Larissa* (c. 160–79)				
		Demetrius Lacon (fl. late 2nd–early 1st cent.)				Meleager (fl. 100)	
1st BCE							
			Cicero (106–43)				Hecato of Rhodes (fl. c. 100)
	Hellenistic Pythagoreanism Pseudonymous Pythagorean and Neopythagorean Letters (1st BCE–2nd CE)	Phaedrus* (c. 140–70)	*Middle Platonism* Antiochus of Ascalon (c. 130–c. 68)	Aristo of Alexandria* (Cont. w/ Antiochus of Ascalon)	*Neopyhronnism* Aenesidemus of Cnossos (fl. c. 100–50)		
		Philodemus of Gadara (c. 110–c. 35)		Staseas of Naples (fl. early 1st cent.)			Posidonius of Apamea (c. 135–c. 50)

		Siro (Cont. w/ Philodemus of Gadara) Amafinius (Cont. w/ Philodemus) Lucretius (c. 94–55)		Androni-cus of Rhodes* (fl. c. 50)			
	Neo-pythagore-anism Nigidius Figulus (fl. c. 50)			Boethus of Sidon* (fl. 27 BCE–14 CE)			Arius the Stoic (= Arius Didymus?) (fl. 27 BCE–14 CE)
			Eudorus of Alexandria (fl. c. 25)	Nicolaus of Damascus (64–post 6 CE)		Pseudo-Diogenes (1st BCE–2nd CE)	
1st CE							
	Apollonius of Tyana (fl. 1st cent.)		Pseudo-Timaeus (c. 25 BCE–100 CE) Thrasyllus (fl. 14–36)		Agrippa (fl. post Aeneside-mus)	Demetrius (fl. 40–80) Pseudo-Cebes (Al-legiance uncertain) (1st cent.)	*Late Stoa* Seneca (c. 4 BCE–65 CE)

	Moderatus of Gades (c. 50–100)		Ammonius (*) (fl. c. 66)				Cornutus (c. 20–post 65) Musonius Rufus (before 30–c. 102)
			Plutarch (c. 50–c. 120)			Dio Chrysostom (Or Stoic) (40–post 112) Pseudo-Socrates (1st cent.) Pseudo-Heraclitus (c. 1–150) Pseudo-Crates (c. 1–200)	
2nd CE							
	Nicomachus of Gerasa (c. 50–150)		Theon of Smyrna (fl. c. 115–140) Calvenus Taurus (fl. c. 145) Apuleius (c. 123–post 161) Maximus of Tyre (c. 125–85)	Aspasius (c. 100–150)		Oenomaus of Gadara (c. 120) Peregrinus Proteus (c. 100–165)	Epictetus (c. 55–c. 135) Hierocles (fl. 100)

Diogenes of Oenoanda (*fl.* 2nd cent.)	Numenius of Apamea (Or Neo-pythagore-an) (*fl.* 2nd cent.)			Demonax of Cyprus (*fl.* 2nd cent.)	
	Albinus (*fl.* c. 150)			Demetrius of Sunium (2nd cent.)	
	Alcinous (*fl.* c. 150)			Theagenes of Patras (2nd cent.)	
	Atticus (c. 150–200)				Marcus Aurelius (121–180)
	Celsus (*fl.* c. 180)				
	Galen (c. 129–99)	Aristocles of Messana (*fl.* late 2nd cent.)		Theodorus (Cynulcus) (*fl.* late 2nd cent.)	
		Alexander of Aphrodisias (*fl.* c. 200)	Sextus Empiricus (*fl.* c. 200)		

JEWISH BACKGROUNDS

PAUL R. TREBILCO

INTRODUCTION

Any study of New Testament texts needs to be informed by an understanding of the Jewish world of the first century. Jesus and his disciples were a part of this world, many details of which feature in the texts, and the main agents of the spread of Christianity into the Gentile world were Jews who continued to see themselves as part of God's chosen people. What was that Jewish world like?

It is now recognized that there was considerable diversity within first-century CE Judaism. At any given time, Jews practised their religion in many different ways. The majority of the people did not belong to any particular group, but were zealous to live according to God's Torah and sought to be faithful to Judaism (see Sanders 1992: 448-51). Within Palestine itself there were different groups: Pharisees, Sadducees, Essenes, Zealots, some of which were far from unified, as well as a number of teachers and holy men, each with their band of followers. In addition, many Jews lived outside Palestine as a minority group in a Gentile city, spoke Greek rather than Hebrew or Aramaic, and may have only visited Jerusalem once in their lives, if at all. These Diaspora communities were far from uniform in practice and belief. This overall diversity is such that some scholars argue it is best to speak of ' Judaisms' in the plural in this period.[1]

While there was considerable diversity within first-century Judaism, we can also identify a central core of beliefs and practices that the great majority of first-century Jews, who followed no particular party, held in common. Further, there was also broad agreement on these beliefs and practices among the various Jewish parties and groups, agreement at a deeper and more fundamental level than the variations of interpretation and practice which divided these groups. These

---

[1]   See for example, J. Neusner, W.S. Green, and E. Fredrichs (eds.), *Judaisms and their Messiahs at the Turn of the Christian Era* (Cambridge: Cambridge University Press, 1987); see also Green in Neusner 1995: 1-10. On diversity in this period see for example Porton in Kraft and Nickelsburg 1986: 57-80; Dunn in Neusner 1995: 236-51.

various areas of broad agreement, to which we will now turn, gave Jews a common identity in very concrete ways.

COMMON JUDAISM[2]

With respect to belief, the following elements can be identified as fundamental and shared by most Jews of this period. There is only one true God, who had chosen the people of Israel and had made a covenant with them (Exod. 19:5-6). God, who alone should be worshipped, had created the world and continued to govern it. In the covenant, God had promised to be their God, and they had promised to be God's people. This relationship was dependent on God's mercy and grace (Exod. 19:4). Belief in election set Israel apart and also led to the solidarity of the Jewish people throughout the world. God had given Israel Torah, the covenant charter for all that Israel was, so that, by keeping it, the people might express their answering fidelity to God. Thus obedience to Torah was the appropriate response to the prior grace of God in election, the proper response to the covenant.[3] Obedience would lead to blessing, blessing connected with the promise of the land (Deut. 6:1-3). Transgression of Torah was punished, but in this regard, God's justice was moderated by mercy and by God's promises. Further, transgression could be forgiven by God through repentance, sacrifice and, if possible, making reparation. Obedience and atonement kept people in the covenant, and thus within God's people.[4] It is through God's people that God will act to restore and heal the world.

Inherent in these beliefs are certain practices, practices decreed by

---

[2]   On common Judaism see Cohen 1987: 62-103; Riches 1990: 30-51; Dunn 1991: 18-36; Sanders 1992: 1-303; Wright 1992: 215-79. Of course, these beliefs could be articulated or developed in different ways, and different beliefs and actions could flow from these basic elements of common Judaism (for example, concerning how the covenant is to be maintained and Torah obeyed), and this led to considerable debate and antagonism between different groups. This will be dealt with in the next section.

[3]   For the importance of covenant ideas in this period, see for example 1 Macc. 2:49-68; 2 Macc. 8:14-18; *Jub.* 15:1-34; Wis. 18:22; Ben Sira 44–50; *4 Ezra* 5:21-30; *Pss. Sol.* 9:9-10; CD 6:19; Sanders 1977: 84-107. For a restatement of his helpful notion of 'covenantal nomism', see Sanders 1992: 262-75.

[4]   Sanders (1992: 274) notes: 'Salvation depends on overall stance, whether or not one is "in"; for non-Christian Jews, salvation depended on being in the covenant'.

God in the Torah revealed to Moses, which encompasses all aspects of life (see *Apion* 2:171). The covenant, which was entered through birth as a Jew or by becoming a proselyte, was sealed for males by circumcision, since this was the covenant sign of the chosen people. Jews were to worship God, above all at the Jerusalem Temple; in order to enter the Temple, Jews had to be in a state of ritual purity. Jews paid the Temple tax that supported the sacrifices, went on pilgrimage to the Temple where they attended the festivals and tithed their produce. They also observed the sabbath and the food laws that regulated what food could be eaten, how it was to be killed and cooked and with whom it could be eaten. In the time of Jesus, Jews also attended the synagogue on the sabbath to study Torah and to pray. In this period, circumcision, sabbath and food and purity laws in particular seem to have functioned as badges or boundary markers that distinguished Jews from non-Jews, and thus reinforced Jewish identity and distinctiveness. The day-to-day praxis of Torah was thus a vital badge of a person's Judaism.[5]

It is likely that the great majority of Jews in the New Testament period observed these elements of Jewish praxis. The evidence suggests that they were sufficiently concerned about their Jewish heritage to take a fair amount of trouble to observe at least the biblical law, to pray, fast, keep the sabbath, go to the synagogue, circumcise their sons, keep the food laws and to travel to Jerusalem for the regular festivals (see Sanders 1992: 47-303; Wright 1992: 213-14).

The reason Jews followed these practices is worth underlining. As Wright notes, it was not

> because Jews in general or Pharisees in particular were concerned merely for outward ritual or ceremony, nor because they were attempting to earn their salvation (within some later sub-Christian scheme!) by virtuous living. It was because they were concerned for the divine Torah, and were therefore anxious to maintain their [G]od-given distinctiveness over against the pagan nations, particularly those who were oppressing them. Their whole *raison-d'être* as a nation depended on it. Their devotion to the one [G]od was enshrined in it. Their coming liberation might perhaps be hastened by it, or conversely postponed by failure in it (Wright 1992: 237). [6]

---

5   Our information for the Diaspora is more limited, and cannot be discussed here, but in many cases we have evidence that Diaspora Jews also shared these elements of common Judaism.

6   Note also Wright 1992: 334: '[A]s Sanders has argued extensively,

Having discussed the broad framework of common Judaism, we will now turn to four facets of first-century Judaism that are particularly significant for New Testament exegesis: Torah, the Temple, the cult and eschatology.

A. Torah[7]

The Torah was the covenant charter for Israel as God's people; obedience to Torah was the appropriate response to the prior grace of God in giving the covenant. One of the unique features of Judaism in the ancient world was that Israel's Torah covered all of life.[8] In the first century, Torah was often divided into two parts: laws that governed relations between people and God, and laws that governed relations amongst people.[9] If Torah was to be kept, it needed to be applied to everyday life in more detail than is found in the Pentateuch. For example, the Pentateuch goes into little detail in prohibiting work on the sabbath (e.g. Deut. 5:12-15); what then constituted 'work'? Thus there was the need for the formulation of interpretations of Torah, which developed Torah where necessary and applied it to everyday life. Although such traditions are normally associated with the Pharisees, the Qumranites and almost certainly the Sadducees and the priests also developed a body of interpretation of Torah, since anyone faced with applying Torah had to make such decisions (see Sanders 1990: 97-108). For all Jewish groups, this was the way of maintaining the relevance of Torah, and of putting it into practice.

Did most Jews of this period keep Torah? Sanders comments helpfully:

---

membership in the covenant is *demonstrated*, rather than *earned*, by possession of Torah and the attempt to keep it. When the age to come dawns, those who have remained faithful to the covenant will be vindicated; this does not mean "those who have kept Torah completely", since the sacrificial system existed precisely to enable Israelites who knew themselves to be sinful to maintain their membership none the less. And the attempt to keep Torah, whether more or less successful, was normally and regularly understood as response, not as human initiative.' See further Sanders 1977; Sanders 1992: 262-78.

7   On Torah see Sanders 1992: 190-240; Schürer 1973-87: II, pp. 464-87.

8   See for example Josephus in *Apion* 2:171: 'Piety governs all our actions and occupations and speech; none of these things did our lawgiver leave unexamined or indeterminate'.

9   See, for example, Philo, *Spec. Leg.* 2:63. The latter category of course had implications for relations with God. We should note that the modern distinction between ritual and ethical Torah is anachronistic and misleading.

What we should not assume is what most scholars do assume: people either obeyed the rabbis (or Pharisees), or they were non-observant. We must always remember the very large number of people who, when push came to shove, were ready to die for Torah and who kept most of it in ordinary circumstances (Sanders 1992: 153-54).[10]

Thus, the evidence, some of which will be discussed below, suggests that people generally followed Torah concerning worship, prayer, keeping the sabbath, circumcision, purity and food laws, and supporting the Temple.[11] While the ordinary people did not obey all the Pharisaic rules, they generally tried to follow Torah in all areas of life. Of course, 'following Torah' meant different things to different people. Even the most basic commandments were subject to varying interpretations, and there was a range of opinions about how strictly people should interpret and follow Torah (Sanders 1992: 236).

As noted above, by the New Testament period some aspects of Torah observance—most notably sabbath, circumcision and food and purity laws—seem to have functioned as cultural, social and religious boundary markers that preserved Jewish identity and thus were the main identifying marks of Jews that distinguished them from their pagan neighbours. The observance of the sabbath was one of the best-known Jewish customs in the ancient world, which suggests, along with other evidence, that Jews faithfully kept the sabbath in this

---

10   Sanders (1992: 238-40) notes the number of passages in which ordinary Jews are said to have been willing to die for their faith and Torah; e.g. *Ant.* 15:248; 18:262; *War* 2:169-74; Dio Cassius, *History of Rome* 37:16:2 (keeping the sabbath led to defeat and death). These passages strongly underline the zeal that ordinary Jews had for God and for God's Torah.

11   Sanders (1992: 237) considers the evidence on these areas sufficient to speak of 'orthopraxy in worldwide Judaism'. We can also note that, in the Diaspora, Jews obtained permission from the Romans and their local cities to assemble, to keep the sabbath, to have their 'ancestral food', to decide their own affairs, to send money to Jerusalem and to 'follow their laws' in general; see Trebilco 1991: 8-20. This enabled Diaspora Jews to maintain a Jewish way of life, and shows that they generally endeavoured to obey Torah. We should also note that, in some writings, the particularly Jewish aspects of Torah were ignored (e.g. Pseudo-Phocylides), allegorized (e.g. Letter of Aristeas 130–69) or otherwise rationalized (e.g. Aristobulus in Eusebius, *P.E.* 13:12:9-16), so as to emphasize to Gentile readers the aspects of Judaism that would be most intelligible to them. This does not necessarily mean that the Jewish authors of these works did not observe Torah, however.

period.[12] Sabbath observance generally involved attending the synagogue, abstaining from work and having a special meal. Circumcision, which for Jews was a sign of the election of Israel and the covenant with Abraham (Genesis 17), was regarded by both Jews and non-Jews alike as a distinctively Jewish practice, even though other ethnic groups also observed it. Despite some possible exceptions,[13] circumcision was regarded as an essential part of Jewish practice.

The food laws forbade Jews from eating certain foods, with abstinence from pork particularly attracting the attention of non-Jews. Comments from non-Jewish authors, and the explicit mention of some food laws in various texts, suggest that most Jews kept these laws in the first century (see *Ant.* 14:245, 259-61; Whittaker 1984: 73-80). Purity laws were also important in the New Testament period and were generally obeyed, although various interpretations were adopted by different people. Impurity resulted from such sources as skin diseases, contact with a corpse, childbirth, menstruation, semen and irregular discharges. Impure people were not, for example, to enter the Temple or handle priests' food, and purity laws also governed when intercourse could occur. Various rituals, generally involving water and the passage of a period of time, resulted in purification (Sanders 1992: 214-30).[14]

Given the importance of Torah, there was the need for some people to become masters of Torah through prolonged study, which was itself seen as a religious duty. The priests were the great teachers and guardians of Torah, but alongside them there developed a body of lay scribes and teachers (see, for example, Ben Sira 38:34b–39:8). They were a revered group who commanded the highest respect.

On the sabbath, Jews gathered for reading and exposition of Torah in the synagogue,[15] although the use of the term 'house of prayer' for

---

[12]   See Sanders 1992: 209-12; note, for example, *Jub.* 2:17-33; *War* 1:145-47; *Ant.* 14:226, 264; 16:45-46; *Apion* 2:40; Seneca, *Ep.* 95:47; Whittaker 1984: 63-73. On the sabbath, see R. Goldenberg, 'The Jewish Sabbath in the Roman World up to the Time of Constantine the Great', *ANRW* II.19.1 (1979), pp. 414-47.

[13]   For example, the allegorizers mentioned by Philo, *Migr. Abr.* 89-93.

[14]   The wide distribution of immersion pools shows that purity rules were generally obeyed, as do the rabbinic passages (given in Sanders 1992: 522 n. 34), which show that the Pharisees thought that ordinary people kept many of the purity laws.

[15]   See, for example, *Apion* 2:175 and the Theodotus inscription from Jerusalem, which tells us that Theodotus built the synagogue 'for reading of the

synagogues, especially in the Diaspora, shows that prayer was also common during the sabbath assembly.[16] Members of the congregation could address the gathering concerning the Scripture readings, as Jesus and Paul did at various times (Mark 1:14-15; 6:1-5; Acts 13:15). We can note that the synagogue also had a range of other functions, and in areas where Jews were in a minority, such as the Diaspora, the synagogue was a community centre that fulfilled a wide range of functions, including meeting educational, social, political, and economic needs.

B. The Temple[17]

The Temple was the central communal institution for Jews in Palestine and throughout the Diaspora and was the basic rallying point of Jewish loyalties. Judaism was unique in the ancient world because it had only one Temple. It portrayed the point that for Israel there was only one God, and only one place was suitable for God's dwelling on earth (see *Apion* 2:23; Matt. 23:21). Because the Temple was in Jerusalem, the city of Jerusalem was the centre of the Jewish nation. It was the place where sacrifices were offered to atone for transgressions and so enable the people to maintain the covenant. Many Jews came on pilgrimage to worship at the Temple at the key festivals of Passover, Weeks and Tabernacles, and it was to the Temple that adult male Jews everywhere paid their Temple tax. The Temple and the city of Jerusalem were thus key unifying elements in Jewish life, both for Jews in Palestine and throughout the Diaspora. Further, the evidence strongly suggests that most first-century Jews regarded the Temple, as well as the requirements of prescribed gifts and offerings, as sacred, and that they respected the priesthood (Sanders 1992: 52-54, 170-89, 441).[18] However, because of its significance, the Temple was also a

---

law and for teaching of the commandments'.

16   Despite continuing debate about the origins of the synagogue, it is clear that synagogues were important in Jewish life and worship in the first century CE. They are often mentioned in the New Testament (e.g. Mark 1:21; Acts 6:9; 13:15) and Josephus and Philo take them for granted (e.g. *War* 2:285-90; *Life* 277, 280, 293; Philo, *Spec. Leg.* 155-56.). On the synagogue see now Urman and Flesher 1995.

17   On the temple see Safrai and Stern 1974-76: II, pp. 865-907; Sanders 1992: 47-145, 306-14; Wright 1992: 224-26.

18   Note the exception found in *Sib. Or.* 4:24-30. Thus the devotion to the Temple that is clearly shown in Luke 1-2 by Zechariah, Mary and Joseph, and Anna and Simeon reflects the attitude of the majority of Jews of this period.

factor in some of the divisions of first-century CE Jewish life. The Qumran community, for example, had a very high regard for the Temple, but rejected the current Temple regime as illegitimate and corrupt and looked forward to a new Temple.

Herod the Great rebuilt the Temple on a vast scale. He began the work in either 23/22 or 20/19 BCE; it was completed around 63 CE. The whole complex, which measured around 450 by 300 metres and was massively imposing, was an extraordinary achievement and displayed an impressive harmony and simplicity of design. It consisted of the Court of the Gentiles, the Women's Court, the Court of the Israelites, the Court of the Priests where the sacrifices were offered, and finally the sanctuary, which consisted of two chambers, the second of which was the Holy of Holies. These areas are listed in order of increasing sanctity, with admission being progressively restricted, underlining how crucial the concept of purity was for the whole Temple.

The key role of the priests was of course to offer the sacrifices ordained by God in the Temple; as those who alone could minister in the Temple, the priests enjoyed considerable prestige.[19] They were not active in the Temple full-time, but rather were divided into twenty-four 'courses', with each course serving for a week in regular rotation. Many priests, the great majority of whom were not aristocrats, lived away from Jerusalem and stayed in the city only when it was the turn of their group to perform the rituals of the Temple. The priests were also expert interpreters of the Scriptures, although they were not the only such experts. Hence, they functioned as magistrates, key legal and religious authorities and as scribes in their local settings to whom ordinary Jews turned for teaching and for advice and judgments in matters relating to Torah (*Apion* 2:184-89, 193-94). These leadership roles in the nation were traditional to the priests, and they continued to fulfil them in the New Testament period (see for example Ben Sira 45:17; *Apion* 2:187; *Ant.* 14:41; see also Sanders 1992: 170-82). Although some priests were Sadducees or Pharisees, the priests did not constitute a party as such, and most shared the beliefs and practices of other Jews, as well as following the laws which applied to priests, and thus were part of common Judaism. Josephus records that

---

[19]   On the priests see Schürer 1973–87: II, pp. 227-308; Safrai and Stern 1974–76: II, pp. 580-600; Sanders 1992: 77-189, 317-40, 388-404. On the charge that the priests were not sufficiently strict in keeping Torah, see Sanders 1992: 182-89, 336.

there were around 20,000 priests and Levites in his time (*Apion* 2:108).

After the conquest of Palestine by the Romans in 63 BCE, the power of the high priest was curtailed (on the high priest, see Safrai and Stern 1974–76: I, pp. 400-404; II, pp. 600-612; Sanders 1992: 319-27). From the time of Herod, the secular ruler controlled the office and appointed whom he wished, which meant that the office did not gain the full confidence and support of the people. Yet the high priest still retained considerable influence on and authority over the people, as holder of the office that really counted to many of the Jews, because the high priest represented the people to God and God to the people. Further, the Romans dealt in the first instance with the high priest and expected him to have some control over the nation and to act as mediator between the Roman power and the people. Under the Roman prefects and procurators who normally stayed in Caesarea, the high priest basically administered Jerusalem, and the Temple was highly significant as a basis for political life and for the limited Jewish self-government of the period. The role of the high priest in the trial of Jesus clearly reflects this situation (see Mark 14:53–15:1; John 18:12-32; see also Acts 5:17-42; 7:1; 23:2-5).

C. The Cult[20]

The sacrificial cult was the God-ordained way of expressing thanksgiving and praise, and of obtaining forgiveness and atonement. Therefore it was a principal aspect of the true worship of God. Sacrifice was crucial, since it was part of the means by which Jews maintained their status as the covenant people. There were also daily and weekly services in the Temple, services that included recitation of Scripture, prayer and the burning of incense.

There were a variety of sacrifices, including the Passover lamb, that signified the past act of God and the future hope of national redemption. These included the individual and corporate sacrifices on the Day of Atonement, in which the nation and individuals recognized that Israel had sinned but could receive forgiveness through sacrifice, and the sin-offerings made by individuals to reaffirm their membership of God's people. Sacrifices atoned for sin, showed thanks and praise to God, enabled communion with God, petitioned God for

---

[20] On the cult see Schürer 1973–87: II, pp. 292-308; Safrai and Stern 1974–76: II, pp. 885-907; Sanders 1992: 103-18, 251-57.

blessing and provided for the feeling of community among all Jews (Sanders 1992: 251-57).

There were also the three major festivals of Passover, Pentecost and Tabernacles (Sanders 1992: 119-45). Each festival celebrated God's blessings upon the Land and the people. In addition, Passover celebrated the exodus from Egypt and Tabernacles celebrated the wilderness wandering on the way to the promised land. They thus focused attention on key aspects of Israel's history and encouraged the people that God would again liberate them. In addition, Hanukkah celebrated the overthrow of Antiochus Epiphanes by the Maccabees and thus emphasized the importance of true worship and the belief that God would rescue the people from tyranny. Purim, which celebrated the story of the book of Esther, underlined the same point. We can also note the Day of Atonement, which was a day of fasting and solemn rest, a time of examination and confession of sins. It was a communal day of worship on which all-inclusive rites of atonement were carried out.

The festivals thus underlined fundamental elements of the nation's faith: that Israel was the covenant people of the one God, that the land was sacred, the Torah was inviolable and redemption was certain. It seems that participation in festivals in this period was widespread, with very large numbers of people gathering in Jerusalem.[21]

D. Eschatology

During the period of the second Temple, there was a flowering of thinking about eschatology, or doctrine concerning the end time or ultimate future. In the first century CE, Israel was dominated politically by the might of Rome, which made inroads into all aspects of Israel's national life. As a result, most Jews longed for 'freedom', although this meant different things to different people.[22] Because of this domination, the longing intensified among many Jews that God would act to reverse the present state of affairs, fulfil the covenant and come to deliver the nation and re-establish the divinely intended order in the world. This longing took a variety of forms, but the hope was widely present that God would act decisively to bring in 'the coming

---

[21]   Note that the Temple could hold 400,000 pilgrims at a festival; see Sanders 1992: 127-28. Sanders estimates that 300,000 to 500,000 pilgrims attended the festivals in Jerusalem; see also Riches 1990: 51.

[22]   Sanders 1992: 279-80. The longing for freedom led to a variety of protests and acts of armed insurrection.

age' and forgive, liberate and redeem his covenant people, and restore their fortunes.[23] This would involve the covenant being renewed, the Temple and Jerusalem being rebuilt or purified and made more glorious, the land cleansed, Torah kept perfectly by the renewed and righteous covenant people and the subjugation or conversion of the Gentiles. Then at last Israel and the world would be set to rights and ruled over in reality by the true king, Israel's God; then at last a restored Israel would live within a restored cosmos. This renewed order would be 'the kingdom of God' (see Cohen 1987: 22-23; Wright 1992: 280-338; Sanders 1992: 279-303). For most Jews, one dimension of this hope was for resurrection, although often this was conceived of very vaguely.[24] In the present Israel was to be patient and faithful, to keep the covenant and trust God to act soon to vindicate them at last.

One dimension of the hope of Israel was for a Messiah. Although there was no single and uniform expectation concerning the Messiah in this period, and the expectation of a Messiah was not the rule, his role as the agent of Israel's God could include to fight the battles that would liberate Israel, to enact God's judgment on Israel's oppressors, to execute true justice within Israel, to rebuild the Temple and otherwise to fulfil Israel's hopes. The number of messianic movements in the first century CE, as well as a number of texts, show that the hope for a coming Messiah was reasonably widespread. However, these messianic hopes remained fragmentary; the wider and far more important strain of thought concerned the expectation of Yahweh's coming kingdom, of which the hope for a Messiah was but one (only occasionally discussed) part in texts from the New Testament period.[25]

---

[23] There was a wide diversity of opinion concerning whether the people should simply wait for God to intervene and liberate the people, or whether they should begin the battle with the oppressors and hope for miraculous intervention, or adopt one of a number of other possible positions.

[24] Sanders 1985: 237; 1992: 298-303. See, for example, *Life of Adam and Eve* 41:3; 43:2-3; 51:2; *1 En.* 51:1-5; *4 Ezra* 7:32; *T.Jud.* 25:1-5; 1QS 4:7-8. The Sadducees rejected this belief.

[25] On the Messiah, see J.H. Charlesworth, 'The Concept of the Messiah in the Pseudepigrapha', *ANRW* II.19.1 (1979), pp. 188-218; Schürer 1973–87: II, pp. 488-554; Sanders 1992: 295-98; Wright 1992: 307-20; Charlesworth 1992; Collins 1995. See for example, 4Q174 (= 4QFlor); 1QSb 5:23-9; *Pss. Sol.* 17:21-32; *4 Ezra* 11:36-46; 12:10-35; *2 Bar.* 39–40.

E. The Importance of these Elements of Common Judaism for New Testament Exegesis

When interpreting the New Testament, it is important to appreciate the elements of common Judaism outlined above. Further, in exegeting the New Testament, the attitude of the early Christians towards Torah and the Temple and its cult and their modification of eschatology are all crucial issues. Some examples will be discussed briefly.

With regard to common Judaism, we can highlight the importance of the covenant for Paul, and the need for us to appreciate his attitude to the Law within the framework of the covenant. Failure to do so has led to much misunderstanding of Paul, as well as a highly distorted understanding of Judaism. Further, in Romans 9–11 Paul notes that 'the adoption, the glory, the covenants, the giving of the law, the worship, and the promises' belong to Israel (Rom. 9:4), and he goes on to state that 'the gifts and call of God to Israel are irrevocable' (Rom. 11:29). In this section of Romans, Paul grapples with the election of Israel, a belief that he will not relinquish, since for him it is self-evident. An understanding of election, and its place within the framework of common Judaism, is crucial to exegesis of the passage. To take one further example, Paul clearly believes that there is only one true God, as the Shema (Deut. 6:4-5), which was said twice a day by Jews, states clearly. Yet in 1 Cor. 8:5-6 Paul modifies the Shema, while clearly remaining a Jew who believes in the One God of Israel (see Gal. 3:20). All Paul says about Jesus Christ must therefore be interpreted against this background.

We have noted that Torah provides the crucial boundary markers for the covenant people. This has great importance for understanding Jesus' controversies about the Law, and Paul's theology. Thus, for example, Paul's phrase 'the works of the law' has often been understood to refer to those things that a Jew did in order to earn salvation. However, this was clearly not how first-century Judaism understood the matter, since for them salvation was a matter of gift and grace (see in particular Sanders 1977: 84-107, 419-23; Dunn 1990: 216-25). How then should we understand the Pharisees' insistence on purity in the Gospels, or Paul's phrase 'the works of the law'? As Wright notes:

> The 'works of Torah' were not a legalist's ladder, up which one climbed to earn the divine favour, but were the badges that one wore as the marks of identity, of belonging to the chosen people in the

present, and hence the all-important signs, to oneself and one's neighbour, that one belonged to the company who would be vindicated when the covenant [G]od acted to redeem his people. They were the present signs of future vindication. This was how 'the works of Torah' functioned within the belief, and the hope, of Jews and particularly of Pharisees (Wright 1992: 238). [26]

The exegete must appreciate this when endeavouring to understand these debates in New Testament texts.

There was a variety of attitudes to the Temple in early Christianity, which is understandable, given the Temple's importance for Judaism. The significance of Paul applying the category of the Temple to people and their immediate relationship with God through the Spirit can only be appreciated when we see how crucial the Temple was for first-century Judaism (see 1 Cor. 3:16-17; 6:19; 2 Cor. 6:16; see also Dunn 1991: 37-97). The Epistle to the Hebrews is dominated by the question of the relationship of Christianity to the Jewish cult, with its priesthood, tabernacle and sacrifices. To appreciate the argument of Hebrews, the way these elements of common Judaism functioned in relation to Jewish practice and belief must be understood. Finally, the view that sacrifices, and the shedding of blood in particular, atone for sin was widespread in Judaism, and was given a prominent place in Christianity (see for example Rom. 3:25; 5:9; Eph. 1:7; Heb. 9:22; 1 John 1:7). Understanding the Jewish concept of sacrifice is crucial for exegesis of passages that, for example, concern the death of Christ.

Finally, an appreciation of the views on eschatology in first-century Judaism is crucial for an informed understanding of Jesus' message about the Kingdom of God (see for example Mark 1:14-15; Luke 11:20 = Matt. 12:28; Matt. 11:2-6) and for exegesis of the many New Testament texts that concern eschatology (see for example Mark 13; Rom. 8:18-30; 1 Thess. 4:13–5:11 and Revelation).

JEWISH PARTIES

By the time of the New Testament, special Jewish groups or parties

---

[26]   See also Sanders 1992: 262-78. These insights have led to an ongoing debate, which cannot be entered into here, concerning the 'new perspective on Paul', a debate that includes the question of Paul's view on the Law. See, for example, Dunn 1991: 117-39; D.A. Hagner, 'Paul and Judaism: The Jewish Matrix of Early Christianity: Issues in the Current Debate', *BBR* 3 (1993), pp. 111-30.

had arisen, each with their own particular views. Most Jews did not belong to a party, and these parties did not constitute Judaism. However, the parties show that Judaism was not controlled by the priests in Jerusalem; others could come to their own views.[27]

A. *The Pharisees*[28]

Our main sources of information for the Pharisees in the time of Jesus are Josephus, the New Testament and rabbinic texts. Each source has a quite distinctive perspective on the Pharisees, which means they each must be used with great care in historical study; in addition, the rabbinic texts must be used with great caution as evidence for the pre-70 period.

The origins of the Pharisees are debated, but it seems that they originated fairly early in the Hasmonean period, probably before 134 BCE,[29] and probably included some people from the ranks of the more general Hasidean movement. They were made up mainly, but not entirely, of non-priests and few of their members were socially and financially prominent. At the time of Herod they numbered over 6,000 (*Ant.* 17:42).[30]

While the Pharisees shared many of the views common to Jews of the period, there were also some distinctive Pharisaic beliefs and practices. It is clear that they were a group committed to accurate and precise interpretation of Torah and to scrupulous obedience to its commands (see *War* 1:110; 2:162; *Ant.* 17:41; Acts 22:3; 26:5). As Josephus tells us, they had 'the reputation of being unrivalled experts in their country's laws' (*Life* 191). The Pharisees attached great importance to the 'traditions of the elders', which supplemented biblical law (*Ant.* 13:297, 408; 17:41; *Life* 198). These traditions,

---

[27] Sanders (1992: 363-64) has noted that Judaism produced parties and sects in this period because Torah covered all of life, and study was encouraged. Thus, through study, people came to different interpretations of Torah, and, given the range of Torah, these differences covered most aspects of life.

[28] On the Pharisees see in particular Neusner 1971; 1973; 1984: 45-61; 1991: 1-15; Saldarini 1988: 79-237, 277-97; Sanders 1990: 97-254; 1992: 380-451; Mason 1991; Wright 1992: 181-203; Grabbe 1992: 467-84.

[29] They probably originated between 164 and 134 BCE; Josephus's first concrete story about them belongs to the period of John Hyrcanus (134–104); see *Ant.* 13:288-98.

[30] But see the discussion in Wright 1992: 196-97, who suggests that this figure does not give us an assessment of the number of Pharisees in the country as a whole, and argues that they were probably far more numerous.

handed down by former generations, helped the Pharisees to interpret and apply the written Torah to the conditions of their age.[31] Sometimes the traditions made the law more difficult, but sometimes less restrictive.[32] They were also noted for their leniency in judgment, which is reflected in the attitude of the Pharisee Gamaliel towards Peter and John in Acts 5:33-40.

A key issue for the Pharisees was purity. As Sanders has shown, the Pharisees aspired to a level of purity above the ordinary, but below that of priests and their families, a level of purity that reflected in some degree the purity proper to priests serving in the Temple.[33] Thus they made minor gestures towards living like priests, thereby intensifying biblical purity regulations, and strove for purity more thoroughly than did most Jews (Sanders 1992: 440).[34] Further, Pharisees would not generally eat with ordinary people, because of the latter's routine impurity, although they did not form a sect that avoided all contact with others.[35] They also went beyond biblical Law in their very strict and scrupulous view of tithing and handling the priests' food, and had particular views, for example, concerning the sabbath year, what constituted work on the sabbath, and on festivals.

We know of two other elements of the Pharisees' belief system. They believed in resurrection (*War* 2:162-63; *Ant.* 18:14; Acts 23:6-8), a view the Sadducees rejected, and they believed that, although

---

[31]   Sanders (1992: 423-24) notes that the Pharisees and early rabbis did not claim that their oral Torah was of equal age and status as the written Torah, but they did defend their traditions by an appeal to their antiquity.

[32]   An example of a less restrictive law is that by constructing doorposts and lintels the Pharisees joined several houses into one, so that food could be carried from one to the other on the sabbath. This distinguished the Pharisees from the Sadducees and the Essenes; see '*Eruvin* 6:2; CD 11:7-9.

[33]   See Sanders (1992: 432) where he argues convincingly that the Pharisees did not think that all food and wine that they consumed should always be kept pure, and that they distinguished the handling of food before the heave offering and first and second tithe were taken from it, from the way food was handled afterwards for their own use.

[34]   See the debate on this between Sanders 1990: 131-254; 1992: 431-40 and Neusner 1992. In my view, Sanders is most convincing. See also Wright 1992: 187-88, 195.

[35]   See Sanders 1992: 428-29, 436-37, 440-43. He also notes on p. 434: 'The Pharisees did not think that the common people were excluded from the sphere of the divine and sacred; they were just one step lower on the purity ladder than the Pharisees themselves, who were one step below priests outside the temple.'

everything was brought about by providence, humans still possessed free will (*War* 2:162-63; *Ant.* 13:172; 18:13). Thus the Pharisees took a middle position between the Essenes who were 'wont to leave everything in the hands of God' (*Ant.* 18:18) and the Sadducees who believed everything depended on the exercise of human free will (*War* 2:164-65). We can also note that, in the Roman period, the Pharisaic movement was divided on some issues, with the great teachers Hillel and Shammai and their schools representing differences of opinion on a number of issues, including the attitude to adopt towards Rome.[36]

During the later Hasmonean period, particularly under Salome Alexandra (76–67 BCE), the Pharisees were also a major political force and were a *de facto* power in the land.[37] While they were not the official teachers of Torah, since this was one of the functions of the priesthood, in this period they did seek to bring pressure to bear on those who had actual power. Faced with the issue of the proper stance to take with respect to the encroachments of non-Jewish ways of life, the Pharisees stood firmly for strict adherence to the covenant.

During the Roman period from 63 BCE to 70 CE, the possibilities of the Pharisees exerting influence on those with political power were greatly reduced. We do, however, know of continuing political and revolutionary activity on the part of some Pharisees at this time; hence their focus was not solely on private piety and they were as active in public and political life as they could be without being crushed.[38] Their agenda remained the same as in the earlier period: 'to purify Israel by summoning her to return to the true ancestral tradition; to restore Israel to her independent theocratic status; and to be, as a pressure-group, in the vanguard of such movements by the study and practice of Torah' (Wright 1992: 189). Hence they still wanted to direct public policy and to be influential in national life, but given the political situation, they had to be very careful in their attempts to do so.[39]

---

[36]   The Hillelites were more ready to accept Roman rule, provided Jews could study and practise Torah, and the Shammaites advocated some form of revolutionary zeal; see Saldarini 1988: 204-11.

[37]   It seems that they led the opposition to Alexander Jannaeus who ruled before Salome Alexandra; see *Ant.* 13:410.

[38]   See for example, *Ant.* 15:370; 17:41-45, 149-67; 18:4-10; 19:332-34; *War* 1:567-73, 648-55; 2:118; see also Saldarini 1988: 95-105; Sanders 1992: 380-85; 409-10; Wright 1992: 190-94; compare Neusner 1973: 45-66; 1983: 61-82.

[39]   We note Herod's fears for his safety and his jealousy that made it very

While the Pharisees did not exercise general supervision of all aspects of life and worship, and rulers did not obey the Pharisees (who would then have been indirectly powerful), as has sometimes been thought,[40] it seems clear that they were generally highly respected and popular amongst most other Jews because of their precision as interpreters of Torah and the devotion and strictness with which they obeyed it.[41] Thus their influence as unofficial *de facto* teachers of many of the people probably remained considerable, and it seems that many people were prepared to take at least some of the Pharisaic positions with some seriousness (see Wright 1992: 195, 212-14; see also Mason 1991: 372-73).[42] However, they should not be thought of as controlling the masses and strict Pharisaic laws were probably observed only by the Pharisees and not by the people at large.

B. The Sadducees[43]

While we have no Sadducean sources, and our other evidence for Sadducees is slight, we do have some information on this group. The origins of the Sadducees are unclear, but the group probably began in the Hasmonean period, perhaps when Simon was ruler. The most likely explanation for the name of the group is that some of its founders were members of the Zadokites, the former high priestly family.

In the first century CE they were a small party that opposed and were opposed by the Pharisees. Some priests were Sadducees (*Ant.*

---

difficult for others to be influential, and that the Romans ruled through the aristocracy, of which the Pharisees were generally not a part.

40 In four passages (*Ant.* 13:288, 298; 18:15, 17) Josephus attributes great authority and indirect power to the Pharisees, and suggests that they controlled the masses. However, these summaries are not borne out by Josephus's account of individual events, which show that they did not control the populace; see Sanders 1992: 388-402.

41 See Sanders 1992: 402-404 and, for example, *War* 2:563; 4:159. Josephus also notes that they practised 'the highest ideals both in their way of living and in their discourse' (*Ant.* 18:15).

42 Sanders (e.g. 1992: 402-404) underestimates the influence of the Pharisees on Jewish society; see M. Hengel and R. Deines, 'E.P. Sanders' "Common Judaism", Jesus, and the Pharisees', *JTS* 46 (1995), pp. 1-70.

43 On the Sadducees see Saldarini 1988: 79-133, 144-237, 298-308; Sanders 1992: 332-40; Wright 1992: 210-13; C. Wassén, 'Sadducees and *Halakah*', in P. Richardson and S. Westerholm (eds.), *Law in Religious Communities in the Roman Period: The Debate over Torah and Nomos in Post-Biblical Judaism and Early Christianity* (Waterloo: Wilfrid Laurier University Press, 1991), pp. 127-46.

18:17), and all or almost all Sadducees were probably aristocrats, although not all aristocrats were Sadducees. They accepted the essential points of common Judaism, such as that God had chosen Israel, and that Israel was to obey Torah. Their principal additional doctrines as a group were that they claimed to follow only the written Torah, and thus rejected the Pharisaic 'tradition of the elders' (*Ant.* 13:297),[44] denied the resurrection (*War* 2:165; *Ant.* 18:16; Mark 12:18) and believed in free will (*War* 2:164-65; *Ant.* 13:173). They were also less lenient in judgment than the Pharisees (*War* 2:166; *Ant.* 20:199), as is shown by them being depicted in Acts 4:1-6, 5:17, 33-39 as the chief persecutors of the early Christians.

C. The Qumran Community[45]

In 1947, the first Dead Sea Scrolls were discovered in caves adjacent to ruins at Khirbet Qumran, to which the scrolls were linked by pottery fragments. The fragmentary documents, which number around eight hundred in total, date from the third century BCE to the first century CE and can be divided into three groups. First, manuscripts of the Hebrew Bible, targums and Greek translations of the Old Testament; secondly, apocryphal and pseudepigraphical works like Tobit, Sirach, *Jubilees* and *1 Enoch*, which originated outside of Qumran; and thirdly, works which were written by the Qumran sect itself, such as commentaries on biblical texts, the Manual of Discipline (also called the Community Rule), the Temple Scroll and the War Scroll. The Qumran ruins were a communal centre that was occupied from around 140 BCE to 68 CE, when they seem to have been destroyed by the Romans.

The group that produced the Qumran scrolls shares many features with the Essenes described by Pliny the Elder, Josephus and Philo—notably geographical location, commonality of property, entry procedures, sacred meals, the emphasis on purity, the non-use of oil, strict community organization and discipline, celibacy and belief in

---

[44]   Sanders 1992: 333-35 notes that Josephus's implication that the Sadducees rejected anything that was not written in Torah is an oversimplification. They rejected the Pharisees' traditions, and probably claimed to follow only the biblical law, but likely had their own oral traditions, since much biblical law needed both interpretation and supplementation; see also Saldarini 1988: 303-304. They also should not be thought of as literal interpreters of Torah.

[45]   On the community and the Scrolls see in particular Davies 1987; Knibb 1987; Sanders 1992: 341-79; VanderKam 1994; Ulrich and VanderKam 1994; Collins 1995; Martínez and Barrera 1995; Maier in Neusner 1995: 84-108.

predestination. Thus, many strong arguments suggest that the members of the Qumran community were Essenes, although some scholars dispute this.[46] It also seems likely that there were two basic types of Essene groups. One form, envisioned in the Manual of Discipline (1QS), was a society of celibate men living in isolation from other Jews, as at Qumran; this group is therefore a sect, since the members considered themselves to be the only true Israel and all other Jews to be apostate. The second type of Essenes, envisioned in the Damascus Document (CD), was a community of men, women and children who lived among non-Essenes; they can be considered as an extremist party within Judaism rather than as an alternative to it (Sanders 1992: 352). Josephus and Philo put the number of Essenes at around four thousand (*Ant.* 18:20; *Quod Omn.* 75). The community resident at Qumran was never bigger than a few hundred, so most members of the Essenes probably lived among non-Essenes.

The origin of the Qumran community can probably be traced to around 152 BCE, when a Zadokite priest, who is called 'the Teacher of Righteousness' in the scrolls, was joined by members of a pietist group, probably the Hasideans mentioned in 1 Maccabees. The Teacher had come into conflict with 'the Wicked Priest', who seems to have been the high priest of the time (see for example 1QpHab 8:9–13:4), and must have been one of the Hasmoneans, most probably Jonathan, although his brother·Simon is also a possibility (see Knibb 1987: 4-10; VanderKam 1994: 100-104). As a result of this dispute, which probably grew from disagreements concerning sacrificial law and ritual purity, the Teacher and his Hasidean followers decided to separate from someone they saw as a corrupt and impure high priest and so departed (perhaps circuitously) to Qumran. They probably chose Qumran because they took literally the command in Isa. 40:3 to prepare the way of the Lord in the wilderness (see 1QS 8:12-16).

The theology of the Qumran community has a number of clear elements. A redefinition of Jewish membership, and thus a shift in understanding of the concepts of election and covenant occurred, which meant that the election of Israel was understood to have been refocused on the group, which now formed the people of the new

---

46 See the discussion in VanderKam 1994: 71-98. The suggestion that the group was Christian is contrary to the archaeological and paleographical evidence that it existed well before the time of Jesus. The suggestions that the residents of Qumran were Sadducees or that the scrolls were hidden in the caves by people fleeing from Jerusalem at the time of the First Jewish Revolt are unlikely.

covenant (CD 6:19; 8:21; 20:12; 1QpHab 2:3-4; 1QH 6:7-8). Members of the community thus saw themselves as the true representatives of Judaism who alone were destined for salvation, the new elect, the 'sons of righteousness', the 'men of the Covenant' ruled by the Prince of Light (1QS 3:20). Those who were not part of the group were not part of the elect, whatever their current status in the eyes of many Jews. The group had been eternally predestined by God and would be brought into the covenant by God's grace and call (see 1QH 2:20-21; 15:13-19; 1QM 13:9-11); related to this was a dualism between the way of light and the way of darkness. Becoming a member of the community was thus seen as separating from people of falsehood and as uniting with those who keep the covenant (1QS 5:1-3). It required a conscious voluntary decision, with full membership occurring after a period of instruction and testing.[47]

As members of the renewed covenant, strict obedience to God's will as understood by the community was required of them. They were stricter than other Jews in their interpretation of Torah on many points; for example, concerning what they could do on the sabbath (see *War* 2:147; CD 10:14–11:18). Acceptance of the discipline of the community was the sign that one belonged. The community also applied to themselves additional purity laws that were derived either from the practice of priests, or from laws governing lay people in connection with the Temple. Thus a higher level of purity than the Torah required was rigorously maintained. The whole community regarded itself as in some sense analogous to priests in the Temple, and the community served in place of the Temple, in which members did not participate, since they regarded it as a polluted institution run by a corrupt and sinful priesthood which followed an incorrect calendar. Hence they saw the obedience and worship of their community as a substitute for the sacrificial and atoning rituals of the Temple (1QS 9:4-5). Yet obedience to the community's rules and observance of purity were not regarded as 'earning' membership, or salvation. Rather, obedience and purity were appropriate expressions of membership in the group, and of election and salvation (see Wright 1992: 207-208; Sanders 1992: 357-79; Maier in Neusner 1995: 102-103). Further, the texts show a strong emphasis on the inability of humans to be righteous; correspondingly, gratitude at being chosen

---

[47]   Clearly, they saw no conflict between predestination and the need for individual choice and commitment; see Sanders 1992: 373-74.

and a total reliance on God's graciousness (see e.g. 1QS 11:2-3; 1QH 7:26-31; 11:3-4).

We can note then that the Qumran community participated in common Judaism in significant ways: they believed in the one God, in divine election, the giving of Torah, and repentance and forgiveness. However, they were radicals in the sense that they believed that only they were truly in the covenant, that they had the one true interpretation of Torah and that only their priests were acceptable.

The community was waiting for the war of the endtimes when their Israelite enemies and then the Gentiles would be destroyed. They would take control of Jerusalem (1QM), rebuild the Temple according to their own plans and restore true worship (11QT). The ordered community would then live pure lives under a rigorous discipline. They would be led by two Messiahs, a Davidic Messiah who would defeat Israel's enemies and execute justice, and a superior priestly Aaronic Messiah who would instruct the Davidic Messiah concerning the teaching of Torah and making judgments according to it and would carry out other priestly duties.[48]

Revelation and scriptural interpretation at Qumran also led to knowledge of the true calendar and the correct times at which to celebrate the festivals. The Qumran calendar called for a solar year of 364 days, which differed from the 354 day lunar calendar in use in the Temple. This meant that the Qumranites observed a unique cycle of festival and effectively distanced themselves from the common pattern of festivals of the period. They also celebrated some festivals that other Jews did not observe.

D. Use and Abuse of our Knowledge of Jewish Parties in Exegesis

The Pharisees figure in the New Testament as opponents of Jesus, and Paul tells us that he himself was a Pharisee. As Sanders has shown, a considerable amount of New Testament scholarship has misjudged the Pharisees and seen them, for example, as those who tried to earn salvation through keeping Torah, or as self-righteous exclusivists who despised the common people (Sanders 1992: 413-51). Neither view does justice to the evidence; working with these views of the Pharisees will distort the New Testament text.

In the Gospels, the Pharisees feature as informed and learned adversaries of Jesus, which is in keeping with what we know of them

---

48   See, for example, 1QSa 2:12-21. Note, however, that there is no Davidic messiah in the War Rule.

as experts in the interpretation of Torah. The statement in Matt. 5:20 that 'unless your righteousness exceeds that of the scribes and Pharisees, you will never enter the kingdom of heaven' reflects the common view of the period that the Pharisees were among the most committed to obedience to Torah (see also Matt. 23:2-3).

In the Gospels, the Pharisees dispute with Jesus over matters that we know from other sources were some of the major concerns of the Pharisees. These include matters such as fasting (Mark 2:18), keeping the sabbath (Mark 2:24; 3:2), purity (Mark 7:1; Matt. 23:25-26), eating with sinners (Mark 2:16) and tithing (Matt. 23:23).[49] In order to appreciate these disputes, we must understand the beliefs and practices of the Pharisees, and also appreciate their motivation for being strict interpreters of Torah. They did not see this as 'earning salvation', nor as being nit-picking, but rather as being fully obedient to God's Torah.[50] The Gospels also present Jesus as criticizing the Pharisees for obeying insignificant rules and not attending to the weightier matters of the law (Matt. 23:23; cf. Mark 2:24). Such passages clearly reflect a situation of polemic. In addition, as Sanders notes:

> others could see their [the Pharisees'] scrupulous definition and fulfilment of the laws as being merely external activity that masked inner hypocrisy and self-righteousness, but they did not themselves see it that way. They thought that God had given them his Torah and bestowed on them his grace, and that it was their obligation within the loving relationship with God to obey Torah precisely (Sanders 1992: 446).

The commitment of the Pharisees to 'the tradition of the elders' is reflected in New Testament passages where Jesus criticizes the Pharisees on this point. In Mark 7:1-8, Jesus criticizes them concerning handwashing, which is not a biblical requirement, and in

---

49   Other matters include divorce (Mark 10:2-9), oaths (Matt. 5:33-37), and Roman taxes (Mark 12:13).

50   I have noted above that purity matters functioned as boundary-setting mechanisms. Saldarini (1988: 150) comments: 'Thus the Pharisees are the defenders of a certain kind of community and Jesus challenged the Pharisees' vision of community by attacking their purity regulations concerning washing and food, as well as sabbath practice. The effect of Jesus' teaching is to widen the community boundaries and loosen the norms for membership in his community. Jesus thus created a new community outside their control and quite naturally provoked their protest and hostility.' This must be connected with Jesus' preaching concerning the Kingdom of God (Mark 1:14-15).

Mark 7:11-13, Jesus rebukes the Pharisees for the way they used the practice of declaring property or goods *korban*, or 'an offering' to God (cf. Matt. 15:1-9; see also Matt. 23:15-26).

We know that Paul had been a Pharisee (Phil. 3:5-6; Acts 22:3; 23:6; 26:5); thus knowledge of the Pharisees helps us to understand some of Paul's presuppositions and theology. For example, Paul tells us that he was zealous for the 'traditions of the elders' (Gal. 1:14) and 'as to the law, a Pharisee' (Phil. 3:5-6); in both cases he is referring to the Pharisees' views on Torah. As a Christian, he faces the issue of the place of the law in relation to Christ. This can be seen as working through one of the most important features of his Pharisaic background in the light of the coming of Christ.[51]

The Scrolls are immensely helpful for New Testament exegesis, since they provide numerous illustrations of contemporary ideas.[52] Clearly there were major differences between the two movements. Two obvious examples are: first, for the early Christians, Jesus, who was believed to be the Messiah, was the central figure whereas the Teacher of Righteousness fulfilled this role at Qumran; secondly, some Jewish Christians launched a Gentile mission in which purity was not observed, whereas the Qumranites formed a pure Jewish community in the wilderness. Yet there are also significant similarities in vocabulary, doctrine, organizational and ritual practices. We note the following examples:[53]

(1) The Scrolls probably give the Semitic original for a number of expressions found in the Greek New Testament. Examples include

---

[51] See also J.H. Neyrey, *Paul in Other Words: A Cultural Reading of His Letters* (Louisville: Westminster/John Knox Press, 1990) who argues that Paul's socialization as a Pharisee led to his passionate concern as a Christian for such categories as order, hierarchy and boundaries with respect to purity.

[52] A number of highly improbable claims have been made with respect to the relationship between the Scrolls and the New Testament, including that the Qumranites were Christians, that some parts of the New Testament have been found at Qumran or that Jesus was the Wicked Priest of the Scrolls. All these views are highly unlikely.

[53] See J.A. Fitzmyer, 'The Qumran Scrolls and the New Testament after Forty Years', *RevQ* 13 (1988), pp. 609-20; J.H. Charlesworth (ed.), *Jesus and the Dead Sea Scrolls* (New York: Doubleday, 1992); C.A. Evans, 'The Recently Published Dead Sea Scrolls and the Historical Jesus', in B. Chilton and C.A. Evans (eds.), *Studying the Historical Jesus: Evaluations of the State of Current Research* (NTTS, 19; Leiden: Brill, 1994), pp. 547-65; VanderKam 1994: 159-85; Collins 1995; Martínez and Barrera 1995: 203-32.

'the majority (οἱ πλείονες)' (2 Cor. 2:6), 'overseer (ἐπίσκοπος)' (Phil. 1:1; 1 Tim. 3:1-7; Titus 1:7-9) and 'works of the law (ἔργα νόμου)' (Gal. 2:16; Rom. 3:20, 28).

(2) Scholars have noted the similarities between John the Baptist and the Qumranites concerning eschatological urgency, teaching and practice. It is possible that John had some contact with Qumran prior to his own independent ministry.

(3) Various elements in the teaching of the two groups are similar, such as the use of dualistic language (1QS 3:19-26; 4:16-18; 2 Cor. 6:14–7:1; John 8:12; 1 John 2:8-11), the belief that group members participated in a new covenant (CD 20:12; 2 Cor. 3:6), that some are given the gift of divine wisdom (1QH 12:12-13; 1QpHab 7:4-5; 1 Cor. 2:7; 12:8) and the ban on divorce (11QT 57:17-19; CD 4:20-21; Mark 10:2-9). Further, in 11QMelch we see something of a parallel to the exalted status and characteristics of Melchizedek in Hebrews.

(4) Both the Qumranites and the early Christians were eschatological communities that were convinced that the end was near and that their community should live accordingly. Both groups shared a number of beliefs about the Messiah, although the Qumranites looked for two Messiahs in the future, and the Christians believed Jesus was the Messiah who would return. Similar titles are used in the different texts (cf. Luke 1:32-33 and 4Q246; Matt. 11:5 and 4Q521).

(5) There are a number of similarities in the practices of the Qumranites and the early Christians. We note the sharing of property (Acts 2:44-45; 4:32; 1QS 6:17-22) and regular participation in a meal with eschatological associations (Mark 14:22-55; 1QS 6:4-6, 16-17; 1QSa 2:11-22).

(6) Similar methods of biblical interpretation were used, with both communities believing that some biblical texts concerned the latter days in which the group was living, and hence referred to contemporary events.

(7) It is also interesting that the three biblical books for which the largest number of copies have been found at Qumran (Psalms, Deuteronomy and Isaiah) are also the three that are most frequently quoted in the New Testament (see VanderKam 1994: 32).

The extent of the parallels between the two movements shows how deeply rooted early Christianity was in Jewish soil and the way in which it borrowed much of the heritage of Judaism in shaping its own life and beliefs. Further, these parallels show that the uniqueness of early Christianity lies not in its eschatology or community practices, but in its central confession that Jesus who taught, healed, suffered, died and rose again was the Messiah, Son of God and Lord.

There are numerous other ways in which the Qumran texts aid exegesis of the New Testament, but one further illustration must suffice here. None of the 11 manuscripts of *1 Enoch* found at Qumran contains anything from the Similitudes of Enoch (*1 Enoch* 37–71). Scholars have debated whether the concept of a super-human son of man who will be involved in the final judgment, and who plays a central role in these chapters of *1 Enoch*, may have been a source used by the evangelists in writing of Jesus as the Son of Man. However, since the Similitudes are not present at Qumran and all the other parts of *1 Enoch* are, it seems likely, though not certain, that the Similitudes are a later composition, which could not have served as a source for the evangelists.

COMPARATIVE INTERPRETATION OF SCRIPTURE

A. *Scriptural Interpretation in Judaism*

The Hebrew Scriptures were fundamental for all Jews of this period. However, a wealth of different interpretations, reflecting a variety of approaches, developed at this time. This diversity of interpretations witnesses to the diversity of Judaism.

Scriptural study and interpretation were central at Qumran, as is shown by the number of texts that are commentaries on Scripture or concern its interpretation.[54] They believed that the purposes of God were revealed in the Scriptures and these had now been made known to the community through its inspired leader, the Teacher of Righteousness. God had revealed to the Teacher the mysteries of the Scriptures and principles and techniques of its interpretation, so that he and subsequent interpreters could instruct the community in the true understanding, clarification and application of the Scripture (CD 1:1–2:1; 1QpHab 7:4-5, 8). Hence they believed that only their interpretation of Scripture was true and certain and that through correct interpretation they were provided with '*the* way of salvation (CD 14:1-2) and *the* knowledge of the divine plan for history (1QpHab 2:6-10)'.[55]

---

[54] On the interpretation of Scripture at Qumran, see Brooke 1985; Fishbane in Mulder 1988: 339-77; Martínez and Barrera 1995: 111-21. On its importance see for example 1QS 6:6-8.

[55] Fishbane in Mulder 1988: 340. One interesting example of the authority

Through its study of Scripture, the community was convinced that the latter days predicted by the prophets had arrived; in addition, the words of some of the prophets spoke about the history of the community. These views were factors that led to the community's pesherim texts[56] being unique within Judaism. Scriptural interpretation also led to the derivation of various specific rules and practices that they believed lay hidden in the words of Torah, by which the members of the community were to live (e.g. CD 3:13). Transgression of these hidden and secret requirements was regarded as sin. Thus, it was not Scripture alone that had authority over the community, but Scripture *and* its interpretation—Scripture as understood through their inspired interpretation of its 'hidden' sense. In this way, Scripture was interpreted so that its meaning was redirected to the community's own day, and it was used so as to relate to their own practices and beliefs. We see then the vital role played by the interpretation of Scripture in shaping the identity of one particular Jewish community.[57]

Interpretation of Scripture was also fundamental to the Pharisees. Through their interpretations, which became called the 'traditions of the elders', they sought to apply the written text to the present and thus to make it relevant. Key teachers were involved in this interpretative enterprise, and there were often disagreements concerning proposed interpretations.

In the Apocrypha and Pseudepigrapha, Scripture is occasionally explicitly quoted and the situation described in the Old Testament text is then equated with the later situation being presented in the new text, thus seeing in the new text the fulfilment of the old.[58] On other

---

given to their own interpretation of Scripture is that, in the Temple Scroll (11QT), the author or redactor presents the text not as an interpretation of Scripture but as an immediate divine revelation by regularly presenting both quotations from Scripture and supplementary legal material as directly spoken by God. Thus the whole text is presented as Torah revealed by God to Moses.

56   In pesher interpretation, the biblical text is read as a prefiguration of contemporary events.

57   Fishbane (in Mulder 1988: 360) notes: 'It was, in fact, precisely in the special way that the old laws were reinterpreted or extended, the old predictions reapplied or decoded, and the institutions of ancient Israel restructured or regenerated, that the covenanters of Qumran saw themselves as distinct from other contemporary Jewish groups'.

58   See, for example, Lev. 26:24 in *3 Macc.* 6:15 and Amos 8:10 in Tob. 2:6; see Divant in Mulder 1988: 389-90. On the interpretation of Scripture in the Apocrypha and Pseudepigrapha, see Divant in Mulder 1988: 379-419; J.H.

occasions, biblical elements are interwoven unobtrusively into a new text using implicit quotations, allusions or motifs from biblical texts, without such elements being formally introduced. Often this leads to new texts in which the biblical text is expanded and rewritten (e.g. *Jubilees*, Pseudo-Philo's *Biblical Antiquities*, *1 Enoch* 6–11). In the process, the biblical text is interpreted, for example, by way of editorial alterations and substitutions, giving the story a new, more explicit and contemporary meaning. Thus we find both dependence and innovation with respect to the biblical text. Further, implicit quotations are often used to imitate biblical styles (e.g. in Tobit, Susanna, 1 Maccabees), or a text employs the biblical text as a pattern (e.g. most of the Testaments use Genesis 49 or Deuteronomy 31–34 in this way).

B. *The Use of Comparative Interpretation in New Testament Exegesis*[59]

Interpretation of Scripture was also of crucial significance for the early Christians. We cannot discuss this in detail here, but two points are noteworthy. First, the early Christians followed presuppositions, perspectives and methods with respect to the interpretation of Scripture that are also found in Jewish writings of the period, so an awareness of these matters is very helpful in exegesis. Thus, for example, in writing the story of Jesus and the early Church, Luke adopted the language and themes of Scripture, and uses Scripture to give shape to the narrative in much the same way as had the authors of *Jubilees* and the Genesis Apocryphon; in addition, the use of interpretative alterations or expansions within Old Testament quotations, which is a form of implicit midrash found in Jewish

---

Charlesworth and C.A. Evans (eds.), *The Pseudepigrapha and Early Biblical Interpretation* (JSPSup, 14; Sheffield: JSOT Press, 1993); see also van der Horst in Mulder 1988: 519-46.

[59] On the interpretation and function of Israel's Scriptures in the New Testament, see, for example, Ellis in Mulder 1988: 691-725; R.B. Hays, *Echoes of Scripture in the Letters of Paul* (New Haven: Yale University Press, 1989); C.A. Evans and J.A. Sanders, *Luke and Scripture: The Function of Sacred Tradition in Luke–Acts* (Minneapolis: Fortress Press, 1993); C.A. Evans and J.A. Sanders (eds.), *Paul and the Scriptures of Israel* (JSNTSup, 83; Sheffield: JSOT Press, 1993); C.A. Evans and W.R. Stegner (eds.), *The Gospels and the Scriptures of Israel* (JSNTSup, 104; Sheffield: JSOT Press, 1994).

texts,[60] occurs in Acts 4:11 (cf. Ps. 118:22) and Rom. 10:11 (cf. Isa. 28:16).

Secondly, it is noteworthy that the most distinctive feature in Christian texts is the thoroughgoing reinterpretation of Scripture in the light of the ministry, death and resurrection of Jesus. Thus, as at Qumran, Old Testament eschatological texts are taken to apply to the present (e.g. Acts 2:16-21), but, in contradistinction to Qumran, the messianic and eschatological orientation of the early Christians is focused on Jesus.

BIBLIOGRAPHY

Boccaccini, G.
1991   *Middle Judaism: Jewish Thought, 300 B.C.E. to 200 B.C.E.* Minneapolis: Fortress Press.
Brooke, G.
1985   *Exegesis at Qumran: 4QFlorilegium in its Jewish Context.* JSOTSup, 29. Sheffield: JSOT Press.
Charlesworth, J.H. (ed.)
1983–85 *The Old Testament Pseudepigrapha.* 2 vols. Garden City, NY: Doubleday.
1992   *The Messiah: Developments in Earliest Judaism and Christianity.* Minneapolis: Fortress Press.
Cohen, S.J.D.
1987   *From the Maccabees to the Mishnah.* Philadelphia: Westminster Press.
Collins, J.J.
1995   *The Scepter and the Star: The Messiahs of the Dead Sea Scrolls and other Ancient Literature.* New York: Doubleday.
Davies, P.R.
1987   *Behind the Essenes: History and Ideology in the Dead Sea Scrolls.* BJS, 94. Atlanta: Scholars Press.
Davies, W.D., and L. Finkelstein
1989   *The Cambridge History of Judaism.* II. *The Hellenistic Age.* Cambridge: Cambridge University Press.
Dunn, J.D.G.
1990   *Jesus, Paul and the Law.* London: SPCK.
1991   *The Partings of the Ways between Christianity and Judaism and their Significance for the Character of Christianity.* London: SCM Press; Philadelphia: Trinity Press International.

---

[60] As for example in 4QTest 22 (cf Josh. 6:26) and 1QpHab 8:3 (cf. Hab. 2:5).

Goodman, M.

1987 *The Ruling Class of Judaea: The Origins of the Jewish Revolt against Rome A.D. 66–70.* Cambridge: Cambridge University Press.

Grabbe, L.L.

1992 *Judaism from Cyrus to Hadrian.* 2 vols. Minneapolis: Fortress Press.

Hengel, M.

1974 *Judaism and Hellenism: Studies in their Encounter in Palestine during the Early Hellenistic Period.* 2 vols. London: SCM Press.

1989 *The 'Hellenization' of Judaea in the First Century after Christ.* London: SCM Press.

Knibb, M.A.

1987 *The Qumran Community.* Cambridge Commentaries on Writings of the Jewish and Christian World, 200 BC–AD 200. Cambridge: Cambridge University Press.

Kraft, R.A., and G.W.E. Nickelsburg (eds.)

1986 *Early Judaism and its Modern Interpreters.* Philadelphia: Fortress Press; Atlanta: Scholars Press.

Martínez, F.G., and J.T. Barrera

1995 *The People of the Dead Sea Scrolls: Their Writings, Beliefs and Practices.* Leiden: Brill.

Mason, S.N.

1991 *Flavius Josephus on the Pharisees: A Composition-Critical Study.* SPB, 39. Leiden: Brill.

Mulder, M.J. (ed.)

1987 *Mikra: Text, Translation, Reading and Interpretation of the Hebrew Bible in Ancient Judaism and Early Christianity.* CRINT, 2.1. Philadelphia: Fortress Press; Assen: Van Gorcum.

Neusner, J.

1971 *The Rabbinic Traditions about the Pharisees Before 70.* 3 vols. Leiden: Brill.

1973 *From Politics to Piety. The Emergence of Rabbinic Judaism.* Englewood Cliffs, NJ: Prentice–Hall.

1983 *Formative Judaism: Religious, Historical and Literary Studies. Third Series. Torah, Pharisees, and Rabbis.* BJS, 46. Chico, CA: Scholars Press.

1984 *Judaism in the Beginning of Christianity.* London: SPCK.

1991 *Jews and Christians: The Myth of a Common Tradition.* London: SCM Press.

1992 *Judaic Law from Jesus to the Mishnah.* South Florida Studies in the History of Judaism, 84. Atlanta: Scholars Press.

Neusner, J. (ed.)

1995 *Judaism in Late Antiquity. Part One: The Literary and Archaeological Sources; Part Two: Historical Syntheses.* 2 vols. Handbuch der Orientalistik Abt 1.16-17. Leiden: Brill.

Neusner, J., W.S. Green, and E. Fredrichs (eds.)

1987 *Judaisms and their Messiahs at the Turn of the Christian Era.* Cambridge: Cambridge University Press.

Riches, J.

1990   *The World of Jesus: First Century Judaism in Crisis*. Cambridge: Cambridge University Press.

Safrai, S., and M. Stern

1974–76 *The Jewish People in the First Century: Historical Geography, Political History, Social, Cultural and Religious Life and Institutions*. 2 vols. CRINT, 1. Philadelphia: Fortress Press; Assen: Van Gorcum.

Saldarini, A.J.

1988   *Pharisees, Scribes and Sadducees in Palestinian Society*. Wilmington, DE: Michael Glazier.

Sanders, E.P.

1977   *Paul and Palestinian Judaism: A Comparison of Patterns of Religion*. London: SCM Press.

1985   *Jesus and Judaism*. London: SCM Press.

1990   *Jewish Law from Jesus to the Mishnah: Five Studies*. London: SCM Press.

1992   *Judaism: Practice and Belief, 63 BCE–66 CE*. London: SCM Press.

Schürer, E.

1973–87 *The History of the Jewish People in the Age of Jesus Christ (175 B.C.– A.D. 135)*. Revised and edited by G. Vermes, F. Millar, M. Black, M. Goodman. 3 vols. Edinburgh: T. & T. Clark.

Stemberger, G.

1995   *Jewish Contemporaries of Jesus: Pharisees, Sadducees, Essenes*. Minneapolis: Fortress Press.

Trebilco, P.R.

1991   *Jewish Communities in Asia Minor*. SNTSMS, 69. Cambridge: Cambridge University Press.

Ulrich, E., and J. VanderKam (eds.)

1994   *The Community of the Renewed Covenant: The Notre Dame Symposium on the Dead Sea Scrolls*. Notre Dame: University of Notre Dame Press.

Urman, D., and P.V.M. Flesher (eds.)

1995   *Ancient Synagogues: Historical Analysis and Archaeological Discovery*. 2 vols. SPB, 47. Leiden: Brill.

VanderKam, J.C.

1994   *The Dead Sea Scrolls Today*. Grand Rapids: Eerdmans.

Vermes, G.

1995   *The Dead Sea Scrolls in English*. London/New York: Penguin, 4th edn.

Whittaker, M.

1984   *Jews and Christians: Graeco-Roman Views*. Cambridge Commentaries on Writings of the Jewish and Christian World. Cambridge: Cambridge University Press.

Wright, N.T.

1992   *The New Testament and the People of God*. I. *Christian Origins and the Question of God*. Minneapolis: Fortress Press.

THE ROMAN EMPIRE AS A CONTEXT FOR THE
NEW TESTAMENT

DAVID W.J. GILL

The New Testament documents were written against the background of the Roman Empire. The Gospel narratives take place within the province of Judaea (Bauckham 1995), and the Acts of the Apostles record the spread of the Church through most of the significant eastern provinces (Gill and Gempf 1994). The epistles were written to the Christian communities in Roman colonies (Corinth, Philippi), Greek cities (Ephesus), and even in the city of Rome. Private individuals lived and travelled in a world dominated by Roman culture and institutions; although at the same time regional differences would have been quite apparent. Control of an empire was often with the consent and indeed co-operation of local elites, and local civic political structures continued under the authority of the provincial governor and ultimately the emperor (Millar 1981: 81-103). Any reading of the New Testament background needs to take account of the local setting as well as the broader issues of empire.

PROVINCES

One of the most important regional structures of the empire was the province. Following Augustus's reforms, there were essentially two main types: those under senatorial control and those under the emperor (imperial). In general, provinces on the frontiers, with significant numbers of troops, tended to be imperial, while the more peaceful regions would be senatorial. The chief person in charge of the province was the governor, and a number appear through the New Testament: for example, Quirinius in Syria (Luke 2:2), Sergius Paullus on Cyprus (Acts 13:7), L. Junius Gallio in Achaea (Acts 18:12), Pontius Pilate (Matt. 27:2; Mark 15:1; Luke 23:1; John 18:28-29), Felix and Festus in Judaea (Acts 24–26). The status of these men is revealed by further details about their careers. For example, Sergius Paullus had earlier served as one of the river commissioners appointed by the emperor Claudius to supervise the banks of the river Tiber, and may have eventually held the consulship under Vespasian (Nobbs 1994). Governors had a small staff to assist them with the administration of the province. One of the most important members was the procurator, who had different functions depending on the status of the province. In an imperial province, the procurator was responsible for the collection of taxes, as well as the payment of those on official duty. Such men were usually of equestrian rank.

An exception to this provincial framework was Judaea itself, which, like Egypt, did not have, at least in the New Testament period, a full governor, but rather a prefect (ἔπαρχος) or procurator (ἐπίτροπος) (Schürer 1973: 358). Thus, when Pontius Pilatus dedicated a temple of the imperial cult at Caesarea (Tiberieium), he was described in the Latin inscription as prefect (Schürer 1973: 358). Such men were drawn from the equestrian class of Roman citizens. They required a property qualification of 400,000 sesterces—a third of that of a senator—as well as having had free status for two generations. Equestrian governors were thus of a slightly lower status than other senatorial governors.

CLIENT KINGDOMS AND THE PLACE OF JUDAEA

Alongside the provinces were a series of client kingdoms which maintained diplomatic relations with Rome. For example, when Paul fled from Damascus (2 Cor. 11:32), he was within the kingdom of Aretas, the king of Nabataea, which later formed part of the province of Arabia (Bowersock 1983: 68).

The status of such kingdoms is well illustrated by Judaea. On Herod's death in 4 BCE, Sabinus the procurator of the adjoining province of Syria intervened to secure the royal treasury at Jerusalem. However, it was not until 6 CE that Archelaus, Herod's heir, was deposed and sent into exile, thus allowing Judaea to become a province under the control of a prefect (Gill 1995a). The first governor was Coponius. At the same time, the tetrarchs Herodes Antipas and Philip were left in charge of their own territories. When Philip died, his territory was incorporated in the province of Syria rather than Judaea.

One of the most important changes was that, in January 41, Agrippa I, who had been at Rome, was rewarded with Judaea for his support of Claudius following the assassination of the emperor Gaius. This change in the status of the region is reflected in Acts (12:20-21), where Agrippa is recorded as receiving an embassy from Tyre and Sidon. However, after his death in 44, instead of the kingdom reverting to his sixteen year old son Agrippa II, Claudius appointed the equestrian Cuspius Fadus as procurator, thus reestablishing Judaea as a province.

Some governors seem to have been quite insensitive to Jewish customs and culture. Thus, Pontius Pilate used money from the 'Corbanus' treasury in order to pay for the construction of an aqueduct, and, on another occasion, caused a riot by introducing images of the emperor into Jerusalem at night. Felix, who appears in the book of Acts, was married to Drusilla, the daughter of Agrippa I. In spite of this, he was high-handed with the Jews, and allowed their homes to be looted by his troops.

Tensions against Rome may in part look back to 63 BCE, when Pompey captured Jerusalem, even entering the Holy of Holies. Suspicion of gentiles can be traced to the interference of the Hellenistic rulers of the region, and their imposition of Greek culture (Schürer 1973: 137-63). For example, Antiochus IV Epiphanes (175–164 BCE) had tried to impose a ruler cult in the Temple at Jerusalem, and there had been an active policy of Hellenization, which had sought to undermine Jewish orthodoxy. It is important to realize that the governor of the province of Judaea had considerable influence over Jewish cult practice (Goodman 1987). Like some of the Hellenistic rulers they had the right to appoint the High Priests. It was only in 36 CE, following intervention by the legate of Syria against Pontius Pilate, that the right of the Jews to control the priestly robes was returned. This right was in fact redemanded by Claudius's new governor Cuspius Fadus when he was appointed in 44 CE. This caused such offence that petitions were sent to the legate of Syria, as well as Claudius himself, and it may have been to appease the Jewish elite that the next governor, Tiberius Julius Alexander (c. 46–48 CE), was from a Jewish family from Alexandria. Even so, the subsequent procurator Cumanus gave considerable offence and the legate of Syria had to intervene and send him to Rome.

One clear way that incorporation into the Roman Empire interfered with those in the province was the imposition of a census mentioned by Luke (2:2), who claimed that it took place when Quirinius was governor of the adjoining province of Syria (but see Schürer 1973: 399-427; Millar 1993: 46). This episode has caused chronological problems since, although Quirinius's survey is likely to have been linked to the incorporation of Judaea in 6 CE, Luke 1:5 also places this in the time of Herod, who died in 4 BCE.

Certain parts of the province of Judaea were more gentilic than others. The port of Caesarea, named in honour of Augustus, was the administrative centre and residence of the governor. Its gentile nature is reflected in the way that the imperial cult was located here; according to Josephus (*Ant.* 15:339), the temple of Roma and Augustus could be seen from out at sea. A temple in honour of the emperor Tiberius was erected during the governorship of Pontius Pilate (Schürer 1973: 358). Indeed, in Josephus (*War* 2:270) it was at Caesarea that the Jews had to mount their protest. Paul himself was imprisoned in Herod's *praetorium*, which reflects the origins of the city (Acts 23:35).

CITIES AND LOCAL ELITES

Cities within the empire did not all have the same legal status. In a province such as Achaea, there were Roman colonies like Corinth that had a very Italian feel to the architecture, sculpture and language, whereas, at the same time, a city like Athens very much retained its Greek feel and structures (Gill 1993a). Thus, the cultural background of a specific community becomes significant when trying to understand the biblical text.

The *pax Romana* enjoyed by the cities at the same time deprived communities of a way to express inter-city rivalry. Thus, in the Roman period there is a noticeable flourishing of agonistic festivals supported by local elites. This imagery is a theme to which Paul returns on several occasions (e.g. 1 Cor. 9:24-27; Phil. 3:14).

Individuals within the empire did not have the same status. Distinctions were made between slave and free, rich and poor, citizen and non-citizen. Paul is a good case in point, in that he was a Roman citizen—and would thus have had a tripartite name—through birth (Acts 22:28) (Rapske 1994b: 71-112). It is no doubt significant that it was in a scene before the governor of Cyprus, Sergius Paullus, that Luke records Saul also being called Paul (Acts 13:9). This probably signifies the way Paul had adopted the use of his patron's name (Nobbs 1994: 287-89). Paul's inherited citizenship is in marked contrast to the arresting tribune at Jerusalem, Claudius Lysias, who claimed to have bought his (Acts 22:26, 28); this man's name suggests that he obtained his citizenship under the emperors Claudius or Nero.

The way that the local civic community, or *polis*, continued to form the framework of each province, meant that the local elites of those communities had a special place. Some of the more prominent members may have been Roman citizens, though, in the New

Testament period, not all. These cities were thus able to continue under their own civic institutions. For example, at Thessalonica Paul was brought before the *politarchs* or civic officials (Acts 17:6) (Horsley 1994). A more detailed example of the way that a legal body in a Greek city continued to function under the empire is provided by Paul's speech before the Areopagos at Athens (Acts 17:19-34). Although at first sight it appears that this is no more than a hearing in front of the Athenian intellectuals, there are elements that imply that this was a legal hearing. Athenian inscriptions of the Roman period show that the city could be addressed in terms of its civic institutions: 'the *boule* of the Areopagos, the *boule* of the Six Hundred and the *demos* of the Athenians'. Indeed, as a body, even in the Roman period, it may have been possible for the Areopagos to exact exile and capital punishment. Barnes (1969) has suggested that, just as Paul was brought before civic magistrates at Philippi and Thessalonica, or the governor at Corinth, in the 'free city' of Athens, the Areopagos was the logical place to lay charges against an individual. He proposed that the charge against Paul was that he was introducing a new religion to the city, and that Paul's speech forms the key elements of his defence.

The riot at Ephesus caused by the silversmiths who were associated with the worship of the civic goddess, Artemis, brings into sharp focus the problems faced by the civic authorities under the Roman Empire (Acts 19:23-41) (Trebilco 1994: 302-57). Paul's companions were seized by the mob, and even the provincial officials, the Asiarchs, advised against Paul intervening (Horsley 1994). Such unruly behaviour might cause an intervention by the governor, and so there is little surprise that the city *grammateus* (secretary) intervened to quieten down the proceedings (Acts 19:35). He pointed out that, if any laws had been broken, then the courts were open and they could take appropriate action. Secondly, he reminded the crowd that the city ran the risk of 'being charged with rioting because of today's events' (Acts 19:40).

It is clear from epigraphic evidence from elsewhere that such behaviour was not tolerated. For example, an inscription, almost certainly relating to a second-century CE riot at Magnesia on the Maeander by the bakers, reveals the threats made by the governor for such behaviour:

> I therefore order the Bakers' Union not to hold meetings as a faction nor to be leaders in recklessness, but strictly to obey the regulations... When from this time forward any one of them shall be caught in the act of

attending a meeting contrary to order, or of starting any tumult and riot, he shall be arrested and shall undergo the fitting penalty.

At the end of the first century CE, Dio Chrysostom (*Or.* 34:21-22) addressed the people of Tarsus and suggested that, if the linen workers caused trouble, 'you should expel them altogether and not admit them to your popular assemblies'.

Elite members of these urban communities do appear in the New Testament documents. For example, Aristarchus from Thessalonica has a name that is suggestive of high status (Gill 1994b). Moreover, the way that he appears at Ephesus as well as on the final voyage to Rome suggests that he belonged to this social group which had the means to travel (Acts 19:29; 20:4; 27:2; Phlm. 24; Col. 4:10).

At Thessalonica some Christians had stopped working and were 'living in idleness' (2 Thess. 3:6; cf. 1 Thess. 4:11). Winter (1994a: 41-60) has argued that the appropriate background to this may have been a food shortage which hit the Mediterranean in the 40s and 50s. Some members of the church had built up a patron/client relationship with the elite members of the church during the crisis, and continued to use it even when the time of need was past. Such shortages may have also influenced the Thessalonian interest in eschatological concerns.

SLAVES AND FREEDMEN

One of the most important institutions of the ancient world was that of slavery. It underpinned much of the ancient economy, including the running of the home and agriculture. Slavery appears at several points in the New Testament documents (e.g. 1 Cor. 12:13; Gal. 3:28; Eph. 6:8; Col. 3:11; Philemon *passim*. It is important to remember that, in some ways, slaves in a good household may have been considerably better off than the urban poor, especially at Rome (Finley 1968; 1980). Former slaves, on obtaining their freedom, could become Roman citizens, an image used by Paul (1 Cor. 7:22-23). In the epigraphic record, they can often be identified either by the omission of their father's name, or the mention that they were the freedman of a named individual, whose name they would take. The children of such individuals obtained full rights. Some of these freedmen could be extremely rich. Take, for example, C. Julius Zoilos at Aphrodisias (in western Asia Minor)—a freedman of either Julius Caesar or more likely Augustus—who is known to have given a series of buildings to his home town (Smith 1993). Freedmen even became governors of Judaea. For example, Felix was a freedman of the emperor Claudius, and may have obtained his position through the influence of his brother Pallas. Although Pallas's full name was Antonius Pallas, as he received his freedom from Antonia the mother of the emperor Claudius, Josephus (*Ant.* 18:6:6) calls his brother Claudius Felix. A tantalizingly incomplete Greek epitaph that was found between Dora and Athlit mentions a procurator called Tiberius Claudius, and Felix must be a possibility (Gill 1995a: 22).

ROMAN AUTHORITY AND CHRISTIANITY

Roman authority appears in the New Testament in several places. The most obvious is the role of Pontius Pilate as prefect of the province of Judaea. Although the charges brought against Jesus came from the Jewish authorities, the governor alone had the responsibility to punish Jesus with a death sentence. At the same time, it has to be realized that, although Pilate had the authority to reject the charges, his position in the province largely rested with the goodwill of the Jewish authorities, in particular members of the Jewish elite (Goodman 1987). Moreover, with only a limited number of troops available to him, the easiest course of action was often one of appeasement.

One of clearest statements about the legal status of Christianity may be found in Acts. The Jews at Corinth brought Paul before the governor, Gallio (the brother of Seneca), and suggested that he was guilty of 'persuading the people to worship God in ways contrary to the law' (Acts 18:13). Gallio came to the conclusion that Christianity was no more than a sub-group of Judaism, and therefore should be accorded similar privileges and rights as the Jews. He thus dismissed the case (Winter 1994a: 142-43). The privileges of the Jews in the empire are well documented, especially from Anatolia (Trebilco 1991). For example, a civic decree at Sardis (c. 49 BCE)—recorded by Josephus (*Ant.* 14:259-61)—declared that Jewish citizens of the city could 'adjudicate suits among themselves' and even that 'the *agoranomoi* (the officials in charge of the markets) shall be charged with the duty of having suitable food...brought in'. Further privileges were granted in 14 BCE, when Rome guaranteed the right of Jewish communities to send money to Jerusalem (Josephus, *Ant.* 16:162-70).

Other governors mentioned in the New Testament include Sergius Paulus on Cyprus, who may have helped Paul's ministry by encouraging him to visit Pisidian Antioch where his family had estates (Mitchell 1993: 6-7; Nobbs 1994). In Judaea, Paul was imprisoned under the governor Felix (Acts 23:35), a state of affairs that continued under his successor Festus. Indeed, Paul identified Festus as being the emperor's representative when he stated, 'I am now standing before Caesar's court, where I ought to be tried' (Acts 25:10).

Finally, behind much of the New Testament stands the shadowy figure of the emperor. It is to him that Paul finally appealed as a citizen (Acts 25:12). It was this appeal that removed him from the authority of the provincial governor, Festus (Rapske 1994b: 85-88; Millar 1992: 510-11).

CHRISTIANITY IN A ROMAN COLONY: CORINTH

Historical and archaeological study of the colony of Corinth has now recognized the Roman nature of the community (Clarke 1993; Gill 1993a). Latin appears to have been the main language for public inscriptions and, until the reign of Trajan, there are only a handful of inscriptions in Greek; for these a special case can be presented, including their link to the Panhellenic Isthmian Games held under the auspices of the city. This is perhaps emphasized by the choice of Latin for a Trajanic inscription honouring Titus Prifernius Paetus (Kent 1966: no. 134), which has an identical text in Greek from Argos. There are nevertheless problems with this, as the excavations have concentrated on the Roman forum where public documents might be expected to have been in Latin. The few published examples of graffiti scratched on pottery show that Greek was also used in the first century CE, and that is, of course, the language of Paul's correspondence to the Corinthian church.

Although Pausanias records that the colony was drawn from Italian freedmen, it is also clear from the epigraphy that the urban elites of the province were drawn to Corinth to fulfil civic and indeed provincial magistracies. A good example is provided by the Euryclid family from Sparta. Members of the family include C. Julius Spartiaticus, son of Laco, who held the post of *duovir quinquennalis* possibly in 47/48, and *agonothetes* in 47 (West 1931: no. 68); the same man is also known from Greek inscriptions at Athens, Epidauros and Sparta (Gill 1993a: 263). Indeed, Pausanias (2:3:5) records that one of the sets of baths in the city was donated by a member of the family, although the baths at Corinth are now thought to be Trajanic not Hadrianic. The donor would be the Trajanic senator C. Iulius

Eurycles Herculanus L. Vibullius Pius (Spawforth 1996: 179). A further example of the links between the minor towns of the province and the colony is represented by the honorific inscription of the Corinthian L. Licinnius Anteros (Spawforth 1996: 180; this inscription has also been published by Foxhall, Gill and Forbes 1997: 273-74 no. 15). This individual was granted the right to graze sheep on the peninsula of Methana (adjoining the Saronic Gulf) in return for acting as *proxenos*, or intermediary, for the community at Corinth. The date of 1 or 2 CE can be linked to the difficulties facing the local communities during the early years of Roman rule, and thus show that elite contacts in the colony itself were of prime importance (Gossage 1954: 56). A further example of mobility is represented by the honorific inscription of Junia Theodora, a Roman citizen resident at Corinth, who was celebrated around 43 CE in a series of decrees by the Lycian league and other cities of that region in 43 CE (Pallas *et al.* 1959; Robert 1960: 324-42).

In a city where status mattered, it is perhaps not surprising to find such issues appearing within the New Testament documents. For example, Paul reminded the church that 'not many of you were wise according to worldly standards, not many were powerful, not many were of noble birth' (1 Cor. 1:26). The implication is clear: some members clearly were well-born, in other words, members of the Corinthian elite. One possible case is the Erastus who is named in Romans (16:23) as the οἰκόνομος τῆς πόλεως (Clarke 1993: 46-56; Gill 1989). There has been considerable debate about whether or not this is the same individual who, in return for being elected as *aedile* of the colony, gave a piazza adjoining the theatre. As the Epistle to the Romans does not provide the *praenomen* or *nomen*, and the inscription is fragmentary, there can be no certainty that they are the same individual. Indeed, a second-century CE inscription on a sundial from Corinth shows that it had been dedicated by Vitellius Erastus along with Vitellius Frontinus, perhaps two freedmen (Clarke 1991). At the same time, there is discussion about whether the Latin *aedile* is the equivalent of the Greek term *oikonomos*. However, given the realization that the Corinthian church is likely to have contained members of the social elite, certain objections can be eliminated.

If the Corinthian correspondence is read against such a Roman elite setting, new issues can be detected. Take, for example, the case of civil litigation (Winter 1994a: 81-121). At face value, this might be seen as an injunction for Christians not to take other Christians to court. Yet, once it is realized that the Roman legal setting needs to be considered, a different view emerges. As the case was over the 'smallest causes', such matters might be considered to be within the scope of a civil rather than a criminal case. As Winter (1994a: 107) has pointed out, this would be within the area of 'legal possession, breach of contract, damages, fraud and injury'. As such cases were between social equals, or against someone of an inferior social status, it is likely that such cases were brought by members of the local social elite. Winter (1994a: 113-15) has argued that personal enmity might lie behind such actions, perhaps within the setting of a young man keen to demonstrate his forensic skills. Clearly such actions would be divisive within the church, and this is why Paul calls for care in such areas.

The issue of sexual immorality within the church was highlighted by Paul, who observed that it was of 'a kind that does not occur even among pagans' (1 Cor. 5:1). The issue was that a man was having a sexual relationship with his stepmother (Clarke 1993: 77-85). There were indeed penalties for such a situation within Roman law—exile to an island. Jewish law also forbade such a relationship. Clarke has raised the possibility that the woman involved was childless, and that this limited her to one-tenth of her inheritance. However, if she could conceive a child—in this case through her stepson—then her financial security was assured. In any case, the fact that the Corinthians knew about the affair (1 Cor. 5:1) suggests that the husband of the woman was no longer living, since, if he had been, he himself would have had to have taken legal actions or be implicated in the crime.

Then there is the advice not to marry in the 'present necessity' (1 Cor. 7:26). Although some have taken this to be advice on not to marry and that celibacy is in fact a better way, it ignores the immediate context. The present 'necessity' (ἀνάγκη) would seem to apply to a contemporary period of unease. A particular issue facing the Mediterranean world at this point in time was famine or food shortage (Winter 1994b). It is recognized that famine had hit the Mediterranean. At Corinth itself, the different 'tribes' of the colony honoured one Tiberius Claudius Dinippus (Spawforth 1996: 177-78) with portrait statues in public spaces, as he had acted as *curator annonae*, or curator of the food supply. This in itself implies that, in c. 51 CE, Corinth was hit by a major food shortage that was relieved only by a member of the local elite helping out with a distribution. Indeed, this period coincides with the apparent development of the harbour facilities at Lechaeum, one of the ports of Corinth (Williams 1993: 46). This picture seems to fit into the wider literary and papyrological testimonia that imply fairly widespread crop failure due to droughts in the Mediterranean region. When it is realized that Corinth at this point in time may have had a population of some 20,000 people, and only had a territory of some 207 km², then it seems likely that the poorer members of society would be hardest hit (Gill 1993b: 333-34). Indeed, there is evidence that food shortages caused urban riots, and it may be this type of civic dislocation that lies behind this part of the epistle. Paul's advice here is clear. Marriage might mean procreation of children, who would be born into a situation where famine was a major and likely risk.

Behind the epistle may lie issues relating to patron–client relationships within the colony. Clearly in a large urban community like Corinth, the poor would have to rely on the generosity of the urban elite either through established patron–client relationships, through public patronage, or through elite members within the church. This probably explains the situation at Corinth where the 'household of Stephanas' was commended by Paul for 'devoting themselves to the service of the saints' (1 Cor. 16:15). Presumably, the resources of the *oikos* or *domus* of this member of the Corinthian elite were being released to the benefit of the new Christian community.

Elite presence in the Church may also be reflected in the very buildings which could be used for times of worship, and, in particular, the commemoration of the Lord's supper (Blue 1994). The factions that Paul notes in the church at Corinth, especially in this celebration, may reflect the social divisions of the church where some ate and drank while other went hungry and thirsty (1 Cor. 11:21). The poorest group are even identified as the 'Have-nots'.

If Corinth was a strongly Roman city, then the issue over head coverings in 1 Corinthians (11:2-16) needs to be reassessed against the Roman evidence (Gill 1990). The notion of men covering their heads is linked to the way that a Roman priest would cover his head with his toga when making a sacrifice, so as to cut out all distractions. One of the most famous examples of this pose is the portrait statue of Augustus, a type found at Corinth. As such priesthoods were often filled by members of the social elite, Paul seems to be challenging the view that a Christian minister was the equivalent of a sacrificial priest, and that he automatically had to be a member of the elite. The covering of the head for women is more problematic, although there are indications that social norms may have influenced Paul's instructions.

The issues that the church faced at Corinth may be similar to those found in the Roman colony of Philippi in the province of Macedonia (Winter 1994a: 81-104). It is no doubt significant that Paul frames the inheritance of Christians in terms of citizenship (πολίτευμα) (Phil. 3:20). As members of a Roman colony and holding Roman citizenship, the members of church would understand the privileges of heavenly citizenship.

CHRISTIANITY AND COMMUNICATIONS

The spread of Christianity as reflected in the New Testament documents reflects the way that the communication routes of the Roman Empire were exploited to the full. Take, for example, Paul's travels through Cyprus (Gill 1995b). Acts (13:6) records that Paul and Barnabas passed through 'the whole of the island', before reaching Paphos where they encountered the provincial governor, Sergius Paulus. An inscribed Roman milestone on the road along the south coast of Cyprus towards Citium shows that the road had been constructed in the Augustan period sometime after 12 BCE. As other evidence suggests that the road system on Cyprus was not developed until the Flavian period, when one inscription records the construction of 'new roads' throughout the province, it seems likely that the south coast was the most likely route for Paul. This would have allowed him to have passed through some of the key cities of the province, each roughly 20 Roman miles apart, the distance that could be travelled in a day.

Likewise, Paul's journey up into central Anatolia would have taken advantage of the newly-constructed road system (French 1980; 1994). Milestones show that the *via Sebaste* was constructed in 6 BCE. Paul and Barnabas are likely to have landed at Attalia, and then used the road constructed under Tiberius—and repaired under Claudius—as far as Perge. From there they joined the *via Sebaste* which passed through *Colonia Comana* and thence to Pisidian Antioch. They would have been able to follow the road to Iconium and Lystra, although the final part of their journey to Derbe may have been on unpaved tracks. In Macedonia, Paul was able to use the *via Egnatia*, constructed in the 140s BCE, which joined the Adriatic (and thus Rome) with Macedonia and the eastern provinces (Gill 1994c: 409-10). Two key churches on this route were established at Philippi and Thessalonica.

Sea journeys also play a large part in Acts (Rapske 1994a). The major church at Corinth was a strategic location, as it lay at the hub of two systems: eastwards via its port of Cenchreae (cf. Rom. 16:1) and the Saronic Gulf to the eastern provinces such as Syria and Egypt, and westwards via Lechaeum and the Corinthian Gulf to Italy. Paul in his trip to Rome made use of one of the grain ships (Acts 27:6) that formed an essential link between Egypt and the ever-hungry city of Rome.

THE RELIGIOUS LANDSCAPE OF THE ROMAN EMPIRE

It is hard to make generalizations about the religious background to the empire. The New Testament documents themselves are remarkably quiet about the religious landscape of the provinces. Acts is perhaps the most explicit. The major civic cult of Artemis at Ephesus sparked the major riot (Acts 19:23-41). Although at first sight Artemis, the equivalent of the Roman Diana, might seem to be a standard classical deity, her iconography reflects her local Anatolian nature. For example instead of images of a huntress, the cult statue, best known from a copy recovered from the *bouleuterion* at Ephesus, shows the goddess with multiple appendages over her body which can either be considered as breasts or possibly bulls' testicles draped around her. Acts (20:35) also records that the cult image was thought to have fallen from the sky; such sacred rocks or *baetyls* are common throughout the eastern empire. Famous examples include the cult of Aphrodite at Paphos on the island of Cyprus, and Artemis at Perge in Pamphylia. An inscription found at Agios Tychon near Amathus records a cult of 'Cyprian Aphrodite' and the sanctuary of 'the Seven within the Stelai', which was patronized by the Roman governor of Cyprus, L. Bruttius Maximus (79/80). This was presumably a *baetyl* cult. The worship of sacred rocks may in fact reflect an interest in aniconic worship, which was derived from the Semitic heartlands. One famous example was the cult of Elagabal at Emesa in Syria; this was the home of the third century CE Roman emperor Elagabalus who transported the sacred rock to Rome (Millar 1993: 300-309).

Other local cults seem to have continued throughout the empire. This is perhaps reflected in Paul and Barnabas's arrival in Lycaonia in central Anatolia. At Lystra, the pair were perceived as gods in human form, and they were identified as Zeus (Barnabas) and Hermes (Paul) (Acts 14:11-13). This episode also recalls the local myth that deities had visited the sea and had been refused hospitality by everyone except one elderly couple, Philemon and Bacis (see Ovid, *Met.* 8:670-724). Both deities could be linked to local cults in this region.

One important Anatolian cult, although not mentioned in the biblical documents, was that of Mên. One of the main cult centres was at Pisidian Antioch, a city visited by Paul. The sanctuary itself lay a little distance from the city in a large classical style temple. In many of the dedications, the deity appears to be linked with the moon—a crescent moon is often used to represent the god—and the Latin version of the cult seems to have been that of Luna, even though Mên was a male god. Members of the local elite seem to have fulfilled priesthoods at the sanctuary and an agonistic festival was founded to honour the deity.

The imperial cult was a major feature of provincial and urban life, yet there is little comment from the biblical documents. In Anatolia, the imperial cult had an extremely high profile, in part building on the earlier divine aspect of Hellenistic rulers (Price 1984). In Galatia, the provincial imperial cult seems to have been established as early as 25 BCE. Mitchell (1993: 100-17) has noted how the construction of elaborate temples changed the urban landscape of these cities. For example, the so-called State Agora at Ephesus contained a series of buildings linked to the imperial cult that included a double temple of Roma and Julius Caesar and temple of Augustus (Price 1984: 139 fig. 3). At Pisidian Antioch, there was an important temple built in honour of Augustus, and indeed a copy of the *Res Gestae* has been found there (Mitchell 1993: 104).

At Athens, a round temple in honour of Augustus and Roma would have dominated the skyline next to the Parthenon on the acropolis. At the same time, the main public space, the agora, was filled with a temple of Ares which may have housed the cult of Augustus's deceased heir, Gaius. At Corinth, there is evidence that there was a provincial imperial cult established c. 54 CE that included an annual festival along with a wild beast show (Spawforth 1994). The first high priest to hold this office was C. Julius Spartiaticus, a member of the influential Spartan family of the Euryclids.

The imperial cult itself would have made an impact on members of the local elite, and for Christians among this group, there would have been certain questions of loyalty raised (Winter 1994a: 123-43). The description of the imperial cult at Narbo in Gaul suggests that three *equites* and three freedmen were each responsible for the sacrifices as well as the provision of wine and incense for the population of the colony. This group of six would change each year, so that each family was not over-burdened. The strain this caused is probably reflected by the situation in Britain where the local members of the elite were expected to service the cult of the divine Claudius at the colony of Camulodunum (Colchester), and were required to take out substantial loans as a result; this formed one of the reasons behind Boudicca's revolt. Presumably in colonies like Pisidian Antioch or Corinth, the turn would come round relatively quickly, and Christians would be faced with the dilemma whether or not to take part. This dilemma may have been resolved by the decision of Gallio which extended to Christians the privileges of a *religio licita* and thus exemption from aspects of the imperial cult.

The imperial cult may lie behind Paul's discussion of 'so-called' gods at Corinth distinct from the 'many gods and many lords' (1 Cor. 8:4-6). As there was an obligation to engage in the imperial cult, it may be argued that the reason why Christians in Galatia were eager to seek circumcision and therefore be identified as Jews would be for the reason that they would obtain the legal privilege of the Jews who were excluded from such cultic activities (Gal. 6:11-18) (Winter 1994a: 123-43).

BIBLIOGRAPHY

Barnes, T.D.
1969 'An Apostle on Trial', *JTS* 22: 407-19.
Bauckham, R. (ed.)
1995 *The Book of Acts in its First Century Setting. IV. The Book of Acts in its Palestinian Setting.* Grand Rapids: Eerdmans.
Blue, B.
1994 'Acts and the House Church', in Gill and Gempf 1994: 119-222.
Bowersock, G.W.
1983 *Roman Arabia.* Cambridge, MA: Harvard University Press.
Clarke, A.D.
1991 'Another Corinthian Erastus Inscription', *TynBul* 42: 146-51.
1993 *Secular and Christian Leadership in Corinth: A Socio-Historical and Exegetical Study of 1 Corinthians 1–6.* AGAJU, 18. Leiden: Brill.
Engels, D.
1990 *Roman Corinth: An Alternative Model for the Classical City.* Chicago: University of Chicago Press.
Finley, M.I. (ed.)
1968 *Slavery in Classical Antiquity: Views and Controversies.* Cambridge: Heffer.
1980 *Ancient Slavery and Modern Ideology.* London: Chatto & Windus.

Foxhall, L., D. Gill and H. Forbes

1997   'The Inscriptions of Methana', in C. Mee and H. Forbes (eds.), *A Rough and Rocky Place: The Landscape and Settlement History of the Methana Peninsula, Greece* (Liverpool: Liverpool University Press: 268-77.

French, D.

1980   'The Roman Road-System of Asia Minor', *ANRW* II.7.2: 698-729.

1994   'Acts and the Roman Roads of Asia Minor', in Gill and Gempf 1994: 49-58.

Gill, D.W.J.

1989   'Erastus the Aedile', *TynBul* 40: 293-301.

1990   'The Importance of Roman Portraiture for Head Coverings in 1 Corinthians 11:2-16', *TynBul* 41: 245-60.

1993a   'Corinth: A Roman Colony of Achaea', *BZ* 37: 259-64.

1993b   'In Search of the Social Elite in the Corinthian Church', *TynBul* 44.2: 323-37.

1994a   'Acts and Roman Religion: A. Religion in a Local Setting', in Gill and Gempf 1994: 79-92.

1994b   'Acts the Urban Elites', in Gill and Gempf 1994: 105-18.

1994c   'Macedonia', in Gill and Gempf 1994: 397-417.

1994d   'Achaia', in Gill and Gempf 1994: 433-53.

1995a   'Acts and Roman Policy in Judaea', in Bauckham 1995: 15-26.

1995b   'Paul's Travels through Cyprus (Acts 13:4-12)', *TynBul* 46.2: 219-28.

Gill, D.W.J., and C. Gempf (eds.)

1994   *The Book of Acts in its First Century Setting. II. The Book of Acts in its Graeco-Roman Setting.* Grand Rapids: Eerdmans.

Goodman, M.

1987   *The Ruling Class of Judaea: The Origins of the Jewish Revolt against Rome AD 66–70.* Cambridge: Cambridge University Press.

Gossage, A.G.

1954   'The Date of *IG* V (2) 516 (*SIG*[3] 800)', *Annual of the British School at Athens* 49: 51-56.

Horsley, G.H.R.

1994   'The Politarchs', in Gill and Gempf 1994: 419-31.

Kearsley, R.A.

1994   'The Asiarchs', in Gill and Gempf 1994: 363-76.

Kent, J.H.

1966   *The Inscriptions, 1926-1950. Corinth*, 8.3. Princeton: American School of Classical Studies at Athens.

Millar, F.

1981   *The Roman Empire and its Neighbours.* London: Duckworth, 2nd edn.

1992   *The Emperor in the Roman World (31 BC–AD 337).* London: Duckworth, 2nd edn.

1993   *The Roman Near East 31 BC–AD 337.* Cambridge, MA: Harvard University Press.

Mitchell, S.
1993   *Anatolia: Land, Men and Gods in Asia Minor.* 2 vols. Oxford: Clarendon Press.

Nobbs, A.
1994   'Cyprus', in Gill and Gempf 1994: 279-89.

Pallas, D.I., S. Charitonidis and J. Venencie
1959   'Inscriptions lyciennes trouvées a Solômos près de Corinth', *Bulletin de Correspondence hellenique* 83: 496-508.

Price, S.R.F.
1984   *Rituals and Power: The Imperial Cult and Asia Minor.* Cambridge: Cambridge University Press.

Rapske, B.
1994a   'Acts, Travel and Shipwreck', in Gill and Gempf 1994: 1-47.
1994b   *The Book of Acts in its First Century Setting. III. The Book of Acts and Paul in Roman Custody.* Grand Rapids: Eerdmans.

Robert, L.
1960   'Décret de la confédération lycienne a Corinth', *Revue des Études Anciennes* 62: 324-42.

Schürer, E.
1973   *The History of the Jewish People in the Age of Jesus Christ (175 BC–AD 135).* Vol. 1. Rev. and ed. G. Vermes and F. Millar. Edinburgh: T. & T. Clark.

Smith, R.R.R.
1993   *The Monument of C. Julius Zoilos.* Mainz am Rhein: P. von Zabern.

Spawforth, A.J.S.
1994   'Corinth, Argos, and the Imperial Cult: A Reconsideration of Pseudo-Julian Letters 198 Bidez', *Hesperia* 63.2: 211-32.
1996   'Roman Corinth: The Formation of a Colonial Elite', in A.D. Rizakis (ed.), *Roman Onomastics in the Greek East: Social and Political Aspects.* Meletemata, 21. Athens: Research Centre for Greek and Roman Antiquity: 167-82.

Trebilco, P.
1991   *Jewish Communities in Asia Minor.* SNTSMS, 69. Cambridge: Cambridge University Press.
1994   'Asia', in Gill and Gempf 1994: 291-362.

West, A.B.
1931   *Latin Inscriptions, 1896–1926. Corinth,* 8.2. Cambridge, MA: American School of Classical Studies at Athens.

Williams, C.K., II
1993   'Roman Corinth as a Commercial Centre', in T.E. Gregory (ed.), *The Corinthia in the Roman Period Including the Papers Given at a Symposium Held at The Ohio State University on 7-9 March, 1991. Journal of Roman Archaeology* Sup, 8. Ann Arbor, MI.

Winter, B.W.
1994a   *Seek the Welfare of the City: Christians as Benefactors and Citizens.* Grand Rapids: Eerdmans.

1994b 'Acts and Food Shortages', in Gill and Gempf 1994: 59-78.
1994c 'Acts and Roman Religion: B. The Imperial Cult', in Gill and Gempf
       1994: 93-103.

EXEGESIS IN THE SECOND CENTURY

THOMAS H. OLBRICHT

It is common for New Testament exegetes to search backgrounds in the Jewish and Greco-Roman worlds in order to better understand New Testament expressions and concepts. Less priority, however, is assigned to scrutinizing succeeding documents, such as those of the second century. In many cases, these documents are instructive in augmenting comprehension. With respect to worship, for example, many valuable insights may be obtained. Ignatius (35–107) wrote of Christians 'no longer observing the Sabbath but living according to the Lord's day' (Ignatius, *Mag.* 9). Pliny (62–113) declared that Christians '...were in the habit of meeting on a certain fixed day before it was light, when they sang in alternate verses a hymn to Christ, as to a god...then reassemble to partake of food' (Pliny, *Ep.* 10:96). Justin Martyr (100–160) described the proceedings at some length:

> The memoirs of the apostles or the writings of the prophets are read, as long as time permits. Then when the reader ceases, the president in a discourse admonishes and urges the imitation of these good things. Next we rise together and send up prayers. And, as I said before, when we cease from our prayer, bread is presented and wine and water. The president in the same manner sends up prayers and thanksgivings according to his ability, and the people sing out their assent saying the 'Amen'. A distribution and participation of the elements for which thanks have been given is made to each person, and to those who are not present it is sent by the deacons. Those who have means and are willing, each according to his own choice, gives what he wills, and what is collected is deposited with the president (Justin Martyr, *Apol.* 1:67).

On this and various other subjects, valuable insights as to New Testament documents may be obtained.

We now take up second-century authors and the aspects of their writings from which help may be obtained. The extant writings from the second century by no means cover all the topics of interest to New Testament exegetes. The documents early in the century relate Christianity to the Greek and Roman worlds. Somewhat later writers evince a breaking off of Christianity from Judaism. Soon persecution of Christians occurred erratically in the empire and some of the writing pertains to martyrdom. After the middle of the century, various authors were consumed with aberrant perspectives on Christianity, both by way of affirmation and refutation. The literary styles and genres differ in these authors, providing interesting comparisons and contrast with New Testament documents. Except for persons with roots in Alexandria, most of these writers eschewed metaphorical and allegorical interpretations.

The writers of the second century of the Christian Era continued, for the most part, the varieties of manner in which the Old Testament Scriptures were employed in the New Testament. But, in addition, they began to incorporate references to the various New Testament documents, though not as often as we in the twentieth century might suppose. The privileged documents cited most frequently by these second-century authors were the Old Testament, the epistles, especially of Paul and James, and the Gospel of Matthew.

THE EPISTLE OF BARNABAS

The *Epistle of Barnabas* was written at the end of the New Testament period. Some of the early churchmen held the letter to be inspired, and were disposed toward including it in the canon of the New Testament. The *Epistle of Barnabas* is found in Codex Sinaiticus after the Old and New Testament texts, along with the *Shepherd of Hermas*. Clement of Alexandria cited the *Epistle of Barnabas* as though it were Scripture, and both Jerome and Clement declared it to be authored by the traveling companion of Paul, who, in Acts, is designated an apostle (Acts 14:14). Authorship by Barnabas of the letter, however, seems doubtful. It seems more likely that the name Barnabas was attached to the document in order to give it apostolic status. The *Epistle of Barnabas* was likely written 96–100 CE, possibly in Alexandria of Egypt.[1]

The main contribution of the *Epistle of Barnabas* to the New Testament exegete is the manner in which it draws upon the Old Testament, and how its rhetoric and hermeneutics compare and contrast with the Letter to the Hebrews, and to a lesser extent with the writings of Paul. The document is more a discourse than a letter, much like Hebrews. The author recommends hope, righteousness according to judgment, and the love of joy in an evil time. He declares that the

---

[1]   L.W. Barnard, 'The Problem of the Epistle of Barnabas', *Church Quarterly Review* 159 (1958), pp. 211-30.

Old Testament prophets (by which he means from Moses on) heralded these latter times and disclosed the means of combating the malfeasance. He ends with the two-way option of embracing light and darkness or life and death. Unlike Hebrews, which sustains a closely reasoned theological argument, the *Epistle of Barnabas* is a discursive marshaling of prophetic utterances.

The *Epistle of Barnabas* has no specific reference to contemporary Judaism. The writer believes that Israel failed in its response to God, but that, more importantly, the real message of the Old Testament prophets anticipates the followers of Jesus. Much like the epistles of the New Testament, the author rarely references or quotes words and deeds of Jesus. By his time, Christians, as evidenced in the writing of the Gospels, relished the words and works of Jesus, but still cited the Old Testament as the authentic word from God. With some frequency, the *Epistle of Barnabas* explicates extended allegorical meaning in texts, for example, in regard to the offering of a heifer in Numbers 18 (*Barn.* 8:1). The sacrifice clearly points ahead to Christ's sacrificial death. While Barnabas clearly employs allegorical interpretation, the application is more practical/theological than philosophical in a Philonic sense.

THE DIDACHE

The full title of the document now designated *The Didache* was *Teaching of the Twelve Apostles*. A subheading identified it as 'The teaching of the Lord through the twelve apostles to the nations'. *The Didache* was highly regarded in the fourth-century Church, and was believed in some quarters to have been composed by or on behalf of the original twelve disciples of Jesus, a conclusion which scholars do not now embrace. It is thought to have been written between 80 and 120 CE, probably in Antioch of Syria, most likely by a Jewish Christian. The work bears comparison with the Pastoral Epistles, and indicates how some New Testament injunctions were later fleshed out.

In this short work, the author contrasts the way of life, which entails love and keeping God's commandments, with the way of death, which is filled with lust and other undesirable traits denounced in Scripture. Thereupon follow instructions with regard to foods, baptism, fasting, prayer, sound teaching, and the roles of apostles and prophets, wandering Christians, bishops and deacons, monetary assistance, assembly, correction and warnings.

These instructions are grounded first of all in the Old Testament, especially in regard to violations that lead to death. The instructions for the believing community incorporate many echoes from the Gospels and some from the epistles, though some of these may be from common sources rather than directly from the New Testament writings. In terms of clear dependence, more allusions may be found to the Gospel of Matthew than to the other three Gospels. References tend to be short phrases and allusions, rather than direct quotations. Their applications tend to be more literal, rather than metaphorical or allegorical. In this manner, the bringing in of biblical materials reflects a different hermeneutic than the *Epistle of Barnabas*. Almost no effort is directed toward showing how the Old Testament was fulfilled in Christ.

THE LETTER OF PLINY THE YOUNGER TO TRAJAN

The letter of Pliny the Younger (c. 62–113) to the emperor Trajan (53–117; emperor 98–117) and Trajan's response comprise an unprecedented imperial insight into second-century Christianity. Pliny, a favorite of Roman emperors, served as governor of Pontus/Bithynia from 111–113 CE. The important letter regarding Christianity is preserved in the tenth book, along with Trajan's reply (10:96, 97). Trajan's father fought in the 70 CE war against the Jews, and was later appointed governor of Syria and then Asia by Vespasian. Trajan was therefore familiar with Jewish concerns and conditions in the near east.

These letters show that no official Roman policy had been enacted with regard to Christians or to their persecution. Pliny was concerned because of the increase of the Christians and the abandonment of the native religions. He therefore demanded that alleged Christians worship the image of the emperor and the statues of the gods. He killed those who refused. Trajan agreed with this policy, but declared that Christians were not to be sought out, nor was Pliny to pursue charges against persons made anonymously. Of interest to New Testament interpretation is that the Christians met before dawn, sang a hymn to Christ as God, and bound themselves to each other by an oath. They reassembled then toward nightfall to eat together.

IGNATIUS (C. 35–107 CE)

Ignatius was reputed to be the second bishop of Antioch. He was singled out for martyrdom and traveled from Antioch to Rome accompanied by ten soldiers. Little is known about his life otherwise. On the journey across Asia Minor, Ignatius wrote seven letters, probably from 105–110 CE. These letters reflect what he considered the most pressing matters for the believers as he anticipated death. He made stops in Smyrna, where he was honored by Polycarp, and Troas. The letters from Smyrna were to Tralles, Magnesia, Ephesus and Rome, and the letters from Troas were to Philadelphia, Smyrna and Polycarp.

These letters are important to the exegete with respect to comparison and contrasts with the canonical epistles. Their purview is somewhat more narrowly conceived. They are, therefore, worth consulting regarding epistolary style and rhetorical features. The tendencies are less metaphorical and allegorical, than, for example, the works of Clement of Alexandria. They are also helpful simply because of the number of topics they cover. Evidence of an early mono-episcopacy may be found in the letters, though the full meaning and implications are, to a degree, problematic. Another topic worthy of pursuit is the creedal material embedded in the letters. This may be compared and contrasted with creedal statements in the New Testament, and with other early creeds, such as the Apostolic Creed in its various versions. Perspectives on servanthood and martyrdom are also worthy of perusal. It should also be noted that Ignatius eschews heresy, but is not too specific as to what sorts of heresy he has in mind. The most obvious seems to be some version of docetism. He also highlights Christian Old Testament foundations over the Jewish, but this is not a major concern. Other topics less developed include perspectives on the baptism of Jesus, the ramifications of the cross, the Lord's Supper, unity, and Onesimus.

THE EPISTLE OF POLYCARP TO THE PHILLIPPIANS

Polycarp was a respected leader (bishop or elder) of the church in Smyrna. He was martyred in Smyrna, probably on February 23, 155 CE. He wrote an epistle to the church in Philippi in conjunction with efforts of Irenaeus and at the church's request. The letter that has survived may, in fact, be the conflation of two of his letters. *Philippians* is of interest because of the manner in which Polycarp cites New Testament epistles. In contrast with *Barnabas*, he refers little to the Old Testament. He refers little to the Gospels, but on occasion does refer to Matthew. His employment of statements from the epistles is mostly straightforward with little metaphorical implication. He cites epistles, not so much by way of shoring up his points, but in a manner of amplification.

Philippians first of all sets out a profile of righteousness. Polycarp mostly provides exterior specifics rather than theological or psychological ramifications, in contrast with Paul's theological reflection upon God, the cross and the parousia. He also rejects a docetic Christology, perhaps with Marcion in mind, but this is not certain. Comparisons and contrasts with the Johannine epistles are of potential exegetical value. In addition, he emphasizes the unity of the Church and the need to respect the leaders.

THE MARTYRDOM OF POLYCARP

The *Martyrdom of Polycarp* was apparently written by an eye-witness, not long after it occurred on February 23, 155 CE. The author clearly parallels the death of Polycarp with that of Jesus. The *Martyrdom of Polycarp* assumes an epistolary form but, aside from the introduction and conclusion, may best be described as a discourse on martyrdom. Little reference is made to Scripture, but a knowledge of the death of Christ in a Gospel or the Gospels is presupposed.

The *Martyrdom of Polycarp* is the first in a catalog of Christian martyrdoms, unless one includes Paul's reflections on death for Christ's sake or certain comments in Revelation. In order to explicate New Testament depictions, a foray into the martyrdom literature should be of value. In the *Martyrdom of Polycarp*, Christians are not encouraged to seek out martyrdom, but neither to resist it if no other avenue is available. The grounds for standing firm according to conviction are expressed in this document. Especially of concern are the previous actions of Christ and the conviction that God will give life anew to those who have witnessed unto death.

1 CLEMENT

1 Clement is normally accepted as an authentic letter from Clement of Rome to the church in Corinth sometime between 81–96 CE. If so, it is among the earliest of the non-canonical Christian materials. The situation assumes rifts in the church at Corinth. It is interesting, however, that the causes are not addressed directly, as, for example, in Paul's 1 Corinthians. The form is epistolary, but incorporates elements of Greek diatribe and synagogue homiletic style. A number of references are made to the Old Testament with occasional quotations, especially of Genesis. The biblical examples are incorporated so as to illustrate the results of jealousy and division. The references to the Gospels are largely from Matthew. Some of the letters of Paul, as well as James, were apparently familiar to Clement. Little allegorical or metaphorical use is found. *1 Clement* was often alluded to by Clement of Alexandria (150–215 CE), and he adduces evidence that various early churchmen considered it inspired and belonging in the canon.

1 Clement focuses on the fractures that appeared in the Corinthian community. The desired church situation exhibits order or peace. The case for peace is expounded not so much from the ramifications of the cross as in 1 Corinthians, but through the advancement of Old Testament examples which display the consequences of jealousy and strife, though the author does emphasize the humility of Christ. Repentance and obedience are the solution. Order, Clement argues, is endemic in nature, almost as in Stoic thought, and all aspects of creation demonstrate obedience. Facets of revived nature likewise establish sufficient grounds for affirming the resurrection of Christ, as does also the legend of the Phoenix, metaphorically.

2 CLEMENT

On the grounds of internal style and the absence of external evidence, *2 Clement* has been assigned to a later unknown author. Clement of Alexandria did not seem to know of *2 Clement*, and the early Church historian Eusebius questioned its authenticity. The style is that of a tractate or homily rather than an epistle. Some have supposed that the letter was in fact to the Corinthian church at a later date, and, since it was stored with *1 Clement*, was therefore presumed to be by the same author. The probable date is between 120 and 140 CE. Many of the references are to Isaiah. The allusions to the New Testament are more than in *1 Clement*. The author obviously knows the epistles as well as the Synoptic Gospels, mostly Matthew and Luke.

The author affirms the divine relationship of Christ and the salvation that he alone provides. Believers therefore need to respond in service and obedience. The Christian life is one of righteousness and holiness, and the wayward are exhorted to heed the call for repentance. The author, for the most part, addresses general problems, rather than specified situations explicitly located in the Corinthian church.

SHEPHERD OF HERMAS

The *Shepherd of Hermas* is of particular value for the study of the apocalyptic genre of biblical materials, but also legal and parabolic writings. It reflects both similarities and differences. The setting for the document is ostensibly Rome during a time of persecution. The date is less certain and if it is in two parts, the first (1–24) is c. 90–110, and the second (25–114) is 100–150. The works falls into three clear parts: (1) Visions (1–25), (2) Commandments (26–49), and (3) Parables (50–113). The work was highly respected, and sometimes regarded as canonical. Jerome and Origen argued that the author was the Hermas of Rom. 16:14. In the second vision (8:3) Clement is mentioned, and so some argue that he is the author of *1 Clement*. Since the author is reporting original visions, he makes no appeal to the Scriptures to authenticate his statements. Few quotations from the Old or New Testaments may be found, but allusions to both are present, especially to the Gospels and James. The allusions are not as clear nor as frequent, however, as in the canonical Revelation. Scriptures are employed in much the same manner as in Revelation, that is, to amplify specific statements with canonical language. The intentional metaphorical use of Scripture is minimal. The visions and parables, however, depend on highly metaphorical or symbolic entities with regard to the Church and heavenly powers. The visions in their narrativity look forward more to John Bunyan's *Pilgrim's Progress* than to prior biblical materials. Key topics in the *Shepherd of Hermas* have to do with repentance, purity, the Church and loyalty to it, the characteristics of the Spirit, and Christology. The author is especially interested in whether forgiveness is possible after having been baptized. He argues that indeed it is, however, only once.

LETTER TO DIOGNETUS

The author of *Diognetus* is unknown, but is most likely a non-Jewish Christian who wrote toward the end of the second century CE. Scholars have suggested various dates between 117 and 310 CE. The consensus view is that the document consists of two separately circulated parts later joined. The first (chs. 1–10) is in the form of a letter. The second (chs. 11–12) is a treatise or homily. Though the document is not a narrative history of Christianity as is Acts, a comparison of the apologetic outlook of each is rewarding.

The author speaks of Christianity as a new way of worship, neither pagan nor Jewish. Christianity is a third way. Pagans, he charges, worship objects made from stone, wood and metal, arguments similar to those of Isaiah 44. It is not certain, however, that he drew on Isaiah. The Jews, in contrast with the pagans, have rules in respect to the Sabbath and other celebrations that impede human welfare and become idolatrous. Christians live as all others in outward appearance, but are pilgrims in the world, a third race. They do not expose their children, that is, abandon them to certain death, and they love all persons. Christians constitute the soul of the people of the world, just as the individual soul sustains the body. Christians are imprisoned in the world, and thereby support the world. The last section of the epistle extols the committed believer, who is consigned to enjoy the fruits that God has provided. Allusions to Scripture mostly borrow biblical language and ideas.

JUSTIN MARTYR (100–165)

Justin Martyr was born of non-Christian parents in Flavia Neapolis, the ancient Shechem in Samaria. After embracing several philosophies, he became a Christian about 130. He taught at Ephesus, where he engaged in discussion Trypho the Jew in an effort to convince him that Jesus was the predicted Messiah, and that Christianity was the new covenant. Later he moved to Rome where he opened a Christian school. His extant works judged authentic are the *First Apology,* the *Second Apology*, and the *Dialogue with Trypho.* The *First Apology* was written about 150 CE and addressed to the emperors Antoninus Pius and Marcus Aurelius. In it, Justin defended Christians against the charge of atheism and hostility to the Roman state. His *Second Apology* was addressed to the Roman senate about 161 CE, in which he argued that Christians were being unjustly punished by Rome. Justin was denounced by the Cynic philosopher Crescens, with others, as a committed Christian in 165. Because they refused to sacrifice to the Roman gods, many believers were scourged and beheaded, as was Justin that same year.

Justin declared that Christianity can be defended not only on the grounds of revelation, especially fulfilled prophecy, but also through reason. His chief contribution lay in setting forth history as the arena in which God brought salvation to fruition through the converging of Old Testament revelation and Hellenistic philosophy or reason so as to form Christianity. The writings of Justin are of interest to the New Testament scholar because in them is an ostensible effort to adapt to the Hellenistic world, an adaptation which goes beyond that of any New Testament writer. Also of interest in Justin are his depictions of early Christian baptism, worship and the celebration of the Lord's supper.

In order to assimilate Greek reason to Christianity, Justin identified the biblical Word (logos) with Platonic or Stoic concepts of logos. When addressing philosophers, logos, for Justin, had a philosophical dimension. But in arguing with Trypho, Justin pinpointed the Hebrew Word (logos) by which God creates and controls. Justin did not, as Philo, explain biblical conceptions by allegorizing them into Platonic forms. Unlike Plato, he believed that sensation continues after death in the world to come. He tended to focus on the predictive aspects of biblical interpretation. He was apparently won to Christianity, in part, because of the allure of ancient documents and the prophetic disclosing of future events. He assigned a significance to prophecy— fulfillment that exceeded that of the biblical documents. Justin interpreted most Old Testament actions and statements as pointing ahead to the coming of Christianity. The first advent of Christ disclosed in some measure the nature and purpose of the second. In the first advent, the institutions and actions were this-worldly and therefore contingent. The New Covenant, in contrast, is eternal. The first advent likewise produced what will ultimately pass away. But what Christ brings at the second advent will be permanent and eternal. The Old Testament therefore presents symbols and parables that point beyond themselves and are fully and inextricably realized in the New Testament. So Justin was given to what Christian thinkers have labeled typology, not allegory. Justin in this manner reflected the typological methods so obvious in Hebrews.

MARCION

Marcion is important for his doctrine of God, the manner in which he interpreted Paul and his perspectives on the canon, which in turn may have initiated canonical discussions among other churchmen. Marcion was born in Sinope in Pontus early in the second century and died about 160 CE, apparently in Rome. His father was the bishop and, according to later statements, excommunicated his son on the grounds of immorality. The son himself had status in the church in Sinope and shared the wealth of the family. He was an owner of ships. About 140 CE, Marcion attached himself to the church in Rome where he influenced various believers and made a large gift to the church. In

144 CE, he was excommunicated by the Roman church and thereafter he expended much energy in establishing a network of counter churches throughout the empire. Many of these churches later assimilated into Manichaeism.

Marcion was greatly influenced by a perspective on God which emphasized his love rather than law, and whose being transcended the confines of material existence. In this belief, he shared with the Platonists and Gnostics a claim as to the superiority of the suprasensible world, but Marcion's outlook was at the same time tinctured by the Hebraic vision of a God who is a loving person. In order to explain the God of the Old Testament who is ostensibly a God of law, he differentiated the God of the Old Testament from the God of Jesus Christ. In this manner, he cut adrift the New Testament from the Old. According to Marcion, the purpose of Jesus was to overthrow the God of the Old Testament. The earliest Christian leader who best understood the contrast of law and love or grace was the apostle Paul. Because of Marcion, Paul's theology drew especial attention in the churches where Marcion's views were known. Without that influence, the churches dwelt on the Old Testament, the Gospel of Matthew and James.

In order to develop his perspective, Marcion found it important to identify the writings that he believed supported his interests. He therefore first of all rejected that the Old Testament could be a word from the God of Jesus Christ. The central documents were the letters of Paul. In his list of acceptable New Testament books, Marcion included ten letters of Paul (the Pastorals were excepted) and an edited version of the Gospel of Luke. It is not clear whether Marcion did not know about the Pastorals, or whether he rejected them. Some have argued that Luke was the Gospel preferred by Marcion because of the traditional relationship of Paul and Luke, but, since Marcion edited the text of Luke by leaving out sections, the reason may be that he found the Gospel the one most useful for his purposes. Clearly an insight into the views of Marcion enhances an understanding of the manner in which the New Testament became Scripture alongside the Old Testament.

ARISTIDES

Aristides was among the early Christian apologists. Little is known about his life. He is important for his early efforts to bolster the superiority of the Christian faith after the manner of the Greek philosophers. According to Eusebius, Aristides delivered his apology to the emperor Hadrian in 124 CE, but J. Rendel Harris argued that it was addressed to Antoninus Pius, who died in 161 CE. Aristides used to good advantage a detailed insight into various concepts of deity in Greek writings having to do with the Middle East and Egypt, as well as writings detailing the exploits of the Hellenistic gods. He therefore detailed the defects of the gods of the major civilizations known to the Greeks up to that time. He criticized the plurality of the gods and the immoral and unethical actions characteristic of them. He gave the Jewish view of deity a stronger recommendation, but presented the Christian view as superior in that, because of Christ, God is more clearly revealed and Christians live a more admirable moral and ethical life. Though he presented short narrative accounts of God both in the Old and New Testaments, he did not quote from the Scriptures. His method of amplification was to identify certain specifics, especially with regard to the Christians' love for God and their life characteristics.

ATHENAGORUS

Another early apologist was Athenagorus, whose dates are also unknown, but who addressed an apology to Marcus Aurelius and his son Commodus about 177 CE, *A Plea for Christianity*. He apparently spent most of his career in Athens. In addition, he wrote a treatise, *Resurrection of the Dead*, which is disputed, but usually held to be authentic. Athenagorus is of interest in observing the manner in which initial efforts by Paul to relate the biblical themes of God, nature, Christ and the resurrection to the Hellenistic world were further developed in the second century.

In his two treatises, Athenagorus was chiefly interested in establishing the reasonableness of Christianity for the Athenian thinker. In *A Plea for Christianity* he sets forth three charges made by opponents against the Christians: atheism, Thyestean feasts, that is, the claim that the Lord's Supper involved eating flesh, and Oedipodean intercourse, that is, incest. Athenagorus denied the charges in each case. In regard to atheism, according to Athenagorus, many Greeks held that matter was eternal and that the gods themselves had emerged from the cosmos. Christians, he declared, distinguish God from matter and declare God the creator of all that exists. They therefore hold that God created all things by the logos and sustains the universe by his Spirit. This means therefore that the created realm is orderly and may be apprehended by reason. His view of reality and creation therefore, though different, shared many of the same presuppositions of those of Plato and Aristotle, and he concluded that these philosophers were not judged to be atheists.

With regard to the resurrection, Athenagorus argued that, since God created the world out of nothing and providentially sustains it, he naturally recreates by resurrection those who have perished. God's creation is always purposeful and orderly, and the resurrection is consonant with logos and natural order as well as God's purpose for man in the universe. Clearly Athenagorus engaged with more fundamental Hellenistic thought from the Christian perspective than those who preceded him.

BASILIDES AND VALENTINUS

Gnosticism may be either a background study for New Testament exegesis, as Rudolf Bultmann and his school argued, or a foreground study, as has been declared by those associated with R.McL. Wilson. Though good grounds exist for rejecting a developed Gnosticism by the New Testament period, incipient Gnosticism lies behind some views opposed by certain New Testament documents. In this essay, the focus is the second century. Two main leaders of Gnosticism emerge in Basilides and Valentinus.

Basilides flourished in Alexandria about 130 CE. He published a commentary on the Scriptures in twenty-four books, and perhaps also a book entitled *The Gospel*, as well as some odes. Only fragments of his writings survive, but he employed secret traditions that he claimed came from Peter and Matthew, as well Platonic and Stoic philosophy. According to Hippolytus, Basilides held that God, who was wholly transcendent, created a good world and an elect race. The God of the Jews was a source of strife, and, in time, heavenly light raised up Jesus to summon the elect and raise them above the Jewish God to heavens appropriate to their abilities. He believed that these higher stages were achieved through suffering. The Scriptures were to be interpreted spiritually through the use of allegory. His disciples founded a separate sect, but were perhaps a part of the ill-defined Alexandrian Christianity.

Valentinus was a younger contemporary of Basilides, also of Alexandria, but who spent much of his later career in Rome about 140–165 CE. According to Clement of Alexandria and Jerome, he was a person of great ability, who was almost appointed bishop at Rome, and is said to have worked under Pope Anicetus (154–165). Four of the Nag Hammadi documents somewhat reflect his thinking (if we may trust Irenaeus's account of his views): *The Gospel of Truth, The Gospel of Philip, The Exegesis on the Soul,* and the *Treatise on Resurrection to Rheginus* as well as another contemporary document, *The Teachings of Silvanus.*

Valentinus proclaimed a transcendent God who originated in the Primal Cause, that of Depth (βυθός). From the Depths, Silence, Understanding (νοῦς) and Truth (ἀλήθεια) also developed. From these arose Word and Life, Man and Church, and thirty aeons, the last being Wisdom (σοφία). Falling into despair, Wisdom gave birth to a child who created the world with its imperfections. Jesus then appeared to Wisdom and, pushing aside her negative attributes, launched salvation. The ideas of Valentinus are more Hellenized than those of other gnostics. A preference was given to a psychic or allegorical interpretation of the Scripture. The gnostics tended more and more to reject the Old Testament, pushing aside the typological for the allegorical. These writings provide the impression that, whatever gnostic elements may be found in the New Testament, they were much less developed than the views of Basilides and Valentinus.

MONTANUS, MAXIMILLA, PRISCA, AND TERTULLIAN

The Montanist movement in Phrygia resulted in continuing claims about the Holy Spirit, prophecy and eschatology. About 172 CE, Montanus, along with two women companions, Prisca and Maximilla, claimed to be inspired by the Paraclete to be prophets to the churches. They announced that the return of Christ would take place some 15 miles east of Philadelphia. It was a new outburst of the Spirit in the wilderness. Many persons were attracted. While these three may have come from certain indigenous religious groups, the perspectives they brought to bear came from biblical materials, especially the Gospel of John and Revelation. This region was a seed-bed for spirit-filled prophecy. The movement had widespread influence, but was rejected by many churchmen on the grounds that the prophecy often arrived in ecstasy or sleep. They were also discredited because the parousia did not occur on their predicted date. Montanism especially flourished in the countryside of North Africa, where interest continued in apocalyptic, prophetic and Holy Spirit-filled activities.

The Montanists were also interested in the moral purity of the Church, as is evidenced in the shift of Tertullian to the movement in

207 CE. Tertullian was born in Carthage and well trained in classical culture. Although he employed the tools of classical argumentation, he attacked what he considered to be the pagan elements of classical culture. He was faithful to the mainline churches in Carthage for ten years, but, after 207 CE attacked them, as well as the pagans, for lack of dedication, integrity among the leadership, and moral purity. Tertullian opposed second marriages, lax rules on fasting, flight in times of persecution and what he perceived as a lenient penitential code. He also emphasized prophetic apocalyptic and a disciplined moral and ethical life. In his lifetime he published a long list of apologetic, theological, controversial and ascetic works. He generally preferred a literal and historical interpretation of Scripture as opposed to a metaphorical or allegorical one.

IRENAEUS (130–200)

A major figure in the life of the second-century mainstream Church was Irenaeus of Lyons. In his works, he opposed heresy and proceeded to flesh out the core of Christianity or the *Regula Fidei*. Since Irenaeus was said to know Polycarp, he apparently was a native of Smyrna. He studied at Rome, but spent his later career as a bishop and author in Lyons of France. His chief work was *Adversus omnes Haereses*, in which he opposed Gnosticism and Montanism. In modern times, an Armenian translation of his *The Demonstration of Apostolic Preaching* has been discovered. He centered in upon the developing polity of the Church and its unity, the canon of Scriptures, and the traditional doctrines handed down by the apostles. These focused upon God, Christ and the Holy Spirit. Irenaeus especially developed an incarnational Christology. Though he considered himself a philosopher, when he went searching for proofs he almost always went to the Scriptures.

Irenaeus wrote systematically on most aspects of Christian theology. He emphasized a historical perspective on the Scriptures, which especially connected the Testaments typologically. In this manner, he set out in a new way to systematize the theological teaching of the Old and New Testaments. The Old Testament was crucial, yet not an embarrassment, because it was superseded by the New Testament. This resulted in a sense of salvation history and a means of responding to what some saw as primitive life and ethic in the Old Testament. Irenaeus for the most part avoided explicit allegorization.

CELSUS

The most significant programmatic antagonist of second-century Christianity was Celsus, who flourished 170–180 CE, and was from somewhere in the region of Palestine. He studied the writings of both the Old and New Testaments, especially the Pentateuch and Matthew. His attack on Christianity was more an intellectual than an irrational one. His central charge was that Christianity was a revolutionary movement which would eventually undercut traditional culture, society and government. Christ, rather than being a miracle worker as presented in the Gospels, was something of a quack who had learned magic in Egypt. Christians should abandon their role as a disruptive force, and support the emperor and the empire. The unity and preservation of the empire rested, he believed, with the embracing of the ancient traditional deities. He attacked the Christians for departing from a monotheism by affirming God the Father, God the Son and God the Holy Spirit. He failed to comprehend how it was possible for the three to be one. Various persons in the third century, including Origen, attempted to answer his charges.

MELITO OF SARDIS (D. 190)

Melito, bishop of Sardis, who flourished 160–180, wrote many documents, all of which were only known in fragments prior to the middle of the twentieth century. Melito attacked the Jews for having crucified Christ. Christ for him could best be described as both God and man, anticipating Chalcedon. He also affirmed the unity of the Old and New Testaments, but tended to find the meaning for everything in the Old Testament as adumbrating the New Testament, and believed that only Christians understood the New Testament correctly. He argued that, while sin destroyed the unity of body and soul in man, the salvation possible in Christ restores this unity. Melito probably influenced Irenaeus and Tertullian. He too interpreted the Scriptures typologically and eschewed allegory.

Many other documents were produced in the second century, but these are the major ones. These works present a rich diversity of approaches and conclusions. The explication of New Testament documents is augmented through an exploration of these successors of New Testament Christianity.

BIBLIOGRAPHY

Altaner, B. *Patrology*. Trans. H.C. Graef. Freiburg: Herder, 1960.

Brown, R.E., and J.P. Meier. *Antioch and Rome: New Testament Cradles of Christianity*. New York: Paulist, 1983.

Cross, F.L. *The Early Christian Fathers*. London: Duckworth, 1960.

Corwin, V. *St Ignatius and Christianity in Antioch*. Yale University Publications in Religion, 1. New Haven: Yale University Press, 1960.

Donfried, K.P. *The Setting of Second Clement in Early Christianity*. NovTSup, 38. Leiden: Brill, 1974.

Ferguson, E. (ed.). *Encyclopedia of Early Christianity*. New York and London: Garland, 1990.

Frend, W.H.C. *Martyrdom and Persecution in the Early Church*. Oxford: Oxford University Press, 1965, pp. 268-302.

Grant, R.M. *The Apostolic Fathers: An Introduction*. New York: Thomas Nelson, 1964.

_____. *Greek Apologists of the Second Century*. Philadelphia: Westminster Press, 1988.

Hagner, D.A. *The Use of the Old and New Testaments in Clement of Rome*. NovTSup, 34. Leiden: Brill, 1973.

Harrison, P.N. *Polycarp's Two Epistles to the Philippians*. Cambridge: Cambridge University Press, 1936.

Jefford, C.N. *Reading the Apostolic Fathers: An Introduction*. Peabody: Hendrickson, 1996.

Koester, H. *Introduction to the New Testament*. 2 vols. Philadelphia: Fortress Press, 1982.

Kraft, R.A. *Barnabas and the Didache*. The Apostolic Fathers, 3. New York: Thomas Nelson, 1965.

Lake, K. *The Apostolic Fathers*. 2 vols. LCL. Cambridge, MA: Harvard University Press; London: Heinemann, 1977.

Meecham, H.G. *The Epistle to Diognetus*. Manchester: Manchester University Press, 1949.

Osiek, C. *Rich and Poor in the Shepherd of Hermas: An Exegetical-Social Investigation*. CBQMS, 15. Washington: Catholic Biblical Association, 1983.

Quasten, J. *Patrology, I–IV*. Westminster, MD: Christian Classics, 1990.

Robinson, J.A. *Barnabas, Hermas and the Didache*. London: SPCK; New York: Macmillan, 1920.

Robinson, T.A. *The Early Church: An Annotated Bibliography of Literature in English*. ATLA Bibliographical Series, 33. London and Metuchen, NJ: American Theological Library Association and Scarecrow, 1993.

Schoedel, W.F., *Ignatius of Antioch: A Commentary on the Letters of Ignatius of Antioch*. Philadelphia: Fortress Press, 1985.

_____. *Polycarp, Martyrdom of Polycarp, Fragments of Papias*. The Apostolic Fathers, 5. New York: Thomas Nelson, 1965, pp. 3-49.

Wilson, J.C. *Toward a Reassessment of the Shepherd of Hermas: Its Date and its Pneumatology*. Lewiston: Edwin Mellen, 1993.

PART TWO

APPLICATION

THE LIFE OF JESUS

CRAIG A. EVANS

My task is to treat the practice of exegesis as it concerns the life of Jesus. In a certain sense, one cannot really exegete the historical Jesus. One exegetes written texts; and Jesus himself wrote nothing. Hence, it is conventional to speak of exegeting the Gospels, which tell us many important things about the life and teaching of Jesus of Nazareth. What then does exegeting the life of Jesus entail? It entails the exegesis of the (historical) story behind the (literary) story. Thus, it is necessary to engage in historical criticism of the Gospels, if we are to make a serious attempt to exegete the life and teaching of Jesus.

Because of the complicated nature of Jesus research, it will be necessary to develop a 'theory of exegesis'; and in doing this, some overlap with the above Chapter on Form, Source, and Redaction Criticism in Part One (on 'Method') of the present volume is unavoidable. My focus, however, has more to do with the historical Jesus, as opposed to the respective theologies and tendencies of the evangelists (as is properly pursued in the above chapter).

A THEORY OF EXEGESIS

We are after the theology of Jesus; to understand it is in fact to engage in exegesis. We have the respective theologies of the four evangelists, to the extent that we are able accurately to infer these theologies from the Gospels. We have the theologies of Paul and the other New Testament writers. Why not attempt to unpack the theology of Jesus? To ask this question, of course, seems to imply that the evangelists have not faithfully preserved the theology of Jesus. I do not mean to imply that. If that were the case, that is, that the evangelists did not preserve the theology of Jesus, then there would be no hope of recovering and interpreting the message of Jesus. I believe that the evangelists, as well as the tradents who went before them, were conservative caretakers, and that the message of Jesus is in fact preserved in the Gospels. However, the message of

Jesus is not the only thing preserved in the Gospels. This is why Jesus research cannot proceed without carefully taking into account the results of source, form, and redaction criticism.

The message of Jesus has been overlaid with later interpretations and applications. The historical Jesus is much like an old painting, which has become overlaid with a patina. We are accustomed to the patina, and without it, the painting may not look familiar to us. Often times art critics do not want to remove the patina. In a certain sense, it has become part of the painting, part of the art itself. Many Christians feel this way about the Gospels and the historical Jesus. They are not too comfortable with the idea of trying to peak behind the Gospels, of trying to catch a glimpse of Jesus in his original setting. If we are willing to undertake this work, we must be prepared to discover a Jesus whose activities and teachings are in places unexpected, perhaps even strange.

There are three critical methods, mentioned above, that impinge directly on Jesus research: (1) source criticism, (2) form criticism, and (3) redaction criticism. The application of these critical methods has had profound implications for Jesus research. For example, at one time form criticism was thought to make the quest of the historical Jesus 'impossible'.[1] Redaction criticism, in its more ambitious and subjective forms, apparently corroborated this judgment. Source criticism, the saviour of the nineteenth-century quest, has today become a hotbed of disagreement and has generated such a diversity of portraits of Jesus, that, in the opinion of some, current Jesus research has been seriously discredited.[2] In use of these

---

[1]   For the classic assessment of the 'old quest', including the important insight that most participants read their theology and personality into their respective portraits of Jesus, see A. Schweitzer, *Von Reimarus zu Wrede: Eine Geschichte des Leben-Jesu-Forschung* (Tübingen: Mohr–Siebeck, 1906; 2nd edn, 1913); ET *The Quest of the Historical Jesus: A Critical Study of its Progress from Reimarus to Wrede* (London: A. & C. Black, 1910; with 'Introduction' by J.M. Robinson; New York: Macmillan, 1968). In the aftermath of Schweitzer's work, a pessimistic mood prevailed in Germany, with many regarding the quest historically 'impossible' and theologically 'illegitimate'. For assessment of this aspect of the quest and of the post-Bultmannian response to it, see J.M. Robinson, *A New Quest of the Historical Jesus* (SBT, 25; London: SCM Press; repr. Missoula, MT: Scholars Press, 1979); repr. *A New Quest of the Historical Jesus and Other Essays* (Philadelphia: Fortress Press, 1983).

[2]   For a colorful statement of this opinion, see J. Neusner, 'Who Needs "The Historical Jesus"?', *BBR* 4 (1994), pp. 113-26.

three methods, various criteria have been invoked to discuss the authenticity of the Jesus tradition. With these issues in mind, let us briefly review the critical methods and then turn to the criteria of authenticity.

A. *Source Criticism*

For New Testament critics, the major source-critical issue concerns the solution of the Synoptic problem. The high degree of verbal and structural agreement among Matthew, Mark, and Luke has convinced virtually everyone that the solution must be in terms of literary dependence. Two hypotheses have been championed in the last two centuries. The oldest of the two is called the Griesbach-Farmer Hypothesis, or, as its advocates prefer to call it, the Two Gospels Hypothesis. The other is called the Two Document Hypothesis (or Two Source Hypothesis, as its advocates nowadays prefer). The first hypothesis proposes that Matthew was written first, that Luke was written second and made use of Matthew, and that Mark was written last of all and made use of both Matthew and Luke. The second hypothesis proposes that Mark was written first and that Matthew and Luke, independently of one another, made use of Mark and another collection of Jesus' sayings (known as 'Q'). The latter hypothesis today remains the majority view, despite William Farmer's unending efforts to unseat it and return the Griesbach Hypothesis to a position of dominance.

The Two Source Hypothesis still claims the support of the majority of New Testament scholars for the following six reasons.[3]

(1) Mark's *literary style* lacks the polish and sophistication that one regularly encounters in Matthew and Luke. Indeed, Markan style is Semitic and non-literary, and sometimes may even be described as primitive. One must wonder, if Farmer is right, why the Markan evangelist would have chosen time after time to rewrite Matthew and Luke in a cruder and less polished form. Why not simply reproduce one version or the other? Why introduce Semitic words (which are often not found in the Matthean and Lukan parallels) only to have to translate them? It is more probable that Matthew and Luke represent improvements upon Mark. Mark's writing style, when compared to

---

3   In the paragraphs that follow, I summarize my arguments found in C.A. Evans, 'Source, Form and Redaction Criticism: The "Traditional" Methods of Synoptic Interpretation', in S.E. Porter and D. Tombs (eds.), *Approaches to New Testament Study* (JSNTSup, 120; Sheffield: JSOT Press, 1995), pp. 17-45.

that of Matthew and Luke, supports Markan priority, not posteriority.

(2) In comparing the Synoptics, one observes that Mark's version of a story is sometimes *potentially embarrassing*. Jesus and the disciples are sometimes portrayed in a manner that appears either undignified or possibly at variance with Christian beliefs. One should compare the three accounts of the notice that Jesus was driven/led by the Spirit into the wilderness (Matt. 4:1 = Mark 1:12 = Luke 4:1), the stilling of the storm (Matt. 8:23-27 = Mark 4:35-41 = Luke 8:22-25), and Jesus' treatment by family and acquaintances (Matt. 12:46-50 = Mark 3:31-35 = Luke 8:19-21). In these parallel accounts, we can observe what appear to be Matthean and Lukan efforts to mitigate or remove altogether Mark's embarrassing way of telling the story.

(3) Where there is no Markan parallel, *Matthean and Lukan divergence* is greatest. This phenomenon is explained best with reference to Markan priority, rather than Matthean. There is significant divergence in two areas involving material not found in Mark. We see this in the distribution of the double tradition (i.e. Q) throughout Matthew and Luke. With a few easily explainable exceptions (such as placing at the same point in the narrative John the Baptist's 'brood of vipers' speech and the story of the three temptations), the double tradition is found in different contexts. This has not been convincingly explained by advocates of the Griesbach hypothesis. Why would Luke follow Matthew's narrative sequence, but break up his collections of Jesus' sayings (such as the Sermon on the Mount) and scatter them throughout his Gospel? We also see such divergence in the material special to Matthew (M) and Luke (L). Although a small and important common core of material can be detected in the Matthean and Lukan versions of Jesus' birth and resurrection, we have here a remarkable amount of divergence. In short, what we observe is that, where there is no Mark to follow, this is where Matthew and Luke go their separate ways. This observation is very difficult to explain assuming Matthean priority, but it is exactly what one should expect assuming Markan priority.

(4) Another indication of Markan priority lies in the observation that in some instances, due to omission of Markan details, *Matthew and Luke have created difficulties*. Stein has provided several

examples that illustrate this feature well.[4] Instructive examples include the healing of the paralytic (Matt. 9:1-8 = Mark 2:1-12 = Luke 5:17-26), Jesus' dialogue with the rich young man (Matt. 19:16-22 = Mark 10:17-22 = Luke 18:18-23), the request of James and John (Matt. 20:20-23 = Mark 10:35-40; Luke omits the episode), and Pilate's Passover pardon (Mark 15:6-14 = Luke 23:17-23, where, because Luke has omitted Mark's explanation of the Passover pardon, the reader has no way of knowing why the crowd shouts for the release of Barabbas).

(5) The small amount of material that is *unique* to the Gospel of Mark also supports Markan priority. This material consists of 1:1; 2:27; 3:20-21; 4:26-29; 7:2-4, 32-37; 8:22-26; 9:29, 48-49; 13:33-37; 14:51-52. In reviewing this material, one should ask which explanation seems the more probable, that Mark added it, or that Matthew and Luke found it in Mark and chose to omit it. The nature of the material supports the latter alternative, for it seems more likely that Matthew and Luke chose to omit the flight of the naked youth (14:51-52), the odd saying about being 'salted with fire' (9:48-49), the strange miracle where Jesus effects healing in two stages (8:22-26), the even stranger miracle where Jesus puts his fingers in a man's ears, spits, and touches his tongue (7:32-37), and the episode where Jesus is regarded as mad and his family attempts to restrain him (3:20-22). If we accept the Griesbach-Farmer Hypothesis, we would then have to explain why Mark would choose to add these odd, potentially embarrassing materials, only to omit the Sermon on the Mount/Plain, the Lord's Prayer, and numerous other teachings and parables found in the larger Gospels. It seems much more likely that Matthew and Luke represent *improvements* upon Mark; in this case, improvements through deletion.

(6) The final consideration that adds weight to the probability of Markan priority has to do with the *results* of the respective hypotheses. The true test of any hypothesis is its effectiveness. In biblical studies, a theory should aid the exegetical task. The theory of Markan priority has provided just this kind of aid. Not only has Synoptic interpretation been materially advanced because of the conclusion, and now widespread assumption, of Markan priority, but the development of critical methods oriented to Gospels research,

---

4   R.H. Stein, *The Synoptic Problem: An Introduction* (Grand Rapids: Baker, 1987), pp. 70-76.

such as form criticism and redaction criticism, which have enjoyed success, has also presupposed Markan priority. In countless studies, whether dealing with a particular pericope, or treating one of the Synoptic Gospels in its entirety, it has been recognized over and over again that Matthew and Luke make the greatest sense as *interpretations of Mark.*[5] If the Griesbach-Farmer Hypothesis was correct, one should expect major breakthroughs in Markan research. After all, we would now know what Mark's sources were. But Farmer's followers have not cast significant light on Mark.

For these reasons (and other lines of argument have not been considered) the Two Source Hypothesis remains the most compelling solution to the Synoptic problem.[6] Of the three Synoptic Gospels, it would appear that Mark is the most primitive. The date of Mark is debated, though most appear willing to assign this Gospel to the late sixties or early seventies. I incline to the former, for I think the Temple of Jerusalem is still standing at the time that the evangelist writes. Either the war with Rome has just gotten under way (66 CE) or the danger of war is sensed to be imminent.

However, even if we agree that the Two Source Hypothesis has solved the Synoptic problem, so that we now know that Mark is the oldest Gospel, the priority of the Synoptic tradition itself has become an uncertainty. Much controversy has been recently generated by the claim, made mostly by members of the Jesus Seminar, a North American phenomenon, that the canonical Gospels are not in fact the oldest and most reliable sources for Jesus research. Jesus Seminar members, particularly John Dominic Crossan, have argued that several extra-canonical (or apocryphal) Gospels contain traditions that predate some of the traditions preserved in the canonical Gospels.[7] The most notable of these extra-canonicals are the *Gospel of Thomas*, the Egerton Papyrus 2, the *Gospel of Peter*, and the *Secret Gospel of Mark.*[8] But critical study of these documents has

---

5   See C.M. Tuckett, *The Revival of the Griesbach Hypothesis* (SNTSMS, 44; Cambridge: Cambridge University Press, 1983), pp. 186-87.

6   See Tuckett, *Revival of the Griesbach Hypothesis*; S.E. Johnson, *The Griesbach Hypothesis and Redaction Criticism* (SBLMS, 41; Atlanta: Scholars Press, 1991).

7   For a major example of the extent to which Crossan is dependent on the extra-canonical Gospels for his research, see his *The Historical Jesus: The Life of a Mediterranean Jewish Peasant* (San Francisco: HarperCollins, 1991).

8   For studies of these Gospels, from the perspective of the Jesus Seminar,

persuaded few scholars that they contain anything of genuine value.[9] Jesus research will not make progress if it relies on these dubious sources.[10]

B. Form Criticism

Form criticism attempts to identify specific literary or sub-literary forms and infer from these forms their function or setting in the life of the early Christian community (i.e. *Sitz im Leben*).[11] It is assumed

---

see R. Cameron, *The Other Gospels: Non-Canonical Gospel Texts* (Philadelphia: Westminster Press, 1982); J.D. Crossan, *Four Other Gospels: Shadows on the Contours of Canon* (New York: Harper & Row, 1985; repr. Sonoma, CA: Polebridge, 1992); and R.J. Miller (ed.), *The Complete Gospels* (Sonoma, CA: Polebridge, 1992).

9   The best statement in defense of the antiquity and independence of the extra-canonical Gospels comes from H. Koester, *Ancient Christian Gospels: Their History and Development* (London: SCM; Philadelphia: Trinity Press International, 1990). But Koester's work still remains problematic at many points. See J.H. Charlesworth and C.A. Evans, 'Jesus in the Agrapha and Apocryphal Gospels', in B.D. Chilton and C.A. Evans (eds.), *Studying the Historical Jesus: Evaluations of the State of Current Research* (NTTS, 19; Leiden: Brill, 1994), pp. 479-533.

10   In my judgment, Crossan's portrait of the historical Jesus is badly flawed because of his heavy reliance on several of the extra-canonical Gospels and fragments.

11   For basic bibliography, see W.G. Doty, 'The Discipline and Literature of New Testament Form Criticism', *ATR* 51 (1969), pp. 257-321; E.V. McKnight, *What is Form Criticism?* (Philadelphia: Fortress, 1969); E.E. Ellis, 'New Directions in Form Criticism', in G. Strecker (ed.), *Jesus Christus in Historie und Theologie* (Tübingen: Mohr–Siebeck, 1975), pp. 299-315; S.H. Travis, 'Form Criticism', in I.H. Marshall (ed.), *New Testament Interpretation* (Grand Rapids: Eerdmans, 1977), pp. 153-64; W. Kelber, *The Oral and Written Gospel* (Philadelphia: Fortress, 1983); K. Berger, *Formgeschichte des Neuen Testaments* (Heidelberg: Quelle & Meyer, 1984); idem, *Einführung in die Formgeschichte* (Tübingen: Franke, 1987); Stein, *Synoptic Problem*, pp. 161-228; S. McKnight, *Interpreting the Synoptic Gospels* (Grand Rapids: Baker, 1988), pp. 71-82; E.P. Sanders and M. Davies, *Studying the Synoptic Gospels* (London: SCM Press; Philadelphia: Trinity Press International, 1989), pp. 123-97; D.L. Bock, 'Form Criticism', in D.A. Black and D.S. Dockery (eds.), *New Testament Criticism and Interpretation* (Grand Rapids: Zondervan, 1991), pp. 175-96; C.L. Blomberg, 'Form Criticism', in J.B. Green *et al.* (eds.), *Dictionary of Jesus and the Gospels* (Downers Grove, IL: InterVarsity, 1992), pp. 243-50; G. Strecker, 'Schriftlichkeit oder Mündlichkeit der synoptischen Tradition? Anmerkungen zur formgeschichtlichen Problematik', in F. Van Segbroeck *et al.* (eds.), *The Four Gospels 1992* (3 vols.; BETL, 100; Leuven: Leuven University Press, 1992), I, pp. 159-72.

that the tradition of the life of Jesus was 'minted by the faith of the primitive Christian community in its various stages'.[12] Of the three traditional criticisms, form criticism is the most problematic. It is problematic because, by its very nature, a great deal of subjectivity comes into play. We really do not know what the practices were of first-century Christians who told and retold the sayings of and stories about Jesus.[13] Therefore, we can never be sure of precisely what setting a piece of tradition may reflect.

The German scholars who applied form criticism to the Gospels assigned a great many of the traditions to the early Church, rather than to Jesus himself.[14] English form critics were less skeptical.[15] Recent discussion has been quite diverse. Harald Riesenfeld and Birger Gerhardsson, taking a different tack, have argued that the tradition is reliable, since Jesus, like the rabbis of old, taught his disciples to memorize his teachings.[16] Rainer Riesner has argued for

---

[12]   E. Käsemann, *Essays on New Testament Themes* (SBT, 41; London: SCM Press; Naperville, IL: Allenson, 1964), p. 15.

[13]   This point has been convincingly made by E.P. Sanders, *The Tendencies of the Synoptic Tradition* (SNTSMS, 9; Cambridge: Cambridge University Press, 1969).

[14]   K.L. Schmidt, *Der Rahmen der Geschichte Jesu: Literarkritische Untersuchungen zur ältesten Jesusüberlieferung* (Berlin: Trowitzsch & Sohn, 1919); M. Dibelius, *Die Formgeschichte des Evangeliums* (Tübingen: Mohr–Siebeck, 1919; 3rd edn, 1959); ET *From Tradition to Gospel* (Cambridge: James Clarke; New York: Scribners, 1934); R. Bultmann, *Die Geschichte der synoptischen Tradition* (FRLANT, 12; Göttingen: Vandenhoeck & Ruprecht, 1921; 3rd edn, 1957 [= FRLANT, 29]); ET *The History of the Synoptic Tradition* (Oxford: Blackwell; New York: Harper & Row, 1963); *idem, Die Erforschung der synoptischen Tradition* (Giessen: Töpelmann, 1925; 2nd edn, 1930); ET 'The Study of the Synoptic Gospels', in R. Bultmann and K. Kundsin, *Form Criticism: Two Essays on New Testament Research* (New York: Willett, Clark, 1934), pp. 11-76.

[15]   V. Taylor, *The Formation of the Gospel Tradition* (London: Macmillan, 1933; 2nd edn, 1935); C.H. Dodd, *The Parables of the Kingdom* (London: Nisbet, 1935); *idem*, 'The Appearances of the Risen Christ: A Study in Form-Criticism of the Gospels', in D.E. Nineham (ed.), *Studies in the Gospels: Essays in Memory of R.H. Lightfoot* (Oxford: Blackwell, 1955), pp. 9-35.

[16]   H. Riesenfeld, *The Gospel Tradition and its Beginnings: A Study in the Limits of 'Formgeschichte'* (London: Mowbray, 1957); B. Gerhardsson, *Memory and Manuscript: Oral Tradition and Written Transmission in Rabbinic Judaism and Early Christianity* (Lund: Gleerup, 1961). Gerhardsson supposes that the words of Jesus may have been carefully preserved as rabbis carefully preserved the words of Scripture.

even greater confidence in the general reliability of the Synoptic Gospels.[17] But their work has been criticized for importing later rabbinic principles of discipleship into the earlier context of the New Testament Gospels.[18] It is argued that we cannot assume that Jesus' followers and the generation that followed them emphasized memorization to the degree that it would appear that many rabbis of later generations did. In any event, comparison of the Synoptic Gospels reveals to what extent the sayings of Jesus have been edited, paraphrased, and diversely contextualized. The very phenomena of the Gospels tell against Gerhardsson and company. Accordingly, the difficult question of how extensive were early Christian editing and expansion of the dominical tradition still remains open.

In general, we can agree with the classic form critics that the sayings and stories of Jesus functioned in various ways in the life of the early Church. Certain traditions served liturgical functions, others served evangelistic and apologetic purposes. But this should remain a general observation. The greater the specificity, the greater the subjectivity.[19]

Some form critics have emphasized the role of prophecy in early Christianity in shaping dominical tradition and in generating it altogether. In my judgment, Eugene Boring's thesis, to the effect that much of dominical tradition arose through early Christian prophecy, is no longer persuasive or widely held.[20] Boring is certainly right in finding that much of the dominical tradition has been reinterpreted, largely through recontextualization, but there is little objective

---

[17] R. Riesner, *Jesus als Lehrer: Eine Untersuchung zum Ursprung der Evangelien-Überlieferung* (WUNT, 2.7; Tübingen: Mohr–Siebeck, 1981; 4th edn, 1994).

[18] See M. Smith, 'A Comparison of Early Christianity and Early Rabbinic Traditions', *JBL* 82 (1963), pp. 169-76; Sanders, *Tendencies of the Synoptic Tradition*, pp. 294-96.

[19] E.P. Sanders (*Jesus and Judaism* [London: SCM Press; Philadelphia: Fortress Press, 1985], p. 16) appropriately comments: 'The form critics were right in thinking that the material changed; they were wrong in thinking that they knew how it changed'. The early Christian community sometimes left behind obvious traces, as seen for example in the parenthetic comment, 'Thus he declared all foods clean' (Mark 7:19). But rarely are such traces this obvious.

[20] M.E. Boring, *Sayings of the Risen Jesus: Christian Prophecy in the Synoptic Tradition* (SNTSMS, 46; Cambridge: Cambridge University Press, 1982); *idem, The Continuing Voice of Jesus* (Louisville: Westminster/John Knox Press, 1991).

evidence of wholesale creation through prophetic utterance or otherwise.[21]

In my judgment, the most prudent position to take is that, on principle, most material ultimately derives from Jesus, but that most material has been edited and recontextualized. Here the assumptions and conclusions of the Jesus Seminar are particularly problematic. The Seminar's color scheme ('red'—Jesus said it; 'pink'—something close to what Jesus said; 'gray'—doubtful that Jesus said it; and 'black'—Jesus definitely did not say it) is unrealistic and misleading.[22]

In a certain sense, most of the material should be rated pink, if we are speaking of the sayings as approximating the utterances of Jesus. But in another sense, most of the material should be gray, or even black, if we are speaking of what the material precisely meant and in what setting(s) it was spoken. It is this latter dimension that vexes Jesus research. But in the case of the historical Jesus, we at least have a pretty good idea of the environment, situation, and principal events of Jesus' life during and at the end of his ministry. In contrast, we know comparatively little about the early Palestinian Church, and not a great deal more about the Church of Asia Minor and Greece. Yet Bultmann and Dibelius (and now the Jesus Seminar) exhibit a remarkable degree of confidence about what early Christians were saying and thinking. In many places these scholars are able, so they tell us, to penetrate behind obscure utterances and find out with what

---

[21]   For criticisms of Boring's conclusions, see D.E. Aune, *Prophecy in Early Christianity and the Ancient Mediterranean World* (Grand Rapids: Eerdmans, 1983), pp. 240-42 (on Jesus tradition, see pp. 153-88); D. Hill, *New Testament Prophecy* (Atlanta: John Knox, 1979), pp. 5-9 (on Jesus tradition, pp. 48-69). Aune and Hill are responding to Boring's dissertation and to earlier studies presented in the *Society of Biblical Literature Seminar Papers* (1973, 1974, 1976, 1977) and *JBL* (1972). For an earlier statement that is compatible with Boring's conclusions, see F.W. Beare, 'Sayings of the Risen Jesus in the Synoptic Tradition', in W.R. Farmer *et al.* (eds.), *Christian History and Interpretation* (Festschrift J. Knox; London: Cambridge University Press, 1967), pp. 161-81.

[22]   See now R.W. Funk and R.W. Hoover (eds.), *The Five Gospels: The Search for the Authentic Words of Jesus* (New York: Macmillan, 1993). This pretentious book is dedicated to Galileo, Thomas Jefferson, and David Strauss. One reviewer thinks it would have been better to have dedicated it to P.T. Barnum, the great American showman; cf. R.B. Hays, 'The Corrected Jesus', *First Things* (May, 1994), pp. 43-48. See also N.T. Wright, 'Taking the Text with Her Pleasure', *Theol* 96 (1993), pp. 303-10; H.C. Kee, *TTod* 52 (1995), pp. 17-28.

the Church of the mid-first century was dealing. There is a disturbing tendency to ignore the literary context of pericopes and their meaning in these contexts (the only real contexts we have) in preference for the highly subjective contexts, or *Sitze im Leben*, in the early Church, in which these pericopes allegedly originated.

The difficulties that form criticism faces should not deter us from engaging in its task. Proper identification of the form of a given pericope plays an important role in exegesis. Ascertaining how a given pericope may have been edited and contextualized by early Christians is appropriate. Understanding the nature of a form that commonly occurs in the Gospels (such as parables) is also very helpful in exegesis and in the complicated task of distinguishing (where it in fact needs to be distinguished) the meaning in the life of Jesus from later meanings invested in the tradition as it was passed on and put to use in Christian circles.

C. Redaction Criticism

Redaction criticism is concerned with the manner in which the respective evangelists and their communities edited the written traditions. It is assumed that much can be learned about the evangelists and their communities by carefully observing what traditions were retained, how they were supplemented, how they were reworded, and how they were recontextualized. The evangelists' literary work was assumed to provide important insights into their respective theologies.[23]

---

23   J. Rohde, *Die redaktionsgeschichtliche Methode: Einführung und Sichtung des Forschungstandes* (Hamburg: Furche, 1966); R.H. Stein, 'What is *Redaktionsgeschichte*?', *JBL* 88 (1969), pp. 45-56; *idem, Synoptic Problem*, pp. 231-72; N. Perrin, *What is Redaction Criticism?* (Philadelphia: Fortress Press, 1974); R.T. Fortna, 'Redaction Criticism, NT', *IDBSup*, pp. 733-35; S.S. Smalley, 'Redaction Criticism', in Marshall (ed.), *New Testament Interpretation*, pp. 181-95; W. Kelber, 'Redaction Criticism: On the Nature and Exposition of the Gospels', *PRS* 6 (1979), pp. 4-16; McKnight, *Interpreting the Synoptic Gospels*, pp. 83-95; E.V. McKnight, 'Form and Redaction Criticism', in E.J. Epp and G.W. MacRae (eds.), *The New Testament and its Modern Interpreters* (Atlanta: Scholars Press, 1989), pp. 149-74; Sanders and Davies, *Studying the Synoptic Gospels*, pp. 201-98; Johnson, *Griesbach Hypothesis and Redaction Criticism*; G.R. Osborne, 'Redaction Criticism', in Black and Dockery (eds.), *New Testament Criticism*, pp. 199-224; *idem*, 'Redaction Criticism', in *Dictionary of Jesus and the Gospels*, pp. 662-69; J.R. Donahue, 'Redaction Criticism: Has the *Hauptstrasse* Become a *Sackgasse*?', in E.S. Malbon and E.V. McKnight (eds.), *The New Literary Criticism and the New Testament* (JSNTSup, 109; Sheffield: JSOT Press,

In its earliest presentation, redaction criticism presupposed the results of source criticism (i.e. the Two Source Hypothesis) and of form criticism (i.e. that the early Church freely shaped, even created, the dominical tradition to serve its needs). Willi Marxsen's pioneering work on the earliest Gospel, the Gospel of Mark, ran into difficulties, because the distinction between tradition and redaction was not always clear.[24] His objectives more than his conclusions

---

1994), pp. 27-57. Donahue's essay traces the development of redaction criticism and explores the ways the method has contributed to the newer forms of literary criticism and sociological readings of the Gospels. He concludes that redaction criticism has not reached a dead end (*Sackgasse*) but a crossroad (*Querstrasse*), 'where different methods continue to intersect' (p. 48).

24   W. Marxsen, 'Redaktionsgeschichtliche Erklärung der sogenannten Parabeltheorie des Markus', *ZTK* 52 (1955), pp. 255-71; repr. in *idem, Der Exeget als Theologe: Vorträge zum Neuen Testament* (Gütersloh: Mohn, 1968), pp. 13-28; *idem, Der Evangelist Markus: Studien zur Redaktionsgeschichte des Evangeliums* (FRLANT, 67; Göttingen: Vandenhoeck & Ruprecht, 1956; 2nd edn, 1959); ET *Mark the Evangelist: Studies on the Redaction History of the Gospel* (Nashville: Abingdon Press, 1969). For criticism of the subjectivity in scholarly attempts to distinguish source and redaction in Mark, see reviews by R. Pesch in *TRev* 72 (1976), pp. 101-102; 73 (1977), pp. 459-60.

For attempts to distinguish Mark's sources from his redaction and to establish criteria for doing so, see R. Pesch, *Naherwartungen: Tradition und Redaktion in Mk 13* (Düsseldorf: Patmos, 1968); J.D. Kingsbury, *The Parables of Jesus in Matthew 13* (Richmond: John Knox, 1969); P.J. Achtemeier, 'Toward the Isolation of Pre-Markan Miracle Catenae', *JBL* 89 (1970), pp. 265-91; *idem*, 'The Origin and Function of Pre-Markan Miracle Catenae', *JBL* 91 (1972), pp. 198-221; K. Kertelge, *Die Wunder Jesu im Markusevangelium: Eine redaktions-geschichtliche Untersuchung* (SANT, 23; Munich: Kösel, 1970); R.H. Stein, 'The Proper Methodology for Ascertaining a Markan Redaction History', *NovT* 13 (1971), pp. 181-98; T.J. Weeden, *Mark—Traditions in Conflict* (Philadelphia: Fortress Press, 1971); J.R. Donahue, *Are You the Christ? The Trial Narrative in the Gospel of Mark* (SBLDS, 10; Missoula, MT: Scholars Press, 1973); F. Neirynck, *Duality in Mark: Contributions to the Study of Markan Redaction* (BETL, 31; Leuven: Leuven University Press, 1973; 2nd edn, 1988); E. Best, 'Mark's Preservation of the Tradition', in M. Sabbe (ed.), *L'évangile selon Marc* (BETL, 34; Leuven: Leuven University Press, 1974), pp. 21-34; W. Schenk, *Der Passionsbericht nach Markus: Untersuchungen zur Überlieferungsgeschichte der Passionstraditionen* (Gütersloh: Mohn, 1974); D. Juel, *Messiah and Temple: The Trial of Jesus in the Gospel of Mark* (SBLDS, 31; Missoula, MT: Scholars Press, 1977); E.J. Pryke, *Redactional Style in the Marcan Gospel: A Study of Syntax and Vocabulary as Guides to Redaction in Mark* (SNTSMS, 33; Cambridge: Cambridge University Press, 1978); U. Luz, 'Markusforschung in der Sackgasse?', *TLZ* 105 (1980), pp. 653-54; F. Neirynck, 'The Redactional Text of Mark', *ETL* 57 (1981),

proved to be of enduring worth. Günther Bornkamm and Hans Conzelmann, who practiced the new method on Matthew and Luke, were able to achieve more convincing and longer lasting results.[25]

In the case of Matthew, we observe a tendency to group Jesus' teachings into five major discourses (chs. 5–7, 10, 13, 18, 24–25), often placing Jesus on a mountain. There is interest in citing Scripture as 'fulfilled'. The word 'righteous' appears to be part of a theme revolving around what it means to believe in Jesus and be a Torah-observant Jew. The infancy story is told in such a way as to be reminiscent of Moses' brush with death as an infant. The Pharisees are singled out for especially harsh criticism (chs. 15, 23). All of this led Bornkamm and his many successors to the various conclusions that the author was in all probability Jewish, that he was fending off charges that Christians did not keep the Law, and that Jesus lacked the necessary credentials to be Israel's awaited Messiah.[26]

---

pp. 144-62; C.C. Black, 'The Quest of Mark the Redactor: Why Has it Been Pursued, and What Has it Taught Us?', *JSNT* 33 (1988), pp. 19-39; *idem, The Disciples according to Mark: Markan Redaction in Current Debate* (JSNTSup, 27; Sheffield: JSOT Press, 1989); Donahue, 'Redaction Criticism', pp. 29-34.

25   G. Bornkamm, 'Enderwartung und Kirche im Matthäusevangelium', in Bornkamm, G. Barth, and H.-J. Held, *Überlieferung und Auslegung im Matthäusevangelium* (WMANT, 1; Neukirchen-Vluyn: Neukirchener Verlag, 1960), pp. 13-53; ET 'End-Expectation and Church in Matthew', in Bornkamm *et al., Tradition and Interpretation in Matthew* (NTL; London: SCM Press; Philadelphia: Westminster Press, 1963), pp. 15-51; H. Conzelmann, *Die Mitte der Zeit: Studien zur Theologie des Lukas* (Tübingen: Mohr–Siebeck, 1954); ET *The Theology of St Luke* (New York: Harper & Row, 1960).

26   Besides the work of Bornkamm and his pupils, see R.H. Gundry, *The Use of the Old Testament in St Matthew's Gospel* (NovTSup, 18; Leiden: Brill, 1967); D.R.A. Hare, *The Theme of Jewish Persecution of Christians in the Gospel according to St Matthew* (SNTSMS, 6; Cambridge: Cambridge University Press, 1967); M.J. Suggs, *Wisdom, Law and Christology in Matthew's Gospel* (Cambridge, MA: Harvard University Press, 1970); W.G. Thompson, *Matthew's Advice to a Divided Community: Mt. 17,22–18,35* (AnBib, 44; Rome: Biblical Institute Press, 1970); O.L. Cope, *Matthew: A Scribe Trained for the Kingdom of Heaven* (CBQMS, 5; Washington: Catholic Biblical Association, 1976); J.P. Meier, *Law and History in Matthew's Gospel* (AnBib, 71; Rome: Biblical Institute Press, 1976); B. Przybylski, *Righteousness in Matthew and his World of Thought* (SNTSMS, 41; Cambridge: Cambridge University Press, 1980); T.L. Donaldson, *Jesus on the Mountain: A Study in Matthean Theology* (JSNTSup, 8; Sheffield: JSOT Press, 1985); S.H. Brooks, *Matthew's Community: The Evidence of his Special Sayings Material* (JSNTSup, 16; Sheffield: JSOT Press, 1987); D.E. Orton, *The Understanding Scribe: Matthew and the Apocalyptic Ideal* (JSNTSup,

We encounter a dramatically different treatment of traditional materials and distinctive features in the material found only in Luke. Luke does not often cite Scripture as fulfilled, but he does weave the language and themes of Scripture into the narratives and speeches of his characters. His version of the infancy narrative is particularly instructive in this regard. Whereas five times Matthew claims that this or that event related to Jesus' birth was in fulfillment of something one prophet or another said, Luke claims no fulfillment, but rather records several canticles (such as the *Magnificat* and the *Nunc Dimittis*) which are laced throughout with important scriptural traditions. Luke's interesting and much disputed Central Section (chs. 10–18 or 19) challenges assumptions held about election, that is, who is saved and who is not, and why. When we take Luke's second volume, Acts, into account, we find a pronounced interest in stewardship and the early Church's success in breaking down the barriers between Jews and Gentiles. All of this has led Lukan interpreters to conclude that this evangelist was probably a Gentile with some personal knowledge of the synagogue, who knew portions of the Greek Old Testament, and who was interested in showing how the Gentile mission stood in continuity with biblical history.[27]

25; Sheffield: JSOT Press, 1989); G.N. Stanton, *A Gospel for a New People: Studies in Matthew* (Edinburgh: T. & T. Clark, 1992); M.P. Knowles, *Jeremiah in Matthew's Gospel: The Rejected-Prophet Motif in Matthaean Redaction* (JSNTSup, 68; Sheffield: JSOT Press, 1993). For commentaries on Matthew that blend traditional redaction criticism with the more recent wholistic approach of literary criticism, see R.H. Gundry, *Matthew—A Commentary on his Literary and Theological Art* (Grand Rapids: Eerdmans, 1982; 2nd edn, 1994); D.A. Hagner, *Matthew* (WBC, 33AB; Dallas: Word, 1993, 1994).

[27] Besides the work of Conzelmann, see H.-W. Bartsch, *Wachet aber zu jeder Zeit! Entwurf einer Auslegung des Lukas-Evangeliums* (Hamburg: Reich Evangelischer Verlag, 1963); H. Flender, *St Luke: Theologian of Redemptive History* (London: SPCK; Philadelphia: Fortress Press, 1967); T. Holtz, *Untersuchungen über die alttestamentlichen Zitate bei Lukas* (TU, 104: Berlin: Akademie Verlag, 1968); S. Brown, *Apostasy and Perseverance in the Theology of Luke* (AnBib, 36; Rome: Biblical Institute Press, 1969); T. Schramm, *Der Markus-Stoff bei Lukas: Eine literarkritische und redaktionsgeschichtliche Untersuchung* (SNTSMS, 14; Cambridge: Cambridge University Press, 1971); S.G. Wilson, *The Gentiles and the Gentile Mission in Luke–Acts* (SNTSMS, 23; Cambridge: Cambridge University Press, 1973); G. Braumann, *Das Lukas-Evangelium: Die redaktions- und kompositionsgeschichtliche Forschung* (WF, 280; Darmstadt: Wissenschaftliche Buchgesellschaft, 1974); P. Zingg, *Das Wachsen der Kirche: Beiträge zur Frage der lukanischen Redaktion und Theologie* (OBO, 3; Fribourg:

Redaction criticism's single greatest vulnerability lies, of course, in whether or not source critics have found the solution to the Synoptic Problem. I have argued above that Markan priority, which is held by most New Testament scholars today, is the most probable solution. If I am wrong, then my redaction-critical judgments are inaccurate and misleading. However, it is redaction criticism itself that lends support to Markan priority, in that, time after time, Matthew and Luke make better sense as revisions and interpretations of Mark, rather than Mark as conflation and interpretation of Matthew and Luke.[28]

D. Criteria of Authenticity

Because our interest here is with the life of Jesus, with his words and activities, it is necessary to ascertain what parts of the material have reasonable claim to authenticity. This must be done if we are to avoid confusing the theology of the early Church with the theology of Jesus, at least in those places where their respective theologies do not completely overlap. This is not the place to indulge in a full-scale treatment of the criteria of authenticity, but a brief review of them would be helpful.

Recently Meier has grouped these criteria into two categories. To the first category he assigns the useful, or valid, criteria and to the

---

Universitätsverlag; Göttingen: Vandenhoeck & Ruprecht, 1974); L.T. Johnson, *The Literary Function of Possessions in Luke–Acts* (SBLDS, 39; Missoula, MT: Scholars Press, 1977); J. Ernst, *Herr der Geschichte: Perspektiven der lukanischen Eschatologie* (SBS, 88; Stuttgart: Katholisches Bibelwerk, 1978); J. Jeremias, *Die Sprache des Lukasevangeliums: Redaktion und Tradition im Nicht-Markusstoff des dritten Evangeliums* (KEK, Sonderband; Göttingen: Vandenhoeck & Ruprecht, 1980); C.H. Giblin, *The Destruction of Jerusalem according to Luke's Gospel: A Historical-Typological Moral* (AnBib, 107; Rome: Biblical Institute Press, 1985); D.L. Bock, *Proclamation from Prophecy and Pattern: Lucan Old Testament Christology* (JSNTSup, 12; Sheffield: JSOT Press, 1987); R.L. Brawley, *Luke– Acts and the Jews: Conflict, Apology, and Conciliation* (SBLMS, 33; Atlanta: Scholars Press, 1987); P.F. Esler, *Community and Gospel in Luke–Acts: The Social and Political Motivations in Lucan Theology* (SNTSMS, 57; Cambridge: Cambridge University Press, 1987). For commentaries on Luke that blend traditional redaction criticism with the more recent wholistic approach of composition criticism, see J.A. Fitzmyer, *The Gospel according to Luke* (AB, 28, 28A; Garden City: Doubleday, 1981–85); J. Nolland, *Luke* (WBC, 35ABC; Dallas: Word, 1989–93).

28　Indeed, I am not sure of any instance where Mark makes sense as a revision of either Matthew or Luke.

second he assigns the dubious criteria.[29] His assessment of these criteria is practical and judicious. Following Meier's lead, though with some modification, I regard the following six criteria as valid.

1. Historical Coherence. Material that coheres with what we know of Jesus' historical circumstances and the principal features of his life should be given priority. This is a point that Sanders has made, and I think it has merit. We may expect authentic material to help explain 'why [Jesus] attracted attention, why he was executed, and why he was subsequently deified'.[30] Material that does not clarify these questions is not automatically excluded, of course, but priority must be given to material that does clarify them.

2. Multiple Attestation. Multiple attestation refers to material that appears in two or more independent sources.[31] This material may be regarded as primitive, though not necessarily authentic. Multiple attestation confirms that material was not generated by one evangelist or another (or their respective communities), but must have been in circulation some years before the Gospels and their sources were composed.[32] Therefore, multiple attestation does not guarantee

---

29   J.P. Meier, *A Marginal Jew: Rethinking the Historical Jesus* (ABRL; New York: Doubleday, 1991), I, pp. 167-95. For further discussion, with more detail and more examples, see R. Latourelle, 'Critères d'authenticité des Évangiles', *Greg* 55 (1974), pp. 609-38; F. Lentzen-Deis, 'Kriterien für die historische Beurteilung der Jesusüberlieferung in den Evangelien', in K. Kertelge (ed.), *Rückfrage nach Jesus: Zur Methodik und Bedeutung der Frage nach dem historischen Jesus* (QD, 63; Freiburg: Herder, 1974), pp. 78-117; R.H. Stein, 'The "Criteria" for Authenticity', in R.T. France and D. Wenham (eds.), *Studies of History and Tradition in the Four Gospels* (Gospel Perspectives, 2; Sheffield: JSOT Press, 1980), pp. 225-63; D. Polkow, 'Method and Criteria for Historical Jesus Research', in K.H. Richards (ed.), *Society of Biblical Literature 1987 Seminar Papers* (SBLSP, 26; Atlanta: Scholars Press, 1987), pp. 336-56; C.A. Evans, 'Authenticity Criteria in Life of Jesus Research', *CSR* 19 (1989), pp. 6-31; *idem, Jesus and his Contemporaries: Comparative Studies* (AGJU, 25; Leiden: Brill, 1995), pp. 13-26.

30   Sanders, *Jesus and Judaism*, p. 7.

31   F.C. Burkitt (*The Gospel History and its Transmission* [Edinburgh: T. & T. Clark, 3rd edn, 1911], pp. 148-66) identified thirty-one multiply attested sayings. See also the recently published H.T. Fleddermann, *Mark and Q: A Study of the Overlap Texts* (BETL, 122; Leuven: Peeters/Leuven University Press, 1995). Fleddermann identifies twenty-nine overlaps.

32   The criterion of multiple forms demonstrates the same thing; cf. C.H. Dodd, *History and the Gospel* (New York: Scribners, 1937), pp. 91-101. Ideas

authenticity; it only guarantees antiquity.[33]

3. Embarrassment. By 'embarrassing', I mean material that is perceived by the evangelists as awkward, as in need of qualification, and perhaps even deletion. It may also be material that is contrary to the editorial tendency of the evangelist himself. Nevertheless, despite the awkwardness and the potential embarrassment, the material is preserved. It is reasoned, and I think cogently, that this material is preserved because it is ancient and widespread.[34] As Meier has put it, 'It is highly unlikely that the Church went out of its way to create the cause of its own embarrassment'.[35] John's baptism of Jesus (Mark 1:9-11) and his later question about whether or not Jesus is 'one who is coming' (Matt. 11:2-6 = Luke 7:18-23) are excellent examples of potentially awkward or embarrassing material that is surely authentic.

4. Dissimilarity. Defined and put into practice as it was during the heyday of redaction criticism, the criterion of dissimilarity (or discontinuity, as it was sometimes called) is problematic. Norman Perrin gave this criterion its classic definition: '[T]he earliest form of a saying we can reach may be regarded as authentic if it can be shown to be dissimilar to characteristic emphases both of ancient Judaism and of the early Church'.[36] In recent years, it has been

---

that appear in two or more forms of tradition (e.g. sayings, parables, stories) may be regarded as ancient and widespread. Examples would include the kingdom of God, association with sinners, and certain halakic disputes.

[33] It has also been argued, and I think rightly in most cases, that the burden of proof shifts in favor of *authenticity* when material is multiply attested; cf. H.K. McArthur, 'The Burden of Proof in Historical Jesus Research', *ExpTim* 82 (1970–71), pp. 116-19.

[34] See D.G.A. Calvert, 'An Examination of the Criteria for Distinguishing the Authentic Words of Jesus', *NTS* 18 (1972), pp. 209-19. Calvert comments: 'The inclusion of material which does not especially serve his purpose may well be taken as a testimony to the authenticity of that material, or at least to the inclusion of it in the tradition of the Church in such a clear and consistent way that the evangelist was loath to omit it' (p. 219). This criterion is not precisely the same as that of the criterion of embarrassment, but it is cognate. In the case of the latter, authenticity is supported when the tradition cannot easily be explained as the creation of the Church in general; in the case of the former, authenticity is supported when the tradition cannot easily be explained as the creation of a given evangelist or his community.

[35] Meier, *A Marginal Jew*, I, p. 169.

[36] N. Perrin, *Rediscovering the Teaching of Jesus* (London: SCM Press; New

soundly criticized.[37] There are at least two problems with this understanding of the criterion: (1) Jesus was a Jew; we should expect his teachings and actions to reflect Jewish ideas and customs. Why must authentic materials be dissimilar to 'characteristic emphases...of ancient Judaism'? This thinking, which is clearly rooted in Bultmann's *History of the Synoptic Tradition* and presupposed in his *Jesus*,[38] in my opinion grows out of a theology that places great emphasis on how Jesus was different from (i.e. 'superior to') Judaism. In essence, what we have in Bultmann and his pupils is apologetics, not history. So far as the requirements of logic are concerned, there are no legitimate grounds for skepticism simply because dominical tradition sometimes reflects characteristic emphases of first-century Judaism.[39] Jesus was, moreover, the

---

York: Harper & Row, 1967), p. 39. For a similar statement of the principle, see Käsemann, *Essays on New Testament Themes*, p. 37.

[37] See the studies by M.D. Hooker, 'On Using the Wrong Tool', *Theol* 75 (1972), pp. 570-81, esp. pp. 574-75; D.L. Mealand, 'The Dissimilarity Test', *SJT* 31 (1978), pp. 41-50; Stein, 'The "Criteria" for Authenticity', pp. 240-45; B.D. Chilton, *A Galilean Rabbi and his Bible: Jesus' Own Interpretation of Isaiah* (London: SPCK, 1984), pp. 86-87; Sanders, *Jesus and Judaism*, pp. 16-17, 252-55; Evans, 'Authenticity Criteria', pp. 15-16; Sanders and Davies, *Studying the Synoptic Gospels*, pp. 301-33.

[38] For example, see Bultmann, *History of the Synoptic Tradition*, pp. 102-108; esp. *idem, Jesus* (Berlin: Deutsche Bibliothek, 1926), esp. pp. 15-18; ET *Jesus and the Word* (New York: Scribners, 1934), esp. pp. 12-15. I refer to these pages in *Synoptic Tradition* because they illustrate Bultmann's skepticism with regard to various proverbial sayings attributed to Jesus *because of their similarities with rabbinic proverbial sayings*. There is simply no good reason for doubting the authenticity of dominical tradition simply because it parallels genres and styles of first-century Palestine. Skepticism must be justified on other grounds.

[39] In sharp contrast to Bultmann and his pupils, Geza Vermes has emphasized the Jewish parallels, not only as authentic in most cases, but as essential for understanding Jesus; cf. G. Vermes, *Jesus the Jew* (London: Collins; Philadelphia: Fortress Press, 1973); *idem, Jesus and the World of Judaism* (London: SCM Press; Philadelphia: Fortress Press, 1983); *idem, The Religion of Jesus the Jew* (London: SCM Press; Minneapolis: Fortress Press, 1993). Other Jewish scholars have emphasized the importance of Jesus' Jewishness; cf. D. Flusser, *Jesus in Selbstzeugnissen und Bilddokumenten* (Rowohlts Monographien, 140; Hamburg: Rowohlt, 1968); ET *Jesus* (New York: Herder & Herder, 1969); P. Lapide, *Der Rabbi von Nazaret: Wandlungen des jüdischen Jesusbildes* (Trier: Spee, 1974). The Jewish interest in Jesus has been recently discussed by D.A. Hagner, *The Jewish Reclamation of Jesus: An Analysis and Critique of Modern Jewish Study of Jesus* (Grand Rapids: Zondervan, 1984).

founder of a movement that was devoted to him and to his teaching. Should we not then expect many of Jesus' emphases to carry over into the movement? It is reasoned that, since much of the Church's teaching is indebted to the teaching of Jesus, it is probable that some of the early Church's emphases likewise grew out of those of Jesus' teaching. Sayings that cohere with early Christian emphases but are in various ways inconsistent with other sayings are appropriate candidates for exclusion. (2) Employment of the criterion of dissimilarity has also been criticized for its tendency to exclude material too readily. Instead, the criterion should be used to ascertain a core of reasonably certain material. In other words, the criterion is valid in a *positive*, not *negative* application.

5. Semiticisms and Palestinian Background. Meier subdivides this criterion into two related criteria: 'Traces of Aramaic' and 'Palestinian Environment'. He admits that they have some value in making negative assessments (i.e. linguistic and environmental elements foreign to first-century Palestine probably do not derive from Jesus, but from later, non-Palestinian segments of the early Church), but he doubts that these criteria have much value for making positive judgments.[40] All that Semiticisms and Palestinian features prove is that a given saying originated in an Aramaic-speaking Palestinian community, not that it necessarily originated with Jesus. To an extent, Meier is right. There is no question that Joachim Jeremias and others sometimes claimed too much on the basis of Aramaic and Palestinian elements.[41] Nevertheless, I think these criteria do make an important contribution, perhaps mostly in a general way.

The Gospels are written in Greek, and yet they purport to record the sayings of Jesus who in all probability spoke primarily in Aramaic. If these Greek sayings in reality represent the utterances of the Aramaic-speaking Jesus,[42] we should expect to find traces of the

---

[40]   Meier, *A Marginal Jew*, I, pp. 178-80. A similar negative evaluation is offered by Sanders and Davies, *Studying the Synoptic Gospels*, pp. 333-34.

[41]   For illustrations, see J. Jeremias, *Neutestamentliche Theologie. I. Die Verkündigung Jesu* (Gütersloh: Mohn, 1971), pp. 14-45; ET *New Testament Theology: The Proclamation of Jesus* (London: SCM Press; New York: Scribners, 1971), pp. 3-37. See also the older work by G. Dalman, *Die Worte Jesu mit Berücksichtung des nach kanonischen jüdischen Schrifttums und der aramäistischen Sprache erörtert* (Leipzig: Hinrichs, 1898), pp. 13-34; ET *The Words of Jesus* (Edinburgh: T. & T. Clark, 1902), pp. 17-42.

[42]   On the question of the language(s) spoken by Jesus, see J.A. Fitzmyer,

Aramaic language. And indeed we do. We find Aramaic words and idioms that are foreign to Greek but at home in Aramaic.[43] Aramaic language and Palestinian elements do not of course prove the authenticity of any given saying, though they add a measure of support and, in general, they instill in the historian the confidence that the tradition is ancient and bears the characteristics one should expect of authentic dominical tradition. I believe that it is therefore appropriate to regard the criterion of Semiticisms and Palestinian background as playing an important supporting role with respect to the other criteria.[44]

6. *Coherence*. Finally, the criterion of coherence (or consistency) should also be considered as a valid canon of authenticity. It justifies the broadening of the core of material established as authentic through appeal to the criteria described above. Accordingly, material that coheres or is consistent with material judged authentic may also be regarded as authentic.[45] However, Meier rightly warns that this criterion should not be applied too rigorously, especially negatively, to exclude material as inauthentic.[46]

PRACTICE OF EXEGESIS

The interpretation of the words and activities of Jesus necessarily involves several aspects of philological, cultural, and historical study. Exegetes of the Jesus tradition must consider (a) linguistic features,

---

'The Languages of Palestine in the First Century A.D.', *CBQ* 32 (1970), pp. 501-31, p. 21, rev. and repr. in S.E. Porter (ed.), *The Language of the New Testament: Classic Essays* (JSNTSup, 60; Sheffield: JSOT Press, 1991), pp. 126-62; J.A. Fitzmyer, 'Methodology in the Study of the Aramaic Substratum of Jesus' Sayings in the New Testament', in J. Dupont (ed.), *Jésus aux origines de la christologie* (BETL, 40; Gembloux: Duculot, 1975), pp. 73-102 rev. and repr. in Fitzmyer, *A Wandering Aramean: Collected Aramaic Essays* (SBLMS, 25; Missoula, MT: Scholars Press, 1979), pp. 1-56; and S.E. Porter, 'Jesus and the Use of Greek in Galilee', in Chilton and Evans (eds.), *Studying the Historical Jesus*, pp. 123-54.

[43]   For a recent study reassessing the criteria used in identifying the presence of Semiticisms, see E.C. Maloney, *Semitic Interference in Marcan Syntax* (SBLDS, 51; Chico, CA: Scholars Press, 1981).

[44]   For a lucid and compelling demonstration of the value of targumic tradition for the identification and clarification of potentially authentic dominical tradition, see Chilton, *Galilean Rabbi*; *idem*, 'Targumic Transmission and Dominical Tradition', in France and Wenham (eds.), *Studies of History and Tradition*, pp. 21-45.

[45]   See Perrin, *Rediscovering the Teaching of Jesus*, p. 43.

[46]   Meier, *A Marginal Jew*, I, pp. 176-77.

(b) teaching conventions, (c) the Scriptures of Israel and the ways in which they were interpreted, and (d) the social, political, and economic context of first-century Palestine. The following examples should illustrate the importance of these aspects of our work.

A. *Linguistic Aspects*

Linguistic study is closely tied to several, and perhaps in some cases all, of the dimensions of Jesus research. This field proves to be difficult and contentious, for no fewer than four languages were alive and well in first-century Palestine: Aramaic, Greek, Hebrew, and Latin (in their probable order of usage among Jews).[47] How many of these languages Jesus himself made use of, and to what extent, continues to be debated.[48] In my judgment, the majority view that Jesus' mother tongue was Aramaic and that he could converse in Greek, but normally did not teach in it, is compelling. That Jesus knew some Latin and Hebrew is probable, but it is impossible to determine how much of these languages he might have known.[49]

The following examples largely reflect the Aramaic language, though in some instances other languages may also be relevant. These examples are intended only to expose the novice to linguistic study and to various ways in which it can sometimes aid the exegetical task.

---

[47]   On the languages of first-century Palestine, see J.M. Grintz, 'Hebrew as the Spoken and Written Language in the Last Days of the Second Temple', *JBL* 79 (1960), pp. 32-47; Fitzmyer, 'Languages of Palestine', pp. 501-31; A.W. Argyle, 'Greek among the Jews of Palestine in New Testament Times', *NTS* 20 (1973–74), pp. 87-89; C. Rabin, 'Hebrew and Aramaic in the First Century', in S. Safrai and M. Stern (eds.), *The Jewish People in the First Century* (2 vols.; CRINT, 1.2; Assen: Van Gorcum; Philadelphia: Fortress, 1974, 1976), II, pp. 1007-39.

[48]   On the language of Jesus, see A.W. Argyle, 'Did Jesus Speak Greek?', *ExpTim* 67 (1955–56), pp. 92-93, 383; J.A. Emerton, 'Did Jesus Speak Hebrew?', *JTS* 12 (1961), pp. 189-202; H. Ott, 'Um die Muttersprache Jesu: Forschungen seit G. Dalman', *NovT* 9 (1967), pp. 1-25; J. Barr, 'Which Language Did Jesus Speak?—Some Remarks of a Semitist', *BJRL* 53 (1970), pp. 9-29; G.R. Selby, *Jesus, Aramaic and Greek* (Gingley-on-the-Hill: Brynmill, 1989); J.M. Ross, 'Jesus's Knowledge of Greek', *IBS* 12 (1990), pp. 41-47; Meier, *A Marginal Jew*, I, pp. 255-68; Porter, 'Jesus and the Use of Greek in Galilee', pp. 123-54.

[49]   A large part of this problem has to do with the fact that we simply do not know what the extent of Jesus' education was. It seems probable that Jesus had some education, because (1) he was a devout Jewish man and (2) he was called 'rabbi' or 'teacher'. On Jesus' education, see Meier, *A Marginal Jew*, I, pp. 268-78.

(1) 'Qorban'. In the context of debate with some Pharisees and scribes Jesus refers to the practice of qorban: 'You say, "If a person should say to his father or mother, 'Whatever from me you might be owed is "Qorban" (which is "Gift")', you no longer permit him to do anything for his father or mother"' (Mark 7:11-12). Mark's κορβᾶν renders קָרְבָּן (or קֻרְבָּן), and is appropriately translated by δῶρον, 'gift' (cf. LXX Leviticus and Numbers).

Commentators in the past have frequently referred to passages in Josephus and in the Mishnah. Passages in the latter may be somewhat misleading, however, in that an imprecatory element often seems to be present (cf. *m. Ned.* 1:2, 4; קָרְבָּן seems to be used as a synonym of קוֹנָם, which means 'forbidden'), while passages in the former are vague and so are not too helpful (cf. Josephus, *Ant.* 4:4:4 §§72-73; *Apion* 1:22 §§166-167: 'Qorban...means God's gift').

Fitzmyer has rightly directed our attention to an ossuary inscription, which provides us with a close parallel to the language found in Mark 7.[50] The late first-century inscription reads:

כל די אנש מתהנה בחלתה דה

קרבן אלה מן דבגוה

Everything that a man will find to his profit in this ossuary
(is) an offering to God from the one within it.

This inscription carries with it no imprecation. It is simply an affirmation that all that is profitable within the ossuary has been given to God as a gift. To take anything from it would be to steal from God. The parallel with the words of Jesus seems apposite. Jesus complains that the Pharisees make a gift to God (which to take back would be stealing from God) of what might have been used in support of their parents. In adhering to this oral tradition, the written command to honor one's parents could often be nullified.[51]

(2) 'Mammon'. Jesus is remembered to have told his disciples, 'You cannot serve God and mammon' (Matt. 6:24 = Luke 16:13).

---

[50] J.A. Fitzmyer, *Essays on the Semitic Background of the New Testament* (London: Chapman, 1971; repr. SBLSBS, 5; Missoula, MT: Scholars Press, 1974), pp. 93-100; *idem, A Wandering Aramean*, pp. 11, 24 n. 56; *idem* and D.J. Harrington, *A Manual of Palestinian Aramaic Texts* (BibOr, 34; Rome: Biblical Institute Press, 1978), pp. 168, 222-23. Also see the discussion in R.A. Guelich, *Mark 1–8:26* (WBC, 34A; Dallas: Word, 1989), pp. 368-71.

[51] The command to honor one's parents (Exod. 20:12 = Deut. 5:16) came to be understood as a command to provide for their physical necessities (cf. Prov. 28:24; 1 Tim. 5:4).

The Lukan evangelist clusters two other mammon sayings around the one he shares with Matthew: 'Make for yourselves friends from the mammon of unrighteousness' (Luke 16:9); 'If then you have not been faithful in the unrighteous mammon, who will entrust to you true (wealth)?' (Luke 16:11). Jesus' use of the word in reference to money or wealth is not remarkable, but his association of it in two of the sayings with unrighteousness calls for comment.

'Mammon' is a transliteration of μαμωνᾶς, which in turn is a transliteration of either the Hebrew מָמוֹן or the Aramaic מָמוֹן (or מָמוֹנָא in the emphatic state), which means 'wealth', 'riches', or 'property' in both languages. There are at least four occurrences of the word in the Dead Sea Scrolls. The first three are found in Hebrew texts. The first is fragmentary and reads: 'He will have no success in anything. Thus, all the good his wealth (מָמוֹנוֹ)...' (1Q27 1 ii 5). It seems to be part of a polemic directed against those who put their faith in wealth. The second example also finds itself in a fragmentary context: '...in property (בְּמָמוֹן) and he knows...' (CD 14:20). In this instance, it is impossible to ascertain the point that is being made, although it is probably a critical one. The third Hebrew occurrence is found in 1QS 6:2: 'And the lesser shall obey the greater in matters of work or property (מָמוֹן)'. The fourth occurrence, which is Aramaic and must be restored in part, is found in 11QtgJob 11:8 (= Job 27:17): 'and the true one will divide his money (ממונה)'. Here 'mammon' has replaced 'silver'.

Perhaps the earliest attested Hebrew usage of מָמוֹן is found in the Hebrew version of Sirach (at 31:8). This part of Hebrew Sirach is not preserved in the fragments found at Masada or in caves 2 and 11 of Qumran, but there is a good chance that it was part of the original Hebrew Sirach (which dates to the early part of the second century BCE). The Hebrew version reads: 'Blessed is the man who is found blameless and after wealth (מָמוֹן) does not turn aside'.

The word is also used in rabbinic literature, usually without any negative associations. 'Rabbi Yose said: "Let the property (מָמוֹן) of your fellow be as dear to you as your own"' (*'Abot* 2:12). More examples could be found in the Talmuds (cf. *b. Ber.* 61b ['a man who values his life more than his money']; *y. Nazir* 5:4; *y. Sanh.* 8:8) and the Midrashim (cf. *Gen. Rab.* 39:11 [on Gen. 12:2]; *Exod. Rab.* 31:3 [on Exod. 22:24]; *Exod. Rab.* 31:11 [on Exod. 22:24]). The later Targums also use the word: 'What profit (מָמוֹן) will we have?' (*Targ. Neof.* Gen. 37:26; cf. 36:6; *Targ. Onq.* Exod. 21:30).

Fitzmyer is critical of Matthew Black's preference for the Aramaic background of the word.[52] Because there are some early examples of מָמוֹן in Hebrew (as reviewed above), Fitzmyer sees no need to have recourse to later Aramaic examples.[53] (The Job Targum from cave 11 of Qumran provides the only indisputably early Aramaic example.) Fitzmyer's criticisms are justified, so far as the evidence adduced by Black goes.

Recently, Bruce Chilton has called our attention to examples in the Isaiah Targum that may force us once again to look to Aramaic as the background against which Jesus' understanding of the word ought to be understood.[54] Chilton has observed that, in the Isaiah Targum, mammon is consistently used in a negative sense (*Targ. Isa.* 5:23; 33:15; 45:13; 55:1; 56:11; 57:17). Two of these examples are potentially quite significant. In 5:23, the Hebrew's 'bribe' becomes in the Aramaic 'mammon of deceit' (מָמוֹן דִּשְׁקָר),[55] while in 57:17 the Hebrew's 'iniquity of his covetousness' becomes in the Aramaic 'sins of their mammon' (חוֹבֵי מָמוֹנְהוֹן). Chilton rightly observes how closely this language approximates the expressions attributed to Jesus: 'from the mammon of unrighteousness (ἐκ τοῦ μαμωνᾶ τῆς ἀδικίας)' (Luke 16:9) and 'with unrighteous mammon (ἐν τῷ ἀδίκῳ μαμωνᾷ)' (Luke 16:11). Chilton does not think that in this instance Jesus has alluded to targumic tradition. He believes rather that the Isaiah Targum 'employs language which corresponds to that of Jesus'.[56]

Given the strong probability that Jesus regularly taught in Aramaic (not Hebrew) and that the use of מָמוֹן in the Isaiah Targum parallels Jesus' language more closely than other sources currently available,

---

[52]   As seen in M. Black, *An Aramaic Approach to the Gospels and Acts* (Oxford: Clarendon Press, 3rd edn, 1967), pp. 139-40.

[53]   Fitzmyer, *A Wandering Aramean*, pp. 11-12.

[54]   Chilton, *Galilean Rabbi*, pp. 117-23.

[55]   This is how Chilton translates it; but see J.F. Stenning (*The Targum of Isaiah* [Oxford: Clarendon Press, 1949], p. 18) who translates 'unjust gain'. The LXX sometimes translates שֶׁקֶר with ἄδικος (Exod. 23:7; 1 Kgs 25:21; Pss. 118:118; 119:2), ἀδικία (Pss. 7:14 [B]; 118:104, 163; 143:34), and ἀδίκως (Lev. 6:3-4; Job 36:4; Pss. 34:19; 37:19; 68:4; 118:78, 86; Ezek. 13:22). The frequent association of ἄδικος with the tongue (Prov. 6:17; 12:19) or with speech (Exod. 23:7; Lev. 19:12; Deut. 19:18; Job 36:4; Pss. 26:12; 62:11; 100:7; Prov. 14:5; 29:12; Isa. 32:7; 59:13; Jer. 5:31; 7:9) suggests that 'deceit' was not an unusual meaning for this word.

[56]   Chilton, *Galilean Rabbi*, p. 123.

it seems prudent, *pace* Fitzmyer, to refer to Aramaic after all.[57]

(3) 'The Lord said to my lord'. Jesus' citation and interpretation of Ps. 110:1 has occasioned a great deal of scholarly discussion. The passage (Mark 12:35-37; cf. Matt. 12:41-46; Luke 20:41-44) reads:

> How do the scribes say that the Christ is the son of David? David himself said in the Holy Spirit, 'The Lord said to my lord, "Sit at my right hand, until I place your enemies beneath your feet"'. David himself calls him 'lord', how is he then his son?

Scholars have asserted that Jesus' exegesis seems to presuppose that the words translated 'Lord/lord' are the same. This is true in the LXX, where κύριος is found (εἶπεν κύριος τῷ κυρίῳ μου), but not in the Hebrew (נאם יהוה לאדני), where it is 'Yahweh' who speaks to David's 'adonai'. Because of this, some scholars question the authenticity of the saying (because, it is assumed, Jesus would not appeal to the Greek version of the Jewish Scriptures). But Fitzmyer has pointed out that, by the time of Jesus, 'adonai' had become a substitute for the divine name, and that the Aramaic מרא was used to translate both יהוה and אדני. Jesus' Aramaic form of the citation of Ps. 110:1 might have gone something like: אֲמַר מָרֵא לְמָרֵאי.[58] Fitzmyer thinks that Jesus meant to imply that the Messiah was greater than the epithet 'son of David' implied. Whereas it may be true that the Messiah would be David's son, it is also true that he would be David's lord.[59]

(4) 'Son of God'. It has been observed that there is no Jewish, Palestinian text in which the Messiah is called the 'son of God'. Thus, Bultmann and others have claimed that calling Jesus 'son of God', as

---

[57] Throughout his work (esp. *Galilean Rabbi*), Chilton has shown how, at many points, Jesus' language and understanding of Scripture reflect traditions preserved in the Isaiah Targum.

[58] In the Targum, Ps. 110:1 is understood to refer to David, and not to an eschatological Messiah: 'A Psalm by the hand of David. The Lord (יהוה) said by his memra that he will make me the master of all Israel. However, he said to me: "Sit and wait until Saul, who is of the tribe of Benjamin, does, so that one kingdom may not crowd out the other. After that I will make your enemies your footstool."'

[59] See Fitzmyer, *Essays on the Semitic Background of the New Testament*, pp. 113-26; *idem, A Wandering Aramean*, p. 90; D. Daube, *The New Testament and Rabbinic Judaism* (London: Athlone, 1956), pp. 158-63; B.D. Chilton, 'Jesus ben David: Reflections on the Davidssohnfrage', *JSNT* 14 (1982), pp. 88-112; repr. in C.A. Evans and S.E. Porter (eds.), *The Historical Jesus: A Sheffield Reader* (BibSem, 33; Sheffield: JSOT Press, 1995), pp. 192-215.

though it were a messianic title, arose in the Greek-speaking Church, under the influence of Hellenism and the Roman emperor cult (in which the emperor was routinely called 'son of god').[60] The discovery of 4Q246, the so-called 'Son of God' text, has forced scholars to reconsider this thinking. This fragmentary text anticipates the coming of one who

> will be called [son of] the [gr]eat [God], and by his name shall he be named. He shall be hailed 'Son of God' (ברה די אל), and they shall call him 'Son of the Most High' (בר עליון)...his kingdom (shall be) an everlasting kingdom, and all his ways (shall be) in truth (4Q246 1:9–2:1, 5-6).

The appearance of this epithet in Luke 1:32-35 (Gabriel's announcement to Mary) significantly suggests that it was understood not only to apply to Davidic tradition, but in a messianic sense as well. The angelic annunciation, moreover, contains unmistakable allusions to the Davidic covenant (cf. 2 Sam. 7:12-16). The relevant parts of the Lukan passage read:

> He shall be great and he shall be called Son of the Most High; and the Lord God will give to him the throne of David his father. And he will reign over the house of Jacob forever; and his kingdom will have no end... The power of the Most High will overshadow you; therefore that which has been conceived will be called holy, Son of God.

The parallels between 4Q246 and the angelic annunciation are stunning, and lend support to the messianic interpretation of this important Aramaic text from Qumran.[61]

---

60   R. Bultmann, *Theology of the New Testament* (2 vols.; New York: Scribners, 1951, 1955), I, pp. 130-31; F. Hahn, *The Titles of Jesus in Christology* (London: Lutterworth; Cleveland: World, 1969), pp. 291, 293.

61   For critical discussion of 4Q246 and its relevance for Luke 1:32-35, see Fitzmyer, *Essays on the Semitic Background of the New Testament*, pp. 127-60; *idem, A Wandering Aramean*, pp. 90-94, 102-107; *idem*, '4Q246: The "Son of God" Document from Qumran', *Bib* 74 (1993), pp. 153-74 (+ pl.). Fitzmyer is not yet persuaded that the 'son of God' in 4Q246 is a messianic personage. Others are convinced that he is such a figure; cf. J.J. Collins, 'The *Son of God* Text from Qumran', in M.C. De Boer (ed.), *From John to Jesus: Essays on Jesus and the New Testament in Honour of Marinus de Jonge* (JSNTSup, 84; Sheffield: JSOT Press, 1993), pp. 65-82; rev. and repr. in Collins, *The Scepter and the Star: The Messiahs of the Dead Sea Scrolls and Other Ancient Literature* (ABRL; New York: Doubleday, 1995), pp. 154-72; Evans, *Jesus and his Contemporaries*, pp. 107-11. Davidic traditions in which God promises to be 'Father' to David's heir and he as 'son' to God (2 Sam. 7:14; 1 Chron. 17:13; Ps. 2:7) are what ultimately lie behind

Moreover, we now see that the Gerasene demoniac's address to Jesus as 'son of the Most High God' (Mark 5:7) is right at home in first-century Palestine. That both epithets, 'son of God' and 'son of the Most High,' occur in a Dead Sea Scroll tells against the suggestion that this language derives from non-Palestinian Hellenistic sources.

(5) There are other dominical words and phrases that find parallels in Aramaic sources from the time of Jesus. Some of these include the following:

'Lord of heaven and earth'. This phrase appears in a prayer attributed to Jesus (κύριε τοῦ οὐρανοῦ καὶ τῆς γῆς; Matt. 11:25 = Luke 10:21) and in Melchizedek's prayer, according to the Aramaic Genesis Apocryphon (מרה שמיא וארעא; 1QapGen 22:16).[62] The use of this epithet in prayer may have further significance, when we remember that, in the Lord's Prayer, Jesus asks that God's will be done 'on earth, as it is in heaven' (Matt. 6:10).

'with desire I desired'. In the words of institution that are found only in Luke, Jesus tells his disciples that 'with desire have I desired (ἐπιθυμίᾳ ἐπεθύμησα) to eat this Passover (meal)' (Luke 22:15). A century ago, Gustaf Dalman thought that Hebrew must underlie this manner of speaking, because the 'Hebrew mode of emphasizing the finite verb by adding its infinitive or cognate substantive[63]...is in the Palestinian Aramaic of the Jews—apart from the Targums—quite unknown'. This opinion was later repeated by Black,[64] but we now have an Aramaic parallel from the approximate time of Jesus: 'and weeping (ובכיה) I Abram wept (בכי)' (1QapGen 20:10-11).[65]

'debtors'. Jesus' understanding of 'debtors' as 'sinners', and vice versa, reflects Aramaic usage, and sheds light on an important aspect of his teaching. The Parable of the Unforgiving Servant (Matt. 18:23-35) and the Parable of the Two Debtors (Luke 7:41-43) presuppose the equation of sins and debts. This equivalency is also seen in the Lord's Prayer (Matt. 6:9-13 = Luke 11:2-4). Matthew's 'forgive us our debts' (τὰ ὀφειλήματα) in Luke becomes 'forgive us our sins'

---

the 'son of God' epithet.

[62] See Fitzmyer, *A Wandering Aramean*, pp. 98-99; *idem, Luke*, II, p. 872.

[63] For example, see Isa. 6:9 ('hearing hear...seeing see').

[64] Dalman, *The Words of Jesus*, p. 34; Black, *An Aramaic Approach*, p. 238.

[65] As noted by Fitzmyer, *A Wandering Aramean*, p. 112 n. 58. On the Aramaic substratum underlying the words of institution (Mark 14:22-23 = Luke 22:19b-20), see Fitzmyer, *Luke*, II, pp. 1394-95.

(τὰς ἁμαρτίας).[66] Jesus' rhetorical question in Luke 13:4 ('were they worse debtors (ὀφειλέται) than all those who dwell in Jerusalem?') refers, of course, to sinners, not to persons who were in financial difficulties.

The Greek phenomena reflect the Aramaic חוֹבָה, which means 'sin' or 'debt'. There are several examples in the Targums, where the Hebrew חֵטְא ('sin') or חַטָּאת ('to sin') is translated with חוֹבָה (cf. MT and *Targ. Neof.* Gen. 18:20-24; Exod. 32:30-33; Num. 12:11; Deut. 15:9; 19:15; 23:23; *Targ. Isa.* 1:18; 31:7; 53:12). The cognates חַיָּיב/חַיָּיבָא also translate חַטָּאת/חֶטְאָה (cf. *Targ. Isa.* 1:28; 13:9; 33:14), as well as various synonyms of 'sinner'. For examples of the latter, see *Targ. Onq.* Gen. 18:23 and *Targ.* Job 38:13 where חַיָּיבָא translates רָשָׁע ('wicked'). One should note also how the Hebrew 'Will you condemn me that you may be justified?' (Job 40:8) becomes in the targum from Qumran 'Will you again set judgment aside and condemn me as a debtor [*or* sinner: ותחיבני] that you may be clean?' (11QtgJob 34:4).[67]

'amen' and 'in truth'. Jesus' habit of introducing many of his pronouncements with 'amen' or 'in truth' is a distinctive feature of his teaching style. Sayings with good claim to authenticity include Mark 8:12 ('Amen, I say to you, no sign shall be given to this generation') and 9:1 ('Amen, I say to you, there are some standing here who will not taste death before they see that the kingdom of God has come in power').[68] What is noteworthy here is that Jesus

---

[66]   It is interesting to observe that in the *Even Bohan* (a medieval work that contains a Hebrew translation of the Gospel of Matthew) 'debts' is translated 'sins' (חטא). For text, translation, and arguments for the antiquity of this Hebrew version of Matthew, see G. Howard, *The Gospel of Matthew according to a Primitive Hebrew Text* (Macon, GA: Mercer University Press, 1987).

[67]   For discussion, see Black, *An Aramaic Approach*, p. 140; Fitzmyer, *Luke*, II, pp. 1007-1008; M. McNamara, *Targum and Testament: Aramaic Paraphrases of the Hebrew Bible* (Shannon: Irish University Press; Grand Rapids: Eerdmans, 1972), pp. 120-21; J.A. Sanders, 'Sins, Debts, and Jubilee Release', in C.A. Evans and J.A. Sanders, *Luke and Scripture: The Function of Sacred Tradition in Luke–Acts* (Minneapolis: Fortress Press, 1993), pp. 84-92.

[68]   A major factor in favor of the authenticity of these lies in the difficulties they created for the early Church. In the case of the first saying, early Christians wanted to claim that Jesus in fact did provide his generation with a sign, namely, the 'sign of Jonah'—the resurrection of Jesus (cf. Matt. 12:38-41). Indeed, in the fourth Gospel, Jesus' entire ministry is described in terms of 'signs'. In the case of the second saying, early Christians struggled to explain in what sense the kingdom of

introduces sayings with 'amen' or 'in truth', while the norm was to conclude a saying or prayer with this word (from the Bible, see Num. 5:22; Deut. 27:15; Neh. 8:6; Ps. 41:13; from sources that date approximately to the time of Jesus, see 1QS 1:20; 2:10; 4QBerakot 10 ii 1, 5, 10; 4Q504 3 ii 3; *passim*).

The word ἀμήν is a transliteration of אָמֵן. The Lukan evangelist, or the tradition that he inherited, sometimes translates with either a prepositional phrase or the adverbial equivalent: 'In truth [ἐπ' ἀληθείας] I say to you, there were many widows in Israel in the days of Elijah...' (4:25; cf. 9:27 [ἀληθῶς]; 12:44; 21:3; 22:59). Greek equivalents are also found elsewhere (cf. Mark 12:14, 32; Dan. 2:47 [translates קְשֹׁט]; *T. Dan.* 2:1). A parallel of this last example is found in 1QapGen. 2:5: ' ...in truth (בקושטא) you make everything known to me' (cf. 2:6, 7, 10, 18, 22). Examples of the asseverative usage of בקושטא can be found in the targums (cf. *Targ. Onq.* Gen. 3:1; 17:19; *Targ. Isa.* 37:18; 45:14, 15). The Hebrew אָמֵן is itself carried over into the targums, including two relatively rare instances of the asseverative usage (1 Kgs 1:36; Jer. 28:6).[69] Chilton wonders if Jesus' distinctive habit of introducing pronouncements with the asseverative 'amen'/'in truth' is yet again another parallel with targumic diction.[70]

B. Teaching Conventions

Jesus' parables, proverbs, and prayers parallel the teaching conventions attested in rabbinic sources (which admittedly derive from sources that postdate the New Testament) and, in some instances, in sources from the time of Jesus. Although the rabbinic materials are from a later time, certain formal and thematic features that closely parallel features found in Jesus' parables may be relevant and may be helpful.[71]

God actually came, before the death of Jesus' contemporaries.

[69] See K. Berger, 'Zur Geschichte des Einleitungsformel "Amen ich sage euch"', *ZNW* 63 (1972), pp. 45-75; B.D. Chilton, '"Amen": An Approach through Syriac Gospels', *ZNW* 69 (1978), pp. 203-11; *idem*, 'Amen', *ABD* 1 (1992), pp. 184-86; J. Strugnell, '"Amen, I say Unto You" in the Sayings of Jesus', *HTR* 67 (1974), pp. 177-82; J.A. Fitzmyer, *The Genesis Apocryphon of Qumran Cave I: A Commentary* (BibOr, 18A; Rome: Biblical Institute Press, 1971), pp. 84-85; *idem, Luke*, I, p. 537.

[70] Chilton, *Galilean Rabbi*, p. 202.

[71] For proposed critical guidelines for making use of rabbinic literature in Jesus research, see C.A. Evans, 'Early Rabbinic Sources and Jesus Research', in

1. Parables. Thematically, the parables of Jesus and the later parables of the rabbis have many things in common. Half of Jesus' parables deal with the 'kingdom of God'; half of the rabbinic parables speak of a 'king' (who is usually understood to be God). In the rabbinic parables, 'kingdom' is sometimes defined as God's dominion or sphere of rule (cf. *Mek.* on Exod. 20:2 [*Baḥodeš* §5]; *Sipra Lev.* §194 [on Lev. 18:1-30]). In Jesus' parables, the kingdom of God seems best understood as 'realm' or 'dominion' (cf. Luke 11:20). The characters of the parables of Jesus and the rabbis often behave in illogical and extreme ways. Finally, the rabbinic parables employ formal terminology and imagery often found in parables attributed to Jesus.

For examples of this last point, consider the following parallels in formal terminology:

אמשול לך משל: למה הדבר דומה: לאדם שנושה בחבירו מנה—'I will give you a parable. To what does this matter compare? To a man who lent his neighbor a mina...' (*b. Roš Haš.* 17b).

משל למלך שזימן את עבדיו לסעודה—'It compares to a king who summoned his servants to a banquet...' (*b. Šabb.* 153a).

ἄλλην παραβολὴν παρέθηκεν αὐτοῖς λέγων, ὡμοιώθη ἡ βασιλεία τῶν οὐρανῶν ἀνθρώπῳ σπείραντι καλὸν σπέρμα...—'He set before them another parable, saying, "The kingdom of Heaven may be compared to a man who sowed good seed..."' (Matt. 13:24).

τίνι ὁμοία ἡ βασιλεία τοῦ θεοῦ καὶ τίνι ὁμοιώσω αὐτὴν ὁμοία ἐστιν κόκκῳ σινάπεως...—'What is the kingdom of God like and to what shall I compare it? It is like a mustard seed...' (Luke 13:18).

כך נעשה למצרים—'Thus it happened to the Egyptians...' (*Mek.* on Exod. 14:5 [*Bešallaḥ* §2]).

כך אמר להם משה לישראל—'Thus did Moses speak to Israel...' (*Sipre Deut.* §53 [on Deut. 11:26]).

οὕτως ἐστὶν ἡ βασιλεία τοῦ θεοῦ—'Thus is the kingdom of God' (Mark 4:26).

οὕτως ἔσται καὶ τῇ γενεᾷ ταύτῃ τῇ πονηρᾷ—'Thus it will be also with this evil generation' (Matt. 12:45).

The parables of the rabbis often portray characters behaving in irrational and illogical ways. Consider the following parable,

---

E.H. Lovering (ed.), *Society of Biblical Literature 1995 Seminar Papers* (SBLSP, 34; Atlanta: Scholars Press, 1995), pp. 53-76.

attributed to Rabbi Yose the Galilean (second century CE):

> The parable, as told by Rabbi Yose the Galilean, concerned a mortal king who had set out for a city far across the sea. As he was about to entrust his son to the care of a wicked guardian, his friends and servants said to him: 'My lord king, do not entrust your son to this wicked guardian'. Nevertheless the king, ignoring the counsel of his friends and servants, entrusted his son to the wicked guardian. What did the guardian do? He proceeded to destroy the king's city, have his house consumed by fire, and slay his son with the sword. After a while the king returned. When he saw his city destroyed and desolate, his house consumed by fire, his son slain with the sword, he pulled out the hair of his head and his beard and broke out into wild weeping, saying: 'Woe is me! How <foolish> I have been, how senselessly I acted in this kingdom of mine in entrusting my son to a wicked guardian!'[72]

In Yose's parable, we have a man who appears utterly to lack common sense. Against the advice of friends and counselors, he entrusts his son to a man known to be a 'wicked guardian'. However, the actions of the guardian are just as difficult to comprehend. We are not told that he stole anything or profited in any way by his actions. He destroys the king's city, burns down his house, and murders his son. What could he possibly have hoped to gain? Did he imagine that he could get away with these crimes? Would not every hearer of this parable suppose that the king would send troops after the guardian and have him executed?

These are the same kinds of questions some critics have from time to time raised in reference to the Parable of the Vineyard Tenants, as well as other parables. How could the owner of the vineyard be so foolish and so reckless with the lives of his servants and especially with the life of his son? What could the tenants realistically have hoped to gain? Did they not know that the owner had the power to come and destroy them? Did they really imagine that they could inherit the vineyard? One may ask similar questions with respect to the rude behavior of the invited guests of the Parable of the Great Banquet (Luke 14:15-24) or the eccentric behavior of the vineyard owner in the Parable of the Laborers (Matt. 20:1-15).

It is significant to observe that Yose applies his parable to God's trusting his exiled people to Nebuchadnezzar! How could God have

---

[72] Trans. by W.G. Braude and I. Kapstein, *Tanna Děbe Eliyyahu: The Lore of the School of Elijah* (Philadelphia: Jewish Publication Society, 1981), p. 369. The translation has been slightly modified.

been so incautious as to entrust his people to the care of such a villain? We should understand the folly of the vineyard owner and the vineyard tenants in a similar light. Their actions are inexplicable. But the shocking details and the questions these parables raise are supposed to lead the hearers to grasp and apply the intended lesson.

2. Proverbs. There are at least forty proverbial sayings attributed to Jesus in the Synoptic Gospels that closely parallel proverbial sayings found in the rabbinic literature.[73] For example, Jesus asks, 'If the salt has lost its flavor, with what is it to be salted?' (Mark 9:50). The proverb is found verbatim in *b. Ber.* 8b. Again, Jesus admonishes his disciples: 'With what measure you measure, it shall be measured to you again' (Matt. 7:2 = Luke 6:38; Mark 4:24). This proverb appears in the Mishnah, the Tosefta, the Talmud, some of the Midrashim, and in some of the targumic tradition. Jesus' humorous proverbial admonition, 'First remove the beam from your own eye; and then you will see clearly to remove the speck from your brother's eye' (Matt. 7:5), finds a close parallel in the Talmud: 'If one say to him, "Remove the speck from between your eyes", he would answer, "Remove the beam from between your eyes!"' (*b. ʿArak.* 16b).

These parallels are interesting and, in a general sense, help us appreciate the various usages of proverbs in the Jewish world of late antiquity, but sometimes a parallel proverb might actually offer some specific help in the task of interpreting the words of Jesus. One thinks of the episode where Jesus observes the poor widow drop her last penny into one of the offering receptacles in the Temple precincts (Mark 12:41-44). Jesus declares: 'Out of her poverty she put in all that she had, even her own life (βίος)' (v. 44). Christian interpretation has traditionally understood his statement as a word of praise, as though Jesus viewed the widow's sacrificial gift as a good thing, worthy of emulation.[74]

Recently, however, a few interpreters have challenged this position. It has been suggested that Jesus uttered a word of lament, not praise.[75] According to this view, Jesus lamented the failure of the

---

[73] For a listing of these parallels, see G. Dalman, *Jesus–Jeshua: Studies in the Gospels* (London: SPCK, 1929; repr. New York: Ktav, 1971), pp. 225-32; Evans, *Jesus and his Contemporaries*, pp. 269-76.

[74] For example, see W.L. Lane, *The Gospel of Mark* (NICNT; Grand Rapids: Eerdmans, 1974), p. 443.

[75] See A.G. Wright, 'The Widow's Mites: Praise or Lament?—A Matter of

Temple establishment to act as guardian and caretaker of the poor (particularly widows and orphans), as the laws of Moses commanded (cf. Exod. 22:22; Deut. 14:28-29). Rather, the Temple had become a burden for the poor, drawing off their last penny, seemingly sucking the life out of them. When the same proverb appears in a later rabbinic text—and in this context also the priesthood is criticized—one suspects that this new interpretation of the dominical tradition may very well be on target. The rabbinic story reads: 'Once a woman brought a handful of fine flour, and the priest despised her, saying, "See what she offers! What is there in this to offer up?" It was shown to him in a dream: "Do not despise her! It is regarded as if she had sacrificed her own life (נפש)"' (*Lev. Rab.* 3:5 [on Lev. 1:17]). The context of Jesus' pronouncement, where he warns of scribes who 'devour the houses of widows' (Mark 12:38-40), supports a critical interpretation, at least as it is contextualized in the Synoptic Gospels. But the function of the parallel pronouncement in the rabbinic passage supports a critical interpretation in a setting similar to that of the Synoptic Gospels, perhaps deriving from Jesus himself.

3. Prayers. The prayers of Jesus are eschatological.[76] In his Prayer of Thanksgiving (Matt. 11:25b-26 = Luke 10:21b), Jesus thanks God because he has 'hidden these things from the wise and understanding and revealed them to infants'. What God has hidden from the wise is the presence and nature of the kingdom, or reign, of God. This language alludes to Dan. 2:21-23, in which Daniel thanks God for revealing the meaning of Nebuchadnezzar's dream.[77] Daniel has learned that the kingdom of God will appear and will crush all opposing kingdoms (Dan. 2:44). Likewise, what has been revealed to Jesus and his followers is the appearance of the promised kingdom.

The Lord's Prayer coheres with this eschatological perspective: 'Father, sanctify your name; may your kingdom come' (Luke 11:2).

Context', *CBQ* 44 (1982), pp. 256-65; Fitzmyer, *Luke*, II, pp. 1320-21.

[76] For defense of this claim, see R.E. Brown, 'The Pater Noster as an Eschatological Prayer', *TS* 22 (1961), pp. 175-208; repr. in Brown, *New Testament Essays* (Garden City: Doubleday, 1967), pp. 217-53; Evans, *Jesus and his Contemporaries*, pp. 286-97.

[77] Thanking God for revelation, in language reminiscent of Daniel, is also found in the Dead Sea Scrolls; for example: 'I thank you, O Lord, because you gave me your truth, you have made me know your wonderful mysteries' (1QH 7:26-27).

These opening petitions parallel closely the ancient Jewish prayer known as the Qaddish (the 'holy'): 'May his great name be glorified and sanctified... May he establish his kingdom...speedily and soon.'[78] The Amida ('standing'), also know as the Shemone Esra ('eighteen'), contains petitions that probably reach back to the time of Jesus (though it is not always easy to identify early material). Many of these petitions are also eschatological. Petition §7 pleads for redemption, §8 pleads for healing, §10 pleads for the sounding of the shofar and the gathering of the exiles of Israel, §11 pleads for the restoration of good government in Israel, §12 pleads for the destruction of Rome, and §14 pleads for mercy on Jerusalem and on David, God's 'righteous Messiah'. The Hebrew version of Sirach, at 51:12 (according to the Greek versification), offers thanks to God, who is described as Israel's redeemer, gatherer of the dispersed, and the one who 'makes a horn sprout for the house of David'.

Jesus' eschatological prayers cohere with these Jewish prayers. We find that there is little in Jesus' prayers that is distinctive. They are marked by simplicity and directness. But their eschatological orientation, the hope expressed in them for Israel's redemption, places them squarely within Jewish piety of late antiquity.

C. Scripture and Interpretative Traditions

Another fruitful area of Jesus research involves study of the way the Scripture of Israel was interpreted in late antiquity. Careful, comparative study enables us to see better to what extent Scripture and interpretive traditions informed Jesus' teaching and activities. We must ask several important questions: To what extent did Scripture lie behind Jesus' proclamation and definition of the kingdom of God? What was Jesus' hermeneutic? Did he view Scripture as fulfilled in his ministry? How did his understanding of Scripture differ from that of his contemporaries?

These are difficult questions, but all of them can be answered, at least in part. Our most important source is the dominical tradition itself. We must look at what Scriptures are cited and alluded to, and how they were interpreted. We must look at the Scriptures themselves, as they existed in the time of Jesus. Here the Dead Sea Scrolls are of immense value. Not only do we have portions of 38 of the 39 books that make up what eventually becomes the Hebrew Bible (and the fullest preserved books—Isaiah, Psalms, and

---

[78]   See the analysis in Fitzmyer, *Luke*, II, pp. 900-901.

Deuteronomy—are the very ones that were the most influential in the teaching of Jesus and the early Church), but we have a host of writings that interpret various Scriptures. The Septuagint is also important, not only because one half of all New Testament quotations of the Old Testament are taken from this Greek translation, but also because it preserves interpretive traditions that give us some indications of how Jews of late antiquity understood their Scriptures. The Aramaic paraphrases are also important, though these targums must be used with care, given their relative late dates of composition. The writings of Josephus and Philo, as well as many of the writings that make up the Old Testament Apocrypha and Pseudepigrapha, are also of great value in our attempts to ascertain what Scriptures were important to Jews of late antiquity and how they were interpreted.

The following three examples will illustrate what is involved in this aspect of the exegetical task. We shall see how the Dead Sea Scrolls and the targums are especially useful. The first example treats the potentially embarrassing question raised by the imprisoned John the Baptist, who wonders if Jesus really is the 'coming one'. The second example shows how the Scrolls and targumic tradition sometimes fill in gaps in some of the debates that Jesus had with his contemporaries. The third example illustrates how important Scripture and its popular interpretation in late antiquity are for understanding certain aspects of Jesus' criticism of the religious authorities of his day.

(1) 'Go and tell John what you have seen and heard.' The exchange between John the Baptist (via his messengers) and Jesus (Matt. 11:2-6 = Luke 7:18-23) is so potentially embarrassing to the early Church that its authenticity is virtually guaranteed. It is impossible to imagine why early Christians would invent a story in which John, a major witness and validator of Jesus, his 'successor', would question Jesus' identity and mission. John asked Jesus, 'Are you the one who is coming, or shall we look for another?' Was this a 'messianic' question; and, more importantly, was Jesus' reply messianic? For years, scholars have debated these questions. But the publication of 4Q521, a fragmentary scroll that speaks of God's 'messiah', may have finally resolved the dispute.

The relevant part of the scroll reads (1 ii 1-14):

> [1][*...the hea*]*vens and the earth* will obey His Messiah, [2][*...and all th*]*at is in them.* He will not turn aside from the commandments of the holy ones. [3]Take strength in His service, (you) who seek the Lord. [4]Will you not find

the Lord in this, all you who wait patiently in your hearts? [5]For the Lord will visit the pious ones, and the righteous ones He will call by name. [6]Over the meek His Spirit will hover, and the faithful He will restore by His power. [7]He will glorify the pious ones on the throne of the eternal kingdom. [8]*He will release the captives, make the blind see, raise up the do[wntrodden.]* [9]For[ev]er I shall cling [to Him...], and [I shall trust] in His lovingkindness, [10]and [His] goo[dness...] of holiness will not delay [...] [11]And as for the wonders that are not the work of the Lord, when He [...] [12]then he will heal the slain, resurrect the dead, and *announce glad tidings to the poor.* [13][...] He will lead the [hol]y ones; he will shepherd [th]em; he will do [...] [14]and all of it ...

This text contains several important allusions to Isaiah and Psalms. We find words and phrases from Ps. 146:6, 8 ('heaven and earth...and all that is in them...the Lord opens the eyes of the blind. The Lord lifts up those who are downtrodden'), and Isa. 61:1-2 ('the Lord has anointed me to bring glad tidings to the poor...to proclaim liberty to the captives'). The reference to 'anoint' in the latter passage may tie in the opening statement that the 'heavens and earth obey his anointed (or Messiah)'.

Shortly after the publication of this text, a remarkable parallel with a saying of Jesus was observed. In reply to the Baptist's question Jesus says: 'Go and tell John what you hear and see: the blind receive their sight and the lame walk, lepers are cleansed and the deaf hear, and the dead are raised up, and the poor have good news preached to them'. Jesus' reply alludes to Isa. 61:1-2 ('the Lord has anointed me to bring glad tidings to the poor...to proclaim liberty to the captives') and Isa. 35:5-6 ('the eyes of the blind shall be opened'), or Ps. 146:6 ('the Lord opens the eyes of the blind'). None of the passages to which Jesus alludes say anything about the dead being raised up. This element is, however, present in 4Q521. The principal elements may be compared as follows:

Q (Matt. 11:5 = Luke 7:22)	Isaiah 35 + 61	4Q521
he cured many of diseases		he will heal the slain
blind receive sight	blind receive sight	make blind see
lame walk	lame walk	
lepers are cleansed		
deaf hear	deaf hear	
dead are raised up		*resurrect the dead*
poor have good news preached	poor have good news preached	poor have good news preached

John Collins has suggested that 4Q521 describes the expected activity of a prophetic Messiah.[79] This seems likely, because Isaiah 61 concerns someone anointed to 'bring good news' and to 'proclaim liberty' and 'the year of the Lord's favor'. These are the responsibilities of the eschatological prophet. Indeed, the Aramaic paraphrase renders Isa. 61:1: 'The Prophet said, "A spirit of prophecy...is upon me...to announce good news..."'

4Q521 is apparently describing the works of God's anointed. In all probability, the text is eschatological. These deeds of healing, including raising the dead, will take place when the anointed one appears. Jesus' answer to the Baptist, in that it parallels some of the same Scripture exploited by 4Q521, seems to be an affirmation of his anointed status. Is Jesus the 'one who is coming'? Yes, he is; and this claim is demonstrated by the fact that he is doing the deeds of the anointed one.

(2) 'Do this and you will live.' On one occasion, an expert in the Mosaic Law asked Jesus, 'What must I do to inherit eternal life?' (Luke 10:25). We are told that Jesus in turn asked him what was written in the Law and how did he understand it? The legal expert summarized the Law with the two great commandments, to love God and to love one's neighbor (Luke 10:26-27; cf. Mark 12:28-34, where it is Jesus who affirms the great commandments). To this affirmation Jesus responded: 'You have answered rightly. Do this and you will live' (Luke 10:28).

Most commentators agree that, in saying this, Jesus has alluded to Lev. 18:5, which, according to the Hebrew, reads: 'You shall keep my statutes and my ordinances; a human will do them and will live by them'. The Septuagint reads: 'And you shall keep all my ordinances and my judgments and you shall do them, which having done, a human will live by them'. Neither version says anything about 'eternal life', which was the point of the legal expert's question. Leviticus 18 is concerned with life in this world: If Israelites obey God's Law, they will enjoy life and well-being in the land that God will give them. Why then did Jesus allude to Lev. 18:5,

---

[79]   J.J. Collins, 'The Works of the Messiah', *DSD* 1 (1994), pp. 98-112; *idem, The Scepter and the Star*, pp. 117-22, 205-206. The association with Isaiah 61 lends support to the eschatological prophet interpretation, but the later reference to 'his scepter' (שבטו) leaves open the possibility that the messianic figure of 4Q521 is a royal figure after all. The relevant, but fragmentary text reads: 'May the earth rejoice in all the places [...] for all Israel in the rejoicing of [...] and his scepter [...]' (2 iii 4-6).

as though, in applying it to the legal expert, his question regarding eternal life had been answered? After all, the legal expert did not ask Jesus what he must do to continue living in the land of Israel.

The Damascus Document and the *Psalms of Solomon* may aid us in answering this question. According to the latter (first century BCE) the commandments are 'for our life' and the 'Lord's devout shall live by (the Law) forever' (*Pss. Sol.* 14:1-5). It is not certain that this text alludes specifically to Lev. 18:5, but the idea that obeying the Law will lead to eternal life seems clear enough. The former writing (second century BCE), which was found in the Cairo synagogue genizah and in fragments at Qumran, refers to God's Law, '"which a man should do and live by"… Those who adhere to it will live forever' (CD 3:12-16, 20). This text appears to have alluded to Lev. 18:5, and understands the promise to 'live' in terms of eternal life, and not simply temporal life.

This understanding of Lev 18:5 is made explicit in the targumic tradition. Onqelos expands the key part of the verse to read: 'he will live by them in eternal life (עלמא בחיי)' (*Targ. Onq.* Lev. 18:5). Pseudo-Jonathan expands the verse with greater elaboration: 'he will live by them in eternal life (עלמא בחיי) and will be assigned a portion with the righteous' (*Targ. Ps.-J.* Lev. 18:5). The equation of obedience to the Law to inheriting eternal life appears elsewhere in the targums (*Targ. Isa.* 4:3; 58:11; *Targ. Ezek.* 20:11, 13, 21).

From this, we probably should assume that, when Jesus alluded to Lev. 18:5 ('You have answered rightly. Do this and you will live'), he and the legal expert understood it in reference to eternal life. What must he do to inherit eternal life? He must keep the great commandments. If he does them, he will live forever.

(3) 'A man planted a vineyard.' The Parable of the Wicked Vineyard Tenants (Mark 12:1-11) affords us another opportunity to observe how the targum and the Dead Sea Scrolls shed important light on the teaching of Jesus. The parable begins with several words taken from Isaiah's Song of the Vineyard (Isa. 5:1-7): 'A man "planted a vineyard, placed a hedge around it, dug out a wine vat, and built a tower". Then he leased it to farmers and went abroad' (Mark 12:1). The well known parable goes on to describe the farmers' refusal to surrender the fruit of the vineyard to the owner. They abuse the owner's servants, even killing some. Finally, in desperation, the owner sends his beloved son, but he too is murdered and cast out of the vineyard. 'What will the owner of the vineyard

do?'. Jesus asks his hearers. 'He will come and destroy the farmers, and give the vineyard to others' (Mark 12:9).

Among Jesus' hearers are ruling priests, scribes, and elders (cf. Mark 11:27). When they heard the parable, they 'perceived that he had told the parable against them' (Mark 12:12). Why did they assume that the parable was directed against them? Isaiah 5, the passage on which the details of the Parable of the Wicked Vineyard Tenants is based, is directed against the *whole* of the nation (against the 'inhabitants of Jerusalem', 'the men of Judah', and 'the house of Israel'; Isa. 5:3, 7). Nothing in Isaiah's song suggests that it was directed against the ruling priests or other religious authorities. Besides, would not ruling priests, given their wealth and social status, have more readily identified with the vineyard owner, not the farmers who lease the vineyard?

The Aramaic paraphrase found in the Isaiah Targum provides an important clue in finding an answer to these questions. According to *Targ. Isa.* 5:2: 'I established them as the plant of a choice vine; and I built my sanctuary in their midst, and I even gave my altar to atone for their sins'. 'Sanctuary' and 'altar' have taken the place of 'tower' and 'wine vat'. Such an identification is made explicit in the Tosefta (*t. Me'il.* 1:16; *t. Sukk.* 3:15). Because of the nation's sin, the Lord says: 'I will take up my Shekhinah from them, and they shall be for plundering; I will break down my sanctuaries, and they will be for trampling' (*Targ. Isa.* 5:5).[80] The prophetic word of judgment, according to the Aramaic tradition, is directed against the Temple establishment. Indeed, the reference to farmers' hopes of gaining the 'inheritance' (Mark 12:7) seems to cohere exegetically with the Targum's description of the 'inheritance on a high hill' (*Targ. Isa.* 5:1).

Jesus' direction of Isaiah 5 against the Temple establishment of his day coheres with what we find in the Isaiah Targum. But was this targumic tradition in circulation in Jesus' day, or is this no more than a coincidence? Referring to the Temple as a 'tower' is attested in *1 Enoch* (89:56, 66-67, 73), and the cultic association of Isaiah 5 itself is documented in 4Q500, whose fragmentary text reads: 'a wine vat built among stones [...] before the gate of the holy height [...] your planting and the streams of your glory [...] your vine[yard...]'

---

80   I am following the translation of B.D. Chilton, *The Isaiah Targum* (ArBib, 11; Wilmington: Glazier, 1987), pp. 10-11.

(lines 3-7). The words 'wine vat', 'built', 'stones', and 'planting' make it evident that the vineyard of Isaiah 5 is in view. The 'gate of the holy height' and the 'streams of your glory' are unmistakable references to the Temple.[81]

Jesus' usage of Isaiah 5 in the telling of his parable seems to have presupposed the exegetical tradition now preserved in the Isaiah Targum. Even the quotation of Ps. 118:22-23, with which the parable concludes (Mark 12:10-11) and which many interpreters assume is a later Christian addition, in order to heighten the christological potential of the parable, takes on added significance when we consider the Aramaic paraphrase preserved in the Psalms Targum: 'The boy which the builders abandoned was among the sons of Jesse, and he is worthy to be appointed king and ruler' (*Targ. Ps.* 118:22). The Aramaic evidently has exploited the potential for a play on words in the Hebrew involving הָאֶבֶן ('the stone') and הַבֵּן ('the son'). Such a wordplay in Hebrew, reflected in the targumic tradition, but not preserved in the LXX (which is what is actually quoted in Mark), suggests that the quotation derives from Jesus and not from the Greek-speaking Church (as many interpreters suppose). The linkage between the quotation and the parable, which tells of a rejected son, becomes much closer. Not only does the Aramaic tradition shed important meaning on the parable itself, but it provides a plausible frame of reference for understanding Mark 12:1-9 + 12:10-11 as a coherent, and original, unity.

D. Historical, Political, and Economic Context

In recent years a great deal of research has focused on the world of first-century Jewish Palestine. Archaeology, historical criticism, and studies in the politics, economics, and cultures of the Mediterranean world of late antiquity have shed light on various aspects of the activities, teachings, and general context of Jesus.[82]

---

[81]   See the discussion in J.M. Baumgarten, '4Q500 and the Ancient Conception of the Lord's Vineyard', *JJS* 40 (1989), pp. 1-6.

[82]   Representative studies include E. Schürer, *The History of the Jewish People in the Age of Jesus Christ* (3 vols.; rev. and ed. by G. Vermes, F. Millar, and M. Black; Edinburgh: T. & T. Clark, 1973–87); M. Hengel, *Judaism and Hellenism* (2 vols.; Philadelphia: Fortress Press, 1974); Safrai and Stern (eds.), *The Jewish People in the First Century*; E.M. Smallwood, *The Jews under Roman Rule: From Pompey to Diocletian* (SJLA, 20; Leiden: Brill, 2nd edn, 1981); H. Koester, *Introduction to the New Testament*. I. *History, Culture and Religion of the Hellenistic Age* (Berlin and New York: de Gruyter, 1982); M. Goodman, *State*

New study in Josephus has been especially helpful.[83] From this first-century apologist, interpreter, and historian we learn much about the events surrounding Jesus and his followers. Three important aspects of Jesus' message and activities will be considered: (1) Jesus' announcement of the kingdom of God, (2) the Pharisees' demand for a confirming sign, and (3) Jesus' debate with the Temple establishment.

1. The Announcement of the Kingdom of God. The Markan evangelist summarizes Jesus' message with the words: 'The time is fulfilled, and the kingdom of God has arrived! Repent, and believe in the Good News' (Mark 1:15).[84] The first part of this statement in all

---

and Society in Roman Galilee, A.D. 132–212 (Oxford Centre for Postgraduate Hebrew Studies; Totowa: Rowman & Allandheld, 1983); E. Bammel and C.F.D. Moule (eds.), *Jesus and the Politics of his Day* (Cambridge: Cambridge University Press, 1984); D.E. Oakman, *Jesus and the Economic Questions of his Day* (SBEC, 8; Lewiston & Queenston: Mellen, 1986); R.A. Horsley, *Jesus and the Spiral of Violence: Popular Jewish Resistance in Roman Palestine* (San Francisco: Harper & Row, 1987); J. Neusner *et al.* (eds.), *Judaisms and their Messiahs at the Turn of the Christian Era* (Cambridge: Cambridge University Press, 1987); S. Freyne, *Galilee, Jesus and the Gospels: Literary Approaches and Historical Investigations* (Philadelphia: Fortress Press, 1988); M. Hengel, *The Zealots: Investigations into the Jewish Freedom Movement in the Period from Herod I until 70 A.D.* (Edinburgh: T. & T. Clark, 1989); J.H. Charlesworth (ed.), *The Messiah: Developments in Earliest Judaism and Christianity* (Minneapolis: Fortress Press, 1992); L.I. Levine (ed.), *The Galilee in Late Antiquity* (Jerusalem and New York: Jewish Theological Seminary of America, 1992); Evans, *Jesus and his Contemporaries*, pp. 53-297.

83   R.J.H. Shutt, *Studies in Josephus* (London: SPCK, 1961); O. Betz *et al.* (eds.), *Josephus-Studien: Untersuchungen zu Josephus, dem antiken Judentum und dem Neuen testament* (Festschrift O. Michel; Göttingen: Vandenhoeck & Ruprecht, 1974); S.J.D. Cohen, *Josephus in Galilee and Rome: His Vita and Development as a Historian* (SCT, 8; Leiden: Brill, 1979); T. Rajak, *Josephus: The Historian and his Society* (London: Duckworth; Philadelphia: Fortress Press, 1983); R.A. Horsley and J.S. Hanson, *Bandits, Prophets, and Messiahs: Popular Movements at the Time of Jesus* (Minneapolis: Winston, 1985; repr. San Francisco: Harper & Row, 1988); L.H. Feldman and G. Hata (eds.), *Josephus, the Bible, and History* (Detroit: Wayne State University Press, 1987); *idem* (eds.), *Josephus, Judaism, and Christianity* (Detroit: Wayne State University Press, 1987).

84   Some scholars suspect that these are not the actual words of Jesus, especially the final words, 'Repent, and believe in the Good News' (e.g. Bultmann, *History of the Synoptic Tradition*, pp. 118, 127); but many suspect that they do summarize the principal components of his message, and, in part, may actually derive from Jesus; cf. Guelich, *Mark*, pp. 41-43; R.H. Gundry, *Mark: A*

probability approximates Jesus' message, for elsewhere he is said to have announced: 'The kingdom of God has come in power!' (Mark 9:1).[85] Even the latter part, which many scholars view as the evangelist's summary of the Christian message, may also derive from Jesus.[86]

Jesus' announcement of the kingdom was evidently echoed by enthusiastic members of his following. When he entered Jerusalem, he was met with the shout: 'Blessed is the coming kingdom of our father David' (Mark 11:10). The political implications of Jesus' ride on the donkey could scarcely have been missed. One immediately thinks of Solomon, who rode the donkey of his father King David down to the Gihon spring in Jerusalem, where he was met by the High Priest and was proclaimed king (1 Kgs 1:32-40). This historical picture would also have received important prophetic impetus as well, when we remember Zechariah's prophecy: 'Your king comes to you...humble and riding on a donkey' (Zech. 9:9). When the people spread their garments on the road before the approaching Jesus (Mark 11:8), we are reminded of the reception given to Jehu, when the Israelites placed their garments on the steps before their new monarch and cried out, 'Jehu is king' (2 Kgs 9:13). Also, the waving of the palm branches is reminiscent of the greeting extended to the victorious Judas Maccabeus (2 Macc. 10:7).

Judging by the biblical precedents, it is evident that Jesus' entrance into Jerusalem carried with it political connotations, connotations his contemporaries could scarcely have missed. But were there other men from this period of time who made claims or were recognized by their respective followings as royal figures, perhaps even messianic claimants? According to Josephus, there were.[87] Following the death of Herod the Great, several men attempted to gain the

---

Commentary on his Apology for the Cross (Grand Rapids: Eerdmans, 1993), pp. 69-71; and esp. B.D. Chilton, God in Strength: Jesus' Announcement of the Kingdom (SNTU, 1; Freistadt: Plöchl, 1979; repr. BibSem, 8; Sheffield: JSOT Press, 1987), pp. 27-95.

[85] Chilton, God in Strength, pp. 251-74; idem, 'The Transfiguration: Dominical Assurance and Apostolic Vision', NTS 27 (1980–81), pp. 115-24.

[86] Gundry, Mark, pp. 466-69.

[87] For critical discussion, see R.A. Horsley, 'Popular Messianic Movements around the Time of Jesus', CBQ 46 (1984), pp. 471-95; idem and Hanson, Bandits, Prophets, and Messiahs: Popular Movements at the Time of Jesus, pp. 88-134; Hengel, The Zealots, pp. 290-302; Evans, Jesus and his Contemporaries, pp. 53-81.

throne. Josephus tells us of the Galilean Judas, son of Hezekiah the brigand chief, who plundered the royal arsenals, attacked other kingly aspirants, and had 'ambition for royal honor' (*Ant.* 17:10:5 §§271-272; *War* 2:4:1 §56). Next we are told of Simon of Perea, a former royal servant, who 'was bold enough to place the diadem on his head, and having got together a body of men, he was himself also proclaimed king by them' (*Ant.* 17:10:6 §§273-276; *War* 2:4:2 §§57-59; cf. Tacitus, *Hist.* 5:9). Josephus also tells us of one Athronges the shepherd of Judea, a man who, acting like a king, 'dared to gain a kingdom' and 'put on the diadem' (*Ant.* 17:10:7 §§278-284; *War* 2:4:3 §§60-65).

Josephus also describes what appear to have been messianic claimants who took action during the great revolt against Rome (66–70 CE). He tells us of the son (or grandson) of Judas the Galilean, Menahem, a man who entered Jerusalem 'like a king' and arrayed himself 'in royal apparel' (*War* 2:17:8-9 §§433-448). Next we are told of John of Gischala, son of Levi, who behaved like a despot and monarch (*War* 4:7:1 §§389-394; 4:9:11 §566), language normally used in reference to kings and emperors. Finally, Josephus describes to us, almost with a hint of admiration, Simon bar Giora of Gerasa, the leader of an army which was 'subservient to his command as to a king' (*War* 4:9:4 §510; 4:9:11 §§570-576; 5:7:3 §309), but the city was captured and the Temple was destroyed. Defeated and for a time in hiding, Simon, dressed in white tunics and a purple mantle, made a dramatic appearance before the Romans on the very spot where the Temple had stood (*War* 7:1:2 §29).

Given the biblical precedents and the parallel, though not identical, actions of some of his contemporaries, it is not surprising that Jesus' entrance into Jerusalem and his subsequent actions in the Temple precincts prompted such questions as, 'By what authority are you doing these things?' (Mark 11:28), and, 'Is it lawful to pay taxes to Caesar?' (Mark 12:14; cf. Luke 23:2, where Jesus is accused of teaching the people not to pay taxes to Caesar). The payment of taxes was a particularly sore spot for Jewish nationalists. According to Josephus, it was the initiation of direct Roman taxation, following the banishment of Archelaus (6 CE), that led to a rebellion inspired by one Judas of Galilee (*War* 2:8:1 §§117-118; *Ant.* 18:1:6 §23).

Other details from the Gospels parallel certain aspects of Jewish messianic actions. The anointing of Jesus (Mark 14:3-9) was in all probability a messianic anointing. Jesus may or may not have spoken of his death and burial, but it does seem probable that, by anointing him, the unnamed woman had in fact recognized Jesus as Israel's true king. Such recognition coheres with Jesus' fate, crucified as 'king of the Jews' (Mark 15:26), 'between two rebels' (Mark 15:27). That ληστaί should be understood as 'rebels' or 'insurrectionists', instead of 'robbers' or (wrongly, as in the KJV) 'thieves', seems quite clear once again thanks to Josephus, who regularly speaks of the Jewish kingly claimants as ληστaί (e.g. *War* 2:3:2 §57; cf. Mark 14:48).

2. *The Demand for a Sign.* The narratives of Josephus provide us with insight into the odd exchange between Jesus and skeptics who demand 'a sign (σημεῖον) from heaven' (Mark 8:11 = Matt. 16:1 = Luke 11:16; cf. John 2:18; 6:30). Jesus' reply is categorical: 'Why does this generation seek a sign? Truly, I say to you, no sign shall be given to this generation!' (Mark 8:12 = Matt. 16:4 = Luke 11:29; cf. John 4:48). That Jews demanded signs seems clear enough from Paul's comment (1 Cor. 1:22: 'Jews demand signs and Greeks seek wisdom') and from the fourth evangelist's deliberate presentation of Jesus' miracles—somewhat in tension with the stance taken by the historical Jesus—as 'signs' (e.g. John 2:11; 4:54; 9:16; 11:47; 20:30).

The demand for signs, together with the later Synoptic warnings concerning those who promise them (Mark 13:22 = Matt. 24:24), is meaningfully illustrated by Josephus. One should consider the attempts at restoration brought on by persons such as Theudas (*Ant.* 20:5:1 §§97-98) and the anonymous Egyptian Jew (*Ant.* 20:8:6 §§169-170). Evidently these men, and probably others as well who saw themselves as Joshua-like figures and successors to Moses (Deut. 18:15-18), anticipated a new conquest of the promised land. In reference to these men and others, Josephus says that they promised the gullible 'signs' (σημεῖα) of salvation (*War* 2:13:4 §260; 6:5:4 §315; *Ant.* 20:8:6 §168). Their promises of signs were taken very seriously by the Romans, who viewed such talk as politically dangerous and responded with violence. Jesus' refusal to offer signs may have been prompted by a desire to distance himself from such persons.

3. *Debate with the Temple Establishment.* Several aspects of Jesus' criticism of the Temple establishment cohere with details that can be gleaned from Josephus, although this historian and apologist had little sympathy for its critics. In disagreement with the Temple's ruling that the half-shekel tax was to be paid annually, Jesus declared that the 'sons are free' (Matt. 17:24-26). On the occasion that Jesus

demonstrated within the Temple precincts, he is remembered to have alluded to two prophetic passages: 'My house shall be called a house of prayer, but you have made it a cave of robbers' (Mark 11:17; cf. Isa. 56:7; Jer. 7:11). Such a demonstration coheres with episodes reported by Josephus (*Ant.* 13:13:5 §§372-373; 17:6:1-4 §§149-167 = *War* 1:33:2-4 §§648-655) and faintly (but imaginatively) recalled in rabbinic sources (*m. Ker.* 1:7; *b. Beṣa* 20a-b).[88]

Of special interest is Jesus' allusion to Jeremiah 7, a harsh and doleful passage that warned the seventh-century BCE priesthood that their Temple would be destroyed. It is this passage that another Jesus, one son of Ananias, who made his public appearance some thirty years after the execution of Jesus of Nazareth, would draw on, making his fateful pronouncements of doom upon Jerusalem and her Temple. Josephus tells us that leading citizens (among whom he surely included the ruling priests) seized this man, beat him, and handed him over to the Roman governor, with demands that he be put to death (*War* 6:5:3 §§300-309).

Jesus' threatening prediction that the administration of God's 'vineyard' (i.e. Israel) would be given 'to others', by which he implied that the ruling priests would lose their position of power and privilege, only exacerbated the already tense situation (Mark 12:1-11). The warning to 'Beware the scribes!' (Mark 12:38-40) and the lament over the poor widow's meager gift (Mark 12:41-44) represent fragments of a deadly controversy between Jesus and the Temple establishment. The resentment and hatred with which many peasants regarded the ruling priesthood are plainly evident in Josephus's account of the burning of the High Priest's house, the murder of the High Priest, the flight of the ruling priests, and the burning of the records of debt on file within the Temple precincts (*War* 2:17:6 §§426-429; 2:17:9 §§441-442).

CONCLUSION

From the foregoing it is apparent that 'exegesis' of the historical Jesus is difficult but rewarding. Perhaps the single most important aspect of Jesus research involves context. Much of the recent popular and sensational work is flawed by a failure to situate Jesus in his

---

88 For critical discussion of these examples, see B. Chilton, *The Temple of Jesus: His Sacrificial Program within a Cultural History of Sacrifice* (University Park: Pennsylvania State University Press, 1992), pp. 100-107, 181-88.

cultural and historical context. We have been treated to Jesuses who champion various (contemporary) causes and who frequently look a lot like late twentieth-century scholars. But the Jesus of history was very much a part of his world, and was very much in tune with the concerns and ambitions of his people.[89]

Jesus prayed and taught in the manner of the popular preachers and teachers of his time. He interpreted Scripture much as did other teachers. In places, Jesus' use of the Old Testament reveals familiarity with the Aramaic paraphrases, suggesting that his understanding of Scripture in large measure took shape in the context of the synagogue. Jesus proclaimed the appearance of the kingdom of God, something longed for by many of his contemporaries, though strongly opposed by many who were secure in positions of power and wealth.

Jesus was a successful exorcist and healer. These healings were understood as indications of the presence of God, which was evidence of the inbreaking of the kingdom of God. Jesus demanded repentance and a return to the ethical laws of the Pentateuch and their applications found in the prophets. These demands carried with them serious implications for the ruling elite. Not surprisingly, Jesus was opposed by the ruling elite; his message and authority were rejected.

This opposition and rejection probably led to an intensification of Jesus' criticism of the ruling elite. He condemned it and predicted dire consequences for the city and the Temple establishment. Jesus' words and actions provoked the religious leaders, and eventually led them to seek his destruction. Following his arrest, Jesus affirmed his messianic identity as he understood it, and in so doing provided the grounds for a Roman execution as 'king of the Jews'.

Some time later the apostles, fully persuaded that Jesus had been resurrected, proclaimed him Israel's Messiah. To be sure, the proclamation itself was the result of Easter, but the *messianic identification* arose from Jesus' teaching and activities. A non-messianic teacher or prophet would not have been proclaimed 'Messiah', even if his followers believed him to have been resurrected. It was Jesus' promise of kingdom and salvation, the essential elements of the

---

[89]   To illustrate in what ways this is true is the principal concern of Evans, *Jesus and his Contemporaries.*

messianic task, that resulted in the emergence of a *Christology*, not the Easter discovery alone.

To unpack the nuances of these elements of Jesus' life and message is the task of Jesus research. This unpacking can only be done by taking into account the historical, linguistic, social, and cultural dimensions of the world in which Jesus lived.

BIBLIOGRAPHY

Aune, D.E. *Prophecy in Early Christianity and the Ancient Mediterranean World.* Grand Rapids: Eerdmans, 1983.

Berger, K. *Formgeschichte des Neuen Testaments.* Heidelberg: Quelle & Meyer, 1984.

Boring, M.E. *Sayings of the Risen Jesus: Christian Prophecy in the Synoptic Tradition.* SNTSMS, 46. Cambridge: Cambridge University Press, 1982.

_____. *The Continuing Voice of Jesus.* Louisville: Westminster/John Knox Press, 1991.

Bultmann, R. *Die Geschichte der synoptischen Tradition.* FRLANT, 12. Göttingen: Vandenhoeck & Ruprecht, 1921; 3rd edn, 1957 [= FRLANT, 29]. ET *The History of the Synoptic Tradition.* Oxford: Blackwell; New York: Harper & Row, 1963.

_____. *Jesus.* Berlin: Deutsche Bibliothek, 1926. ET *Jesus and the Word.* New York: Scribners, 1934.

Charlesworth, J.H., and C.A. Evans. 'Jesus in the Agrapha and Apocryphal Gospels', in B.D. Chilton and C.A. Evans (eds.), *Studying the Historical Jesus: Evaluations of the State of Current Research.* NTTS, 19. Leiden: Brill, 1994, pp. 479-533.

Chilton, B.D. *A Galilean Rabbi and his Bible: Jesus' Own Interpretation of Isaiah.* London: SPCK, 1984.

_____. *The Temple of Jesus: His Sacrificial Program within a Cultural History of Sacrifice.* University Park: Pennsylvania State University Press, 1992.

Chilton, B.D., and C.A. Evans (eds.). *Studying the Historical Jesus: Evaluations of the State of Current Research.* NTTS, 19. Leiden: Brill, 1994.

Crossan, J.D. *The Historical Jesus: The Life of a Mediterranean Jewish Peasant.* San Francisco: HarperCollins, 1991.

Dalman, G. *Die Worte Jesu mit Berücksichtung des nach kanonischen jüdischen Schrifttums und der aramäistischen Sprache erörtert.* Leipzig: Hinrichs, 1898. ET *The Words of Jesus.* Edinburgh: T. & T. Clark, 1902.

_____. *Jesus–Jeshua: Studies in the Gospels.* London: SPCK, 1929; repr. New York: Ktav, 1971.

Dodd, C.H. *The Parables of the Kingdom.* London: Nisbet, 1935.

Epp, E.J., and G.W. MacRae (eds.). *The New Testament and its Modern Interpreters.* Atlanta: Scholars Press, 1989.

Evans, C.A. *Jesus and his Contemporaries: Comparative Studies.* AGJU, 25. Leiden: Brill, 1995.

_____. 'Source, Form and Redaction Criticism: The "Traditional" Methods of Synoptic Interpretation', in S.E. Porter and D. Tombs (eds.), *Approaches to New Testament Study*. JSNTSup, 120. Sheffield: JSOT Press, 1995, pp. 17-45.

Evans, C.A., and S.E. Porter (eds.). *The Historical Jesus: A Sheffield Reader*. BibSem, 33. Sheffield: JSOT Press, 1995.

France, R.T., and D. Wenham (eds.). *Studies of History and Tradition in the Four Gospels*. Gospel Perspectives, 2. Sheffield: JSOT Press, 1980.

Gerhardsson, B. *Memory and Manuscript: Oral Tradition and Written Transmission in Rabbinic Judaism and Early Christianity*. Lund: Gleerup, 1961.

Hagner, D.A. *The Jewish Reclamation of Jesus: An Analysis and Critique of Modern Jewish Study of Jesus*. Grand Rapids: Zondervan, 1984.

Hahn, F. *The Titles of Jesus in Christology*. London: Lutterworth; Cleveland: World, 1969.

Jeremias, J. *Neutestamentliche Theologie*. I. *Die Verkündigung Jesu*. Gütersloh: Mohn, 1971. ET *New Testament Theology: The Proclamation of Jesus*. London: SCM Press; New York: Scribners, 1971.

Koester, H. *Ancient Christian Gospels: Their History and Development*. London: SCM Press; Philadelphia: Trinity Press International, 1990.

McKnight, E.V. *What is Form Criticism?* Philadelphia: Fortress Press, 1969.

McKnight, S. *Interpreting the Synoptic Gospels*. Grand Rapids: Baker, 1988.

Malbon, E.S., and E.V. McKnight (eds.). *The New Literary Criticism and the New Testament*. JSNTSup, 109. Sheffield: JSOT Press, 1994.

Meier, J.P. *A Marginal Jew: Rethinking the Historical Jesus*. Vols. 1–2. ABRL. New York: Doubleday, 1991, 1994.

Perrin, N. *Rediscovering the Teaching of Jesus*. London: SCM Press; New York: Harper & Row, 1967.

_____. *What is Redaction Criticism?* Philadelphia: Fortress Press, 1974.

Porter, S.E. 'Jesus and the Use of Greek in Galilee', in B.D. Chilton and C.A. Evans (eds.), *Studying the Historical Jesus: Evaluations of the State of Current Research*. NTTS, 19. Leiden: Brill, 1994, pp. 123-54.

Riesner, R. *Jesus als Lehrer: Eine Untersuchung zum Ursprung der Evangelien-Überlieferung*. WUNT, 2.7. Tübingen: Mohr–Siebeck, 1981; 4th edn, 1994.

Robinson, J.M. *A New Quest of the Historical Jesus*. SBT, 25. London: SCM Press; repr. Missoula, MT: Scholars Press, 1979; repr. *A New Quest of the Historical Jesus and Other Essays*. Philadelphia: Fortress Press, 1983.

Sanders, E.P. *The Tendencies of the Synoptic Tradition*. SNTSMS, 9. Cambridge: Cambridge University Press, 1969.

Sanders, E.P., and M. Davies. *Studying the Synoptic Gospels*. London: SCM Press; Philadelphia: Trinity Press International, 1989.

Schweitzer, A. *Von Reimarus zu Wrede: Eine Geschichte des Leben-Jesu-Forschung*. Tübingen: Mohr–Siebeck, 1906; 2nd edn, 1913. ET *The Quest of the Historical Jesus: A Critical Study of its Progress from Reimarus to Wrede*. London: Black, 1910. With 'Introduction' by J.M. Robinson; New York: Macmillan, 1968.

Stein, R.H. *The Synoptic Problem*. Grand Rapids: Baker, 1987.

Taylor, V. *The Formation of the Gospel Tradition.* London: Macmillan, 1933; 2nd edn, 1935.

Vermes, G. *Jesus and the World of Judaism.* London: SCM Press; Philadelphia: Fortress Press, 1983.

_____. *Jesus the Jew.* London: Collins; Philadelphia: Fortress Press, 1973.

_____. *The Religion of Jesus the Jew.* London: SCM Press; Minneapolis: Fortress Press, 1993.

THE SYNOPTIC GOSPELS AND ACTS

CHRISTOPHER M. TUCKETT

INTRODUCTORY ISSUES AND INTERPRETATION

The aim of this chapter is to show how some of the so-called 'introductory' problems concerning the Synoptic Gospels and Acts relate to the interpretation of the texts themselves. By 'introductory' issues, I mean issues concerned with the date, authorship or provenance of the documents concerned, the projected audiences of the texts, the problem of synoptic interrelationships, as well as the relationship between the Synoptic Gospels and other (non-canonical) sources, etc. The aim here is not to try to solve these issues in and for themselves. Such attempts can be found elsewhere, for example, in standard introductions to the New Testament, such as that of Kümmel (1975). Rather, the aim is to see how possible solutions to these problems affect, and are affected by, the interpretation and understanding of the texts and of specific exegetical issues.

In relation to, say, the Pauline corpus, it may be that we can deal with at least some of the 'introductory' issues independently of the exegesis of significant parts of the texts themselves. With a Pauline letter, for example, we can sometimes make important deductions about certain aspects of its circumstances on the basis of some of the personal greetings that come at the end of the letter, after the great doctrinal and ethical discussions. The Gospels and Acts simply do not have such personal details. For the most part, we are dependent on the interpretation of individual passages, or groups of passages, to make decisions about introductory issues; and in turn any decisions we make may well have an important bearing on our understanding of the passages concerned. We are thus frequently drawn into a form of circular argument from which it is not easy to escape.

One possible way of avoiding such circularity might be provided by evidence from outside the texts themselves. There is a certain amount of such external evidence from patristic sources about the authors of the Synoptic Gospels and their circumstances. However, much if not all of it is now regarded as highly suspect, if only because it is so often difficult to square with the evidence of the texts themselves. For example, the patristic evidence that Mark was a follower of Peter, or

Luke a companion of Paul, has been held to be questionable precisely because it does not seem to fit the evidence of the Gospels themselves. Nevertheless, even that claim is far too black-and-white, and the issues are by no means so clear cut. But on any showing, it remains the case that the resolution of such issues is integrally related to the interpretation of the texts themselves, and the relationship between exegesis and 'introduction' is one of continuous interplay and interaction. This can be illustrated in a number of ways and at many levels. I consider first, therefore, questions of date, authorship and provenance in relation to the Synoptic evangelists.

A. Mark

I do not propose here to discuss the issue of the specific identity of the author of the Gospel we attribute to 'Mark'. Patristic tradition probably intended to identify this Mark as the John Mark of Acts, and hence as a member of the primitive Jerusalem church. This seems very doubtful in view of the author's well-known apparent lack of knowledge of Palestinian geography (cf. Mark 5:1; 7:31) and of Jewish legal practice (cf. Mark 7:3-4; 10:11-12; though see also below for this in relation to Mark's trial narrative).[1] Much more uncertain is the question of the date of Mark, and this is connected in an integral way with exegesis of Mark 13, especially vv. 14-20.

1. Mark 13 and the Date of Mark's Gospel. Mark 13 is an extraordinarily complex chapter. Usually called the 'apocalyptic discourse', it purports to be a speech of Jesus predicting what is to come in the future. For Mark writing some years later, no doubt some of the events predicted have already happened. Thus what is future for Mark's Jesus is partly past or present for Mark himself. The problem (as with the interpretation of much 'apocalyptic' writing, which often uses a similar genre of having a revered figure of the writer's past predict what is to come in the 'future') is to know where the discourse slides over from the writer's past or present to the writer's future.

---

[1]   In Mark 5:1, the author seems to assume that Gerasa is near the Sea of Galilee, when it is in fact c. 30 miles away; in 7:31, he apparently assumes that a direct journey from Tyre to the Sea of Galilee would involve going through Sidon and the region of the Decapolis, when such a route would in fact involve long detours to the north and south respectively. In 7:3-4, Mark states that handwashing was obligatory on all Jews at the time, when all our information indicates otherwise; and in 10:11-12, Mark's Jesus presupposes the conditions of Roman law, not Jewish law, in apparently assuming that a woman could divorce her husband. For details, see the commentaries on Mark at these points.

In Mark 13, the issue is complicated further by what appears to be deliberately cryptic and veiled language used in v. 14, referring to the 'desolating sacrilege' standing where 'he' ought not to stand. (The noun used for 'desolating sacrilege' in Greek is neuter, though the participle 'standing' which qualifies it is masculine.) Mark's diction here seems to echo quite deliberately language from the book of Daniel, especially Dan. 9:27 and 12:11, where the seer refers to the desecration of the Temple during the period of the persecutions under Antiochus Epiphanes. Most commentators have therefore assumed that Mark is referring to a similar kind of desecration of the Temple by non-Jewish intruders coming into the most holy parts of the Temple building.

Some have argued that Mark's warning here reflects the danger that developed in 40 CE when Roman troops threatened to enter the Temple building and put up a statue of Caligula in the sanctuary (Theissen 1992: 125-65). On the other hand, this danger was averted: after the pleas of Jews, and an almost incredible display of silent protest, the legate Petronius was persuaded not to enter the Temple, and the threat finally ended with Caligula's murder. If Mark 13:14 refers to this, then it must be a genuine prophecy, since the presence of the 'desolating sacrilege' in the Temple never occurred. Hence, Mark 13:14 must predate the Caligula crisis of 40 CE. For the dating of Mark, this must mean that either Mark's Gospel as a whole is to be dated prior to 40, or the source used by Mark here is to be dated prior to 40.

An alternative way to read the evidence would, however, be to argue that such a date seems impossibly early for Mark himself; and if this is a pre-Markan source, why has Mark failed to contemporize a tradition that surely cried out for some up-dating? Hence, another interpretation would relate these verses not to the threat to the Temple under Caligula, but to the destruction of the Temple in 70 CE by the forces of Titus, when the Roman standards were set up in the sanctuary. Certainly the structure of the chapter as a whole suggests that the events alluded to in v. 14 are past, not future, for Mark. Mark gives two warnings of outsiders who may mislead the Christian community (vv. 5-6, 21-22), and almost certainly these reflect what Mark regards as real dangers in his own day. But the close similarity (though not identity) of the warnings suggests that both are thought to be real and present by Mark. This suggests that, even at v. 22, the discourse has not yet moved into Mark's future. Thus the event alluded to in v. 14 is probably past for Mark. If this is the correct way to interpret the chapter, it provides perhaps the clearest indication that Mark is to be dated *after* 70 CE (cf. Hooker 1982, 1991).

However, one may simply note here the element of inevitable circularity in the argument. *If* we knew Mark was writing prior to 70, then we would have to change our exegesis of the passage: if we interpret v. 14 as referring to a (for Mark) future destruction of the Temple, this will entail placing the shift, from Mark's past or present to Mark's future, much earlier in the chapter. On the other hand, if we could be sure of the referent in the verse, this could have direct implications for the dating question. Hence the introductory issue of the date of Mark is integrally related to the exegesis of a key passage in the Gospel.

2. Provenance of Mark. The dating question may also be connected in part with the problem of the general provenance of Mark. The question of Mark's provenance, and the situation of the community for which he is writing, is a very wide-ranging one. Here I wish to focus on one aspect of that problem, namely, the question of whether Mark's Gospel is written for a suffering community. The Gospel is well-known for its great stress on the necessity of Jesus' suffering, as well as that of the disciples (cf. 8:34–10:52, especially 8:34-38). What situation within the community for whom Mark is writing might this presuppose?

Many have argued that such stress on the necessity of suffering reflects a situation of a Christian community which is itself suffering. This is in turn often connected with a possible date for Mark: the Gospel may reflect the situation of the Roman Christian community suffering in the mid-60s during the fierce outbreak of persecution under Nero, following the fire of Rome. (This is a standard view adopted in many older commentaries on Mark: cf. Taylor 1952: 31-32. This does, of course, run counter to the argument of the previous section which suggested that Mark was writing after 70, not in the mid-60s.)

At one level, the 'exegesis' of the passages on suffering in Mark is unaffected by the issue. The words, and the sentences, can be translated and understood whatever the precise situation.[2]

---

2   This is not to say that the exegesis is always straightforward, even at this level. For example, the language in 8:34 about 'bearing one's cross' is notoriously difficult to interpret precisely: is this meant literally or metaphorically?

Nevertheless, the nature of the exhortations about the necessity of suffering is radically affected by the situation in which they are read. If they are read by a suffering community, they may provide assurance that any sufferings now being endured are not to be regarded as unexpected. If read by a community that is not suffering, they would be taken as perhaps dire warnings to Christians to take seriously the possibility of suffering: they could thus function as rather unpleasant jolts to a community that is in danger of becoming somewhat complacent (Hooker 1983: 116).

Given the fact that, in Mark, the warnings about the disciples' suffering hardly ever give any explanation of why such suffering would take place, the second of the two possibilities outlined above is perhaps the more plausible. It does not necessarily help those being persecuted very much to tell them simply that they must suffer. (Interpretations of Jesus' suffering in Mark are also notoriously infrequent [cf. only 10:45; 14:24], but even here such explanations apply to Jesus' sufferings alone, not those of his followers.) However, the alternative way of reading Mark is still well established, and this example shows once again the close connection between the interpretation of some passages in Mark and one's decision about introductory issues.

3. Mark's Knowledge of Judaism: The Sanhedrin Trial. Another area where similar issues are important concerns Mark's knowledge of Judaism and his account of the trial of Jesus. It is well known that Mark's account of the Sanhedrin trial of Jesus has the Jewish authorities acting in ways that seem to break a number of their own rules for conducting a capital trial (see Brown 1994: 357-63). Such a claim of course begs a number of questions. Our evidence for such rules comes from a later period, and we do not know if these rules were in force at the time of Jesus. We do not even know for certain if the Jews were allowed to hold such trials at all: their right to carry out a death sentence at this period is also much disputed (Brown 1994: 363-72). Thus it is not even clear that the hearing of the Sanhedrin was ever intended to be a formal 'trial' at all.[3] Nevertheless, we can

---

3   It is well known that the Lukan account of the Sanhedrin 'trial' presents what appears to be more of an informal hearing than a formal trial (though see Brown 1994: 389). It may also be independent of the Markan account and represent a more reliable tradition of the events concerned (Catchpole 1970: chap. 3). Some of the alleged breaches in the legal procedure do not appear in the Lukan account (the trial held at night, the problem of the blasphemy charge when

say that, if our knowledge is at all accurate, Mark's account of the
Jewish authorities, conducting what appears to be a formal trial of
Jesus, has them acting illegally at a number of levels.

But how far is Mark himself aware of this, and how should we then
read his narrative of the trial scenes? Could we say that Mark was
aware of the legal 'shortcomings' of the Sanhedrin trial, and his story
of the trial is intended to vilify even more the characters of the Jewish
leaders? They do not of course appear in a good light in Mark's
narrative anyway: they are the archetypal 'villains' who act as the foil
for Jesus as the 'hero' of the story. But perhaps their failure to observe
even their own rules shows them to be that much worse. Thus Hooker
writes: 'The proceedings are a farce—and Mark has probably
deliberately presented them as such. It is not Jesus who is guilty of
breaking the Law, but his opponents, who claim to uphold it!' (1991:
357).[4]

This is certainly possible, though it does presuppose a certain
amount of knowledge on Mark's part of such Jewish legal niceties. I
have earlier noted in passing that Mark seems elsewhere in his Gospel
to be rather ignorant about some details within Jewish Law (see n. 1
above). It might fit this evidence from elsewhere in the Gospel better
if Mark were unlikely to have known any of the finer details of Jewish
legal procedures. Hence, the apparent irregularities of the Sanhedrin
trial of Jesus may be irrelevant for interpreting the story at the level of
Mark's understanding or intention.[5]

At the level of any underlying history, the question remains
unresolved. To address the question at that level requires detailed
discussion of the regulations themselves and their possible dates. The
issue I have raised relates only to understanding Mark's narrative
within its own story world. At this level, the argument is probably
circular (though other evidence from within the Gospel, but outside
the passion narrative, may be relevant). Nevertheless, it may have a

---

Jesus does not appear to have blasphemed since he has not uttered the divine
name).

4   Cf. more generally Lührmann 1981: 459: 'Der Prozeß...ist von Anfang an
als unfair beschrieben' (though it is not quite so clear if this is intended as in
relation to the Jewish Law).

5   More generally, cf. Brown 1994: 387: 'While [Mark's] portrayal [of the
Jewish authorities here] is highly unsympathetic, it is primarily one of fanatical
intolerance, rather than of hypocrisy'.

significant effect on our understanding of the present form of the narrative.

B. Luke

A range of similar problems, with the same inherent circularity, arises in the case of the Lukan writings. (I assume here without question that Luke's Gospel and Acts belong together as the two-volume work of a single author.)

1. Date/Authorship. Tradition identifies the author of Luke–Acts as Luke, the companion of Paul mentioned at times in the Pauline corpus (Col. 4:14; 2 Tim. 4:11; Phlm. 24). One's decision about the accuracy of this may then affect, and be affected by, one's understanding and interpretation of key parts of the book of Acts, notably the picture of Paul which emerges from Acts and also the ending of Acts. I consider these issues briefly in turn.

(a) The Portrait of Paul in Acts. It is well known that there are discrepancies at many levels between the picture of Paul in Acts and the picture of Paul that emerges from Paul's own letters. These range from relatively insignificant details about chronology, travelling companions, etc., through to aspects of 'theology', the understanding of apostleship and Paul's presentation of himself.[6]

At first sight, it might appear that the issue of the authorship of Acts would be crucially significant in interpreting these apparent differences. For example, a decision that the author of Acts was in fact a companion of Paul might make one more inclined to seek to reconcile any apparent differences between Acts and Paul's letters, and to seek to build up a composite picture of Paul from the two sets of sources giving as much weight to Acts as to the letters. A decision the other way on the authorship question might make one more inclined to discount the evidential value of Acts in interpreting Paul as an historical figure.

In fact, the authorship question is probably not very significant in this context. Whatever one decides about Acts, the fact remains that the primary evidence for discovering information about Paul is his own letters; Acts is at best secondary evidence, written probably some time after the event. Moreover, even if the author of Acts were a companion of Paul, this would not *ipso facto* guarantee Luke's reliability or accuracy. Eye-witnesses are not always accurate;

---

[6]   See the survey in Haenchen 1971: 112-16; a classic treatment remains that of Vielhauer 1968.

conversely, accurate and reliable information can often be purveyed by a non-eye-witness. Thus, any theory about the identity of the author of Acts does not necessarily imply anything clearly about the accuracy of the portrayal of Paul in Acts. For this we are driven to the texts themselves, and to a comparison of Acts with Paul's own letters, and the troublesome lack of correspondence between the two bodies of evidence at a number of key points. The greater one judges the disparity between Acts and the letters to be, the more one might be inclined to decide against identifying 'Luke' (that is, the author of Acts) as a companion of Paul. But one must remember that, if Luke, as a companion of Paul, got Paul wrong and failed to understand key aspects of his thought, he was probably neither the first nor the last to do so![7]

(b) *The Date of Acts and the Ending of Acts.* The issue of dating can also have a significant effect on one's interpretation of Luke–Acts. One aspect of this issue, which has potentially far-reaching significance for the interpretation of Luke's two-volume work, concerns the ending of Acts.

The last two-thirds of the book of Acts is dominated by the figure of Paul, recounting various of his travels and exploits, and the last quarter of the book is taken up with Paul's trials before various authorities, his appeal to Caesar, his journey to Rome to make that appeal, and his arrival in Rome. Acts looks very much like a 'life of Paul'. However, Acts breaks off without telling us directly what many assume should be the expected ending, namely the outcome of Paul's appeal and the end of Paul's life. Some have argued that this is clearly what the narrative should give us if Luke knew what had happened; since Acts stops where it does, the best explanation is that this is the chronological position of the author as well. In other words, the ending of Acts implies that Luke is writing in the early 60s; subsequent events in Paul's life have not yet happened and this is why they are not narrated (Bruce 1951: 11; Robinson 1976: 91).

All this does, however, is make a number of assumptions about the nature of Acts as a whole, and what Luke 'must' have written if he

---

[7]   In any case, as Fitzmyer points out, if the question of the authorship of Acts is related to the 'we-passages' in Acts, so that the latter are taken as implying that the author was present at the events described in these passages, this would suggest that Luke was an eye-witness of a relatively limited amount of Paul's career, and this might also explain some of the discrepancies (e.g. in ideas) between Paul and Acts (Fitzmyer 1989: 5).

had had the chance to do so. In fact, there is more than one hint that Luke is writing after 70 CE (cf. Luke 21:20);[8] moreover, the words of Paul in his farewell speech to the Ephesian elders at Miletus in Acts 20:25 ('you shall see my face no more') have seemed to many to indicate quite clearly that Luke is aware that Paul's final journey to Rome will end in his death (Haenchen 1971: 592, and many others). Hence it seems very unlikely that Acts can be dated in the early 60s, and Luke probably does know of some of the events that come after the point where his story ends in Acts. All this may therefore suggest that Acts is *not* a 'life of Paul'. Luke's interest in writing Acts is not primarily biographical, in the sense of giving a biography of his hero Paul. What exactly his purpose might be is another issue, for which there is not time or space to discuss here. Probably it would be wrong to tie Luke down to a single 'aim' or 'purpose'. But perhaps the issue of dating and the phenomenon of the ending of Acts should alert us to the probability that Luke's aim in writing Acts is certainly more than to give (just) an account of his hero Paul.

(c) Luke 6:22 and the Date of Luke. The issue of dating can also affect the detailed exegesis of individual words and phrases. For example, in Luke's version of the final beatitude in the Great Sermon (Luke 6:22), Jesus pronounces a blessing on those who will be 'separated': 'Blessed are you when men hate you and when they separate (ἀφορίσωσιν) you'. Most would agree that what is mostly future for Jesus may well be, at least in part, past or present for the evangelist. What then is the significance of Luke's reference to 'separation' here?

Some have argued that what Luke has in mind is the formal separation of Christians from Jewish synagogues as a result of the so-called *Birkath-ha-minim*, the 'blessing on the heretics', which may have been incorporated into Jewish synagogues around 85 CE (Goulder 1989: 352-53). According to this interpretation, Luke thus represents a relatively late stage in the developing history of

---

8   Luke here replaces Mark's reference to the 'desolating sacrilege standing where he ought not to stand' (Mark 13:14) by 'When you see Jerusalem surrounded by armies'. (I am assuming here, and for the most of this rest of this chapter, the validity of the Two Source theory as the solution to the Synoptic problem, though I am fully aware that this is not accepted by all: see the discussion in section D below.) Most would see this as a clear indication of Luke's interpreting the enigmatic Markan verse by a reference to the fall of Jerusalem in 70 CE which, for him, lies in the past.

Christian–Jewish relationships, and reflects a situation of well-established formal separation at the social level.[9]

On the other hand, such an interpretation of the key word ἀφορίσωσιν in Luke 6:22 is by no means certain. The word is fairly general, and may in fact simply refer to a more general, and more informal, social ostracism experienced by Christians (Hare 1967: 53). It is certainly not clear that any formal synagogue ban was in mind.[10] The dating of the *Birkath-ha-minim* is itself notoriously uncertain, but even if we could date it with precision, we probably cannot use the diction of Luke 6:22 to date the formulation of this verse more precisely after this date.

2. Provenance of Luke. The question of the relationship between Christianity and Judaism, or of that between Christians and Jews, is also related to another 'introductory' issue relating to the Lukan writings, namely, the provenance of Luke. What kind of a person was Luke? To or from what situation is he writing? These questions can be considered at a number of levels. Here I consider two aspects: Luke's relationship to Judaism, and his social status.

(a) Luke and the Jews. It is clearly an important part of Luke's aim in writing at least to address the question of the relationship between Christians and Jews. What precisely Luke's attitude is to Judaism has been a matter of considerable debate.[11] At one level, Luke seems to present a thoroughly positive picture of Judaism and Jewish institutions in relation to the new Christian movement. The Lukan birth narratives present the key characters in the Christian story as models of Jewish piety; the early Church in Acts remains focused in its piety on the Jewish Temple in Jerusalem; Paul's own travels all seem to start from, and return to, Jerusalem as a base; and (notoriously!) Paul is consistently presented in Acts as the pious Jew

---

[9]   In Goulder's overall theory, the interpretation of this verse is connected with his views about the Synoptic Problem: according to Goulder, Luke is directly dependent on Matthew for the non-Markan material they share, and hence the Lukan verse here is due to Lukan redaction. As we shall see below, Luke's whole work probably does reflect a situation of sharp social separation between the Jewish and Christian communities of his day; but it is another matter whether the language of Luke 6:22 itself implies this.

[10]   For those holding some form of Q hypothesis, this verse in Luke may reflect Q's language and a situation of far closer contact between the Christian and Jewish communities concerned: see Tuckett 1996: 297-300.

[11]   See the various views represented in Tyson 1988.

par excellence, especially in relation to his observance of the Jewish Law.

On the other hand, other aspects of Luke's narrative, especially the story in Acts, present a rather different picture. For Acts also shows an increasing level of alienation between Christians and Jews. As the Christian mission spreads to various cities in the empire, the Jews are regularly portrayed as hostile and increasingly violent towards the Christians. Hence the regular refrain of Paul that, if the Jews reject the gospel, the mission will go to the Gentiles (Acts 13:46; 18:6; 28:28). And the final climactic scene in Acts 28 can be interpreted as in some sense representing the final break between Christians and Jews (Haenchen 1971: 729; Sanders 1987: 296-99). By the end of the story, Luke seems to show no sympathy at all for the Jews—there appears to be only implacable hostility. Is then Luke's account in some sense 'anti-Semitic'?[12]

Such language is probably not very helpful. Whatever the feelings reflected in the New Testament of Christians about Jews, there is no suggestion of their being 'anti-Semitic' in any sense of what that term might imply in a post-Holocaust era (though cf. Gager 1983). No Christian in the New Testament ever advocates physical violence against, and total extinction of, the Jewish people. But how far does Luke's work suggest implacable hostility to the Jewish nation as a whole?

Much depends on how one regards Luke himself. Was Luke himself a Jew or a Gentile (see Salmon 1988)? Certainly any language of hostility against Jews, or some Jews, depends critically for its interpretation on whether the author was himself Jewish or not. Tirades against Jews by other Jews are a stock part of the Jewish tradition ever since the days of the prophets. Any accusations against Jews, however harsh the language, are thus in no sense inherently anti-Semitic unless one wants to tar Isaiah, Amos, Jeremiah *et al.* with that brush. Language about the definitive rejection of the Jewish people by a non-Jew might however have greater significance in this context.

The situation is, however, probably not so black-and-white. The tradition about Luke suggests that he was a Gentile; but the category of 'Gentiles', or 'non-Jews', was almost certainly not a uniform one.

---

12   Cf. the discussion in Sanders 1987, especially his Preface, p. xvii: 'I do not know what to call that hostility [i.e. Luke's hostility to the Jews] if not antisemitism'.

Some Gentiles were clearly hostile to Judaism, but others were clearly attracted to it and adopted positions of varying levels of attachment to Judaism (see the survey in De Boer 1995). That Luke is in some sense very positive about Judaism seems undeniable in view of the positive picture of various aspects of Judaism already noted. Further, it is clearly of vital importance for Luke to show that Christianity is in some real sense the direct continuation of the Judaism of the pre-Christian era (cf. the emphases on the fulfilment of Old Testament texts in Luke 4:18-19; 24:24, 44, etc.). Luke is thus in many ways thoroughly positive about Judaism as an institution or religion.

Clearly, however, the negative picture in Acts remains, and it seems very likely that the force of the final scene in Acts 28 is indeed to show that, at the social level at least, the break between Christians and Jews is final. Luke does not seem to envisage any positive relationship between the Christian Church and non-Christian Jews in his own day. But this does not make Luke 'anti-Semitic'. Luke is also aware of many Jewish members of the Christian Church. He is also very keen to affirm the positive links between the Christian movement and the ancestral Jewish faith. Perhaps the picture that best fits the evidence is of Luke as a close Jewish sympathizer, but aware of the break that has already occurred between Christians and Jews. Yet, as with so many of the issues we have looked at in this chapter, the relationship between the interpretation of the text and one's understanding of the introductory problems is a dialectical one: one issue feeds into, and is informed by, the other.

(b) Luke and Poverty/Possessions. A similar problem is raised by the issue of Luke's evident concern about the question of money and possessions. Luke's two-volume work is well known for its commendation for the poor and its attacks on the rich,[13] and in the early chapters in Acts, the earliest Christian community adopts a life-style involving each individual renouncing any personal possessions (cf. Acts 2:44, etc.). Similarly, Luke's Gospel is renowned for the way in which the author seems to go out of his way to claim that disciples of Jesus give up 'everything' when they start to follow Jesus.[14]

In terms of the detailed 'exegesis' of individual sentences, or even

---

[13]Cf. passages peculiar to Luke such as Luke 1:51-53; 6:24-26; 12:16-21; 16:19-31, as well as Q passages such as Luke 6:20-23, etc.

[14] Cf. Luke 5:11; 5:28 (Luke adds to Mark the note that Levi 'left everything' to follow Jesus); 14:33; 18:22 (Luke adds to Mark that the rich young man must sell 'everything' he has).

whole pericopes, there is little problem here. However, as in the case
of the issue of Luke and Judaism, the interpretation of the broader
picture, and how—if at all—the individual elements fit into a broader
coherent pattern, can crucially depend on one's decisions about more
'introductory' problems: what kind of person Luke was and the nature
and situation of his audience. The interpretation of material in a text
such as Luke–Acts will critically depend on whether it is addressed to,
or read by, a community which is itself materially destitute, or which
is economically well-off. In the first case, the attacks on the rich and
the promises to the poor would be interpreted as providing consolation
and hope to an economically beleaguered community. In a way, this is
very similar to the manner in which apocalyptic writings have
sometimes been thought to provide hope for persecuted and
marginalized groups in a society where they are in a situation of deep
pessimism about the present world order (Hanson 1975). On the other
hand, if Luke–Acts is read by people who are materially comfortable,
the notes about poverty, possessions and the like become a sharp
challenge to the listeners/readers to reassess their priorities and to
reflect upon their life-style. Rather than providing comfort and hope,
Luke's Gospel becomes a highly uncomfortable challenge.

It is probably fair to say that the majority opinion within Lukan
scholarship today is that Luke is addressing an audience that is
reasonably well-to-do and not economically destitute. The parable of
the rich fool (Luke 12:16-21) seems to be addressed specifically to
property owners, not to the destitute—Luke's (probable) redaction of
the material on love-of-enemies and non-retaliation in Luke 6:32-35
adds in v. 34 an exhortation to lend to all those who ask, presupposing
that the readers/hearers do have the wherewithal to make monetary
loans.[15] So too, in the parable of the rich man and Lazarus (Luke
16:19-31), the focus of attention is primarily the rich man himself:
despite the fact that Lazarus is (unusually) given a name in the
parable, he is very much a dumb actor in the story and functions
primarily as a foil to highlight the situation of the rich man. Similarly,
the consistent theme running through the whole of Luke–Acts on the
importance of practical charitable giving (cf. Luke 3:11; 6:30; 10:29-
36; 11:5-8; 11:41; 19:1-10; Acts 9:36; 10:2; 24:17) again presupposes
that Luke is addressing a community that has some material resources

---

[15]   Luke's third exhortation here—to lend to, as well as to love and to greet,
everyone indiscriminately—is widely taken as a redactional addition, slightly
overloading the structure of the sequence.

with which to be generous. It looks very much then as if Luke's community is *not* economically destitute (i.e. 'poor'); the parts of Luke's two-volume work dealing with the themes of poverty and possessions seem to be primarily addressed to those who are not poor, challenging them to use the material possessions they may have wisely and responsibly.

This in turn may then significantly affect the more detailed interpretation of specific passages. Thus the parable of the rich man and Lazarus may be less of a statement about what will be, come what may (thus providing assurance to the 'Lazaruses' of the audience), and more of a warning to the rich in the audience of what might be if they do not change their ways in some respects (Bauckham 1991). Further, Luke gives no real justification for a model of poverty itself as an ideal. For Luke, what is promised is an end to poverty (cf. Luke 6:20-23). The model of discipleship as entailing giving up everything seems to be one that is confined to the lifetime of Jesus. Those who become Christians in the later parts of Acts do not make such radical renunciation, and there is never any implied criticism of them for not doing so. Similarly, the economic situation and set-up of the earliest Jerusalem church is not replicated in the later Pauline communities, and there is no hint that this is in any way reprehensible. The one thing that remains constant throughout Luke–Acts is the importance and value placed on the action of charitable giving (cf. above). But this again presumes that Christians are regarded primarily as potential 'givers' rather than 'receivers' (cf. Acts 20:35).

It is hopefully clear that the wider interpretation of some key parts of Luke–Acts is integrally connected with one's decision about the identity[16] and situation of both Luke and his readers.

C. Matthew

A number of problems, very similar to those we have already discussed in relation to Luke, arise in the case of the interpretation of Matthew's Gospel as well. In particular, there is the issue of Matthew's relationship to Judaism. I consider this in general terms first, and then in relation to one specific text.

1. Matthew and Judaism. Even more than in the case of Luke, the question of Matthew's relationship to Judaism has been a key question

---

[16] That is, 'identity' in a very broad sense of what kind of a person, 'religiously' or socially, Luke was. The issue of his precise identity, or his name, is one of the less important issues.

in Matthean studies, with the constantly recurring issue of how far Matthew may be regarded as 'anti-Semitic'. This arises above all from the very violent forms of the denunciations placed on the lips of Jesus (and others) by Matthew to vilify some—or perhaps even all—Jews. The diatribe against the scribes and Pharisees in Matthew 23 is well known. So too the famous (or infamous) elements in Matthew where the Jews (by implication) seem to be singled out for implied rejection and condemnation are equally well known (cf. Matt. 8:11-12; 21:43; 22:7, etc.), culminating in Matthew's account of the trial of Jesus before Pilate where Matthew has the Jewish crowds (not just the leaders!) claim responsibility for Jesus' death by shouting 'His blood be on us and on our children' (Matt. 27:25).

Now, as with Luke, the question of authorship (at least in a very general sense) is vitally important here to interpret such language. Is Matthew himself a Jew? On any showing, Matthew is closely related to Judaism. As is well known, he takes great care to try to rewrite some of the Markan stories that seem to show Jesus in conflict with the Law, so that Jesus is less polemical. At the very least, Matthew tries to argue his case on presuppositions that would be shared by a Torah-observant Jewish partner in any possible dialogue.[17] So too Matthew's vocabulary and mind-set seem to be typically Jewish. It is thus probably somewhat precarious to try to read out of Matthew's polemic about 'the Jews' a cold and sober statement about a 'theology' or 'ideology' of the nature of the relationship between Christianity and Juda*ism* from one who is uninvolved in either side of the argument.

Many Matthean scholars today would agree that Matthew probably reflects a situation of direct confrontation between two social groups who, at the social level at least, are either at the point of, or have already, separated (Stanton 1992: 146-68). Yet this separation is probably not very great as far as spatial geography is concerned: the two groups are probably still confronting each other and perhaps are being extremely rude about each other. Indeed, the very intensity of the conflict may, paradoxically, be an indication of how close in many ways—ideologically as well as geographically—the two groups are.[18] Hence the nature of Matthew's polemic against 'the Jews' has to be read in the light of Matthew's own (probable) situation, as well as

---

[17]   This is well established in Matthean studies. Cf. the programmatic study of Barth 1963.

[18]   Cf. Stanton 1992: 98-100, citing Coser 1956.

with the insights that a more sociological approach to conflict and 'sectarianism' (in a broad sense) can bring to bear.

2. *Matthew's Knowledge of Judaism: Matt. 12:11-12.* A more specific problem of exegesis arises in relation to the more concrete question of whether Matthew himself was a Jew. We have already noted that Matthew's Gospel is in many respects very Jewish. Yet at times Matthew seems surprisingly ignorant about aspects of Judaism. As is well known, he does not distinguish between different Jewish groups (Pharisees, scribes, Sadducees), and runs them together almost indiscriminately.

A peculiar problem arises in this respect in relation to a couple of verses in Matthew: Matt. 12:11-12. These verses constitute Matthew's addition to Mark's account of Jesus' healing the man with the withered hand on the sabbath, and are probably part of Matthew's attempt to alleviate the offence which Mark's Jesus might appear to cause in relation to sabbath law. In Mark, Jesus poses the blunt rhetorical questions 'Is it lawful to do good on the sabbath or to do evil? To save life or to destroy it?' (Mark 3:4) as apparent 'justification' for the action of healing the man on the sabbath in a way that it is assumed will breach sabbath law by constituting 'work'. (There is debate about whether Jesus' actions really would have constituted work [Harvey 1982: 38]. However, the fact remains that, in both Mark and Matthew, it is assumed without question that Jesus' action does constitute 'work'.) As is well known, the rhetorical questions do not settle the issue. The general rule at the time was that sabbath law could be broken to save life, but not otherwise. Here the man's life is clearly not in danger. Hence Jesus should not work on the sabbath; 'doing good' on the sabbath in these circumstances should then involve respecting the sabbath legislation and not working.

Matthew clearly sees these problems and tries then to rescue Jesus from what he seems to regard as a potentially dangerous and damaging stance in relation to the Jewish Law. Thus he has Jesus give a further argument to justify his proposed action by appealing to the example of rescuing a sheep from a pit on the sabbath. He claims that this is a legitimate breach of sabbath law, and asserts that the situation of a man in difficulties is both analogous and also more important: hence what one does for a sheep one will do for a human being. Thus 'it is lawful' (v. 12) to do good on the sabbath, and by implication to heal the man with the withered hand.

The major exegetical problem arises from the fact that, as far as we can tell from our available evidence, rescuing a sheep from a pit on the sabbath was *not* regarded as a legitimate breach of sabbath law. On the other hand, our knowledge is very fragmentary and its value uncertain: there is a later rabbinic ruling, and also a text from Qumran, explicitly forbidding this (see *b. Sanh.* 128b; CD 11:13); but the rabbinic evidence is late (well after the time of Matthew), and the Qumran evidence may only show what one small pocket of Judaism at the time thought, not what all Jews followed. Further, the fact that the case is explicitly ruled upon in the texts we have may imply that such a case was contested by some.

How then are we to interpret the evidence of Matthew? One could say, if we assumed that Matthew were a Jew, that the evidence of Matthew's Gospel itself could constitute evidence that this was regarded as a legitimate breach of sabbath law at the time (cf. by implication Jeremias 1971: 209). Alternatively, one could argue that, since all our available evidence (such as it is) is consistent in saying that such action was not allowed on the sabbath, then Matthew must be wrong here, and hence it is unlikely that Matthew himself was a Jew (Strecker 1962: 19). A third possibility is that Matthew's Jesus is appealing to common practice among Galilean farmers who may not have been so concerned about the letter of the Law when dealing with such a precious commodity as a sheep in a situation of precarious agrarian economic existence (Manson 1949: 188-89). On the other hand, while this might explain the saying on the lips of Jesus, or in an earlier stratum of the tradition,[19] Matthew seems to understand it as part of a legal argument to justify breaking sabbath law. Hence Matthew may have misunderstood the nature of the appeal, but this then simply highlights even more the question of how extensive Matthew's knowledge of Judaism actually was.

There is thus no clear right or wrong answer to the issues raised by these two verses in Matthew. The argument is circular, and one can go round the circle in different ways, or break into the circle at different points with different initial assumptions. However, I hope that it is clear that theories about the identity of the author of a text[20] are integrally related to the problem of how to interpret aspects of the text: one issue affects the other, and in turn is affected by the other so

---

[19] The saying almost certainly goes back to Q: cf. the parallel in Luke 14:5.

[20] As before, 'identity' here is meant in a relatively general sense. The specific name of the author is perhaps one of the less important issues.

that there can be no neat division of labour into the tasks of 'introduction' and 'exegesis', as if the former can be carried out independently of the latter or vice versa.

D. The Synoptic Problem

Another standard 'introductory' problem concerns the relationship between the three Synoptic Gospels, the so-called 'Synoptic problem'. What difference does a particular solution to the Synoptic problem make to exegesis or interpretation? Again the problems probably arise more at the level of the interpretation of broader issues than detailed exegesis of individual words or phrases. Certainly at such a broad level, the solution to the Synoptic problem that is adopted may affect one's understanding of the text significantly.

I focus here on two particular solutions to the Synoptic problem to illustrate the issues that may arise. One very widely-held solution to the Synoptic problem is the so-called Two Source Theory. According to this, Mark's Gospel was written first and was then used as a source by Matthew and Luke; Matthew and Luke also had access to another body of source material, now lost but usually known as Q. One major rival to this theory is the so-called Griesbach Hypothesis, according to which Matthew was written first, Luke came second using Matthew, and Mark's Gospel was written last using both Matthew and Luke as sources. How then is one's understanding of the Gospels affected by the solution adopted to the Synoptic problem?

In some ways it may be that there is little difference. The text of each Gospel stands as a literary entity, worthy of study in its own right, whatever the nature of the interrelationships between the Gospels. However, a great deal of interpretation of the Synoptic Gospels takes place via a comparison of the text with the alleged source(s) used by each evangelist. In this approach, a different decision about the nature of Gospel interrelationships can become quite critical. Nevertheless, the two approaches should be complementary to each other. Indeed, the extent to which the two approaches mesh, or fail to mesh, may be a measure of the correctness or otherwise of the source theory presupposed. To illustrate this, I take two issues, one in relation to Mark, the other in relation to Matthew and Luke.

1. Mark's Purpose. The first question concerns the interpretation of the Gospel of Mark. What was Mark's purpose in writing? What were Mark's concerns?

According to the Two Source Theory, Mark's was the first Gospel to be written, and there are no extant predecessors or sources with which to compare Mark. On this basis, one has to take the Gospel as it stands to try to discover what the writer thought was important about Jesus. There is not space here to discuss this in any more than an extremely cursory and superficial way. However, most would argue that a feature of paramount concern in Mark's Gospel is the issue of Christology and the centrality of the cross: Jesus is the one whose appointed role is to suffer and to die, and whose true identity, as 'Son of God', is revealed fully in the light of the cross. Hence too, perhaps, the element of secrecy that surrounds Jesus' person prior to the events of the passion (cf. Räisänen 1990).

Using the Griesbach Hypothesis, a potentially very different picture of Mark emerges. Mark is one who is clearly anxious to preserve some (though not all) elements common to both his sources, Matthew and Luke. He appears to be one who is positively disinterested in Jesus' teaching since he cuts a lot of it out (e.g. all the material usually ascribed to 'Q' in the Two Source Theory, including the ethical teaching of the Sermon on the Mount/Plain), with the result that relatively more space is devoted to Jesus' miracles. He tones down some of Matthew's or Luke's high Christology: for example, at Caesarea Philippi, Peter in Mark no longer confesses Jesus as 'Son of God' (as in Matthew); and in the rejection scene in Nazareth, Mark writes in the fact that Jesus *could* not perform many miracles (Mark 6:5, cf. Matt. 13:58). Any secrecy elements are mostly taken from his sources. In all, Mark is something of an irenic writer, seeking perhaps to reconcile and unite potentially conflicting accounts in his two sources, Matthew and Luke, but with little new to add of his own.[21]

It seems clear that the two pictures of Mark that emerge here are not easily compatible. Indeed one could argue that the apparent failure of the two interpretations of Mark to mesh with each other is a serious drawback to the Griesbach Hypothesis. The Mark of the Two Source Theory is effectively the same as the Mark who emerges from a 'straight' reading of the Gospel as an undifferentiated whole, since *ex hypothesi* this is the only way the Gospel can be read. However, such a way of reading Mark, taking the text as a literary unity, should relate positively to the way in which a text is read on the basis of a source-critical theory. There should be some positive correlation between the

---

[21] Such a portrait may be a slight caricature, but modern defenders of the Griesbach Hypothesis have not yet developed a clear profile of Mark's Gospel as a whole on the basis of their theory.

two readings. The fact that there is not is in some measure an indication that the source theory in question fails to convince. Nevertheless, as with the other 'introductory' issues we looked at, the problem of interrelationships and the broader interpretative problem of understanding Mark are clearly intertwined and cannot be easily separated. Thus it could be that, *if* the Griesbach Hypothesis is correct, then Mark must be interpreted in a certain way, and this would also determine our more 'literary' reading of Mark as well.

2. *Wisdom Christology.* A second problem concerns the (relatively few) texts in Luke's Gospel where Wisdom appears in almost personified form (Luke 7:35; 11:49). According to the Two Source Theory, these are Q texts, and Luke's version probably reproduces the Q version more accurately than Matthew's parallel.[22] Further, these texts show a characteristic, and in part distinctive, feature of the ideas emerging from the Q material: here Wisdom is portrayed as the one who sends the prophets who in turn suffer violence; among these prophetic messengers are, by implication, Jesus and John the Baptist, so that this schema represents a distinct christological pattern (Tuckett 1983: 164-65; also 1996: chap. 7).

Using the Griesbach Hypothesis, or indeed any theory that makes Luke directly dependent on Matthew,[23] a quite different interpretation is suggested. In at least one of the passages, Luke has the reference to Wisdom where Matthew does not (Luke 11:49; cf. Matt. 23:34). Hence, if Matthew is Luke's source (as the Griesbach Hypothesis postulates), this reference in Luke must be due to Luke's deliberate redaction. The difference between the two Gospels is thus not a reflection of any Q Christology but reflects Luke's own concerns. On this hypothesis, then, a significant aspect of Luke's Christology would be opened up.

One could, of course, turn all this around as an argument (as with the consideration of Mark's Gospel) and argue conversely: part of the reason why the Wisdom reference in Luke 11:49 is thought in the Two Source Theory to represent Q's wording is because this idea

---

[22] For those espousing some kind of Q theory, Luke's reference to 'Wisdom' in Luke 11:49 is uniformly taken as the Q wording. (Matthew has 'I'.) See Tuckett 1983: 160, and many others. Luke 7:35 and Matthew's parallel (Matt. 11:19) both contain the reference to Wisdom.

[23] As, for example, in the theories of Goulder 1989, who argues that Mark came first, but that Luke is directly dependent on Matthew, not on some lost Q source.

seems so unlike anything else in Luke. Apart from these few Q passages, Luke shows no interest in ideas of personified Wisdom. There is nothing comparable in Luke's redaction of Mark (using the Two Source Theory) or Matthew (using the Griesbach Theory) elsewhere, and no evidence of such ideas anywhere in Acts, especially in the speeches of Acts (where Luke's ideas might most likely be in evidence). The implicit claim of the Griesbach Hypothesis in relation to Luke 11:49 thus effectively has to postulate a positive christological concern by Luke, for which there is very little evidence elsewhere in Luke's writings. Hence some would argue that this text is a positive reason for casting doubt on any theory that Luke is dependent on Matthew (cf. Tuckett 1996: 25).

However, we should note how, yet again, introductory issues and broader interpretative problems interrelate with each other. The former affect the latter; but equally we have to use the broader issues to influence our solution to the 'introductory' issues. The two are never separable from each other.

E. Non-Canonical Sources

In a final section, I consider briefly the question of other sources, from outside the New Testament, as possible evidence for the traditions found in the Synoptic Gospels. In this context, the most obvious such source for consideration is the *Gospel of Thomas*. In one sense, the issues posed by such a source as the *Gospel of Thomas* belong more within a consideration of problems of the historical Jesus, and these are dealt with in the chapter, 'Life of Jesus'. However, decisions about the nature and relevance of a text such as the *Gospel of Thomas* can have a significant effect on the study of the Synoptic Gospels themselves.

Ever since the discovery of its full text in 1945, a key point in discussions about the *Gospel of Thomas* has been the problem of its relationship to the Synoptic Gospels. The *Gospel of Thomas* contains a string of sayings of Jesus, some of which are closely parallel to sayings of Jesus found in the Synoptics. Is then the *Gospel of Thomas* an independent line of the tradition, giving us independent attestation for these sayings? Or does it represent a line of the tradition which develops out of or from our Synoptic Gospels? The relevance of the issue to study of Jesus is presumably clear. What though of the Gospels themselves?

If the *Gospel of Thomas* is dependent on our Gospels (at however many stages removed), then the *Gospel of Thomas* has little to contribute to the study of the canonical Gospels. The *Gospel of Thomas* is in this view a witness to how the tradition develops after this stage. With the alternative view, the *Gospel of Thomas* is an independent witness to the tradition, or at least diverging from the Synoptic 'trajectories' before the stage of the canonical Gospels. It might then assist us in making exegetical decisions about Synoptic texts. For example, in cases where there are parallel versions of a tradition or saying in the *Gospel of Thomas* and in the Synoptics, the *Gospel of Thomas* might help us in determining which is the earlier form of the tradition. Thus Koester has argued that, if a 'Q' tradition appears in Matthew and Luke and also in the *Gospel of Thomas*, the version that is closer to that in the *Gospel of Thomas* may be more original (Koester 1990a: 61; more generally 1990b). Thus, one's theories about the nature of the *Gospel of Thomas*, and its relationship to the Synoptic Gospels, can have a significant effect on decisions about the Synoptic evidence itself, in particular the relative dating of parallel versions. A similar situation could arise in the case of Markan traditions, as the following example shows.

The Gospel of Thomas 14//Matt. 15:11//Mark 7:15. Part of saying 14 in the *Gospel of Thomas* reads: 'What goes into your mouth will not defile; rather, it is what comes out of your mouth that will defile you'. This is clearly very close to the Synoptic tradition found in Mark 7:15 and Matt. 15:11. Further, it is apparently much closer to the Matthean version in explicitly mentioning the 'mouth', a feature that Mark lacks. The evidence is (as ever!) open to more than one interpretation.

If one starts with the Synoptic evidence alone, then Matthew's version seems to be due to Matthew's redaction of Mark. The 'mouth' is thus due to Matthew's editing. The *Gospel of Thomas* then shows knowledge of Matthew's edited form of the saying and hence is to be judged to be secondary to Matthew, that is, it must represent a post-Matthean development (McArthur 1960: 286).

On the other hand, one could equally well argue that the reference to the 'mouth' is a very obvious addition and could have been added independently by *Thomas* and Matthew (Patterson 1993: 25). Alternatively, if one starts from a premise that the *Gospel of Thomas* is independent of the Synoptics, one could argue that the *Gospel of Thomas* is itself positive evidence for the possibility that Matt. 15:11 is not due to Matthew's editing of Mark, but represents an independent form of the saying (Dunn 1985: 263). If one's concern is to recover the earliest form of the saying in the tradition, then the evidence from the *Gospel of Thomas* might be crucially important in opening up the possibility that Jesus' words are reflected in Matthew's version of the saying, not Mark's.[24]

For what it is worth, I find it difficult to assume a global theory about the *Gospel of Thomas*'s independence and to then use this to get round a piece of data that, on the surface, would appear to be clear evidence to the contrary, namely, an element of the redactional activity of one of the Synoptic evangelists reappearing in the *Gospel of Thomas*. Thus, the evidence from this parallel between the *Gospel of Thomas* and Matthew's Gospel may be part of a body of evidence indicating that the *Gospel of Thomas* is *not* independent for the Synoptics, but represents a *post*-Synoptic development of the tradition (Tuckett 1988). But, as with so many of these issues we have looked at in this chapter, one is involved in potentially circular arguments where the point at which one breaks into the circle, and the initial starting point one adopts, are crucial.

CONCLUSION

The aim of this chapter has been to try to illustrate some of the ways in which one's understanding of aspects of a text are integrally related to 'introductory' issues associated with that text. On several occasions, we have seen that the relationship is often a dialectical one: the question of interpretation is affected by the solutions adopted to an introductory problem, but it can also itself affect the latter. Very often, as we have seen, there are no clear right or wrong answers to the problems concerned. At the very least, then, all those seeking to interpret and understand the New Testament texts should be aware of the circular nature of many of the arguments used in several critical discussions, and of the unavoidably provisional nature of any 'conclusions' drawn. For some, such indeterminacy is a disappointment; for others, it is a refreshing corrective to over-dogmatic claims by others and a welcome challenge to continue the exploration of seeking to discover what these texts may mean.

---

[24]   The saying is of immense potential significance in relation to the question of Jesus' attitude to the Law, since Jesus in Mark 7:15 appears at first sight to be jettisoning all the food laws of Leviticus. Matthew's version is more susceptible to the interpretation that Jesus is simply placing different concerns in a relative order of priorities, but without rejecting the Law itself.

BIBLIOGRAPHY

Barth, G.
1963 'Matthew's Understanding of the Law', in G. Bornkamm, G. Barth and H.J. Held, *Tradition and Interpretation in Matthew*. ET London: SCM Press: 58-164.

Bauckham, R.J.
1991 'The Rich Man and Lazarus: The Parable and the Parallels'. *NTS* 37: 225-46.

De Boer, M.C.
1995 'God-Fearers in Luke–Acts', in C.M. Tuckett (ed.), *Luke's Literary Achievement*. JSNTSup, 116. Sheffield: Sheffield Academic Press: 50-71.

Brown, R.E.
1994 *The Death of the Messiah*. 2 vols. New York: Doubleday.

Bruce, F.F.
1951 *The Acts of the Apostles*. London: Tyndale.

Catchpole, D.R.
1970 *The Trial of Jesus*. SPB, 18. Leiden: Brill.

Coser, L.
1956 *The Functions of Social Conflict*. London: Routledge & Kegan Paul.

Dunn, J.D.G.
1985 'Jesus and Ritual Purity. A Study of the Tradition History of Mk 7,15', in *A Cause de l'Evangile*. Festschrift J. Dupont. Paris: Cerf: 251-76.

Fitzmyer, J.A.
1989 'The Authorship of Luke–Acts Reconsidered', in *Luke the Theologian: Aspects of his Teaching*. New York: Paulist: 1-26.

Gager, J.
1983 *The Origins of Anti-Semitism*. New York and Oxford: Oxford University Press.

Goulder, M.D.
1989 *Luke—A New Paradigm*. 2 vols. JSNTSup, 20. Sheffield: JSOT Press.

Haenchen, E.
1971 *The Acts of the Apostles*. ET Oxford: Blackwell.

Hanson, P.D.
1975 *The Dawn of Apocalyptic*. Philadelphia: Fortress Press.

Hare, D.R.A.
1967 *The Theme of Jewish Persecution of Christians in the Gospel according to St Matthew*. SNTSMS, 6. Cambridge: Cambridge University Press.

Harvey, A.E.
1982 *Jesus and the Constraints of History*. London: Duckworth.

Hooker, M.D.
1982 'Trial and Tribulation in Mark XIII'. *BJRL* 65: 78-99.
1983 *The Message of Mark*. London: Epworth.
1991 *The Gospel according to St Mark*. London: A. & C. Black.

Jeremias, J.
1971 *New Testament Theology. I. The Proclamation of Jesus.* ET London: SCM Press.

Koester, H.
1990a 'Q and its Relatives', in J.E. Goehring *et al.* (eds.), *Gospel Origins and Christian Beginnings.* Festschrift J.M. Robinson. Sonoma, CA: Polebridge: 49-63.
1990b *Ancient Christian Gospels.* London: SCM Press; Philadelphia: Trinity Press International.

Kümmel, W.G.
1975 *Introduction to the New Testament.* ET London: SCM Press.

Lührmann, D.
1981 'Markus 14.55-64: Christologie und Zerstörung des Tempels im Markusevangelium'. *NTS* 27: 457-74.

McArthur, H.K.
1960 'The Dependence of the Gospel of Thomas on the Synoptics'. *ExpTim* 71: 286-87.

Manson, T.W.
1949 *The Sayings of Jesus.* London: SCM Press.

Patterson, S.J.
1993 *The Gospel of Thomas and Jesus.* Sonoma, CA: Polebridge.

Räisänen, H.
1990 *The 'Messianic Secret' in Mark's Gospel.* ET Edinburgh: T. & T. Clark.

Robinson, J.A.T.
1976 *Redating the New Testament.* London: SCM Press.

Salmon, M.
1988 'Insider or Outsider? Luke's Relationship with Judaism', in J.B. Tyson (ed.), *Luke–Acts and the Jewish People.* Minneapolis: Augsburg, 1988: 76-82.

Sanders, J.T.
1987 *The Jews in Luke–Acts.* London: SCM Press.

Stanton, G.N.
1992 *A Gospel for a New People: Studies in Matthew.* Edinburgh: T. & T. Clark.

Strecker, G.
1962 *Der Weg der Gerechtigkeit.* Göttingen: Vandenhoeck & Ruprecht.

Taylor, V.
1952 *The Gospel according to St Mark.* London: Macmillan.

Theissen, G.
1992 *The Gospels in Context: Social and Political History in the Synoptic Tradition.* ET Edinburgh: T. & T. Clark.

Tuckett, C.M.
1983 *The Revival of the Griesbach Hypothesis.* Cambridge: Cambridge University Press.
1988 'Thomas and the Synoptics'. *NovT* 30: 132-57.
1996 *Q and the History of Early Christianity.* Edinburgh: T. & T. Clark.

Tyson, J.B. (ed.)
1988   *Luke–Acts and the Jewish People*. Minneapolis: Augsburg.
Vielhauer, P.
1968   'On the "Paulinism" of Acts'. ET in L.E. Keck and J.L. Martyn (eds.),
       Studies in Luke–Acts. London: SPCK: 33-50.

EXEGESIS OF THE PAULINE LETTERS, INCLUDING THE DEUTERO-PAULINE LETTERS

STANLEY E. PORTER

1. INTRODUCTION

For some reason, the notion persists that exegesis of the Pauline letters is easier than that of the Gospels. The thought is that matters of language are more self-evident in the Pauline letters, due to lack of translation from Aramaic (as Jesus' words purportedly are), and matters of background are less complex, due to a lack of issues raised by synoptic comparison. Only a moment of reflection will reveal that this notion is greatly mistaken, or at least no more true of the Pauline letters than of the Gospels.

Two examples will suffice to illustrate the difficulties of Pauline exegesis. The first considers a matter of language. Paul quotes the Old Testament on numerous occasions. It is difficult to calculate the exact numbers, but the direct quotations in his major letters number around 80 instances.[1] In several of these places, he appears to change the wording significantly. Why? What does he mean by these changes? What do they imply about the text he is using? What does his quotation of the Old Testament imply when he writes to predominantly Gentile churches? These are not easy questions to answer, but they have large exegetical significance for understanding Paul's message and his argumentative strategy. It is difficult to understand major sections of such a fundamental letter to the Pauline corpus as Romans without addressing this and related questions. The second example considers a matter of context. Related to the example cited above is the debate over how much about the historical Jesus Paul appeared to know, with the range of opinion running from much to very little. Discussion often involves exegesis of two or three key, though disputed, passages in 1 Corinthians (7:10; 9:14; possibly

---

[1]   On issues related to this, see S.E. Porter, 'The Use of the Old Testament in the New Testament: A Brief Comment on Method and Terminology', in *Early Christian Interpretation of the Scriptures of Israel: Investigations and Proposals* (ed. C.A. Evans and J.A. Sanders; SSEJC, 5; JSNTSup, 148; Sheffield: Sheffield Academic Press, 1997), pp. 79-96.

11:23-25).[2] Scholars have found it difficult to delimit the passages for consideration, to say nothing of determining their significance for understanding Paul's relation to the historical Jesus. All of this is not to say that Paul's letters are not understandable without delving into complex linguistic and contextual exegetical matters. On a superficial level they certainly are. They are, I would contend, as understandable as any other writings of the New Testament—probably no more or no less.

To provide as complete an exegesis of a passage in a Pauline letter as is possible, however, the exegete needs to consider a host of issues regarding authorship, language, culture, religion and theology, literary genre—far too many to discuss here in any detail—that form the necessary interpretative context for analysis of a particular passage. In light of the importance of these various issues, a chapter such as this could approach the Pauline letters in a number of ways. One would be to discuss the individual letters, singling out the particular questions that apply to a given book and showing how they apply to exegesis of particular passages. Much of this information can already be found in numerous introductions to the New Testament (see the Biblio-graphical Essay above, for description of some of these sources), as well as commentaries that provide exegesis of particular passages, and is not necessary to repeat here. Instead, the topics below constitute a select number of fundamental exegetical issues that form the foundation for exegesis of particular passages in the Pauline letters. This number is not complete, but is designed to sensitize the interpreter to the issues involved in Pauline exegesis. Discussion of issues of this sort is necessary for informed and informative exegesis, even though the exegetical implications of these topics is often ignored when exegesis becomes merely a matter of describing the grammar of a given passage, as if it did not matter whether the passage was found in Paul, the Gospels or another New Testament writer. I assume that the exegete has sufficient linguistic understanding to grasp the basic structure of a passage. Rigorous exegesis, however, demands a larger interpretative context in terms of issues specific to the Pauline letters to become useful.

---

2   For a recent discussion, see F. Neirynck, 'The Sayings of Jesus in 1 Corinthians', in *The Corinthian Correspondence* (ed. R. Bieringer; BETL, 125; Leuven: Leuven University Press/Peeters, 1996), pp. 141-76.

2. PAUL'S JEWISH AND HELLENISTIC BACKGROUNDS

An important first step in exegesis of the Pauline letters is to place them in their proper larger context, that is, with regard to their cultural, religious and theological background. Therefore, a fundamental set of assumptions in much discussion of the Pauline letters attaches to whether Paul reflects a Jewish or a Hellenistic background.[3] Although it is rarely stated as baldly as that, discussion in the secondary literature often reflects such a dichotomy, attempting to classify various elements of Paul's thought on the basis of whether the Jewish or Greek elements predominate.

Those who wish to argue for the importance of Paul's Jewish background begin from several programmatic statements that Paul makes regarding his Jewish background, including Phil. 3:5-6. Also brought into the equation is the tradition found in Acts that Paul, although born in Tarsus in Silicia, was educated in Jerusalem under the Rabbi Gamaliel I. This would harmonize with his becoming a Pharisee and then becoming a persecutor of the Church because of its acceptance of Jesus as the Messiah. Those who wish to argue for the importance of Paul's Hellenistic background often begin with a distinction between Palestinian and Diaspora Judaism. Paul's being born outside of the Land and travelling extensively in the Mediterranean world, using the Greek language and the Greek letter-form as his major means of communication with the churches that he founded, all play into the hands of these scholars.

To a large extent, however, each of these characterizations is in need of correction. The simple opposition between Jewish and Hellenistic backgrounds is unsupportable in light of recent research. Much of this research has been promoted by Martin Hengel, but he is only one of the latest of a number of scholars who have seen the first-century world in broader terms.[4] The first-century Mediterranean

---

3   This issue is discussed in some detail in L.M. McDonald and S.E. Porter, *Early Christianity and its Sacred Literature* (Peabody: Hendrickson, forthcoming), chap. 9.

4   See M. Hengel, *Judaism and Hellenism* (trans. J. Bowden; 2 vols.; London: SCM Press; Philadelphia: Fortress Press, 1974); *idem, The 'Hellenization' of Judaea in the First Century after Christ* (trans. J. Bowden; London: SCM Press; Philadelphia: Trinity Press International, 1989); *idem, Jews, Greeks and Barbarians* (trans. J. Bowden; London: SCM Press, 1980), etc. He follows in the tradition of such scholars as E.J. Bickerman (e.g. *The Jews in the Greek Age* [Cambridge, MA: Harvard University Press, 1988]) and V.

world was essentially Greco-Roman in nature, even at its fringes, such as the Roman near east, where Greco-Roman customs, law and language prevailed. In other words, as an aftermath of the conquests of Alexander the Great (late 4th century BCE), and the subsequent unification of the Greek states and other territories under Roman rule from the time of Augustus (late 1st century BCE), from Arabia in the east to Spain in the west, and as far north as Britain and south as the north of Africa, the world was in many respects one. This is not to say that there were not regional differences in culture, religion and even local languages, since there were. These were determined by such matters as cultural and ethnic background, language, history of conquest and politics. The framework in which these regional differences were allowed to continue, however, was Greco-Roman, that is, Greek culture as mediated through Roman rule. Several of the most noticeable elements of this were, for example, the fact that Greek was the *lingua franca* of this empire. Regional languages continued in a few places (e.g. Phrygian in northern Asia Minor, Aramaic in Palestine and Syria, and Nabatean in Arabia, etc.), and eventually Latin became a second *lingua franca* from the second century on, but the major language that held this empire together was Greek, even in Palestine. An additional Greco-Roman element of life throughout the Roman east was the establishment of many cities built on Greek and Roman plans, such as Caesarea Maritima, or other immense building projects of Herod the Great in Palestine.[5]

The Roman world was also highly religious and very syncretistic. Roman religion was apparently originally based upon the Greek pantheon, but had readily embraced a large number of regional cults as well.[6] With the perception of the overwhelming largeness of the contemporary world, privatistic religion also increased, with the result that mystery cults spread throughout the empire, such as Mithraism,

---

Tcherikover (*Hellenistic Civilization and the Jews* [Philadelphia: Jewish Publication Society of America, 1959]).

[5]   See F.W. Walbank, *The Hellenistic World* (London: Fontana, 1981); W. Tarn and T.G. Griffith, *Hellenistic Civilisation* (London: Edward Arnold, 3rd edn, 1952); and M. Cary, *A History of Rome down to the Reign of Constantine* (London: Macmillan, 2nd edn, 1954), for details of what is summarized above.

[6]   See J. Ferguson, *The Religions of the Roman Empire* (Ithaca: Cornell University Press, 1970), for an excellent discussion that places Judaism within the context of Roman religion; cf. J.H.W.G. Liebeschuetz, *Continuity and Change in Roman Religion* (Oxford: Clarendon Press, 1979).

which was largely spread by the Roman army. Judaism was one of these cults, with its own meeting places (synagogues) and writings (the Old Testament, usually in its Greek form, the Septuagint). Many people were apparently attracted to some of the tenets of Judaism (called God-fearers),[7] but most of them without formal allegiance. Judaism probably did not have formal recognition, but, because Jews tended to be exclusive and to live in concentrated ghettos in certain places, such as Rome, they received certain religious considerations and some resultant privileges. These were perhaps not much different from considerations given to other religious cults. One potentially troublesome area was worship of the emperor, but this practice did not develop more formally until late in the first century and into the second century CE (Pliny, *Ep.* 10:96).[8] Most Greco-Roman life did not exclude Jews from functioning in various ways in the empire. Sometimes they lived in large enough numbers to attract undue attention, or were thought to cause disruptions, which brought punishment (e.g. the expulsion from Rome in 49 or 41 CE—the date is uncertain). Of course, Judaism maintained a number of distinctive beliefs, especially regarding the coming of a messiah. Even in many of its beliefs, however, there are more than a few traces of influence from the larger Greco-Roman world. However, it was merely one religious-ethnic people group—albeit a significant one—within the larger Greco-Roman world.

What difference does this perspective make in exegeting the Pauline letters? The most important consideration is that interpretation of Paul's writings must occur within this conceptual framework. Paul is sometimes viewed as unique because he combined being an ethnic Jew with being a citizen of the Greco-Roman world. To the contrary, although his literary and theological contribution was undeniably unique, Paul was in many ways a typical member of the Greco-Roman world—a large number of, if not most, people had a similar bi-unitary background and set of allegiances. It is not known how many Jews were Roman citizens,[9] but in this regard Paul was almost assuredly not

---

7   For recent discussion of this controversial topic, see I. Levinskaya, *The Book of Acts in its First Century Setting. V. Diaspora Setting* (Grand Rapids: Eerdmans; Exeter: Paternoster, 1996), esp. pp. 1-126.

8   See L.J. Kreitzer, *Striking New Images: Roman Imperial Coinage and the New Testament World* (JSNTSup, 134; Sheffield: Sheffield Academic Press, 1996), pp. 69-98, for a recent discussion of the emperor cult.

9   Even though statements that Paul was a Roman citizen are only found in

unique (note that Paul's father also was a citizen; Acts 25:28). Paul both had a specific ethnic heritage, and was a 'citizen' of the larger Greco-Roman world. This world was truly cosmopolitan, as, for the first time, people were able to travel relatively extensively and communicate over broad expanses of territory previously for the most part out of reach. Paul was not unreasonable in hoping that he could travel to Spain (see Rom. 15:24, 28), and his many travels around the eastern side of the Mediterranean bear witness to the extensive travel and shipping lines available. Many of these were based upon the importance of supplying food for the empire, especially grain shipments from Egypt and Africa.[10] When Paul wrote his letters in Greek to various groups of Christians throughout the Roman empire, he wrote them with the reasonable expectation that these letters could and would be understood by those to whom they were transmitted.

An example that well illustrates the interconnectedness of the Greco-Roman world, of which Judaism was a part, is the suggestion that Paul uses forms of rabbinic argumentation at certain places in his letters. For example, at Rom. 5:8-9 he states that, if God was able to reconcile humanity when humanity was an enemy of God, how much more will he be able to save humanity in the end. This seems to reflect the Rabbinic form of argumentation of the lesser to the greater (*t. Sanh.* 7:11). In other words, God's being able to accomplish the harder task of overcoming human animosity implies that he can perform the easier task of saving those who have been reconciled. This indeed resembles what has come to be known as rabbinic argumentation, and Paul may have learned this form of argumentation during the time of his study with Gamaliel in Jerusalem. However, one must examine the larger question of the origins of rabbinic exegesis. David Daube, the Jewish legal historian, has convincingly argued that 'the Rabbinic methods of interpretation derive from Hellenistic rhetoric. Hellenistic rhetoric is at the bottom both of the fundamental ideas, presuppositions, from which the Rabbis proceeded

---

Acts (16:38; 22:25), they are probably accurate. See B. Rapske, *The Book of Acts in its First Century Setting. III. Paul in Roman Custody* (Grand Rapids: Eerdmans; Exeter: Paternoster, 1994), pp. 72-90; A.N. Sherwin-White, *Roman Society and Roman Law in the New Testament* (Oxford: Clarendon Press, 1963), pp. 144-93 and *idem, The Roman Citizenship* (Oxford: Clarendon Press, 2nd edn, 1973), p. 273, who provides much documentation on this issue.

10   See G. Rickman, *The Corn Supply of Ancient Rome* (Oxford: Clarendon Press, 1980), esp. pp. 231-35.

and of the major details of application, the manner in which these ideas were translated into practice.'[11] Rhetoric was very important in the ancient world, and led to a set of more or less formalized principles by which those who were engaged in public discussion and disputation crafted their statements. Rhetoric was of great importance from the fourth century BCE on, and led to a number of important formulations of its principles by such writers roughly contemporary with Paul as Cicero and Quintilian, among others.[12] Within this world, it is not surprising to find that Jewish forms of exegesis may well have been influenced in their development by Greco-Roman rhetoric. Thus, it is unwise to draw a bifurcation between Jewish and Greco-Roman influence upon Paul. Rather, what is often seen here as a Jewish feature should be seen within the larger sphere of Hellenistic influence.

A similar situation is found in the use of the Old Testament by Paul. This is an issue that must be discussed on two levels. The first level concerns why Paul even uses the Old Testament, especially when writing to predominantly Gentile churches, and the second is how to account for his exegetical techniques when he cites the Old Testament. For example, the book of Romans has more direct quotations of the Old Testament than any other of Paul's books— around 55 instances. Paul was probably writing to a church of mixed Jewish and Gentile background, though probably with more Gentiles than Jews (see below).[13] This makes it difficult to understand why Paul relies so heavily upon the Old Testament to structure his argument. At Rom. 1:17, he quotes Hab. 2:4 as the 'thematic' statement that governs his entire conception of the book. When he undertakes to justify the faithfulness of God, in light of the situation with Israel (Romans 9–11), he creates a veritable pastiche of Old Testament quotations (see the *UBSGNT*[4] list). As a further example, it is even less readily understandable why Paul uses the Old Testament at probably at least three places in Philippians (1:19; 2:9-11; 4:18), a

---

[11]   D. Daube, 'Rabbinic Methods of Interpretation and Hellenistic Rhetoric', *HUCA* 22 (1949), pp. 239-64 (240).

[12]   A recent survey of the history of rhetoric is to be found in G.A. Kennedy, 'Historical Survey of Rhetoric', in *Handbook of Classical Rhetoric in the Hellenistic Period (330 B.C.–A.D. 400)* (ed. S.E. Porter; Leiden: Brill, 1997), pp. 3-42.

[13]   See discussion of this and related issues in K.P. Donfried (ed.), *The Romans Debate* (Peabody: Hendrickson, 2nd edn, 1991), *passim*.

letter addressed to a church with probably very little Jewish membership. Certainly the city of Philippi itself did not have much of a Jewish population.

Several observations of exegetical significance can be made concerning Paul's use of the Old Testament. The first is with regard to Paul himself and the second is with regard to how Paul uses the Old Testament. The first factor to keep in mind is that Paul's argument (see below on the letter form) should be assessed at least in the first instance in terms of how he wishes it to be constructed, rather than how it would have come across to his listeners. We know from others of Paul's letters (e.g. the Corinthian correspondence—see below) that Paul was not always conceptually understood by his audience, so much so that he was required to write other letters to rectify situations that earlier correspondence may have even aggravated. Paul's worldview, including his theological perspective, was oriented toward seeing the Scriptures fulfilled in the coming of Christ. This framework provides the basis for his thought and his argumentation. As a result, he often structures his argument around the Old Testament. This is especially, but by no means always, true when he is dealing with the Jewish people, as Romans 9–11 illustrates. The key is to appreciate why and in what way Paul invokes the Old Testament in his thought. In some instances, his readers may have been familiar with the Jewish Scriptures and could have informed those who were not so informed of added significance. His invoking of sacred texts, even if they were not familiar to his audience, would probably have been seen as providing a form of rhetorical proof to his argument. This technique of argumentation was well-known in the ancient world (e.g. quotation of Homer by later Greek writers), and the words of authorities were often seen as carrying special weight in support of an argument.

How was it that Paul used these texts in support of his argument? There has been much recent discussion of Paul's exegetical technique, but the majority of this discussion has been inclined to argue that Paul's exegetical technique is dependent upon some form of Jewish exegesis.[14] Christopher Stanley has argued that Paul's technique is similar to that of other Jewish exegetes of his time, as opposed to those of the Greco-Roman world. Stanley's analysis is revealing, however. He divides up the categories for comparison into two. He

---

[14]   See C.D. Stanley, *Paul and the Language of Scripture: Citation Technique in the Pauline Epistles and Contemporary Literature* (SNTSMS, 74; Cambridge: Cambridge University Press, 1992), esp. pp. 8-28.

then explores citation techniques in Greco-Roman literature and in early Judaism. He divides those of early Judaism into two major categories, with writers such as Philo of Alexandria in one category and the Qumran texts in another. Stanley's conclusion is that Paul's exegesis of the Old Testament falls most comfortably into that of the Jewish interpreters such as Philo. In light of the comments above, one can readily see that there are problems with such a categorization, however. The first is the neat bifurcation between Greco-Roman and early Jewish interpreters, since the writers of early Judaism, especially Philo, were very much a part of the Greco-Roman world; the second is the failure to take seriously the fact that Paul writes in Greek, and has that in common with Philo, as opposed to those interpreting the Old Testament in Semitic languages such as those at Qumran; and the third is the lack of recognition of Greek influence upon some, if not most, of the Jewish interpreters of the time, including Philo.[15] Philo's so-called allegorical method of interpretation of the Old Testament, which amounts to an expanded paraphrase of especially the Torah, is fully consonant with Greek-based citation and interpretation of important literary texts (especially Homer), typical of the Alexandrian literary tradition.[16] In other words, as argued above, what one might characterize as Jewish exegesis of the Old Testament is, instead, exegesis within the larger context of the Greco-Roman interpretative tradition of venerated texts, a tradition that he has in common with a host of other ancient writers of the Hellenistic world. The kinds of changes to the text that Paul makes—such as expansion, contraction, grammatical alteration, etc.—are much like that of both other Jewish interpreters as well as many Greco-Roman writers. Comparison of Paul's practice with that of other writers helps the exegete of the New Testament to realize that the kinds of changes that Paul makes are consistent with the broad textual interpretative tradition of the ancient world, in which venerated texts were invoked for a variety of important reasons. Sometimes these texts provided the philosophical foundation for a particular position, other times they offered argumentative support for such a position, and other times they only illustrated the terms in which the discussion or thought-processes took

---

15   Again, see Daube, 'Rabbinic Methods of Interpretation', *passim*, on the Greco-Roman origins of rabbinic exegetical technique.

16   R. Lamberton, *Homer the Theologian: Neoplatonist Allegorical Reading and the Growth of the Epic Tradition* (Berkeley: University of California Press, 1986), esp. pp. 44-54 on Philo.

place for a particular writer. Paul displays all of these tendencies in his use of the Old Testament, an element of his own exegesis that has not been fully explored in recent scholarship.

Thus, the matter of Paul's background has important exegetical implications. His use of the Old Testament, traditionally seen as an area that reveals his Jewish background, provides confirmatory evidence for analysis of Paul within the larger Greco-Roman world of which he was an active participant.

3. PAUL'S OPPONENTS

A second issue relevant for exegesis of a number, if not virtually all, of Paul's letters is the issue of the opposition that he faced in a given Christian community and that elicited his epistolary response. There are a few letters in which Paul does not apparently face opponents in a strict sense, such as the book of Romans, Philemon, and possibly Philippians. Even for letters such as Romans or Philemon, however, the letter reveals that Paul is facing a potentially divisive and/or contentious situation. Analysis of the points of contention, often in terms of specific opposition, is an important part of Pauline exegesis, and the nature of Paul's opponents is a matter of recurring yet unresolved debate. Not only does virtually every New Testament introduction discuss this topic, but there have been a number of important studies of the subject.[17] One of the most exegetically difficult situations to analyze is the one that Paul confronted at Corinth. The situation is difficult because, despite the relative abundance of evidence available, there is much that is simply not expressed or known, and exegesis of the letters requires extensive historical and theological reconstruction to provide an appropriate interpretative framework. As a result, there are varying reconstructions that must be weighed, some of them with more and others with less plausibility. In this section, exploration of the

---

[17] See, for example, J.J. Gunther, *St Paul's Opponents and their Background: A Study of Apocalyptic and Jewish Sectarian Teaching* (NovTSup, 35; Leiden: Brill, 1973); E.E. Ellis, 'Paul and his Opponents: Trends in the Research', in *Prophecy and Hermeneutic in Early Christianity: New Testament Essays* (WUNT, 18; Tübingen: Mohr–Siebeck, 1978; repr. Grand Rapids: Eerdmans, 1978), pp. 80-115; and the important methodological statements found in J.L. Sumney, *Identifying Paul's Opponents: The Question of Method in 2 Corinthians* (JSNTSup, 40; Sheffield: JSOT Press, 1990), esp. pp. 75-112.

opponents at Corinth will provide an opportunity to evidence the exegetical significance of this important category of investigation.

The first stage in analysis, however, must be the establishment of the proper historical and temporal context. This includes the gathering of significant data that must be explained by any exegetical hypothesis. In other words, what is the relationship between the composition of 1 and 2 Corinthians, and the issues that seem to have warranted their being written? There is much disagreement on this. I will offer one plausible historical scenario, but also try to indicate in recounting it where there are major points of dispute (minor points of dispute will not be included here, even though there are plenty that could be). It must be noted that my reconstruction admits evidence where appropriate from the book of Acts, an admission that many scholars would dispute and wish to exclude from their exegesis.

Paul appears to have planted a church in Corinth on what has come to be characterized as his second missionary journey (probably c. 50-52 CE) (cf. Acts 18:1-18), staying in Corinth for a year and a half. During this time, probably around 50-51 CE, he appeared before the Roman proconsul Gallio, who dismissed charges brought by the Jews against him, and may have, through his verdict, helped to guarantee Paul's safety in Corinth (1 Cor. 3:6; 2 Cor. 1:19). The dating of Gallio's term as proconsul, on the basis of the so-called Gallio inscription, is one of most secure dates of New Testament chronology.[18] Leaving Corinth, Paul returned to Antioch by way of Ephesus, Caesarea and Jerusalem, thus ending his second missionary journey. During the earlier part of his third missionary journey (probably 53-55 CE), probably during an extended stay at Ephesus (Acts 19:1-41), Paul sent his first letter to the Corinthian church. Some scholars think that 2 Cor. 6:14–7:1 is part of this now lost letter, although recent scholarship has tended away from this position.[19] Paul apparently then received information about problems in the church

---

[18]   On matters of New Testament chronology, see the summary and bibliography in S.E. Porter, 'New Testament Chronology', in *Eerdmans Dictionary of the Bible* (ed. D.N. Freedman; Grand Rapids: Eerdmans, 1998). The Gallio inscription is conveniently discussed in G. Ogg, *The Chronology of the Life of Paul* (London: Epworth, 1968), pp. 104–10, along with other relevant inscriptions.

[19]   See M.E. Thrall, *A Critical and Exegetical Commentary on the Second Epistle to the Corinthians* (2 vols.; ICC; Edinburgh: T. & T. Clark, 1994–), I, pp. 25-36, for discussion of this hypothesis.

(1 Cor. 1:11), as well as a letter from the church asking for advice on certain issues (see 1 Cor. 5:1; 7:1). Paul responded with what we call 1 Corinthians. Timothy was then sent on a special mission to Corinth (1 Cor. 4:17; 16:10), where he discovered that there was a crisis, apparently including attacks on Paul's authority (2 Cor. 2:5-11; 7:8-12). Timothy was unable to deal with this crisis, and returned to Ephesus to tell Paul. Upon hearing of these difficulties, Paul apparently visited Corinth briefly, but he was rebuffed. This visit is apparently referred to by Paul as the 'painful visit' (2 Cor. 2:1; 12:14; 13:1, 2), not recorded in Acts. After his visit, Paul sent a powerful letter in response, probably carried by Titus, to deal with this crisis involving his apostleship. This letter is probably that referred to as the 'tearful/severe' letter (2 Cor. 2:4; 7:8-12). Many scholars have maintained that 2 Corinthians 10–13 is a part of this letter, a hypothesis often based on, among other arguments, the use of the verb tenses in the two sections. For example, there are some pairs of verbs where the so-called present tense is found in 2 Corinthians 10–13 and a so-called past tense is found in 2 Corinthians 1–9. The implication in some scholars' minds is that the events described in the past tense occurred before those in the present tense (see 2 Cor. 10:6 and 2 Cor. 2:9, 2 Cor. 13:2 and 2 Cor. 1:23, and 2 Cor. 13:10 and 2 Cor. 2:3). Unfortunately for this part of the theory, the verb tenses in Greek, according to the latest discussion of Greek verb structure, do not refer primarily to time, and will not sustain such an argument.[20] Nevertheless, differences in tone between 2 Corinthians 1–9 and 10–13 may still indicate that the two portions were at least written at different times. Many scholars, if not most, however, would now claim that this third letter to the Corinthians is now lost. After writing this letter to the Corinthians, Paul departed Ephesus and went toward Macedonia (1 Cor. 16:5-9; cf. Acts 20:1-2). Delayed along the way by a visit to Troas, he waited for Titus, but could not find him (2 Cor. 2:12-13). Going on to Macedonia, he met Titus there, who informed him that the worst of the crisis in Corinth was over (2 Cor. 7:6-16), in response to which Paul wrote 2 Corinthians, his fourth and final Corinthian letter, carried by Titus and two other 'brothers in Christ'. Many scholars think that chs. 10–13 may have been sent separately from the rest of the letter, probably later if they were separate, but

---

[20]   See S.E. Porter, *Verbal Aspect in the Greek of the New Testament, with Reference to Tense and Mood* (SBG, 1; New York: Lang, 1989), esp. pp. 75-108, and the Chapter on the Greek Language of the New Testament.

being sent earlier may help to account for their stronger tone. Paul then traveled on to Corinth (cf. Acts 20:3), from which, within a year, he probably wrote the letter to the Romans, apparently without any difficulties. This indicates the likelihood that the Corinthian crisis was finally resolved in Paul's favor.

This basic chronology, along with some observations about surrounding events, already includes a surprisingly large number of exegetical judgments. These include, among others, estimations of the number of letters, the events precipitating their being sent, some motivations on both Paul's and the Corinthians' parts, and the forms of the letters and their contents. One could conclude differently on several of these matters, and it would have consequences for exegesis. However, this historical–chronological fact-finding stage is merely the first, leading to a necessary further step in the exegetical task. This step involves gathering exegetical data from the letters themselves regarding the kind of opposition Paul encountered, and then constructing a plausible explanation regarding these data in terms of identifying the opponents. In some instances, it is better to separate this into two tasks, although it is difficult to think of individual data outside of a conceptual framework. One must grapple at this point with the importance of an exegetical spiral. That is, from the situation and data at hand one creates a reconstruction of the Corinthian situation. This reconstruction is then used to re-interpret the data in the text. Out of the interplay of the data and one's further analysis, one hopes to gain insight into the Pauline letter situation and the content of the letter. What is to be avoided is simply reading pre-conceived ideas into the data, and finding 'confirmation' of one's hypotheses in them.

This stage of exegesis is best handled in terms of the individual letters, but must then be brought together in light of the multiple Corinthian-letter situation. The second stage can begin with the simple question—what could have been so cataclysmic to elicit these events as just recounted, including multiple letters and multiple trips back and forth between Ephesus and other places, and Corinth? There has been much scholarly debate regarding the conflict at Corinth that brought forth this series of correspondence. By recounting the several major proposals regarding the opponents at Corinth, one can begin to see how one's exegetical decisions in just one area have significant effects upon interpretation. The situation is compounded by the fact that there are (at least) two Corinthian letters to be analyzed. I begin with 1 Corinthians, before discussing 2 Corinthians.

The traditional view regarding the issue at Corinth has been that, initially, it was about unity and disunity within the church. Indications in the letters are that Paul was informed that the church was divided into a variety of factions, with controversial issues or practices going on that warranted a series of comments from him. Since Paul's first letter (1 Cor. 5:9), he had apparently received further communication from the Corinthian church, including specific information regarding their various quarrels and divisions (1:10-17). At 5:1, then, Paul turns from the brief body of his letter regarding the larger issue of church unity to a lengthy parenetic section dealing with specific issues that are dividing the Corinthian church. He treats them serially, sometimes indicating a change in topics by use of the phrase περὶ δέ, 'now concerning' (7:1, 25; 8:1; 12:1; 16:1).[21]

The following four issues appear to have been causing division at Corinth: (1) sexual behavior (5:1-13; 6:12-20; 7:1, 28); (2) controversy between those who were scrupulous in not eating food that may have been offered to idols, and those who held no scruple regarding eating this meat in places where it was known to be served (8:10; 10:27-28), possibly resulting in behavior that led to Corinthian Christians getting involved in court cases with each other (6:1-11), along with social divisions creeping into celebration of the Lord's Supper (11:17-34); (3) practices of worship, including a number of women having been particularly vocal during services, as well as undue emphasis being put on the charismatic gifts, such as speaking in divine or heavenly languages (chs. 12, 14); and (4) the resurrection (ch. 15), whether the Corinthian church held that the resurrection of Christ had not occurred, or whether they were disputing that there would be a resurrection of believers, especially if some members believed that they had already entered the eschaton.

A major problem with this position is that one must wonder whether there was some sort of larger outside influence that had penetrated the Corinthian church to cause such strife over these issues. If not, the matter of disunity may not indicate what can rationally be called Pauline 'opposition' apart from the kinds of internal squabbles one might expect in a growing and developing organization, such as the Church was in the first century. As a result, some have argued that

---

21   See M.M. Mitchell, 'Concerning ΠΕΡΙ ΔΕ in 1 Corinthians', *NovT* 31 (1989), pp. 229-56. Paul also uses conditional clauses (1 Cor. 7:17; 13:1; 15:12), a knowledge formula (10:1), a strong adversative (15:35), and an emphatic cataphoric pronoun (11:17; 15:50).

there was a wide variety of divisive groups in Corinth, none of which was pre-eminent (although many may have thought of themselves as such), and maybe none of which was attempting to wrest control of the church from Paul. For example, the evidence may support the idea that there were some libertines, who had misunderstood the concept of Christian freedom as an excuse for excessive indulgence (5:1-13, 6:12-20). Others may have been ascetics, who viewed such practices as marriage to be sinful (7:1-28). Still others may have been ecstatics, who were allowing spiritual experience to lead to disorderly behavior in the church (ch. 14). Some of these may have had a realized eschatology, thinking that they had already attained the eschaton, which condition justified their behavior. Each of these groups may have been associated with a particular individual or recognizable group in Corinth, or there may also have been people siding with various individuals, including the Paul group, the Apollos group, the Cephas group, and the Christ group (1:12).[22]

A second hypothesis has tended to dominate much recent exegesis of 1 Corinthians, and that is that there were Jewish-Christian gnostics in the church.[23] These gnostics, so the hypothesis goes, disparaged the earthly and the fleshly realms, and elevated the spiritual realm with its esoteric knowledge (see 1:18–2:16, 3:18-23 for references to 'knowledge'). Their set of beliefs that freed them from the constraints of this world may well have resulted in overindulgence (see 5:1–6:20; 11:17-34). These Jewish-Christian gnostics were concerned to mediate the otherworldly realm to this world, but it raised some direct questions regarding their Christology, responded to most directly in what Paul says in ch. 15 regarding Christ and the resurrection. If Christ was God, the question might be asked, how could he also be a man? This bifurcation in thought and formulation would have tended toward a position in which Christ's humanness would have been merely an appearance of being human.

But is the gnostic hypothesis that exegetically convincing? Several factors should be considered. One is that it does not appear to address the range of issues mentioned in the letter, only focusing on certain sections. Furthermore, most recent research has come to acknowledge the fact that there is a significant difference between 'proto-gnostic

---

22   See C.K. Barrett, 'Christianity at Corinth', in his *Essays on Paul* (Philadelphia: Westminster Press, 1981), pp. 3-6.

23   See, for example, W. Schmithals, *Gnosticism in Corinth: An Investigation of the Letters to the Corinthians* (trans. J.E. Steely; Nashville: Abingdon, 1971).

tendencies' and full-blown Gnosticism. As Gnosticism emerged in the second and third centuries with its myth of the heavenly redeemer, full of all sorts of emanations and manifestations, it probably reflected the influence of Christian thought, rather than the other way around. As a result, the most that can probably be argued is that some proto-gnostic tendencies, perhaps common to Judaism and wider Hellenistic thought, were to be found at Corinth. For example, heavenly knowledge took an exalted place over the earthly, but without the gnostic Christology or worldview that later developed.[24] Much of what is often cited as gnostic may reveal other influences, such as Jewish wisdom thought, rather than full-blown Gnosticism.[25] Thus the gnostic hypothesis, though not without some appeal, fails to be convincingly well established as the best explanation of the situation at Corinth.

As a result, a somewhat related and more specific view has been proposed that the major problems at Corinth stemmed from the outworkings of an over-realized eschatology.[26] In the mind of the Corinthians, according to this hypothesis, a mystical or magical element seemed to attach to the various practices in which those in the church were engaged, including baptism and the Lord's Supper. Those practicing them apparently thought quite highly of their spiritual status, depreciating earthly things and status. Thinking of themselves as already having entered the eschaton, they lived accordingly. This kind of thinking may well have derived from wisdom speculation or some other form of Hellenistic thought. Rather than positing that Hellenistic Judaism was responsible for these influences, the emphasis should probably be on Hellenistic thought in general. The general exaltation of esoteric knowledge was emphasized, perhaps in conjunction with the Platonic thought promoted by Hellenistic philosophy.[27] As noted above, it is precarious to try to create a divide

---

[24]   See R.McL. Wilson, 'Gnosis at Corinth', in *Paul and Paulinism: Essays in Honour of C.K. Barrett* (ed. M.D. Hooker and S.G. Wilson; London: SPCK, 1985), pp. 102-14.

[25]   See B.A. Pearson, *The Pneumatikos-Psychikos Terminology* (SBLDS, 12; Missoula, MT: Scholars Press, 1973).

[26]   See A.C. Thiselton, 'Realized Eschatology at Corinth', *NTS* 24 (1977–78), pp. 510-26, for the standard discussion of this issue.

[27]   See G.W. Bowersock (ed.), *Approaches to the Second Sophistic* (University Park, PA: American Philological Association, 1974); cf. D. Litfin, *St Paul's Theology of Proclamation: 1 Corinthians 1–4 and Greco-Roman Rhetoric* (SNTSMS, 79; Cambridge: Cambridge University Press, 1994), esp. pp. 109-34.

between Hellenistic Judaism and the encompassing phenomenon of Hellenism.

These previous characterizations of the opponents tend to emphasize divisive struggles within the Corinthian church, often fomented by outside agitation. However, it has recently been argued that the major problem at Corinth was one between the church and Paul, its founder, over his authority and the nature of the gospel.[28] In 1 Cor. 9:1-14, for example, Paul rigorously defends himself, rejecting the church's judgment of him. 1 Corinthians is also Paul's response to their letter to him, in which they had taken exception to several of Paul's positions in his previous letter (1 Cor. 5:9). Paul responds by re-asserting his authority (3:5-9; 4:1-5), and correcting the Corinthians as a whole church, using the second person (1:10-12; 3:4-5; 11:18-19). The problem in the church does not seem to stem from outside opposition having infiltrated the group (so the term 'opponents' may be the wrong one), but seems to stem from anti-Pauline sentiment started by a few who had eventually infected the whole congregation. These people thought of themselves as being wise. Paul's preaching was 'milk' compared to their mature teaching (2:8; 3:1), and his behavior was seen to be weak or vacillating with respect to such issues as food offered to idols (8:1–11:1). When Paul emphasized how he was writing on spiritual things (14:37), it was to respond to people who thought of themselves as being 'spiritual', but who did not consider Paul as such, since they had fantastic experiences to back their claims (chs. 12–14) and he did not. Their spiritual endowment was related to their knowledge and wisdom (chs. 1–4, 8–10). They went even further, however, contending that they were already experiencing the Spirit in full measure, probably including some eschatologically exuberant women who thought they had entered the new age (chs. 7, 11), contrary to the weak Paul, who had not.

This exegetical position provides a unified depiction of the problem, and rightly focuses it upon the apostle Paul and his defense of his apostleship (1 Cor. 9:1-14). Several factors must be considered further, however. One is whether the issue of Paul's personal apostleship is really at the heart of the letter, especially in terms of the variety of issues raised in chs. 5–11. These problems seem rather to reflect issues of practice and behavior rather than personal

---

28   See G.D. Fee, *The First Epistle to the Corinthians* (NICNT; Grand Rapids: Eerdmans, 1987), p. 6.

confrontation. Evidence of outside factors, such as mention of the Apollos and Cephas parties (1:12), points to some form of outside agitation. This solution, while perhaps right in recognizing that personal opposition to Paul as an apostle might constitute a partial explanation of the situation, is probably not a sufficient analysis of the data.

The predominant scholarly position regarding 1 Corinthians posits that Paul is responding to behavior in the Corinthian church that originates with influences from the surrounding Hellenistic world, even if the specific nature of that outside influence cannot be adequately and fully described. But how does that help us to understand the possible opponents in 2 Corinthians? The historical reconstruction offered above would seem to imply continuity regarding the situations of the two letters. Nevertheless, the data do not necessarily indicate this, and it is difficult to pin down those who seem to stand behind 2 Corinthians. Part of the problem might be alleviated if one separates 2 Corinthians 1–9 from 10–13, inferring that chs. 10–13, with a harsher tone, were sent before chs. 1–9, but arguments for separating the two, especially in light of their unity in the text-critical tradition (i.e. no extant text of 2 Corinthians separates the two), are not entirely convincing.[29] If the occasion that prompted the first two letters to the Corinthians was the possible fragmentation of the church, in 2 Corinthians it appears that much of the disunity has been overcome. Consequently, the opponents that elicited 2 Corinthians have often been separately characterized in terms of the specific nature of their attack. As noted above, Paul's fourth letter to the Corinthians (no matter how much of it is found in our 2 Corinthians) apparently dealt sufficiently with the problem, reinforcing the view that these opponents represent a minority position that was finally rejected by the church at Corinth.

The nature of the attack against Paul reflected in 2 Corinthians seems to have consisted of a number of wide-ranging accusations brought by outsiders. He was accused of being unstable, as evidenced by a change of plans and vacillation (1:15-18), being unclear as to what he meant (1:13-14), being ineffective (10:10), being a tyrant (10:8), abandoning the Corinthians (2:1; 13:2), his gospel not being clear (4:3), and his speech being pitiful (10:11; 11:6; this last point

---

[29]   Besides Thrall (*Second Corinthians*, pp. 5-20), who surveys opinion, for bibliography see L.L. Welborn, 'The Identification of 2 Corinthians 10–13 with the "Letter of Tears"', *NovT* 37 (1995), pp. 138-53.

probably indicates that he was not trained in rhetoric as some of them may have been). Paul was also apparently denigrated for a number of reasons concerning his claim to being a representative of Christ, or an apostle. These include the fact that he had no formal letters of recommendation, as perhaps did other itinerant preachers and teachers (3:1; 4:2); his claims regarding belonging to Christ were apparently seen as unsupported, perhaps because he had not actually seen Christ (10:7); he arrived in Corinth without a clear mandate (10:13-14); and he was said to be inferior to the 'super apostles' (11:5; 12:11), a position that Paul himself may well have indirectly re-enforced by being seen as having distanced himself from the Corinthians by refusing to be supported by the congregation (11:7-9). All of this may well have indicated to some that Paul was not even to be considered an apostle (12:12, 14), and that Christ was not speaking through him (13:3). Paul may also have been accused of having a deleterious effect upon the congregation, because his behavior seemed to be offensive, including praising himself (3:1, 5; 4:5; 5:11-15; 6:3-5; 10:2, 8; 11:16-18; 12:1, 11). He may have been accused of working duplicitously for gain (7:1; 12:17-18) even by using the collection (8:20-21), being a coward (1:23; 8:2; 10:1, 10; 11:32-33), and harming the Christian community by abandoning the Corinthians (2:1; 13:2) and exploiting the situation for his own benefit (7:2; 12:16).

In his response, Paul had to find a suitable tone in the letter and make his perspective clear. For example, he says that his opponents were a paid minority (2:6; 10:2), implying that they readily accepted financial compensation (2:17; 11:20; something he believed that he was entitled to, even if he did not use it; 1 Cor. 9:3-11), and had gained entrance into the church by letters of recommendation and self-commendation (3:1; 10:12, 18). They apparently boasted of their own excellence (5:12; 11:12, 18), emphasized ecstatic experience (that Paul counters with his own) (5:13; 12:1-6), and overtly claimed both the apostolic office (11:5, 13; 12:11) and superiority to Moses (3:4-11), although without making known their own Jewish heritage (11:22). Paul claims that these people were in fact preaching another gospel (11:4), had encroached on others' missionary territory (10:15-16), were immoral (12:21; 13:2), were boastful (10:12-13), and were led by a particular person (2:5; 7:12; 11:4). As a result, he calls them Satan's servants (11:13-15). By contrast, Paul regarded himself as an apostle (1:1), and the proof of this lay in the Corinthians themselves

(3:2-3), among whom he had done mighty things (12:12), reflecting his appointment from God (3:5, 6; 4:7).

These two full paragraphs provide a summary of at least some of the data gleaned from 2 Corinthians regarding its situation. Can these false preachers be more definitively characterized, and then correlated with the situation of 1 Corinthians?[30] There has been much speculation, often focusing upon 2 Corinthians 11. Some have characterized his opponents as Judaizers such as were involved in the Galatian situation, on the basis of their emphasis upon their Jewish heritage (3:4-7; 11:22).[31] However, Paul's response in 2 Corinthians is not nearly as strong as that in Galatians. Some have thought that the opponents were 'gnostics'.[32] One sees their willingness to emphasize ecstatic experience, but this position would require a fuller development of Gnosticism than is likely for the first century (see above). A third proposal is that these were Hellenistic Jews who were making claims regarding their miraculous powers.[33] This theory of 'divine men' (θεῖος ἀνήρ) lacks evidence for its existence before Christianity had taken firm root, with the best parallels coming from the third century and later (see Apollonius of Tyana).

It is even possible that these false preachers were followers of Apollos, and reflected the Hellenistic Judaism of Alexandria. Consequently, they may well have been educated and articulate spokesmen who were formidable opponents for Paul. The merit for this suggestion, especially in light of 1 Corinthians (e.g. 1:12, 18-31; 2:1-5), is mitigated by the quite different ways in which Paul seems to handle the two situations. He is more conciliatory in 1 Corinthians, but more confrontative in 2 Corinthians. There is no hard evidence that the situation had escalated, and it is difficult to form a hard line of connection between the two. Perhaps this implies that the problems

---

[30]   See Sumney, *Identifying Paul's Opponents*, esp. pp. 13-73 for summary of the positions noted below, and pp. 187-91 for his own conclusions.

[31]   C.K. Barrett, 'Paul's Opponents in 2 Corinthians', in *Essays on Paul*, pp. 60-86; *idem*, 'ΨΕΥΔΑΠΟΣΤΟΛΟΙ (2 Cor. 11:13)', in *Essays on Paul*, pp. 87-107; Gunther, *St Paul's Opponents*, pp. 1-94.

[32]   R. Bultmann, *The Second Letter to the Corinthians* (trans. R.A. Harrisville; Minneapolis: Augsburg, 1985), *passim*; Schmithals, *Gnosis in Corinth, passim*.

[33]   D. Georgi, *The Opponents of Paul in Second Corinthians* (Philadelphia: Fortress Press, 1986), *passim*; contra C. Holladay, *Theios Aner in Hellenistic-Judaism: A Critique of the Use of this Category in New Testament Christology* (SBLDS, 40; Missoula, MT: Scholars Press, 1977).

reflected in 2 Corinthians were attributable to a minority of people who were personally attacking Paul, perhaps a new group of outsiders questioning Paul's apostolic authority in a potentially persuasive way. Arguably the most likely explanation is that this group of false preachers originated in Palestine, quite possibly as emissaries (whether legitimate or otherwise) of the Jerusalem leaders or 'super apostles' (see 11:5, 13, 23; 12:11),[34] or as itinerant preachers who claimed to have been with Jesus. The Jerusalem leaders were not necessarily directly opposing Paul at Corinth, but one must not dismiss the degree of suspicion that apparently existed between the Jerusalem and Antiochian missionary efforts (see Acts 15:1-5; 21:20-21). Paul suggests that the Corinthians have been too quick to accept the false preachers' claims to have the authority and endorsement of the 'super apostles'. As a result, he asserts his equal standing and authority with any other apostles, including those in Jerusalem—anyone who says otherwise is a false apostle (2 Cor. 11:5, 12-15).

The exegetical importance of establishing the possible opposition to Paul in a letter is clearly of importance, but the issues cannot always be clearly resolved, as the above discussion illustrates. For example, the two (to my mind) most likely scenarios regarding 1 and 2 Corinthians (the traditional view regarding disunity and that of outsiders from Jerusalem) seems to be consistent with readings of the individual letters involved, but is in tension with the reconstructed scenario above. The solution that posits a gnostic influence behind the problems of both letters resolves the problem of contradiction, but is far from being the most obvious understanding of the data in the individual letters, especially in light of problems with the concept of Gnosticism itself. Nevertheless, as I hope that this example illustrates, discussion of the opponents of Paul in a given letter certainly has exegetical significance, and must be approached in a systematic way. This significance can be seen in the area of interpretation of the individual letters, but extends more broadly to include understanding the larger life and ministry of the apostle.

---

[34]   Cf. R.P. Martin, 'The Opponents of Paul in 2 Corinthians: An Old Issue Revisited', in *Tradition and Interpretation in the New Testament: Essays in Honor of E. Earle Ellis* (ed. G.F. Hawthorne with O. Betz; Grand Rapids: Eerdmans, 1987), pp. 279-87.

4. THE OCCASION AND PURPOSE OF THE PAULINE LETTERS

A further factor to consider in exegesis of the Pauline letters is the issue of the occasion and purpose of the letters. Interpreters of the Pauline letters often fail to make an important distinction between the occasion of a letter or the situation that elicited it, and the purpose that might have been served by the writing of the letter.[35] The discussion above regarding the opponents at Corinth is to a large extent a discussion of the occasion of those letters. The purpose of a letter reflects the perspective of the author in relation to the occasion. It is entirely possible that a given occasion could result in writings with varying purposes, depending upon the given author and his motivations. Some idea of the purpose of a literary work, such as a Pauline letter, would seem to be necessary to serve as a means of arbitrating between various possible interpretations of passages in any book.

There is perhaps no more widely disputed Pauline letter regarding its purpose than the book of Romans. The circumstances that elicited the letter to the Romans seem to be encapsulated in a number of important passages that occur at the beginning and the end of the letter. These passages require sustained analysis, in light of how they relate to the rest of the letter and the re-constructed historical circumstances, in order to establish the purpose of the letter. Paul states in Rom. 1:13-15 that he had planned to come to Rome, and that he was eager to preach the gospel to those in Rome, but that he had been prevented from doing so. In Rom. 15:22, he clarifies why he had been prevented—he had been preaching in the eastern part of the Mediterranean. He had now preached from Jerusalem all the way to Illyricum (Rom. 15:19) and had no place further to preach in the east (15:23), so he set his sights on Spain (15:24, 28). He intended to visit the church in Rome in the course of his westward movement (15:23, 28-29), but first had to go to Jerusalem to deliver the collection that he had gathered from the churches in Macedonia and Greece (15:26). This was the occasion or situation in the apostle's life when the letter was written, but what was the purpose of the letter?[36] In other words,

---

[35]   This is an important distinction used in McDonald and Porter, *Early Christianity and its Sacred Literature*, chap. 10. This section is based on treatment of Romans in that chapter, where a fuller discussion may be found.

[36]   A summary of various positions is found in A.J.M. Wedderburn, *The Reasons for Romans* (Edinburgh: T. & T. Clark, 1988); L.A. Jervis, *The Purpose of Romans: A Comparative Letter Structure Investigation* (JSNTSup, 55;

just because his situation or circumstances were as depicted does not mean that he had to write a letter to Rome. Much less, it does not dictate that he had to write a letter like the one now in our New Testament. Whereas it may be agreed that the occasion of Paul's proposed visit to Rome was part of the westward expansion of his preaching ministry, the purpose or motivation for his writing the letter to the Romans is far from agreed, and has elicited an incredible amount of debate.

The element of contingency in the Pauline letters has become important in recent scholarly discussion. In other words, Paul as a writer is addressing in each letter a unique set of circumstances that warrants a response to that particular situation.[37] So much is true of any communication; however, that does not help to decide the purpose of a given letter. Determining a letter's purpose requires examination of the content of the letter in the light of its situation. As a result, there have been a number of proposals worth considering regarding the book of Romans, several of them mutually contradictory, or at opposite ends of the spectrum.

Melanchthon's judgment that Romans is a compendium of the Christian religion summarizes the traditional view of the purpose of Romans—that is, the letter is as close to a systematic theology as is found in Paul's writings. Paul is writing to a church that he has not visited, but that figures in his future travel plans, as a means of setting out the major tenets of what he believes constitutes Christian belief. He does so in a highly systematic and organized way, using the letter form. This position tends to minimize the contingent elements of Paul's presentation, including the relevance of specific contextual issues (e.g. Romans 14–15), and emphasizes the major doctrines that constitute the Pauline gospel (e.g. justification by faith, human sinfulness, the role of Adam and Christ, sanctification, reconciliation, the relations of Jews and Gentiles, the role of the state, etc.). This position was virtually unchallenged until the work of F.C. Baur in the early nineteenth century, and still has significant supporters.[38]

Sheffield: JSOT Press, 1991); R. Morgan, *Romans* (NTG; Sheffield: Sheffield Academic Press, 1995), pp. 60-77.

37 J.C. Beker, *Paul the Apostle: The Triumph of God in Life and Thought* (Philadelphia: Fortress Press, 1980), pp. 23-36; 'Paul's Theology: Consistent or Inconsistent?', *NTS* 34 (1988), pp. 364-77.

38 See F.C. Baur, *Paul the Apostle of Jesus Christ: His Life and Work, his Epistles and his Doctrine* (2 vols.; London: Williams & Norgate, 2nd edn, 1876),

Two major objections to this position are that it minimizes the context and circumstances surrounding the writing of the letter, to the point that this book could apparently have been written to virtually any Christian community anywhere at any time; and that many of what some scholars would consider major Christian doctrines are lacking in Romans, making it at best an incomplete, and hence flawed, compendium. The doctrines often cited as lacking are eschatology, Christology, the doctrine of the Church, the Lord's Supper/Eucharist and marriage. There are responses to these objections, but it is sufficient here to note that they provide substantial reasons against accepting this proposal.

A purpose for the letter has been proposed that addresses one of the major objections to the first position above regarding the contingency of the letter. T.W. Manson claimed that the book of Romans was sent originally to the churches both at Rome (chs. 1–15:23 or 33) and at Ephesus (chs. 1–16). Thus, it reflects the ideas that were deepest in Paul's thought. It is not a full-orbed compendium of all major Christian doctrine, but rather a manifesto of Paul's deepest convictions.[39] Paul, unable to visit Ephesus on his way to Jerusalem and then Rome, sent this letter to both, in a larger form for the Ephesians. This would account for inclusion of the names in ch. 16 that seem to be associated with Ephesus, and the fact that, in some later manuscripts, the Roman destination is missing. Thus, the letter is expanded in its scope from being a letter addressed to a single church to a type of circular letter.

Unfortunately for this position, there is not a strong case to be made for the book of Romans circulating in a form that only included chs. 1–15, since this would make for a somewhat abrupt close and an unnatural ending. This raises the further question of why Paul would convey his deepest convictions to the church at Rome, a city he had never visited. It is understandable that a revised form would be sent to the church at Ephesus, but why not Corinth or Antioch, churches that he knew, rather than Rome? It is perhaps more understandable that Paul would send a compendium of Christian belief to a church that he anticipated visiting, rather than an exposition of his deepest beliefs.

I, pp. 331-65; D.J. Moo, *The Epistle to the Romans* (NICNT; Grand Rapids: Eerdmans, 1996), esp. pp. 22-24; N.T. Wright, *The Climax of the Covenant: Christ and the Law in Pauline Theology* (Edinburgh: T. & T. Clark, 1991), p. 234.

[39]   T.W. Manson, 'St Paul's Letter to the Romans—and Others', in *Romans Debate*, pp. 3-15.

A further proposal regarding the purpose of Romans recognizes that Paul was facing an unknown future on his contemplated journey to Jerusalem. He was carrying the collection from the churches in Greece and Macedonia, not knowing how it would be received in Jerusalem, so Bornkamm argued that Paul wrote his last will and testament to the Roman Christians.[40] The record in Acts 21:17-26 indicates that Paul had good reason to wonder about his Jerusalem reception (Rom. 15:31) (it seems very likely that this account in Acts is reliable, since it creates a very plausible course of events in which the Jerusalem church is implicated in Paul's arrest). Paul took this occasion to write to the Christians at Rome to provide a permanent record of his message, as a forecast of the preaching and missionary ministry he wished to continue. A balance is maintained in the letter that reflects one of his persistent battles, and perhaps one of the issues to be faced in Jerusalem—legalism and antinomianism. Although he had been accused of being an antinomian, he was anxious to show that he, as well as the Christian faith, was neither antinomian nor legalistic.

Why did Paul choose to write this kind of a letter to Rome, a church he had never visited? Bornkamm insists that this letter is not a last will and testament with Paul not anticipating being able to carry on his ministry. In what sense then is it a *last* will and testament? Furthermore, if it were to be his last, Paul could have been expected to pour out his theological heart to his friends, such as one of the churches that could have been expected to maintain the Pauline mission. There is the further difficulty that the unsettled state that Bornkamm posits does not appear in the letter. There is reference to uncertainty regarding the church at Jerusalem (Rom. 15:31), but this is mitigated by Paul's conviction that he is determined to make his way to Rome on his way to Spain after having visited Jerusalem (Rom. 15:24). Romans has none of the gloom found in letters such as 2 Corinthians 10–13 or especially 2 Tim. 4:6-7 (which Bornkamm considers deutero-Pauline), where Paul seems genuinely exhausted and concerned regarding the future.

The distinguishing mark of all of the genuine Pauline letters, it has been maintained, is mention of the collection (e.g. 1 Cor. 16:1-4; 2 Cor. 8:1–9:15).[41] The collection is important in Paul's thinking,

---

40   G. Bornkamm, 'The Letter to the Romans as Paul's Last Will and Testament', in *Romans Debate*, pp. 16-28.

41   M. Kiley, *Colossians and Pseudepigraphy* (Sheffield: JSOT Press, 1986), p. 46.

even though this framework seems to be predicated upon a previous presumption of which are the authentic letters. Consequently, it has been posited that Romans, though addressed to the Roman churches, is in fact a letter that is 'addressed to Jerusalem'.[42] In other words, it was written as if it were being overheard by the church at Jerusalem, so that they would accept both Paul's ministry and his collection, and he could overcome their possible objections regarding what he had been teaching. What he is writing in the letter may even constitute a dress rehearsal for the kind of speech or apology that he would deliver to the leaders of the church in Jerusalem.

Despite the validity of Paul's concern regarding his reception in Jerusalem, Romans is probably not best seen as an apology to Jerusalem. This letter can be only an indirect way of offering an apology to them, since it is sent in the completely opposite direction, that is, to Rome. The reference to Jerusalem in Rom. 15:31 is insufficient to suggest that Paul is concerned that his letter might reach Jerusalem. Furthermore, there is material in the letter that would hardly appeal to Jews, especially an audience that Paul was trying to please (see Romans 4, 11). The collection might offer a suitable occasion for writing the letter, but it hardly provides a sufficient purpose to write such a lengthy and involved one, especially since references to the collection in Romans are minimal.

A more realistic option, in conjunction with the hypothesis above, is that Paul wrote this letter as a letter of self-introduction, possibly verging on an apologetic letter.[43] Paul wrote to the Christians in Rome so that they would welcome him and help him on his way to Spain (Rom. 1:11-15; 15:24, 28). Rapport was needed with that church, so that they would receive him and his gospel, with the idea that he may well have been in need of financial support (his mention of the collection and his work on behalf of the church in Jerusalem would have prepared them for this). In keeping with this theory, Paul uses many of the techniques of a teacher or an apologist. For example, he uses the dialogue form typical of diatribe, in which he writes both sides of the dialogue in order to raise issues, explain ideas, raise

---

42   J. Jervell, 'The Letter to Jerusalem', in *Romans Debate*, pp. 53-64.

43   F.F. Bruce, 'The Romans Debate—Continued', in *Romans Debate*, pp. 175-93; A.J.M. Wedderburn, 'Purpose and Occasion of Romans Again', in *Romans Debate,* pp. 195-202; P. Stuhlmacher, 'The Purpose of Romans', in *Romans Debate*, pp. 231-42. On the apologetic or protreptic letter, see D.E. Aune, 'Romans as a *Logos Protreptikos*', in *Romans Debate*, pp. 278-96.

objections and respond to them—all as a way of leading his audience through his argument. Just as Corinth, Ephesus and Antioch had provided platforms for his work in the eastern Mediterranean, Paul envisioned Rome as his platform for moving westward.

Paul seems, nevertheless, to be engaging in an awful lot of very heavy theology simply to introduce himself to the Roman church. Paul would appear to be running a serious risk of jeopardizing his plans if he were to touch on some disputed issue or pronounce on a sensitive issue such as Jewish and Gentile relations. This approach is not one used elsewhere by Paul; he does not lay out his gospel for others to examine and approve. The church at Rome was unique in Paul's experience, since he had at least had important contacts with the church at Colossae, another church that he may not have visited. Nevertheless, it is hard to accept that Paul was so unknown to the church at Rome, thus hardly warranting such an extended introduction. In the letter itself, his plans seem to center more on Spain, and less on Rome, a city which seems to be only incidental to his plans.

One scholar has gone so far as to argue that Paul wrote Romans as an instrument to re-found the church so that it would have an apostolic grounding to which it could point for authority.[44] According to this position, Paul viewed some churches as full and complete, and others he did not. Paul says in Rom. 15:20 that he does not build upon another's foundation, but this can be reconciled with Rom. 1:15 and his eagerness to preach in Rome if it is seen that the church does not in fact have the kind of foundation that he sees as necessary for an apostolic church.

This solution to the purpose of Romans is perhaps indicative of the variety of approaches offered, many of them perhaps borne out of frustration that there is no more definitive solution. Nevertheless, it is difficult to quantify what exactly the Roman church would have lacked by not having an apostolic foundation. Paul in fact says in the letter that they are full of knowledge, capable, and proclaimers of the faith (Rom. 1:6-16; 15:14-23). In Rom. 1:6, Paul favorably describes the Romans as being 'among' the Gentiles who have become obedient to the faith, making it unlikely that he is distinguishing them in any meaningful way. Even if Paul is forcefully asserting his apostolic

---

44   G. Klein, 'Paul's Purpose in Writing the Epistle to the Romans', in *Romans Debate*, pp. 29-43.

authority in the letter (something he does not appear to be emphasizing; see Rom. 1:12), that would not necessarily mean that he is founding or re-founding the church there. The evidence of such a re-founding is lacking, here and elsewhere in the New Testament.

Several scholars have more realistically proposed that the purpose of Romans is tied up with Gentile and Jewish relations. There are two forms of this position. The first sees a divide in early Christianity between Petrine or Jewish and Pauline or Hellenistic elements.[45] According to this position, the letter was the earliest support for the great Gentile church in Rome, opposing the Jewish Christians there. Paul wanted to be able to deliver the picture of a unified Gentile Christianity when he presented his collection in Jerusalem. This letter has nothing to do with Rome per se, but with Rome as a church of Gentiles to which Paul can point as a noteworthy success in support of his position as representative of Hellenistic Christianity.

It is true that there was conflict in the early Church between parties that have been called 'Jewish' and 'Hellenistic' (whether these are the most appropriate labels requires further examination), but this position still fails to explain the purpose of Paul's writing Romans. There are too many specific references in the letter for it to be unconcerned with the church at Rome (see e.g. 1:8-15; 13:1-7 and chs. 14–15). There are also too many references to the Jews, including lengthy discussion in chs. 9–11, for a letter that is merely designed to present a unified picture of Gentile Christianity. There is no other letter that does this. If the dispute in the early Church is primarily an ethnic-cultural one, why is the issue not addressed in that way? Much of the language is too comprehensive, including description of Jews and Gentiles, to provide an argument for this being a picture concerned only to promote the Hellenistic side of Jewish and Gentile Christian relations.

The second form of the Jew and Gentile proposal argues that there were divergent communities that are being addressed, possibly the weak (Jewish) and the strong (Gentile), or various groups involved in the question of status. This theory takes seriously the conditional and

---

45 This view is held in various ways by R. Jewett, 'Following the Argument of Romans', in *Romans Debate*, pp. 265-77; W.S. Campbell, 'Romans III as a Key to the Structure and Thought of Romans', in *Romans Debate*, pp. 251-64, chap. 3 in his *Paul's Gospel in an Intercultural Context* (Studies in the Intercultural History of Christianity, 69; Frankfurt: Lang, 1992), pp. 25-42; K.P. Donfried, 'False Presuppositions in the Study of Romans', in *Romans Debate*, pp. 102-24; M. Goulder, *A Tale of Two Missions* (London: SCM Press, 1994).

contingent nature of the Pauline writings, as well as the specific references within the book, especially those in the parenetic section. Paul perhaps offers something encouraging to each side in the dispute. The Jews, for example, are allowed to retain pride in Abraham, while the Gentiles can see themselves as grafted onto the tree that Israel once occupied alone.

This theory does not seem to offer much regarding the purpose of Romans until chs. 14–15, where the discussion of the weak and the strong is introduced, thus leaving the bulk of the letter unexplained. However, it is not clear that the 'weak' and the 'strong' are being addressed in ethnic terms. What it means to be 'in Christ' is being addressed, but not enough is known of the composition of the church to make firm equations with particular groups.

As this brief survey of exegetical options has shown, there is no consensus regarding the purpose of Paul's writing the letter to the Romans. This has several important exegetical consequences. First, in interpreting the letter, every exegete must have some idea of the purpose that generated the letter. This is necessary to offer some form of control over exegetical decisions taken in the course of study of individual passages in the letter. For example, one must have some purpose in mind that is able to understand both the discussion of the weak and strong in chs. 14–15, the theological ideas regarding the Jews in ch. 9 and the statements regarding Gentiles in chs. 2–8. Without such an overall conception, the result will be fragmentary exegesis that may have no correlation with its larger context. Various proposals for individual passages may be put forward, but no larger sense of the whole book will be maintained. Secondly, one's conception of purpose must be open to being shaped by exegesis of individual passages. This is a description of the exegetical spiral, in which the part (i.e. individual passages) influences the whole (i.e. one's conception of the purpose of Romans), and vice versa. Thus one's sense of purpose is informed by the text. Each of the proposals above attempts to reflect such a weighing of alternative viewpoints in light of exegesis of particular passages. Nevertheless, larger exegetical decisions must be made, often with inadequate evidence to hand, which have consequences for subsequent understanding.

5. PSEUDONYMY AND EXEGESIS OF THE PAULINE LETTER CORPUS

This discussion of exegesis has so far treated the entire Pauline letter corpus, with little specific attention to issues of authorship.

Nevertheless, this is probably a far more important issue in exegesis than many scholars realize, since it has a variety of implications. These can be readily observed by tracing the response to F.C. Baur and his followers when, in the early nineteenth century, they proposed that the authentic Pauline letters were only four, not the entire thirteen in the New Testament. Today Pauline scholars have tended to settle for a middle ground, most of them recognizing the authenticity of at least seven letters: Romans, 1 and 2 Corinthians, Galatians, Philippians, 1 Thessalonians and Philemon. This means that there are various levels of dispute over the remaining letters: 2 Thessalonians, Colossians and Ephesians, and the Pastoral Epistles. Some scholars would maintain that one or more of these is also authentically written by Paul, while others would dispute that any of them could be. The question here is what difference pseudonymity makes for exegesis of the Pauline letters.[46]

In light of numerous recent episodes in which purportedly authentic documents have proven to be forgeries, we tend to think of the issue of pseudonymy as, for the most part, a modern issue, or at least one on which the ancients had a different perspective. However, pseudonymy was a problem throughout the ancient world—it is certainly not merely a problem of the biblical and related literature (e.g. apocalyptic literature such as *1 Enoch*). These pseudonymous writings included letters.[47]

Before exploring the implications for exegesis of the New Testament, it is worth noting how pseudepigraphal literature was handled in the ancient world, as well as in the early Church. Ancient writers, both Christian and secular, were apparently aware that some of the writings with which they were dealing were pseudonymous. For example, among non-biblical writers, Suetonius describes a letter of Horace as spurious, Galen took only thirteen out of the sixty or eighty Hippocratic texts as genuine, and was concerned that his own corpus of works was being infiltrated by those he did not write, Philostratus disputes a work by Dionysius, and Livy reports that, when discovered, pseudonymous books attributed to Numa were burned. One of the most complex situations in the ancient world was the corpus of

---

[46]   Some of the following arguments were originally developed with regard to issues of canon, rather than exegesis, in S.E. Porter, 'Pauline Authorship and the Pastoral Epistles: Implications for Canon', *BBR* 5 (1995), pp. 105-23.

[47]   See L.R. Donelson, *Pseudepigraphy and Ethical Argument in the Pastoral Epistles* (HUT, 22; Tübingen: Mohr–Siebeck, 1986), esp. pp. 9-42.

Lysias's speeches. Although over 420 were ascribed to him, many ancients knew that many were not genuine, and they formulated various lists indicating this and attempting to determine those that were genuine. For example, one list includes as many speeches as possible, but indicates questions regarding authenticity for a third of them.[48]

A very similar situation apparently held in Christian circles. The general, if not invariable, pattern was that, if a work was known to be pseudonymous, it was excluded from any group of authoritative writings. For example, Tertullian in the early third century tells of the author of '3 Corinthians' (mid second century) being removed from the office of presbyter (Tertullian, *On Baptism* 17).[49] Bishop Salonius rejected Salvian's pamphlet written to the church in Timothy's name.[50] The best known example is the instance where Bishop Serapion in c. 200 reportedly rejected the *Gospel of Peter*. According to Eusebius (*H.E.* 6.12.1-6), Serapion, Bishop of Antioch, wrote to the church at Rhossus in Cilicia, after he had discovered the *Gospel of Peter* being read. He is reported as saying, 'we receive both Peter and the other Apostles as Christ; but as experienced men we reject the writings falsely inscribed with their names, since we know that we did not receive such from our fathers' (LCL). Although the process that led to the Gospel's rejection is complex, involving doctrinal and ecclesiastical issues, it was, in any case, rejected, despite initial tolerance because of its seeming innocuousness.

---

48   See Kiley, *Colossians as Pseudepigraphy*, p. 18 and nn. 9, 10, 11, 12, cf. pp. 17-23, for reference to and citation of primary sources for the above; B.M. Metzger, 'Literary Forgeries and Canonical Pseudepigrapha', *JBL* 91 (1972), p. 6 and *passim*, who discusses many instances of exposed pseudepigrapha; and K.J. Dover, *Lysias and the Corpus Lysiacum* (Berkeley: University of California Press, 1968).

49   See D.A. Carson, D.J. Moo and L. Morris, *An Introduction to the New Testament* (Grand Rapids: Zondervan, 1992), pp. 368-69, who also cite the example of the Epistle to the Laodiceans, which was clearly rejected by the early Church, along with a letter to the Alexandrians, according to the Muratorian fragment (see G.M. Hahneman, *The Muratorian Fragment and the Development of the Canon* [OTM; Oxford: Clarendon Press, 1992], pp. 196-200).

50   Donelson, *Pseudepigraphy and Ethical Argument*, pp. 20-22; E.E. Ellis, 'Pseudonymity and Canonicity of New Testament Documents', in *Worship, Theology and Ministry in the Early Church: Essays in Honor of Ralph P. Martin* (ed. M.J. Wilkins and T. Page; JSNTSup, 87; Sheffield: JSOT Press, 1992), p. 218.

The several means and reasons by which pseudepigrapha were exposed and excluded are admittedly diverse. But as Donelson observes, on the basis of a thorough study of pseudepigraphical writings in the ancient world, both Christian and secular, 'No one ever seems to have accepted a document as religiously and philosophically prescriptive which was *known to be forged*. I do not know a single example.'[51] He includes both Christian and non-Christian documents in this assessment. Therefore, in assessing the implications for exegesis, the interpreter must recognize that the recognition and establishment of pseudonymy for a given Pauline letter puts the letter concerned into a different category of analysis, one separate from the authentic writings of the author.

The question remains, however, what are the specific implications for exegesis? One approach, which has become widely accepted, is to treat the introduction of pseudepigrapha in the Pauline corpus as a phenomenon in harmony with the history of formation of other parts of the scriptural corpus. For example, one scholar has suggested that, within the Old Testament, there is a tradition of pseudonymous literature, in which traditions were supplemented, interpreted and expanded in the names of earlier authors.[52] According to this analysis, there are three major traditions, the prophetic tradition, the wisdom tradition and the apocalyptic tradition. The wisdom tradition in the Old Testament is essentially confined to anonymous literature and the apocalyptic tradition is confined to Daniel, for whom there is no tradition of his being an illustrious hero. Thus the only tradition with direct relevance to the New Testament writings is the prophetic tradition. According to this view, in the prophetic tradition, in particular Isaiah, the tradition was developed by anonymous writers whose writings were attached to the earlier authentic Isaiah. Hence Second Isaiah is not by the historical figure of Isaiah, attested in First Isaiah itself and elsewhere in the Old Testament, but can still only be understood in terms of First Isaiah. The implications of this view of pseudonymity for exegesis would seem to be minimal, with the pseudonymous Pauline letters to be exegeted as part of the larger Pauline corpus, of which the undisputed authentic letters (Romans, 1 and 2 Corinthians, and Galatians, along with Philippians, 1 Thessalonians and Philemon) stand at the center.

---

51   Donelson, *Pseudepigraphy and Ethical Argument*, p. 11 (italics mine).
52   See D. Meade, *Pseudonymity and Canon* (WUNT, 39; Tübingen: Mohr–Siebeck, 1986), pp. 17-43, esp. pp. 26-42 on growth of the Isaiah tradition.

This interpretative framework must be considered further before this pattern can be applied to the Pauline letters, however. It at first appears to present a situation parallel to that in the Pauline letters—there is a pattern of attributing writings to a recognized figure, quite possibly and even probably after the person was dead, and this practice was known to the audience. But this is only a superficial similarity. The type of literature is different. Isaiah is anonymous literature, which purports to contain the words of Isaiah, and is better compared with, for example, the Gospels, which purport to contain the words of Jesus. The Pauline letters are directly attributed to a known author, and appear to be his words, not merely to contain them. The process of literary production is quite different, as well. In the Isaianic writings, the tradition is expanded and compiled over a relatively long period of time, and the document itself grows. In the Pauline letters, the argument would be that the tradition grows, but by adding new documents to the corpus, not merely by expanding others. This would imply that the corpus had already been gathered together—something not sufficiently well known to use as evidence in this discussion—and that the theology of the added letters posed no problem when placed side by side with the authoritative and undisputed Pauline letters. If such a process truly occurred, inclusion must have been early, since attestation of many if not most of the now-disputed Pauline letters in the Church Fathers ranges from as early as *1 Clement* in the late first century to the third quarter of the second century.

Others treat pseudonymy as if it made no difference to exegesis. In his commentary on Ephesians, Lincoln argues that pseudonymy does not detract from the validity or authority of the particular pseudonymous document as part of the New Testament canon. He argues that to worry about such a thing is committing what he calls the 'authorial fallacy', which he defines as setting more store by who wrote a document than by what it says.[53] This argument requires further scrutiny, since the question of authorship does have serious implications, especially for exegesis. First of all, each of the Pauline letters in the New Testament is ascribed to a particular author, one who is well-known in the New Testament and reasonably well-connected to a series of historical events. These letters are not anonymous, without any line of definite authorial connection. The convention of pseudepigraphal writing seems to demand ascription to

---

53   A.T. Lincoln, *Ephesians* (WBC, 42; Dallas: Word, 1990), p. lxxiii.

an important and illustrious figure, of whom a certain number of facts are known. These facts are missing for the pseudepigraph of the disputed Pauline letters, however. Secondly, even if one may have some sense of how to read a letter but not know who the particular author is, for Ephesians—as well as any other disputed Pauline letter—authorship does make a difference for exegesis that addresses the range of questions necessary for understanding a text. Authorship is important for determining whether the situation being addressed is one in the 50s or the 180s, whether one is reading a letter confronting problems at the beginning of the Christian movement or one responding to developed problems of Church order, whether the theology reflects an author formulating and developing profound concepts for the first time or merely repeating what have become accepted dogmas, etc. A clear case in point is Hebrews. Since so little is known of such issues as authorship, date of composition, addressees, and situation, the range of proposals is very wide, and the certainty of conclusions highly elusive. Thirdly, the evaluation of whether any disputed Pauline letter is pseudonymous is often done in terms of evaluating it with reference to the authentic Pauline letters. If Lincoln really believes that authorship makes no difference, then perhaps even asking the question of authorship at all is unnecessary or committing the 'authorial fallacy', for these as well as any other books of the New Testament. Thus, one of the most important links to a particular historical, and hence theological, situation is decisively broken, and exegesis must be altered accordingly.

Therefore, it appears that establishing whether a document is pseudonymous or authentic does indeed make a significant difference to exegesis, and some of these factors have important further implications as well. For example, in attempting to establish which letters are pseudonymous, it is not so simple to establish this for any of the Pauline letters merely by appealing to other New Testament letters that are disputed or even highly doubted, such as the Pastoral Epistles, Ephesians or possibly 2 Thessalonians and Colossians, or, outside the Pauline corpus, 2 Peter. Such an appeal introduces a circularity to the argumentation, which can only be solved by discovery of some sort of firm criteria that can adjudicate the issues. There are apparently no known explicit statements from the first several centuries of the Church to the effect that someone knew that any of the Pauline letters were pseudonymous, so this line of enquiry does not resolve the issue. Nor is it sufficient to cite a number of non-canonical Jewish or especially Christian documents as examples of pseudonymous literature, as if this proves its existence in the New Testament.[54] The fact that these documents are non-canonical is apparent confirmation of the fact that documents that were found to be pseudonymous did not make it into the canon, even if this process of 'discovery' took some time.[55] One is clearly left with internal arguments, but matters such as style, language and theology are highly contentious and ultimately inconclusive, as the history of discussion of these issues well illustrates.

One last issue to raise with regard to exegesis of pseudonymous literature is that of deception. This has been a particularly sensitive issue in the discussion. The matter of deception has more implications than simply casting a shadow of doubt over the process by which a given book was accepted as authoritative. There are also two major results for exegesis.

The first is with regard to the integrity of what can be believed by the author who writes under the name of another. A common argument in defense of pseudepigraphal writings is the so-called 'noble lie', that is, that it is in the best interests of the readers that they not know or are deceived regarding authorship by someone other than the purported author. As Donelson says, the noble lie is still a lie, and all of the attendant moral implications attend to it.[56] Kiley rightly claims that this gives valuable insight into pseudepigraphers' motives.[57] As Davies admits in her discussion of the Pastoral Epistles, the letters make a claim to a high moral standard but she believes that they are pseudonymous and are thus in some sense fraudulent. She admits that there is no simple explanation.[58] As Donelson states, 'We are forced to admit that in Christian circles pseudonymity was considered a dishonorable device and, if discovered, the document

---

54   As does Lincoln, *Ephesians*, pp. lxx-lxxi.

55   Works to be mentioned here would include the Jewish works *4 Ezra* and *1, 2 Enoch*, and the Christian works *Didache, 2 Clement, Epistle of Barnabas*, and the *Apostolic Constitutions*, which (6:16) accuses certain books of being forgeries, while itself being pseudepigraphal. Admittedly, some of these documents remained on the edges of various corpora of authoritative writings for some time.

56   Donelson, *Pseudepigraphy and Ethical Argument*, pp. 18-22. The noble lie refers to Plato's acceptance of a lie that is useful for the one to whom the lie is told (see *Rep.* 2.376e-382b, 3.389b, 414ce).

57   Kiley, *Colossians*, p. 21.

58   M. Davies, *The Pastoral Epistles* (NTG; Sheffield: Sheffield Academic Press, 1996), pp. 113-17.

was rejected and the author, if known, was excoriated'.[59] There were, nevertheless, all sorts of encouragements for skillful pseudepigraphal writing in the ancient world, including pietistic motives prompting those in the Church to speak for an earlier figure,[60] and self-serving motives, such as the money paid by libraries for manuscripts by particular authors.[61]

The second result of pseudonymy for exegesis concerns the circumstances surrounding the production and then acceptance of the pseudepigraph. This can be conveniently explored in terms of the circumstances surrounding the production of the Pastoral Epistles, in particular with reference to their personal features and the original audience or receivers of the letters. Whereas many scholars have struggled with the difficulties surrounding the situation of these letters if they are authentic, the same questions must arise regarding pseudonymous authorship. As Meade has recognized, if they are pseudonymous, there is a 'double pseudonymity' of both *author* and *audience*.[62] What sort of a situation was at play when these letters were received into the Church? It is undecided, even by those who take the Pastoral Epistles as pseudonymous, when the letters were written and/or regarded as authoritative, with dates ranging from an early date of 80–90 to the last half of the second century. The original audience would almost assuredly have known that Paul was dead. Were the letters introduced as new letters from Paul, or at the least inspired by the situation such that Paul would have said these things had he been there? Many have argued that these pseudonymous writings are transparent fictions, and no one would have thought them actually to have been written by Paul. This proposal encounters the problem of why they were acknowledged in the first instance in light of the apparently universal response by the early Church to known pseudepigrapha, which, as we have demonstrated, were rejected *carte blanche*. In any case, any information regarding original context and audience that the original recipients would have known has been lost, as the letters are represented in the New Testament as being a part of the Pauline corpus.

---

[59]   Donelson, *Pseudepigraphy and Ethical Argument*, p. 16.

[60]   It is questionable whether this motive can be equated with an innocent motive. See Donelson, *Pseudepigraphy and Ethical Argument*, p. 10.

[61]   See M.L. Stirewalt, Jr, *Studies in Ancient Greek Epistolography* (SBLRBS, 27; Atlanta: Scholars Press, 1993), pp. 31-42.

[62]   Meade, *Pseudonymity in the New Testament*, p. 127.

With regard to exegesis, there are a number of further implications regarding Pauline pseudepigrapha. First, they cannot be used in any way in the establishment of a Pauline chronology, since the lack of grounding in a specific historical and authorial context removes this point of stability. Secondly, in light of theological development and possible pseudepigraphal authorship, the disputed or pseudonymous Pauline Epistles must be handled delicately in establishing Pauline theology. 'Pauline theology' is here a slippery term, but one that must be defined at least in part. For some, it may mean a theology of all of the letters attributed to Paul, whether genuine or not. The exegetical significance of the disputed letters would constitute evidence for the diversity and development of early Pauline theology so defined. For those concerned with trying to establish a Pauline theology based on what Paul may have actually thought and written, pseudonymous letters cannot be used to create a Pauline theology in this sense. They are instead part of a record of how some people responded to Paul, how others developed his thought, how some people applied his ideas to later situations, or even how some people wished Paul could have spoken—they can never be more than only one interpretation among many others. The fact that they were included in the group of Pauline letters has enhanced their apparent authority, and may mean that they represent the most influential or powerful followers of Paul, but it does not raise their level of authenticity.

As discussed above, a factor not as fully appreciated as it might be is the difference that the issue of authorship ultimately makes for exegesis. Even for the authentic letters there are problems of interpretation with regard to such issues as occasion and purpose. Without attributable authorship, there is even less information available. The letters must be interpreted in light of the double pseudonymy of author and audience, and thus cannot constitute evidence for the life and teachings of Paul. In other words, questions of authorship have serious exegetical implications.

6. RHETORICAL CRITICISM AND THE PAULINE LETTER FORM

Paul was a letter writer in an age of letter writing.[63] The joining

---

[63]   On the Pauline letter form, see McDonald and Porter, *Early Christianity and its Sacred Literature*, chap. 9; and on the issue of Pauline rhetoric, see S.E. Porter, 'Paul of Tarsus and His Letters', in *Handbook of Classical Rhetoric in the Hellenistic Period*, pp. 533-85.

together of the world surrounding the Mediterranean during the Hellenistic period, regularized under the Roman empire, brought a sense of unity to the region, and also created the functional need for communication between people who were sometimes removed by great distances from each other. This includes the need to communicate between the apostle and the small Christian assemblies he had founded, or with which he wished to communicate. As a result, the letter became very important, not only for general communication, but as an important form of communication in the early Church. The exegetical implications of this form of communication must always be considered when analyzing the Pauline writings, since letters are the only literary genre that Paul used.

Thousands upon thousands of letters from the Greco-Roman period have been found as a part of a vast quantity of papyrus documents from the ancient world. The vast majority of these papyrus documents were found in Egypt, although others of significance have been found east of the Mediterranean. The kinds of documents found include wills, land surveys, reports, receipts for various financial transactions, contracts (especially regarding agriculture and related services), personal letters, and a variety of judicial, legal and official documents and letters, as well as numerous literary and theological works.[64] Twenty-one of the twenty-seven books of the New Testament have been identified as letters of various sorts, and all of Paul's writings are letters. The same pattern was continued by the Apostolic Fathers, of whom twelve of the fifteen texts of the Apostolic Fathers by the nine authors included are letters.

Adolf Deissmann, one of the first to appreciate the importance of the papyrus letters for study of the New Testament, observed that the Egyptian letters tend to be short, with the average being somewhere around 275 words. Paul's letters, however, are much longer. Only Philemon, at 335 words, approximates the length of the average

---

[64]   Collections of these letters useful for New Testament study are to be found in, for example, A.S. Hunt and C.C. Edgar, *Select Papyri* (vols. 1–2; LCL; London: Heinemann; Cambridge, MA: Harvard University Press, 1932, 1934); G.H.R. Horsley and S. Llewelyn, *New Documents Illustrating Early Christianity* (7 vols. to date; New South Wales: Macquarie University, 1981–); J.L. White, *Light from Ancient Letters* (FFNT; Philadelphia: Fortress Press, 1986); for background information, see E.G. Turner, *Greek Papyri: An Introduction* (Oxford: Clarendon Press, 2nd edn, 1980), and R.S. Bagnall, *Reading Papyri, Writing Ancient History* (AAW; London: Routledge, 1995).

Egyptian letter (and even it is longer by a few words). However, there are a number of letters attributed to literary figures, such as Plato, Isocrates, Demosthenes, Cicero and Seneca. As a result of observing these various kinds of letters, Deissmann distinguished the 'true letters' of the papyri from 'literary letters' or 'epistles', concluding that Paul's letters were true letters (except for the Pastoral Epistles), since they were addressed to a specific situation and specific people, and reflected Paul's genuine and unaffected thoughts and ideas, and were written in the language of the people of the day, rather than some artificial literary style.[65] Most studies of the letters of the New Testament are responses to Deissmann's analysis.

The general consensus among scholars today is that a variety of factors must be considered, rather than simply length and supposed genuineness. Better than seeing a disjunction between letter and epistle is the idea that there is a continuum, which depends on at least the following factors: language, whether the letters have a formal or informal style; content, whether their subject matter is one of business, personal recommendation, praise or blame, or instruction; and audience, including whether they are public or private. Some of the other factors to consider in analyzing Paul's letters are that these, unlike most true letters, are not private in the conventional sense, but neither are they for any and all who might be interested in reading them. They are for groups of followers of Christ, or churches, hence the frequent use of the second person plural form of address. Barring Philemon, Paul's letters are significantly longer than the average papyrus letter, and they have some unique features of organization, discussed below. The body of the Pauline letter is recognizably that of the ancient personal letter, although the topics discussed are not usually personal commendations, but rather instructions in the Christian faith. With this essential framework regarding the letter in place, more specific exegetical issues regarding Paul's letters can be examined.

In recent exegesis of the Pauline letters, classical rhetorical criticism

---

[65]　See especially A. Deissmann, *Bible Studies* (trans. A. Grieve; Edinburgh: T. & T. Clark, 1901; 2nd edn, 1909), pp. 1-59. For an important critique of Deissmann's hypothesis, as well as a discussion of recent research in Greek epistolography, see S.K. Stowers, *Letter Writing in Greco-Roman Antiquity* (LEC; Philadelphia: Westminster Press, 1986), pp. 17-26, and the Chapter on the Genres of the New Testament in this volume.

has been frequently drawn upon.[66] Before proposing a method of exegeting the letters on the basis of epistolary theory, I wish to subject the concept of rhetorical criticism as an exegetical method of the Pauline letters to critical scrutiny.[67] Some scholars seem to suggest, even if implicitly, that the application of the categories from classical rhetoric to ancient letters was something with which the ancients themselves would have been familiar, that they would have recognized, and that Paul would have intended to use. These kinds of suppositions seem to be particularly useful to those who wish to find a firm basis for their exegesis by appealing to the ancients themselves. When such support is sought among the ancients, however, it is conspicuously missing. After his thorough study of ancient epistolary theory, Abraham Malherbe states, 'Epistolary theory in antiquity belonged to the domain of the rhetoricians, but it was not originally part of their theoretical systems. It is absent from the earliest extant rhetorical handbooks, and it only gradually made its way into the genre.' He states further, 'It is thus clear that letter writing was of interest to rhetoricians, but it appears only gradually to have attached itself to their rhetorical systems'.[68] These conclusions certainly offer little theoretical justification for the kind of rhetorical analysis that is found in many commentators on the rhetoric of the Pauline letters. A survey of the primary sources confirms Malherbe's conclusions. It is not until Julius Victor (fourth century CE), in an appendix to his *Ars rhetorica* (27), that letter writing is discussed in a rhetorical handbook, although confined to comments on style. Thus, although categories of ancient rhetoric may have been 'in the air' of the Greco-Roman world, their use in the writing or analysis of letters cannot be substantiated. Only matters of style, and some forms of argumentation, appear to have been discussed in any significant or extended way, though not systematically, with letters virtually always mentioned in contrast to oratory.

---

66   One of the major proponents is G.A. Kennedy, *New Testament Interpretation through Rhetorical Criticism* (Chapel Hill and London: University of North Carolina Press, 1984).

67   See S.E. Porter, 'The Theoretical Justification for Application of Rhetorical Categories to Pauline Epistolary Literature', in *Rhetoric and the New Testament: Essays from the 1992 Heidelberg Conference* (ed. S.E. Porter and T.H. Olbricht; JSNTSup, 90; Sheffield: JSOT Press, 1993), pp. 100-122.

68   A.J. Malherbe, *Ancient Epistolary Theorists* (SBLSBS, 19; Atlanta: Scholars Press, 1988), pp. 2, 3.

The above conclusion does not preclude exegeting the Pauline letters in terms of the categories of ancient rhetoric, however, as long as it is kept in mind that these categories, especially those regarding the arrangement of the parts of the speech, probably did not consciously influence the writing of the letters and almost assuredly did not figure significantly in their earliest interpretation. Rhetorical analyses are one form of exegesis to which these texts can be subjected, but they are not the only ones, and should not necessarily enjoy a privileged status among interpretative methods. This is not to say, however, that there is no relationship between ancient rhetorical and epistolary theory—some functional correspondence between them may be established.[69] These functional correspondences are related to the various uses to which the various literary forms were put, and how these uses correlate with their literary structures.

The major importance of the study of the ancient Greek letter form for exegesis is seen in relation to the structure of the letter. Scholars are divided over whether Paul's letters fall into three, four or five parts.[70] The question revolves around whether two of the parts are seen, on functional grounds, to be separate and distinct units within the letter, or whether these are subsumed in the other parts of the letter. Without wishing to distance Paul's letters from those of the Hellenistic world, especially in light of how Paul enhanced the letter form, it is appropriate to expand the traditional form-based three-part structure, and talk in terms of five formal parts to the Pauline letter: opening, thanksgiving, body, parenesis and closing. This is not, however, to say that each of the Pauline letters has all five of these elements. Nevertheless, when one of these sections is missing, it is worth asking whether there is a reason for this departure from his standard form.

Since presentation of content is based on the defined structure of the genre, the Pauline letter form provides one of the best guides to exegesis of the Pauline letters. Comments on each of the five

---

[69]   See J.T. Reed, 'Using Ancient Rhetorical Categories to Interpret Paul's Letters: A Question of Genre', in *Rhetoric and the New Testament*, pp. 297-314.

[70]   The three-part letter is defended by J.L. White, 'Ancient Greek Letters', in *Greco-Roman Literature*, pp. 85-105, esp. p. 97; the four-part letter by J.A.D. Weima, *Neglected Endings: The Significance of the Pauline Letter Closings* (JSNTSup, 101; Sheffield: JSOT Press, 1994), p. 11; and the five-part letter by W.G. Doty, *Letters in Primitive Christianity* (GBS; Philadelphia: Fortress Press, 1973), pp. 27-43. I tend to follow Doty below.

epistolary parts will provide examples of exegetical significance. This is where an expanded concept of rhetoric might well illustrate functional overlap between rhetoric and epistolary theory.

A. Opening

The usual (though certainly not unvaried) opening of a letter in the Hellenistic world from the third century BCE to the third century CE included three elements: the sender, the recipient and a greeting, often formalized as 'A to B, greetings (χαίρειν)', although the form 'to B from A, greetings' was also found. The formal features of the epistolary opening, such as the greeting, perform certain functions in the letter. These include establishing and maintaining contact between the sender and recipients, and clarifying their respective statuses and relationships.

Paul, while including all three formal elements in his standard opening, introduces several modifications. For example, Paul often includes others as co-authors or co-senders of his letters. Only Romans, Ephesians and the Pastoral Epistles do not include a co-sender, usually Timothy. There are several possible exegetical implications for Paul's including another person or persons in the opening. Perhaps these people should be seen as co-senders. By mentioning them, such as his longstanding companion Timothy (and Silas), Paul shows that his gospel is not his alone; what he is saying comes from a Christian community to another Christian community. Timothy is also seen to be as a letter-carrier in Acts, as well as in the Pauline letters, so the specification at the beginning of the letter probably helped to establish the authority of the letter-carrier, possibly responsible for reading (and interpreting?) the letter to the audience. Romans and Ephesians do not have co-senders, perhaps because these letters were being sent under different circumstances than the other Pauline letters, the first to a church Paul had never visited, located outside his immediate sphere of influence (Paul may not have been to Colossae either, but it was within his sphere of influence), and the second perhaps to no specific church but to a number of churches in Asia (if Paul wrote the letter at all). The Pastorals also include no co-sender, but if they are authentic and if they are sent to Timothy and Titus, two of Paul's close associates, they would have no need of a co-sender as defined above.

Paul also often expands the specification of the sender or recipient of a letter, including information of potential exegetical and even theological significance. For example, in Rom. 1:1-6 Paul designates himself as set apart for the gospel of God, which leads to a lengthy expansion on the nature of this gospel and its relation to Jesus Christ. In 1 Cor. 1:2, Paul expands upon the designation of the recipients, defining the church of God in Corinth in terms of those who are sanctified and called to be holy. Whereas designation of the title or position of the sender or recipient in a letter was known in the ancient world, Paul's kind of expansion is virtually unknown before his writings.

Paul has also apparently modified the word of greeting. All of Paul's letters include the words 'grace' (χάρις) and 'peace' (εἰρήνη), with the word 'mercy' (ἐλεημοσύνη) added in 1 and 2 Timothy, rather than the verb 'greet' (χαίρειν) found in Hellenistic letters. The word for 'grace' is cognate with the word 'greet', so it is easy to see that Paul is apparently playing upon the standard convention for greeting, probably in a sense theologizing the letter opening in a distinctly Christian way. The suggestion that Paul includes 'peace' as a translation of the Hebrew word *shalom*, and that this reflects his integration of Greek and Jewish elements into his letter, is probably to be dismissed as over-theologizing the opening.

B. Thanksgiving

Many Greco-Roman letters then include a health wish, in which a prayer or word of thanks was offered for the well-being of the addressee. This was often addressed to one of the Egyptian gods, such as Serapis. Paul also uses a formula in which a verb of thanksgiving (εὐχαριστῶ) is addressed to God, with a reason for his thanks.[71] Paul has again adapted the Hellenistic letter form to his epistolary and theological purposes. Galatians, however, lacks a thanksgiving, creating a jarring transition from the opening to the body of the letter, in which Paul expresses his astonishment that the Galatians have so quickly deserted their calling. 1 Thessalonians, on the other hand, is full of thanksgiving by Paul for the Thessalonian Christians, with words of thanksgiving spread throughout the letter.

One must, however, be cautious in exegeting the thanksgiving portion of the letter, in light of the theory of many scholars that Paul

---

71   On the relation of the Pauline thanksgiving to other thanksgivings, see J.T. Reed, 'Are Paul's Thanksgivings "Epistolary"?', *JSNT* 61 (1996), pp. 87-99; cf. G.P. Wiles, *Paul's Intercessory Prayer: The Significance of the Intercessory Prayer Passages in the Letters of Paul* (SNTSMS, 24; Cambridge: Cambridge University Press, 1974), who analyzes prayers in the thanksgiving, as well as the other parts of the letter.

utilizes the thanksgiving section to forecast the topics that are to be discussed in the letter. For example, most if not all of the ideas introduced in the thanksgiving of 1 Thessalonians (1:2-10) are developed in various ways in the rest of the letter: their work (1 Thess. 2:1-16), being imitators (3:6-10), being models (4:1-12), and the return of Christ (5:1-11). To the contrary, however, only two of the many themes discussed in 1 Corinthians are introduced in its thanksgiving, spiritual gifts and eschatology (1 Cor. 1:7).[72] A more accurate assessment of the relationship between the thanksgiving and the content of a letter is to say that the thanksgiving provides a general orientation to the relationship between Paul and the particular church, a relationship which is then developed in various ways in the rest of the letter.

C. Body

The Hellenistic letter body has been the least studied part of the Hellenistic letter form. The same is true of the body of the Pauline letter, with much more attention being devoted to exegeting individual theological ideas in isolation rather than appreciating the unfolding of Paul's argument. For Paul, the body of the letter tends to deal with one or both of two subjects: Christian doctrine and, like Hellenistic letters of friendship, Paul's personal situation. Letters such as Romans, Galatians and 1 Corinthians tend to be concerned in their bodies to outline and develop important Pauline theological concepts. Paul's personal situation, especially in relation to a particular church, is discussed in Philippians, as well as in 1 and 2 Corinthians. In the Pauline letter corpus, the epistolary body typically follows the friendship letter convention, in which various issues regarding the personal relationship of those involved are broached (these may include theological issues). In that sense, Christian teaching and issues of belief fall within the scope of the personal letter form, although Paul has clearly developed and applied this form in an extended way.

Like other Hellenistic letters, the body of the Pauline letter is usually divided into three parts: the body opening, the body middle or body proper, and the body closing. These formal locations in the body of the letter serve various functions in introducing and concluding the matter at hand. Like other letter writers, Paul relies upon a number of formulas to mark the beginnings and endings of various portions of

---

[72]   See J. Bailey and L.D. Vander Broek, *Literary Forms in the New Testament* (London: SPCK, 1992), p. 24.

the body and to draw attention to the significance of various ideas that he introduces. For exegetical purposes, these formulas can serve as important markers to indicate logical shifts in the argument and in terms of the conclusion and introduction of new ideas.

The following introductory formulas are worth noting: the verb 'beseech' (παρακαλῶ) in a transitionary request or appeal formula (e.g. 1 Cor. 4:16; 16:15; Phlm. 8, 10), often, though not always, as a transition from the thanksgiving to the body of the letter (e.g. 1 Cor. 1:10); disclosure formulas, such as 'I want you to know' or 'I don't want you to be ignorant', indicating that the sender believes the recipients should know what he is about to tell them, often used near the beginning of the body of the letter (see e.g. Rom. 1:13; 2 Cor. 1:8; 1 Thess. 2:1; Phil. 1:12; Gal. 1:11); expressions of astonishment (e.g. Gal. 1:6), indicating that Paul completely objects to what it is that the recipients are doing or saying (usually in relation to what is being disclosed); and compliance formulas, in which he restates something that places an obligation of action upon his readers (e.g. Gal. 1:9, 13-14).

Body closing formulas are designed to bring the argument of the body together and close this portion of the letter. The following closing formulas are worth noting: confidence formulas, in which Paul expresses confidence that his recipients will have understood what he has said and will act appropriately upon it (e.g. Rom. 15:14; 2 Cor. 7:4, 16; 9:1-2; Gal. 5:10; 2 Thess. 3:4; Phlm. 21); and an eschatological conclusion, in which Paul places what he has been saying in the larger framework of the imminent return of Christ (e.g. Rom. 8:31-39; 11:25-26; 1 Cor. 4:6-13; Gal. 6:7-10; Phil. 2:14-18; 1 Thess. 2:13-16). Belief in the imminent return of Christ was used by Paul as a serious motivation for proper Christian action and belief. Paul also occasionally uses a travelogue near the close of the body portion of his letter (e.g. 1 Thess. 2:17–3:13), characterized as the 'apostolic parousia' or apostolic presence.[73] Paul indicates his reason

---

[73] See R.W. Funk, 'The Apostolic Parousia: Form and Significance', in *Christian History and Interpretation: Studies Presented to John Knox* (ed. W.R. Farmer, C.F.D. Moule and R.R. Niebuhr; Cambridge: Cambridge University Press, 1967), pp. 249-68. Funk tries to identify a formal category, but the apostolic presence is better seen as a functional convention. See also M.M. Mitchell, 'New Testament Envoys in the Context of Greco-Roman Diplomatic and Epistolary Conventions: The Example of Timothy and Titus', *JBL* 111 (1992), pp. 641-62, who questions some of Funk's conclusions.

for writing or his intention to send an emissary or even pay a personal visit to his recipients. In effect, the letter is a temporary substitute for the apostle's (or his designated representative's) presence. The travelogue outlining the apostle's plans usually occurs near the end of the body or even the parenesis (Rom. 15:14-33; Phlm. 21-22; 1 Cor. 4:14-21; 1 Thess. 2:17–3:13; 2 Cor. 12:14–13:13; Gal. 4:12-20; Phil. 2:19-24), but it is not necessarily only found at the close (see Rom. 1:10; 1 Cor. 4:21; Phil. 2:24).

D. Parenesis

The parenesis section of the Pauline letter is concerned with proper Christian behavior. The parenesis often specifies what is proper Christian behavior, and expresses this using various traditional forms of moral instruction. These include moral maxims, vice and virtue lists, and household codes (German *Haustafeln*) that specify mutual submission between members of the household (e.g. Eph. 5:21–6:9; Col. 3:18–4:1). In creating his parenesis, Paul draws upon a variety of sources, including the Old Testament, contemporary Jewish thinking, Greco-Roman thought and Hellenistic moral traditions. Paul's best known parenetic sections are those in Rom. 12:1–15:13, Gal. 5:13–6:10, and 1 Thess. 4:1–5:22.

E. Closing

The typical Hellenistic letter closing expressed a health wish, often in terms of a closing imperative, a word of farewell, and the word 'good-bye' (ἔρρωσο or ἔρρωσθε). Paul, however, includes a number of different elements in his closings, showing significant differences from the typical Hellenistic letter closing. The Pauline letter closing might consist of any number of the following elements: greetings, to the recipients or conveyed from those who are with him to the recipients (Rom. 16:3-23, with the longest list; 1 Cor. 16:19-21; 2 Cor. 13:12-13; Phil. 4:21-22; 1 Thess. 5:26; Phlm. 23-25); doxology at the end of his letter (one is included earlier at Gal. 1:5), often containing exalted language of praise and glory to God (e.g. Rom. 16:25-27; Phil. 4:20; 1 Thess. 5:23); benediction, which takes several different forms, depending upon whether it is a grace or a peace benediction (Rom. 15:33; 16:20; 1 Cor. 16:23; 2 Cor. 12:14; Gal. 6:18; Phil. 4:22; 1 Thess. 5:28; Phlm. 25); and occasionally greeting of each other with a holy kiss (Rom. 16:16; 1 Cor. 16:20; 2 Cor. 3:12; 1 Thess. 5:26).[74]

---

[74]   On these and other features of the Pauline closing, see H. Gamble, Jr, *The Textual History of the Letter to the Romans: A Study in Textual and Literary*

As in the epistolary opening, some of the ideas and themes presented in the letter are also summarized in the closing, but the function of the closing is not best described as a summary of the contents of the letter. The closing of the letter is simply a way of concluding the correspondence, often not by adding to or even recapitulating what has already been said, but by providing suitable words of closing. Paul has again theologized the closing in a Christian way, in order to leave his recipients with a closing that offers praise and glory to God (Rom. 16:25-27) and grace or peace to the recipients (2 Cor. 13:14).

Thus the structure of the Pauline letter provides exegetical guidance as to what one might expect when one confronts the letter form. The letter form can set legitimate parameters for the kinds of exegetical conclusions that can be drawn from the various sections of the letter. A poignant example can be found in the book of 1 Corinthians. Because of statements that are made, especially in chs. 12 and 14 regarding women in worship and spiritual gifts, in particular the gift of tongues, this book has been invoked in much recent theological discussion. A factor that is often overlooked in this discussion, however, and one relevant to matters of exegesis as discussed above, is where these chapters appear in the book itself. The body of 1 Corinthians extends from 1:10–4:21, and is concerned with Church unity. Perhaps the most plausible explanation of the occasion for the letter was a conflict over unity that elicited this letter addressed to that issue. In his argument, developed in the body of the letter, Paul first discusses the problem of disunity (1:10-17). He then turns to a discussion of the gospel (1:18–2:5), which consists of the message of Christ crucified, a concept that is foolishness to most (1:18-25), including the Corinthians, who were called to faith when they were unwise (1:26-31). Paul's message is based upon the power of the Spirit (2:1-5). The Spirit is the source of God's wisdom (2:6-16). Turning specifically to the question of divisiveness in the Church (3:1-23), Paul sees disunity as a sign of spiritual immaturity (3:1-4), and he discusses how the work of various people contributes to God's larger purpose of building the Church (3:5-17), leading to his call for unity among the Corinthians (3:18-23). Paul concludes the body of the letter with a justification of himself as Christ's faithful servant (4:1-

---

Criticism (SD, 42; Grand Rapids: Eerdmans, 1977), pp. 56-83; Weima, *Neglected Endings, passim.*

23). After elucidating these general concepts, though illustrated through specific statements regarding Paul and his situation as an apostle, Paul turns to the parenetic section of the letter (5:1–16:12). The parenetic section is much larger than the body of the letter; however, this does not mean that the relative functions of the sections involved are to be viewed differently. In this section, Paul responds to particular problems of the Corinthian church. Many, if not most, of them seem to have threatened their church unity in some way, and in that sense they are specific instantiations of the more general truths discussed in the body of the letter. However, the nature of parenesis is exhortative, that is, to describe how Christians are to behave in light of their Christian faith. Therefore, parenesis is not focused upon doctrine except as doctrine is worked out in behavior. Hence Paul has words regarding questions of morality (5:1–6:20), marriage (7:1-40), food sacrificed to idols (8:1–11:1), worship (11:2-34), spiritual gifts (12:1–14:40), and the resurrection (15:1-58), closing with words on the collection. Any didactic material in the parenesis must be taken in light of the particular situation that is being addressed regarding the Corinthian church. This can be clearly seen in the passage in 5:1-13, where a case of incest in the church is being addressed. The particular steps to be taken are addressed to that particular case. The same kind of exegetical framework should also be employed when examining the more controversial passages in chs. 12 and 14, seeing the problems discussed there in the first instance as examples of behavior that threatened the larger concept of unity in the church at Corinth.

7. CONCLUSION

The importance of Pauline exegesis cannot be minimized. The ability to linguistically analyze a given passage of one of the Pauline letters is of course not to be minimized. However, exegesis involves much more than being able to parse word-forms and string together syntactical units, or find lexical glosses in a dictionary. Exegesis requires knowledge and application of the issues specific to exegesis of a given author. For Paul, this requires the placement of this intriguing figure of the ancient world into his appropriate historical, cultural, religious and theological contexts, weighing all of the various aspects of the world in which he lived. This also requires consideration of the implications whether Paul actually wrote any of the given letters being exegeted. Once this has been established, consideration must be given to the specific issues being faced, often in terms of Paul's opponents. Once the occasion of the letter is reconstructed, one can attempt to assess the specific purpose of Paul's writing the given letter. This determination of purpose, in conjunction with analysis of any given passage in terms of how it fits within the format of the Pauline letter form, provides a useful set of parameters for determining the exegetical significance of a passage. In this sense, one can speak of exegesis of the Pauline letters.

BIBLIOGRAPHY

This bibliography does list commentaries on individual Pauline letters, or most specialized studies, but concentrates on books about Paul's life and thought.

Anderson, C.A.A. *Christianity according to St Paul*. Cambridge: Cambridge University Press, 1939.

Barrett, C.K. *From First Adam to Last: A Study in Pauline Theology*. London: A. & C. Black, 1962.

_____. *Paul: An Introduction to his Thought*. London: Chapman, 1994.

Bassler, J.M. (ed.). *Pauline Theology*. I. *Thessalonians, Philippians, Galatians, Philemon*. Minneapolis: Fortress Press, 1991.

Beare, F.W. *St Paul and his Letters*. London: A. & C. Black, 1962.

Beker, J.C. *Heirs of Paul: Paul's Legacy in the New Testament and in the Church Today*. Minneapolis: Fortress Press, 1991.

Best, E. *Ephesians*. NTG. Sheffield: JSOT Press, 1993.

Bornkamm, G. *Paul*. New York: Harper & Row, 1971.

Bruce, F.F. *Paul: Apostle of the Heart Set Free*. Grand Rapids: Eerdmans, 1977.

Conybeare, W.J., and J.S. Howson. *The Life and Epistles of St Paul*. London: Longmans, Green, new edn, 1883.

Davies, M. *The Pastoral Epistles*. NTG. Sheffield: Sheffield Academic Press, 1996.

Davies, W.D. *Paul and Rabbinic Judaism: Some Rabbinic Elements in Pauline Theology*. Philadelphia: Fortress Press, 4th edn, 1980.

Deissmann, A. *Paul: A Study in Social and Religious History*. London: Hodder & Stoughton, 2nd edn, 1927.

Donfried, K.P., and I.H. Marshall. *The Theology of the Shorter Pauline Letters*. Cambridge: Cambridge University Press, 1993.

Dunn, J.D.G. *1 Corinthians*. NTG. Sheffield: Sheffield Academic Press, 1995.

_____. *The Theology of Paul's Letter to the Galatians*. Cambridge: Cambridge University Press, 1993.

Elliott, N. *Liberating Paul: The Justice of God and the Politics of the Apostle*. Sheffield: Sheffield Academic Press, 1995.

Ellis, E.E. *Paul and his Recent Interpreters*. Grand Rapids: Eerdmans, 1961.

_____. *Paul's Use of the Old Testament*. Edinburgh: Oliver & Boyd, 1957.

Glover, T.R. *Paul of Tarsus*. London: SCM Press, 1925.

Hay, D.M. (ed.). *Pauline Theology*. II. *1 & 2 Corinthians*. Minneapolis: Fortress Press, 1993.

Hay, D.M., and E.E. Johnson (eds.). *Pauline Theology*. III. *Romans*. Minneapolis: Fortress Press, 1995.

Hays, R.B. *Echoes of Scripture in the Letters of Paul*. New Haven: Yale University Press, 1989.

Hengel, M. *The Pre-Christian Paul*. London: SCM Press, 1991.

Hock, R.F. *The Social Context of Paul's Ministry: Tentmaking and Apostleship*. Philadelphia: Fortress Press, 1980.

Holmberg, B. *Paul and Power: The Structure and Authority in the Primitive Church Reflected in the Pauline Epistles*. Philadelphia: Fortress Press, 1978.

Hunter, A.M. *Paul and his Predecessors*. London: SCM Press, rev. edn, 1961.

Jewett, R. *Dating Paul's Life*. London: SCM Press, 1979.

Kim, S. *The Origin of Paul's Gospel*. Grand Rapids: Eerdmans, 1981.

Knox, J. *Chapters in a Life of Paul*. Macon, GA: Mercer University Press, rev. edn, 1989.

Knox, W.L. *St Paul and the Church of Jerusalem*. Cambridge: Cambridge University Press, 1925.

———. *St Paul and the Church of the Gentiles*. Cambridge: Cambridge University Press, 1939.

Lake, K. *The Earlier Epistles of St Paul: Their Motive and Origin*. London: Rivingtons, 1911.

Lincoln, A.T., and A.J.M. Wedderburn. *The Theology of the Later Pauline Epistles*. Cambridge: Cambridge University Press, 1993.

Lüdemann, G. *Paul, Apostle to the Gentiles: Studies in Chronology*. Philadelphia: Fortress Press, 1984.

Machen, J.G. *The Origin of Paul's Religion*. Grand Rapids: Eerdmans, 1947.

Malherbe, A.J. *Paul and the Popular Philosophers*. Minneapolis: Fortress Press, 1989.

Meeks, W.A. *The First Urban Christians: The Social World of the Apostle Paul*. New Haven: Yale University Press, 1983.

Morgan, R. *Romans*. NTG. Sheffield: Sheffield Academic Press, 1995.

Munck, J. *Paul and the Salvation of Mankind*. London: SCM Press, 1959.

Murphy-O'Connor, J. *Paul the Letter-Writer: His World, his Options, his Skills*. Collegeville, MN: Liturgical Press, 1995.

Ogg, G. *The Chronology of the Life of Paul*. London: Epworth, 1968.

Plevnik, J. *What are They Saying about Paul?* New York: Paulist Press, 1986.

Porter, S.E., and C.A. Evans (eds.). *The Pauline Writings: A Sheffield Reader*. Sheffield: Sheffield Academic Press, 1995.

Ramsay, W.M. *The Cities of St Paul: Their Influence on his Life and Thought*. London: Hodder & Stoughton, 1907.

———. *St Paul the Traveller and the Roman Citizen*. London: Hodder & Stoughton, 1895.

Ridderbos, H. *Paul: An Outline of his Theology*. Grand Rapids: Eerdmans, 1975.

Roetzel, C.J. *The Letters of Paul: Conversations in Context*. Louisville: Westminster/John Knox Press, 3rd edn, 1981.

Sanders, E.P. *Paul and Palestinian Judaism: A Comparison of Patterns of Religion*. Philadelphia: Fortress Press, 1977.

_____. *Paul, the Law and the Jewish People*. Philadelphia: Fortress Press, 1983.

Schoeps, H.J. *Paul: The Theology of the Apostle in the Light of Jewish Religious History*. Philadelphia: Westminster Press, 1959.

Schreiner, T.R. *Interpreting the Pauline Epistles*. Grand Rapids: Baker, 1990.

Segal, A. *Paul the Convert: The Apostolate and Apostasy of Saul the Pharisee*. New Haven: Yale University Press, 1990.

Stanley, C.D. *Paul and the Language of Scripture: Citation Technique in the Pauline Epistles and Contemporary Literature*. Cambridge: Cambridge University Press, 1992.

Wedderburn, A.J.M. (ed.). *Paul and Jesus: Collected Essays*. Sheffield: JSOT Press, 1989.

Wenham, D. *Paul: Follower of Jesus or Founder of Christianity?* Grand Rapids: Eerdmans, 1995.

Westerholm, S. *Israel's Law and the Church's Faith: Paul and his Recent Interpreters*. Grand Rapids: Eerdmans, 1988.

Whiteley, D.E.H. *The Theology of St Paul*. Oxford: Blackwell, 2nd edn, 1974.

Witherington, B., III. *Paul's Narrative Thought World: The Tapestry of Tragedy and Triumph*. Louisville: Westminster/John Knox Press, 1994.

Young, F. *The Theology of the Pastoral Epistles*. Cambridge: Cambridge University Press, 1994.

THE JOHANNINE LITERATURE

JOHN PAINTER

THE JOHANNINE CORPUS

The Johannine literature consists of the Gospel of John, the Epistles of John and Revelation or the Apocalypse. While contemporary scholars generally recognize that the Gospel and Epistles came from the Johannine school, if not from the same author, few would set Revelation in the same context. For most Johannine scholars the views of Schüssler Fiorenza concerning the relationship of Revelation to the rest of the Johannine literature are to the point. Schüssler Fiorenza is of the view that Revelation is closer to Pauline than Johannine Christianity (Schüssler Fiorenza 1976–77). Revelation does not share the common language exhibited by the other Johannine books, which differ greatly from Revelation's apocalyptic genre. While Revelation combines the form of letters and prophecy, the apocalyptic genre is dominant. The element that is thought most to distinguish Revelation from the rest of the Johannine literature is its dominant imminent future eschatology. This eschatology is set in the context of a dualistic worldview, which portrays the present world as under the power of evil. The expectation in the hoped-for coming of the Lord is that he will overthrow the power of evil.

Differences in the Johannine literature should not be ignored, but connections often go unnoticed and differences are exaggerated because no allowance is made for the influence of genre in the construction of Gospel and Apocalypse. Revelation shares with the Gospel the concentration on the language of 'witness', the identification of Jesus as 'the Word of God', and the focus on the role of the Spirit and the theme of 'abiding'. Both authors quote Zech. 12:10 using ἐξεκέντησαν, which is not in the LXX. Both use the phrases 'to keep the word' or 'to keep the commandments', 'whoever thirsts let him come', and the term 'to overcome (conquer)'. The Christ of the Gospel and Apocalypse is a pre-existent being, a judge who knows the hearts and thoughts of people.

Further, the dualistic worldview of Revelation is not foreign to the Gospel and epistles, which refer to the prince of this world (John 12:31) and assert that the whole world lies in the power of the evil one

(1 John 5:19). While the main focus is on present fulfilment, the Gospel and epistles also maintain a future eschatological perspective (John 5:28-29; 6:39, 40, 44, 54; 11:24; 14:3; 1 John 2:18, 28; 3:2; 4:17). Revelation is oriented to the imminent future, but present fulfilment is assumed, though it is obscured by the symbolic mode of communication that is common to apocalypses.

Certainly there is a shift of balance to the present, especially in the Gospel, but this difference may not be as great as at first seems to be the case. The major difference is between the Gospel genre and letter genre as distinct from that of an apocalypse. We are not dealing with pure, hermetically-sealed genres, but apocalyptic dominates Revelation, while the narrative of the ministry of Jesus dominates the Gospel. 1 John is something of a cross between a letter and a tract. It lacks the address and signature of a letter, but is addressed to a more specific group of readers than is normally the case with a tract.

Showing that Revelation is not in conflict with the thought of the Gospel does not demonstrate common authorship. At most, it shows that the case against common authorship is not conclusive. But what is the case for common authorship? It is first the testimony of Irenaeus (c. 180 CE), who claims to have his information from the elders of Asia Minor of whom he names Polycarp of Smyrna and Papias of Hierapolis (*A.H.* 3:3:3; 5:33:3-4; *Ep. ad Flor.*). The validity of this evidence has been challenged, as much on the basis of contemporary criticism as on a presumed misunderstanding of the evidence by Irenaeus. He supposedly confused two Johns, one the apostle and the other the elder (Eusebius, *H.E.* 3:39:1-10). His conclusion concerning the common authorship of all five Johannine books and the identification of the author as John the son of Zebedee is far from secure. The reasons for recognizing the Johannine corpus are more certain and provide grounds for recognizing a Johannine school, if not a single author. Recognition that the Gospel and epistles share something of a common point of view is widely accepted, and recognition of Revelation as part of this corpus is not without its supporters (Barrett 1978; Bernard 1928: lxviii; Brown 1982: 56 n. 131).

REVELATION

A. Author

Only in Revelation does the author identify himself as John (1:1, 4,

9; 22:8). On the assumption that the same author wrote all five Johannine books, the author of all of them has been identified as John. Even if this is correct the question needs to be asked, 'Which John?'. Since the time of Irenaeus (c. 180 CE) it has commonly been accepted that John the son of Zebedee (*A.H.* 4:30:4; 5:26:1), identified as the beloved disciple, was the author of the Johannine corpus (*A.H.* 3:16:5), though there are early dissenting views (Dionysus of Alexandria) when it comes to Revelation. Certainly the John of Revelation makes no claim to be an apostle (see 1:1, 9) and when he writes of the apostles, he seems to distinguish himself from them (21:14). Once Revelation is separated from the other Johannine books, there is no internal evidence for the name of John in relation to the author of the Gospel and the epistles. The conclusion could be drawn on the assumption that all five books were by the same author, named as John in Revelation, but in Revelation there is no reason to think that this John was an apostle or was even intended to be thought as such. Hence, unlike many apocalyptic books, Revelation does not appear to be pseudonymous. Rather, the author John is identified simply as 'your brother', although he clearly held a position of some authority and is, by implication of writing a prophetic book, a prophet (1:3; 22:9).

B. Date of Composition

The most likely time for the composition of Revelation is the reign of Domitian (81–96 CE). From the time of Melito of Sardis, Domitian was regarded as the next great persecutor after Nero and a date of c. 95 CE has thus been commonly accepted for Revelation. But this assumes that Domitian was a severe persecutor of the early Christians, a view found in the early Christian sources (Eusebius, *H.E.* 3:17-20), but not supported by Roman evidence or Roman historians. Nevertheless, the Christian evidence is probably to be accepted. Thus, while there has been some support for the composition of Revelation in the reign of Nero, a date around 95 CE seems much more likely. The persecution of Christians by Domitian need not mean that he was not considered a good emperor like the rest of the Flavians.

C. Language

The Greek of the Apocalypse is unusual, and quite different from that of the Gospel. While both books have limited vocabularies, the vocabulary of Revelation is the more limited, using only 866 words of which only 441 words (just over half) are common to the Gospel. That means that more than half (478) of John's words are not used by

Revelation. Many of the differences in language can be explained in terms of the subject matter of the Gospel and the nature of the Apocalypse. But differences in the use of prepositions, adverbs, particles and syntax set the works quite widely apart. Charles (1920: I, pp. cxvii-clix) has demonstrated the Hebraic character of the grammar of the Apocalypse. The awkward use of Greek seems to indicate an author who instinctively thought in Aramaic or Hebrew. On the other hand, while the author of the Gospel betrays a Semitic mind-set, he was perfectly at home in the use of Greek, and displays a subtle and nuanced mastery of the language in the writing of his book.

D. Provenance and Situation

The author indicates that he was exiled to Patmos because of his witness to Jesus (1:9). The revelation was made to him and he was told to write down in a book what he saw (1:2-3, 11; 2:1, 8, 12, 18; 3:1, 7, 14; 22:18-19). What he writes is entitled 'The revelation (ἀποκάλυψις) of Jesus Christ which God gave to him to show to his servants...and he signified having sent by his messenger (ἀγγέλου) to his servant John' (1:1). Exile on Patmos for the witness of Jesus suggests a time of persecution. The letters to the seven churches each conclude by reference 'to the one who conquers' (τῷ νικῶντι; 1:7, 11, 17, 25; 2:5, 12, 21). Those who conquered are later portrayed (in a vision) as a great multitude out of every nation, tribe, people and tongue dressed in white robes and standing before the throne of God (in heaven). When asked by one of the elders who they are, John replies, 'You know', and then is told, 'These are those coming out of great tribulation and who have washed their robes and made them white in the blood of the Lamb' (7:13-14). These are the martyrs. Thus there is good reason to think that Revelation was written in a time of severe persecution and as a response to it. Another aspect of persecution is the attraction of avoiding it either by sheltering under the protection afforded to Jews or by submitting to the divine claims of the empire and the emperor. Indeed, both of these attractions appear to be confronted by the author of Revelation in the letters to the seven churches. Consequently the book as a whole and the letters in particular are a call to faithful witness where other options appear to be more enticing.

The letters to the seven churches of Asia Minor (Ephesus, Smyrna, Pergamum, Thyatira, Sardis, Philadelphia and Laodicea; 1:11; chs. 2–3) are said to be addressed to them by John from his exile on the isle of Patmos, close to the southwestern coast (1:9). There is no reason to think that this locale is fictitious, hence the internal evidence of Revelation locates the book in Asia Minor. Nor is there any reason to doubt that the author was John: no extravagant claims are made about his identity.

E. Influences and Sources

Underlying Revelation is the apocalyptic discourse of Jesus, especially as it appears in Matthew 24. This discourse is associated with the Jewish war, the destruction of Jerusalem and the Temple. The war began in the time of Nero, under whom there was severe persecution *in Rome* (see the evidence in Tacitus, *Annals* 15:44 and Suetonius, *Vita Neronis* 16:2), but there is no evidence that persecution of Christians was more widespread. Naturally, Jewish believers in Palestine would have been caught up in the events of the Jewish war. Thus Nero became the image of the anti-Christ, the number 666 is the equivalent of 'Nero Caesar' when the Greek characters are transliterated into Hebrew letters (*gematria*), and there was a recurring expectation of the return of Nero. Using various methods of calculation, the textual variants on the number of the beast confirm Nero's identification with it. Both the Jewish war and the expectations concerning Nero form a background to the writing of Revelation, but not the direct situation for which it was a response. It is possible that the tradition in Revelation was originally shaped around the time of the Jewish war, perhaps in Palestine, but was reworked into its present form in Asia Minor in the time of Domitian (Barrett 1978: 133-34).

Revelation, like apocalyptic literature in general, is a scribal production. That is, it is a self-conscious literary production in which the author is instructed to write the book as a means of conveying the message. As a scribal writing, it is produced with a self-conscious use of the Scriptures, especially Daniel, Ezekiel, Zechariah and Genesis. But it is a *reworking* of the sources, not a mere copy of them. It is a transformation of the images, the symbols of the tradition, which had already been taken up in the apocalyptic discourse of Jesus, especially in the form in which it appears in Matthew 24. That discourse is recycled over and again in the development of Revelation.

A convincing structure of Revelation is set out by John Sweet, and his outline is the basis of what follows (1990: 52-54).

F. Outline

Parallel verses from Matthew 24 are noted. Each of the four main divisions of Revelation is divided into seven sections: seven letters,

seven seals, seven trumpets, seven bowls. The characterization of the
seven churches, set out in chs. 2–3, provides elements from two of the
seven churches to be featured in each of the four sections, so that the
seventh church (Laodicea) is featured twice. The two churches
featured in each part are shown in brackets.

Introduction and Opening Vision (Rev. 1:1-20)
1:1-11	opening address
1:12-20	vision of Son of Man

The Seven Letters to the Seven Churches (Rev. 2:1–3:22)
(Ephesus, Sardis)
State of churches: deception, lawlessness   (Matt. 24:4-5, 9-12)

2:1-7	Ephesus—false apostles, Nicolaitans
2:8-11	Smyrna—false Jews, tribulation
2:12-17	Pergamum—witness, idolatry
2:18-29	Thyatira—Jezebel, fornication
3:1-6	Sardis—sleep, soiled garments
3:7-13	Philadelphia—false and true Jews
3:14-22	Laodicea—affluence, nakedness

The Seven Seals (Rev. 4:1–8:1)
(Smyrna, Philadelphia)
Assurance and endurance   (Matt. 24:13)

4:1–5:14	*preface to the breaking of the seven seals*	
4:1-11	vision of God the Lord of creation—rainbow and sea	
5:1-14	vision of God the redeemer—the Lamb slain in the midst of the throne	
	worthy to break the seals and read the book	
6:1-8	*first four seals: four horsemen—*	
	beginnings of birth pangs	(Matt. 24:6-8)
6:1-2	first seal—conquest	
6:3-4	second seal—war	
6:5-6	third seal—famine	
6:7-8	fourth seal—death (pestilence)	
6:9–8:1	*fifth, sixth and seventh seals*	
6:9-11	fifth seal—comfort for martyrs	(Matt. 24:13-14)
6:12-17	sixth seal—cosmic demolition	
	('wrath of the lamb')	(Matt. 24:29-30)
7:1-8	sealing of true Israel (144,000)	
7:9-17	final ingathering from all nations	(Matt. 24:31)
8:1	seventh seal—silence (birth of the new age)	

The Seven Trumpets (Three Woes) (Rev. 8:2–14:20)
(Pergamum, Laodicea)
Idolatry and witness   (Matt. 24:14-15)

8:2-5	heavenly altar of incense	
8:6-12	*first four trumpets*: destruction of nature	(Matt. 24:29)
8:13–14:5	*eagle—three woes (fifth, sixth and seventh trumpets)*	
8:13	eagle—three woes	
9:1-12	*fifth trumpet—first woe*: locust-scorpions	
9:13-21	*sixth trumpet—second woe*: lion-cavalry	
	self-destruction of idolatry; impenitence	
10:1-11	little scroll (symbol of the gospel)	
11:1-13	measuring of Temple; two witnesses	(Matt. 24:14)
	Church's witness; penitence	(Mark 13:9-13)
11:14–13:18	*seventh trumpet—third woe (Rev. 12:12)*	
11:15-19	heavenly worship	
12:1-12	defeat of the dragon in heaven leads to—	
12:13-17	flight of the woman (symbol for the Church)	(Matt. 24:16-20)
13	kingdom of beasts on earth	(Matt. 24:15)
13:1-10	sea beast: war on the saints	(Matt. 24:21-22)
13:11-18	land beast: deception	(Matt. 24:23-26)
14:1-5	144,000—first fruits	
14:6-11	eternal gospel; consequence of refusal	
14:12-20	coming of Son of Man	(Matt. 24:30-31)
	final ingathering: harvest and vintage	

The Seven Bowls (Rev. 15:1–22:5)
(Thyatira, Laodicea)
Fornication and purity: Bridegroom comes   (Matt. 24:30-31)

15:1-4	song of Moses and the Lamb	
15:5-8	heavenly Temple	
16:1-9	*first four bowls of wrath* (cf. trumpets and seals)	
16:10-11	*fifth bowl*: beast's kingdom darkened	(Matt. 24:29)
16:12-16	*sixth bowl*: Armageddon	
16:17–22:5	*seventh bowl*: beast's city destroyed; the coming of the city of God	
17	harlot destroyed by beast	
18	doom of harlot = Babylon = Rome	(Matt. 24:37-40)
19:1-10	marriage supper of the Lamb	(Matt. 25:1-13)
19:11-16	coming of Son of Man, as Word of God	(Matt. 24:30)
19:17-21	destruction of beasts	
20:1-6	binding of Satan, rule of saints	
	(millennium = thousand years)	
20:7-10	release and final destruction of Satan	
20:11-15	last judgment	

21:1-8	new creation expounded as:
21:9-21	adornment of bride—holy city
21:22–	
22:5	ingathering of the nations
	tree of life–paradise restored

Final Attestation and Warning (22:6-21)

This outline suggests four series of sevens set between a prologue (1:1-20) and an epilogue (22:6-21). Careful attention to this outline helps to make clear that Revelation does not provide a detailed prediction of the future. Repetition of the pattern of seven letters to seven churches, seven seals, seven trumpets, and seven bowls leads the reader fairly naturally to the conclusion that we are dealing with a recurrent theme of judgment and renewal or redemption. Recognition of the symbolism of numbers and strange beasts and living creatures is of a part with the awareness of this symbolism as a reworking of certain strands of Jewish tradition (Court 1979; Caird 1966). Stories about the end, like those of the beginning, were told because of their relevance for the present. Thus, although there is a recurring assertion about the imminence of the end (1:1, 3, 19; 22:6, 10, 20), this is not inconsistent with a recognition of an element of inaugurated eschatology. But this inaugurated eschatology is expressed in a way appropriate to the chosen medium of an apocalypse; thus the present reality is affirmed through the medium of the heavenly vision.

G. Apocalyptic Ideology

Revelation is immediately recognizable as an apocalyptic book by its opening words. By this means, writers in the ancient world gave *de facto* titles to their works, supplying the words by which the 'book' would be known. But the term ἀποκάλυψις had not yet become a technical term. It was through John's coining of it that it became the identifier of the apocalyptic genre. Consequently, there are other recognizable features of Revelation that draw attention to its similarity to other books. Yet writers of such books did not set out to conform to set criteria or to produce books belonging to a pure genre. Revelation is presented in terms of letters addressed to the seven churches of Asia, which are self-consciously described as part of a book John was commanded to write, a book of *prophecy* from which nothing was to be taken away and nothing was to be added (1:11; 22:7, 9-10, 18-19). The connection between prophecy (1:3; 22:7, 10, 18) and apocalyptic is important. Apocalypse should be seen as the continuation of prophecy in a new form. Revelation defines 'the spirit of prophecy' as 'the witness to Jesus'. There is a discernible new depth to the term μαρτυρία so that the 'witness' (μάρτυς) is also perceived as a 'martyr' (11:1-14). Through his two witnesses, God addresses his prophetic word to the world, and Revelation embodies that prophetic word. It may be that Peter and Paul, who are believed to have given a good witness in Rome in the reign of Nero, are portrayed representatively of the witness of the Church.

While the message of the prophets was written down, it was ideally and generally oral in the first place. Apocalypse was essentially a written message. John was instructed to write down what he saw (1:11, 19; [cf. 2:1, 8, 12, 18; 3:1, 7, 14] 14:13; 19:9; 21:5). Unlike the direct prophetic proclamation of 'Thus says the Lord', apocalypses take the form of the *record* of visions and dreams. This is mainly a difference in the mode of communication. Further, the visions and dreams frequently needed to be interpreted, and this task was performed by heavenly messengers (ἄγγελοι) or angels (1:1; 7:13-17; 19:9-10; 22:6-11). The visions and dreams of the heavenly realm accentuate the *sense* of the absence of God from the world. This is reinforced by the role of intermediaries who interpret the visions. The *sense* of the absence of God is associated with the experience of evil, and the world dominated by the powers of evil. Apocalypse provided a means of acknowledging evil without giving up faith in God who reigns over all without compromising his goodness.

In a world where the powers of the empire were turned against the believers and those powers were seductively attractive, there was a *sense* of the absence of God. 'Eternal Rome' appeared to be divine, and the emperor was the personal embodiment of it. The problem was not simply one of severe persecution where believers were put to death for witness to the name of Jesus. Because Judaism was legal, a permitted religion in the empire, there was also an attraction for believers to be sheltered from persecution under the protective wing of Judaism. It is probable that the synagogue was a reluctant shelter for those who believed in Jesus, because the Jews were themselves seeking to redefine their own boundaries. There was also the seduction to the worship of the divine powers of the empire. But for John, the empire was the embodiment of evil. Thus the believers experienced the world as dominated by evil and only a vision of the heavenly realities could restore balance to the sense of reality and counteract the sinister attraction of the anti-Christ. The Apocalypse is thus a direct response to the problem of theodicy.

H. Compositional Techniques: Clues to Interpreting the Visions

1. The Opening Greeting from God (1:4, 8). The opening vision of ch. 1 is the key to much that follows. It describes the book as 'the revelation of Jesus Christ which God gave to him to show to his servants'. We are probably right in taking 'of Jesus Christ' as both an objective and a subjective genitive. Because the revelation was given to him by God, it is his. Thus, even in the work of revelation, which originates with God, God is distanced from those who receive the revelation. Indeed, the process of distancing is taken further because Jesus Christ sent his messenger (ἀγγέλου) to signify the revelation to John. But the revelation also has Jesus Christ as its subject. The things which must happen soon, because the time is near, concern the coming Son of Man (1:7, 13).

The sense, introduced in the opening verses, that Jesus is identified with God and yet God is distanced from him, continues in the initial address to the seven churches (1:4-8). The greeting addressed to the seven churches has God as its source, who is designated 'the one who is and who was and who is coming' (1:4, 8). It is also 'from the seven Spirits before his throne and from Jesus Christ, the faithful witness, the firstborn of the dead and the ruler of the kings of the earth'. The formula of God, Spirits, Jesus Christ suggests that Spirits in the formula 'from the seven Spirits' should be given a capital indicating the divine side of reality. But this is an unconventional form of trinitarian formula. The emphasis on seven is consistent with the use of numbers in Revelation, stressing the perfection, in spite of appearances, of God's relationship with his creation through the seven Spirits. Further, in spite of appearances, Jesus Christ, the firstborn from the dead, is the ruler of the kings of the earth.

The greeting has its source in God, who is described in terms which introduce the vision of God in Revelation 4. He is the one who is, who was and is coming; and the seven Spirits are before his throne. This description is further elaborated in 1:8, where God announces 'I am the Alpha and Omega, the one who is and who was and is coming, the Almighty (παντοκράτωρ)'. This self-revelation should be compared with 1:17 where Christ is the subject, 21:6 where God is again subject, and 22:13 where Christ is again subject. In the first instance, the speaker is God, and this leads into the vision of the throne of God.

2. The Vision of the Throne of God (4:1-11). Revelation 4 emphasizes that a heavenly vision is in view by stating that a door is opened in heaven and a voice calls John to 'Come up here and I will show you what must be after these things'. John travels in the spirit to heaven and what he sees is reminiscent of the visions of Dan. 7:9-14, Ezek. 1:4-28, especially at this point 1:26-27, and Isa. 6:1-13. John draws on a rich tradition concerning the transcendent almighty power of God on his throne, a tradition that maintains the mystery of God even in the context of the revealing vision. This vision provides an alternative to the perception of the world as it seems to be. There is an *epistemic* distance between God and the world. To the senses, God appears to be absent. The world appears to be out of control, at least beyond the control of God and in the control of the powers of evil. The vision opens up a view of another reality. In spite of appearances in the world, God is on his throne. The heavenly reality is rich in the worship of God. Around the throne are the twenty-four elders, the seven Spirits of God, the sea of glass-like crystal, and the four living creatures who ceaselessly cry out in praise to God, 'Holy, holy, holy Lord God almighty, who was and who is and who is coming'. All focus of attention is on the one on the throne, and the twenty-four elders cast their crowns before him saying, 'You are worthy, our Lord and God, to receive glory and honour and power, because you created all things and by your will they were and were created'. The world as now experienced by John and his readers seems incompatible with the God of creation. Yet the vision of heaven is of God on the throne surrounded by heavenly worshippers confessing him as creator. This is, however, something of a mystery.

3. The Opening Greeting from Jesus Christ (1:5, 6). Jesus Christ is first introduced as the faithful witness, the firstborn of the dead and the ruler of the kings of the earth. Reference to the faithful witness draws attention to the martyr status of Jesus, which is reinforced by reference to him as the firstborn of the dead. Thus the call to faithful witness is based on the example of the one who was a faithful witness to death and had been raised to life. As the firstborn of the dead, he is the ruler of the kings of the earth.

Thus far, the role of Jesus is understood in relation to the world. Now the ascription, 'To the one who loves us and loosed us from our sins by his blood, and made us kings and priests to his God and father, to him be glory and might for ever and ever, amen', interprets his role directly in relation to those who believe in him. One such believer is the spokesman who refers to Jesus as the one who *loves* us. The present tense is noticeable, as is the writer's inclusive language, 'us'. The understanding of the present situation is built on the act in the past when Jesus 'loosed us from our sins by his blood', that is, by his death. Because of what he is and has done, glory and might are his for ever and ever. This prepares the way for the continuing vision of God in ch. 5.

4. The Vision of the Lamb in the Midst of the Throne (5:1-14). The vision of the throne of God comes to focus on the book which no one could be found who was worthy to open and read, until one of the elders announced that the lion of the tribe of Judah had conquered, and the root of David would open the book. The figure is then elaborated in terms of the vision, in the midst of the throne, in the midst of the elders, a lamb standing as having been slaughtered. Again the vision leads to the worship of heaven in which the lamb is praised as worthy to take the book and open the seals because 'you were slaughtered and you redeemed [saints] to God by your blood from every tribe and tongue and people and nation and made them kings and priests to our God and they shall reign upon earth'. The whole company of heaven then takes up the praise: 'Worthy is the lamb that was slain to receive power and riches and wisdom and strength and honour and glory and blessing'. Then the whole creation joins in, 'To him who sits upon the throne and to the lamb be blessing and honour and glory and might for ever and ever'. At this, the four living creatures say, 'Amen', and the elders fall down and worship.

As the faithful witness and as the firstborn from the dead, Jesus was ruler of the kings of the earth; now as the lamb who was slain he is worthy to take the book and open the seals. As the one who loves us and loosed us from our sins by his blood, he has redeemed to God saints from every tribe. Consequently, it seems that at the heart of the mystery of the world dominated by evil is the lamb who was slain. Only from this perspective could the vision of heaven with God on his throne remain credible. Thus chs. 4–5, building on the vision of ch. 1, provide the context in which the cycles of judgment must be understood.

With chs. 4–5, the reader is introduced to the worship of heaven which will be encountered again and again throughout the book. It is uncertain whether John has taken over the language of praise and worship from his communities, or whether the inspired language that he has used has become the language of worship for succeeding generations of Christians.

5. The Inaugural Vision and the Letters to the Seven Churches (1:7, 9–3:22). The latter part of the inaugural vision introduces the letters to the seven churches. In 1:7, the coming of one like a Son of Man is alluded to by reference to his coming with clouds (Dan. 7:13; Matt. 24:30; Mark 13:26; Luke 21:27; 1 Thess. 4:17). This has been combined with reference (drawn from Zech. 12:10, 12, 14; see Matt. 24:30; John 19:34, 37) to what is interpreted as the awareness of all people on earth to the coming in judgment of the one they had 'pierced', which John must take as an equivalent of 'slain'. It is his coming in judgment that produces mourning. Jesus as redeemer, who is a comforting figure to those who have suffered for his sake, is also, consequently, a threatening figure.

The inaugural vision then reveals *one like a Son of Man* moving in the midst of seven golden candle sticks. The description is clearly a reference to the figure of Dan. 7:13. But in the description of his hair as white as wool, John has described him in terms of the one who sits on the throne in Dan. 7:9. Other features are drawn from the throne chariot vision of God in Ezek. 1:24 and other parts of Ezekiel. That we are meant to understand him as a fearsome figure is confirmed by the response of John who, when he sees him, falls at his feet as one dead (1:17).

Aspects of the vision are explained: the seven golden candlesticks are the seven churches; the seven stars are the seven messengers (ἄγγελοι) of the seven churches, and are probably to be understood as the 'ministers' of the churches. In each of the letters to the seven churches that follow in chs. 2 and 3, some aspect of the inaugural vision of Jesus is featured. In these letters, there is an element of assurance and an element of threat; the balance varies from letter to letter. Overall, the situation of Christians in Asia is covered, and there is preparation for the following visions with their threats and promises.

THE FOURTH GOSPEL

A. *Title and Author*

The title, 'The Fourth Gospel', is not traditional. The traditional title is 'According to John' or 'Gospel according to John'. The variant titles show that they were not original, but there is no evidence that the Gospel was attributed to any other author and the titles are no later than the early second century. Irenaeus, writing around 180 CE, asserts the authenticity of the title identifying the author as John the son of Zebedee, called the beloved disciple in the Gospel (*A.H.* 2:22:5; 3:1:1). But his view is questionable, not only because his testimony is quite late, but the *basis* for his view (especially the testimony of Papias now in Eusebius, *H.E.* 3:39:1-10) remains ambiguous, and he asserts more than his own understanding of the Papias testimony justifies. *If* Papias claims the *apostle* John wrote the Gospel, Irenaeus asserts he also wrote the three epistles and Revelation. It now seems more likely that these books were the product of a 'school' which we may, on the basis of the naming of the author of Revelation, call 'the Johannine school'. But if the Gospel emanates from the Johannine school, that is no reason to think that the author of the Gospel was John or that the John in question was the apostle.

The title, 'The Fourth Gospel', may well have reflected the view that John was the fourth Gospel to have been written ('Last of all John...', Irenaeus, *A.H.* 3:1:1). However, it is no longer possible to hold this view with any probability. Indeed, there is no reason to think that John is any later than Matthew. Many of the factors used in the dating of John are equally relevant to the dating of Matthew. Yet John remains the fourth Gospel in canonical order. In the absence of strong evidence of the identity of the author, the title 'The Fourth Gospel' remains the most useful.

The Fourth Gospel is strictly anonymous. Recognition that John 21:24 identifies the beloved disciple as author does nothing to lift the veil of anonymity, because there are no clear clues to his identity. The beloved disciple, literally 'the disciple whom Jesus loved', appears for the first time at the last supper shared by Jesus with his disciples. There he appears in a privileged position in a contrast with Peter (13:23-24), a contrast which probably continues in the account of Jesus before the high priest (18:15), certainly in the narrative of the empty tomb (20:1-10) and in the epilogue (21:7, 20-24). He was also present at the crucifixion (19:26-27, 35). It may be that he is to be identified with one of the two disciples of John 1:35ff., one of whom is identified as Andrew, the brother of Simon Peter. The other remains anonymous—to be revealed in due course as the beloved disciple? But who is the beloved disciple? While a case can be made for identifying him with John the son of Zebedee, there is no compelling reason for identifying him with any one of 'the Twelve'. Thus there are advocates for identifying him with Lazarus (Mark Stibbe), John Mark (Pierson Parker), Paul (B.W. Bacon and Michael Goulder), Thomas (James Charlesworth), Matthias (Eric L. Titus), the rich young ruler (H.B. Swete), Benjamin (Paul Minear), the elder of 2 and 3 John (H. Thyen), while others suggest that he is an *ideal* rather than an actual disciple. Thus he is said to represent the Johannine Christians (Alv Kragerud) or Gentile Christianity, while the mother of Jesus, with whom he is associated at the crucifixion, represents Jewish Christianity (Rudolf Bultmann).

It is difficult to dismiss the case for recognizing that the beloved disciple is an ideal figure, though not straightforwardly representative of any particular ethnic group. He is, rather, representative of Johannine Christianity, which appears to have had a changing ethnic make-up. This need not mean that he is not also an historical figure or the characterization of an historical figure. 21:24 identifies the beloved disciple as the author of the Gospel. It is unlikely that any author would describe himself in these terms. The portrayal of the beloved disciple can be seen as an attempt to give ideal status to the Gospel by attributing authorship to him. There are broadly two ways in which this is thought to be done. One simply has the actual author 'create' the figure of the beloved disciple and attribute the Gospel to him. The other takes account of the probability that ch. 21 is an epilogue to the Gospel, added by hands other than those that wrote chs. 1–20. The figure of the beloved disciple was found in chs. 1–20, and those who added ch. 21 *mistakenly* attributed the Gospel to him. But if those who added ch. 21 did not know the identity of such a notable member as the one who wrote the Gospel, it would strain our understanding of the Johannine school.

A more likely alternative is that those who added ch. 21 (members of the Johannine school) correctly identified the beloved disciple as the author of the Gospel. They were responsible for introducing this characterization of the author into the body of the Gospel where the author had originally referred to himself in a way that preserved his anonymity such as in 1:35ff. and 18:15. Yet, given that he was well known at the time, knowing readers needed no prompting to identify his role in the Gospel story where he was identified simply as 'the other disciple'. Probably two developments changed this situation. First, the beloved disciple died and, secondly, it became necessary for the Johannine community to relate to wider groups of Christian communities where the beloved disciple was not well known. The epilogue set out to make clear the outstanding (ideal) and distinctive role played by the author of the Gospel, and this was caught in the title which others had given to him in recognition of his special relation to Jesus. When using this title, he is first described as one of Jesus' disciples (13:23-24) and then, at his crucifixion, Jesus sets him in a special relationship with his mother as they are portrayed as ideal disciples. There is a bridging passage in 20:2 where he is called 'the other disciple' and the one whom Jesus loved, linking these two descriptions. The Johannine school was responsible for the introduction of this 'title' and the identification of the beloved disciple as author. Given that the Johannine school professes intimate knowledge of the author, we should suppose that the identification is correct. Yet the author of the Fourth Gospel remains anonymous to us, because the identity of the beloved disciple remains a secret.

This reading best takes account of the fact that those responsible for 21:24 add their stamp of approval to the truth of what the beloved disciple has written, 'and we know that his witness is true'. Given the role and status of the beloved disciple, we would not expect that his witness would need this attestation. Certainly those who corroborate his witness have provided no credentials to add any weight to his word. Their testimony is meaningful only in a context where they are known and the beloved disciple is no longer present—no longer alive—which seems to be the point of 21:20-23. Against this view, some think, is the use of the present participle in 21:24, 'This is the disciple *who bears witness* concerning these things and has written these things'. But the disciple need not still be alive because he continues to bear witness through what he has written.

If we accept that the hands that added ch. 21 were also responsible for introducing references to the beloved disciple into chs. 1–20, we have opened the way for recognizing other explanatory comments as additions made at the same time to prepare the Gospel for a wider and not necessarily Jewish audience. The explanations of Jewish terms and customs were probably introduced when the Gospel was prepared for this expanded audience and sent out with ch. 21 as an integral part. While it is not impossible that extensive changes were made to chs. 1–20 at the time, it now seems impossible to isolate them in detail. It is perhaps more likely that the integrity of the Gospel was respected, and only necessary changes were made for the adaptation of the Gospel to a broader group. The wider audience also stands at some little temporal distance from the work of the beloved disciple. This is likely because it was necessary to introduce him and his role to the wider group of readers now envisaged in 21:24.

B. *Provenance and Date*

Given that we have identified a two-stage production of the Gospel, it may be necessary to deal with the question of provenance also in two (or more) stages. Some scholars have long drawn attention to aspects of the Gospel which make best sense in a pre-70 CE Palestinian setting. Such features include the use of transliterated Hebrew terms, and the evidence of some aspects of topography now given support by archaeology such as the pool described in John 5 and the 'pavement' of 19:13. Perhaps more important are the close associations between the Gospel and some aspects of the Qumran texts. John's Gospel shares with some of the Qumran writings the attraction to the central symbolism found in the antithesis of light and darkness. While there are other antitheses, such as truth and falsehood, light and darkness provides the central symbol set for the Gospel and the sect of Qumran. Each sees themselves as belonging to the light while all others belong to the darkness. Thus, there is strong evidence for understanding the influences shaping the language and thought of the Gospel in the context of a form of Judaism not unlike that of the community of Qumran. Of course, in this context, Judaism means pre-70 CE Judaean Judaism.

But it is unlikely that the Gospel reached even its *earliest* written form in that period and place. The Gospel was written in Greek and reflects a post-70 CE point of view, in that there is a tendency to dissolve the differences of pre-70 CE Judaism into the all-embracing category, 'the Jews'. The Pharisees sometimes appear as an alternative description for 'the Jews', and this seems to reflect the fact that the Pharisees survived the catastrophe of the Jewish war and emerged as the leaders responsible for shaping what was to become rabbinic Judaism. This concentration on them reflects the reality of a later time. The only other Jewish groups mentioned are the chief priests or high priest and rulers. Notably absent are the Sadducees, who were the dominant political and priestly group in the time of Jesus.

From John 5 onwards, the Gospel depicts Jesus and his followers in conflict with the Jewish leaders. From John 5:16-18 Jesus is persecuted, and there are attempts to kill him because of his failure to keep the sabbath, and because it is understood that he claimed to be equal with God. In John 9:22, we are told that the Jews had decided to 'excommunicate from the synagogue' (ἀποσυνάγωγος γένηται) anyone who confessed Christ. This is extraordinary for a number of reasons. That Jesus is *the Christ* had not to this point been a particularly prominent or contentious issue in the Gospel. In terms of the story of Jesus, this decision seems to come from nowhere. It is notable too that the decision is directed not against Jesus but against his followers, and in the long run, the man healed of blindness by Jesus was cast out of the synagogue (9:34). In the process, he has become the model of true discipleship in the face of persecution. Such persecution emerges as the formidable context shaping the Gospel. Even many of the rulers who believed in Jesus feared the Pharisees and did not confess Jesus as the Christ lest they should become excommunicated from the synagogue (12:42). While this is expressed in terms of present realities, in the farewell discourses Jesus predicts what is coming upon those who believe in and follow him (16:2). There he says 'They *will* make you excommunicated from the synagogue' (ἀποσυναγώγους ποιήσουσιν ὑμᾶς). Thus, what is described as happening to the disciple of Jesus in the narrative of the Gospel is spoken of in terms of warnings of the future in the farewell discourses. Here there is also the warning that those who kill his disciples will think of that as an act of serving God. While in the narrative of the Gospel none of Jesus' disciples is put to death, Jesus himself is put to death, and, from 5:17 onwards, there are continuing plots to arrest or execute/assassinate him. There is also a plot not only to kill Jesus but also to kill Lazarus (12:9-11). That Jesus warns his disciples in the farewell discourses of what the narrative already describes as happening to the disciple suggests that the narrative is a conflation of the story of Jesus with the story of the Johannine community, so that Jesus' own conflict has been interpreted in relation to the conflict experienced later by the community. Naturally, the terms of the conflict have changed. In the later period, focus is on the confession of Jesus as the Christ.

While we cannot locate precisely where and when the crisis of the Johannine community took place, J.L. Martyn's thesis (1979) concerning the way the conflict of the community has been caught up in the narrative of the conflict of Jesus and his disciples with the Jewish authorities is persuasive. The conflict is often described in terms more appropriate to the conflict of the community. What seems clear is that exclusion from the synagogue for the confession that Jesus is the Christ did not happen during his ministry and almost certainly belongs to the period subsequent to the Jewish war when

Judaism was drawing new lines of self-definition. Without Jerusalem and the Temple, there was less room for flexibility and diversity. In this period, Jewish believers in Jesus as the Messiah were ostracized. While no precise date can be put on this conflict, which is not at all concerned with the terms of the admission of Gentiles as Paul was, a time closer to the end of the first century than to the Jewish war is likely. Threats against Paul were not expressed in terms of excommunication.

Much of the Gospel has been shaped to deal with the trauma of exclusion from the synagogue, and to prepare believers for the crises it would cause. Part of this is concerned with timid or secret believers who sought to avoid confessing Jesus and to remain within the synagogue. For them, the Gospel is a call to a courageous confession. But the Gospel looks beyond the breach with the synagogue. Being written in Greek is not only an indication that the community was somewhere beyond Palestine, perhaps Asia Minor; it is also a signal of the wider readership brought about by the community finding itself cut loose from its Jewish roots. Thus, the Gospel has already begun to make some adjustment to this new environment by attempting to explain a Gospel with thoroughly Jewish roots in terms that would be meaningful for Hellenistic readers. While there is no way to be certain of the date, somewhere close to the end of the first century is probable, and an Asia Minor location in the region of Ephesus is certainly no less probable than any other situation.

C. Purposes

Given that the Gospel was shaped over a lengthy period of time, probably coming to its canonical form only around 85–90 CE, it is likely that we should talk of purposes rather than a single purpose. The earliest purpose was to persuade Jews that Jesus was the Messiah, and it did this using the narratives of the signs of Jesus. Then, in the debate with the synagogue, which opposed Moses to Jesus, the Gospel sought to show that eternal life came through Jesus, not through Moses. Nevertheless, there were those who believed in Jesus, yet, by keeping their faith secret, they remained within the synagogue. The Gospel was then designed to persuade them to make a public confession of faith and to join the Johannine community 'in exile'. Essential to Johannine theology is a view of God who loves the world and wills that his love should be known by the world and that the world should believe (3:16; 17:20-26, especially 21 and 23).

Consequently, the Gospel provides a basis for a universal mission which, in principle, was a law-free mission.

D. Structure

The overall structure of the Gospel is fairly clear and is generally recognized. An outline can be set out as follows:

1. Prologue (1:1-18)
2. Public Ministry of Jesus (1:19–12:50)
   a. the quest for the Messiah (1:19–4:54)
   b. the rejection of the Messiah (5:1–12:50)
3. Farewell Discourses: The Farewell of the Messiah (13:1–17:26)
   a. setting (13:1-30)
   b. first discourse (13:31–14:31)
   c. second discourse (15:1–16:4a)
   d. third discourse (16:4b-33)
   e. farewell prayer (17:1-26)
4. Passion and Resurrection Narratives (18:1–20:29)
   a. betrayal, arrest, trial and condemnation of Jesus (18:1–19:16a)
   b. crucifixion, death and burial of Jesus (19:16b-42)
   c. resurrection appearances of Jesus and commissioning of disciples (20:1-29)
5. Concluding Statement of the Purpose of the Book (20:30-31)
6. Epilogue (21:1-25)
   a. the appearance of Jesus to seven disciples on the Sea of Tiberius (21:1-14)
   b. Jesus and Peter: the reinstatement of Peter (21:15-19)
   c. Jesus and Peter: the role of the beloved disciple (21:20-23)
   d. attestation of authorship: the truth of the witness (21:24)
   e. relativizing the book in relation to the works of Jesus (21:25)

E. Language and Worldview

The Fourth Gospel is written in simple but correct Hellenistic Greek, using a limited and repetitive vocabulary so that the language is characteristic of the Gospel. The Gospel uses only 919 words, of which 84 are exclusive to the Gospel and epistles in the New Testament and, of these, 74 are used in the Gospel alone (Bernard 1928: I, p. lxv). Many of these terms are used only once and in specific contexts so that they are not as important as Johannine markers as might be expected. Instead, words used elsewhere as well take on Johannine significance by their frequency and distinctiveness of use. John uses the verbs 'to believe' (98 times), 'to know' (γινώσκω 56 times; οἶδα 85 times), 'to love' (ἀγαπάω 37 times;

φιλέω 13 times and the noun 'love' 7 times), 'to bear witness' (33 times) and the noun 'witness' (14 times).

The Gospel is especially marked by certain characteristic sets of symbols, most notably the antithesis of light and darkness. This language unveils the worldview within which the Gospel story takes place. Underlying the Johannine dualism is the perception that, in spite of the creation of all things by God through his *logos,* the world is dominated by the powers of evil (12:31; 14:30; 16:11). This apocalyptic understanding is expressed in terms of Johannine dualism, which has three important aspects:

1. the spatial antithesis between above and below;
2. the temporal tension between this age and the age to come; and
3. the ethical conflict between good and evil, God and the devil, the children of God (of light) and children of the devil (the darkness).

The Fourth Gospel stands with those (apocalyptic) works that see a conflict between above and below, this age and the age to come; that see this world/age dominated by the forces of evil which would be overcome in the coming age. The coming of Jesus is portrayed as the divine approach to resolve the dualism. The coming of Jesus is marked by references to the coming hour (7:30; 8:20), which arrives at the end of his ministry in the triumphant 'Now...!' of 12:31-33. The complexity of the struggle between the light and darkness is clear from the beginning (1:5; 3:19-21), where the distinctive Johannine theme of the triumph of the revelation is stamped on traditional apocalyptic themes. John has modified the apocalyptic vision in that Jesus, as the emissary from above, has entered this present world or age as the revelation of the age to come. But he is more than this; he is already, in his coming and going, the decisive intervention of God in this world. This does not, however, exhaust or completely fulfil the purpose of God for this world. Because of this, John's eschatological views are complex, and the perspective of future fulfilment remains important (see Painter 1993a).

In the context of this worldview, the 'works' of Jesus are portrayed as 'signs' that reveal the presence of the light in the world of darkness. The light reveals the goal of the creation in the midst of the confusion that is caused by the power of darkness. Jesus also speaks in a distinctive way, revealing himself in solemn 'I am' sayings that echo the sayings of divine Wisdom or of *Yahweh* himself. Consequently, his words are the decisive clue revealing the meaning and purpose of his signs. His words are not empty or meaningless, but full of divine power; his actions are not merely demonstrations of divine power but are also full of meaning (Bultmann 1971: 114, 452, 696).

F. Tradition and Sources

There are broadly three, perhaps four, hypotheses concerning the composition of the Gospel. These can be further reduced to two types when looked at in terms of the question of whether the distinctive character of the Gospel comes from the evangelist's interpretation or from sources that are quite different from the Synoptics. While Bultmann's overall source theory now has few supporters, variations based on his *semeia* or signs source continue to be supported as a basis for understanding the narrative of the Gospel. The most important proponent of this hypothesis is Robert Fortna, whose major works on this subject span 1970 to 1988. Fortna advocates the view that a Signs Gospel, which already included the passion narrative, was the basis of the evangelist's composition. Fortna expresses no views concerning the origin and development of the discourse material. Given the distinctive character and importance of the Johannine discourses, it must be said that failure to deal with this problem leaves the mystery of the Gospel largely unresolved. Fortna thinks that the narrative material is primary in the Gospel. A natural progression from this point is to assert that the evangelist himself was responsible for the distinctive character of the discourses. Fortna would then need to have argued that the evangelist worked differently (creatively) in the discourses while he remained faithful to his source when working with the narrative.

A second distinctive source theory attributes the Gospel, or its major source, to an eyewitness of the ministry of Jesus. The author himself is thought to be responsible for the transmission of a distinctive source, and stress falls on a distinctive tradition rather than the creative and interpretative role of the evangelist. Few authors today make this view basic to their understanding of the Gospel.

Two types of theory make the distinctive nature of the Gospel the work of the evangelist. First, there are those who think that John was dependent on the Synoptics. A long and important tradition of interpretation has adopted this position, which has the support of such important scholars as C.K. Barrett and F. Neirynck. Indeed, Neirynck has carried the Leuven school with him in a long advocacy of John's dependence on the Synoptics. The argument for dependence is based on two kinds of evidence: evidence from agreement in order and detailed evidence of agreement in wording. The evidence of the agreement in order is all the more impressive in the light of overall radical differences in order. Barrett (1978: 43) sets out an impressive, though incomplete, list of the evidence.

	Mark	John
a. the work and witness of the Baptist	1:4-8	1:19-36
b. departure to Galilee	1:14-15	4:3
c. feeding of the multitude	6:34-44	6:1-13
d. walking on the Lake	6:45-52	6:16-21
e. Peter's confession	8:29	6:68-69
f. departure to Jerusalem	9:30-31	7:10-14
	10:1, 32, 46	
g. the entry (transposed in John)	11:1-10	12:12-15
and the anointing	14:3-9	12:1-8
h. the last supper, with predictions of		
betrayal and denial	14:17-26	13:1–17:26
i. the arrest	14:43-52	18:1-11
j. the passion and resurrection	14:53–16.8	18:12–20:29

Barrett correctly notes that it is unlikely that Mark and John would both independently follow the sequence of the feeding miracle with the narrative of the walking on the lake. But this need not mean that John used Mark as the most important source for his Gospel, because it is likely that the sequence was already in the source used by Mark. This hypothesis helps to explain why Mark includes a second feeding miracle which is not tied to a following narrative of Jesus walking on the lake. The hypothesis of John's dependence on Mark makes full use of agreements between Mark and John, but it does not do justice to the differences in order, detailed content and language. For example, the so called 'cleansing of the Temple' occurs at the beginning of Jesus' ministry in John and at the end in Mark. The details of both the feeding miracle and the sea crossing are quite different in Mark and John. While it is true that *if we knew* that John had used Mark as his source we could find ways of explaining what John had done, this is not the only or the most persuasive hypothesis.

Following the lead of P. Gardner-Smith, C.H. Dodd (1963) argued that John made use of Synoptic-like tradition that was nevertheless independent of the Synoptic Gospels. His hypothesis does justice not only to the similarities to, but also to the differences from the Synoptics. It does not provide a basis for outlining in detail the full extent of the sources used by John. Rather, this approach brings to light Synoptic-like tradition as it surfaces from time to time. Contact with the Synoptics is one important criterion for recognition of the evangelist's use of tradition. On this basis, the evangelist is perceived to be a profound and radical theological interpreter of the Gospel tradition.

G. Exegetical Issues

The Gospel contains a variety of material. Recognition of this variety is important for the interpretation of the Gospels. The genre of stories and sayings functions specifically, providing clues for the interpretation of the Gospel as a whole.

1. The Prologue (1:1-18). The Prologue is an unusual beginning, even for a Gospel, as can be seen from a comparison with the other Gospels. While John is different from them in many ways, the Prologue is not simply different in language, order or extent; it is altogether different from anything in the other Gospels. This should alert the reader to the special demands placed on the interpreter. Two related questions emerge as a guide to the reader: (1) To what genre does the Prologue belong? (2) What functions does the Prologue perform within the Gospel as a whole?

First, the opening words of the Prologue set up a resonance with the opening words of Genesis. Genesis provides the 'pre-understanding' that the implied reader brings to the text. But the skilful (expert) reader also needs to be ready for surprises in the text. At the beginning, recognition of the resonance with Genesis signals that what follows is language about God, language in dialogue with the foundational Jewish language about God. That is, the story of Jesus that follows is to be understood as the evangelist's way of talking about God. Surprises in the text that follows, however, make some modifications to Jewish language about God. Secondly, like Genesis 1, the Prologue provides a worldview, a basis for understanding the world in which the following story takes place. The evangelist uncompromisingly affirms that God is the creator of all things through his Word or *logos*. In spite of this, the world and human history are dominated by the darkness. The Prologue thus sets the Gospel in a context that confronts the problem of evil, and should be understood as a contribution to theodicy. The purpose of God cannot be 'read' from the world as it is, dominated by the darkness. In this world, the incarnation of the *logos* in Jesus of Nazareth is the key to the understanding of the *purpose* of God in the world. In the body of the Gospel, the *signs* provide the clearest indication of that purpose. The creation story of the Prologue does not provide a picture of an ideal world, but rather an understanding that enables the believer to perceive the purpose of God in a world presently dominated by darkness.

The Prologue is not an unbiased description of the world. It is rather a *confession* of faith, a vision of the world from the perspective of faith arising from the manifestation of glory in the *logos* made flesh (1:14-18). Much of the Prologue appears to have been derived from an early Christian *hymn* in praise of Jesus as creator and revealer of God, a hymn that might have been developed on the basis of a Jewish hymn in praise of Wisdom (Law). In the Christian version, the revelation in Jesus is set over against the Law given through Moses. While there is conflict between Jesus and Moses, the resonance set up by the opening of the Prologue with Genesis 1 asserts a continuity between Jesus and God revealed in creation. Thus, already in the Prologue, the reader is alerted to the way the Law of Moses has been set against Jesus.

Three important clues are given to the reader, drawing attention to important aspects that should guide any significant reading of the Prologue. Resonance with the Genesis 1 creation story provides the first important clue. Secondly, in Genesis, God's creative acts are initiated by his speech, 'And God said...' This is either the basis or an expression of the tradition of the creative Word of God (Ps. 33:6), and is closely related to the tradition of Wisdom (Wis. 9:1-2, 10; 18:15; Sir. 24:1-3), where Wisdom and Word are understood as synonyms for the Law. It has long been recognized that what is said of the Word in the Prologue has been drawn from Jewish tradition about Wisdom (Harris 1917; Dodd 1953: 274-75; Painter 1993b: 145-52). Thirdly, the Prologue bears the marks of having been developed out of 'a hymn in praise of Christ as (a) God', such as was known to Pliny, Roman Governor of Bithynia in the early second century CE. Thus, the clues point to a confrontation between Jesus and the Jewish Law, a conflict that becomes explicit by the conclusion of the Prologue and is worked out in some detail in the body of the Gospel.

2. The Quest for the Messiah: Act One (1:19-51). The first four chapters focus on the theme of the quest for the Messiah, which is introduced by the first act (1:19-51) of the public ministry of Jesus. A sequence of scenes makes up the first act. The first scene shows an embassy from the Jews of Jerusalem in search of the Messiah. Because of John the Baptist's activity, they inquire of him if perchance he is the Messiah. Rather, he asserts, his baptizing mission was commissioned to reveal the Messiah to Israel (1:19-28). In due course (two days and two scenes later; 1:35-42), he reveals Jesus to two of his own disciples, who are in quest of the Messiah. In response to their initiative, Jesus inquires, 'What are you seeking?'. This language, which expresses quest, recurs in the Gospel. In this chapter, there is the important sequence of 'following', 'seeking' and 'finding'. The importance of this theme of 'seeking' is brought out by a number of observations. The first words spoken by Jesus (the first words of the incarnate Word) in this Gospel are, 'What are you seeking?'. Jesus himself draws attention to the initiative of the first disciples who attach themselves to him; thus the 'seeking' can hardly be a triviality. That this is a distinctively Johannine feature becomes apparent by a comparison with the other Gospels, where Jesus invariably takes the initiative, calling his disciple with his authoritative, 'Follow me'. In John, it is the first disciples who seek out Jesus and the nature and success of their quest is affirmed in a refrain, 'We have found the Messiah' (1:41), 'We have found the one of whom Moses wrote in the Law and the prophets' (1:45). They, like the embassy and John himself, were in quest of the Messiah.

There is continuity between the various scenes of the first act that are linked by the expression 'On the next day...' (1:29, 35, 43). The continuity carries over into the first scene of the next chapter (2:1-11), which happens 'On the third day' (2:1), probably counting the last day in the previous sequence as the first. The continuity in the sequence is reinforced by the way at least one character from each scene reappears in the following scene. In each case the focus moves—from the embassy to John, from John to Jesus, from Jesus to one of the two disciples, from that disciple to another. In the final scene of the sequence, Jesus and his disciples, who now constitute a group, are together and another important character, the mother of Jesus, is introduced. Continuity is also seen in the way the diverse messianic expectations of the embassy lead on to the revelation of Jesus as the one about whom they are unwittingly inquiring. John's revelation of Jesus as 'the lamb of God' is not final, any more than are the confessions of 'Jesus as Messiah' and the 'one of whom Moses wrote', made by the disciples. These developing confessions find their fulfilment in Jesus, though there is also a transformation that culminates, in the first act, in the self-revelation of Jesus in terms of the 'Son of Man' (1:51 and compare the developing confessions of the once blind man in John 9 that culminate in the self-revelation of Jesus to him as 'Son of Man' in 9:35). The transformation can be expressed in terms of the relationship of messianic expectations to the development of Johannine Christology (Painter 1993b: 16-20).

If the first words of Jesus in *John* are 'What are you seeking?', the first words of the risen Jesus, spoken to Mary outside the empty tomb, are, 'Woman, why are you weeping? Whom are you seeking?' (20:15). She is seeking Jesus, whom she thinks to be dead, and does not know him as the risen one. The quest for the Messiah continues, even when Jesus is found, because the reality of his messiahship remains a mystery to her. Thus also for the reader, the quest for the Messiah continues because the mystery of the Messiah is bound up with the mystery of God.

3. The Signs of John 5 and 9. In John, miracle stories are described as *signs* (see the section on Language and Worldview above). Three important narratives describe miracles of healing. Two of these are found in John 5 and 9. The other (4:46-54) is an expression of the quest for the Messiah and concerns the 'nobleman' who took the initiative in the quest to find healing for his ailing/dying son. But in John 5 and 9 a brief narrative describes the healing (5:1-9a; 9:1-12) in which Jesus takes the initiative, and after the healing narrative has been completed the reader is told that 'it was the sabbath on that day' (5:9b; 9:14). The marks that distinguish the healings of John 5 and 9 from John 4 are the conflict of Jesus with the Jews and their rejection of him and his followers.

Given the sabbath context, each incident (John 5 and 9) leads to conflict with 'the Jews', and is presented by the opponents of Jesus as a conflict between Jesus and Moses. In 5:16-18, Jesus himself is the object of persecution, and there is an attempt to kill him, the first of repeated descriptions of attempts to arrest or kill him. The remainder of John 5 contains Jesus' defense of his position in relation to God and as opposed by the Jews. In John 9, the sabbath conflict leads to a series of scenes culminating in the excommunication of the once-blind man from the synagogue because of his loyalty to Jesus (not Moses). The blind man is portrayed in such a way that he becomes the model disciple, one who comes to *see* and obey the truth, in a context of the *blindness* of Jewish persecution. The chapter concludes with Jesus' condemnation of those Pharisees who have rejected him, declaring them to be blind, in the darkness.

These two signs provide essential clues for the recognition of a two-level history, enabling the reader to better understand Johannine theology (see Martyn 1979). It is the history of the conflict of the

Johannine community with the synagogue that enables the reader to understand the way the Gospel presents the conflict of Jesus with the Jews. At the same time, the signs are presented as the means by which those who are willing to take account of them are enabled to see the truth about Jesus and the world, bringing out the continuity of creation and redemption *in the purpose of God.*

4. The Farewell Discourses (John 13–17). The discourses in John are quite distinctive. Of these, the farewell discourses call for special attention. The style of the discourses is similar to the epistles, and there are grounds for suspecting that, even more than with the narratives, the evangelist has framed the teaching of Jesus in his own words, though there is evidence that he has built on fragments of the Jesus tradition. The discourses appear to be interpretative elaborations of key themes from the Jesus tradition. In John, these are understood in ways that make them relevant to the Johannine situation.

Recognition of the farewell scene is important for the interpretation of John 13–17. *The Testaments of the Twelve Patriarchs,* which is based on Genesis (especially 29:30–31:24; ch. 34; 35:16-26; and chs. 37–50), provides important clues for understanding John's farewell scene. In the genre of the farewell scene, on the eve of departure, the central character gives warnings and promises and prays for those who are to follow him, which is precisely the way Jesus is portrayed in John. Thus his farewell is portrayed in terms characteristic of the great figures from the past.

Recognition of the genre of the farewell scene alerts the reader to the interpretative role of the evangelist in developing chs. 13–17. This interpretative role is justified by the introduction of the teaching of the unique role of the Paraclete or Spirit of Truth. In this way, John justifies the distinctive language of the Gospel, and provides a rationale for the development of the Johannine Christology. Again, in the farewell discourses the focus is not on the situation of Jesus but on that of the disciples (Johannine community) in later periods.

THE JOHANNINE EPISTLES

Nothing in the Johannine Epistles provides clear evidence of their date of composition or authorship. Theories concerning these matters arise from conclusions drawn concerning the relation of the letters to each other, to the Gospel and to Revelation. Once the testimony of Irenaeus has been brought into question, these and many other questions are left unanswered. There is nothing in the letters that *directly* links them to the Fourth Gospel or Revelation, though the Prologue of 1 John appears to be based on the Prologue of the Gospel. The language of 1 John shares the characteristic vocabulary of the Gospel.

A. Authorship

Nothing in the epistles *specifically* identifies the author(s). The author of 1 John presents himself as an authoritative bearer of the tradition that is from the beginning (1:1-5). In the second and third epistles, the author addresses himself to his readers as 'the elder' (2 John 1; 3 John 1), giving the impression that the same author is responsible for both letters. But this is little evidence to go on because we are dealing with very short works. 2 John consists of just 13 verses or 244 words, while 3 John has 15 verses or 219 words. If we were to conclude that these letters stood alone, it would be difficult to know how to read them. Most scholars conclude that, even if the three letters are not the work of a single author, they all derive from the same 'school' that produced the Fourth Gospel. Some scholars continue to maintain common authorship of these works, and many think it probable that at least the epistles had a single author.

The author's reference to himself as 'the elder' (ὁ πρεσβύτερος) in 2 and 3 John could be a reference to his age or, more likely, draws attention to his position of authority. He presents himself as an authoritative teacher in the letters and, in the first letter, he appears to be an authoritative bearer of tradition. This understanding is confirmed by the references to 'elders' in the Papias fragment concerning John (Eusebius, *H.E.* 3:39:1-10), and in Irenaeus's treatment of the elders of Asia Minor (*A.H.* 3:3:3; 5:33:3-4; *Ep. ad Flor.*). If these are by a common author, it is a puzzle that 1 John is not addressed in the same way as the other letters. 1 John is more like the Epistle to the Hebrews. It has no personal address at the beginning, though, like Hebrews, it has something of a personal closing, 'Little children, guard yourselves from idols'. The personal force is reduced by recognition that 'Little children' is a stylized form of address.

B. Provenance

1 John contains direct address to the readers, not by name, but in collective and general terms, as 'Children' (τεκνία; 2:1, 12, 28; 3:7; 5:21; παιδία; 2:14, 18), 'Beloved' (ἀγαπητοί; 2:7, 15; 3:21; 4:1, 7, 11), 'Fathers' (πατέρες; 2:13, 14), 'Young men' (νεανίσκοι; 2:13,

14). There are numerous appeals introduced by 'I write [wrote] to you' (plural) (2:1, 7, 12, 13, 14 [3 times], 26; 5:13). In the second letter, the addressees are identified as the 'elect lady and her children', while the third letter is addressed to 'Gaius, the beloved, whom I love in truth'. A possible way of understanding this is to see 2 and 3 John as covering letters sent with 1 John, which was a circular 'message' to a group of 'house churches'. The 'elect lady' (ἐλεκτῇ κυρίᾳ) might be some notable lady, though more likely it is a personification of the Church viewed collectively. Reference to the children takes account of the Church in terms of her individual members.

Just where such a circle of house churches might have been is not hinted at in the letters. Tradition places all of the Johannine writings in Asia Minor, and this is in harmony with the milieu portrayed by Revelation. It is reasonable to think that a circle of churches around Ephesus was the place of origin for the Johannine Epistles; there is no compelling evidence suggesting any other situation.

C. Structure

There are considerable problems concerning the structure of 1 John. Brooke put this down to the 'aphoristic character of the writer's meditations' (1912: xxxii-xxxviii). Nevertheless, he recognized that Theodor Häring (1892) had made the most successful attempt to show the underlying sequence of thought in the epistle and followed his analysis generally in his own commentary. A summary of Häring's analysis follows:

1. Introduction   1:1-4
2. First presentation of the two tests   1:5–2:27
   The two tests of fellowship with God (the ethical and
   christological theses)
   a. The ethical test: Walking in the light as the true sign of
   fellowship with God; Refutation of the first lie   1:5–2:17
   b. The christological test: Faith in Jesus Christ as the test of
   fellowship with God; Refutation of the second lie   2:18-27
3. Second presentation of the two tests   2:28–4:6
   Emphasizing the connection between the two tests   3:22-24
   a. The ethical test: Doing righteousness (= love of the
   brethren) as the sign by which we may know that
   we are born of God   2:28–3:24
   b. The christological test: The Spirit from God
   confesses Jesus Christ has come in the flesh   4:1-6
4. Third presentation of the two tests   4:7–5:12
   Stressing the inseparable relation between the two tests
   a. Love based on faith in the revelation of love is

Häring's analysis of 1892 is largely followed by Robert Law (1909) although he appears not to have known Häring's article at the time. There are three differences. First, Law refers to 'three cycles', whereas Häring refers to 'theses' though I have preferred the term 'tests', a term taken from Law's title, *The Tests of Life*. Secondly, Law has three tests—righteousness, love, belief—whereas Häring sees love as the expression of righteousness. Thirdly, Law fails to distinguish the 'Conclusion' or 'Epilogue' from the third cycle. On the substantial differences, Häring's analysis is to be preferred, though Law's work remains a stimulating interpretation.

This analysis of the letter emphasizes the controversial nature of the letter. The tests of life were necessary because the author of the letter perceived that counterfeit claims were abroad in the Church. Such claims needed to be tested so that the true ones may be recognized and the false ones rejected. Critical analysis of the epistle that emphasizes the way it is constructed, to refute false affirmations and to affirm what was falsely denied, implies that the epistle was written with a specific problem in mind that was confronting a church or circle of churches.

D. Date and Context

Given the lack of specific evidence concerning authorship and provenance, it is not surprising that the letters lack clear indication of date. It would be helpful to know whether the letters were written at the same time, which would fit the theory that 2 and 3 John were written to accompany 1 John. But were they written before or after the Gospel? This is a key question. It has been argued that the epistles were written to affirm that Jesus is the Christ (Messiah) against objections that Jesus did not fulfil the messianic expectations. Thus, the epistles are seen in terms of Jewish and Jewish–Christian controversy and this is sometimes seen in relation to Cerinthus who is understood to be a Jewish Christian (see Hengel 1989; Lieu 1986; Okure 1988). This approach owes too much to reading the epistles in the light of the Gospel, on the assumption that they were written at the same time for the same situation.

Alternatively, it is noted that there are no quotations from the Old Testament in the epistles, and the final warning in 1 John, 'guard yourselves from idols', is more appropriately addressed to a predominantly Gentile audience. While the Gospel was shaped in relation to Judaism, the epistles reflect Christianity adrift from Judaism.

Most of the evidence concerning the situation addressed comes from 1 John, where it is apparent that the letter concerns an internal problem that led to a schism (2:19). But is this evidence of the author's rhetoric, rather than a reflection on actual historical conflict? Reference to the schism makes the rhetoric option unlikely, and other evidence enables us to build up a cohesive picture of the author's opponents. The author refers to what his opponents affirmed (1:6, 8, 10; 2:4, 6, 9; 4:20), what they denied (4:1-6), and, in a series of antitheses expressed using different syntactical constructions, sets out the position opposed (2:29b; 3:3a, 4a, 6a, 6b, 9a, 10b, 15; 5:4, 18; also 3:7, 8, 10, 14-15; 4:8; 5:6, 10, 12, 19; 2:23). This conflict, evident in the text itself, should not be ignored. The cohesiveness of the position confirms that this deals with a single group of opponents who are described as anti-Christs (2:18-19).

The interpreter needs to exercise caution in reading the author's unsympathetic treatment of his opponents. With caution, the following can be said: they were opposed to the affirmation that Jesus Christ had come in the flesh. Minimally, this means that they saw no revelatory or saving value in the humanity of Jesus. Rather, Jesus was the model of their own experience. As he is from above, has knowledge and is without sin, so are they. How could such a position emerge in the Johannine community? It was a result of one reading of tradition in the Fourth Gospel. Thus the author of the epistle(s) and his opponents were separated from each other by their differing interpretations of that tradition. What led to this was the author's participation in the conflict of the Johannine community with the synagogue, which provided one context of interpretation, while the opponents coming into the Johannine community, after the breach from Judaism, interpreted the tradition from the context of their own religious experience, which was influenced by the mystery cults.

While the Gospel is the canonical culmination of a developing tradition over more than half a century, the epistles represent a single response at a particular moment in time to one specific problem. It is likely that the problem had appeared before the Gospel was published. It has even been suggested that the schism of 1 John 2:19 is reflected in Jesus' reference to the many disciples who no longer followed him (6:60-66). This is unlikely, because the controversy there concerns the bread from heaven, Jesus' heavenly origin. That schism concerned the divinity of Jesus, and reflects the controversy with the Jews. Those who no longer followed were the secret 'believers' for whom the Gospel's presentation of Jesus as the one from above and superior to Moses did not persuade them to confront the threat of exclusion from the synagogue as a consequence of their confession of faith.

The opponents confronted by the Johannine letters cannot be identified by name, though they have often been related to Cerinthus who apparently rejected the identity of Jesus with the Christ. Certainly what we know of him fits the teaching refuted in the letters. But that falls short of proving identity. Nevertheless we are not wrong to see the opponents as some form of docetists, who at least denied the significance of the humanity of Jesus. They also rejected the need to express their faith in terms of love for the brethren. It is not likely that this meant only a failure to love those recognized as brothers by 'the elder'. Rather, their religious experience made such ethical behaviour irrelevant.

E. Purpose of the Letters

The purpose of the *first letter* is to refute the position of the opponents by reaffirming that what the author asserts is the correct interpretation of the tradition in the Gospel. Naturally, we should not expect the opponents and their position to be treated sympathetically. On the other hand, the purpose of the letter is to persuade his adherents not to follow his opponents into schism; the position of the opponents would have been well known to them. Thus it is not likely to grossly distort the schismatics' views.

The *second letter* is addressed to 'the elect lady and her children', which is probably a symbolic reference to the Church. As a covering letter, it briefly summarizes the main teaching of the first letter: the correctness of the confession of faith in Jesus Christ come in the flesh and the outworking of faith in love for one another. This is the basis of the call for the readers to refuse hospitality to those who do not share the correct teaching (9-11).

The *third letter* is addressed to an individual named Gaius, whom the author says he loves and who is perhaps a 'disciple' of the author. This letter is also about hospitality in the mission. It opposes the work of Diotrophes, who may side with the opponents of the author and refuses hospitality to those who support him.

There is a good case for seeing 2 and 3 John as supporting covering letters sent with 1 John. 3 John appears to have been sent to one particular person, while 2 John is a general covering letter accompanying 1 John. Its point is to crystallize the two main points of 1 John and to call on his supporters to refuse hospitality to the opponents. 3 John indicates that the opponents and their reporters have already withdrawn hospitality to our author and his supporters.

Exegetically, it is crucial that the nature and purpose of the letters be recognized. Only when the letters are read as the expression of a bitter internal controversy can they be adequately appreciated. The community that resulted as a consequence of being excluded from the synagogue was itself subjected to a schism in which a large and powerful group left the Johannine community. Those who left appear to have interpreted the Johannine tradition from the perspective of the experience of the mystery religions, and were on the road to what we have come to call Gnosticism.

BIBLIOGRAPHY

Abbott, E.A.
1905   *Johannine Vocabulary*. London: A. & C. Black.
1906   *Johannine Grammar*. London: A. & C. Black.
Barrett, C.K.
1978   *The Gospel according to St John*. London: SPCK, 2nd edn.
Bauckham, R.
1992   *The Climax of Prophecy: Studies on the Book of Revelation*. Edinburgh: T. & T. Clark.
1993   *The Theology of the Book of Revelation*. Cambridge: Cambridge University Press.
Bernard, J.H.
1928   *A Critical and Exegetical Commentary on the Gospel according to St John*. 2 vols. ICC. Edinburgh: T. & T. Clark.
Brooke, A.E.
1912   *A Critical and Exegetical Commentary on the Johannine Epistles*. ICC. Edinburgh: T. & T. Clark.
Brown, R.E.
1966–70 *The Gospel according to John*. AB, 29, 29A. New York: Doubleday.
1982   *The Epistles of John*. AB, 30. New York: Doubleday.
Bultmann, R.
1971   *The Gospel of John*. Oxford: Blackwell.
Caird, G.B.
1966   *The Revelation of St John the Divine*. New York: Harper & Row.
Charles, R.H.
1920   *A Critical and Exegetical Commentary on the Revelation of St John*. 2 vols. ICC. Edinburgh: T. & T. Clark.

Court, J.M.
1979   *Myth and History in the Book of Revelation.* London: SPCK.
1994   *Revelation.* NTG. Sheffield: JSOT Press.
Culpepper, R.A.
1983   *Anatomy of the Fourth Gospel.* Philadelphia: Fortress Press.
1994   *John the Son of Zebedee: The Life of a Legend.* Columbia: University of
        South Carolina Press.
Denaux, A. (ed.)
1992   *John and the Synoptics.* Leuven: Leuven University Press.
Dodd, C.H.
1953   *The Interpretation of the Fourth Gospel.* Cambridge: Cambridge
        University Press.
1963   *Historical Tradition and the Fourth Gospel.* Cambridge: Cambridge
        University Press.
Fortna, R.T.
1970   *The Gospel of Signs.* Cambridge: Cambridge University Press.
1988   *The Fourth Gospel and its Predecessor.* Philadelphia: Fortress Press.
Häring, T.
1892   'Gedankengang und Grundgedanke des ersten Johannesbriefs', in
        Theologische Abhandlungen Carl von Weizäcker...gewidmet. Freiburg:
        Mohr: 171-200.
Harris, J.R.
1917   *The Origin of the Prologue to St John's Gospel.* Cambridge: Cambridge
        University Press.
Hengel, M.
1989   *The Johannine Question.* London: SPCK.
Jonge, M. de (ed.)
1977   *L'Evangile de Jean: Sources, redaction, theologie.* Leuven: Leuven
        University Press.
Kysar, R.
1975   *The Fourth Evangelist and his Gospel.* Minneapolis: Augsburg.
Law, R.
1909   *The Tests of Life.* Edinburgh: T. & T. Clark.
Lieu, J.
1986   *The Second and Third Epistles of John.* Edinburgh: T. & T. Clark.
Martyn, J.L.
1979   *History and Theology of the Fourth Gospel.* Nashville: Abingdon, 2nd
        edn.
Neirynck, F.
1977   'John and the Synoptics', in M. de Jonge (ed.), *L'Evangile de Jean:
        Sources, redaction, theologie.* Leuven: Leuven University Press.
1992   'John and the Synoptics: 1975–1990', in A. Denaux (ed.), *John and the
        Synoptics.* Leuven: Leuven University Press: 3-62.
Okure, T.
1988   *The Johannine Approach to Mission: A Contextual Study of John 4:1-42.*
        Tübingen: Mohr–Siebeck.

Painter, J.

1986   *John: Witness and Theologian*. Melbourne: Beacon Hill Books, 3rd edn.

1993a 'Theology and Eschatology in the Prologue of John'. *SJT* 46: 27-42.

1993b *The Quest for the Messiah: The History, Literature and Theology of the Johannine Community*. Edinburgh: T. & T. Clark; Nashville: Abingdon, 2nd edn.

Schüssler Fiorenza, E.

1976–77 'The Quest for the Johannine School: The Apocalypse and the Fourth Gospel'. *NTS* 23: 402-27.

Segovia, F.

1991   *The Farewell of the Word: The Johannine Call to Abide*. Minneapolis: Fortress Press.

Smith, D.M.

1984   *Johannine Christianity: Essays on its Setting, Sources and Theology*. Columbia: University of South Carolina Press.

1992   *John among the Gospels: The Relationship in Twentieth-Century Research*. Minneapolis: Fortress Press.

Sweet, J.

1990   *Revelation*. London: SCM Press.

NEW TESTAMENT EXEGESIS OF HEBREWS AND THE CATHOLIC EPISTLES

GEORGE H. GUTHRIE

Several years ago at a Society of Biblical Literature meeting in the United States, I arose one morning before sunrise to get an early start on the day. Since my colleagues were still sleeping, I dressed without turning on the lights, took my watch and glasses from the table, and turned to leave the room. Suddenly, the room took on a strange appearance, the furniture, pictures on the wall, and my colleagues shifting slightly out of focus. The effect was disorienting, but I attributed the phenomenon to the surreal aspect of the room, lit dimly as it was by artificial light filtering through the thick curtains on the window. I grabbed my attaché, made my way to the door, and, thankfully, entered a well-lit hallway leading to the elevators. I had taken only a few steps when the disorientation hit me again. As I approached the elevators I was contemplating the maladies which might be behind my blurred vision. Then I saw the problem in the mirrored image of the elevator door. Looking at the reflection, I realized I had picked up the wrong pair of glasses on the table. My roommate's pair was the same shape as mine, slightly different in color, but of course differing greatly in prescription. Having on the wrong glasses had a powerful, image-skewing effect.

Basic to the enterprise of exegesis is the dictum, 'There exists no presuppositionless exegesis' (Conzelmann and Lindemann 1985: 2). We all come with a set of 'glasses' which affect what we see in the text, and viewing the text through these lenses can be both distorting and disorienting. These glasses are made of our own histories of thinking (or lack of thinking) about the text, our traditions, be they critical or ecclesiastical, our communities, and our experiences—and should be acknowledged as one takes up the task of interpreting any passage. These presuppositions may or may not be valid, but they must be identified. Moreover, an understanding of this condition can infuse the process with both vigor and integrity, and raises the possibility that the exegete's presuppositions may be informed and modified in the process of study. Reminder of this need serves not only the initiate, but also those practiced in the art of New Testament criticism. Although rigor in employing the historical-critical method can help guard against eisegesis, its use does not assure objectivity.

Integral to the historical-critical method are questions of a book's structure, language, date, authorship, and provenance, and presuppositions held regarding these issues carry great weight in interpretation and, at points, set parameters for conclusions that may be drawn. Therefore, the need to examine freshly these matters from time to time, in light of recent thinking and research, seems all the more necessary. The current essay seeks to demonstrate how presuppositions regarding these introductory questions influence the exegesis of passages in five New Testament books: Hebrews, James, 1 Peter, 2 Peter, and Jude. I first deal with the text-oriented dynamics of structure and language and then turn to background issues of date, authorship, and provenance.

STRUCTURE

One needs only to examine introductions to several commentaries on any New Testament book to see divergence of structural assessments offered for that book. Often one's understanding or misunderstanding of a book's structure influences exegesis of specific passages. Decisions made concerning the structure of a discourse should be based on sound exegesis, but decisions made concerning structure also influence further exegesis. Thus in discourse analysis there exists an interplay between decisions made at the micro- and macro-levels of the text (Guthrie 1994: 45-58).

Exegetical errors may arise from a lack of attention to structural dynamics in a book. For example, at Heb. 1:4 the author introduces the comparison of Christ with the angels, a theme that pervades the first two chapters of the work. Some commentators have interpreted the comparison with the angels in chapter one to indicate that the readers were adrift theologically, toying with the worship of angels (Manson 1962: 242) or, perhaps, a form of aberrant Christology in which Christ was considered subordinate to an angel (Yadin 1958). Commenting on the verse, P.E. Hughes states, 'It follows, then, that those to whom this letter was sent were entertaining, or being encouraged to entertain, teaching which elevated angels, or particular angels, to a position which rivaled that of Christ himself' (Hughes 1977: 51-52).

Although speculation concerning angels seemed to present a

problem in some New Testament communities, and was known in various Jewish and, later, gnostic circles (Ellingworth 1993: 103), William L. Lane rightly points out the misdirection of this exegesis, and does so on the basis of structural considerations (Lane 1991a: 17). First, the reference to angels in 1:4 provides a structural parallel to the reference to the prophets earlier in 1:1-2. Both the prophets and the angels served as agents of the older covenant revelation (1:1-2; 2:2). Secondly, comparison with the angels in 1:1-14 sets up the *a fortiori* argument of 2:1-4 (Hughes 1979: 7-9). The author strongly supports the superiority of the Son over the angels with the string of Old Testament texts in 1:5-14. Having established this relationship, he proceeds to argue that (a) those who rejected the revelation given through the angels were severely punished; since the Son is greater than the angels it follows that (b) those who reject the revelation given through the superior Son deserve even greater punishment than those disobedient to the older revelation through angels. In 2:1-4, the author casts the angels in a positive, though inferior, role (Lane 1991a: 17). This positive role is foundational to the rhetorical argument that the hearers need to take seriously the revelation delivered through the Son.

Thirdly, in Heb. 2:5-9 the author makes a transition to the next major unit (2:10-18), which deals with the Son's incarnation, an event that, for our author, fulfills the words of Ps. 8:5-7: ἠλάττωσας αὐτὸν βραχύ τι παρ' ἀγγέλους (2:9). Is it likely that an author, wishing to counter a heresy by which Christ was deemed less than pre-eminent, would introduce a text stressing the positional subordination of the Son to the angels? No. In Hebrews 1–2, the angels play a very specific and important role in the development of the discourse. They are a reference point from which to magnify both the exaltation and incarnation of the Son. Therefore, it is both unnecessary and ill-advised to describe the author's use of angels as polemical. In this case an understanding of structural dynamics in the broader context corrects a misreading of Hebrews.

By their approaches to the structure of James, Peter Davids and Martin Dibelius offer a second example of the role structural assessments play in the exegetical enterprise. Specifically, their different approaches illustrate how a commentator's attitude concerning structure can influence the data that are chosen when dealing with a text. Davids follows those who understand James as organized around a double opening (1:2-27), a body (2:1–5:6), and a closing (5:7-20). In the body, the redactor recapitulates the themes of testing, wisdom, and wealth introduced in the double opening, and the closing statement provides a final summary of these three major themes (Davids 1982: 22-29). Dibelius, on the other hand, posits the sayings and proverbs of James to be a stringing together of unrelated units that lack continuity in thought (Dibelius 1976: 2).

For Davids, an analysis of 5:7-20 can be carried through in light of insights mined earlier in James. Introducing this unit he comments, 'there is a real sense of unity with the rest of the book as themes are resumed and brought into dynamic relationship with one another' (Davids 1982: 181). Thus he comments on the theme of patience in 5:7-11 with reference to 1:2-4, 12. The topic of harmony he considers in light of 4:11-12, 3:1-18, and 1:19-21, and the author's common concern over the use of the tongue (e.g. 1:26; 3:1-17) is revisited in the 'rejection of oaths' of 5:12 (Davids 1982: 181-89). Dibelius, on the other hand, reads Jas 5:7-20, for the most part, in isolation from the rest of the work. Thus for Davids the dynamic of broader literary context plays a vital role, while for Dibelius, broader contextual concerns are practically nonexistent. Needless to say, these divergent approaches to the structure of James affect the way each commentator understands particular dynamics in Jas 5:7-20.

A third example of the relationship between structural assessment and exegesis may be found in the influence that a critical methodology wields on exegesis. In recent years, rhetorical criticism, the analysis of New Testament texts in light of ancient Greek literary and oratorical conventions, has been on the rise. The rationale for the methodology goes as follows. The New Testament literature developed in a Greek cultural context. Rhetoric stood in a highly systematized form at the educational center of that culture and was extensively documented in handbooks of the day. The writers of the New Testament would have been influenced by this approach to public address, even if they did not have the benefit of formal training. Therefore, the New Testament displays patterns of rhetorical argumentation as expounded in the Greco-Roman handbooks.

Although in practice rhetorical criticism examines the text at the micro-discourse level, seeking to identify features of style, it also involves whole-discourse analyses of New Testament documents. By labeling portions of these documents in terms of Greco-Roman rhetoric, the analysis reflects interpretative decisions concerning the role played by units in the discourse. In rhetorical criticism, the role of each unit in turn affects how the critic analyzes specific constituents in that unit, and constituents are analyzed mostly in terms of their effect on the hearers. In the conclusion to his rhetorical analysis of Jude and 2 Peter, Duane F. Watson states

> This study also shows that rhetorical criticism is an important tool for the interpretation of the New Testament. A specific pericope can be reasonably assigned to an element of arrangement, be placed in the inventional scheme, and be investigated for stylistic features. The ability of the interpreter to analyze the pericope is enhanced by the wealth of knowledge derived from the rhetoric of the whole (Watson 1988: 189).

In his analysis of the text, Watson assigns rhetorical labels to units in Jude and 2 Peter and consistently analyzes these texts in terms of what one would expect to find there based on descriptions given in the rhetorical handbooks. He outlines 2 Peter as having an epistolary prescript (or quasi-*exordium*), an *exordium* (1:3-15), a *probatio* (1:16–3:13), and a *peroratio* (3:14-18).

Watson identifies 2 Peter as deliberative rhetoric. He explains that this form of rhetoric need not have an *exordium* per se, but may have one based on the circumstance being addressed. Also, he informs the reader that a simple case, as with 2 Peter, requires only a short *exordium*. Against the rhetorical critic's expectation, 2 Peter has a lengthy *exordium*, a fact Watson attributes to the author's incorporation of the testament genre. Watson further suggests that the length of the *exordium* may be due to a lack of awareness or preparation on the part of the audience. It may be that they do not understand the dire straits in which the author sees them (Watson 1988: 88).

Watson notes further that the *exordium*, when judged in terms of the deliberative rhetoric of the day, seems wanting. The negative rebuttal of charges made against the faith by the heretics found in the *probatio* and *peroratio*, according to Watson, should be found in the *exordium* to prepare for what follows. This negative feature is lacking from the *exordium* and, therefore, 'the *exordium* produces only half the results that the case requires, and so is faulty' (Watson 1988: 94). Why the lack? Because the testament genre forces the *exordium* to be a positive presentation of the Christian faith.

Rhetorical critics quite literally interpret the New Testament text with the text itself in one hand and the rhetorical handbooks in the other, which proves productive in identifying stylistic features in the text. Certain rhetorical dynamics have prevailed across many literatures of the ancient world. However, the exegete evaluating various methodologies to utilize in analysis of the New Testament needs to consider whether pegging the whole of 2 Peter and other New Testament books as species of Greco-Roman rhetoric, and using that identification as a starting point for exegesis, elucidates or skews interpretation. Such a methodological decision certainly affects the way one understands the structure of a book and, therefore, affects that book's interpretation.

LANGUAGE

As we turn to consider language as used by New Testament authors, we must consider dynamics in both the ancient and modern horizons. First, an understanding of an author's style of writing, that is, the crafting of phrases, sentences, and paragraphs, is especially important for analysis of the New Testament text. The exegete may examine patterns of sentence structure, whether the author uses identifiable forms of argument, strategic use of vocabulary and idioms, and the possible presence of Semitisms or Septuagintalisms. Secondly, students of the text neglect to their peril recent advances in the study of language, most notably the redirection brought about by James Barr in *The Semantics of Biblical Language* (1961). In this regard, certain exegetical fallacies must be avoided.

One author criticized harshly by Barr was T.F. Torrance, whose book *Royal Priesthood* offered Barr numerous examples of exegetical missteps. For example, Torrance argued against Platonic philosophy as an interpretative grid for Hebrews, and did so on the following bases. The Old Testament word for 'pattern', תאבנית, is translated by the LXX either by παράδειγμα or by εἶδος, and these terms, according to Torrance, are philosophically loaded to communicate the Platonic idea of eternal forms. Hebrews, on the other hand, corrects the Septuagintal importation of Platonism by using the term ὑπόδειγμα in place of these 'Platonic' terms (Torrance 1955: 20-21, 90-91).

Among Barr's criticisms of this line of linguistic reasoning are, first, that it cannot be shown that uses of παράδειγμα in the LXX are meant to refer to Platonic concepts, nor can it be inferred that the author of Hebrews rejects such concepts by not using the word. Torrance's arguments in this regard are based on dictionary treatments of the terms in question rather than a serious study of the texts. Secondly, in the LXX there occur examples of παράδειγμα translating תאבנית to communicate 'plan' or 'design' of a building, a straightforward meaning found in broader Greek literature. Thirdly, Torrance's arguments present words as theologically loaded in and of themselves, separate from any context (Barr 1961: 152-56).

It is interesting to note that many commentators have addressed Hebrews' use of ὑπόδειγμα as *supporting* a Platonic interpretation of the book, an intention exactly opposite to that of Torrance. However, ὑπόδειγμα, as used in Heb. 8:5 and 9:23, is considered Platonic on false grounds (Hurst 1990: 13-17). Commentators draw parallels to Platonic thought on the false understanding of the term as meaning 'copy', roughly synonymous to Plato's use of μίμημα or εἰκών. Yet, there are no instances in known Greek literature where ὑπόδειγμα can be shown to have this meaning. In ancient literature, the word signifies an 'example', 'prototype', or perhaps 'outline'—that is, something to *be* copied, rather than the copy itself. In this case, a false understanding of a word's meaning again skews interpretation of a specific text and points to the danger of carrying an exegetical argument on the back of individual terms divorced from a thorough study of their uses in context.

Turning to the ancient horizon, an understanding of the general features of an author's style can aid in the process of exegesis. For example, features in James, such as careful attention to word order, the lack of anacolutha, the use of the gnomic aorist, and choice of words, point to a highly developed Koine literary style. In addition, the book is replete with qualities pointing to the orality of this text; for example, alliteration, rhyme, short sentence structure, and forms of direct address. James also contains an undercurrent of Semitic influence, perhaps most prominently derived from the language of the LXX (Martin 1988: lxx-lxxi; Davids 1982: 58-59). Therefore, the student attempting exegesis on James must be aware of these features and how they affect one's understanding of the text.

The phrase ἐν ταῖς πορείαις αὐτοῦ in Jas 1:11 may be regarded as a Semitism meaning 'pattern of life'. The statement here is proverbial, and is meant to present a generalized truth about the misjudgment committed by those who take pride in riches. When commentators such as Mayor relate the phrase to the specific life situation of traveling merchants mentioned in Jas 4:13-16, they show too little recognition of its proverbial style, and the interpretation is skewed (Davids 1982: 78).

A third way in which sensitivity to language affects exegesis is in the attempt to identify traditional material in New Testament books.

The process is somewhat circular, in that a critic identifies language in the book as indicating traditional material, then interprets aspects of the text in light of that identification. For example, the question of the Gospel tradition in 1 Peter has fostered a robust discussion. R.H. Gundry has catalogued numerous allusions to the teachings of Jesus in 1 Peter (Gundry 1966-67; 1974). Although many of Gundry's suggestions have come under fire (Best 1982: 52-53), he has furthered consideration of possible links between the book and traditional Gospel material. Thus, for example, the phrase 'have no fear of them' in 1 Pet. 3:14 may prompt reflection as both a quotation of Isa. 8:12 LXX and echoing Jesus' words (Michaels 1988: 186-87).

At points, a theory of traditional material, derived from the use of language in a text, can strongly influence the exegesis of particular words and phrases. F.L. Cross designates 1 Pet. 1:3–4:11 as part of a baptismal rite associated with Easter, the Paschal celebration (Cross 1954). Cross draws connections between Easter and Passover and finds significance in that 1 Peter uses the Greek word for suffering, πασχεῖν, more than other pieces of New Testament literature. Thus Cross interprets the theme of joy running through the book as related to Easter. In 1:18-19, Jesus is interpreted as the new Passover lamb, and the exhortation of 1:13, 'gird up', for Cross harks back to Exod. 12:11 and the first Passover. Cross's exegesis of 1 Peter at these points provides a poignant example of a theory casting a strong influence over the exegesis of specific passages.

AUTHORSHIP AND DATE

The questions of authorship and date of the Catholic Epistles are notoriously difficult, and provide rich examples of the impact that introductory questions have on exegesis. Through the years, certain positions on authorship and dating of these books have reached, in some circles, a level of 'orthodoxy', whether that orthodoxy be traditional or critical. Yet these issues are complex and demand an ongoing assessment of the data in light of critical discussion. Although swimming against the current of majority opinion, works such as J.A.T. Robinson's *Redating the New Testament* (1976), which challenge commonly-held positions, should be considered carefully in light of the New Testament texts. One can rush too quickly to an assumption as to dating or authorship, which will have vast implications for the process of thinking about the New Testament literature (Ellis 1979-80).

Notice, for example, the assumptions underlying the following statement by Hans Conzelmann and Andreas Lindemann concerning the dating of Hebrews:

> The statement in 13:7, about the 'leaders' whose example is to be followed and who had proclaimed the word of God, further indicates *clearly* that the apostolic era already belongs to the past. Likewise, the difference between Jewish Christians and Gentile Christians is *quite obviously* already history; the dispute with Jewish Christianity is merely theoretical (Conzelmann and Lindemann 1988: 265) (italics mine).

Yet, is the case really 'clear' and 'quite obvious'? First, the term ἡγούμενοι was used in the broader culture of state officials and had been used in the LXX of religious, political, and military leaders (e.g. Sir. 17:17; 33:19; 1 Macc. 9:30; 2 Macc. 14:16). In Acts 15:22, the word occurs adjectivally to designate Judas and Silas as ἄνδρες ἡγούμενοι, and Luke 22:26 speaks to the role of ὁ ἡγούμενος as servant among the disciples (Lane 1991b: 526; Ellingworth 1993: 702-703). The term, used in a Christian context for a Church office, finds expression in *1 Clement* and *The Shepherd of Hermas*, documents related to the church at Rome and normally dated between 80 and 150 CE. However, there is no reason why ἡγούμενοι could not have been used to designate a Church office earlier, and if, as many suppose, Hebrews is associated with the Roman church, the usage may be due to geographical rather than temporal concerns. Even if one understands Heb. 13:7 to indicate that the leaders had died (Lane 1991b: 526), this does not necessitate a post-apostolic date, since church leaders certainly died prior to the end of the apostolic era.

Secondly, to suggest that the 'theoretical' nature of Hebrews somehow indicates that a time of dispute between Jewish and Gentile branches of the Church is past must be questioned. Whatever one's opinion on relations between Jews and Gentiles in primitive Christianity, this argument rests on the shaky foundation of silence. Supposedly, since the author did not raise practical concerns about strained relations between these groups, he must have known of no such concerns. Besides, Hebrews has no dispute (theoretical or otherwise) with Jewish Christianity, but rather shows the inferiority of the older covenant institutions.

The much-loved question concerning the authorship of Hebrews has prompted commentators to spill buckets of ink in pursuit of an unanswerable question. Spicq, along with many others, has argued strongly for Apollos, a suggestion that originated with Luther (Spicq

1952–53: I, pp. 209-19). However, in Spicq's case, the discussion interplays with his conviction that Hebrews has highly Philonic overtones. That Apollos was from Alexandria, therefore, is deemed quite significant. For Spicq, the identification of Apollos as author of the book becomes another piece of evidence supporting a Platonic interpretation of Hebrews.

Turning to 1 Peter, the discussion of authorship and date has implications for specific points of exegesis. For those such as F.W. Beare who take a late date and pseudonymous authorship of the epistle, 1:1 and 5:1 are part of the apparatus of pseudepigraphy. Beare interprets the author's description of himself with συμπρεσβύτερος (5:1) as mock modesty, which when coupled with the claim to 'unique experience and peculiar privilege would ill become Peter himself' (Beare 1947: 172). J.R. Michaels, while stressing the tentative nature of any position on authorship, is more comfortable speaking of the apostolic overtones established by 1:1 and echoed in 5:1-2. This is due to an openness to the possibility of Peter's influence on the letter, whether before or after his death (Michaels 1988: lxii-lxvii, 280). W. Grudem, who holds to the apostle Peter's authorship of the letter, goes a step further and interprets μάρτυς τῶν τοῦ Χριστοῦ παθημάτων of 5:1 as 'eyewitness' of the events surrounding the death of Christ (Grudem 1988: 186). The term, governed by the article before συμπρεσβύτερος, more probably refers to the ministry of Christian preaching shared by the author and the elders being addressed (Michaels 1988: 280-81).

A final example further demonstrates how one's understanding of authorship and date may have an impact upon interpretation of the New Testament text. E. Earle Ellis, in his work *Prophecy and Hermeneutic in Early Christianity*, understands Jude to be midrashic in character, that is, a commentary on Old Testament texts, or apocryphal elaborations of Old Testament texts, and he provides a portrayal of Jude's structure on this basis (Ellis 1993: 221-23). He points to the formal similarity that Jude has with other New Testament texts such as 1 Corinthians 1–4 and Romans 1–4, 9–11, and partially on this basis places Jude in mid-first century. Ellis understands the book to be a product of the prophet Jude, one of the 'brothers' (i.e. co-workers) of James mentioned in Acts 15 (Ellis 1993: 229-32). The false teachers excoriated by Jude are not gnostics, as suggested by some commentators proposing a late date for the book, but are identical with the Judaizing counter-mission opposed by Paul. Ellis supports this argument by showing idiomatic parallels between Paul's treatment of the Judaizers and the description of the false teachers in Jude.

On the basis of Ellis's arguments he denies that ἡ πίστις (Jude 3, 20) must refer to a later, post-apostolic conception of formally transmitted tradition. Rather, he suggests that it fits well with Pauline thought (e.g. 2 Thess. 2:15, 3:6; 1 Cor. 15:3; Rom. 16:17). Furthermore, Ellis interprets the apostolic prophecy of Jude 17-18 to indicate that the readers are contemporaries of the apostles from whom they have received instruction concerning the fate of disobedient persons (vv. 5-15) and the future arrival of scoffers (v. 18) (Ellis 1993: 234).

PROVENANCE

In addition to authorship and date, the background question of provenance may carry some weight in exegetical decisions. William L. Lane identifies the recipients of Hebrews as members of a house church in or near the city of Rome (Lane 1991a: lviii-lx). Thus he cautiously interprets Heb. 10:32-34 in light of the Claudian expulsion of Jews from Rome in 49 CE. For the Jewish Christians, this persecution perhaps meant banishment, loss of property, imprisonment, injury, or other indignities (Lane 1991b: 301). Furthermore, recent research has affirmed the multiplicity of house churches throughout Rome in the first century. This may suggest why the church struggled with the twin problems of disunity and a tendency toward independence. When read in this light, Heb. 13:17 is understandable. A tension existed between the church leaders and members of the audience due, in part, to their fragmentary social situation. The author wishes to remind the audience that they are not autonomous, free to isolate themselves from others in the Christian community. In exhorting them to have an attitude of common respect for and submission to their leaders, he offers them a remedy to the problem of disunity. They are further exhorted to greet 'all the saints' (13:24a), not just those of a particular faction (Lane 1991a: lx).

Provenance also plays a pivotal role in F.W. Beare's interpretation of 1 Peter. As foundational to dating 1 Peter, Beare points to the region of address designated in the book's opening (1:1). It was in Bithynia and Pontus, Beare explains, that persecution against Christians broke out during the reign of Trajan (98–117 CE). Thus, he uses the specific social context of the addressees to date the letter (Beare 1947: 9-24).

For Beare, the 'fiery trial' of 1 Pet. 4:12-16 reflects an official state persecution of the Church, focused in Pontus and Bithynia under the governor Pliny the Younger about 111–12 CE (Beare 1947: 13-14, 19-24). This in turn affects the commentator's interpretation of specific terms in the passage. The 'astonishment' of the letter's recipients at the 'strange' situation they are encountering (4:12) stems from the fact that, for the first time in their experience, persecution has risen to the level of a painful crisis, well beyond the normal trials of the Christian life. Commentators who opt for a less critical social situation, however, understand the passage to deal with trials addressed throughout 1 Peter as common to those living for Christ in a pagan culture (Davids 1990: 164; Kelly 1969: 183). The point is that provenance has a great impact on Beare's dating and placing of the letter, and thus on the interpretation of 1 Pet. 4:12-16.

EXEGETICAL ISSUES AND DIFFICULTIES

Several years ago, I was presenting a lecture on 'Matters of Introduction' to a class on 'Hebrews and General Epistles', speaking eloquently on the subjects of authorship, date, and so on. The students were so enthralled, so deeply engrossed in thoughtful meditation, that a couple in the back even looked as though they were asleep. In the midst of this significant academic moment, one bright student had the audacity to ask, 'What difference does all this make anyway?'. Hopefully, this essay has offered some small defense of the difference made by one's thinking on matters introductory to these New Testament books. It remains for us to consider certain issues and difficulties surrounding the exegesis of Hebrews, James, 1 Peter, 2 Peter, and Jude. This essay concludes with general observations concerning the study of these books, rather than citing conundrums related to particular passages.

First, the importance of introductory topics to the task of exegesis vindicates ongoing, critical examination of these matters. Someone has affectionately designated Hebrews and the Catholic Epistles as 'the Leftovers', due to their neglect, comparatively speaking, in New Testament criticism. Certainly the volume of research on the Gospels or Paul dwarfs that accomplished on the documents under consideration. However, their stars seem to be rising. This is important, since effective exegesis demands good tools, be they commentaries, articles, monographs, or other reference works.

Since 1980 Hebrews, once considered the 'Cinderella' of New Testament scholarship, has experienced a 'mini revival' in interest (McCullough 1994a: 66). Weighty commentaries such as those by Lane and Attridge have offered the student of Hebrews up-to-date, razor-sharp tools to aid in exegesis. Although ground has been gained on the questions of authorship (that is, a general profile of the author), date, provenance, thought-world, and structure, much remains to be done.

Work on James, 1 Peter, 2 Peter, and Jude has also advanced, though not with the intensity of work on Hebrews. Helpful commentaries, such as those by Davids, Laws, and Martin, while benefiting from the earlier work of Dibelius, have blown fresh breezes through the exegetical study of James. The same may be said of Michaels on 1 Peter and Bauckham on 2 Peter and Jude. Yet, the study of this branch of New Testament literature warrants increased attention from New Testament scholars.

Secondly, exegetical difficulties sometimes relate to the sparsity of evidence that Hebrews and the General Epistles offer for assessing certain topics of introduction. The person-specific authorship of Hebrews and the provenance of Jude or 2 Peter are merely representative. This fact has frequently generated arguments from silence, which, at best, offer poor speculation and, at worst, a distortion of what evidence lies at hand. Harold Attridge has noted wisely, 'The beginning of sober exegesis is a recognition of the limits of historical knowledge...' (Attridge 1989: 5). At times, the confession, 'we do not know', represents a judicious point of departure for exegesis.

Thirdly, investigation of intersecting streams of tradition in early Christianity has born some fruit in the exegesis of Hebrews and the Catholic Epistles, and this dynamic deserves further attention. Some scholars suggest, for example, that Hebrews has strong affinities with traditional material used in 1 Peter (Attridge 1989: 31). The same may be true of 1 Peter and James, both of which seem to include forms of Gospel tradition. Too often, New Testament criticism has presented primitive Christian 'schools' or 'communities' as if they were isolated, developing alone in the Greco-Roman world without the benefit of interaction with other communities and streams of tradition, yet this perspective seems to be changing where warranted by details of the text. The difficulty here, of course, lies in going beyond verbal similarities to the question of meaning. What controls are needed to help the exegete guard against reading one document's use of tradition into the use made by another?

Fourthly, the process of exegesis should include consideration of meaning relationships within and above the sentence level in a text. Traditional exegetical concerns with backgrounds, word meanings, and syntax are mandatory to the process and staple fare in good commentaries. Yet, more needs to be done to address sense relations between various parts of a discourse unit and relations between units (Cotterell and Turner 1989: 188-256). For example, 1 Pet. 4:1-2 could be analyzed as follows:

basis of the exhortation:	Χριστοῦ οὖν παθόντος σαρκὶ
EXHORTATION:	καὶ ὑμεῖς τὴν αὐτὴν ἔννοιαν ὁπλίσασθε
purpose:	ὅτι ὁ παθὼν σαρκὶ πέπαυται ἁμαρτίας
result:	εἰς τὸ μηκέτι ἀνθρώπων ἐπιθυμίαις ἀλλὰ θελήματι θεοῦ τὸν ἐπίλοιπον ἐν σαρκὶ βιῶσαι χρόνον.

Every phrase in every unit of every meaningful text has a function. The same is true of every unit in a discourse. Perhaps the day will come when enough of a consensus will be reached concerning possible phrase and unit functions within a discourse that meaningful interaction on these matters will be common to commentaries, as is the case now with Greek syntax.

Finally, as demonstrated by this handbook, in recent years scholars have set forth numerous new methodologies for study of the New Testament. Most taking up these new approaches, as well as those holding to more traditional criticisms, feel strongly about their particular approach to reading the text. Albeit unintentionally, this state of affairs can lead to the fragmentation of New Testament studies. What is needed is work from all sides to integrate the strengths of these various methods (Pearson 1989: 387-88). Perhaps in the coming decades, as those of various methodological persuasions have meaningful interaction, study of Hebrews and the Catholic Epistles will be advanced greatly, and so also the task of New Testament exegesis.

BIBLIOGRAPHY

Attridge, H.
1989   *To the Hebrews*. Hermeneia. Philadelphia: Fortress Press.

Barr, J.
1961   *The Semantics of Biblical Language.* Oxford: Oxford University Press.

Bauckham, R.J.
1983   *Jude, 2 Peter.* WBC, 50. Dallas: Word.

Beare, F.W.
1947   *The First Epistle of Peter.* Oxford: Blackwell.

Best, E.
1982   *1 Peter.* NCB. London: Marshall, Morgan & Scott.

Conzelmann, H., and A. Lindemann
1988   *Interpreting the New Testament: An Introduction to the Principles and Methods of N.T. Exegesis.* Trans. S.S. Schatzmann. Peabody: Hendrickson.

Cotterell, P., and M. Turner
1989   *Linguistics and Biblical Interpretation.* Downers Grove, IL: InterVarsity Press.

Cross, F.L.
1954   *1 Peter, A Paschal Liturgy.* London: Mowbray.

Davids, P.
1982   *The Epistle of James: A Commentary on the Greek Text.* NIGTC. Grand Rapids: Eerdmans.
1990   *The First Epistle of Peter.* NICNT. Grand Rapids: Eerdmans.

Dibelius, M.
1976   *James.* Trans. M.A. Williams. Hermeneia. Philadelphia: Fortress Press.

Ellingworth, P.
1993   *The Epistle to the Hebrews: A Commentary on the Greek Text.* NIGTC. Grand Rapids: Eerdmans.

Ellis, E.E.
1979–80 'Dating the New Testament'. *NTS* 26: 487-502.
1993   *Prophecy and Hermeneutic in Early Christianity.* Grand Rapids: Baker.

Grudem, W.A.
1988   *The First Epistle of Peter: An Introduction and Commentary.* TNTC. Leicester: InterVarsity Press.

Gundry, R.H.
1966–67 '"Verba Christi" in 1 Peter: Their Implications Concerning the Authorship of 1 Peter and the Authenticity of the Gospel Tradition'. *NTS* 13: 336-50.
1974   'Further Verba on Verba Christi in First Peter'. *Bib* 55: 211-32.

Guthrie, G.H.
1994   *The Structure of Hebrews: A Text-Linguistic Analysis.* NovTSup, 73. Leiden: Brill.

Hughes, G.
1979   *Hebrews and Hermeneutics: The Epistle to the Hebrews as a New Testament Example of Biblical Interpretation.* Cambridge: Cambridge University Press.

Hughes, P.E.
1977   *A Commentary on the Epistle to the Hebrews.* Grand Rapids: Eerdmans.

Hurst, L.D.

1990   *The Epistle to the Hebrews: Its Background and Thought*. SNTSMS, 65. Cambridge: Cambridge University Press.

Kelly, J.N.D.

1969   *A Commentary on the Epistles of Peter and of Jude*. HNTC. New York: Harper & Row.

Lane, W.L.

1991a   *Hebrews 1–8*. WBC, 47A. Dallas: Word.

1991b   *Hebrews 9–13*. WBC, 47B. Dallas: Word.

Manson, T.W.

1949   'The Problem of the Epistle to the Hebrews'. *BJRL* 32: 1-17.

Martin, R.P.

1988   *James*. WBC, 48. Dallas: Word.

Mayor, J.B.

1897   *The Epistle of St James*. London: Macmillan.

McCullough, J.C.

1994a   'Hebrews in Recent Scholarship'. *IBS* 16: 66-86.

1994b   'Hebrews in Recent Scholarship (Part 2)'. *IBS* 16: 108-20.

Michaels, J.R.

1988   *1 Peter*. WBC, 49. Dallas: Word.

Osborne, G.R.

1991   *The Hermeneutical Spiral: A Comprehensive Introduction to Biblical Interpretation*. Downers Grove, IL: InterVarsity Press.

Pearson, B.A.

1989   'James, 1–2 Peter, Jude', in E.J. Epp and G.W. MacRae (eds.), *The New Testament and its Modern Interpreters*. Philadelphia: Fortress Press: 371-406.

Robinson, J.A.T.

1976   *Redating the New Testament*. Philadelphia: Westminster Press.

Spicq, C.

1952–53 *L'Épître aux Hébreux*. 2 vols. Paris: Gabalda.

Torrance, T.F.

1955   *Royal Priesthood*. Edinburgh: Oliver & Boyd.

Watson, D.F.

1988   *Invention, Arrangement, and Style: Rhetorical Criticism of Jude and 2 Peter*. SBLDS, 104. Atlanta: Scholars Press.

Yadin, Y.

1958   'The Dead Sea Scrolls and the Epistle to the Hebrews', in C. Rabin and Y. Yadin (eds.), *Aspects of the Dead Sea Scrolls*. Jerusalem: Magnes.

INDEX OF BIBLICAL WRITINGS

INDEX OF MODERN AUTHORS

NEW TESTAMENT
TOOLS AND STUDIES

edited by

Bruce M. Metzger, Ph.D., D.D., L.H.D., D. Theol., D. Litt.

and

Bart D. Ehrman, Ph.D.